A
HISTORY OF PHILOSOPHY
GREECE AND ROME

A
HISTORY OF PHILOSOPHY

Volume I
GREECE AND ROME

BY

FREDERICK COPLESTON, S.J.

*Professor of the History of Philosophy
at Heythrop College*

NEW REVISED EDITION

THE NEWMAN PRESS
Westminster, Maryland
1960

First published 1946
Second printing 1948
Second Edition 1950
Reprinted 1953
Reprinted 1955
Reprinted 1957
Reprinted 1959
Reprinted 1960

De Licentia Superiorum Ordinis:
    FRANCISCUS MANGAN, S.J.

Praep. Prov. Angliae

Nihil Obstat:
    C. LATTEY, S.J.

Censor Deputatus

Imprimatur:
    ✠ THOMAS

Archiepiscopus Birmingamiensis

Die 17 Martii 1944

TO MY BROTHER

Printed in the United States of America

PREFACE

THERE are so many histories of philosophy already in existence that it seems necessary to give some explanation why one has added to their number. My chief motive in writing this book, which is designed to be the first volume of a complete history of philosophy, has been that of supplying Catholic ecclesiastical seminaries with a work that should be somewhat more detailed and of wider scope than the text-books commonly in use and which at the same time should endeavour to exhibit the logical development and inter-connection of philosophical systems. It is true that there are several works available in the English language which (as distinct from scientific monographs dealing with restricted topics) present an account, at once scholarly and philosophical, of the history of philosophy, but their point of view is sometimes very different from that of the present writer and of the type of student whom he had in mind when writing this book. To mention a "point of view" at all, when treating of the history of philosophy, may occasion a certain lifting of the eyebrows; but no true historian can write without some point of view, some standpoint, if for no other reason than that he must have a principle of selection, guiding his intelligent choice and arrangement of facts. Every conscientious historian, it is true, will strive to be as objective as possible and will avoid any temptation to distort the facts to fit a preconceived theory or to omit the mention of certain facts simply because they will not support his preconceived theory; but if he attempts to write history without any principle of selection, the result will be a mere chronicle and no real history, a mere concatenation of events or opinions without understanding or *motif*. What would we think of a writer on English history who set down the number of Queen Elizabeth's dresses and the defeat of the Spanish Armada as facts of equal importance, and who made no intelligent attempt to show how the Spanish venture arose, what events led to it and what its results were? Moreover, in the case of an historian of philosophy, the historian's own personal philosophical outlook is bound to influence his selection and presentation of facts or, at least, the emphasis that he lays on certain facts or aspects. To take a simple example. Of two historians of ancient philosophy,

v

each may make an equally objective study of the facts, e.g. of the history of Platonism and Neo-Platonism; but if the one man is convinced that all "transcendentalism" is sheer folly, while the other firmly believes in the reality of the transcendental, it is hardly conceivable that their presentation of the Platonic tradition should be exactly the same. They may both narrate the opinion of the Platonists objectively and conscientiously; but the former will probably lay little emphasis on Neo-Platonic metaphysics, for instance, and will indicate the fact that he regards Neo-Platonism as a sorry ending to Greek philosophy, as a relapse into "mysticism" or "orientalism," while the other may emphasise the syncretistic aspect of Neo-Platonism and its importance for Christian thought. Neither will have distorted the facts, in the sense of attributing to philosophers opinions they did not hold or suppressing certain of their tenets or neglecting chronology or logical interconnection, but all the same their pictures of Platonism and Neo-Platonism will be unmistakably different. This being so, I have no hesitation in claiming the right to compose a work on the history of philosophy from the standpoint of the scholastic philosopher. That there may be mistakes or misinterpretations due to ignorance, it would be presumptuous folly to deny; but I do claim that I have striven after objectivity, and I claim at the same time that the fact that I have written from a definite standpoint is an advantage rather than a disadvantage. At the very least, it enables one to give a fairly coherent and meaningful account of what might otherwise be a mere jumble of incoherent opinions, not as good as a fairy-tale.

From what has been said, it should be clear that I have written not for scholars or specialists, but students of a certain type, the great majority of whom are making their first acquaintance with the history of philosophy and who are studying it concomitantly with systematic scholastic philosophy, to which latter subject they are called upon to devote the greater part of their attention for the time being. For the readers I have primarily in mind (though I should be only too glad if my book should prove of any use to others as well) a series of learned and original monographs would be of less use than a book which is frankly designed as a text-book, but which may, in the case of some students, serve as an incentive to the study of the original philosophical texts and of the commentaries and treatises on those texts by celebrated scholars. I have tried to bear this in mind, while writing the

present work, for *qui vult finem, vult etiam media*. Should the work, therefore, fall into the hands of any readers who are well acquainted with the literature on the history of ancient philosophy, and cause them to reflect that this idea is founded on what Burnet or Taylor say, that idea on what Ritter or Jaeger or Stenzel or Praechter have said, let me remind them that I am possibly quite well aware of this myself, and that I may not have agreed uncritically or unthinkingly with what the scholar in question says. Originality is certainly desirable when it means the discovery of a truth not hitherto revealed, but to pursue originality for the sake of originality is not the proper task of the historian. I willingly acknowledge my debt, therefore, to those men who have shed lustre on British and Continental scholarship, to men like Professor A. E. Taylor, Sir David Ross, Constantin Ritter, Werner Jaeger and others. In fact, it is one of my excuses for writing this book that some of the manuals which are in the hands of those for whom I am writing have paid but scant attention to the results of modern specialist criticism. For my own part, I should consider a charge of making insufficient use of such sources of light a more reasonable ground for adverse criticism, than a charge of making too much use of them.

Grateful thanks are due to the Encyclopaedia Britannica Co., Ltd., for permission to use diagrams taken from Sir Thomas Little Heath's article on Pythagoras (14th edit.); to Professor A. E. Taylor (and Messrs. Macmillan & Co., Ltd.) for his generous permission to utilise so freely his study on Forms and Numbers in Plato (reprinted from *Mind in Philosophical Studies*); to Sir David Ross and Messrs. Methuen & Co. for kind permission to incorporate his table of the moral virtues according to Aristotle (from *Aristotle*, p. 203); to Messrs. George Allen & Unwin, Ltd., for permission to quote a passage from the English translation of Professor Nicolai Hartmann's *Ethics* and to utilise a diagram from that work; to the same publishers and to Dr. Oscar Levy to make some quotations from the authorised English translation of Nietzsche's works (of which Dr. Levy is editor); to Messrs. Charles Scribner's Sons (U.S.A.) for permission to quote the translation of Cleanthes' Hymn to Zeus by Dr. James Adam (from Hicks' *Stoic and Epicurean*); to Professor E. R. Dodds and the S.P.C.K. for permission to utilise translations found in *Select Passages Illustrating Neo-platonism* (S.P.C.K. 1923); and to

Messrs. Macmillan & Co., Ltd., for permission to quote from
R. L. Nettleship's *Lectures on the Republic of Plato*.

References to the pre-Socratic philosophers are given according
to the fifth edition of Diels' *Vorsokratiker* (D. in text). Some of
the fragments I have translated myself, while in other cases I
have (with the kind permission of Messrs. A. & C. Black, Ltd.)
adopted the English translation given by Burnet in his *Early
Greek Philosophy*. The title of this work is abbreviated in reference
to E.G.P., and *Outlines of the History of Greek Philosophy*, by
Zeller—Nestle—Palmer, appear generally as *Outlines*. Abbreviations for the titles of Platonic dialogues and the works of Aristotle
should be sufficiently obvious; for the full titles of other works
referred to recourse may be had to the first Appendix at the end
of the volume, where the abbreviations are explained. I have
mentioned a few works, by way of recommendation, in the third
Appendix, but I do so simply for the practical convenience of the
type of student for whom I have primarily written; I do not
dignify the short list of books with the title of bibliography and
I disclaim any intention of giving a bibliography, for the simple
reason that anything approaching a full bibliography (especially
if it took into account, as it ought to do, valuable articles in
learned periodicals) would be of such an enormous size that it
would be quite impracticable to include it in this work. For a
bibliography and a survey of sources, the student can turn to
e.g. Ueberweg-Praechter's *Die Philosophie des Altertums*.

AUTHOR'S FOREWORD
TO REVISED EDITION

My thanks are due to the Rev. T. Paine, S.J., the Rev.
J. Woodlock, S.J., and the Reader of Messrs. Burns Oates and
Washbourne, Ltd., for their valuable assistance in the correction
of misprints and other errors of form which disfigured the first
impression, and for their suggestions in regard to the improvement of the index. Some slight additions to the text have been
made, as on p. 126, and for these I am entirely responsible.
The necessity of producing a second edition without delay has
prevented me from making more extensive changes in the text.

CONTENTS

CONTENTS

PART IV
ARISTOTLE

PART V
POST-ARISTOTELIAN PHILOSOPHY

APPENDICES

CHAPTER I

INTRODUCTION

1. *Why Study the History of Philosophy?*

1. WE would scarcely call anyone "educated" who had no knowledge whatsoever of history; we all recognise that a man should know something of the history of his own country, its political, social and economic development, its literary and artistic achievements—preferably indeed in the wider setting of European and, to a certain extent, even World history. But if an educated and cultured Englishman may be expected to possess some knowledge of Alfred the Great and Elizabeth, of Cromwell and Marlborough and Nelson, of the Norman invasion, the Reformation, and the Industrial Revolution, it would seem equally clear that he should know something at least of Roger Bacon and Duns Scotus, of Francis Bacon and Hobbes, of Locke, Berkeley and Hume, of J. S. Mill and Herbert Spencer. Moreover, if an educated man is expected to be not entirely ignorant of Greece and Rome, if he would be ashamed to have to confess that he had never even heard of Sophocles or Virgil, and knew nothing of the origins of European culture, he might equally be expected to know something of Plato and Aristotle, two of the greatest thinkers the world has ever known, two men who stand at the head of European philosophy. A cultured man will know a little concerning Dante and Shakespeare and Goethe, concerning St. Francis of Assisi and Fra Angelico, concerning Frederick the Great and Napoleon I: why should he not be expected also to know something of St. Augustine and St. Thomas Aquinas, Descartes and Spinoza, Kant and Hegel? It would be absurd to suggest that we should inform ourselves concerning the great conquerors and destroyers, but remain ignorant of the great creators, those who have really contributed to our European culture. But it is not only the great painters and sculptors who have left us an abiding legacy and treasure: it is also the great thinkers, men like Plato and Aristotle, St. Augustine and St. Thomas Aquinas, who have enriched Europe and her culture. It belongs, therefore, to a cultured education to know something at least of the course of European philosophy, for it is our thinkers,

as well as our artists and generals, who have helped to make our time, whether for good or ill.

Now, no one would suppose that it is waste of time to read the works of Shakespeare or contemplate the creations of Michelangelo, for they have intrinsic value in themselves which is not diminished by the number of years that have elapsed between their deaths and our own time. Yet no more should it be considered a waste of time to study the thought of Plato or Aristotle or St. Augustine, for their thought-creations abide as outstanding achievements of the human spirit. Other artists have lived and painted since the time of Rubens, but that does not lessen the value of Rubens' work: other thinkers have philosophised since the time of Plato, but that does not destroy the interest and beauty of his philosophy.

But if it is desirable for all cultured men to know something of the history of philosophic thought, so far as occupation, cast of mind and need for specialisation permit, how much more is this not desirable for all avowed students of philosophy. I refer especially to students of the Scholastic Philosophy, who study it as the *philosophia perennis*. That it is the *philosophia perennis* I have no wish to dispute; but it did not drop down from Heaven, it grew out of the past; and if we really want to appreciate the work of St. Thomas Aquinas or St. Bonaventure or Duns Scotus, we should know something of Plato and Aristotle and St. Augustine. Again, if there is a *philosophia perennis*, it is only to be expected that some of its principles should be operative in the minds even of philosophers of modern times, who may seem at first sight to stand far from St. Thomas Aquinas. And even if this were not so, it would be instructive to observe what results follow from false premisses and faulty principles. Nor can it be denied that the practice of condemning thinkers whose position and meaning has not been grasped or seen in its true historic setting is greatly to be deprecated, while it might also be borne in mind that the application of true principles to all spheres of philosophy was certainly not completed in the Middle Ages, and it may well be that we have something to learn from modern thinkers, e.g. in the field of Aesthetic theory or Natural Philosophy.

2. It may be objected that the various philosophical systems of the past are merely antique relics; that the history of philosophy consists of "refuted and spiritually dead systems, since each has

killed and buried the other."[1] Did not Kant declare that Metaphysic is always "keeping the human mind in suspense with hopes that never fade, and yet are never fulfilled," that "while every other science is continually advancing," in Metaphysic men "perpetually revolve round the same point, without gaining a single step"?[2] Platonism, Aristotelianism, Scholasticism, Cartesianism, Kantianism, Hegelianism—all have had their periods of popularity and all have been challenged: European Thought may be "represented as littered with metaphysical systems, abandoned and unreconciled."[3] Why study the antiquated lumber of the chamber of history?

Now, even if all the philosophies of the past had been not only challenged (which is obvious) but also refuted (which is not at all the same thing), it still remains true that "errors are always instructive,"[4] assuming of course that philosophy is a possible science and is not *of itself* a will-o'-the-wisp. To take an example from Mediaeval Philosophy, the conclusions to which Exaggerated Realism lead on the one hand and those to which Nominalism lead on the other hand indicate that the solution of the problem of universals is to be sought in a mean between the two extremes. The history of the problem thus serves as an experimental proof of the thesis learnt in the Schools. Again, the fact that Absolute Idealism has found itself incapable of providing any adequate explanation of finite selves, should be sufficient to deter anyone from embarking on the monistic path. The insistence in modern philosophy on the theory of knowledge and the Subject-Object relation should, despite all the extravagances to which it has led, at any rate make it clear that subject can no more be reduced to object than object to subject, while Marxism, notwithstanding its fundamental errors, will teach us not to neglect the influence of technics and man's economic life on higher spheres of human culture. To him especially who does not set out to learn a given system of philosophy but aspires to philosophise *ab ovo*, as it were, the study of the history of philosophy is indispensable, otherwise he will run the risk of proceeding down blind alleys and repeating the mistakes of his predecessors, from which a serious study of past thought might perhaps have saved him.

3. That a study of the history of philosophy may tend to

---

[1] Hegel, *Hist. Phil.*, I, p. 17.　　　　[2] *Proleg.*, p. 2 (Mahaffy).
[3] A. N. Whitehead, *Process and Reality*, p. 18. Needless to say, the antihistorical attitude is not Professor Whitehead's own attitude.
[4] N. Hartmann, *Ethics*, I, p. 119.

induce a sceptical frame of mind is true, but it must be remembered that the fact of a succession of systems does not prove that any one philosophy is erroneous. If X challenges the position of Y and abandons it, that does not by itself prove that the position of Y is untenable, since X may have abandoned it on insufficient grounds or have adopted false premises, the development of which involved a departure from the philosophy of Y. The world has seen many religions—Buddhism, Hinduism, Zoroastrianism, Christianity, Mohammedanism, etc., but that does not prove that Christianity is not the true Religion; to prove that, a thorough refutation of Christian Apologetics would be necessary. But just as it is absurd to speak as if the existence of a variety of Religions *ipso facto* disproved the claim of any one religion to be the true Religion, so it is absurd to speak as though the succession of philosophies *ipso facto* demonstrated that there is no true philosophy and can be no true philosophy. (We make this observation, of course, without meaning to imply that there is no truth or value in any other religion than Christianity. Moreover, there is this great difference between the true (revealed) Religion and the true philosophy, that whereas the former, as revealed, is necessarily true in its totality, in all that is revealed, the true philosophy may be true in its main lines and principles without reaching completion at any given moment. Philosophy, which is the work of the human spirit and not the revelation of God, grows and develops; fresh vistas may be opened up by new lines of approach or application to new problems, newly discovered facts, fresh situations, etc. The term "true philosophy" or *philosophia perennis* should not be understood to denote a static and complete body of principles and applications, insusceptible of development or modification.)

II. *Nature of the History of Philosophy*

1. The history of philosophy is certainly not a mere congeries of opinions, a narration of isolated items of thought that have no connection with one another. If the history of philosophy is treated "only as the enumeration of various opinions," and if all these opinions are considered as of equal value or disvalue, then it becomes "an idle tale, or, if you will, an erudite investigation."[1] There is continuity and connection, action and reaction, thesis and antithesis, and no philosophy can really be understood fully

[1] Hegel, *Hist. Phil.*, I, p. 12.

unless it is seen in its historical setting and in the light of its connection with other systems. How can one really understand what Plato was getting at or what induced him to say what he did, unless one knows something of the thought of Heraclitus, Parmenides, the Pythagoreans? How can one understand why Kant adopted such an apparently extraordinary position in regard to Space, Time and the Categories, unless one knows something of British empiricism and realises the effect of Hume's sceptical conclusions on the mind of Kant?

2. But if the history of philosophy is no mere collection of isolated opinions, it cannot be regarded as a continual progress or even a spiral ascent. That one can find plausible instances in the course of philosophic speculation of the Hegelian triad of thesis, antithesis and synthesis is true, but it is scarcely the task of a scientific historian to adopt an *a priori* scheme and then to fit the facts into that scheme. Hegel supposed that the succession of philosophic systems "represent the necessary succession of stages in the development" of philosophy, but this can only be so if the philosophic thought of man is the very thinking of the "World-Spirit." That, practically speaking, any given thinker is limited as to the direction his thought will take, limited by the immediately preceding and the contemporary systems (limited also, we might add, by his personal temperament, his education, the historical and social situation, etc.) is doubtless true; none the less he is not determined to choose any particular premisses or principles, nor to react to the preceding philosophy in any particular way. Fichte believed that his system followed logically on that of Kant, and there is certainly a direct logical connection, as every student of modern philosophy is aware; but Fichte was not *determined* to develop the philosophy of Kant in the particular way he did. The succeeding philosopher to Kant might have chosen to re-examine Kant's premisses and to deny that the conclusions which Kant accepted from Hume were true conclusions; he might have gone back to other principles or excogitated new ones of his own. Logical sequence there undoubtedly is in the history of philosophy, but not *necessary* sequence in the strict sense.

We cannot, therefore, agree with Hegel when he says that "the final philosophy of a period is the result of this development, and is truth in the highest form which the self-consciousness of spirit affords of itself."[1] A good deal depends, of course, on how you

[1] *Hist. Phil.*, III, p. 552.

divide the "periods" and what you are pleased to consider the
final philosophy of any period (and here there is ample scope for
arbitrary choice, in accordance with preconceived opinion and
wishes); but what guarantee is there (unless we first adopt the
whole Hegelian position) that the final philosophy of any period
represents the highest development of thought yet attained? If
one can legitimately speak of a Mediaeval period of philosophy,
and if Ockhamism can be regarded as the final main philosophy
of that period, the Ockhamist philosophy can certainly not be
regarded as the supreme achievement of mediaeval philosophy.
Mediaeval philosophy, as Professor Gilson has shown,[1] represents
a *curve* rather than a straight line. And what philosophy of the
present day, one might pertinently ask, represents the synthesis
of all preceding philosophies?

3. The history of philosophy exhibits man's search for Truth
by the way of the discursive reason. A Neo-Thomist, developing
St. Thomas' words, *Omnia cognoscentia cognoscunt implicite Deum
in quolibet cognito*,[2] has maintained that the judgment always
points beyond itself, always contains an implicit reference to
Absolute Truth, Absolute Being.[3] (We are reminded of F. H.
Bradley, though the term "Absolute" has not, of course, the same
meaning in the two cases.) At any rate we may say that the
search for truth is ultimately the search for Absolute Truth, God,
and even those systems of philosophy which appear to refute this
statement, e.g. Historical Materialism, are nevertheless examples
of it, for they are all seeking, even if unconsciously, even if they
would not recognise the fact, for the ultimate Ground, the
supremely Real. Even if intellectual speculation has at times led
to bizarre doctrines and monstrous conclusions, we cannot but
have a certain sympathy for and interest in the struggle of the
human intellect to attain Truth. Kant, who denied that Metaphysics in the traditional sense were or could be a science, none
the less allowed that we cannot remain indifferent to the objects
with which Metaphysics profess to deal, God, the soul, freedom;[4]
and we may add that we cannot remain indifferent to the human
intellect's search for the True and the Good. The ease with which
mistakes are made, the fact that personal temperament, education
and other apparently "fortuitous" circumstances may so often

[1] Cf. *The Unity of Philosophical Experience.*   [2] *De Verit.*, 22, 2, ad 1.
[3] J. Maréchal, S.J., *Le Point de Départ de la Metaphysique: Cahier V*
[4] Pref. to 1st Ed. of *Critique of Pure Reason.*

lead the thinker up an intellectual cul-de-sac, the fact that we are not pure intelligences, but that the processes of our minds may frequently be influenced by extraneous factors, doubtless shows the need for religious Revelation; but that should not cause us to despair altogether of human speculation nor make us despise the *bona-fide* attempts of past thinkers to attain Truth.

4. The present writer adheres to the Thomistic standpoint that there is a *philosophia perennis* and that this *philosophia perennis* is Thomism in a wide sense. But he would like to make two observations on this matter: (*a*) To say that the Thomist system is the perennial philosophy does not mean that that system is closed at any given historical epoch and is incapable of further development in any direction. (*b*) The perennial philosophy after the close of the Mediaeval period does not develop merely alongside of and apart from "modern" philosophy, but develops also in and through modern philosophy. I do not mean to suggest that the philosophy of Spinoza or Hegel, for instance, can be comprehended under the term Thomism; but rather that when philosophers, even if they would by no means call themselves "Scholastic," arrive by the employment of true principles at valuable conclusions, these conclusions must be looked on as belonging to the perennial philosophy.

St. Thomas Aquinas certainly makes some statements concerning the State, for example, and we have no inclination to question his principles; but it would be absurd to expect a developed philosophy of the modern State in the thirteenth century, and from the practical point of view it is difficult to see how a developed and articulate philosophy of the State on scholastic principles could be elaborated in the concrete, until the modern State had emerged and until modern attitudes towards the State had shown themselves. It is only when we have had experience of the Liberal State and of the Totalitarian State and of the corresponding theories of the State, that we can realise all the implications contained in the little that St. Thomas says on the State and develop an elaborated Scholastic political philosophy applicable to the modern State, which will expressly contain all the good contained in the other theories while renouncing the errors. The resultant State-philosophy will be seen to be, when looked at in the concrete, not simply a development of Scholastic principle in absolute isolation from the actual historical situation and from intervening theories, but rather a development of these principles in the light of the historical situation, a development achieved in and through opposing theories of the State. If this point of view be adopted, we shall be enabled to maintain the idea of a perennial philosophy without committing ourselves, on the one hand, to a very narrow outlook whereby the perennial philosophy is confined to a given century, or, on the other hand, to an Hegelian view of philosophy, which necessarily implies (though Hegel himself seems to have thought otherwise—inconsistently) that Truth is never attained at a given moment.

III. *How to Study the History of Philosophy*

1. The first point to be stressed is the need for seeing any philosophical system in its historical setting and connections. This point has already been mentioned and does not require further elaboration: it should be obvious that we can only grasp adequately the state of mind of a given philosopher and the *raison d'être* of his philosophy if we have first apprehended its historical *point de départ*. The example of Kant has already been given; we can understand his state of mind in developing his theory of the *a priori* only if we see him in his historical situation *vis-à-vis* the critical philosophy of Hume, the apparent bankruptcy of Continental Rationalism and the apparent certainty of mathematics and the Newtonian physics. Similarly, we are better enabled to understand the biological philosophy of Henri Bergson if we see it, for example, in its relation to preceding mechanistic theories and to preceding French "spiritualism."

2. For a profitable study of the history of philosophy there is also need for a certain "sympathy," almost the psychological approach. It is desirable that the historian should know something of the philosopher as a man (this is not possible in the case of *all* philosophers, of course), since this will help him to feel his way into the system in question, to view it, as it were, from inside, and to grasp its peculiar flavour and characteristics. We have to endeavour to put ourselves into the place of the philosopher, to try to see his thoughts from within. Moreover, this sympathy or imaginative insight is essential for the Scholastic philosopher who wishes to understand modern philosophy. If a man, for example, has the background of the Catholic Faith, the modern systems, or some of them at least, readily appear to him as mere bizarre monstrosities unworthy of serious attention, but if he succeeds, as far as he can (without, of course, surrendering

his own principles), in seeing the systems from within, he stands much more chance of understanding what the philosopher meant.

We must not, however, become so preoccupied with the psychology of the philosopher as to disregard the truth or falsity of his ideas taken in themselves, or the logical connection of his system with preceding thought. A *psychologist* may justly confine himself to the first viewpoint, but not an *historian* of philosophy. For example, a purely psychological approach might lead one to suppose that the system of Arthur Schopenhauer was the creation of an embittered, soured and disappointed man, who at the same time possessed literary power and aesthetic imagination and insight, and *nothing more*; as though his philosophy were simply the manifestation of certain psychological states. But this viewpoint would leave out of account the fact that his pessimistic Voluntaristic system is largely a reaction to the Hegelian optimistic Rationalism, as it would also leave out of account the fact that Schopenhauer's aesthetic theory may have a value of its own, independent of the *kind of man* that propounded it, and would also neglect the whole problem of evil and suffering which is raised by Schopenhauer's system and which is a very real problem, whether Schopenhauer himself was a disappointed and disillusioned man or not. Similarly, although it is a great help towards the understanding of the thought of Friedrich Nietzsche if we know something of the personal history of the man, his ideas can be looked at in themselves, apart from the man who thought them.

3. To work one's way into any thinker's system, thoroughly to understand not only the words and phrases as they stand, but also the shade of meaning that the author intended to convey (so far as this is feasible), to view the details of the system in their relation to the whole, fully to grasp its genesis and its implications, all this is not the work of a few moments. It is but natural, then, that specialisation in the field of the history of philosophy should be the general rule, as it is in the fields of the various sciences. A specialist knowledge of the philosophy of Plato, for instance, requires besides a thorough knowledge of Greek language and history, a knowledge of Greek mathematics, Greek religion, Greek science, etc. The specialist thus requires a great apparatus of scholarship; but it is essential, if he is to be a true historian of philosophy, that he should not be so overwhelmed with his scholarly equipment and the details of learning, that he fails

to penetrate the spirit of the philosophy in question and fails to make it live again in his writings or his lectures. Scholarship is indispensable but it is by no means enough.

The fact that a whole lifetime might well be devoted to the study of one great thinker and still leave much to be done, means that anyone who is so bold as to undertake the composition of a continuous history of philosophy can hardly hope to produce a work that will offer anything of much value to specialists. The author of the present work is quite conscious of this fact, and as he has already said in the preface, he is not writing for specialists but rather utilising the work of specialists. There is no need to repeat again here the author's reasons for writing this work; but he would like once more to mention that he will consider himself well repaid for his work if he can contribute in some small degree, not only to the instruction of the type of student for whom the work is primarily designed, but also to the broadening of his outlook, to the acquirement of a greater understanding of and sympathy with the intellectual struggle of mankind, and of course to a firmer and deeper hold on the principles of true philosophy.

iv. *Ancient Philosophy*

In this volume we treat of the philosophy of the Greeks and Romans. There can scarcely be much need for dwelling on the importance of Greek culture: as Hegel says, "the name of Greece strikes home to the hearts of men of education in Europe."[1] No one would attempt to deny that the Greeks left an imperishable legacy of literature and art to our European world, and the same is true in regard to philosophic speculation. After its first beginnings in Asia Minor, Greek philosophy pursued its course of development until it flowered in the two great philosophies of Plato and Aristotle, and later, through Neo-Platonism, exercised a great influence on the formation of Christian thought. Both in its character as the first period of European speculation and also for its intrinsic value, it cannot but be of interest to every student of philosophy. In Greek philosophy we watch problems come to light that have by no means lost their relevance for us, we find answers suggested that are not without value; and even though we may discern a certain *naïveté*, a certain over-confidence and precipitation, Greek philosophy remains one of the glories of European achievement. Moreover, if the philosophy of the

[1] *Hist. Phil.*, I, p. 149.

Greeks must be of interest to every student of philosophy for
its influence on subsequent speculation and for its own intrinsic
value, still more should it be of interest to students of Scholastic
philosophy, which owes so much to Plato and to Aristotle. And
this philosophy of the Greeks was really their own achievement,
the fruit of their vigour and freshness of mind, just as their
literature and art were their own achievement. We must not
allow the laudable desire of taking into account possible non-
Greek influence to lead us to exaggerate the importance of that
influence and to underestimate the originality of the Greek mind:
"the truth is that we are far more likely to underrate the originality of the Greeks than to exaggerate it."[1] The tendency of the
historian always to seek for "sources" is, of course, productive of
much valuable critical investigation, and it would be folly to
belittle it; but it remains true that the tendency can be pushed
too far, even to lengths when criticism threatens to be no longer
scientific. For instance, one must not assume *a priori* that every
opinion of every thinker is borrowed from a predecessor: if this
is assumed, then we should be logically compelled to assume the
existence of some primeval Colossus or Superman, from whom all
subsequent philosophic speculation is ultimately derived. Nor
can we safely assume that, whenever two succeeding contemporary thinkers or bodies of thinkers hold similar doctrines, one
must have borrowed from the other. If it is absurd, as it is, to
suppose that if some Christian custom or rite is partially found in
Asiatic Eastern religion, Christianity must have borrowed that
custom or rite from Asia, so it is absurd to suppose that if Greek
speculation contains some thought similar to that appearing in
an Oriental philosophy, the latter must be the historical source of
the former. After all, the human intellect is quite capable of
interpreting similar experiences in a similar way, whether it be
the intellect of a Greek or an Indian, without its being necessary
to suppose that similarity of reaction is an irrefutable proof of
borrowing. These remarks are not meant to depreciate historical
criticism and research, but rather to point out that historical
criticism must rest its conclusions on historical proofs and not
deduce them from *a priori* assumptions, garnishing them with a
pseudo-historical flavour. Legitimate historical criticism would
not, as yet at least, seem to have seriously impaired the claim to
originality made on behalf of the Greeks.

[1] Burnet, *G.P.*, I, p. 9

Roman philosophy, however, is but a meagre production compared with that of the Greeks, for the Romans depended in large
part on the Greeks for their philosophic ideas, just as they
depended on the Greeks in art and, to a great extent at least, in
the field of literature. They had their own peculiar glory and
achievements (we think at once of the creation of Roman Law
and the achievements of Roman political genius), but their glory
did not lie in the realm of philosophical speculation. Yet, though
the dependence of Roman Schools of philosophy on Greek predecessors is undeniable, we cannot afford to neglect the philosophy
of the Roman world, since it shows us the sort of ideas that
became current among the more cultured members of the class
that was Master of the European civilised world. The thought of
the later Stoa, for example, the teaching of Seneca, Marcus
Aurelius and Epictetus, affords in many respects an impressive
and noble picture which can hardly fail to arouse admiration and
esteem, even if at the same time we are conscious of much that is
lacking. It is desirable too that the Christian student should
know something of the best that paganism had to offer, and should
acquaint himself with the various currents of thought in that
Greco-Roman world in which the Revealed Religion was implanted and grew. It is to be regretted if students should be
acquainted with the campaigns of Julius Caesar or Trajan, with
the infamous careers of Caligula or Nero, and yet should be
ignorant of the philosopher-Emperor, Marcus Aurelius, or the
influence at Rome of the Greek Plotinus, who though not a
Christian was a deeply religious man, and whose name was so
dear to the first great figure of Christian philosophy, St. Augustine
of Hippo.

PART I

PRE-SOCRATIC PHILOSOPHY

CHAPTER II

THE CRADLE OF WESTERN THOUGHT: IONIA

THE birthplace of Greek philosophy was the sea-board of Asia Minor and the early Greek philosophers were Ionians. While Greece itself was in a state of comparative chaos or barbarism, consequent on the Dorian invasions of the eleventh century B.C., which submerged the old Aegean culture, Ionia preserved the spirit of the older civilisation,[1] and it was to the Ionian world that Homer belonged, even if the Homeric poems enjoyed the patronage of the new Achaean aristocracy. While the Homeric poems cannot indeed be called a philosophical work (though they are, of course, of great value through their revelation of certain stages of the Greek outlook and way of life, while their educational influence on Greeks of later times should not be underestimated), since the isolated philosophical ideas that occur in the poems are very far from being systematised (considerably less so than in the poems of Hesiod, the epic writer of mainland Greece, who portrays in his work his pessimistic view of history, his conviction of the reign of law in the animal world and his ethical passion for justice among men), it is significant that the greatest poet of Greece and the first beginnings of systematic philosophy both belong to Ionia. But these two great productions of Ionian genius, the poems of Homer and the Ionian cosmology, did not merely follow on one another; at least, whatever view one holds of the authorship, composition and date or dates of the Homeric poems, it is clear enough that the society reflected in those poems was not that of the period of the Ionian cosmology, but belonged to a more primitive era. Again, the society depicted by Hesiod, the later of the "two" great epic poets, is a far cry from that of

[1] "It was in Ionia that the new Greek civilisation arose: Ionia in whom the old Aegean blood and spirit most survived, taught the new Greece, gave her coined money and letters, art and poesy, and her shipmen, forcing the Phoenicians from before them, carried her new culture to what were then deemed the ends of the earth." Hall, *Ancient History of the Near East*, p. 79.

the Greek *Polis*, for between the two had occurred the breakdown of the power of the noble aristocracy, a breakdown that made possible the free growth of city life in mainland Greece. Neither the heroic life depicted in the *Iliad* nor the domination of the landed nobility depicted in the poems of Hesiod was the setting in which Greek philosophy grew up: on the contrary, early Greek philosophy, though naturally the work of individuals, was also the product of the City and reflected to a certain extent the reign of law and the conception of law which the pre-Socratics systematically extended to the whole universe in their cosmologies. Thus in a sense there is a certain continuity between the Homeric conception of an ultimate law or destiny or will governing gods and men, the Hesiodic picture of the world and the poet's moral demands, and the early Ionian cosmology. When social life was settled, men could turn to rational reflection, and in the period of philosophy's childhood it was Nature as a whole which first occupied their attention. From the psychological standpoint this is only what one would expect.

Thus, although it is undeniable that Greek philosophy arose among a people whose civilisation went back to the pre-historic times of Greece, what we call early Greek philosophy was "early" only in relation to subsequent Greek philosophy and the flowering of Greek thought and culture on the mainland; in relation to the preceding centuries of Greek development it may be looked on rather as the fruit of a mature civilisation, marking the closing period of Ionian greatness on the one hand and ushering in on the other hand the splendour of Hellenic, particularly of Athenian, culture.[1]

We have represented early Greek philosophic thought as the ultimate product of the ancient Ionian civilisation; but it must be remembered that Ionia forms, as it were, the meeting-place of West and East, so that the question may be raised whether or not Greek philosophy was due to Oriental influences, whether, for instance, it was borrowed from Babylon or Egypt. This view has been maintained, but has had to be abandoned. The Greek philosophers and writers know nothing of it—even Herodotus, who was so eager to run his pet theory as to the Egyptian origins of Greek religion and civilization—and the Oriental-origin theory is due mainly to Alexandrian writers, from whom it was taken

---

[1] For what Julius Stenzel calls *Vortheoretische Metaphysik* cf. Zeller, *Outlines*, Introd. ss 3; Burnet, *E.G.P.*, Introd.; Ueberweg-Praechter, pp. 28–31; Jaeger, *Paideia*; Stenzel, *Metaphysik des Altertums*, I, pp. 14 ff., etc.

over by Christian apologists. The Egyptians of Hellenistic times, for instance, interpreted their myths according to the ideas of Greek philosophy, and then asserted that their myths were the origin of the Greek philosophy. But this is simply an instance of allegorising on the part of the Alexandrians: it has no more objective value than the Jewish notion that Plato drew his wisdom from the Old Testament. There would, of course, be difficulties in explaining *how* Egyptian thought could be transmitted to the Greeks (traders are not the sort of people we would expect to convey philosophic notions), but, as has been remarked by Burnet, it is practically waste of time to inquire whether the philosophical ideas of this or that Eastern people could be communicated to the Greeks or not, unless we have first ascertained that the people in question really possessed a philosophy.[1] That the Egyptians had a philosophy to communicate has never been shown, and it is out of the question to suppose that Greek philosophy came from India or from China.[2]

But there is a further point to be considered. Greek philosophy was closely bound up with mathematics, and it has been maintained that the Greeks derived their mathematics from Egypt and their astronomy from Babylonia. Now, that Greek mathematics were influenced by Egypt and Greek astronomy by Babylon is more than probable: for one thing, Greek science and philosophy began to develop in that very region where interchange with the East was most to be expected. But that is not the same as saying that Greek scientific mathematics *derive* from Egypt or their astronomy from Babylon. Detailed arguments left aside, let it suffice to point out that Egyptian mathematics consisted of empirical, rough and ready methods of obtaining a practical result. Thus Egyptian geometry largely consisted of practical methods of marking out afresh the fields after the inundation of the river Nile. Scientific geometry was not developed by them, but it was developed by the Greeks. Similarly Babylonian astronomy was pursued with a view to divination: it was mainly astrology, but among the Greeks it became a scientific pursuit. So even if we grant that the practical gardener-mathematics of the Egyptians and the astronomical observations of Babylonian

---

[1] *E.G.P.*, pp. 17–18.

[2] "*Nel sesto secolo A.C. ci si presenta, in Grecia, uno dei fenomeni meravigliosi della coltura umana. La Scuola di Mileto crea la ricerca scientifica: e le linee fondamentali, stabilite in quei primi albori, si perpetuano attraverso le generazioni e i secoli.*" Aurelio Covotti, *I Presocratici*, p. 31 (Naples, 1934).

astrologers influenced the Greeks and supplied them with preliminary material, this admission is in no way prejudicial to the originality of the Greek genius. Science and Thought, as distinct from mere practical calculation and astrological lore, were the result of the Greek genius and were due neither to the Egyptians nor to the Babylonians.

The Greeks, then, stand as the uncontested original thinkers and scientists of Europe.[1] They first sought knowledge for its own sake, and pursued knowledge in a scientific, free and unprejudiced spirit. Moreover, owing to the character of Greek religion, they were free from any priestly class that might have strong traditions and unreasoned doctrines of their own, tenaciously held and imparted only to a few, which might hamper the development of free science. Hegel, in his history of philosophy, dismisses Indian philosophy rather curtly, on the ground that it is identical with Indian religion. While admitting the presence of philosophical *notions*, he maintains that these do not take the form of *thought*, but are couched in poetical and symbolic form, and have, like religion, the practical purpose of freeing men from the illusions and unhappiness of life rather than knowledge for its own sake. Without committing oneself to agreement with Hegel's view of Indian philosophy (which has been far more clearly presented to the Western world in its purely philosophic aspects since the time of Hegel), one can agree with him that Greek philosophy was from the first *thought* pursued in the spirit of free science. It may with some have tended to take the place of religion, both from the point of view of belief and conduct; yet this was due to the inadequacy of Greek religion rather than to any mythological or mystical character in Greek philosophy. (It is not meant, of course, to belittle the place and function of "Myth" in Greek thought, nor yet the tendency of philosophy at certain times to pass into religion, e.g. with Plotinus. Indeed as regards myth, "In the earlier cosmologies of the Greek physicists the mythical and the rational elements interpenetrate in an as yet undivided unity." So Professor Werner Jaeger in *Aristotle, Fundamentals of the History of His Development*, p. 377.)

Professor Zeller emphasises the impartiality of the Greeks as they regarded the world about them, which in combination with

[1] As Dr. Praechter points out (p. 27), the religious conceptions of the Orient, even if they had been taken over by the Greeks, would not explain the peculiar characteristic of Greek philosophy, free speculation on the essence of things. As for Indian philosophy proper, it would not appear to be earlier than the Greek.

their sense of reality and power of abstraction, "enabled them at a very early date to recognise their religious ideas for what they actually were—creations of an artistic imagination."[1] (This, of course, would scarcely hold good for the Greek people at large— the non-philosophical majority.) From the moment when the proverbial wisdom of the Wise Men and the myths of the poets were succeeded by the half-scientific, half-philosophic reflections and investigations of the Ionian cosmologists, art may be said to have been succeeded (logically, at any rate) by philosophy, which was to reach a splendid culmination in Plato and Aristotle, and at length in Plotinus to reach up to the heights where philosophy is transcended, not in mythology, but in mysticism. Yet there was no abrupt transition from "myth" to philosophy; one might even say that the Hesiodic theogony, for example, found a successor in Ionian cosmogonic speculation, the myth-element retreating before growing rationalisation yet not disappearing. Indeed it is present in Greek philosophy even in post-Socratic times.

The splendid achievement of Greek thought was cradled in Ionia; and if Ionia was the cradle of Greek philosophy, Miletus was the cradle of Ionian philosophy. For it was at Miletus that Thales, the reputedly earliest Ionian philosopher, flourished. The Ionian philosophers were profoundly impressed with the fact of change, of birth and growth, decay and death. Spring and Autumn in the external world of nature, childhood and old age in the life of man, coming-into-being and passing-away—these were the obvious and inescapable facts of the universe. It is a great mistake to suppose that the Greeks were happy and careless children of the sun, who only wanted to lounge in the porticoes of the cities and gaze at the magnificent works of art or at the achievements of their athletes. They were very conscious of the dark side of our existence on this planet, for against the background of sun and joy they saw the uncertainty and insecurity of man's life, the certainty of death, the darkness of the future. "The best for man were not to have been born and not to have seen the light of the sun; but, if once born (the second best for him is) to pass through the gates of death as speedily as may be," declares Theognis,[2] reminding us of the words of Calderón (so dear to Schopenhauer), *"El mayor delito del hombre, Es haber nacido."* And the words of Theognis are re-echoed in the words of Sophocles

---

[1] *Outlines of the History of Greek Philosophy*, by Eduard Zeller, 13th edit., revised by Nestle, translated by L. R. Palmer, pp. 2-3.   [2] 425-7.

in the *Oedipus Coloneus*, "Not to have been born exceeds every reckoning" . . . μή φῦναι τὸν ἄπαντα νικᾷ λόγον.[1]

Moreover, although the Greeks certainly had their ideal of moderation, they were constantly being lured away from it by the will to power. The constant fighting of the Greek cities among themselves, even at the heyday of Greek culture, and even when it was to their obvious interest to unite together against a common foe, the constant uprisings within the cities, whether led by an ambitious oligarch or a democratic demagogue, the venality of so many public men in Greek political life—even when the safety and honour of their city was at stake—all manifest the will to power which was so strong in the Greek. The Greek admired efficiency, he admired the ideal of the strong man who knows what he wants and has the power to get it; his conception of ἀρετή was largely that of ability to achieve success. As Professor De Burgh remarks, "The Greek would have regarded Napoleon as a man of pre-eminent aretê."[2] For a very frank, or rather blatant, acknowledgment of the unscrupulous will to power, we have only to read the report that Thucydides gives of the conference between the representatives of Athens and those of Melos. The Athenians declare, "But you and we should say what we really think, and aim only at what is possible, for we both alike know that into the discussion of human affairs the question of justice only enters where the pressure of necessity is equal, and that the powerful exact what they can, and the weak grant what they must." Similarly in the celebrated words, "For of the Gods we believe, and of men we know, that by a law of their nature wherever they can rule they will. This law was not made by us, and we are not the first who have acted upon it; we did but inherit it, and shall bequeath it to all time, and we know that you and all mankind, if you were as strong as we are, would do as we do."[3] We could hardly ask for a more unashamed avowal of the will to power, and Thucydides gives no indication that he disapproved of the Athenian conduct. It is to be recalled that when the Melians eventually had to surrender, the Athenians put to death all those who were of military age, enslaved the women and children, and colonised the island with their own settlers—and all this at the zenith of Athenian splendour and artistic achievement.

---

[1] 1224.   [2] *The Legacy of the Ancient World*, p. 83, note 2.
[3] From Benjamin Jowett's translation of Thucydides (Oxford Un. Press).

In close connection with the will to power stands the conception of ὕβρις. The man who goes too far, who endeavours to be and to have more than Fate destines for him, will inevitably incur divine jealousy and come to ruin. The man or the nation who is possessed by the unbridled lust for self-assertion is driven head-long into reckless self-confidence and so to destruction. Blind passion breeds self-confidence, and overweening self-confidence ends in ruin.

It is as well to realise this side of the Greek character: Plato's condemnation of the "Might is Right" theory becomes then all the more remarkable. While not agreeing, of course, with Nietzsche's valuations, we cannot but admire his perspicacity in seeing the relation between the Greek culture and the will to power. Not, of course, that the dark side of Greek culture is the only side—far from it. If the drive of the will to power is a fact, so is the Greek ideal of moderation and harmony a fact. We must realise that there are two sides to the Greek character and culture: there is the side of moderation, of art, of Apollo and the Olympian deities, and there is the side of excess, unbridled self-assertion, of Dionysian frenzy, as seen portrayed in the *Bacchae* of Euripides. As beneath the splendid achievements of Greek culture we see the abyss of slavery, so beneath the dream-world of Olympian religion and Olympian art we see the abyss of Dionysian frenzy, of pessimism and of all manner of lack of moderation. It may, after all, not be entirely fanciful to suppose, inspired by the thought of Nietzsche, that there can be seen in much of the Olympian religion a self-imposed check on the part of the Dionysian Greek. Driven on by the will to power to self-destruc-tion, the Greek creates the Olympian dream-world, the gods of which watch over him with jealousy to see that he does not transgress the limits of human endeavour. So does he express his consciousness that the tumultuous forces in his soul would be ultimately ruinous to him. (This interpretation is not of course offered as an account of the origin of the Greek Olympian religion from the scientific viewpoint of the historian of religion: it is only meant to suggest psychological factors—provisions of "Nature," if you like—that may have been operative, even if unconsciously, in the soul of the Greek.)

To return from this digression. In spite of the melancholic side of the Greek, his perception of the constant process of change, of transition from life to death and from death to life, helped to lead him, in the person of the Ionian philosophers, to a beginning of philosophy; for these wise men saw that, in spite of all the change and transition, there must be something permanent. Why? Because the change is from something into something else. There must be something which is primary, which persists, which takes various forms and undergoes this process of change. Change cannot be merely a conflict of opposites; thoughtful men were convinced that there was something behind these opposites, something that was primary. Ionian philosophy or cosmology is therefore mainly an attempt to decide what this primitive element or *Urstoff*[1] of all things is, one philosopher deciding for one element, another for another element. What particular element each philosopher decided on as his *Urstoff* is not so important as the fact that they had in common this idea of Unity. The fact of change, of motion in the Aristotelian sense, suggested to them the notion of unity, though, as Aristotle says, they did not explain motion.

The Ionians differed as to the character of their *Urstoff*, but they all held it to be material—Thales plumping for water, Anaximenes for air, Heraclitus for fire. The antithesis between spirit and matter had not yet been grasped; so that, although they were *de facto* materialists—in that they assigned a form of matter as the principle of unity and primitive stuff of all things —they can scarcely be termed materialists in our sense of the word. It is not as though they conceived a clear distinction between spirit and matter, and then denied it; they were not fully conscious of the distinction, or at least they did not realise its implications.

One might be tempted, therefore, to say that the Ionian thinkers were not philosophers so much as primitive scientists, trying to account for the material and external world. But it must be remembered that they did not stop short at *sense*, but went beyond appearance to *thought*. Whether water or air or fire be assigned as the *Urstoff*, it certainly does not *appear* as such, i.e. as the ultimate element. In order to arrive at the conception of any of these as the ultimate element of all things it is necessary to go beyond appearance and sense. And they did not arrive at their conclusions through a scientific, experimental approach, but by means of the speculative reason: the unity posited is indeed a

---

[1] The German word *Urstoff* is here employed, simply because it expresses the notion of primitive element or substrate or "stuff" of the universe in one short word.

material unity, but it is a unity posited by thought. Moreover, it is abstract—abstracting, that is to say, from the data of appearance—even if materialist. Consequently we might perhaps call the Ionian cosmologies instances of *abstract materialism*: we can already discern in them the notion of unity in difference and of difference as entering into unity: and this is a philosophic notion. In addition the Ionian thinkers were convinced of the reign of law in the universe. In the life of the individual ὕβρις, the overstepping of what is right and proper for man, brings ruin in its train, the redressing of the balance; so, by extension to the universe, cosmic law reigns, the preservation of a balance and the prevention of chaos and anarchy. This conception of a law-governed universe, a universe that is no plaything of mere caprice or lawless spontaneity, no mere field for lawless and "egoistic" domination of one element over another, formed a basis for a scientific cosmology as opposed to fanciful mythology.

From another point of view, however, we may say that with the Ionians science and philosophy are not yet distinguished. The early Ionian thinkers or wise men pursued all sorts of scientific considerations, astronomical for instance, and these were not clearly separated from philosophy. They were Wise Men, who might make astronomical observations for the sake of navigation, try to find out the one primary element of the universe, plan out feats of engineering, etc., and all without making any clear distinction between their various activities. Only that mixture of history and geography, which was known as ἱστορίη, was separated off from the philosophico-scientific activities, and that not always very clearly. Yet as real philosophic notions and real speculative ability appear among them, as since they form a stage in the development of the classical Greek philosophy, they cannot be omitted from the history of philosophy as though they were mere children whose innocent babblings are unworthy of serious attention. The first beginnings of European philosophy cannot be a matter of indifference to the historian.

CHAPTER III

THE PIONEERS: EARLY IONIAN PHILOSOPHERS

1. *Thales*

THE mixture of philosopher and practical scientist is seen very clearly in the case of Thales of Miletus. Thales is said to have predicted the eclipse of the sun mentioned by Herodotus[1] as occurring at the close of the war between the Lydians and the Medes. Now, according to the calculations of astronomers, an eclipse, which was probably visible in Asia Minor, took place on May 28th, 585 B.C. So if the story about Thales is true, and if the eclipse which he foretold is the eclipse of 585, then he must have flourished in the early part of the sixth century B.C. He is said to have died shortly before the fall of Sardis in 546/5 B.C. Among other scientific activities ascribed to Thales are the construction of an almanac and the introduction of the Phoenician practice of steering a ship's course by the Little Bear. Anecdotes narrated about him, which may be read in the life of Thales by Diogenes Laërtius, e.g. that he fell into a well or ditch while star-gazing, or that, foreseeing a scarcity of olives, he made a corner in oil, are probably just tales of the type easily fathered on a Sage or Wise Man.[2]

In the *Metaphysics* Aristotle asserts that according to Thales the earth is superimposed upon water (apparently regarding it as a flat floating disc). But the most important point is that Thales declared the primary stuff of all things to be water . . . indeed, that he raised the question of the One at all. Aristotle conjectures that observation may have led Thales to this conclusion, "getting the notion perhaps from seeing that the nutriment of all things is moist, and that heat itself is generated from the moist and kept alive by it (and that from which they come to be is a principle of all things). He got his notion from this fact, and from the fact that the seeds of all things have a moist nature, and water is the origin of the nature of moist things."[3] Aristotle also suggests, though with diffidence, to be sure, that Thales was influenced by the older theologies, wherein water—as the Styx of the poets—was the object of adjuration among the gods. However

---

[1] *Hist.*, I, 74. [2] Diog. Laërt, *Lives of the Philosophers*, 1, 22–44.
[3] *Metaphysics* (trans. by J. A. Smith and W. D. Ross).

this may be, it is clear that the phenomenon of evaporation suggests that water may become mist or air, while the phenomenon of freezing might suggest that, if the process were carried further, water could become earth. In any case the importance of this early thinker lies in the fact that he raised the question, what is the ultimate nature of the world; and not in the answer that he actually gave to that question or in his reasons, be they what they may, for giving that answer.

Another statement attributed to Thales by Aristotle, that all things are full of gods, that the magnet has a soul because it moves iron,[1] cannot be interpreted with certainty. To declare that this statement asserts the existence of a world-soul, and then to identify this world-soul with God[2] or with the Platonic Demiurge[3] —as though the latter formed all things out of water—is to go too far in freedom of interpretation. The only certain and the only really important point about Thales' doctrine is that he conceived "things" as varying forms of one primary and ultimate element. That he assigns *water* as this element is his distinguishing historical characteristic, so to speak, but he earns his place as the First Greek philosopher from the fact that he first conceives the notion of Unity in Difference (even if he does not isolate the notion on to the logical plane), and, while holding fast to the idea of unity, endeavours to account for the evident diversity of the many. Philosophy naturally tries to understand the plurality that we experience, its existence and nature, and to understand in this connection means, for the philosopher, to discover an underlying unity or first principle. The complexity of the problem cannot be grasped until the radical distinction between matter and spirit has been clearly apprehended: before this has been apprehended (and indeed even after its apprehension, if, once "apprehended," it is then denied), *simpliste* solutions of the problem are bound to suggest themselves: reality will be conceived as a material unity (as in the thought of Thales) or as Idea (as in certain modern philosophies). Justice can be done to the complexity of the problem of the One and the Many only if the essential degrees of reality and the doctrine of the analogy of being are clearly understood and unambiguously maintained: otherwise the richness of the manifold will be sacrificed to a false and more or less arbitrarily conceived unity.

[1] *De Anima*, A 5, 411 a 7; 2, 405 a 19.   [2] So Aëtius, I, 7, XI (D. 11 A 23).
[3] Cicero: *De Nat. D.*, I, 10, 25 (D *ibid.*).

It is indeed possible that the remark concerning the magnet being alive, attributed by Aristotle to Thales, represents the lingering-on of a primitive animism, in which the concept of the anima-phantasma (the shadowy double of a man that is perceived in dreams) came to be extended to sub-human organic life, and even to the forces of the inorganic world; but, even if this is so, it is but a relic, since in Thales we see clearly the transition from myth to science and philosophy, and he retains his traditional character as initiator of Greek philosophy, ἀλλὰ Θαλῆς μὲν ὁ τῆς τοιαύτης ἀρχηγὸς φιλοσοφίας.[1]

II. *Anaximander*

Another philosopher of Miletus was Anaximander. He was apparently a younger man than Thales, for he is described by Theophrastus as an "associate" of Thales.[2] Like him, Anaximander busied himself with practical scientific pursuits, and is credited with having constructed a map—probably for the Milesian sailors on the Black Sea. Participating in political life, as so many other Greek philosophers, he led a colony to Apollonia.

Anaximander composed a prose-work on his philosophical theories. This was extant in the time of Theophrastus, and we are indebted to the latter for valuable information as to the thought of Anaximander. He sought, like Thales, for the primary and ultimate element of all things; but he decided that it could not be any one particular kind of matter, such as water, since water or the moist was itself one of the "opposites," the conflicts and encroachments of which had to be explained. If change, birth and death, growth and decay, are due to conflict, to the encroachment of one element at the expense of another, then— on the supposition that everything is in reality water—it is hard to see why the other elements have not long ago been absorbed in water. Anaximander therefore arrived at the idea, the primary element, the *Urstoff*, is indeterminate. It is more primitive than the opposites, being that out of which they come and that into which they pass away.[3]

This primary element (ἀρχή) was called by Anaximander— and, according to Theophrastus, he was the first so to call it—the material cause. "It is neither water nor any other of the so-called

---

[1] *Metaph.*, 983 b 18.
[2] *Phys. Opin.*, fr. 2 (D. 12 A 9). Cf. Ps. Plut. *Strom.*, 2 (D. 12 A 10).
[3] Frag. 1.

elements, but a nature different from them and infinite, from which arise all the heavens and worlds within them." It is τὸ ἄπειρον, the substance without limits. "Eternal and ageless" it "encompasses all the worlds."[1]

The encroachments of one element on another are poetically represented as instances of injustice, the warm element committing an injustice in summer and the cold in winter. The determinate elements make reparation for their injustice by being absorbed again into the Indeterminate Boundless.[2] This is an instance of the extension of the conception of law from human life to the universe at large.

There is a plurality of co-existent worlds which are innumerable.[3] Each is perishable, but there seems to be an unlimited number of them in existence at the same time, the worlds coming into being through eternal motion. "And in addition there was an eternal motion in which the heavens came to be."[4] This eternal motion seems to have been an ἀπόκρισις or "separating off," a sort of sifting in a sieve, as we find in the Pythagorean doctrine represented in the *Timaeus* of Plato. Once things had been separated off, the world as we know it was formed by a vortex movement or ʼδίνη—the heavier elements, earth and water, remaining in the centre of the vortex, fire going back to the circumference and air remaining in between. The earth is not a disc, but a short cylinder "like the drum of a pillar."[5]

Life comes from the sea, and by means of adaptation to environment the present forms of animals were evolved. Anaximander makes a clever guess as to the origin of man. ". . . he further says that in the beginning man was born from animals of another species, for while other animals quickly find nourishment for themselves, man alone needs a lengthy period of suckling, so that had he been originally as he is now, he could never have survived."[6] He does not explain—a perennial difficulty for evolutionists—how man survived in the transition stage.

The Doctrine of Anaximander shows an advance, then, on that of Thales. He proceeds beyond the assignation of any one determinate element as primary to the conception of an Indeterminate Infinite, out of which all things come. Moreover, he makes

[1] Frags. 1-3.   [2] Frag. 1.
[3] D. 12 A 17. Simpl. *Phys.*, 1121, 5: Aët. II, 1, 3: Cic. *De Nat. D.*, 1, 10, 25: Aug. *C.D.*, viii, 2.
[4] Cf. Hippol., *Ref.*, 16, 2 (D. 12 A 11).
[5] Frag. 5. Ps. Plut. *Strom.*, 2 (D. 12 A 10).
[6] Ps. Plut. *Strom.*, fr. 2 (D. 12 A 10).

some attempt at least to answer the question *how* the world developed out of this primary element.

III. *Anaximenes*

The third philosopher of the Milesian School was Anaximenes. He must have been younger than Anaximander—at least Theophrastus says that he was an "associate" of Anaximander. He wrote a book, of which a small fragment has survived. According to Diogenes Laërtius, "he wrote in the pure unmixed Ionic dialect."

The doctrine of Anaximenes appears, at first sight at any rate, to be a decided retrogression from the stage reached by Anaximander, for Anaximenes, abandoning the theory of τὸ ἄπειρον, follows Thales in assigning a determinate element as the *Urstoff*. This determinate element is not water, but *Air*. This may have been suggested to him by the fact of breathing, for man lives so long as he breathes, and it might easily appear that air is the principle of life. In fact, Anaximenes draws a parallel between man and nature in general. "Just as our soul, being air, holds us together, so do breath and air encompass the whole world."[1] Air then is the *Urstoff* of the world, from which the things that are and have been and shall be, the gods and things divine, arose, while other things come from its offspring."[2]

But there is obviously a difficulty in explaining how all things came from air, and it is in his proffered solution to this difficulty that Anaximenes shows a trace of genius. In order to explain how concrete objects are formed from the primitive element, he introduces the notion of condensation and rarefaction. Air in itself is invisible, but it becomes visible in this process of condensation and rarefaction, becoming fire as it is dilated or rarefied; wind, cloud, water, earth and finally stones, as it is condensed. And indeed this notion of condensation and rarefaction suggests another reason why Anaximenes fixed on air as the primary element. He thought that, when air becomes rarefied, it becomes warmer and so tends to fire; while when it becomes condensed, it grows colder and tends towards the solid. Air then stands midway between the circumambient ring of flame and the cold, moist mass within it, and Anaximenes fixes on air as a sort of half-way house. The important point in his doctrine, however, may be said to be his attempt to found all quality on quantity—for that

---

[1] Frag. 2. [2] Hippol. *Ref.*, i, 7 (D. 13 A 7).

is what his theory of condensation and rarefaction amounts to in modern terminology. (We are told that Anaximenes pointed out that when we breathe with the mouth open, the air is warm; while when we breathe with the mouth shut, the air is cold—an experimental proof of his position.)[1]

As with Thales, the earth is conceived as flat. It floats on the air like a leaf. In the words of Professor Burnet, "Ionia was never able to accept the scientific view of the earth, and even Democritus continued to believe it was flat."[2] Anaximenes gave a curious explanation of the rainbow. It is due to the sun's rays falling on a thick cloud, which they cannot penetrate. Zeller remarks that it is a far cry from Iris, Homer's living messenger of the gods, to this "scientific" explanation.[3]

.   .   .   .   .

With the fall of Miletus in 494, the Milesian School must have come to an end. The Milesian doctrines as a whole came to be known as the philosophy of Anaximenes, as though in the eyes of the ancients he was the most important representative of the School. Doubtless his historical position as the last of the School would be sufficient to explain this, though his theory of condensation and rarefaction—the attempt to explain the properties of the concrete objects of the world by a reduction of quality to quantity—was probably also largely responsible.

In general we may once more repeat that the main importance of the Ionians lies in the fact that they raised the question as to the ultimate nature of things, rather than in any particular answer which they gave to the question raised. We may also point out that they all assume the eternity of matter: the idea of an absolute beginning of this material world does not enter into their heads. Indeed for them *this* world is the only world. It would scarcely be correct, however, to regard the Ionian cosmologists as dogmatic materialists. The distinction between matter and spirit had as yet not been conceived, and, until this happened, there could hardly be materialists in our sense. They were materialists in the sense that they tried to explain the origin of all things out of some material element: but they were not materialists in the sense of deliberately denying a distinction between matter and spirit, for the very good reason that the distinction had not been so clearly conceived that its formal denial was possible.

[1] (Plut., *De prim. frig.*, 947 f.), Frag. 1.   [2] *G.P.*, I, p. 9.   [3] *Outlines*, p. 31.

It scarcely needs to be indicated that the Ionians were "dogmatists," in the sense that they did not raise the "critical problem." They assumed that we could know things as they are: they were filled with the *naïveté* of wonder and the joy of discovery.

CHAPTER IV

THE PYTHAGOREAN SOCIETY

It is important to realise that the Pythagoreans were not merely a crowd of disciples of Pythagoras, more or less independent and isolated from one another: they were members of a religious society or community, which was founded by Pythagoras, a Samian, at Kroton in South Italy in the second half of the sixth century B.C. Pythagoras himself was an Ionian, and the earlier members of the School spoke the Ionic dialect. The origins of the Pythagorean Society, like the life of the founder, are shrouded in obscurity. Iamblichus, in his life of Pythagoras, calls him "leader and father of divine philosophy," "a god, a 'demon' (i.e. a superhuman being), or a divine man." But the Lives of Pythagoras by Iamblichus, Porphyry and Diogenes Laërtius, can hardly be said to afford us reliable testimony, and it is doubtless right to call them romances.[1]

To found a school was probably not new in the Greek world. Although it cannot be proved definitely, it is highly probable that the early Milesian philosophers had what amounted pretty well to Schools about them. But the Pythagorean School had a distinguishing characteristic, namely, its ascetic and religious character. Towards the end of the Ionian civilisation there took place a religious revival, attempting to supply genuine religious elements, which were catered for neither by the Olympian mythology nor by the Milesian cosmology. Just as in the Roman Empire, a society verging towards its decline, its pristine vigour and freshness lost, we see a movement to scepticism on the one hand and to "mystery religions" on the other hand, so at the close of the rich and commercial Ionian civilisation we find the same tendencies. The Pythagorean Society represents the spirit of this religious revival, which it combined with a strongly marked scientific spirit, this latter of course being the factor which justifies the inclusion of the Pythagoreans in a history of philosophy. There is certainly common ground between Orphicism and Pythagoreanism, though it is not altogether easy to determine the precise relations of the one to the other, and the degree of

[1] *"Ben, invero, possono dirsi romanzi, le loro 'Vite.'"* Covotti, *I Presocratici*, p. 66.

29

influence that the teaching of the Orphic sect may have had on
the Pythagoreans. In Orphicism we certainly find an organisa-
tion in communities bound together by initiation and fidelity to
a common way of life, as also the doctrine of the transmigration
of souls—a doctrine conspicuous in Pythagorean teaching—and
it is hard to think that Pythagoras was uninfluenced by the
Orphic beliefs and practices, even if it is with Delos that Pythagoras is to be connected, rather than with the Thracian Dionysian
religion.[1]

The view has been held that the Pythagorean communities
were *political* communities, a view, however, that cannot be
maintained, at least in the sense that they were essentially
political communities—which they certainly were not. Pythagoras, it is true, had to leave Kroton for Metapontum on the
instance of Cylon; but it seems that this can be explained without
having to suppose any specifically political activities on the part
of Pythagoras in favour of any particular party. The Pythagoreans did, however, obtain political control in Kroton and other
cities of Magna Graecia, and Polybius tells us that their "lodges"
were burnt down and they themselves subjected to persecution
—perhaps about 440–430 B.C.,[2] though this fact does not necessarily mean that they were an essentially political rather than a
religious society. Calvin ruled at Geneva, but he was not primarily
a politician. Professor Stace remarks: "When the plain citizen of
Crotona was told not to eat beans, and that under no circumstances could he eat his own dog, this was too much"[3] (though
indeed it is not certain that Pythagoras prohibited beans or even
all flesh as articles of food. Aristoxenus affirms the very opposite
as regards the beans.[4] Burnet, who is inclined to accept the
prohibitions as Pythagorean, nevertheless admits the possibility
of Aristoxenus being right about the taboo on beans).[5] The
Society revived after some years and continued its activities in
Italy, notably at Tarentum, where in the first half of the fourth
century B.C. Archytas won for himself a reputation. Philolaus
and Eurytus also worked in that city.

As to the religious-ascetic ideas and practices of the Pythagoreans, these centred round the idea of purity and purification,
the doctrine of the transmigration of souls naturally leading to the
promotion of soul-culture. The practice of silence, the influence

[1] Cf. Diog. Laërt., 8, 8.   [2] Polybius, ii, 39 (D. 14, 16).
[3] Stace, *Critical History of Greek Philosophy*, p. 33.
[4] ap. Gell., iv, II, 5 (D. 14, 9).   [5] *E.G.P.*, p. 93, note 5.

of music and the study of mathematics were all looked on as valuable aids in tending the soul. Yet some of their practices were of a purely external character. If Pythagoras really did forbid the eating of flesh-meat, this may easily have been due to, or at least connected with, the doctrine of metempsychosis; but such purely external rules as are quoted by Diogenes Laërtius as having been observed by the School can by no stretch of the imagination be called philosophical doctrines. For example, to abstain from beans, not to walk in the main street, not to stand upon the parings of your nails, to efface the traces of a pot in the ashes, not to sit down on a bushel, etc. And if this were all that the Pythagorean doctrines contained, they might be of interest to the historian of religion, but would hardly merit serious attention from the historian of philosophy. However, these external rules of observance by no means comprise all that the Pythagoreans had to offer.

(In discussing briefly the theories of the Pythagoreans, we cannot say how much was due to Pythagoras himself, and how much was due to later members of the School, e.g. to Philolaus. And Aristotle in the *Metaphysics* speaks of the Pythagoreans rather than of Pythagoras himself. So that if the phrase, "Pythagoras held . . ." is used, it should not be understood to refer necessarily to the founder of the School in person.)

In his life of Pythagoras, Diogenes Laërtius tells us of a poem of Xenophanes, in which the latter relates how Pythagoras, seeing somebody beating a dog, told him to stop, since he had recognised the voice of a friend in the yelping of a dog. Whether the tale be true or not, the ascription to Pythagoras of the doctrine of metempsychosis may be accepted. The religious revival had brought to fresh life the old idea of the power of the soul and its continued vigour after death—a contrast to the Homeric conception of the gibbering shades of the departed. In such a doctrine as that of the transmigration of souls, the consciousness of personal identity, self-consciousness, is not held in mind or is not regarded as bound up with soul, for in the words of Dr. Julius Stenzel: ". . . *die Seele wandert von Ichzustand zu Ichzustand, oder, was dasselbe ist, von Leib zu Leib; denn die Einsicht, dass zum Ich der Leib gehort, war dem philosophischen Instinkt der Griechen immer selbstverständlich.*"[1] The theory of the soul as the harmony of the body, which is proposed by Simmias in Plato's *Phaedo* and

---

[1] *Metaphysik des Altertums*, Teil I, p. 42.

attacked by Plato, would hardly fit in with the Pythagorean view
of the Soul as immortal and as undergoing transmigration; so the
ascription of this view to the Pythagoreans (Macrobius refers
expressly to Pythagoras and Philolaus)[1] is at least doubtful.
Yet, as Dr. Praechter points out, it is not out of the question if
the statement that the soul was harmony of the body, or *tout
simple* a harmony, could be taken to mean that it was the principle
of order and life in the body. This would not necessarily compromise the soul's immortality.[2]

(The similarity in several important points between Orphicism
and Pythagoreanism may be due to an influence exerted by the
former on the latter; but it is very hard to determine if there
actually was any direct influence, and if there was, how far it
extended. Orphicism was connected with the worship of Dionysus,
a worship that came to Greece from Thrace or Scythia, and was
alien to the spirit of the Olympian cult, even if its "enthusiastic"
and "ecstatic" character found an echo in the soul of the Greek.
But it is not the "enthusiastic" character of the Dionysian
religion which connects Orphicism with Pythagoreanism; rather
is it the fact that the Orphic initiates, who, be it noted, were
organised in communities, were taught the doctrine of the transmigration of souls, so that for them it is the soul, and not the
imprisoning body, which is the important part of man; in fact,
the soul is the "real" man, and is not the mere shadow-image of
the body, as it appears in Homer. Hence the importance of soul-
training and soul-purification, which included the observance of
such precepts as avoidance of flesh-meat. Orphicism was indeed
a religion rather than a philosophy—though it tended towards
Pantheism, as may be seen from the famous fragment Ζεὺς
κεφαλή, Ζεὺς μέσσα, Διὸς δ' ἐκ πάντα τέτυκται[3]; but, in so far as
it can be called a philosophy, it was a *way of life* and not mere
cosmological speculation, and in this respect Pythagoreanism was
certainly an inheritor of the Orphic spirit.)

To turn now to the difficult subject of the Pythagorean
mathematico-metaphysical philosophy. Aristotle tells us in the
Metaphysics that "the Pythagoreans, as they are called, devoted
themselves to mathematics, they were the first to advance this
study, and having been brought up in it they thought its principles
were the principles of all things . . ."[4] They had the enthusiasm

---

[1] *Somn. Scip.*, I, 14, 19 (D. 44 A 23).   [2] Ueberweg-Praechter, p. 69.
[3] D. 21 a.   [4] *Metaph.*, 985, b 23–6.

of the early students of an advancing science, and they were
struck by the importance of number in the world. All things are
numerable, and we can express many things numerically. Thus
the relation between two related things may be expressed according to numerical proportion: order between a number of ordered
subjects may be numerically expressed, and so on. But what
seems to have struck them particularly was the discovery that
the musical intervals between the notes on the lyre may be
expressed numerically. Pitch may be said to depend on number,
in so far as it depends on the lengths, and the intervals on the
scale may be expressed by numerical ratios.[1] Just as musical
harmony is dependent on number, so it might be thought that the
harmony of the universe depends on number. The Milesian cosmologists spoke of a conflict of opposites in the universe, and the
musical investigations of the Pythagoreans may easily have
suggested to them the idea of a solution to the problem of the
"conflict" through the concept of number. Aristotle says: "since
they saw that the attributes and the ratios of the musical scales
were expressible in numbers; since then all other things seemed in
their whole nature to be modelled after numbers, and numbers
seemed to be the first things in the whole of nature, and the
whole heaven to be a musical scale and a number."[2]

Now Anaximander had produced everything from the Unlimited or Indeterminate, and Pythagoras combined with this
notion that of the Limit, or τὸ πέρας, which gives form to the
Unlimited. This is exemplified in music (in health too, where the
limit is the "tempering," which results in the harmony that is
health), in which proportion and harmony are arithmetically
expressible. Transferring this to the world at large, the Pythagoreans spoke of the cosmical harmony. But, not content with
stressing the important part played by numbers in the universe,
they went further and declared that things *are* numbers.

This is clearly not an easy doctrine to understand, and it is a
hard saying that all things are numbers. What did the Pythagoreans mean by this? First of all, what did they mean by
numbers, or how did they think of numbers? This is an

---

[1] It seems certain that the Pythagorean acoustic ratios were ratios of lengths
and not of frequencies, which the Pythagoreans would hardly be in a position to
measure. Thus the longest harpstring was called ἡ ὑπάτη, though it gave our
"lowest" note and frequency, and the shortest was called ἡ νεάτη, though it gave
our "highest" note and frequency.

[2] *Metaph.*, 985, b 31–986 a 3.

important question, for the answer to it suggests one reason why the Pythagoreans said that things are numbers. Now, Aristotle tells us that (the Pythagoreans) hold that the elements of number are the even and the odd, and of these the former is unlimited and the latter limited; and the I proceeds from both of these (for it is both even and odd), and number from the I; and the whole heaven, as has been said, is numbers."[1] Whatever precise period of Pythagorean development Aristotle may be referring to, and whatever be the precise interpretation to be put on his remarks concerning the even and the odd, it seems clear that the Pythagoreans regarded numbers spatially. One is the point, two is the line, three is the surface, four is the solid.[2] To say then that all things are numbers, would mean that "all bodies consist of points or units in space, which when taken together constitute a number."[3] That the Pythagoreans regarded numbers in this way is indicated by the "tetraktys," a figure which they regarded as sacred.

This figure shows to the eye that ten is the sum of one, two, three and four; in other words, of the first four integers. Aristotle tells us that Eurytus used to represent numbers by pebbles, and it is in accord with such a method of representation that we get the "square" and the "oblong" numbers.[4] If we start with one and add odd numbers successively in the form of "gnomons," we get square numbers,

while if we start with two and add even numbers, we then get oblong numbers.

This use of figured numbers or connection of numbers with geometry clearly makes it easier to understand how the Pythagoreans regarded things as being numbers, and not merely as

---

[1] *Metaph.*, 986 a 17–21.
[2] Cf. art. *Pythagoras,*, Enc. Brit., 14th edit., by Sir Thos. Little Heath.
[3] Stöckl, *Hist. Phil.*, I, p. 48 (trans. by Finlay, 1887).
[4] *Metaph.*, 1092, b 10–13.

being numerable. They transferred their mathematical conceptions to the order of material reality. Thus "by the juxtaposition of several points a line is generated, not merely in the scientific imagination of the mathematician, but in external reality also; in the same way the surface is generated by the juxtaposition of several lines, and finally the body by the combination of several surfaces. Points, lines and surfaces are therefore the real units which compose all bodies in nature, and in this sense all bodies must be regarded as numbers. In fact, every material body is an expression of the number Four (τετρακτύς), since it results, as a fourth term, from three constituent elements (Points, Lines, Surfaces)."[1] But how far the identification of things with numbers is to be ascribed to the habit of representing numbers by geometrical patterns, and how far to an extension to all reality of Pythagorean discoveries in regard to music, it is extremely difficult to say. Burnet thinks that the original identification of things with numbers was due to an extension of the discovery that musical sounds can be reduced to numbers, and not to an identification of numbers with geometrical figures.[2] Yet if objects are regarded—as the Pythagoreans apparently regarded them—as sums of material quantitative points, and if, at the same time, numbers are regarded geometrically as sums of points, it is easy to see how the further step, that of identifying objects with numbers, could be taken.[3]

Aristotle, in the above-quoted passage, declares that the Pythagoreans held that "the elements of number are the even and the odd, and of these the former is unlimited and the latter limited." How do the limited and the unlimited come into the picture? For the Pythagoreans the limited cosmos or world is surrounded by the unlimited or boundless cosmos (air) which it "inhales." The objects of the limited cosmos are thus not pure limitation, but have an admixture of the unlimited. Now, the Pythagoreans, regarding numbers geometrically, considered that they also (composed of the even and the odd) are products of the limited and the unlimited. From this point of view too, then, it is but an easy step to the identification of numbers with things, the even being identified with the unlimited and the odd with the limited. A contributory explanation may be seen in the fact that the odd gnomons (cf. figures) conserve a fixed quadratic

---

[1] Stöckl, *Hist. Phil.*, I, pp. 43–9.   [2] *E.G.P.*, p. 107.
[3] Philolaus (as we learn from the fragments) insisted that nothing could be known, nothing would be clear or perspicuous, unless it had or was number.

shape (limited), while the even gnomons present a continually changing rectangular shape (unlimited).[1]

When it came to assigning definite numbers to definite things, scope was naturally allowed for all manner of arbitrary caprice and fancy. For example, although we may be able to see more or less why justice should be declared to be four, it is not so easy to see why καιρός should be seven or animation six. Five is declared to be marriage, because five is the product of three—the first masculine number, and two—the first feminine number. However, in spite of all these fanciful elements the Pythagoreans made a real contribution to mathematics. A knowledge of "Pythagoras' Theorem" as a geometrical fact is shown in Sumerian computations: the Pythagoreans, however, as Proclus remarked,[2] transcended mere arithmetical and geometrical facts, and digested them into a deductive system, though this was at first, of course, of an elementary nature. "Summing up the Pythagorean geometry, we may say that it covered the bulk of Euclid's Books i, ii, iv, vi (and probably iii), with the qualification that the Pythagorean theory of proportion was inadequate in that it did not apply to incommensurable magnitudes."[3] The theory which did solve this last arose under Eudoxus in the Academy.

To the Pythagoreans, not only was the earth spherical,[4] but it is not the centre of the universe. The earth and the planets revolve—along with the sun—round the central fire or "hearth of the Universe" (which is identified with the number One). The world inhales air from the boundless mass outside it, and the air is spoken of as the Unlimited. We see here the influence of Anaximenes. (According to Aristotle—De Caelo, 293, a 25–7—the Pythagoreans did not deny geocentricism in order to explain phenomena, but from arbitrary reasons of their own.)

The Pythagoreans are of interest to us, not only because of their musical and mathematical investigations; not only because of their character as a religious society; not only because through their doctrine of transmigration of souls and their mathematical metaphysic—at least in so far as they did not "materialise"

---

[1] Cf. Arist. Physics, 203 a 10–15.   [2] In Eukleiden, Friedlein, 65, 16–19.

[3] Heath, art. cit.

[4] Cf. the words of the Russian philosopher, Leo Chestov: "It has happened more than once that a truth has had to wait for recognition whole centuries after its discovery. So it was with Pythagoras' teaching of the movement of the earth. Everyone thought it false, and for more than 1,500 years men refused to accept this truth. Even after Copernicus savants were obliged to keep this new truth hidden from the champions of tradition and of sound sense." Leo Chestov, In Job's Balances, p. 168 (trans. by C. Coventry and Macartney).

numbers[1]—they tended to break away from the *de facto* materialism of the Milesian cosmologists; but also because of their influence
on Plato, who was doubtless influenced by their conception of the
soul (he probably borrowed from them the doctrine of the tripartite nature of the soul) and its destiny. The Pythagoreans were
certainly impressed by the importance of the soul and its right
tendance, and this was one of the most cherished convictions of
Plato, to which he clung all his life. Plato was also strongly
influenced by the mathematical speculations of the Pythagoreans—even if it is difficult to determine the precise extent of
his debt to them in this respect. And to say of the Pythagoreans
that they were one of the determining influences in the formation
of the thought of Plato, is to pay them no mean tribute.

[1] As a matter of fact the Pythagorean mathematisation of the universe cannot
really be regarded as an "idealisation" of the universe, since they regarded number
geometrically. Their identification of things and numbers is thus not so much
an idealisation of things as a materialisation of numbers. On the other hand, in
so far as "ideas," such as justice, are identified with numbers, one may perhaps
speak with justice of a tendency towards idealism. The same theme recurs in
the Platonic idealism.

It must, however, be admitted that the assertion that the Pythagoreans
effected a geometrisation of number would scarcely hold good for the later
Pythagoreans at least. Thus Archytas of Tarentum, a friend of Plato, was clearly
working in the very opposite direction (cf. Diels, B 4), a tendency to which
Aristotle, believing in the separation and irreducible character of both geometry
and arithmetic, firmly objected. On the whole it might be better perhaps to
speak of a Pythagorean discovery (even if incompletely analysed) of *isomorphisms*
between arithmetic and geometry rather than of an interreduction.

CHAPTER V

THE WORD OF HERACLITUS

HERACLITUS was an Ephesian noble and flourished, according to Diogenes, about the 69th Olympiad, i.e. *c.* 504–501 B.C.; his dates cannot be accurately determined. The office of *Basileus* was hereditary in his family, but Heraclitus relinquished it in favour of his brother. He was, we gather, a melancholy man, of aloof and solitary temperament, who expressed his contempt for the common herd of citizens, as also for the eminent men of the past. "The Ephesians," he said of the citizens of his own city, "would do well to hang themselves, every grown man of them, and leave the city to beardless lads; for they have cast out Hermodorus, the best man among them, saying, "We will have none who is best among us; if there be any such, let him be so elsewhere and among others."[1] Again he comments: "In Priene lived Bias, son of Teutamas, who is of more account than the rest." (He said: "Most men are bad.")[2]

Heraclitus expresses his opinion of Homer in the saying: "Homer should be turned out of the lists and whipped, and Archilochus likewise." Similarly he observed: "The learning of many things does not teach understanding, otherwise it would have taught Hesiod and Pythagoras, and again Xenophanes and Hecataeus." As for Pythagoras, he "practised scientific inquiry beyond all other men, and making a selection of these writings, claimed for his own wisdom what was but a knowledge of many things and an imposture."[3]

Many of Heraclitus' sayings are pithy and pungent in character, if somewhat amusing on occasion. For example: "Physicians who cut, burn, stab and rack the sick, demand a fee for it which they do not deserve to get"; "Man is called a baby by God, even as a child by man"; "Asses prefer straw to gold"; "Man's character is his fate."[4] In regard to Heraclitus' attitude to religion, he had little respect for the mysteries, and even declares that "The mysteries practised among men are unholy mysteries."[5] Moreover, his attitude towards God was pantheistic, in spite of the religious language he employed.

[1] Frag. 121. [2] Frag. 39. [3] Frags. 42, 40, 129 (latter doubtful, acc. to D).
[4] Frags. 58, 79, 9, 119. [5] Frag. 14.

The style of Heraclitus seems to have been somewhat obscure for he gained in later time the nickname of ὁ σκοτεινός. This practice appears to have been not altogether unintentional: at least we find among the fragments sentences such as: "Nature loves to hide"; "The lord whose is the oracle by Delphi neither utters not hides its meaning, but shows it by a sign." And of his own message to mankind he says: "Men are as unable to understand it when they hear it for the first time, as before they have heard it at all."[1] Burnet points out that Pindar and Aeschylus possess the same prophetic tone, and attributes it in part to the contemporary religious revival.[2]

Heraclitus is known to many for the famous saying attributed to him, though apparently not his own: "All things are in a state of flux, πάντα ῥεῖ." Indeed this is all that many people know about him. This statement does not represent the kernel of his philosophic thought, though it does indeed represent an important aspect of his doctrine. Is he not responsible for the saying: "You cannot step twice into the same river, for fresh waters are ever flowing in upon you"?[3] Moreover, Plato remarks that "Heraclitus says somewhere that all things pass and nought abides; and comparing things to the current of a river, he says you cannot step twice into the same stream."[4] And Aristotle describes Heraclitus' doctrine as affirming that "All things are in motion, nothing steadfastly is."[5] In this respect Heraclitus is a Pirandello in the ancient world, crying out that nothing is stable, nothing abides, proclaiming the unreality of "Reality."

It would be a mistake, however, to suppose that Heraclitus meant to teach that there is nothing which changes, for this is contradicted by the rest of his philosophy.[6] Nor is the proclamation of change even the most important and significant feature of his philosophy. Heraclitus lays stress on his "Word," i.e. on his special message to mankind, and he could scarcely feel himself justified in doing this if the message amounted to no more than the truth that things are constantly changing; a truth seen by the other Ionian philosophers and hardly bearing the character of novelty. No, Heraclitus' original contribution to philosophy is

---

[1] Frags. 123, 93, 1 (cf. 17, 34). Cf. Diog. Laërt., 9, 6.   [2] *E.G.P.*, p. 132.
[3] Cf. Frags. 12 and 91.   [4] *Crat.* 402 a.   [5] *De Caelo*, 298 b 30 (III, i).
[6] Heraclitus does indeed teach that Reality is constantly changing, that it is its essential nature to change; but this should not be interpreted as meaning that for him there is no changing Reality at all. Heraclitus has often been compared to Bergson, but Bergson's thought too has, not infrequently, been grossly, if understandably, misinterpreted.

to be found elsewhere: it consists in the conception of unity in diversity, difference in unity. In the philosophy of Anaximander, as we have seen, the opposites are regarded as encroaching on one another, and then as paying in turn the penalty for this act of injustice. Anaximander regards the war of the opposites as something disorderly, something that ought not to be, something that mars the purity of the One. Heraclitus, however, does not adopt this point of view. For him the conflict of opposites, so far from being a blot on the unity of the One, is essential to the being of the One. In fact, the One only exists in the tension of opposites: this tension is essential to the unity of the One.

That Reality is One for Heraclitus is shown clearly enough by his saying: "It is wise to hearken, not to me, but to my Word, and to confess that all things are one."[1] On the other hand, that the conflict of opposites is essential to the existence of the One is also shown clearly by such statements as: "We must know that war is common to all and strife is justice, and that all things come into being and pass away through strife,"[2] and Homer was wrong in saying: "Would that strife might perish from among gods and men!" He did not see that he was praying for the destruction of the universe, for, if his prayer were heard, all things would pass away.[3] Again, Heraclitus says positively: "Men do not know how what is at variance agrees with itself. It is an attune-ment of opposite tensions, like that of the bow and the lyre."[4]

For Heraclitus, then, Reality is One; but it is many at the same time—and that not merely accidentally, but essentially. It is essential to the being and existence of the One that it should be one and many at the same time; that it should be Identity in Difference. Hegel's assignment of Heraclitus' philosophy to the category of Becoming is therefore based on a misconception—and also errs by putting Parmenides earlier than Heraclitus, for Parmenides was a critic as well as a contemporary of Heraclitus, and must be the later writer.[5] The philosophy of Heraclitus corresponds much more to the idea of the concrete universal, the One existing in the many, Identity in Difference.

But what is the One-in-many? For Heraclitus, as for the Stoics of later times, who borrowed the notion from him, the essence of all things is Fire. Now, it might seem at first sight that Hera-clitus is merely ringing the changes on the old Ionian theme—as

---

[1] Frag. 50.   [2] Frag. 80.
[3] Numenius. Frag. 16, apud Chalcidium, c. 297 (D. 22 A 22).
[4] Frag. 51.   [5] Hegel, *Hist. Phil.*, vol. I.

though because Thales made Reality to be Water and Anaximenes Air, Heraclitus, simply in order to find something different from his predecessors, fixed on Fire. Naturally, the wish to find a different *Urstoff* may have operated to a certain extent, but there was something more in his choice of Fire than that: he had a positive reason, and a very good reason for fixing on Fire, a reason bound up with the central thought of his philosophy.

Sense-experience tells us that fire lives by feeding, by consuming and transforming into itself heterogeneous matter. Springing up, as it were, from a multitude of objects, it changes them into itself, and without this supply of material it would die down and cease to exist. The very existence of the fire depends on this "strife" and "tension." This is, of course, a sensual symbolism of a genuine philosophic notion, but it clearly bears a relation to that notion that water or air will not so easily bear. Thus Heraclitus' choice of Fire as the essential nature of Reality was not due simply to arbitrary caprice on his part, nor merely to the desire for novelty, to the necessity of differing from his predecessors, but was suggested by his main philosophic thought. "Fire," he says, "is want and surfeit"—it is, in other words, all things that are, but it is these things in a constant state of tension, of strife, of consuming, of kindling and of going out.[1] In the process of fire Heraclitus distinguished two paths—the upward and the downward paths. "He called change the upward and the downward path and said that the cosmos comes into being in virtue of this. When fire is condensed it becomes moist, and under compression it turns to water; water being congealed is turned to earth, and this he calls the downward path. And, again, the earth is itself liquefied and from it water comes, and from that everything else; for he refers almost everything to the evaporation from the sea. This is the upward path."[2]

However, if it be maintained that all things are fire, and are consequently in a constant state of flux, it is clear that some explanation must be offered of what appears at least to be the stable nature of things in the world. The explanation offered by Heraclitus is in terms of measure: the world is "an ever-living Fire, with measures of it kindling and measures going out."[3] So if Fire takes from things, transforming into itself by kindling, it also gives as much as it takes. "All things are an exchange for Fire, and Fire for all things, even as wares for gold and gold for

[1] Frag. 65.   [2] Diog. Laërt., 9, 8–9.   [3] Frag. 30.

wares."[1] Thus, while the substance of each kind of matter is always changing, the aggregate quantity of that kind of matter remains the same.

But it is not only the relative stability of things that Heraclitus tries to explain, but also the varying preponderance of one kind of matter over another, as seen in day and night, summer and winter. We learn from Diogenes that Heraclitus explained the preponderance of different elements as due to "the different exhalations." Thus "the bright exhalation, when ignited in the circle of the sun, produced day; and the preponderance of the opposite exhalation produced night. The increase of warmth proceeding from the bright exhalation produced summer; and the preponderance of moisture from the dark exhalation produced winter."[2]

There is, as we have seen, constant strife in the universe, and there is also a relative stability of things, due to the different measures of Fire, kindling or going out in more or less equal proportions. And it is the fact of this measure, of the balance of the upward and downward paths, which constitutes what Heraclitus calls the "hidden attunement of the Universe," and which he declares is "better than the open."[3] "Men," says Heraclitus in an already-quoted fragment, "do not know how what is at variance agrees with itself. It is an attunement of opposite tensions, like that of the bow and the lyre."[4] The One, in short, is its differences, and the differences are themselves one, they are different aspects of the one. Neither of the aspects, neither the upward nor the downward path, can cease: if they were to cease, then the One itself would no longer exist. This inseparability of opposites, the essential character of the different moments of the One, comes out in such sayings as: "The way up and the way down is the same," and "It is death to souls to become water, and death to water to become earth. But water comes from earth, and from water, soul."[5] It leads, of course, to a certain relativism, as in the statements that "Good and ill are one"; "The sea is the purest and the impurest water. Fish can drink it and it is good for them: to men it is undrinkable and destructive"; "Swine wash in the mire, and barnyard fowls in the dust."[6] However, in the One all tensions are reconciled, all differences harmonised: "To God all things are fair and good and right, but men hold some

---

[1] Frag. 90.   [2] Diog. Laërt., 9, 11.   [3] Frag. 54.   [4] Frag. 51.
[5] Frags. 60, 36.   [6] Frags. 58, 61, 37.

things wrong and some right."[1] This is, of course, the inevitable conclusion of a pantheistic philosophy—that everything is justified *sub specie aeternitatis*.

Heraclitus speaks of the One as God, and as wise: "The wise is one only. It is unwilling and willing to be called by the name of Zeus."[2] God is the universal Reason (Λόγος), the universal law immanent in all things, binding all things into a unity and determining the constant change in the universe according to universal law. Man's reason is a moment in this universal Reason, or a contraction and canalisation of it, and man should therefore strive to attain to the viewpoint of reason and to live by reason, realising the unity of all things and the reign of unalterable law, being content with the necessary process of the universe and not rebelling against it, inasmuch as it is the expression of the all-comprehensive, all-ordering Λόγος or Law. Reason and consciousness in man—the fiery element—are the valuable element: when the pure fire leaves the body, the water and earth which are left behind are worthless, a thought which Heraclitus expresses in the saying: "Corpses are more fit to be cast out than dung."[3] A man's interest, then, is to preserve his soul in as dry a state as possible: "The dry is the wisest and best."[4] It may be pleasure to souls to become moist, but all the same "it is death to soul to become water."[5] Souls should strive to rise above the private worlds of the 'sleeping" to the common world of the "waking," i.e. to the common world of thought and reason. This thought is of course the Word of Heraclitus. There is, then, one immanent law and Reason in the universe, of which human laws should be the embodiment, though at best they can be but its imperfect and relative embodiment. By stressing universal law and man's participation in Reason, Heraclitus helped to pave the way for the universalist ideals of Stoicism.

This conception of universal, all-ordering Reason appears in the system of the Stoics, who borrowed their cosmology from Heraclitus. But we are not entitled to suppose that Heraclitus regarded the One, Fire, as a *personal* God, any more than Thales or Anaximenes regarded Water or Air as a personal God: Heraclitus was a pantheist, just as the Stoics in later times were pantheists. It is, however, true that the conception of God as the immanent, ordering Principle of all things, together with the moral attitude of acceptance of events as the expression of divine

---

[1] Frag. 102.   [2] Frag. 32.   [3] Frag. 96.   [4] Frag. 118.   [5] Frags. 77, 36.

Law, tends to produce a psychological attitude that is at variance with what would seem to be logically demanded by the theoretical identification of God with the cosmic unity. This discrepancy between psychological attitude and the strict demands of theory became very clear in the Stoic School, the members of which so often betray a mental attitude and employ language that would suggest a theistic conception of God, rather than the pantheistic conception logically demanded by the cosmological system—a discrepancy which was aggravated among the later Stoics especially, owing to their increasing concentration on ethical questions.

Did Heraclitus teach the doctrine of a universal conflagration recurring periodically? As the Stoics certainly held this doctrine, and as they borrowed from Heraclitus, the doctrine of the periodic and universal conflagration has been attributed to Heraclitus too; but, for the following reasons, it does not seem possible to accept this attribution. In the first place, Heraditus, as we have seen, insisted on the fact that the tension or conflict of opposites is essential to the very existence of the One. Now, if all things were periodically to relapse into pure fire, the fire itself should logically cease to exist. In the second place, does not Heraclitus expressly say that the "sun will not go beyond his measures; otherwise the Erinyes, the handmaids of Justice, will find him out,"[1] and "this world was ever, is now, and ever shall be an ever-living Fire, with measures of it kindling and measures going out"? In the third place, Plato contrasts Heraclitus and Empedocles on the ground that, according to Heraclitus, the One is always Many, while, according to Empedocles, the One is many and one by turns.[2] When Professor Zeller says: "It is a contradiction which he, and probably Plato too, has not observed," he is making an unwarrantable supposition. Of course, if it were clear from certain evidence that Heraclitus actually did teach the doctrine of a periodic general conflagration, then we should indeed have to conclude that the contradiction involved was unobserved by both Heraclitus himself and by Plato; but as evidence goes to show that Heraclitus did not teach this doctrine, we cannot reasonably be called upon to attribute a mistake to Plato in this matter. Moreover, it was apparently the Stoics who first stated that Heraclitus maintained the doctrine of a general conflagration;[3] and even the Stoics are divided on the subject. Does not Plutarch

[1] Frag. 94.   [2] *Soph.*, 242 d.   [3] Cf. *E.G.P.*, pp. 159–60.

make a character say; "I see the Stoic conflagration spreading over the poems of Hesiod, just as it does over the writings of Heraclitus and the verses of Orpheus"?[1]

What are we to say of the doctrine of Heraclitus, the notion of unity in difference? That there is a many, a plurality, is clear enough. But at the same time the intellect constantly strives to conceive a unity, a system, to obtain a comprehensive view to link things up; and this goal of thought corresponds to a real unity in things: things are interdependent. Even man, with his immortal soul, depends on the rest of creation. His body depends, in a very real sense, on the whole past history of the world and of the human race: he depends on the material universe for life —bodily life through air, food, drink, sunlight, etc.—for his intellectual life too, through sensation as the starting-point of knowledge. He depends also for his cultural life on the thought and culture, the civilisation and development of the past. But though man is right in seeking a unity, it would be wrong to assert unity to the detriment of plurality. Unity, the only unity that is worth having, is a unity in difference, identity in diversity, a unity, that is to say, not of poverty, but of richness. Every material thing is a unity in diversity (consisting of molecules, atoms, electrons, etc.), every living organism also—even God Himself, as we know by Revelation, is Unity in Distinction of Persons. In Christ there is unity in diversity—unity of Person in diversity of Natures. The union of the Beatific Vision is a union in distinction—otherwise it would lose its richness (apart of course, from the impossibility of a "simple" unity of identification between God and creature).

Can we look on the created universe as a unity? The universe is certainly not a substance: it comprises a plurality of substance. It is, however, a totality in our idea of it, and if the law of the conservation of energy be valid, then it is in a sense a physical totality. The universe, then, may to a certain degree be considered a unity in diversity; but we may perhaps go further and suggest with Heraclitus that the conflict of opposites—change—is necessary to the existence of the material universe.

(i) As far as inorganic matter is concerned, change—at the very least in the sense of locomotion—is necessarily involved, at any rate if modern theories of the composition of matter, the theory of light, etc., are to be accepted.

[1] De def. orac., 415 f.

(ii) This, too, is clear, that if there is to be finite, materially-conditioned life, then change is essential. The life of a bodily organism must be sustained by respiration, assimilation, etc., all of which processes involve change, and so the "conflict of opposites." The preservation of specific life on the planet involves reproduction, and birth and death may well be termed opposites.

(iii) Would it be possible to have a material universe in which there was no conflict of opposites, absolutely no change at all? In the first place, there could be no life in such a universe, for embodied life, as we have seen involves change. But would it be possible to have a material universe—in which there was no life—that was entirely static, entirely without change and movement? If matter be regarded in terms of energy, it is very hard to see how there could be any such purely static material universe. But, prescinding from all physical theories, even if such a universe were physically possible, could it be rationally possible? We could at least discover no possible function for such a universe—without life, without development, without change, a sort of primitive chaos.

A purely material universe seems, then, to be inconceivable not only *a posteriori* but also *a priori*. The idea of a material universe, in which organic life is present, demands change. But change means diversity on the one hand, for there must be a *terminus a quo* and a *terminus ad quem* of the change, and stability on the other hand, for there must be *something which changes*. And so there will be identity in diversity.

We conclude, then, that Heraclitus of Ephesus conceived a genuine philosophic notion, even though he pursued the same way of sensual symbolism as his Ionian predecessors, and this notion of the One as essentially many can be clearly discerned beneath all the sensual symbolism. Heraclitus did not indeed rise to the conception of substantial thought, the νόησις νοήσεως of Aristotle, nor did he sufficiently account for the element of stability in the universe as Aristotle tried to do; but, as Hegel says, "if we wish to consider fate so just as always to preserve to posterity what is best, we must at least say of what we have of Heraclitus, that it is worthy of this preservation."[1]

[1] *Hist. Phil.*, I, pp. 297–8.

CHAPTER VI

THE ONE OF PARMENIDES AND MELISSUS

THE reputed founder of the Eleatic School was Xenophanes. However, as there is no real evidence that he ever went to Elea in Southern Italy, it is unlikely that he is to be accounted anything more than a tutelary founder, a patron of the School. It is not difficult to see why he was adopted as a patron by the School that held fast to the idea of the motionless One, when we consider some of the sayings attributed to him. Xenophanes attacks the anthropomorphic Greek deities: "If oxen and horses or lions had hands, and could paint with their hands, and produce works of art as men do, horses would paint the forms of the gods like horses, and oxen like oxen, and make their bodies in the image of their several kinds":[1] and substitutes in their place, "One god, the greatest among Gods and men, neither in form like unto mortals, nor in thought," who "abideth ever in the selfsame place, moving not at all; nor doth it befit him to go about now hither now thither."[2] Aristotle tells us in the *Metaphysics* that Xenophanes, "referring to the whole world, said the One was god."[3] Most probably, then, he was a monist and not a monotheist, and this interpretation of his "theology" would certainly be more compatible with the Eleatic attitude towards him than a theistic interpretation. A really monotheistic theology may be a familiar enough notion to us, but in the Greece of the period it would have been something exceptional.

But whatever the opinions of Xenophanes may have been, the real founder of the Eleatic School from a philosophical and historical viewpoint was undoubtedly Parmenides, a citizen of Elea. Parmenides seems to have been born towards the close of the sixth century B.C., since round about 451–449 B.C., when 65 years old, he conversed with the young Socrates at Athens. He is said to have drawn up laws for his native city of Elea, and Diogenes preserves a statement of Sotion to the effect that

---

[1] Frag. 15. One might compare the words of Epicharmus (Frag. 5): "For the dog seems to the dog to be the most beautiful creature, and the ox to the ox, the donkey to the donkey, and the swine to the swine."
[2] Frags. 23 and 26.
[3] *Metaph.*, A 5, 986 b 18.

Parmenides began by being a Pythagorean, but afterwards abandoned that philosophy in favour of his own.[1]

Parmenides wrote in verse, most of the fragments we possess
being preserved by Simplicius in his commentary. His doctrine
in brief is to the effect that Being, the One, *is*, and that Becoming,
change, is illusion. For if anything comes to be, then it comes
either out of being or out of not-being. If the former, then it
already is—in which case it does not come to be; if the latter,
then it is nothing, since out of nothing comes nothing. Becoming
is, then, illusion. Being simply *is* and Being is One, since plurality
is also illusion. Now, this doctrine is obviously not the type of
theory that rises immediately to the mind of the man in the
street, and so it is not surprising to find Parmenides insisting on
the radical distinction between the Way of Truth and the Way
of Belief or Opinion. It is very probable that the Way of Opinion
exposed in the second part of the poem, represents the cosmology
of the Pythagoreans; and since the Pythagorean philosophy would
itself scarcely occur to the man who went *merely* by sense-
knowledge, it should not be maintained that Parmenides' distinction between the two Ways has all the formal generality of Plato's
later distinction between Knowledge and Opinion, Thought and
Sense. It is rather the rejection of one definite philosophy in
favour of another definite philosophy. Yet it is true that Parmenides rejects the Pythagorean philosophy—and, indeed, every
philosophy that agrees with it on the point—because it admits
change and movement. Now change and movement are most
certainly phenomena which appear to the senses, so that in
rejecting change and movement, Parmenides is rejecting the way
of sense-appearance. It is, therefore, not incorrect to say that
Parmenides introduces the most important distinction between
Reason and Sense, Truth and Appearance. It is true, of course,
that even Thales recognised this distinction to a certain extent,
for his supposed truth, that all is Water, is scarcely perceptible
immediately to the senses: it needs reason, which passes beyond
appearance, in order to be conceived. The central "truth" of
Heraclitus is, again, a truth of reason and far exceeds the common
opinion of men, who trust in everything to sense-appearance. It
is also true that Heraclitus even makes the distinction partly
explicit, for does he not distinguish between mere common sense
and his Word? Yet it is Parmenides who first lays great and

[1] Diog. Laërt., 9, 21.

explicit stress on the distinction, and it is easy enough to understand why he does so, when we consider the conclusions to which he came. In the Platonic philosophy the distinction became of cardinal importance, as indeed it must be in all forms of idealism.

Yet though Parmenides enunciates a distinction which was to become a fundamental tenet of idealism, the temptation to speak of him as though he were himself an idealist is to be rejected. As we shall see, there is very good reason for supposing that in Parmenides' eyes the One is sensual and material, and to turn him into an objective idealist of the nineteenth-century type is to be guilty of an anachronism: it does not follow from the negation of change that the One is Idea. We may be called upon to follow the way of thought, but it does not follow that Parmenides regarded the One, at which we arrive by this way, as actually being Thought itself. If Parmenides had represented the One as self-subsistent Thought, Plato and Aristotle would hardly have failed to record the fact, and Socrates would not have found the first sober philosopher in Anaxagoras, with his concept of Mind or Nous. The truth really seems to be that though Parmenides does assert the distinction between Reason and Sense, he asserts it not to establish an idealist system, but to establish a system of Monistic Materialism, in which change and movement are dismissed as illusory. Only Reason can apprehend Reality, but the Reality which Reason apprehends is material. This is not idealism but materialism.

To turn now to the doctrine of Parmenides on the nature of the world. His first great assertion is that "It is." "It," i.e. Reality, Being, of whatever nature it may be, is, exists, and cannot not be. It is, and it is impossible for it not to be. Being can be spoken of and it can be the object of my thought. But that which I can think about and speak of can be, "for it is the same thing that can be thought and that can be." But if "It" *can* be, then it *is*. Why? Because if it could be and yet were not, then it would be nothing. Now, nothing cannot be the object of speech or thought, for to speak about nothing is not to speak, and to think about nothing is the same as not thinking at all. Besides, if it merely *could be*, then, paradoxically, it could never come to be, for it would have to come out of nothing, and out of nothing comes nothing and not something. Being, then, Reality, "It" was not first possible, i.e. nothing, and then existent: it was always existent—more accurately, "It is."

Why do we say "more accurately, It is?" For this reason: If something comes into being, it must arise either out of being or out of not-being. If it arises out of being, then there is no real arising, no coming-to-be; for if it comes out of being, it already is. If, however, it arises out of not-being, then not-being must be already something, in order for being to be able to arise out of it. But this is a contradiction. Being therefore, "It" arises neither out of being nor out of not-being: it never came into being, but simply *is*. And as this must apply to all being, nothing ever becomes. For if anything ever becomes, however trifling, the same difficulty always recurs: does it come out of being or out of not-being? If the former, then it already is; if the latter, then you fall into a contradiction, since not-being is nothing and cannot be the source of being. Change, therefore, becoming and movement are impossible. Accordingly "It is." "One path only is left for us to speak of, namely, that *It is*. In this path are very many tokens that what is, is uncreated and indestructible, for it is complete, immovable and without end."[1]

Why does Parmenides say that "It" is complete, i.e. one Reality, which cannot be added to? Because if it is not one but divided, then it must be divided by something other than itself. But Being cannot be divided by something other than itself, for besides being there is nothing. Nor can anything be added to it, since anything that was added to being would itself be being. Similarly, it is immovable and continuous, for all movement and change, forms of becoming, are excluded.

Now, of what nature is this "It," Being, according to Parmenides? That Parmenides regarded Being as material, seems to be clearly indicated by his assertion that Being, the One, is finite. Infinite for him must have meant indeterminate and indefinite, and Being, as the Real, cannot be indefinite or indeterminate, cannot change, cannot be conceived as expanding into empty space: it must be definite, determinate, complete. It is temporarily infinite, as having neither beginning nor end, but it is spatially finite. Moreover, it is equally real in all directions, and so is spherical in shape, "equally poised from the centre in every direction: for it cannot be greater or smaller in one place than in another."[2] Now, how could Parmenides possibly think of Being as spherical, unless he thought of it as material? It would seem, then, that Burnet is right when he aptly says: "Parmenides is

[1] Frag. 8.   [2] Frag. 8.

not, as some have said, 'the father of idealism'; on the contrary, all materialism depends on his view of reality."[1] Professor Stace has to admit that "Parmenides, Melissus and the Eleatics generally did regard Being as, in some sense, material"; but he still tries to make out that Parmenides was an idealist in that he held the "cardinal thesis of idealism," "that the absolute reality, of which the world is a manifestation, consists in thought, in concepts."[2] It is perfectly true that the Being of Parmenides can be grasped only by thought, but so can the reality of Thales or Anaximenes be grasped only by thought, in concepts. But to equate "being grasped in thought" with "being thought" is surely a confusion.

As an historical fact, then, it would seem that Parmenides was a materialist and nothing else. However, that does not prevent there being an unreconciled contradiction in Parmenides' philosophy, as affirmed by Professor Stace,[3] so that, though a materialist, his thought contains also the germs of idealism, or would at any rate form the *point de départ* for idealism. On the one hand Parmenides asserted the unchangeability of Being, and, in so far as he conceived of Being as material, he asserted the indestructibility of matter. Empedocles and Democritus adopted this position and used it in their atomistic doctrine. But while Parmenides felt himself compelled to dismiss change and becoming as illusion, thus adopting the very opposite position to that of Heraclitus, Democritus could not reject what appears to be an inescapable fact of experience, which needs more explanation than a curt dismissal. Democritus, therefore, while adopting Parmenides' thesis that being can neither arise nor pass away— the indestructibility of matter—interpreted change as due to the aggregation and separation of indestructible particles of matter. On the other hand, it is an historical fact that Plato seized on the thesis of Parmenides concerning the unchangeability of Being, and identified the abiding being with the subsistent and objective Idea. To that extent, therefore, Parmenides may be called the father of idealism, in that the first great idealist adopted a cardinal tenet of Parmenides and interpreted it from an idealistic standpoint. Moreover, Plato made great use of Parmenides' distinction between the world of reason and the world of sense or appearance. But if in that historical sense Parmenides may rightly be described as the father of idealism, through his undoubted influence on Plato, it must be understood at the same

[1] E.G.P., p. 182.   [2] Crit. Hist., pp. 47 and 48.   [3] Crit. Hist., pp. 49-52.

time that Parmenides himself taught a materialistic doctrine, and that materialists like Democritus were his legitimate children.

Heraclitus, in his theory of the πάντα ῥεῖ, laid stress on *Becoming*. As we have seen, he did not assert Becoming to the total exclusion of Being, saying that there is becoming, but nothing which becomes. He affirmed the existence of the One— Fire, but held that change, becoming, tension, are essential to the existence of the One. Parmenides, on the other hand, asserted Being even to the exclusion of Becoming, affirming that change and movement are illusory. Sense tells us that there is change, but truth is to be sought, not in sense, but in reason and thought. We have, therefore, two tendencies exemplified in these two philosophers, the tendency to emphasise Becoming and the tendency to emphasise Being. Plato attempted a synthesis of the two, a combination of what is true in each. He adopts Parmenides' distinction between thought and sense, and declares that sense-objects, the objects of sense-perception, are not the objects of true knowledge, for they do not possess the necessary stability, being subject to the Heraclitean flux. The objects of true knowledge are stable and eternal, like the Being of Parmenides; but they are not material, like the Being of Parmenides. They are, on the contrary, ideal, subsistent and immaterial Forms, hierarchically arranged and culminating in the Form of the Good.

The synthesis may be said to have been worked out further by Aristotle. Being, in the sense of ultimate and immaterial Reality, God, is changeless, subsistent Thought, νόησις νοήσεως. As to material being, Aristotle agrees with Heraclitus that it is subject to change, and rejects the position of Parmenides; but Aristotle accounts better than Heraclitus did for the relative stability in things by making Plato's Forms or Ideas concrete, formal principles in the objects of this world. Again, Aristotle solves the dilemma of Parmenides by emphasising the notion of potentiality. He points out that it is no contradiction to say that a thing is X actually but Y potentially. It *is* X, but is going to be Y in the future in virtue of a potentiality, which is not simply nothing, yet is not actual being. Being therefore arises, not out of not-being nor out of being precisely as being *actu*, but out of being considered as being *potentia*, δυνάμει. Of the second part of the poem of Parmenides, *The Way of Belief*, it is unnecessary to say anything, but it is as well to say a few words concerning Melissus, as he supplemented the thought of his master, Parmenides.

Parmenides had declared that Being, the One, is spatially finite; but Melissus, the Samian disciple of Parmenides, would not accept this doctrine. If Being is finite, then beyond being there must be nothing: being must be bounded or limited by nothing. But if being is limited by nothing, it must be infinite and not finite. There cannot be a void outside being, "for what is empty is nothing. What is nothing cannot be."[1]

Aristotle tells us that the One of Melissus was conceived as material.[2] Now, Simplicius quotes a fragment to prove that Melissus did *not* look upon the One as corporeal, but as incorporeal. "Now, if it were to exist, it must needs to be one; but if it is one, it cannot have body; for if it had body, it would have parts, and would no longer be one."[3] The explanation seems to be indicated by the fact that Melissus is speaking of an hypothetical case. Burnet, following Zeller, points out the similarity of the fragment to an argument of Zeno, in which Zeno is saying that if the ultimate units of the Pythagoreans existed, then each would have parts and would not be one. We may suppose, therefore, that Melissus, too, is speaking of the doctrine of the Pythagoreans, is trying to disprove the existence of their ultimate units, and is not talking of the Parmenidean One at all.

[1] Frag. 7.   [2] *Metaph.*, 986 b 18–21.   [3] Frag. 9.   (Simplic. *Phys.*, 109, 34).

CHAPTER VII

THE DIALECTIC OF ZENO

ZENO is well known as the author of several ingenious arguments to prove the impossibility of motion, such as the riddle of Achilles and the tortoise; arguments which may tend to further the opinion that Zeno was no more than a clever riddler who delighted in using his wits in order to puzzle those who were less clever than himself. But in reality Zeno was not concerned simply to display his cleverness—though clever he undoubtedly was—but had a serious purpose in view. For the understanding of Zeno and the appreciation of his conundrums, it is therefore essential to grasp the character of this purpose, otherwise there is danger of altogether misapprehending his position and aim.

Zeno of Elea, born probably about 489 B.C., was a disciple of Parmenides, and it is from this point of view that he is to be understood. His arguments are not simply witty toys, but are calculated to prove the position of the Master. Parmenides had combated pluralism, and had declared change and motion to be illusion. Since plurality and motion seem to be such evident data of our sense-experience, this bold position was naturally such as to induce a certain amount of ridicule. Zeno, a firm adherent of the theory of Parmenides, endeavours to prove it, or at least to demonstrate that it is by no means ridiculous, by the expedient of showing that the pluralism of the Pythagoreans is involved in insoluble difficulties, and that change and motion are impossible even on their pluralistic hypothesis. The arguments of Zeno then are meant to refute the Pythagorean opponents of Parmenides by a series of clever *reductiones ad absurdum*. Plato makes this quite clear in the *Parmenides*, when he indicates the purpose of Zeno's (lost) book. "The truth is that these writings were meant to be some protection to the arguments of Parmenides against those who attack him and show the many ridiculous and contradictory results which they suppose to follow from the affirmation of the one. My writing is an answer to the partisans of the many and it returns their attack with interest, with a view to showing that the hypothesis of the many, if examined sufficiently in detail, leads to even more ridiculous results than the hypothesis of the

One."[1] And Proclus informs us that "Zeno composed forty proofs to demonstrate that being is one, thinking it a good thing to come to the help of his master."[2]

1. Proofs against Pythagorean Pluralism

1. Let us suppose with the Pythagoreans that Reality is made up of units. These units are either with magnitude or without magnitude. If the former, then a line for example, as made up of units possessed of magnitude, will be infinitely divisible, since, however far you divide, the units will still have magnitude and so be divisible. But in this case the line will be made up of an infinite number of units, each of which is possessed of magnitude. The line, then, must be infinitely great, as composed of an infinite number of bodies. Everything in the world, then, must be infinitely great, and *a fortiori* the world itself must be infinitely great. Suppose, on the other hand, that the units are without magnitude. In this case the whole universe will also be without magnitude, since, however many units you add together, if none of them has any magnitude, then the whole collection of them will also be without magnitude. But if the universe is without any magnitude, it must be infinitely small. Indeed, everything in the universe must be infinitely small.

The Pythagoreans are thus faced with this dilemma. Either everything in the universe is infinitely great, or everything in the universe is infinitely small. The conclusion which Zeno wishes us to draw from this argument is, of course, that the supposition from which the dilemma flows is an absurd supposition, namely, that the universe and everything in it are composed of units. If the Pythagoreans think that the hypothesis of the One is absurd and leads to ridiculous conclusions, it has now been shown that the contrary hypothesis, that of the many, is productive of equally ridiculous conclusions.[3]

2. If there is a many, then we ought to be able to say *how many* there are. At least, they should be numerable; if they are not numerable, how can they exist? On the other hand, they cannot possibly be numerable, but must be infinite. Why? Because between any two assigned units there will always be other units, just as a line is infinitely divisible. But it is absurd to say that the many are finite in number and infinite in number at the same time.[4]

[1] *Parmen.*, 128 b. [2] Procl., *in Parmen.*, 694, 23 (D. 29 A 15).
[3] Frags. 1, 2. [4] Frag. 3.

3. Does a bushel of corn make a noise when it falls to the ground? Clearly. But what of a grain of corn, or the thousandth part of a grain of corn? It makes no noise. But the bushel of corn is composed only of the grains of corn or of the parts of the grains of corn. If, then, the parts make no sound when they fall, how can the whole make a sound, when the whole is composed only of the parts?[1]

II. *Arguments against the Pythagorean Doctrine of Space*

Parmenides denied the existence of the void or empty space, and Zeno tries to support this denial by reducing the opposite view to absurdity. Suppose for a moment that there is a space in which things are. If it is nothing, then things cannot be in it. If, however, it is something, it will itself be in space, and *that* space will itself be in space, and so on indefinitely. But this is an absurdity. Things, therefore, are not in space or in an empty void, and Parmenides was quite right to deny the existence of a void.[2]

III. *Arguments Concerning Motion*

The most celebrated arguments of Zeno are those concerning motion. It should be remembered that what Zeno is attempting to show is this: that motion, which Parmenides denied, is equally impossible on the pluralistic theory of the Pythagoreans.

1. Let us suppose that you want to cross a stadium or race-course. In order to do so, you would have to traverse an infinite number of points—on the Pythagorean hypothesis, that is to say. Moreover, you would have to travel the distance in finite time, if you wanted to get to the other side at all. But how can you traverse an infinite number of points, and so an infinite distance, in a finite time? We must conclude that you *cannot* cross the stadium. Indeed, we must conclude that no object can traverse any distance whatsoever (for the same difficulty always recurs), and that all motion is consequently impossible.[3]

2. Let us suppose that Achilles and a tortoise are going to have a race. Since Achilles is a sportsman, he gives the tortoise a start. Now, by the time that Achilles has reached the place from which the tortoise started, the latter has again advanced to

---

[1] Arist., *Phys.*, H, 5,250 a 19; Simplic., 1108, 18 (D. 29 A 29).
[2] Arist., *Phys.*, Δ 3,210 b 22; 1,209 a 23. Eudem., *Phys.*, Frag. 42 (D. 29 A 24)
[3] Arist., *Phys.*, Z 9,239 b 9; 2,233 a 21; *Top.*, Θ 8,160 b 7.

another point; and when Achilles reaches *that* point, then the tortoise will have advanced still another distance, even if very short. Thus Achilles is always coming nearer to the tortoise, but never actually overtakes it—and never *can* do so, on the supposition that a line is made up of an infinite number of points, for then Achilles would have to traverse an infinite distance. On the Pythagorean hypothesis, then, Achilles will never catch up the tortoise; and so, although they assert the reality of motion, they make it impossible on their own doctrine. For it follows that the slower moves as fast as the faster.[1]

3. Suppose a moving arrow. According to the Pythagorean theory the arrow should occupy a given position in space. But to occupy a given position in space is to be at rest. Therefore the flying arrow is at rest, which is a contradiction.[2]

4. The fourth argument of Zeno, which we know from Aristotle[3] is, as Sir David Ross says, "very difficult to follow, partly owing to use of ambiguous language by Aristotle, partly owing to doubts as to the readings."[4] We have to represent to ourselves three sets of bodies on a stadium or race-course. One set is stationary, the other two are moving in opposite directions to one another with equal velocity.

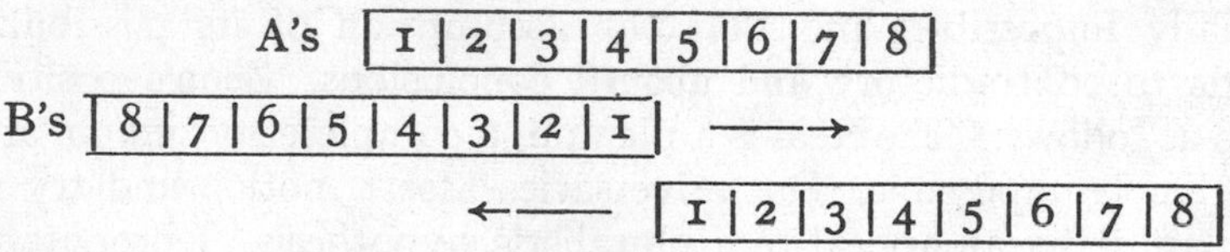

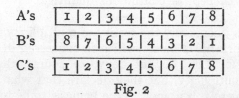

Fig. 1

The A's are stationary; the B's and C's are moving in opposite directions with the same velocity. They will come to occupy the following position:

A's | 1 | 2 | 3 | 4 | 5 | 6 | 7 | 8 |

B's | 8 | 7 | 6 | 5 | 4 | 3 | 2 | 1 |

C's | 1 | 2 | 3 | 4 | 5 | 6 | 7 | 8 |

Fig. 2

[1] Arist., *Phys.*, Z 9,239 b 14. [2] Arist., *Phys.*, Z 9,239 b 30.
[3] Arist., *Phys.*, Z 9,239 b 33. [4] Ross, *Physics*, p. 660.

In attaining this second position the front of B1 has passed four of the A's, while the front of C1 has passed all the B's. If a unit of length is passed in a unit of time, then the front of B1 has taken half the time taken by the front of C1 in order to reach the position of Fig. 2. On the other hand the front of B1 has passed all the C's, just as the front of C1 has passed all the B's. The time of their passage must then be *equal*. We are left then with the absurd conclusion that the half of a certain time is equal to the whole of that time.

———

How are we to interpret these arguments of Zeno? It is important not to let oneself think: "These are mere sophistries on the part of Zeno. They are ingenious tricks, but they err by supposing that a line is composed of points and time of discrete moments." It may be that the solution of the riddles is to be found in showing that the line and time are continuous and not discrete; but, then, Zeno was not concerned to hold that they are discrete. On the contrary, he is concerned to show the absurd consequences which flow from supposing that they are discrete. Zeno, as a disciple of Parmenides, believed that motion is an illusion and is impossible, but in the foregoing arguments his aim is to prove that even on the pluralistic hypothesis motion is equally impossible, and that the assumption of its possibility leads to contradictory and absurd conclusions. Zeno's position was as follows: "The Real is a plenum, a complete continuum and motion is impossible. Our adversaries assert motion and try to explain it by an appeal to a pluralistic hypothesis. I propose to show that this hypothesis does nothing to explain motion, but only lands one in absurdities." Zeno thus reduced the hypothesis of his adversaries to absurdity, and the real result of his dialectic was not so much to establish Parmenidean monism (which is exposed to insuperable objections), as to show the necessity of admitting the concept of continuous quantity.

———

The Eleatics, then, deny the reality of multiplicity and motion. There is one principle, Being, which is conceived of as material and motionless. They do not deny, of course, that we *sense* motion and multiplicity, but they declare that what we sense is illusion: it is mere appearance. True being is to be found, not by sense but by thought, and thought shows that there can be no plurality, no movement, no change.

The Eleatics thus attempt, as the earlier Greek philosophers attempted before them, to discover the one principle of the world. The world, however, as it presents itself to us, is clearly a pluralistic world. The question is, therefore, how to reconcile the one principle with the plurality and change which we find in the world, i.e. the problem of the One and the Many, which Heraclitus had tried to solve in a philosophy that professed to do justice to both elements through a doctrine of Unity in Diversity, Identity in Difference. The Pythagoreans asserted plurality to the practical exclusion of the One—there are many ones; the Eleatics asserted the One to the exclusion of the many. But if you cling to the plurality which is suggested by sense-experience, then you must also admit change; and if you admit change of one thing into another, you cannot avoid the recurring problem as to the character of the common element in the things which change. If, on the other hand, you start with the doctrine of the One, you must—unless you are going to adopt a one-sided position like that of the Eleatics, which cannot last—deduce plurality from the One, or at least show how the plurality which we observe in the world is consistent with the One. In other words, justice must be done to both factors—the One and the Many, Stability and Change. The one-sided doctrine of Parmenides was unacceptable, as also was the one-sided doctrine of the Pythagoreans. Yet the philosophy of Heraclitus was also unsatisfactory. Apart from the fact that it hardly accounted sufficiently for the stable element in things, it was bound up with materialistic monism. Ultimately it was bound to be suggested that the highest and truest being is immaterial. Meanwhile it is not surprising to find what Zeller calls "compromise-systems," trying to weld together the thought of their predecessors.

Note on "Pantheism" in pre-Socratic Greek Philosophy

(i) If a Pantheist is a man who has a subjective religious attitude towards the universe, which latter he identifies with God, then the Pre-Socratics are scarcely to be called pantheists. That Heraclitus speaks of the One as Zeus is true, but it does not appear that he adopted any religious attitude towards the One—Fire.

(ii) If a pantheist is a man who, while denying a Transcendent Principle of the universe, makes the universe to be ultimately *Thought* (unlike the materialist, who makes it Matter alone), then the Pre-Socratics again scarcely merit the name of pantheists, for they conceive or speak of the One in material terms (though it is true that the spirit-matter distinction had not yet been so clearly conceived that they could deny it in the way that the modern materialistic monist denies it).

(iii) In any case the One, the universe, could not be identified with the Greek gods. It has been remarked (by Schelling) that there is no supernatural in Homer, for the Homeric god is part of nature. This remark has its application in the present question. The Greek god was finite and anthropomorphically conceived; he could not possibly be identified with the One, nor would it occur to anyone to do so literally. The *name* of a god might be sometimes transferred to the One, e.g. Zeus, but the one is not to be thought of as identified with the "actual" Zeus of legend and mythology. The suggestion may be that the One is the only "god" there is, and that the Olympian deities are anthropomorphic fables; but even then it seems very uncertain if the philosopher ever *worshipped* the One. Stoics might with justice be called pantheists; but, as far as the early Pre-Socratics are concerned, it seems decidedly preferable to call them monists, rather than pantheists.

CHAPTER VIII

EMPEDOCLES OF AKRAGAS

EMPEDOCLES was a citizen of Akragas, or Agrigentum, in Sicily. His dates cannot be fixed, but it appears that he visited the city of Thurii shortly after its foundation in 444–43 B.C. He took part in the politics of his native city, and seems to have been the leader of the democratic party there. Stories were later circulated about Empedocles' activities as magician and wonder-worker, and there is a story that he was expelled from the Pythagorean Order for "stealing discourses."[1] Apart from thaumaturgic activities, Empedocles contributed to the growth of medicine proper. The death of the philosopher has been made the subject of several entertaining fables, the best known being that he jumped into the crater of Etna in order to make people think that he had gone up to heaven and esteem him as a god. Unfortunately, he left one of his slippers on the brink of the volcano, and, as he used to wear slippers with brazen soles, it was easily recognised.[2] Diogenes, however, who recounts this story, also informs us that "Timaeus contradicts all these stories, saying expressly that he departed into Peloponnesus, and never returned at all, on which account the manner of his death is uncertain."[3] Empedocles, like Parmenides and unlike the other Greek philosophers, expressed his philosophical ideas in poetical writings, more or less extensive fragments of which have come down to us.

Empedocles does not so much produce a new philosophy, as endeavour to weld together and reconcile the thought of his predecessors. Parmenides had held that Being is, and that being is material. Empedocles not only adopted this position, but also the fundamental thought of Parmenides, that being cannot arise or pass away, for being cannot arise from not-being, nor can being pass into not-being. Matter, then, is without beginning and without end; it is indestructible. "Fools!—for they have no far-reaching thoughts—who deem that what before was not comes into being, or that aught can perish and be utterly destroyed. For it cannot be that aught can arise from what in no way is, and

---

[1] Diog. Laërt., 8, 54.   [2] Diog. Laërt., 8, 69.
[3] Diog. Laërt., 8, 71. (The great Germanic classical poet Hölderlin wrote a poem on the legendary death of Empedocles, also an unfinished poetic play.)

it is impossible and unheard of that what *is* should perish, for it
will always *be*, wherever one may keep putting it."[1] And again:
"And in the All there is naught empty and naught too full," and
"In the All there is naught empty. Whence, then, could aught
come to increase it?"[2]

So far, then, Empedocles agrees with Parmenides. But on the
other hand, change is a fact which cannot be denied, and the
dismissal of change as illusory could not long be maintained. It
remained, then, to find a way of reconciling the fact of the
existence of change and motion with the principle of Parmenides,
that Being—which, be it remembered, is material according to
Parmenides—neither comes into being nor passes away. This
reconciliation Empedocles tried to effect by means of the principle
that objects as wholes begin to be and cease to be—as experience
shows they do—but that they are composed of material particles,
which are themselves indestructible. There is "only a mingling
and interchange of what has been mingled. Substance (Φυσις) is
but a name given to these things by men."[3]   P hy $s

Now, though Thales had believed all things to be ultimately
water and Anaximenes air, they believed that one kind of matter
can become another kind of matter, at least in the sense that,
e.g., water becomes earth and air becomes fire. Empedocles, however, interpreting Parmenides' principle of the unchangeability
of being in his own way, held that one kind of matter cannot
become another kind of matter, but that there are fundamental
and eternal kinds of matter or elements—earth, air, fire and
water. The familiar classification of the four elements was therefore invented by Empedocles, though he speaks of them, not as
elements but as "the roots of all."[4] Earth cannot become water,
nor water, earth: the four kinds of matter are unchangeable and
ultimate particles, which form the concrete objects of the world
by their mingling. So objects come into being through the
mingling of the elements, and they cease to be through the
separation of the elements: but the elements themselves neither
come into being nor pass away, but remain ever unchanged.
Empedocles, therefore, saw the only possible way of reconciling
the materialistic position of Parmenides with the evident fact of
change, the way of postulating a multiplicity of ultimate material
particles, and may thus be called a mediator between the system
of Parmenides and the evidence of the senses.

[1] Frag. 11.   [2] Frag. 14.   [3] Frag. 8.   [4] Frag. 7 (ἀγένητα i.e. στοιχεῖα).

Now the Ionian philosophers had failed to explain the process of Nature. If everything is composed of air, as Anaximenes thought, how do the objects of our experience come into being? What force is responsible for the cyclical process of Nature? Anaximenes assumed that air transforms itself into other kinds of matter through its own inherent power; but Empedocles saw that it is necessary to postulate active forces. These forces he found in Love and Hate, or Harmony and Discord. In spite of their names, however, the forces are conceived by Empedocles as physical and material forces, Love or Attraction bringing the particles of the four elements together and building up, Strife or Hate separating the particles and causing the cessation of the being of objects.

According to Empedocles the world-process is circular, in the sense that there are periodic world-cycles. At the commencement of a cycle the elements are all mixed up together—not separated out to form concrete objects as we know them—a general mixture of particles of earth, air, fire and water. In this primary stage of the process Love is the governing principle, and the whole is called a "blessed god." Hate, however, is round about the sphere, and when Hate penetrates within the sphere the process of separation, the disuniting of the particles, is begun. Ultimately the separation becomes complete: all the water particles are gathered together, all the fire particles, and so on. Hate reigns supreme, Love having been driven out. Yet Love in turn begins its work, and so causes gradual mingling and uniting of the various elements, this process going on until the element-particles are mixed up together as they were in the beginning. It is then the turn of Hate to start its operations anew. And so the process continues, without first beginning and without last end.[1]

As to the world as we know it, this stands at a stage half-way between the primary sphere and the stage of total separation of the elements: Hate is gradually penetrating the sphere and driving out Love as it does so. As our earth began to be formed out of the sphere, air was the first element to be separated off; this was followed by fire, and then came earth. Water is squeezed out by the rapidity with which the world rotates. The primary sphere, i.e. primary in the cyclical process, not primary in an absolute sense, is described in what appear to us somewhat

[1] This theme of an unending cyclic process reappears in the philosophy of Nietzsche under the name of the Eternal Recurrence.

amusing terms. "There" (i.e. in the sphere) "are distinguished
neither the swift limbs of the sun; no, nor the shaggy earth in its
might, nor the sea—so fast was the god bound in the close covering
of Harmony, spherical and round, rejoicing in his circular solitude."[1] The activity of Love and Strife is illustrated in various
ways. "This" (i.e. the contest between them) "is manifest in the
mass of mortal limbs. At one time all the limbs that are the
body's portion are brought together by Love in blooming life's
high season; at another, severed by cruel Strife, they wander each
alone by the breakers of life's sea. It is the same with plants and
the fish that make their homes in the waters, with the beasts that
have their lairs on the hills and the seabirds that sail on wings."[2]

The doctrine of transmigration of souls is taught by Empedocles
in the book of the Purifications. He even declares: "For I have
already been in the past a boy and a girl, a shrub and a bird and
a fish which lives in the sea."[3] It can scarcely be said, however,
that this doctrine fits in well with the cosmological system of
Empedocles, since, if all things are composed of material particles
which separate at death, and if "the blood round the heart is the
thought of men,"[4] there is little room left for immortality. But
Empedocles may not have realised the discrepancy between his
philosophical and religious theories. (Among the latter are
certainly some very Pythagorean-sounding prescriptions, such as:
"Wretches, utter wretches, keep your hands from beans!")[5]

Aristotle remarks that Empedocles made no distinction
between thought and perception. His actual theory of vision is
given by Theophrastus, a theory used by Plato in the *Timaeus*.[6]
In sense-perception there is a meeting between an element in us
and a similar element outside us. All things are constantly giving
off effluences, and when the pores of the sense-organs are the right
size, then these effluences enter in and perception takes place.
In the case of vision, for example, effluences come to the eyes
from things; while, on the other hand, the fire from inside the eye
(the eye is composed of fire and water, the fire being sheltered
from the water by membranes provided with very small pores,
which prevent water getting through, but allow fire to get out)
goes out to meet the object, the two factors together producing
sight.

[1] Frag. 27. [2] Frag. 20. [3] Frag. 117. [4] Frag. 105. [5] Frag. 141.
[6] Arist., *De An.*, 427 a 21. Theoph., *de sensu*, 1 ff. Plat., *Tim.*, cf. 67 c ff.
(D. 31 A 86).

In conclusion, we may remind ourselves that Empedocles tried to reconcile the thesis of Parmenides, that being can neither come to be nor pass away, with the evident fact of change by postulating ultimate particles of the four elements, the mingling of which forms the concrete objects of this world and the separation of which constitutes the passing-away of such objects. He failed, however, to explain how the material cyclic process of Nature takes place, but had recourse to mythological forces, Love and Hate. It was left to Anaxagoras to introduce the concept of Mind as the original cause of the world-process.

CHAPTER IX

THE ADVANCE OF ANAXAGORAS

ANAXAGORAS was born at Clazomenae in Asia Minor about 500 B.C., and, although a Greek, he was doubtless a Persian citizen, for Clazomenae had been reduced after the suppression of the Ionian Revolt; and it may even be said that he came to Athens in the Persian Army. If this is so, it would certainly explain why he came to Athens in the year of Salamis, 480/79 B.C. He was the first philosopher to settle in the city, which was later to become such a flourishing centre of philosophic study.[1]

From Plato[2] we learn that the young Pericles was a pupil of Anaxagoras, an association which afterwards got the philosopher into trouble, for after he had resided about thirty years in the city, Anaxagoras was brought to trial by the political opponents of Pericles, i.e. about 450 B.C. Diogenes tells us that the charges were those of impiety (he refers to Sotion) and Medism (referring to Satyros). As to the first charge, Plato relates, it was based on the fact that Anaxagoras taught that the sun is a red-hot stone and the moon is made of earth.[3] These charges were doubtless trumped up, mainly in order to get a hit at Pericles through Anaxagoras. (Pericles' other teacher, Damon, was ostracised.) Anaxagoras was condemned, but was got out of prison, probably by Pericles himself, and he retired to Ionia where he settled at Lampsacus, a colony of Miletus. Here he probably founded a school. The citizens erected a monument to his memory in the market-place (an altar dedicated to Mind and Truth), and the anniversary of his death was long observed as a holiday for school children, at his own request, it is said.

Anaxagoras expressed his philosophy in a book, but only fragments of this remain, and these appear to be confined to the first part of the work. We owe the preservation of the fragments we possess to Simplicius (A.D. sixth century).

.   .   .   .   .

Anaxagoras, like Empedocles, accepted the theory of Parmenides that Being neither comes into being nor passes away,

---

[1] Anax. is said to have had property at Claz. which he neglected in order to follow the theoretic life. Cf. Plato, *Hipp. M.*, 283 a.

[2] *Phaedrus*, 270 a.

[3] *Apol.*, 26 d.

but is unchangeable. "The Hellenes do not understand rightly coming into being and passing away, for nothing comes into being or passes away, but there is a mingling and a separation of things which are" (i.e. persist).[1] Both thinkers, then, are in agreement as to the indestructibility of matter, and both reconcile this theory with the evident fact of change by positing indestructible material particles, the mingling of which forms objects, the separation of which explains the passing away of objects. But Anaxagoras will not agree with Empedocles that the ultimate units are particles corresponding to the four elements—earth, air, fire and water. He teaches that everything which has parts qualitatively the same as the whole is ultimate and underived. Aristotle calls these wholes, which have qualitatively similar parts, τὰ ὁμοιομερῆ; τὸ ὁμοιομερές being opposed to τὸ ἀνομοιομερές. This distinction is not difficult to grasp if one takes an example. If we suppose that a piece of gold is cut in half, the halves are themselves gold. The parts are thus qualitatively the same as the whole, and the whole can be said to be ὁμοιομερές. If, however, a dog, a living organism, be cut in half, the halves are not themselves two dogs. The whole is in this case therefore ἀνομοιομερές. The general notion is thus clear, and it is unnecessary to confuse the issue by introducing considerations from modern scientific experiment. Some things have qualitatively similar parts, and such things are ultimate and underived (as regards *kind*, that is to say, for no given conglomeration of particles is ultimate and underived). "How can hair come from what is not hair, or flesh from what is not flesh?" asks Anaxagoras.[2] But it does not follow that everything which seems to be ὁμοιομερές is really so. Thus it is related by Aristotle that Anaxagoras did not hold Empedocles' elements—earth, air, fire and water—to be really ultimate; on the contrary, they are mixtures composed of many qualitatively different particles.[3]

In the beginning, particles—there is no indivisible particle, according to Anaxagoras—of all kinds were mingled together. "All things were together, infinite both in number and in smallness; for the small too was infinite. And, when all things were together, none of them could be distinguished for their smallness."[4] "All things are in the whole." The objects of experience arise, when ultimate particles have been so brought together that in the resulting object particles of a certain kind predominate. Thus in the original mixture particles of gold were scattered about and mixed with all sorts of other particles; but when particles of gold have been so brought together—with other particles—that the resultant visible object consists predominantly of gold-particles, we have the gold of our experience. Why do we say "with other particles"? Because in concrete objects of experience there are, according to Anaxagoras, particles of *all* things; yet they are combined in such a way that one kind of particle predominates and from this fact the whole object gets its denomination. Anaxagoras held the doctrine that "in everything there is a portion of everything,"[1] apparently because he did not see how he could otherwise explain the fact of change. For instance, if grass becomes flesh, there must have been particles of flesh in the grass (for how can "flesh" come "from what is not flesh"?), while on the other hand in the grass the grass-particles must predominate. Grass, therefore, consists predominantly of grass, but it also contains other kinds of particles, for "in everything there is a portion of everything," and "the things that are in one world are not divided nor cut off from one another with a hatchet, neither the warm from the cold nor the cold from the warm."[2] In this way Anaxagoras sought to maintain the Parmenidean doctrine concerning being, while at the same time adopting a realist attitude towards change, not dismissing it as an illusion of the senses but accepting it as a fact, and then trying to reconcile it with the Eleatic theory of being. Later on Aristotle would attempt to solve the difficulties raised by the doctrine of Parmenides in regard to change by means of his distinction between potency and act.

Burnet does not think that Anaxagoras considered, as the Epicureans supposed him to, "that there must be minute particles in bread and water which were like the particles of blood, flesh and bones."[3] In his opinion it was of the opposites, the warm and the cold, the dry and the moist, that everything contained a portion according to Anaxagoras. Burnet's view has certainly much to support it. We have already seen the fragment in which Anaxagoras declares that "the things that are in one world are not cut off from one another with a hatchet, neither the warm from the cold, nor the cold from the warm." Moreover, since according to Anaxagoras, there are no indivisible particles, there

---

[1] Frag. 11.   [2] Frag. 8.   [3] *G.P.*, I., pp. 77–8.

cannot be any ultimate particles in the sense of what cannot be further divided. But it would not seem to follow necessarily from the indivisibility of the particles that, in the philosopher's opinion, there were no ultimate *kinds* which could not be qualitatively resolved. And does not Anaxagoras explicitly ask how hair can come from what is not hair? In addition to this we read in fragment 4 of the mixture of all things—"of the moist and the dry, and the warm and the cold, and the bright and the dark, and of much earth that was in it, and a multitude of innumerable seeds in no way like each other. For none of the other things either is like any other. And these things being so, we must hold that all things are in the whole." This fragment scarcely gives the impression that the "opposites" stand in any peculiar position of privilege. While admitting, therefore, that Burnet's view has much to be said for it, we prefer the interpretation already given in the text.[1]

So far Anaxagoras' philosophy is a variant from Empedocles' interpretation and adaptation of Parmenides, and offers no particularly valuable features. But when we come to the question of the power or force that is responsible for the forming of things out of the first mass, we arrive at the peculiar contribution of Anaxagoras to philosophy. Empedocles had attributed motion in the universe to the two physical forces of Love and Strife, but Anaxagoras introduces instead the principle of Nous or Mind. 'With Anaxagoras a light, if still a weak one, begins to dawn, because the understanding is now recognised as the principle."[2] "Nous," says Anaxagoras, "has power over all things that have life, both greater and smaller. And Nous had power over the whole revolution, so that it began to revolve at the start. . . . And Nous set in order all things that were to be, and all things that were and are now and that will be, and this revolution in which now revolve the stars and the sun and the moon and the air and the aether which are separated off. And the revolution itself caused the separating off, and the dense is separated off from the rare, the warm from the cold, the bright from the dark, and the dry from the moist. And there are many portions in many things. But no thing is altogether separated off from anything else except Nous. And all Nous is alike, both the greater and the smaller; but nothing else is like anything else, but each

[1] Cf. Zeller, *Outlines*, p. 62; Stace, *Crit. Hist.*, pp. 95 ff.; Covotti, *I Presocratici*, ch. 21.
[2] Hegel, *Hist. Phil.*, I, p. 319.

single thing is and was most manifestly those things of which there are most in it."[1]

Nous "is infinite and self-ruled, and is mixed with nothing, but is alone, itself by itself."[2] How then did Anaxagoras conceive of Nous? He calls it "the finest of all things and the purest, and it has all knowledge about everything and the greatest power . . ." He also speaks of Nous being "there where everything else is, in the surrounding mass."[3] The philosopher thus speaks of Nous or Mind in material terms as being "the thinnest of all things," and as occupying space. On the strength of this Burnet declares that Anaxagoras never rose above the conception of a corporeal principle. He made Nous purer than other material things, but never reached the idea of an immaterial or incorporeal thing. Zeller will not allow this, and Stace points out how "all philosophy labours under the difficulty of having to express non-sensuous thought in language which has been evolved for the purpose of expressing sensuous ideas."[4] If we speak of a mind as "clear" or as someone's mind as being "greater" than that of another, we are not on that account to be called materialists. That Anaxagoras conceived of Nous as occupying space is not sufficient proof that he would have declared Nous to be corporeal, had he ever conceived the notion of a sharp distinction between mind and matter. The non-spatiality of the mind is a later conception. Probably the most satisfactory interpretation is that Anaxagoras, in his concept of the spiritual, did not succeed in grasping clearly the radical difference between the spiritual and the corporeal. But that is not the same as saying that he was a *dogmatic* materialist. On the contrary, he first introduces a spiritual and intellectual principle, though he fails to understand fully the essential difference between that principle and the matter which it forms or sets in motion.

Nous is present in all living things, men, animals and plants, and is the same in all. Differences between these objects are due, then, not to essential differences between their souls, but to differences between their bodies, which facilitate or handicap the fuller working of Nous. (Anaxagoras, however, does not explain the human consciousness of independent selfhood.)

Nous is not to be thought of as *creating* matter. Matter is eternal, and the function of Nous seems to be to set the rotatory movement or vortex going in part of the mixed mass, the action

---

[1] Frag. 12.   [2] Frag. 12.   [3] Frag. 14.   [4] *Crit. Hist.*, p. 99.

of the vortex itself, as it spreads, accounting for the subsequent motion. Thus Aristotle, who says in the *Metaphysics* that Anaxagoras "stood out like a sober man from the random talkers that had preceded him,"[1] also says that "Anaxagoras uses Mind as a *deus ex machina* to account for the formation of the world; and whenever he is at a loss to explain why anything necessarily is, he drags it in. But in other cases he makes anything rather than Mind the cause."[2] We can easily understand, then, the disappointment of Socrates who, thinking that he had come upon an entirely new approach when he discovered Anaxagoras, found "my extravagant expectations were all dashed to the ground when I went on and found that the man made no use of Mind at all. He ascribed no causal power whatever to it in the ordering of things, but to airs, and aethers, and waters, and a host of other strange things."[3] Nevertheless, though he failed to make full use of the principle, Anaxagoras must be credited with the introduction into Greek philosophy of a principle possessed of the greatest importance, that was to bear splendid fruit in the future.

---

[1] *Metaph.*, A 3, 984 b 15–18. [2] *Metaph.*, A 4, 985 a 18–21.
[3] *Phaedo*, 97 b 8.

CHAPTER X

THE ATOMISTS

THE founder of the Atomist School was Leucippus of Miletus. It has been maintained that Leucippus never existed,[1] but Aristotle and Theophrastus make him to be the founder of the Atomist philosophy, and we can hardly suppose that they were mistaken. It is not possible to fix his dates, but Theophrastus declares that Leucippus had been a member of the School of Parmenides, and we read in Diogenes' *Life of Leucippus* that he was a disciple of Zeno (οὗτος ἤκουσε Ζήνωνος). It appears that the *Great Diakosmos*, subsequently incorporated in the works of Democritus of Abdera, was really the work of Leucippus, and no doubt Burnet is quite right when he compares the Democritean *corpus* with the Hippocritean, and remarks that in neither case can we distinguish the authors of the various component treatises.[2] The whole *corpus* is the work of a School, and it is most unlikely that we shall ever be in a position to assign each work to its respective author. In treating of the Atomist philosophy, therefore, we cannot pretend to distinguish between what is due to Leucippus and what is due to Democritus. But since Democritus is of considerably later date and cannot with historical accuracy be classed among the Pre-Socratics, we will leave to a later chapter his doctrine of sense-perception, by which he attempted to answer Protagoras, and his theory of human conduct. Some historians of philosophy, indeed, treat of Democritus' views on these points when dealing with the Atomist philosophy in the section devoted to the Pre-Socratics, but in view of the undoubtedly later date of Democritus, it seems preferable to follow Burnet in this matter.

The Atomist philosophy is really the logical development of the philosophy of Empedocles. The latter had tried to reconcile the Parmenidean principle of the denial of the passage of being into not-being or vice versa, with the evident fact of change by postulating four elements which, mixed together in various proportions, form the objects of our experience. He did not, however, really work out his doctrine of particles, nor did he

[1] Epicurus, for instance, denied his existence, but it has been suggested that this denial was due to Epicurus' determination to claim originality.
[2] *E.G.P.*, p. 331.

72

THE ATOMISTS 73

carry the quantitative explanation of qualitative differences to its logical conclusion. The philosophy of Empedocles formed a transitional stage to the explanation of all qualitative differences by a mechanical juxtaposition of material particles in various patterns. Moreover, Empedocles' forces—Love and Strife—were metaphorical powers, which would have to be eliminated in a thorough-going mechanical philosophy. The final step to complete mechanism was attempted by the Atomists.

According to Leucippus and Democritus there are an infinite number of indivisible units, which are called atoms. These are imperceptible, since they are too small to be perceived by the senses . The atoms differ in size and shape, but have no quality save that of solidity or impenetrability. Infinite in number, they move in the void. (Parmenides had denied the reality of space. The Pythagoreans had admitted a void to keep their units apart, but they identified it with the atmospheric air, which Empedocles showed to be corporeal. Leucippus, however, affirmed at the same time the non-reality of space and its existence, meaning by non-reality, non-corporeity. This position is expressed by saying that "what is not" is just as much real as "what is." Space, then, or the void, is not corporeal, but it is as real as body.) The later Epicureans held that the atoms all move downwards in the void through the force of *weight*, probably influenced by Aristotle's idea of absolute weight and lightness. (Aristotle says that none of his predecessors had held this notion.) Now Aëtius expressly says that while Democritus ascribed size and shape to the atoms, he did not ascribe to them weight, but that Epicurus added weight in order to account for the movement of the atoms.[1] Cicero relates the same, and also declares that according to Democritus there was no "top" or "bottom" or "middle" in the void.[2] If this is what Democritus held, then he was of course quite right, for there is no absolute up or down; but how in this case did he conceive the motion of the atoms? In the *De Anima*[3] Aristotle attributes to Democritus a comparison between the motions of the atoms of the soul and the motes in a sunbeam, which dart hither and thither in all directions, even when there is no wind. It may be that this was also the Democritean view of the original motion of the atoms.

However, in whatever way the atoms originally moved in the

[1] Aët., i, 3, 18 and 12, 6 (D. 68 A 47).
[2] De Fato, 20, 46 and De Fin., i, 6, 17 (D. 68 A 47 and 56).
[3] De An., A, 2, 403 b 28 ff.

void, at some point of time collisions between atoms occurred, those of irregular shape becoming entangled with one another and forming groups of atoms. In this way the vortex (Anaxagoras) is set up, and a world is in process of formation. Whereas Anaxagoras thought that the larger bodies would be driven farthest from the centre, Leucippus said the opposite, believing, wrongly, that in an eddy of wind or water the larger bodies tend towards the centre. Another effect of the movement in the void is that atoms which are alike in size and shape are brought together as a sieve brings together the grains of millet, wheat and barley, or the waves of the sea heap up together long stones with long and round with round. In this way are formed the four "elements"—fire, air, earth and water. Thus innumerable worlds arise from the collisions among the infinite atoms moving in the void.

It is at once noticeable that neither Empedocles' forces, Love and Strife, nor the Nous of Anaxagoras appear in the Atomist philosophy: Leucippus evidently did not consider any moving force to be a necessary hypothesis. In the beginning existed atoms in the void, and that was all: from that beginning arose the world of our experience, and no external Power or moving Force is assumed as a necessary cause for the primal motion. Apparently the early cosmologists did not think of motion as requiring any explanation, and in the Atomist philosophy the eternal movement of the atoms is regarded as self-sufficient. Leucippus speaks of everything happening ἐκ λόγου καὶ ὑπ' ἀνάγκης[1] and this might at first sight appear inconsistent with his doctrine of the unexplained original movement of the atoms and of the collisions of the atoms. The latter, however, occur necessarily owing to the configuration of the atoms and their irregular movements, while the former, as a self-sufficient fact, did not require further explanation. To us, indeed, it may well seem strange to deny chance and yet to posit an eternal unexplained motion—Aristotle blames the Atomists for not explaining the source of motion and the kind of motion[2]—but we ought not to conclude that Leucippus meant to ascribe the motion of the atoms to *chance*: to him the eternal motion and the continuation of motion required no explanation. In our opinion, the mind boggles at such a theory and cannot rest content with Leucippus' ultimate; but it is an interesting

[1] Frag. 2 (Aët., I, 25, 4).
[2] *Phys.*, Θ i, 252 a 32; *De Caelo*, Γ 2, 300 b 8; *Metaph.*, A, 4, 985 b 19-20.

historical fact, that he himself was content with this ultimate and sought no "First Unmoved Mover."

It is to be noted that the atoms of Leucippus and Democritus are the Pythagorean monads endowed with the properties of Parmenidean being—for each is as the Parmenidean One. And inasmuch as the elements arise from the various arrangements and positions of the atoms, they may be likened to the Pythagorean "numbers," if the latter are to be regarded as patterns or "figurate numbers." This can be the only sense to be attached to Aristotle's dictum that "Leucippus and Democritus virtually make all things number too and produce them from numbers."[1]

In his detailed scheme of the world, Leucippus was somewhat reactionary, rejecting the Pythagorean view of the spherical character of the earth and returning, like Anaxagoras, to the view of Anaximenes, that the earth is like a tambourine floating in the air. But, though the details of the Atomist cosmology do not indicate any new advance, Leucippus and Democritus are noteworthy for having carried previous tendencies to their logical conclusion, producing a purely mechanical account and explanation of reality. The attempt to give a complete explanation of the world in terms of mechanical materialism has, as we all know, reappeared in a much more thorough form in the modern era under the influence of physical science, but the brilliant hypothesis of Leucippus and Democritus was by no means the last word in Greek philosophy: subsequent Greek philosophers were to see that the richness of the world cannot in all its spheres be reduced to the mechanical interplay of atoms.

[1] *De Caelo,* Γ 4, 303 a 8.

CHAPTER XI

PRE-SOCRATIC PHILOSOPHY

1. It is often said that Greek philosophy centres round the problem of the One and the Many. Already in the very earliest stages of Greek philosophy we find the notion of unity: things change into one another—therefore there must be some common substratum, some ultimate principle, some unity underlying diversity. Thales declares that water is that common principle, Anaximenes air, Heraclitus fire: they choose different principles, but they all three believe in one ultimate principle. But although the fact of change—what Aristotle called "substantial" change—may have suggested to the early Cosmologists the notion of an underlying unity in the universe, it would be a mistake to reduce this notion to a conclusion of physical science. As far as strict scientific proof goes, they had not sufficient data to warrant their assertion of unity, still less to warrant the assertion of any particular ultimate principle, whether water, fire or air. The fact is, that the early Cosmologists leapt beyond the data to the intuition of universal unity: they possessed what we might call the power of metaphysical intuition, and this constitutes their glory and their claim to a place in the history of philosophy. If Thales had contented himself with saying that out of water earth is evolved, "we should," as Nietzsche observes, "only have a scientific hypothesis: a false one, though nevertheless difficult to refute." But Thales went beyond a mere scientific hypothesis: he reached out to a metaphysical doctrine, expressed in the metaphysical doctrine, that *Everything is One.*

Let me quote Nietzsche again. "Greek philosophy seems to begin with a preposterous fancy, with the proposition that *water* is the origin and mother-womb of all things. Is it really necessary to stop there and become serious? Yes, and for three reasons: Firstly, because the proposition does enunciate something about the origin of things; secondly, because it does so without figure and fable; thirdly and lastly, because in it is contained, although only in the chrysalis state, the idea—Everything is one. The first-mentioned reason leaves Thales still in the company of religious and superstitious people; the second, however, takes

76

him out of this company and shows him to us as a natural philosopher; but by virtue of the third, Thales becomes the first Greek philosopher."[1] This holds true of the other early Cosmologists; men like Anaximenes and Heraclitus also took wing and flew above and beyond what could be verified by mere empirical observation. At the same time they were not content with any mythological assumption, for they sought a real principle of unity, the ultimate substrate of change: what they asserted, they asserted in all seriousness. They had the notion of a world that was a whole, a system, of a world governed by law. Their assertions were dictated by reason or thought, not by mere imagination or mythology; and so they deserve to count as philosophers, the first philosophers of Europe.

2. But though the early Cosmologists were inspired by the idea of cosmic unity, they were faced by the fact of the Many, of multiplicity, of diversity, and they had to attempt the theoretical reconciliation of this evident plurality with the postulated unity —in other words, they had to account for the world as we know it. While Anaximenes, for example, had recourse to the principle of condensation and rarefaction, Parmenides, in the grip of his great theory that Being is one and changeless, roundly denied the facts of change and motion and multiplicity as illusions of the senses. Empedocles postulated four ultimate elements, out of which all things are built up under the action of Love and Strife, and Anaxagoras maintained the ultimate character of the atomic theory and the quantitative explanation of qualitative difference, thus doing justice to plurality, to the many, while tending to relinquish the earlier vision of unity, in spite of the fact that each atom represents the Parmenidean One.

We may say, therefore, that while the Pre-Socratics struggled with the problem of the One and the Many, they did not succeed in solving it. The Heraclitean philosophy contains, indeed, the profound notion of unity in diversity, but it is bound up with an over-assertion of Becoming and the difficulties consequent on the doctrine of Fire. The Pre-Socratics accordingly failed to solve the problem, and it was taken up again by Plato and Aristotle, who brought to bear on it their outstanding talent and genius.

3. But if the problem of the One and the Many continued to exercise Greek philosophy in the Post-Socratic period, and received much more satisfactory solutions at the hands of Plato

[1] *Philosophy during the Tragic Age of the Greeks*, in sect. 3.

and Aristotle, it is obvious that we cannot characterise Pre-Socratic philosophy by reference to that problem: we require some other note of characterisation and distinction. Where is it to be found? We may say that Pre-Socratic philosophy centres round the external world, the Object, the not-self. Man, the Subject, the self, is of course not excluded from consideration, but the interest in the not-self is predominant. This can be seen from the question which the successive Pre-Socratic thinkers set themselves to answer: "Of what is the world ultimately composed?" In their answers to this question the early Ionian philosophers certainly went beyond what the empirical data warranted, but, as already remarked, they tackled the question in a philosophic spirit and not in the spirit of weavers of mythological fancies. They had not differentiated between physical science and philosophy, and combined "scientific" observations of a purely practical character with philosophic speculations; but it must be remembered that a differentiation between physical science and philosophy was hardly possible at that early stage—men wanted to know something more about the world, and it was but natural that scientific questions and philosophical questions should be mingled together. Since they were concerned with the *ultimate* nature of the world, their theories rank as philosophical; but since they had not yet formed any clear distinction between spirit and matter, and since their question was largely prompted by the fact of material change, their answer was couched for the most part in terms and concepts taken from matter. They found the ultimate "stuff" of the universe to be some kind of matter—naturally enough—whether the water of Thales, the Indeterminate of Anaximander, the air of Anaximenes, the fire of Heraclitus, or the atoms of Leucippus, and so a large part of their subject-matter would be claimed by physical scientists of to-day as belonging to their province.

The early Greek philosophers are then rightly called Cosmologists, for they were concerned with the nature of the Cosmos, the object of our knowledge, and man himself is considered in his objective aspect, as one item in the Cosmos, rather than in his subjective aspect, as the subject of knowledge or as the morally willing and acting subject. In their consideration of the Cosmos, they did not reach any final conclusion accounting for all the factors involved; and this apparent bankruptcy of Cosmology, together with other causes to be considered presently, naturally

led to a swing-over of interest from Object to Subject, from the
Cosmos to Man himself. This change of interest, as exemplified in
the Sophists, we will consider in the following section of this book.

4. Although it is true that Pre-Socratic philosophy centres
round the Cosmos, the external world, and that this cosmological
interest is the distinguishing mark of Pre-Socratic as contrasted
with Socratic philosophy, it must also be remarked that one
problem at any rate connected with man as the knowing subject
was raised in Pre-Socratic philosophy, that of the relation between
sense-experience and reason. Thus Parmenides, starting with the
notion of the One, and finding himself unable to explain coming-
to-be and passing-away—which are given in sense-experience—set
aside the evidence of the senses as illusion, and proclaimed the
sole validity of reason, which alone is able to attain the Real and
Abiding. But the problem was not treated in any full or adequate
manner, and when Parmenides denied the validity of sense-
perception, he did so because of a metaphysical doctrine or
assumption, rather than from any prolonged consideration of
the nature of sense-perception and the nature of non-sensuous
thought.

5. Since the early Greek thinkers may justly be termed philosophers, and since they proceeded largely by way of action and
reaction, or thesis and antithesis (e.g. Heraclitus over-emphasising
Becoming and Parmenides over-stressing Being), it was only to
be expected that the germs of later philosophical tendencies and
Schools would already be discernible in Pre-Socratic philosophy.
Thus in the Parmenidean doctrine of the One, when coupled with
the exaltation of Reason at the expense of sense-perception, we
can see the germs of later idealism; while in the introduction of
Nous by Anaxagoras—however restricted his actual use of Nous
may have been—we may see the germs of later philosophical
theism; and in the atomism of Leucippus and Democritus we may
see an anticipation of later materialistic and mechanistic philosophies which would endeavour to explain all quality by quantity
and to reduce everything in the universe to matter and its
products.

6. From what has been said, it should be clear that Pre-Socratic
philosophy is not simply a pre-philosophic stage which can be
discounted in a study of Greek thought—so that we should be
justified in starting immediately with Socrates and Plato. The
Pre-Socratic philosophy is *not* a pre-philosophic stage, but is the

first stage of Greek philosophy: it may not be pure and unmixed philosophy, but it is philosophy, and it deserves to be studied for the sake of its own intrinsic interest as the first Greek attempt to attain a rational understanding of the world. Moreover, it is not a self-contained unit, shut off from succeeding philosophic thought in a watertight compartment; rather is it preparatory to the succeeding period, for in it we see problems raised which were to occupy the greatest of Greek philosophers. Greek thought develops, and though we can hardly over-estimate the native genius of men like Plato and Aristotle, it would be wrong to imagine that they were uninfluenced by the past. Plato was profoundly influenced by Pre-Socratic thought, by the Heraclitean, Eleatic and Pythagorean systems; Aristotle regarded his philosophy as the heir and crown of the past; and both thinkers took up philosophic problems from the hands of their predecessors, giving, it is true, original solutions, but at the same time tackling the problems in their historic setting. It would be absurd, therefore, to start a history of Greek philosophy with a discussion of Socrates and Plato without any discussion of preceding thought, for we cannot understand Socrates or Plato—or Aristotle either —without a knowledge of the past.

We must now turn to the next phase of Greek philosophy, which may be considered the antithesis to the preceding period of Cosmological speculation—the Sophistic and Socratic period.

PART II
THE SOCRATIC PERIOD

CHAPTER XII
THE SOPHISTS

THE earlier Greek philosophers had been chiefly interested in the Object, trying to determine the ultimate principle of all things. Their success, however, did not equal their philosophic sincerity, and the successive hypotheses that they advanced easily led to a certain scepticism as to the possibility of attaining any certain knowledge concerning the ultimate nature of the world. Add to this that doctrines such as those of Heraclitus and Parmenides would naturally result in a sceptical attitude in regard to the validity of sense-perception. If being is static and the perception of movement is an illusion, or if, on the other hand, all is in a state of constant change and there is no real principle of stability, our sense-perception is untrustworthy, and so the very foundations of Cosmology are undermined. The systems of philosophy hitherto proposed excluded one another: there was naturally truth to be found in the opposing theories, but no philosopher had yet arisen of sufficient stature to reconcile the antitheses in a higher synthesis, in which error should be purged away and justice done to the truth contained in rival doctrines. The result was bound to be a certain mistrust of cosmologies. And, indeed, a swing-over to the Subject as point of consideration was necessary if real advance was to be made. It was Plato's consideration of thought that made possible a truer theory in which justice should be done to the facts of both stability and mutability; but the reaction from Object to Subject, which made possible the advance, first appears among the Sophists, and was largely an effect of the bankruptcy of the older Greek philosophy. In face of the dialectic of Zeno, it might well appear doubtful if advance in the study of cosmology was really possible.

Another factor besides the scepticism consequent on the former Greek philosophy, which directed attention to the Subject, was the growing reflection on the phenomena of culture and civilisation, due in large part to extended acquaintance on the part of the Greeks with foreign peoples. Not only did they know something of the civilisations of Persia, Babylon and Egypt, but they had also come into contact with people of a much less advanced stage, such as the Scythians and Thracians. This being so, it was but natural that a highly intelligent people like the Greeks should begin to ask themselves questions; e.g. Are the various national and local ways of life, religious and ethical codes, merely conventions or not? Was Hellenic culture, as contrasted with non-Hellenic or barbarian cultures, a matter of νόμος, man-made and mutable, existing νόμῳ, or did it rest on Nature, existing Φύσει? Was it a sacred ordinance, having divine sanction, or could it be changed, modified, adapted, developed? Professor Zeller points out in this connection how Protagoras, most gifted of the Sophists, came from Abdera, "an advanced outpost of Ionic culture in the land of the Thracian barbarian."[1]

Sophism,[2] then, differed from the older Greek philosophy in regard to the matter with which it dealt, namely, man and the civilisation and customs of man: it treated of the microcosm rather than the macrocosm. Man was becoming self-conscious: as Sophocles says, "Miracles in the world are many, there is no greater miracle than man."[3] But Sophism also differed from previous Greek philosophy in its *method*. Although the method of the older Greek philosophy by no means excluded empirical observation, yet it was characteristically deductive. When a philosopher had settled on his general principle of the world, its ultimate constituent principle, it then remained to explain particular phenomena in accordance with that theory. The Sophist, however, sought to amass a wide store of particular observations and facts; they were Encyclopaedists, Polymaths. Then from these accumulated facts they proceeded to draw conclusions, partly theoretical, partly practical. Thus from the store of facts they accumulated concerning differences of opinion and belief, they might draw the conclusion that it is impossible to have any certain knowledge. Or from their knowledge of various nations and ways of life, they might form a theory as to the origin of civilisation or the beginning of language. Or again they might

[1] *Outlines*, p. 76.
[2] In using the term "Sophism" I do not mean to imply that there was any Sophistic system: the men whom we know as the Greek Sophists differed widely from one another in respect both of ability and of opinions: they represent a trend or movement, not a school.　　　　[3] *Antigone*, 332 ff.

draw practical conclusions, e.g. that society would be most efficiently organised if it were organised in this or that manner. The method of Sophism, then, was "empirico-inductive."[1]

It is to be remembered, however, that the practical conclusions of the Sophists were not meant to establish objective norms, founded on necessary truth. And this fact points to another difference between Sophism and the older Greek philosophy, namely, difference of end. The latter was concerned with objective truth: the Cosmologists wanted to find out the objective truth about the world, they were in the main disinterested seekers after truth. The Sophists, on the other hand, were not primarily intent on objective truth: their end was practical and not speculative. And so the Sophists became instruments of instruction and training in the Greek cities, aiming at teaching the art and control of life. It has been remarked that while a band of disciples was more or less accidental for the Pre-Socratic philosophers—since their primary aim was *finding out* the truth—it was essential for the Sophists, since they aimed at *teaching*.

In Greece, after the Persian Wars, political life was naturally intensified, and this was particularly the case in democratic Athens. The free citizen played some part, at any rate, in political life, and if he wanted to get on he obviously had to have some kind of training. The old education was insufficient for the man who wished to make his way in the State; the old aristocratic ideal was, whether intrinsically superior to the new ideals or not, incapable of meeting the demands made on leaders in the developing democracy: something more was needed, and this need was met by the Sophists. Plutarch says that the Sophists put a theoretical training in the place of the older practical training, which was largely an affair of family tradition, connection with prominent statesmen, practical and experiential training by actual participation in political life. What was now required was courses of instruction, and the Sophists gave such courses in the cities. They were itinerant professors who travelled about from city to city, thus gathering a valuable store of knowledge and experience, and they gave instruction on various themes—grammar, the interpretation of poets, the philosophy of mythology and religion, and so on. But, above all, they professed to teach the art of *Rhetoric*, which was absolutely necessary for political life. In the Greek city-state, above all at Athens, no one could hope to make

[1] Zeller, *Outlines*, p. 77.

his mark as a politician unless he could speak, and speak well. The Sophists professed to teach him to do so, training him in the chief expression of political "virtue," the virtue of the new aristocracy of intellect and ability. There was, of course, nothing wrong in this in itself, but the obvious consequence—that the art of rhetoric might be used to "get across" a notion or policy which was not disinterested or might be definitely harmful to the city or merely calculated to promote the politician's career—helped to bring the Sophists into bad repute. This was particularly the case with regard to their teaching of Eristic. If a man wanted to make money in the Greek democracy, it had to be done mainly by lawsuits, and the Sophists professed to teach the right way of winning these lawsuits. But clearly that might easily mean in practice the art of teaching men how to make the unjust appear the just cause. Such a procedure was obviously very different from the procedure of the old truth-seeking attitude of the philosophers, and helps to explain the treatment meted out to the Sophists at the hands of Plato.

The Sophists carried on their work of instruction by the education of the young and by giving popular lectures in the cities; but as they were itinerant professors, men of wide experience and representative of a, as yet, somewhat sceptical and superficial reaction, the idea became current that they gathered together the young men from their homes and then pulled to pieces before them the traditional ethical code and religious beliefs. Accordingly the strict adherents of tradition regarded the Sophists with some suspicion, though the young were their enthusiastic supporters. Not that the levelling-out tendencies of the Sophists were all weakening to Greek life: their breadth of view generally made them advocates of Panhellenism, a doctrine sorely needed in the Greece of the city-state. But it was their sceptical tendencies that attracted most attention, especially as they did not put anything really new and stable in place of the old convictions which they tended to unsettle. To this should be added the fact that they took payment for the instruction which they imparted. This practice, however legitimate in itself, was at variance with the practice of the older Greek philosophers, and did not agree with the Greek opinion of what was fitting. It was abhorrent to Plato, while Xenophon says that the Sophists speak and write to deceive for their gain, and they give no help to anyone.[1]

---

[1] Xen., *Cyneg.*, 13, 8 (D. 79, 2 a).

THE SOPHISTS 85

From what has been said, it is clear that Sophism does not deserve any sweeping condemnation. By turning the attention of thinkers to man himself, the thinking and willing subject, it served as a transition stage to the great Platonic-Aristotelian achievement. In affording a means of training and instruction, it fulfilled a necessary task in the political life of Greece, while its Panhellenistic tendencies certainly stand to its credit. And even its sceptical and relativist tendencies, which were, after all, largely the result of the breakdown of the older philosophy on the one hand, and of a wider experience of human life on the other, at least contributed to the raising of problems, even if Sophism itself was unable to solve these problems. It is not fanciful to discern the influence of Sophism in the Greek drama, e.g. in Sophocles' hymn to human achievement in the *Antigone* and in the theoretical discussions contained in plays of Euripides, and in the works of the Greek historians, e.g. in the celebrated Melian dialogue in the pages of Thucydides. The term Σοφιστής took some time to acquire its disparaging connotation. The name is applied by Herodotus to Solon and Pythagoras, by Androtion to the Seven Wise Men and to Socrates, by Lysias to Plato. Moreover, the older Sophists won for themselves general respect and esteem, and, as historians have pointed out, were not infrequently selected as "ambassadors" of their respective cities, a fact which hardly points to their being or being regarded as charlatans. It was only secondarily that the term "Sophist" acquired an unsavoury flavour—as in Plato; and in later times the term seems to have reacquired a good sense, being applied to the professors of rhetoric and prose writers of the Empire, without the significance of quibbler or cheat. "It is particularly through the opposition to Socrates and Plato that the Sophists have come into such disrepute that the word now usually signifies that, by false reasoning, some truth is either refuted and made dubious, or something false is proved and made plausible."[1]

On the other hand, the relativism of the Sophists, their encouragement of Eristic, their lack of stable norms, their acceptance of payment, and the hair-splitting tendencies of certain later Sophists, justify to a great extent the disparaging signification of the term. For Plato, they are "shopkeepers with spiritual wares";[2] and when Socrates is represented in the *Protagoras*[3] as asking Hippocrates, who wanted to receive instruction from

[1] Hegel, *Hist. Phil.*, I, p. 354.   [2] *Protag.*, 313 c 5–6.   [3] *Protag.*, 312 a 4–7.

Protagoras, "Wouldn't you be ashamed to show yourself to the Greeks as a Sophist?", Hippocrates answers: "Yes, truly, Socrates, if I am to say what I think." We must, however, remember that Plato tends to bring out the bad side of the Sophists, largely because he had Socrates before his eyes, who had developed what was good in Sophism beyond all comparison with the achievements of the Sophists themselves.

CHAPTER XIII

SOME INDIVIDUAL SOPHISTS

1. *Protagoras*

PROTAGORAS was born, according to most authors, about 481 B.C., a native of Abdera in Thrace,[1] and seems to have come to Athens about the middle of the century. He enjoyed the favour of Pericles, and we are told that he was entrusted by that statesman with the task of drawing up a constitution for the Panhellenic colony of Thurii, which was founded in 444 B.C. He was again in Athens at the outbreak of the Peloponnesian War in 431 and during the plague in 430, which carried off two of Pericles' sons. Diogenes Laërtius relates the story that Protagoras was indicted for blasphemy because of his book on the gods, but that he escaped from the city before trial and was drowned on the crossing to Sicily, his book being burnt in the market-place. This would have taken place at the time of the oligarchic revolt of the Four Hundred in 411 B.C. Burnet is inclined to regard the story as dubious, and holds that if the indictment did take place, then it must have taken place before 411. Professor Taylor agrees with Burnet in rejecting the prosecution story, but he does so because he also agrees with Burnet in accepting a much earlier date for the birth of Protagoras, namely 500 B.C. The two writers rely on Plato's representation of Protagoras in the dialogue of that name as an elderly man, at least approaching 65, in about the year 435. Plato "must have known whether Protagoras really belonged to the generation before Socrates, and could have no motive for misrepresentation on such a point."[2] If this is correct, then we ought also to accept the statement in the *Meno* that Protagoras died in high repute.

The best-known statement of Protagoras is that contained in his work, Ἀλήθεια ἢ Καταβάλλοντες (λόγοι), to the effect that "man is the measure of all things, of those that are that they are, of those that are not that they are not."[3] There has been a considerable controversy as to the interpretation which should be put on this famous saying, some writers maintaining the view that by "man" Protagoras does not mean the individual man,

[1] *Protag.*, 309 c; *Rep.*, 600 c; Diog. Laërt., 9, 50 ff.   [2] *Plato*, p. 236, note.
[3] Frag. 1.

but man in the specific sense. If this were so, then the meaning of the dictum would not be that "what appears to you to be true is true for you, and what appears to me to be true is true for me," but rather that the community or group or the whole human species is the criterion and standard of truth. Controversy has also turned round the question whether things—Χρήματα— should be understood exclusively of the objects of sense-perception or should be extended to cover the field of values as well.

This is a difficult question and it cannot be discussed at length here, but the present writer is not prepared to disregard the testimony of Plato in the *Theaetetus*, where the Protagorean dictum, developed it is true, as Plato himself admits, is certainly interpreted in the individualistic sense in regard to sense-perception.[1] Socrates observes that when the same wind is blowing, one of us may feel chilly and the other not, or one may feel slightly chilly and the other quite cold, and asks if we should agree with Protagoras that the wind is cold to the one who feels chilly and not to the other. It is quite clear that in this passage Protagoras is interpreted as referring to the individual man, and not at all to man in the specific sense. Moreover, it is to be noted that the Sophist is not depicted as saying that the wind merely *appears* chilly to the one and not to the other. Thus if I have come in from a run in the rain on a cold day, and say that the water is warm; while you, coming from a warm room, feel the same water as cold, Protagoras would remark that neither of us is mistaken—the water *is* warm in reference to my sense-organ, and *is* cold in reference to your sense-organ. (When it was objected to the Sophist that geometrical propositions are constant for all, Protagoras replied that in actual concrete reality there are no geometrical lines or circles, so that the difficulty does not arise.[2])

Against this interpretation appeal is made to the *Protagoras* of Plato, where Protagoras is not depicted as applying the dictum in an individualistic sense to ethical values. But even granting that Protagoras must be made consistent with himself, it is surely not necessary to suppose that what is true of the objects of sense-perception is *ipso facto* true of ethical values. It may be pointed out that Protagoras declares that man is the measure of πάντων χρημάτων (*all* things), so that if the individualistic interpretation be accepted in regard to the objects of sense-perception, it should also be extended to ethical values and judgments, and

<hr>

[1] *Theaet.*, 151 e, 152 a.   [2] Arist., *Metaph.*, B 2, 997 b 32–998 a 6.

that, conversely, if it is not accepted in regard to ethical values and judgments, it should not be accepted in regard to the objects of sense-perception: in other words, we are forced to choose between the *Theaetetus* and *Protagoras*, relying on the one and rejecting the other. But in the first place it is not certain that πάντων χρημάτων is meant to include ethical values, and in the second place it might be well that the objects of the special senses are of such character that they *cannot* become the subject of true and universal knowledge, while on the other hand ethical values are of such a kind that they *can* become the subject of true and universal knowledge. This was the view of Plato himself, who connected the Protagorean saying with the Heraclitean doctrine of flux, and held that true and certain knowledge can only be had of the supersensible. We are not trying to make out that Protagoras held the Platonic view on ethical values, which he did not, but to point out that sense-perception and intuition of values do not *necessarily* stand or fall together in relation to certain knowledge and truth for all.

What, then, was Protagoras' actual teaching in regard to ethical judgments and values? In the *Theaetetus* he is depicted as saying both that ethical judgments are relative ("For I hold that whatever practices seem right and laudable to any particular State are so for that State, so long as it holds by them") and that the wise man should attempt to substitute sound practices for unsound.[1] In other words, there is no question of one ethical view being true and another false, but there is question of one view being "sounder," i.e. more useful or expedient, than another. "In this way it is true both that some men are wiser than others and that no one thinks falsely." (A man who thinks that there is no absolute truth, is hardly entitled to declare absolutely that "no one thinks falsely.") Now, in the *Protagoras*, Plato depicts the Sophist as maintaining that αἰδώς and δίκη, have been bestowed on *all* men by the gods, "because cities could not exist if, as in the case of other arts, few men only were partakers of them." Is this at variance with what is said in the *Theaetetus*? It would appear that what Protagoras means is this: that Law in general is founded on certain ethical tendencies implanted in all men, but that the individual varieties of Law, as found in particular States, are relative, the law of one State, without being "truer" than that of another State, being perhaps "sounder" in the sense

[1] *Theaet.*, 166 ff.

of more useful or expedient. The State or city-community would be the determiner of law in this case and not the individual, but the relative character of concrete ethical judgments and concrete determinations of Nomos would be maintained. As an upholder of tradition and social convention, Protagoras stresses the importance of education, of imbibing the ethical traditions of the State, while admitting that the wise man may lead the State to "better" laws. As far as the individual citizen is concerned, he should cleave to tradition, to the accepted code of the community —and that all the more because no one "way" is truer than another. αἰδώς and δίκη incline him to this, and if he has no share in these gifts of the gods and refuses to hearken to the State, the State must get rid of him. While at first sight, therefore, the "relativistic" doctrine of Protagoras might seem intentionally revolutionary, it turns out to be used in support of tradition and authority. No one code is "truer" than another, therefore do not set up your private judgment against the law of the State. Moreover, through his conception of αἰδώς and δίκη Protagoras gives at least some hints of the unwritten or natural law, and in this respect contributed to the broadening of the Greek outlook.

In a work, Περὶ θεῶν, Protagoras said: "With regard to the gods, I cannot feel sure either that they are or that they are not, nor what they are like in figure; for there are many things that hinder sure knowledge, the obscurity of the subject and the shortness of human life."[1] This is the only fragment of the work that we possess. Such a sentence might seem to lend colour to the picture of Protagoras as a sceptical and destructive thinker, who turned his critical powers against all established tradition in ethics and religion; but such a view does not agree with the impression of Protagoras which we receive from Plato's dialogue of that name, and would doubtless be mistaken. Just as the moral to be drawn from the relativity of particular codes of law is that the individual should submit himself to the traditional education, so the moral to be drawn from our uncertainty concerning the gods and their nature is that we should abide by the religion of the city. If we cannot be certain of absolute truth, why throw overboard the religion that we inherit from our fathers? Moreover, Protagoras' attitude is not so extraordinary or destructive as the adherents of a dogmatic religion might naturally suppose, since, as Burnet remarks, Greek religion did not consist

[1] Frag. 4.

"in theological affirmations or negations" but in worship.[1] The effect of the Sophists, it is true, would have been to weaken men's trust in tradition, but it would appear that Protagoras personally was conservative in temper and had no intention of educating revolutionaries; on the contrary, he professed to educate the good citizen. There are ethical tendencies in all men, but these can develop only in the organised community: if a man is to be a good citizen, therefore, he must absorb the whole social tradition of the community of which he is a member. The social tradition is not absolute truth, but it is the norm for a good citizen.

From the relativistic theory it follows that on every subject more than one opinion is possible, and Protagoras seems to have developed this point in his Ἀντιλογίαι. The dialectician and rhetorician will practise himself in the art of developing different opinions and arguments, and he will shine most brightly when he succeeds τὸν ἥττω λόγον κρείττω ποιεῖν. The enemies of the Sophists interpreted this in the sense of making the *morally worse* cause to prevail,[2] but it does not necessarily possess this morally destructive sense. A lawyer, for example, who pleaded with success the just cause of a client who was too weak to protect himself or the justice of whose cause it was difficult to substantiate, might be said to be making the "weaker argument" prevail, though he would be doing nothing immoral. In the hands of unscrupulous rhetoricians and devotees of eristic, the maxim easily acquired an unsavoury flavour, but there is no reason to father on Protagoras himself a desire to promote unscrupulous dealing. Still, it cannot be denied that the doctrine of relativism, when linked up with the practice of dialectic and eristic, very naturally produces a desire to succeed, without much regard for truth or justice.

Protagoras was a pioneer in the study and science of grammar. He is said to have classified the different kinds of sentence[3] and to have distinguished terminologically the genders of nouns.[4] In an amusing passage of the *Clouds* Aristophanes depicts the Sophist as coining the feminine ἀλεκτρύαινα from the masculine ἀλεκτρυών (cock).[5]

II. *Prodicus*

Prodicus came from the island of Ceos in the Aegean. The

inhabitants of this island were said to be pessimistically inclined, and Prodicus was credited with the tendencies of his countrymen, for in the pseudo-Platonic dialogue *Axiochus* he is credited with holding that death is desirable in order to escape the evils of life. Fear of death is irrational, since death concerns neither the living nor the dead—the first, because they are still living, the second, because they are not living any more.[1] The authenticity of this quotation is not easy to establish.

Prodicus is perhaps chiefly remarkable for his theory on the origin of religion. He held that in the beginning men worshipped as gods the sun, moon, rivers, lakes, fruits, etc.—in other words, the things which were useful to them and gave them food. And he gives as an example the cult of the Nile in Egypt. This primitive stage was followed by another, in which the inventors of various arts—agriculture, viniculture, metal work, and so on—were worshipped as the gods Demeter, Dionysus, Hephaestus, etc. On this view of religion prayer would, he thought, be superfluous, and he seems to have got into trouble with the authorities at Athens.[2] Prodicus, like Protagoras, was noted for linguistic studies,[3] and he wrote a treatise on synonyms. He seems to have been very pedantic in his forms of expression.[4]

(Professor Zeller says:[5] "Although Plato usually treats him with irony, it nevertheless speaks well for him that Socrates occasionally recommended pupils to him (*Theaet.*, 151b), and that his native city repeatedly entrusted him with diplomatic missions (*Hipp. Maj.*, 282 c)." As a matter of fact, Zeller seems to have missed the point in the *Theaetetus* passage, since the young men that Socrates has sent to Prodicus are those who, he has found, have not been "pregnant" with thoughts when in his company. He has accordingly sent them off to Prodicus, in whose company they have ceased to be "barren.")

III. *Hippias*

Hippias of Elis was a younger contemporary of Protagoras and was celebrated particularly for his versatility, being acquainted with mathematics, astronomy, grammar and rhetoric, rhythmics and harmony, history and literature and mythology—in short, he was a true Polymath. Not only that, but when present at a certain Olympiad, he boasted that he had made all his own

---

[1] 366 c ff.   [2] Frag. 5.   [3] Cf. *Crat.*, 384 b.   [4] Cf. *Protag.*, 337 a f.
[5] *Outlines*, pp. 84–5.

clothes. His list of the Olympic victors laid the foundation for the later Greek system of dating by means of the Olympiads (first introduced by the historian Timaeus).[1] Plato, in the *Protagoras*, makes him say that "law being the tyrant of men, forces them to do many things contrary to nature."[2] The point seems to be that the law of the city-state is often narrow and tyrannical and at variance with the natural laws (ἄγραφοι νόμοι).

iv. *Gorgias*

Gorgias of Leontini, in Sicily, lived from about 483 to 375 B.C., and in the year 427 he came to Athens as ambassador of Leontini, in order to ask for help against Syracuse. On his travels he did what he could to spread the spirit of Panhellenism.

Gorgias seems to have been at first a pupil of Empedocles, and to have busied himself with questions of natural science, and may have written a book on Optics. He was led, however, to scepticism by the dialectic of Zeno and published a work entitled *On Not-being or Nature* (Περὶ τοῦ μὴ ὄντος ἢ περὶ Φύσεως), the chief ideas of which can be gathered from Sextus Empiricus and from the pseudo-Aristotelian writing *On Melissus, Xenophanes and Gorgias*. From these accounts of the contents of Gorgias' work it is clear that he reacted to the Eleatic dialectic somewhat differently to Protagoras, since while the latter might be said to hold that everything is true, Gorgias maintained the very opposite. According to Gorgias, (i) Nothing exists, for if there were anything, then it would have either to be eternal or to have come into being. But it cannot have come into being, for neither out of Being nor out of Not-being can anything come to be. Nor can it be eternal, for if it were eternal, then it would have to be infinite. But the infinite is impossible for the following reason. It could not be in another, nor could it be in itself, therefore it would be nowhere. But what is nowhere, is nothing. (ii) If there were anything, then it could not be known. For if there is knowledge of being, then what is thought must be, and Not-being could not be thought at all. In which case there could be no error, which is absurd. (iii) Even if there were knowledge of being, this knowledge could not be imparted. Every sign is different from the thing signified; e.g. how could we impart knowledge of colours by word, since the ear hears tones and not colours? And how could the same representation of being

[1] Frag. 3.   [2] 337 d, 2–3.

be in the two persons at once, since they are different from one another?[1]

While some have regarded these astonishing ideas as expressing a seriously meant philosophical Nihilism, others have thought that the doctrine constitutes a joke on the part of Gorgias, or, rather, that the great rhetorician wanted to show that rhetoric or the skilful use of words was able to make plausible even the most absurd hypothesis. (Sic H. Gomperz.) But this latter view hardly agrees with the fact that Isocrates sets Gorgias' opinions besides those of Zeno and Melissus, nor with the writing Πρὸς τὰ Γοργίου, which treats Gorgias' opinions as worth a philosophical criticism.[2] In any case a treatise on Nature would scarcely be the place for such rhetorical tours de force. On the other hand, it is difficult to suppose that Gorgias held in all seriousness that nothing exists. It may be that he wished to employ the Eleatic dialectic in order to reduce the Eleatic philosophy to absurdity.[3] Afterwards, renouncing philosophy, he devoted himself to rhetoric.

Rhetorical art was regarded by Gorgias as the mastery of the art of persuasion, and this necessarily led him to a study of practical psychology. He deliberately practised the art of suggestion (ψυχαγωγία), which could be used both for practical ends, good and bad, and for artistic purposes. In connection with the latter Gorgias developed the art of justifiable deception (δικαία 'απάτη), calling a tragedy "a deception which is better to cause than not to cause; to succumb to it shows greater powers of artistic appreciation than not to."[4] Gorgias' comparison of the effects of tragedy to those of purgatives reminds us of Aristotle's much-discussed doctrine of the κάθαρσις.

The fact that Plato places the might-is-right doctrine in the mouth of Callicles,[5] while another disciple, Lycophron, asserted that nobility is a sham and that all men are equal, and that the law is a contract by which right is mutually guaranteed,[6] while yet another disciple demanded the liberation of slaves in the name of natural law,[7] we may ascribe with Zeller to Gorgias' renunciation of philosophy, which led him to decline to answer questions of truth and morality.[8]

Other Sophists whom one may briefly mention are Thrasymachus

---

[1] Cf. Frags. 1, 3.   [2] Aristotle or Theophrastus?   [3] Cf. Zeller, Outlines, p. 87.
[4] Frag. 23 (Plut., de gloria Athen., 5, 348 c).
[5] Gorgias, 482 e ff.   [6] Frags. 3 and 4.
[7] Alcidamas of Elaea. Cf. Aristot., Rhet., III, 3, 1406 b; 1406 a. Schol. on I 13, 1373 b.   [8] Outlines, p. 88.

of Chalcedon, who is presented in the *Republic* as the brutal champion of the rights of the stronger,[1] and Antiphon of Athens, who asserts the equality of all men and denounces the distinction between nobles and commons, Greeks and barbarians, as itself a barbarism. He made education to be the most important thing in life, and created the literary *genre* of Τέχνη ἀλυπίας λόγοι παραμυθητικοί, declaring that he could free anyone from sorrow by oral means.[2]

v. *Sophism*

In conclusion I may observe again that there is no reason for ascribing to the great Sophists the intention of overthrowing religion and morality; men like Protagoras and Gorgias had no such end in view. Indeed, the great Sophists favoured the conception of a "natural law," and tended to broaden the outlook of the ordinary Greek citizen; they were an educative force in Hellas. At the same time it is true that "in a certain sense every opinion is true, according to Protagoras; every opinion is false, according to Gorgias."[3] This tendency to deny the absolute and objective character of truth easily leads to the consequence that, instead of trying to *convince* anyone, the Sophist will try to *persuade* him or talk him over. Indeed, in the hands of lesser men Sophism soon acquired an unpleasant connotation—that of "Sophistry." While one can only respect the cosmopolitanism and broad outlook of an Antiphon of Athens, one can only condemn the "Might-is-Right" theory of a Thrasymachus on the one hand and the hair-splitting and quibbling of a Dionysodorus on the other. The great Sophists, as we have said, were an educative force in Hellas; but one of the chief factors in the Greek education which they fostered was rhetoric, and rhetoric had its obvious dangers, inasmuch as the orator might easily tend to pay more attention to the rhetorical presentation of a subject than to the subject itself. Moreover, by questioning the absolute foundations of traditional institutions, beliefs and ways of life, Sophism tended to foster a relativistic attitude, though the evil latent in Sophism lay not so much in the fact that it raised problems, as in the fact that it could not offer any satisfactory intellectual solution to the problems it raised. Against this relativism Socrates and Plato reacted, endeavouring to establish the sure foundation of true knowledge and ethical judgments.

---

[1] *Rep.*, 338 c.   [2] Cf. Plut., apud Diels. Frag. 44 and 87 A 6.
[3] Ueberweg-Praechter, p. 122.

CHAPTER XIV

SOCRATES

1. *Early Life of Socrates*

THE death of Socrates fell in the year 399 B.C., and as Plato
tells us that Socrates was seventy years old or a little more at
the time of his death, he must have been born about 470 B.C.[1]
He was the son of Sophroniscus and Phaenarete of the Antiochid
tribe and the *deme* of Alopecae. Some have said that his father
was a worker in stone,[2] but A. E. Taylor thinks, with Burnet,
that the story was a misunderstanding which arose from a playful
reference in the *Euthyphro* to Daedalus as the ancestor of Socrates.[3]
In any case, Socrates does not seem to have himself followed his
father's trade, if it was his father's trade, and the group of Graces
on the Akropolis, which were later shown as the work of Socrates,
are attributed by archaeologists to an earlier sculptor.[4] Socrates
cannot, however, have come from a very poor family, as we find
him later serving as a fully-armed hoplite, and he must have
been left sufficient patrimony to enable him to undertake such
a service. Phaenarete, Socrates' mother, is described in the
Theaetetus[5] as a midwife, but even if she was, this should not be
taken to imply that she was a professional midwife in the modern
sense, as Taylor points out.[6] Socrates' early life thus fell in the
great flowering of Athenian splendour. The Persians had been
defeated at Plataea in 479 and Aeschylus had produced the *Persae*
in 472: Sophocles and Euripides were still boys.[7] Moreover,
Athens had already laid the foundation of her maritime empire.

In Plato's *Symposium* Alcibiades describes Socrates as looking
like a satyr or Silenus,[8] and Aristophanes said that he strutted

---

[1] *Apol.*, 17 d.
[2] Cf. Diog. Laërt. (Thus Praechter says roundly: *Der Vater des Sokrates war
Bildhauer*, p. 132.)
[3] *Euthyphro*, 10 c.
[4] Diog. Laërt. remarks that "Some say that the Graces in the Akropolis are
his work."
[5] *Theaet.*, 149 a.
[6] Taylor, *Socrates*, p. 38.
[7] "All the great buildings and works of art with which Athens was enriched
in the Periclean age, the Long Walls which connected the city with the port of
Peiraeus, the Parthenon, the frescoes of Polygnotus, were begun and completed
under his eyes." *Socr.*, p. 36.
[8] *Sympos.*, 215 b 3 ff.

like a waterfowl and ridiculed his habit of rolling his eyes.[1] But we also know that he was possessed of particular robustness of body and powers of endurance. As a man he wore the same garment winter and summer, and continued his habit of going barefoot, even on a winter campaign. Although very abstemious in food and drink, he could drink a great deal without being any the worse for it. From his youth upwards he was the recipient of prohibitory messages or warnings from his mysterious "voice" or "sign" or *daimon*. The *Symposium* tells us of his prolonged fits of abstraction, one lasting the whole of a day and night— and that on a military campaign. Professor Taylor would like to interpret these abstractions as ecstasies or rapts, but it would seem more likely that they were prolonged fits of abstraction due to intense mental concentration on some problem, a phenomenon not unknown in the case of some other thinkers, even if not on so large a scale. The very length of the "ecstasy" mentioned in the *Symposium* would seem to militate against its being a real rapture in the mystico-religious sense,[2] though such a prolonged fit of abstraction would also be exceptional.

When Socrates was in his early twenties, thought, as we have seen, tended to turn away from the cosmological speculations of the Ionians towards man himself, but it seems certain that Socrates began by studying the cosmological theories of East and West in the philosophies of Archelaus, Diogenes of Apollonia, Empedocles and others. Theophrastus asserts that Socrates was actually a member of the School of Archelaus, the successor of Anaxagoras at Athens.[3] In any case Socrates certainly suffered a disappointment through Anaxagoras. Perplexed by the disagreement of the various philosophical theories, Socrates received a sudden light from the passage where Anaxagoras spoke of Mind as being the cause of all natural law and order. Delighted with the passage, Socrates began to study Anaxagoras, in the hope that the latter would explain how Mind works in the universe, ordering all things for the best. What he actually found was that Anaxagoras introduced Mind merely in order to get the vortex-movement going. This disappointment set Socrates on his own line of investigation, abandoning the Natural Philosophy which seemed to lead nowhere, save to confusion and opposite opinions.[4]

[1] *Clouds*, 362 (cf. *Sympos.*, 221).
[2] It is true, however, that the history of mysticism does record instances of prolonged ecstatic states. Cf. Poulain, *Grâces d' oraison*, p. 256.
[3] *Phys. Opin.*, fr. 4. [4] *Phaedo*, 97–9.

A. E. Taylor conjectures that on Archelaus' death, Socrates was to all intents and purposes his successor.[1] He tries to support this contention with the aid of Aristophanes' play, *The Clouds*, where Socrates and his associates of the notion-factory or Φροντιστήριον are represented as addicted to the natural sciences and as holding the air-doctrine of Diogenes of Apollonia.[2] Socrates' disclaimer, therefore, that he ever took "pupils"[3] would, if Taylor's conjecture be correct, mean that he had taken no paying pupils. He had had ἑταῖροι, but had never had μαθηταί. Against this it may be urged that in the *Apology* Socrates expressly declares: "But the simple truth is, O Athenians, that I have nothing to do with physical speculations."[4] It is true that at the time when Socrates was depicted as speaking in the *Apology* he had long ago given up cosmological speculation, and that his words do not necessarily imply that he *never* engaged in such speculations; indeed, we know for a fact that he *did*; but it seems to the present writer that the whole tone of the passage militates against the idea that Socrates was ever the professed head of a School dedicated to this kind of speculation. What is said in the *Apology* certainly does not prove, in the strict sense, that Socrates was not the head of such a School before his "conversion," but it would seem that the natural interpretation is that he never occupied such a position.

The "conversion" of Socrates, which brought about the definite change to Socrates the ironic moral philosopher, seems to have been due to the famous incident of the Delphic Oracle. Chaerephon, a devoted friend of Socrates, asked the Oracle if there was any man living who was wiser than Socrates, and received the answer "No." This set Socrates thinking, and he came to the conclusion that the god meant that he was the wisest man because he recognised his own ignorance. He then came to conceive of his mission as being to seek for the stable and certain truth, true wisdom, and to enlist the aid of any man who would consent to listen to him.[5] However strange the story of the Oracle may appear, it most probably really happened, since it is unlikely that Plato would have put a mere invention into the mouth of Socrates in a dialogue which obviously purports to give an historical account of the trial of the philosopher, especially as the *Apology* is of early date, and many who knew the facts were still living.

Socrates' marriage with Xanthippe is best known for the stories

[1] *Socr.*, p. 67. [2] *Clouds*, 94. [3] *Apol.*, 19. [4] *Apol.*, 19. [5] *Apol.*, 20 ff.

about her shrewish character, which may or may not be true. Certainly they are scarcely borne out by the picture of Socrates' wife given in the *Phaedo*. The marriage probably took place some time in the first ten years of the Peloponnesian War. In this war Socrates distinguished himself for bravery at the siege of Potidaea, 431/30, and again at the defeat of the Athenians by the Boeotians in 424. He was also present at the action outside Amphipolis in 422.[1]

II. *Problem of Socrates*

The problem of Socrates is the problem of ascertaining exactly what his philosophical teaching was. The character of the sources at our disposal—Xenophon's Socratic works (*Memorabilia* and *Symposium*), Plato's dialogues, various statements of Aristotle, Aristophanes' *Clouds*—make this a difficult problem. For instance, were one to rely on Xenophon alone, one would have the impression of a man whose chief interest was to make good men and citizens, but who did not concern himself with problems of logic and metaphysics—a popular ethical teacher. If, on the other hand, one were to found one's conception of Socrates on the Platonic dialogues taken as a whole, one would receive the impression of a metaphysician of the highest order, a man who did not content himself with questions of daily conduct, but laid the foundations of a transcendental philosophy, distinguished by its doctrine of a metaphysical world of Forms. Statements of Aristotle, on the other hand (if given their natural interpretation), give us to understand that while Socrates was not uninterested in theory, he did not himself teach the doctrine of subsistent Forms or Ideas, which is characteristic of Platonism.

The common view has been that though Xenophon's portrayal is too "ordinary" and "trivial," mainly owing to Xenophon's lack of philosophical ability and interest (it has indeed been held, though it seems unlikely, that Xenophon deliberately tried to make Socrates appear more "ordinary" than he actually was and than he knew him to be, for apologetic purposes), we cannot reject the testimony of Aristotle, and are accordingly forced to conclude that Plato, except in the early Socratic works, e.g. the *Apology*, put his own doctrines into the mouth of Socrates. This view has the great advantage that the Xenophontic and the Platonic

---

[1] *Apol.*, 28 e. Burnet suggests that the fighting at the foundation of Amphipolis (some fifteen years earlier) may be referred to.

Socrates are not placed in glaring opposition and inconsistency (for the shortcomings of Xenophon's picture can be explained as a result of Xenophon's own character and predominant interests), while the clear testimony of Aristotle is not thrown overboard. In this way a more or less consistent picture of Socrates is evolved, and no unjustified violence (so the upholders of the theory would maintain) is done to any of the sources.

This view has, however, been challenged. Karl Joel, for example, basing his conception of Socrates on the testimony of Aristotle, maintains that Socrates was an intellectualist or rationalist, representing the Attic type, and that the Xenophontic Socrates, a *Willensethiker*, representing the Spartan type, is unhistorical. According to Joel, therefore, Xenophon gave a Doric colouring to Socrates and misrepresented him.[1]

Döring, on the contrary, maintained that we must look to Xenophon in order to obtain our historical picture of Socrates. Aristotle's testimony simply comprises the summary judgment of the Old Academy on Socrates' philosophical importance, while Plato used Socrates as a peg on which to hang his own philosophical doctrines.[2] Another view has been propagated in this country by Burnet and Taylor. According to them the historic Socrates is the *Platonic* Socrates.[3] Plato no doubt elaborated the thought of Socrates, but, all the same, philosophical teaching which is put into his mouth in the dialogues substantially represents the actual teaching of Socrates. If this were correct, then Socrates would himself have been responsible for the metaphysical theory of Forms or Ideas, and the statement of Aristotle (that Socrates did not "separate" the Forms) must be either rejected, as due to ignorance, or explained away. It is most unlikely, say Burnet and Taylor, that Plato would have put his own theories into the mouth of Socrates if the latter had never held them, when people who had actually known Socrates and knew what he really taught, were still living. They point out, moreover, that in some of the later dialogues of Plato, Socrates no longer plays a leading part, while in the *Laws* he is left out altogether—the inference

[1] *Der echte und der Xenophontische Sokrates*, Berlin, 1893, 1901.
[2] *Die Lehre des Sokrates als sozialesreform system. Neuer Versuch zur Lösung des Problems der sokratischen Philosophie.* München, 1895.
[3] "While it is quite impossible to regard the Socrates of Aristophanes and the Socrates of Xenophon as the same person, there is no difficulty in regarding both as distorted images of the Socrates we know from Plato. The first is legitimately distorted for comic effect, the latter, not so legitimately, for apologetic reasons. Burnet, *G.P.*, I, p. 149.

being that where Socrates *does* play the leading part, it is his own ideas, and not simply Plato's, that he is giving, while in the later dialogues Plato is developing independent views (independent of Socrates at least), and so Socrates is allowed to drop into the background. This last argument is undoubtedly a strong one, as is also the fact that in an "early" dialogue, such as the *Phaedo*, which deals with the death of Socrates, the theory of Forms occupies a prominent place. But, if the Platonic Socrates is the historic Socrates, we ought logically to say that in the *Timaeus*, for example, Plato is putting into the mouth of the chief speaker opinions for which he, Plato, did not take the responsibility, since, if Socrates does not stand for Plato himself, there is no compelling reason why Timaeus should do so either. A. E. Taylor indeed does not hesitate to adopt this extreme, if consistent, position; but not only is it *prima facie* extremely unlikely that we can thus free Plato from responsibility for most of what he says in the dialogues, but also, as regards the *Timaeus*, if Taylor's opinion is true, how are we to explain that this remarkable fact first became manifest in the twentieth century A.D.?[1] Again, the consistent maintenance of the Burnet-Taylor view of the Platonic Socrates involves the ascription to Socrates of elaborations, refinements and explanations of the Ideal Theory which it is most improbable that the historic Socrates really evolved, and which would lead to a complete ignoring of the testimony of Aristotle.

It is true that much of the criticism levelled against the Ideal Theory by Aristotle in the *Metaphysics* is directed against the mathematical form of the theory maintained by Plato in his lectures at the Academy, and that in certain particulars there is a curious neglect of what Plato says in the dialogues, a fact which might appear to indicate that Aristotle only recognised as Platonic the unpublished theory developed in the Academy; but it certainly would not be adequate to say that there was a complete dichotomy between the version of the theory that Aristotle gives (whether fairly or unfairly) and the evolving theory of the dialogues. Moreover, the very fact that the theory undergoes evolution, modification and refinement in the dialogues would imply that it represents, in part at least, Plato's own reflections on his position. Later writers of Antiquity certainly believed that we can look to

[1] Cf. pp. 245–7 of this book; *v.* also Cornford's *Plato's Cosmology*, where he discusses Professor Taylor's theory.

the dialogues for Plato's own philosophy, though they differ concerning the relation of the dialogues to the teaching of Socrates, the earlier among them believing that Plato introduced much of his own thought into the dialogues. Syrianus contradicts Aristotle, but Professor Field observes that his reasons appear to be "his own sense of what was fitting in the relation of teacher and disciple."[1]

An argument in favour of the Burnet-Taylor hypothesis is constituted by the passage in the second Letter, where Plato affirms that what he has said in writing is nothing but Socrates "beautified and rejuvenated."[2] In the first place, however, the genuineness of the passage, or even of the whole letter, is not certain, while in the second place it could be perfectly well explained as meaning that the dialogues give what Plato considered the metaphysical superstructure legitimately elaborated by himself on the basis of what Socrates actually said. (Field suggests that it might refer to the application of the Socratic method and spirit to "modern" problems.) For no one would be so foolish as to maintain that the dialogues contain nothing of the historic Socrates. It is obvious that the early dialogues would naturally take as their point of departure the teaching of the historic Socrates, and if Plato worked out the epistemological and ontological theories of succeeding dialogues through reflection on this teaching, he might legitimately regard the results attained as a justifiable development and application of Socrates' teaching and method. His words in the Letter would gain in point from his conviction that while the Ideal Theory as elaborated in the dialogues might, without undue violence, be regarded as a continuation and development of the Socratic teaching, this would not be equally true of the mathematical form of the theory given in the Academy.

It would, of course, be ridiculous to suggest that a view sponsored by such scholars as Professor Taylor and Professor Burnet could be lightly dismissed, and to make any such suggestion is very far from the mind of the present writer; but in a general book on Greek philosophy it is impossible to treat of the question at any considerable length or to give the Burnet-Taylor theory the full and detailed consideration that it deserves. I must, however, express my agreement with what Mr. Hackforth, for

[1] *Plato and his Contemporaries*, p. 228, Methuen, 1930. Cf. Field's summary of the evidence on the Socratic question, pp. 61–3.

[2] 314 c, καλοῦ καὶ νέου γεγονότος.

example, has said[1] concerning the lack of justification for ignoring the testimony of Aristotle that Socrates did not separate the Forms. Aristotle had been for twenty years in the Academy and interested as he was in the history of philosophy, can scarcely have neglected to ascertain the origin of such an important Platonic doctrine as the theory of Forms. Add to this the fact that the extant fragments of the Dialogues of Aeschines give us no reason to differ from the view of Aristotle, and Aeschines was said to have given the most accurate portrait of Socrates. For these reasons it seems best to accept the testimony of Aristotle, and, while admitting that the Xenophontic Socrates is not the complete Socrates, to maintain the traditional view, that Plato did put his own theories into the mouth of the Master whom he so much reverenced. The short account of Socrates' philosophical activity now to be given is therefore based on the traditional view. Those who maintain the theory of Burnet and Taylor would, of course, say that violence is thereby done to Plato; but is the situation bettered by doing violence to Aristotle? If the latter had not enjoyed personal intercourse with Plato and his disciples over a long space of time, we might have allowed the possibility of a mistake on his part; but in view of his twenty years in the Academy this mistake would appear to be ruled out of court. However it is unlikely that we shall ever obtain absolute certainty as to the historically accurate picture of Socrates, and it would be most unwise to dismiss all conceptions save one's own as unworthy of consideration. One can only state one's reasons for accepting one picture of Socrates rather than another, and leave it at that.

(Use has been made of Xenophon in the following short account of Socrates' teaching: we cannot believe that Xenophon was either a nincompoop or a liar. It is perfectly true that while it is difficult—sometimes, no doubt, impossible—to distinguish between Plato and Socrates, "it is almost as hard to distinguish between Socrates and Xenophon. For the *Memorabilia* is as much a work of art as any Platonic dialogue, though the manner is as different as was Xenophon from Plato."[2] But, as Mr. Lindsay points out, Xenophon wrote much besides the *Memorabilia*, and consideration of his writings in general may often show us what is Xenophon, even if it does not always show us what is Socrates.

[1] Cf. article by R. Hackforth on Socrates in *Philosophy* for July 1933.
[2] A. D. Lindsay in Introd. to *Socratic Discourses* (Everyman), p. viii.

The *Memorabilia* gives us the impression that Socrates made on Xenophon, and we believe that it is in the main trustworthy, even if it is always as well to remember the old scholastic adage, *Quidquid recipitur, secundum modum recipientis recipitur.*)

III. *Philosophical Activity of Socrates*

1. Aristotle declares that there are two improvements in science which we might justly ascribe to Socrates—his employment of "inductive arguments and universal definitions" (τούς τ'ἐπακτικούς λόγους καὶ τὸ ὁρίζεσθαι καθόλου).[1] The last remark should be understood in connection with the following statement, that "Socrates did not make the universals or the definitions exist apart; his successor, however, gave them separate existence, and this was the kind of thing they called Ideas."

Socrates was therefore concerned with universal definitions, i.e. with the attaining of fixed concepts. The Sophists propounded relativistic doctrines, rejecting the necessarily and universally valid. Socrates, however, was struck by the fact that the universal concept remains the same: particular instances may vary, but the definition stands fast. This idea can be made clear by an example. The Aristotelian definition of man is "rational animal." Now, individual men vary in their gifts: some are possessed of great intellectual gifts, others not. Some guide their lives according to reason: others surrender without thought to instinct and passing impulse. Some men do not enjoy the unhampered use of their reason, whether because they are asleep or because they are "mentally defective." But all animals who possess the gift of reason—whether they are actually using it or not, whether they can use it freely or are prevented by some organic defect—are men: the definition of man is fulfilled in them, and this definition remains constant, holding good for all. If "man," then "rational animal"; if "rational animal," then "man." We cannot now discuss the precise status or objective reference of our generic and specific notions: we simply want to illustrate the contrast between the particular and the universal, and to point out the constant character of the definition. Some thinkers have maintained that the universal concept is purely subjective, but it is very difficult to see how we could form such universal notions, and why we should be compelled to form them, unless there was a foundation for them in fact. We shall have to return later to the question of

[1] *Metaph.*, M. 1078 b 27–9.

the objective reference and metaphysical status of universals: let it suffice at present to point out that the universal concept or definition presents us with something constant and abiding that stands out, through its possession of these characteristics, from the world of perishing particulars. Even if all men were blotted out of existence, the definition of man as "rational animal" would remain constant. Again, we may speak of a piece of gold as being "true gold," implying that the definition of gold, the standard or universal criterion, is realised in this piece of gold. Similarly we speak of things as being more or less beautiful, implying that they approach the standard of Beauty in a greater or less degree, a standard which does not vary or change like the beautiful objects of our experience, but remains constant and "rules," as it were, all particular beautiful objects. Of course, we might be mistaken in supposing that we knew the standard of Beauty, but in speaking of objects as more or less beautiful we imply that there *is* a standard. To take a final illustration. Mathematicians speak of and define the line, the circle, etc. Now, the perfect line and the perfect circle are not found among the objects of our experience: there are at best only approximations to the definitions of the line or the circle. There is a contrast, therefore, between the imperfect and changeable objects of our everyday experience on the one hand and the universal concept or definition on the other hand. It is easy to see, then, how Socrates was led to attach such importance to the universal definition. With a predominant interest in ethical conduct, he saw that the definition affords a sure rock on which men could stand amidst the sea of the Sophist relativistic doctrines. According to a relativistic ethic, justice, for example, varies from city to city, community to community: we can never say that justice is this or that, and that this definition holds good for all States, but only that justice in Athens is this and in Thrace that. But if we can once attain to a universal definition of justice, which expresses the innermost nature of justice and holds good for all men, then we have something sure to go upon, and we can judge not only individual actions, but also the moral codes of different States, in so far as they embody or recede from the universal definition of justice.

2. To Socrates, says Aristotle, may rightly be ascribed "inductive arguments." Now, just as it is a mistake to suppose that in occupying himself with "universal definitions" Socrates was concerned to discuss the metaphysical status of the universal, so it

would be a mistake to suppose that in occupying himself with "inductive arguments" Socrates was concerned with problems of logic. Aristotle, looking back on Socrates' actual practice and method, sums it up in logical terms; but that should not be taken to imply that Socrates developed an explicit theory of Induction from the standpoint of a logician.

What was Socrates' practical method? It took the form of "dialectic" or conversation. He would get into conversation with someone and try to elicit from him his ideas on some subject. For instance, he might profess his ignorance of what courage really is, and ask the other man if he had any light on the subject. Or Socrates would lead the conversation in that direction, and when the other man had used the word "courage," Socrates would ask him what courage is, professing his own ignorance and desire to learn. His companion had used the word, therefore he must know what it meant. When some definition or description had been given him, Socrates would profess his great satisfaction, but would intimate that there were one or two little difficulties which he would like to see cleared up. Accordingly he asked questions, letting the other man do most of the talking, but keeping the course of the conversation under his control, and so would expose the inadequacy of the proposed definition of courage. The other would fall back on a fresh or modified definition, and so the process would go on, with or without final success.

The dialectic, therefore, proceeded from less adequate definitions to a more adequate definition, or from consideration of particular examples to a universal definition. Sometimes indeed no definite result would be arrived at;[1] but in any case the aim was the same, to attain a true and universal definition; and as the argument proceeded from the particular to the universal, or from the less perfect to the more perfect, it may truly be said to be a process of induction. Xenophon mentions some of the ethical phenomena which Socrates sought to investigate, and the nature of which he hoped to enshrine in definitions—e.g. piety and impiety, just and unjust, courage and cowardice.[2] (The early dialogues of Plato deal with the same ethical values—the *Euthyphron* with piety (no result); the *Charmides* with temperance (no result); the *Lysis* with friendship (no result).) The investigation

---

[1] The early dialogues of Plato, which may safely be considered "Socratic" in character, generally end without any determinate and positive result having been attained.

[2] *Mem.*, I, I, 16.

is, for instance, concerning the nature of injustice. Examples are brought forward—to deceive, to injure, to enslave, and so on. It is then pointed out that it is only when these things are done to friends that they are unjust. But the difficulty arises that if one, for example, steals a friend's sword when he is in a passing state of despair and wishes to commit suicide, no injustice is committed. Nor is it unjust on a father's part if he employs deception in order to induce his sick son to take the medicine which will heal him. It appears, therefore, that actions are unjust only when they are performed *against friends with the intention of harming them*.[1]

3. This dialectic might, of course, prove somewhat irritating or even disconcerting or humiliating to those whose ignorance was exposed and whose cocksureness was broken down—and it may have tickled the fancy of the young men who congregated round Socrates to hear their elders being "put in the sack"—but the aim of Socrates was not to humiliate or to disconcert. His aim was to discover the truth, not as matter of pure speculation, but with a view to the good life: in order to act well, one must know what the good life is. His "irony," then, his profession of ignorance, was sincere; he did not know, but he wanted to find out, and he wanted to induce others to reflect for themselves and to give real thought to the supremely important work of caring for their souls. Socrates was deeply convinced of the value of the soul, in the sense of the thinking and willing subject, and he saw clearly the importance of knowledge, of true wisdom, if the soul is to be properly tended. What are the true values of human life which have to be realised in conduct? Socrates called his method "midwifery," not merely by way of playful allusion to his mother, but to express his intention of getting others to produce true ideas in their minds, with a view to right action. This being so, it is easy to understand why Socrates gave so much attention to definition. He was not being pedantic, he was convinced that a clear knowledge of the truth is essential for the right control of life. He wanted to give birth to true ideas in the clear form of definition, not for a speculative but for a practical end. Hence his preoccupation with ethics.

4. I have said that Socrates' interest was predominantly ethical. Aristotle says quite clearly that Socrates "was busying himself about ethical matters."[2] And again, "Socrates occupied

---

[1] *Mem.*, 4, 2, 14 ff. [2] *Metaph.*, A 987 b 1-3.

himself with the excellences of character, and in connection with them became the first to raise the problem of universal definitions."[1] This statement of Aristotle is certainly borne out by the picture of Socrates given by Xenophon.

Plato in the *Apology* relates the profession of Socrates at his trial, that he went where he could do the greatest good to anyone, seeking "to persuade every man among you that he must look to himself, and seek virtue and wisdom before he looks to his private interests, and look to the State before he looks to the interests of the State; and that this should be the order which he observes in all his actions."[2] This was the "mission" of Socrates, which he regarded as having been imposed upon him by the god of Delphi, to stimulate men to care for their noblest possession, their soul, through the acquisition of wisdom and virtue. He was no mere pedantic logician, no mere destructive critic, but a man with a mission. If he criticised and exposed superficial views and easy-going assumptions, this was due not to a frivolous desire to display his own superior dialectical acumen, but to a desire to promote the good of his interlocutors and to learn himself.

Of course it is not to be expected in a member of a Greek City state that an ethical interest should be completely severed from a political interest, for the Greek was essentially a citizen and he had to lead the good life within the framework of the city. Thus Xenophon relates that Socrates inquired τί πόλις, τί πολιτικός τί ἀρχὴ ἀνθρώπων, τί ἀρχηγὸς ἀνθρώπων, and we have seen Socrates' statement in the *Apology* about looking to the State itself before looking to the interests of the State.[3] But, as the last remark implies, and as is clear from Socrates' life, he was not concerned with party politics as such, but with political life in its ethical aspect. It was of the greatest importance for the Greek who wished to lead the good life to realise what the State is and what being a citizen means, for we cannot care for the State unless we know the nature of the State and what a good State is. Knowledge is sought as a means to ethical action.

5. This last statement deserves some development, since the Socratic theory as to the relation between knowledge and virtue is characteristic of the Socratic ethic. According to Socrates knowledge and virtue are one, in the sense that the wise man, he who *knows* what is right, will also *do* what is right. In other

---

[1] *Metaph.*, M 1,078 b 17–19.　　[2] *Apol.*, 36.
[3] Xen., *Mem.*, i, 1, 16; *Apol.*, 36.

words, no one does evil knowingly and of set purpose; no one chooses the evil *as such*.

This "ethical intellectualism" seems at first sight to be in blatant contradiction with the facts of everyday life. Are we not conscious that we ourselves sometimes deliberately do what we know to be wrong, and are we not convinced that other people act sometimes in the same way? When we speak of a man as being responsible for a bad action, are we not thinking of him as having done that act with knowledge of its badness? If we have reason to suppose that he was not culpably ignorant of its badness, we do not hold him to be morally responsible. We are therefore inclined to agree with Aristotle, when he criticises the identification of knowledge and virtue on the ground that Socrates forgot the irrational parts of the soul and did not take sufficient notice of the fact of moral weakness, which leads a man to do what he knows to be wrong.[1]

It has been suggested that, as Socrates was himself singularly free from the influence of the passions in regard to moral conduct, he tended to attribute the same condition to others, concluding that failure to do what is right is due to ignorance rather than to moral weakness. It has also been suggested that when Socrates identified virtue with knowledge or wisdom he had in mind not any sort of knowledge but a real personal conviction. Thus Professor Stace points out that people may go to church and say that they believe the goods of this world to be worth nothing, whereas they *act* as if they were the only goods they valued. This is not the sort of knowledge Socrates had in mind: he meant a real personal conviction.[2]

All this may well be true, but it is important to bear in mind what Socrates meant by "right." According to Socrates that action is right which serves man's true utility, in the sense of promoting his true happiness (εὐδαιμονία). Everyone seeks his own good as a matter of course. Now, it is not every kind of action, however pleasant it may appear at the time, which promotes man's true happiness. For instance, it might be pleasant to a man to get drunk constantly, especially if he is suffering from some overwhelming sorrow. But it is not to the true good of man. Besides injuring his health, it tends to enslave him to a habit, and it goes counter to the exercise of man's highest possession, that

[1] *Eth. Nic.*, 1145 b.
[2] *Crit. Hist.*, pp. 147–8. Professor Stace considers, however, that "Aristotle's criticism of Socrates is unanswerable."

which differentiates him from the brute—his reason. If a man constantly gets drunk, believing this to be his true good, then he errs from ignorance, not realising what his true good is. Socrates would hold that if he knew that it was to his own true good and conducive to his happiness *not* to get drunk, then he would not get drunk. Of course we would remark with Aristotle that a man might well know that to contract a habit of drunkenness is not conducive to his ultimate happiness, and yet still contract the habit. This is doubtless true; it does not seem that Aristotle's criticism can be gainsaid; but at this point we might observe (with Stace) that if the man had a *real personal conviction* of the evil of the habit of drunkenness, he would not contract it. This does not dispose of Aristotle's objection, but it helps us to understand how Socrates could say what he did. And, as a matter of fact, is there not a good deal in what Socrates says, when viewed from the psychological standpoint? A man might know, intellectually, that to get drunk is not conducive to his ultimate happiness and dignity as a man, but when the impulse comes upon him, he may turn his attention away from this knowledge and fix it on the state of intoxication as seen against the background of his unhappy life, until this state and its desirability engage all his attention and take on the character of a true good. When the exhilaration has worn off, he recalls to mind the evil of drunkenness and admits: "Yes, I did wrong, knowing it to be wrong." But the fact remains, that at the moment when he surrendered to the impulse, that knowledge had slipped from the field of his mental attention, even if culpably.

Of course, we must not suppose that the utilitarian standpoint of Socrates envisages the following of whatever is pleasurable. The wise man realises that it is more advantageous to be self-controlled, than to have no self-control; to be just, rather than to be unjust; courageous, rather than cowardly—"advantageous" meaning what is conducive to true health and harmony of soul. Socrates certainly considered that pleasure is a good, but he thought that true pleasure and lasting happiness attend the moral rather than the immoral man, and that happiness does not consist in having a great abundance of external goods.

While we cannot accept the over-intellectualist attitude of Socrates, and agree with Aristotle that ἀκρασία or moral weakness is a fact which Socrates tended to overlook, we willingly pay tribute to the ethic of Socrates. For a rational ethic must be founded on human nature and the good of human nature as such. Thus when Hippias allowed ἄγραφοι νόμοι, but excepted from their number laws which varied from State to State, remarking that the prohibition of sexual intercourse between parents and children is not a universal prohibition, Socrates rightly answered that racial inferiority which results from such intercourse justifies the prohibition.[1] This is tantamount to appealing to what we would call "Natural Law," which is an expression of man's nature and conduces to its harmonious development. Such an ethic is indeed *insufficient*, since the Natural Law cannot acquire a morally binding force, obligatory in conscience—at least in the sense of our modern conception of "Duty"—unless it has a metaphysical basis and is grounded in a transcendental Source, God, Whose Will for man is expressed in the Natural Law; but, although insufficient, it enshrines a most important and valuable truth which is essential to the development of a rational moral philosophy. "Duties" are not simply senseless or arbitrary commands or prohibitions, but are to be seen in relation to human nature as such: the Moral Law expresses man's true good. Greek ethics were predominantly eudaemonological in character (cf. Aristotle's ethical system), and though, we believe, they need to be completed by Theism, and seen against the background of Theism, in order to attain their true development, they remain, even in their incomplete state, a perennial glory of Greek philosophy. Human nature is constant and so ethical values are constant, and it is Socrates' undying fame that he realised the constancy of these values and sought to fix them in universal definitions which could be taken as a guide and norm in human conduct.[2]

6. From the identification of wisdom and virtue follows the unity of virtue. There is really only one virtue, insight into what is truly good for man, what really conduces to his soul's health and harmony. A more important consequence, however, is the teachability of virtue. The Sophists, of course, professed to teach the art of virtue, but Socrates differed from them, not only in the fact that he declared himself to be a learner, but also in the fact that his ethical inquiries were directed to the discovery of universal

---

[1] Xen., *Mem.*, IV, 4, 19 ff.

[2] Not all thinkers have been willing to admit that human nature *is* constant. But there is no real evidence to show that "primitive" man differed essentially from modern man; nor have we justification for supposing that a type of man will arise in the future who will be *essentially* different from the man of to-day.

and constant moral norms. But though Socrates' method was dialectic and not lecturing, it necessarily follows from his identification of virtue with knowledge that virtue can be taught. We would make a distinction: intellectual knowledge of what virtue is can be imparted by instruction, but not virtue itself. However, if wisdom as real personal conviction is stressed, then *if* such wisdom can be taught, perhaps virtue could be taught too. The chief point to remark is that "teaching" for Socrates did not mean mere notional instruction, but rather leading a man to a real insight. Yet although such considerations undoubtedly render Socrates' doctrine of the teachability of virtue more intelligible, it remains true that in this doctrine the over-intellectualism of his ethic is again apparent. He insisted that as, e.g., the doctor is the man who has learnt medicine, so the just man is he who has learnt what is just.

7. This intellectualism was not likely to make Socrates particularly favourable to democracy as practised at Athens. If the doctor is the man who has learnt medicine, and if no sick man would entrust himself to the care of one who had no knowledge of medicine, it is unreasonable to choose public officials by lot or even by vote of the inexperienced multitude.[1] True rulers are those who know how to rule. If we would not appoint as pilot of a vessel a man devoid of all knowledge of the pilot's art and of the route to be traversed, why appoint as ruler of the State one who has no knowledge of ruling and who does not know what is to the good of the State?

8. In regard to religion, Socrates seems to have spoken generally of "gods" in the plural and to have meant thereby the traditional Greek deities; but one can discern a tendency towards a purer conception of Deity. Thus, according to Socrates, the knowledge of the gods is not limited, they are everywhere present and know all that is said and done. As they know best what is good, man should simply pray for the good and not for particular objects like gold.[2] Occasionally belief in one God comes to the fore,[3] but it does not appear that Socrates ever paid much attention to the question of monotheism or polytheism. (Even Plato and Aristotle find a place for the Greek gods.)

Socrates suggested that as man's body is composed of materials gathered from the material world, so man's reason is a part of the universal Reason or Mind of the world.[4] This notion was to be

[1] *Mem.*, I, 2, 9; 3, 9, 10. [2] *Mem.*, I, 3, 2. [3] *Mem.*, I, 4, 5, 7. [4] *Mem.*, I, 4, 8.

developed by others, as was also his teaching on teleology, anthropocentric in character. Not only are sense-organs given to man in order to enable him to exercise the corresponding senses, but anthropocentric teleology is extended to cosmic phenomena. Thus the gods give us the light without which we cannot see, and Providence is displayed in the gifts of food made to man by the earth. The sun does not approach so near the earth as to`wither up or to scorch man, nor is it set so far away that he cannot be warmed thereby. These and suchlike considerations are natural in a man who studied in the School of the Cosmologists and was disappointed at the little use that Anaxagoras made of his principle of Mind; but Socrates was not a Cosmologist or a Theologian, and though he may be called "the real founder of Teleology in the consideration of the world,"[1] he was, as we have seen, primarily interested in human conduct.[2]

9. The picture that Aristophanes gives of Socrates in the *Clouds* need not detain us.[3] Socrates had been a pupil of the old philosophers, and he had admittedly been influenced by the teaching of Anaxagoras. As to the "Sophistic" flavouring imparted to his character in the *Clouds*, it is to be remembered that Socrates like the Sophists, concentrated his attention on the Subject, on man himself. He was a public and familiar figure, known to all the audience for his dialectical activity, and to some he undoubtedly seemed to be "rationalistic," critically destructive and anti-traditionalist in tendency. Even if it were to be assumed that Aristophanes himself realised the difference that existed between Socrates and the Sophists—which is not at all clear—it would not necessarily follow that he would express this realisation before a public audience. And Aristophanes is known to have been a traditionalist and an opponent of the Sophists.

IV. *Trial and Death of Socrates*

In 406 B.C. Socrates showed his moral courage by refusing to agree to the demand that the eight commanders who were to be impeached for their negligence at Arginusae should be tried together, this being contrary to the law and calculated to evoke a hasty sentence. He was at this time a member of the Committee

---

[1] Ueb.-Praechter, p. 145; *der eigentliche Begründer der Teleologie in der Betrachtung der Welt.*
[2] Cf. e.g. *Mem.*, I, 1, 10–16.
[3] It is, as Burnet observes, a caricature which—like any caricature, if it is to have point—possesses a foundation in fact.

of the πρυτάνεις or Committee of the Senate. His moral courage
was again shown when he refused, at the demand of the Thirty
in 404/3, to take part in the arrest of Leon of Salamis, whom the
Oligarchs intended to murder, that they might confiscate his
property. They wished to incriminate as many prominent citizens
as possible in their doings, doubtless with a view to the eventual
day of reckoning. Socrates, however, simply refused to take any
part in their crimes, and would probably have paid for his refusal
with his life, had not the Thirty fallen.

In the year 400/399 Socrates was brought to trial by the leaders
of the restored democracy. Anytus, the politician who remained
in the background, instigated Meletus to carry on the prosecution.
The indictment before the court of the King Archon is recorded
as follows[1]: "Meletus, son of Miletus, of the deme of Pitthus,
indicts Socrates, son of Sophroniscus, of the deme of Alopecae,
on his oath, to the following effect. Socrates is guilty (i) of not
worshipping the gods whom the State worships, but introducing
new and unfamiliar religious practices; (ii) and, further, of corrupting the young. The prosecutor demands the death penalty."

The first charge was never explicitly defined, the reason seem-
ing to be that the prosecutor was relying on the jury's recollection
of the reputation of the old Ionian cosmologists and perhaps of
the profanation of the mysteries in 415, in which Alcibiades had
been involved. But no reference could be made to the profanation
in view of the Amnesty of 404/3, of which Anytus had himself
been the chief promoter. The second charge, that of corrupting
the young, is really a charge of infusing into the young a spirit
of criticism in regard to the Athenian Democracy. At the back of
it all was doubtless the thought that Socrates was responsible for
having "educated Alcibiades and Critias—Alcibiades, who had
for a time gone over to Sparta and who led Athens into such
straits, Critias, who was the most violent of the Oligarchs. This
again could not be explicitly mentioned because of the Amnesty
of 404/3, but the audience would have grasped easily enough
what was meant. That is why Aeschines could say, some fifty
years later: "You put Socrates the Sophist to death, because he
was shown to have educated Critias."[2]

The accusers no doubt supposed that Socrates would go into
voluntary exile without awaiting trial, but he did not. He
remained for trial in 399 and defended himself in court. In the

---

[1] Diog. Laërt., 2, 40.   [2] i, 173.

trial Socrates might have made much of his military service and of his defiance of Critias in the time of the Oligarchy, but he merely brought the facts in, coupling them with his defiance of the democracy in the matter of the trial of the commanders. He was condemned to death by a majority of either 60 or 6 votes by a jury of 500 or 501.[1] It then rested with Socrates to propose an alternative penalty, and it was obviously the wisest course to propose a sufficiently substantial penalty. Thus if Socrates had proposed exile, this alternative to the death penalty would doubtless have been accepted. Socrates, however, proposed as his proper "reward" free meals in the Pryntaneum, after which he consented to propose a small fine—and all this without any attempt to influence the jury, as was usual, by bringing a weeping wife and children into court. The jury was annoyed at Socrates' cavalier behaviour, and he was sentenced to death by a larger majority than the one that had found him guilty.[2] The execution had to be delayed for about a month, to await the return of the "sacred boat" from Delos (in memory of Theseus' deliverance of the city from the tribute of seven boys and girls imposed by Minos of Knossos), and there was plenty of time to arrange an escape, which the friends of Socrates did in fact arrange. Socrates refused to avail himself of their kind offers, on the ground that such a course would be contrary to his principles. Socrates' last day on earth is recounted by Plato in the *Phaedo*, a day that was spent by Socrates in discoursing on the immortality of the soul with his Theban friends, Cebes and Simmias.[3] After he had drunk the hemlock and lay dying, his last words were: "Crito, we owe a cock to Aesculapius; pay it, therefore, and do not neglect it." When the poison reached his heart there was a convulsive movement and he died, "and Crito, perceiving it, closed his mouth and eyes. This, Echecrates, was the end of our friend, a man, we should say, who was the best of all his time that we have known, and, moreover, the most wise and just."[4]

[1] Cf. *Apol.*, 36 a (the reading of which is not absolutely certain), and Diog. Laërt., 2, 41. Burnet and Taylor, understanding Plato as saying that Socrates was condemned by a majority of 60 votes, suppose that the voting was 280 to 220, out of a jury of 500.

[2] Diog. Laërt (2, 42) says that the majority was 80 votes in excess of the first majority. According to Burnet and Taylor, the second voting would thus be 360 in favour of the death penalty as against 140.

[3] This remark is not meant to prejudice my view that the theory of Forms is not to be ascribed to Socrates.

[4] *Phaedo*, 118.

CHAPTER XV

MINOR SOCRATIC SCHOOLS

THE term "Minor Socratic Schools" should not be taken to indicate that Socrates founded any definite School. He hoped, no doubt, that others would be found to carry on his work of stimulating men's minds, but he did not gather round him a band of disciples to whom he left a patrimony of definite doctrine. But various thinkers, who had been disciples of Socrates to a greater or less extent, emphasised one or other point in his teaching, combining it also with elements culled from other sources. Hence Dr. Praechter calls them *Die einseitigen Sokratiker*, not in the sense that these thinkers only *reproduced* certain sides of Socrates' teaching, but in the sense that each of them was a *continuation* of Socratic thought in a particular direction, while at the same time they modified what they took from earlier philosophising, in order to harmonise it with the Socratic legacy.[1] In some ways, then, the use of a common name, Minor Socratic Schools, is unfortunate, but it may be used, if it is understood that the connection of some of these thinkers with Socrates is but slender.

1. *The School of Megara*

Euclid of Megara (not to be confused with the mathematician) seems to have been one of the earliest disciples of Socrates, as— if the story be genuine—he continued his association with Socrates in spite of the prohibition (of 431/2) of Megarian citizens entering Athens, coming into the city at dusk dressed as a woman.[2] He was present at the death of Socrates in 400/399, and after that event Plato and other Socratics took refuge with Euclid at Megara.

Euclid seems to have been early acquainted with the doctrine of the Eleatics, which he so modified under the influence of the Socratic ethic as to conceive of the One as the Good. He also regarded virtue as a unity. According to Diogenes Laërtius, Euclid asserted that the One is known by many names, identifying the One with God and with Reason.[3] The existence of a

---

[1] Ueberweg-Praechter, p. 155.   [2] Gell, *Noct. Att.*, 6, 10.
[3] Diog. Laërt., 2, 106.

principle contrary to the Good he naturally denied, as that principle would be multiplicity, which is illusory on the Eleatic view. We may say that he remained an adherent of the Eleatic tradition, in spite of the Socratic influence that he underwent.

The Megaric philosophy, particularly under the influence of Eubulides, developed into an Eristic which concocted various ingenious arguments, designed to disprove a position through a *reductio ad absurdum*. For example, the famous difficulty: "One grain of corn is not a heap: add a grain and there is yet no heap: when does the heap begin?" was designed to show that plurality is impossible, as Zeno wanted to show that motion was impossible. Another conundrum is that ascribed by some to Diodorus Cronus, another Megaric: "That which you have not lost, you still have; but you have not lost horns; therefore you still have horns." Or again: "Electra knows her brother, Orestes. But Electra does not know Orestes (who stands before her, disguised). Therefore Electra does not know what she knows."[1]

Another philosopher of the Megaric School, Diodorus Cronus (mentioned above), identified the actual and the possible: only the actual is possible. His argument was as follows: The possible cannot become the impossible. Now, if of two contradictories one has actually come to pass, the other is impossible. Therefore, if it had been possible before, the impossible would have come out of the possible. Therefore it was not possible before, and only the actual is possible; (e.g. "The world exists," and "The world does not exist," are contradictory propositions. But the world actually exists. Therefore it is impossible that the world does not exist. But if it were ever possible that the world should not exist a possibility has turned into an impossibility. This cannot be so. Therefore it was never possible that the world should not exist.) This proposition has been taken up in recent times by Professor Nicolai Hartmann of Berlin, who has identified the actual with the possible on the ground that what actually happens depends on the totality of given conditions, and—given those conditions— nothing else could have happened.[2]

A noted adherent of the School was Stilpo of Megara, who taught at Athens about 320, but was afterwards banished. He applied himself chiefly to ethics, developing the point of self-sufficiency in a theory of "apathy." When asked what he had lost in the plundering of Megara, he replied that he had not seen

[1] Cf. Diog. Laërt., 2, 108. [2] *Möglichkeit und Wirklichkeit*, Berlin, 1938.

anyone carrying off wisdom or knowledge.[1] Zeno (the Stoic) was a pupil of Stilpo.

II. *The Elean-Eretrian School*

This School was named after Phaedo of Elis (the Phaedo of Plato's Dialogue) and Menedemus of Eretria. Phaedo of Elis seems to have resembled the Megarians in his use of dialectic, while Menedemus was chiefly interested in ethics, holding the unity of virtue and knowledge.

III. *The Early Cynic School*

The Cynics, or disciples of the dog, may have got their name from their unconventional mode of life or from the fact that Antisthenes, the founder of the School, taught in the gymnasium known as the *Kynosarges*. Perhaps both factors had something to do with the nickname.

Antisthenes (*c.* 445–*c.* 365) was born of an Athenian father and of a Thracian slave mother.[2] This might explain why he taught in the *Kynosarges*, which was reserved for those who were not of pure Athenian blood. The Gymnasium was dedicated to Heracles, and the Cynics took the hero as a sort of tutelary god or patron. One of Antisthenes' works was named after Heracles.[3]

At first a pupil of Gorgias, Antisthenes afterwards became an adherent of Socrates, to whom he was devoted. But what he chiefly admired in Socrates was the latter's independence of character, which led him to act in accordance with his convictions, no matter what the cost. Neglecting the fact that Socrates had been independent of earthly riches and the applause of men only in order to obtain the greater good of true wisdom, Antisthenes set up this independence and self-sufficiency as an ideal or end in itself. Virtue in his eyes was simply independence of all earthly possessions and pleasures: in fact, it was a negative concept— renunciation, self-sufficiency. Thus the negative side of Socrates' life was changed by Antisthenes into a positive goal or end. Similarly, Socrates' insistence on ethical knowledge was exaggerated

---

[1] Diog. Laërt., 2, 115. Senec., *Ep.*, 9, 3.   [2] Diog. Laërt., 6, 1.

[3] It has been suggested that it was Diogenes who founded the Cynic School or "Movement," and not Antisthenes: Arist. refers to the followers of Antisthenes as 'Αντισθενείοι (*Metaph.*, 1043 b 24). But the nickname of "Cynics" seems to have been accepted, only in the time of Diogenes and Arist.'s use of the term 'Αντισθενείοι would not appear to prove anything against Antisthenes having been the real fountain-head of the Cynic School.

by Antisthenes into a positive contempt for scientific learning and art. Virtue, he said, is sufficient by itself for happiness: nothing else is required—and virtue is the absence of desire, freedom from wants, and complete independence. Socrates, of course, had been independent of the opinion of others simply because he possessed deep convictions and principles, the sur-render of which, to satisfy popular opinion, he regarded as treason to the Truth. He did not, however, set out to flout popular opinion or public convictions simply for the sake of doing so, as the Cynics, particularly Diogenes, seem to have done. The philosophy of the Cynics was thus an exaggeration of one side of Socrates' life and attitude, and that a negative one or at least one consequent on a much more positive side. Socrates was ready to disobey the Oligarchy at the risk of his life, rather than commit an act of injustice; but he would not have lived in a tub like Diogenes merely to flaunt his disregard for the ways of men.

Antisthenes was strongly opposed to the theory of Ideas, and maintained that there are only individuals. He is said to have remarked: "O Plato, I see a horse, but I do not see horseness."[1] To each thing only its own name should be applied: e.g. we can say "Man is man" or "The good is good," but not "The man is good." No predicate should be attributed to a subject other than the subject itself.[2] With this goes the doctrine that we can only predicate of an individual its own individual nature; one cannot predicate of it membership of a class. Hence the denial of the theory of Ideas. Another logical theory of Antisthenes was that of the impossibility of self-contradiction. For if a man says different things, he is speaking of different objects.[3]

Virtue is wisdom, but this wisdom consists principally in "seeing through" the values of the majority of mankind. Riches, passions, etc., are not really good, nor are suffering, poverty, contempt, really evil: independence is the true good. Virtue, then, is wisdom and it is teachable, though there is no need of long reasoning and reflection in order to learn it. Armed with this virtue, the wise man cannot be touched by any so-called evil of life, even by slavery. He stands beyond laws and conventions, at least those of the State that does not recognise true virtue. The ideal state or condition of life in which all would live in

[1] Simplic. in Arist., *Categ.*, 208, 29 f.; 211, 17 f.
[2] Plat., *Soph.*, 251 b; Arist., *Metaph.*, Δ 29, 1024 b 32–25 a 1.
[3] Arist., *Top.*, A xi, 104 b 20; *Metaph.*, Δ 29, 1024 b 33–4.

5

independence and freedom from desire, is of course incompatible with wars.[1]

Socrates had, indeed, placed himself in opposition on occasion to the authority of the Government, but he was so convinced of the rightness of the State's authority as such and of the Law, that he would not take advantage of the opportunity presented to him of escape from prison, but preferred to suffer death in accordance with the Law. Antisthenes, however, with his usual one-sided exaggeration denounced the historic and traditional State and its Law. In addition he renounced the traditional religion. There is only one God; the Greek pantheon is only a convention. Virtue is the only service of God: temples, prayers, sacrifices, etc., are condemned. "By convention there are many gods, but by nature only one."[2] On the other hand, Antisthenes interpreted the Homeric myths allegorically, trying to get moral applications and lessons out of them.

Diogenes of Sinope (d. c. 324 B.C.) thought that Antisthenes had not lived up to his own theories and called him a "trumpet which hears nothing but itself."[3] Banished from his country, Diogenes spent most of his life in Athens, though he died in Corinth. He called himself the "Dog," and held up the life of animals as a model for mankind. His task was the "recoining of values,"[4] and to the civilisation of the Hellenic world he opposed the life of animals and of the barbaric peoples.

We are told that he advocated community of wives and children and free love, while in the political sphere he declared himself a citizen of the world.[5] Not content with Antisthenes' "indifference" to the external goods of civilisation, Diogenes advocated a positive asceticism in order to attain freedom. Connected therewith is his deliberate flouting of convention, doing in public what it is generally considered should be done in private—and even what should not be done in private.

Disciples of Diogenes were Monimus, Onesicritus, Philiscus Crates of Thebes. The latter presented his considerable fortune to the city, and took up the Cynic life of mendicancy, followed by his wife Hipparchia.[6]

[1] Cf. Vita Antisth., apud Diog. Laërt.
[2] Cf. Cic., De Nat., 1, 13, 32; Clem. Alex., Protrep., 6, 71, 2; Strom., 5, 14, 108, 4.
[3] Dion. Chrys., 8, 2.   [4] Diog. Laërt., 6, 20.   [5] Diog. Laërt., 6, 72.
[6] Diog. Laërt., Lives of Crates and Hipparchia.

IV. *The Cyrenaic School*

Aristippus of Cyrene, founder of the Cyrenaic School, was born about 435 B.C. From 416 he was in Athens, from 399 in Aegina, from 389/388 with Plato at the court of the elder Dionysius, and then again after 356 in Athens. But these dates and order of events cannot be regarded as beyond dispute, to say the least of it.[1] It has even been suggested that Aristippus never founded the Cyrenaic "School" at all, but was confused with his grandson, a later Aristippus. But in view of the statements of Diog. Laërt., Sotion and Panaetius (cf. D.L., 2, 84 f.), it does not seem possible to accept the statement of Sosicrates and others (D.L.) that Aristippus wrote nothing at all, while the passage in Eusebius' *Praeparatio Evangelica* (14, 18, 31) can be explained without having to suppose that Aristippus never laid a foundation for the Cyrenaic philosophy.

In Cyrene Aristippus seems to have become acquainted with the teaching of Protagoras, while afterwards at Athens he was in relation with Socrates. The Sophist may have been largely responsible for Aristippus' doctrine, that it is our sensations alone that give us certain knowledge:[2] of things in themselves they can give us no certain information, nor about the sensations of others. Subjective sensations, then, must be the basis for practical conduct. But if my individual sensations form the norm for my practical conduct, then, thought Aristippus, it follows as a matter of course that the end of conduct is to obtain pleasurable sensations.

Aristippus declared that sensation consists in movement. When the movement is gentle, the sensation is pleasurable; when it is rough, there is pain; when movement is imperceptible or when there is no movement at all, there is neither pleasure nor pain. The rough movement cannot be the ethical end. Yet it cannot consist in the mere absence of pleasure or pain, i.e. be a purely negative end. The ethical end must, therefore, be pleasure, a positive end.[3] Socrates had indeed declared that virtue is the one path to happiness, and he held out happiness as a motive for the practice of virtue, but he did not maintain that pleasure is the end of life. Aristippus, however, seized on the one side of the Socratic teaching and disregarded all the rest.

[1] Dates from Heinrich von Stein's *De philos. Cyrenaica*, part I, *De Vita Aristippi*, Gött, 1858.

[2] Cf. Sext. Emp. *adv. mathemat.*, 7, 191 ff.   [3] Diog. Laërt., 2, 86 ff.

Pleasure, then, according to Aristippus, is the end of life. But what kind of pleasure? Later on for Epicurus it would be rather painlessness, negative pleasure, that is the end of life; but for Aristippus it was positive and present pleasure. Thus it came about that the Cyrenaics valued bodily pleasure above intellectual pleasure, as being more intense and powerful. And it would follow from their theory of knowledge that the quality of the pleasure does not come into account. The consequential following-out of this principle would obviously lead to sensual excesses; but, as a matter of fact, the Cyrenaics, no doubt adopting the hedonistic elements in Socrates' doctrine, declared that the wise man will, in his choice of pleasure, take cognisance of the future. He will, therefore, avoid unrestrained excess, which would lead to pain, and he will avoid indulgence that would occasion punishment from the State or public condemnation. The wise man, therefore, needs judgment in order to enable him evaluate the different pleasures of life. Moreover, the wise man in his enjoyments will preserve a certain measure of independence. If he allows himself to be enslaved, then to that extent he cannot be enjoying pleasure, but rather is he in pain. Again, the wise man, in order to preserve cheerfulness and contentment, will limit his desires. Hence the saying attributed to Aristippus, ἔχω (Λαΐδα), καὶ οὐκ ἔχομαι ἐπεὶ τὸ κρατεῖν καὶ μὴ ἡττᾶσθαι ἡδονῶν ἄριστον, οὐ τὸ μὴ χρῆσθαι.[1]

This contradiction in the teaching of Aristippus between the principle of the pleasure of the moment and the principle of judgment, led to a divergence of views—or an emphasis on different sides of his doctrine—among his disciples. Thus *Theodorus the Atheist* declared indeed that judgment and justness are goods (the latter only because of the external advantages of a just life), and that individual acts of gratification are indifferent, the contentment of the mind being true happiness or pleasure, but he asserted too that the wise man will not give his life for his country and that he would steal, commit adultery, etc., if circumstances allowed it. He also denied the existence of any god at all.[2] *Hegesias* also demanded indifference towards individual acts of gratification, but he was so convinced of the miseries of life and of the impossibility of attaining happiness, that he emphasised a negative concept of the end of life, namely, absence of pain and sorrow.[3] Cicero and other sources tell us that Hegesias'

---

[1] Diog. Laërt., 2, 75. [2] Diog. Laërt., 2, 97; Cic., *De Nat. D.*, 1, 1, 12.
[3] Diog. Laërt., 2, 94–6.

lectures at Alexandria led to so many suicides on the part of his hearers, that Ptolemy Lagi forbade their continuance![1] *Anniceris*, on the other hand, stressed the positive side of Cyrenaicism, making positive pleasure and, indeed, individual acts of gratification the end of life. But he limited the logical conclusions of such a view by giving great weight to love of family and country, friendship and gratitude, which afford pleasure even when they demand sacrifice.[2] In the value he placed on friendship he differed from Theodorus, who declared (D.L.) that the wise are sufficient for themselves and have no need of friends.

Diogenes Laërtius clearly implies that these philosophers had their own peculiar disciples: for example, he speaks of "Hegesiakoi," though he also classes them together as "Cyrenaics." Thus, while Aristippus the Cyrenaic laid the foundation of the "Cyrenaic" or pleasure-philosophy (*v. sup.*), he can hardly be said to have founded a closely-knit philosophical School, comprising Theodorus, Hegesias, Anniceris, etc., as members. These philosophers were part-heirs of Aristippus the elder, and represent a philosophical tendency rather than a School in the strict sense.

---

[1] Cic., *Tusc.*, 1, 34, 83.
[2] Diog. Laërt., 2, 96 f.; Clem. Alex., *Strom.*, 2, 21, 130, 7 f.

CHAPTER XVI

DEMOCRITUS OF ABDERA

THIS would seem to be the right place to say something of the epistemological and ethical theories of Democritus of Abdera. Democritus was a disciple of Leucippus and, together with his Master, belongs to the Atomist School; but his peculiar interest for us lies in the fact that he gave attention to the problem of knowledge raised by Protagoras and to the problem of conduct which relativistic doctrines of the Sophists had rendered acute. Nowhere named by Plato, Democritus is frequently mentioned by Aristotle. He was head of a School at Abdera, and was still alive when Plato founded the Academy. The reports of his journeys to Egypt and Athens cannot be accepted with certainty.[1] He wrote copiously, but his writings have not been preserved.

1. The account of sensation given by Democritus was a mechanical one. Empedocles had spoken of "effluences" from objects which reach the eye, for example. The Atomists make these effluences to be atoms, images (δείκελα, εἴδωλα), which objects are constantly shedding. These images enter through the organs of sense, which are just passages (πόροι) and impinge on the soul, which is itself composed of atoms. The images, passing through the air, are subject to distortion by the air; and this is the reason why objects very far off may not be seen at all. Differences of colour were explained by differences of smoothness or roughness in the images, and hearing was given a like explanation, the stream of atoms flowing from the sounding body causing motion in the air between the body and the ear. Taste, smell and touch were all explained in the same way. (Secondary qualities would, therefore, not be objective.) We also obtain knowledge of the gods through such εἴδωλα; but gods denote for Democritus higher beings who are not immortal, though they live longer than men. They are δύσφθαρτα but not ἄφθαρτα. Strictly speaking, of course, the Atomist system would not admit of God, but only of atoms and the void.[2]

Now, Protagoras the Sophist, a fellow-citizen of Democritus, declared all sensation to be equally true for the sentient subject:

---

[1] Diog. Laërt., 9, 34 f. Cf. Burnet, *G.P.*, I, p. 195.

[2] According to Diog. Laërt. (9, 35), quoting Favorinus, Democritus ridiculed the assertions of Anaxagoras concerning Mind.

thus an object might be truly sweet for X, truly bitter for Y. Democritus, however, declared that all the sensations of the special senses are false, for there is nothing real corresponding to them outside the subject. "Νόμῳ there is sweet, νόμῳ there is bitter; νόμῳ there is warm and νόμῳ there is cold; νόμῳ there is colour. But ἐτεῇ there are atoms and the void."[1] In other words, our sensations are purely subjective, though they are caused by something external and objective—the atoms, namely—which, however, cannot be apprehended by the special senses. "By the senses we in truth know nothing sure, but only something that changes according to the disposition of the body and of the things that enter into it or resist it."[2] The special senses, then, give us no information about reality. Secondary qualities, at least, are not objective. "There are two forms of knowledge (γνώμη), the trueborn (γνησίη) and the bastard (σκοτίη). To the bastard belong all these: sight, hearing, smell, taste, touch. The trueborn is quite apart from these."[3] However, as the soul is composed of atoms, and as all knowledge is caused by the immediate contact with the subject of atoms coming from the outside, it is evident that the "trueborn" knowledge is on the same footing as the "bastard," in the sense that there is no absolute separation between sense and thought. Democritus saw this, and he comments: "Poor Mind, it is from us" (i.e. from the senses), "thou hast got the proofs to throw us with. Thy throw is a fall."[4]

2. Democritus' theory of conduct, so far as we can judge from the fragments, did not stand in scientific connection with his atomism. It is dominated by the idea of happiness or εὐδαιμονίη, which consists in εὐθυμίη or εὐεστώ. Democritus wrote a treatise on cheerfulness (Περὶ εὐθυμίης), which was used by Seneca and Plutarch. He considers that happiness is the end of conduct, and that pleasures and pain determine happiness; but "happiness dwelleth not in herds nor in gold; the soul is the dwelling-place of the 'daimon.' "[5] "The best thing for a man is to pass his life so as to have as much joy and as little trouble as may be."[6] However, just as sense-knowledge is not true knowledge, so the pleasures of sense are not true pleasures. "The good and the true are the same for all men, but the pleasant is different for different people."[7] We have to strive after well-being (εὐεστώ) or cheerfulness (εὐθυμίη), which is a state of soul, and the attainment of

---

[1] Frag. 9. [2] Frag. 9. [3] Frag. 11. [4] Frag. 125.
[5] Frag. 171. (Almost "fortune.") [6] Frag. 189. [7] Frag. 69.

which requires a weighing, judging and distinguishing of various pleasures. We should be guided by the principle of "symmetry" or of "harmony." By the use of this principle we may attain to calm of body—health, and calm of soul—cheerfulness. This calm or tranquillity is to be found chiefly in the goods of the soul. "He who chooses the goods of the soul, chooses the more divine; he who chooses the goods of the tabernacle (σκῆνος), chooses the human."[1]

3. It appears that Democritus exercised an influence on later writers through a theory of the evolution of culture.[2] Civilisation arose from need (χρεία) and prosecution of the advantageous or useful (σύμφερον), while man owes his arts to the imitation of nature, learning spinning from the spider, house-building from the swallow, song from the birds, etc. Democritus also (unlike Epicurus) emphasised the importance of the State and of political life, declaring that men should consider State affairs more important than anything else and see to it that they are well managed. But that his ethical ideas postulated freedom, whereas his atomism involved determinism, apparently did not occur to Democritus in the form of a problem.

4. It is clear from what has been said that Democritus, in carrying on the cosmological speculation of the older philosophers (in his philosophic atomism he was a follower of Leucippus), was hardly a man of his period—the Socratic period. His theories concerning perception, however, and the conduct of life, are of greater interest, as showing at least that Democritus realised that some answer was required to the difficulties raised by Protagoras. But, although he saw that some answer was required, he was personally unable to give any satisfactory solution. For an incomparably more adequate attempt to deal with epistemological and ethical problems, we have to turn to Plato.

---

[1] Frag. 37.   [2] Frag. 154.

PART III

PLATO

CHAPTER XVII

LIFE OF PLATO

PLATO, one of the greatest philosophers of the world, was born at Athens (or Aegina), most probably in the year 428/7 B.C., of a distinguished Athenian family. His father was named Ariston and his mother Perictione, sister of Charmides and niece of Critias, who both figured in the Oligarchy of 404/3. He is said to have been originally called Aristocles, and to have been given the name Plato only later, on account of his robust figure,[1] though the truth of Diogenes' report may well be doubted. His two brothers, Adeimantus and Glaucon, appear in the *Republic*, and he had a sister named Potone. After the death of Ariston, Perictione married Pyrilampes, and their son Antiphon (Plato's half-brother) appears in the *Parmenides*. No doubt Plato was brought up in the home of his stepfather; but although he was of aristo-cratic descent and brought up in an aristocratic household, it must be remembered that Pyrilampes was a friend of Pericles, and that Plato must have been educated in the traditions of the Periclean régime. (Pericles died in 429/8.) It has been pointed out by various authors that Plato's later bias against democracy can hardly have been due, at any rate solely, to his upbringing, but was induced by the influence of Socrates and still more by the treatment which Socrates received at the hands of the democracy. On the other hand, it would seem possible that Plato's distrust of democracy dated from a period very much earlier than that of the death of Socrates. During the later course of the Pelopon-nesian War (it is highly probable that Plato fought at Arginusae in 406) it can hardly have failed to strike Plato that the democracy lacked a truly capable and responsible leader, and that what leaders there were were easily spoiled by the necessity of pleasing the populace. Plato's final abstention from home politics no doubt dates from the trial and condemnation of his Master; but the

[1] Diog. Laërt., 3, 4.

formulation of his conviction that the ship of State needs a firm pilot to guide her, and that he must be one who *knows* the right course to follow, and who is prepared to act conscientiously in accordance with that knowledge, can hardly fail to have been laid during the years when Athenian power was passing to its eclipse.

According to a report of Diogenes Laërtius, Plato "applied himself to the study of painting, and wrote poems, dithyrambics at first, and afterwards lyric poems and tragedies."[1] How far this is true, we cannot say; but Plato lived in the flourishing period of Athenian culture, and must have received a cultured education. Aristotle informs us that Plato had been acquainted in his youth with Cratylus, the Heraclitean philosopher.[2] From him Plato would have learnt that the world of sense-perception is a world of flux, and so not the right subject-matter for true and certain knowledge. That true and certain knowledge is attainable on the conceptual level, he would have learnt from Socrates, with whom he must have been acquainted from early years. Diogenes Laërtius indeed asserted that Plato "became a pupil of Socrates" when twenty years old,[3] but as Charmides, Plato's uncle, had made the acquaintance of Socrates in 431,[4] Plato must have known Socrates at least before he was twenty. In any case we have no reason for supposing that Plato became a "disciple" of Socrates, in the sense of devoting himself wholly and professedly to philosophy, since he tells us himself that he originally intended to embark on a political career—as was natural in a young man of his antecedents.[5] His relatives in the Oligarchy of 403–4 urged Plato to enter upon political life under their patronage; but when the Oligarchy started to pursue a policy of violence and attempted to implicate Socrates in their crimes, Plato became disgusted with them. Yet the democrats were no better, since it was they who put Socrates to death, and Plato accordingly abandoned the idea of a political career.

Plato was present at the trial of Socrates, and he was one of the friends who urged Socrates to increase his proposed fine from one to thirty *minae*, offering to stand security;[6] but he was absent from the death-scene of his friend in consequence of an illness.[7] After the death of Socrates, Plato withdrew to Megara and took shelter with the philosopher Euclid, but in all probability he soon returned to Athens. He is said by the biographers to have

---

[1] Diog. Laërt., 3, 5.   [2] *Metaph.*, A 6, 987 a 32–5.   [3] Diog. Laërt., 3, 6.
[4] At least, this is what the reference to Potidaea (*Charmides*, 153) implies.
[5] *Ep.*, 7, 324 b 8–326 b 4.   [6] *Apol.*, 34 a 1, 38 b 6–9.   [7] *Phaedo*, 59 b 10.

travelled to Cyrene, Italy and Egypt, but it is uncertain what truth there is in these stories. For instance, Plato himself says nothing of any visit to Egypt. It may be that his knowledge of Egyptian mathematics, and even of the games of the children, indicate an actual journey to Egypt; on the other hand, the story of the journey may have been built up as a mere conclusion from what Plato has to say about the Egyptians. Some of these stories are obviously legendary in part; e.g. some give him Euripides as a companion, although the poet died in 406. This fact makes us rather sceptical concerning the reports of the journeys in general; but all the same, we cannot say with certainty that Plato did *not* visit Egypt, and he may have done so. If he did actually go to Egypt, he may have gone about 395 and have returned to Athens at the outbreak of the Corinthian wars. Professor Ritter thinks it very probable that Plato was a member of the Athenian force in the first years of the wars (395 and 394).

What is certain, however, is that Plato visited Italy and Sicily, when he was forty years old.[1] Possibly he wished to meet and converse with members of the Pythagorean School: in any case he became acquainted with Archytas, the learned Pythagorean. (According to Diogenes Laërtius, Plato's aim in undertaking the journey was to see Sicily and the volcanoes.) Plato was invited to the court of Dionysius I, Tyrant of Syracuse, where he became a friend of Dion, the Tyrant's brother-in-law. The story goes that Plato's outspokenness excited the anger of Dionysius, who gave him into the charge of Pollis, a Lacedaemonian envoy, to sell as a slave. Pollis sold Plato at Aegina (at that time at war with Athens), and Plato was even in danger of losing his life; but eventually a man of Cyrene, a certain Anniceris, ransomed him and sent him to Athens.[2] It is difficult to know what to make of this story, as it is not mentioned in Plato's *Epistles*: if it really happened (Ritter accepts the story) it must be dated 388 B.C.

On his return to Athens, Plato seems to have founded the Academy (388/7), near the sanctuary of the hero Academus. The Academy may rightly be called the first European university, for the studies were not confined to philosophy proper, but extended over a wide range of auxiliary sciences, like mathematics, astronomy and the physical sciences, the members of the School joining in the common worship of the Muses. Youths came to the Academy, not only from Athens itself, but also from abroad;

[1] *Ep.*, 7, 324 a 5-6. [2] Diog. Laërt., 3, 19-20.

and it is a tribute to the scientific spirit of the Academy and a proof that it was not simply a "philosophical-mystery" society, that the celebrated mathematician Eudoxus transferred himself and his School from Cyzicus to the Academy. It is as well to lay stress on this scientific spirit of the Academy, for though it is perfectly true that Plato aimed at forming statesmen and rulers, his method did not consist in simply teaching those things which would be of immediate practical application, e.g. rhetoric (as did Isocrates in his School), but in fostering the disinterested pursuit of science. The programme of studies culminated in philosophy, but it included as preliminary subjects a study of mathematics and astronomy, and no doubt harmonics, in a disinterested and not purely utilitarian spirit. Plato was convinced that the best training for public life is not a merely practical "sophistic" training, but rather the pursuit of science for its own sake. Mathematics, apart of course from its importance for Plato's philosophy of the Ideas, offered an obvious field for disinterested study, and it had already reached a high pitch of development among the Greeks. (The studies seem also to have included biological, e.g. botanical, researches, pursued in connection with problems of logical classification.) The politician so formed will not be an opportunist time-server, but will act courageously and fearlessly in accordance with convictions founded on eternal and changeless truths. In other words, Plato aimed at producing statesmen and not demagogues.

Besides directing the studies in the Academy, Plato himself gave lectures and his hearers took notes. It is important to notice that these lectures were not published, and that they stand in contrast to the dialogues, which were published works meant for "popular" reading. If we realise this fact, then some of the sharp differences that we naturally tend to discern between Plato and Aristotle (who entered the Academy in 367) disappear, at least in part. We possess Plato's popular works, his dialogues, but not his lectures. The situation is the exact opposite in regard to Aristotle, for while the works of Aristotle that are in our hands represent his lectures, his popular works or dialogues have not come down to us—only fragments remain. We cannot, therefore, by a comparison of Plato's dialogues with Aristotle's lectures, draw conclusions, without further evidence, as to a strong opposition between the two philosophers in point of literary ability, for instance, or emotional, aesthetic and "mystical" outlook. We are told that Aristotle used to relate how those who came to hear Plato's lecture on the Good, were often astonished to hear of nothing but arithmetic and astronomy, and of the limit and the One. In *Ep*. 7, Plato repudiates the accounts that some had published of the lecture in question. In the same letter he says: "So there is not, and may there never be, any treatise by me at least on these things, for the subject is not communicable in words, as other sciences are. Rather is it that after long association in the business itself and a shared life that a light is lit in the soul, kindled, as it were, by a leaping flame, and thenceforward feeds itself." Again, in *Ep*. 2: "Therefore I have never myself written a word on these matters, and there neither is nor ever shall be any written treatise of Plato; what now bears the name belongs to Socrates, beautified and rejuvenated."[1] From such passages some draw the conclusion that Plato had not much opinion of the value of books for really educative purposes. This may well be so, but we should not put undue emphasis on this point, for Plato, after all, *did* publish books—and we must also remember that the passages in question may not be by Plato at all. Yet we must concede that the Ideal Theory, in the precise form in which it was taught in the Academy, was not given to the public in writing.

Plato's reputation as teacher and counsellor of statesmen must have contributed to bringing about his second journey to Syracuse in 367. In that year Dionysius I died, and Dion invited Plato to come to Syracuse in order to take in hand the education of Dionysius II, then about thirty years old. Plato did so, and set the Tyrant to a course of geometry. Soon, however, Dionysius' jealousy of Dion got the upper hand, and when Dion left Syracuse, the philosopher after some difficulty managed to return to Athens, whence he continued to instruct Dionysius by letter. He did not succeed in bringing about a reconciliation between the Tyrant and his uncle, who took up residence at Athens, where he consorted with Plato. In 361, however, Plato undertook a third journey to Syracuse at the earnest request of Dionysius, who wished to continue his philosophical studies. Plato apparently hoped to draft a constitution for a proposed confederation of Greek cities against the Carthaginian menace, but opposition proved too strong: moreover, he found himself unable to secure the recall of Dion, whose fortune was confiscated by his nephew.

---

[1] *Ep*. 7, 341 c 4–d 2; *Ep*. 2, 314 c 1–4.

In 360, therefore, Plato returned to Athens, where he continued his activities in the Academy until his death in the year 348/7.[1] (In 357 Dion succeeded in making himself master of Syracuse, but he was murdered in 353, to the great grief of Plato, who felt that he had been disappointed in his dream of a philosopher-king.)

[1] *Uno et octogesimo anno scribens est mortuus.* Cic., *De Senect.*, 5, 13.

CHAPTER XVIII

PLATO'S WORKS

A. *Genuineness*

IN general it may be said that we possess the entire corpus of Plato's works. As Professor Taylor remarks: "Nowhere in later antiquity do we come on any reference to a Platonic work which we do not still possess."[1] We may suppose, then, that we possess all Plato's published dialogues. We do not, however, as already remarked, possess a record of the lectures that he delivered in the Academy (though we have more or less cryptic references in Aristotle), and this would be all the more to be regretted if those are right who would see in the dialogues popular work designed for the educated laymen, to be distinguished from the lectures delivered to professional students of philosophy. (It has been conjectured that Plato lectured without a manuscript. Whether this be the fact or not, we have not got the manuscript of any lectures delivered by Plato. All the same, we have no right to draw an oversharp distinction between the doctrines of the dialogues and the doctrine delivered within the precincts of the Academy. After all, not all the dialogues can easily be termed "popular" work, and certain of them in particular show evident signs that Plato is therein groping after the clarification of his opinions.) But to say that we most probably possess all the dialogues of Plato, is not the same as to say that all the dialogues that have come down to us under the name of Plato are actually by Plato himself: it still remains to sift the genuine from the spurious. The oldest Platonic MSS. belong to an arrangement attributed to a certain Thrasyllus, to be dated round about the beginning of the Christian era. In any case this arrangement, which was by "tetralogies," seems to have been based on an arrangement in "trilogies" by Aristophanes of Byzantium in the third century B.C. It would appear, then, that the thirty-six dialogues (reckoning the Epistles as one dialogue) were generally admitted by scholars of that period to be the work of Plato. The problem can thus be reduced to the question: "Are the thirty-six dialogues all genuine or are some of them spurious; and, if so, which?"

[1] *Plato*, p. 10.

Doubts were cast upon some of the dialogues even in antiquity. Thus from Athenaeus (*flor. c.* 228 B.C.) we learn that some ascribed the *Alcibiades II* to Xenophon. Again, it would seem that Proclus not only rejected the *Epinomis* and *Epistles*, but even went so far as to reject the *Laws* and *Republic*. The assigning of spurious works was carried much further, as might be expected, in the nineteenth century, especially in Germany, the culmination of the process being reached under Ueberweg and Schaarschmidt. "If one includes the attacks of ancient and modern criticism, then of the thirty-six items of the tetralogies of Thrasyllus, only five have remained free from all attack."[1] Nowadays, however, criticism runs in a more conservative direction, and there is general agreement as to the genuineness of all the important dialogues, as also a general agreement as to the spurious character of certain of the less important dialogues, while the genuineness of a few of the dialogues remains a matter of dispute. The results of critical investigation may be summed up as follows:

(i) Dialogues which are generally rejected are: *Alcibiades II, Hipparchus, Amatores* or *Rivales, Theages, Clitophon, Minus.* Of this group, all except the *Alcibiades II* are probably contemporary fourth-century work, not deliberate forgeries but slighter works of the same character as the Platonic dialogues; and they may be taken, with some degree of justification, as contributing something to our knowledge of the conception of Socrates current in the fourth century. The *Alcibiades II* is probably later work.

(ii) The genuineness of the following six dialogues is disputed: *Alcibiades I, Ion, Menexenus, Hippias Maior, Epinomis, Epistles.* Professor Taylor thinks that the *Alcibiades I* is the work of an immediate disciple of Plato[2] and Dr. Praechter, too, thinks that it is probably not the authentic work of the Master.[3] Praechter considers the *Ion* to be genuine, and Taylor remarks that it "may reasonably be allowed to pass as genuine until some good reason for rejecting it is produced."[4] The *Menexenus* is clearly taken by Aristotle to be of Platonic origin, and modern critics are inclined to accept this view.[5] The *Hippias Maior* is most probably to be taken as the genuine work of Plato, as it seems to be alluded to, though not by name, in the *Topics* of Aristotle.[6] As to the *Epinomis*, though Professor Jaeger ascribes it to Philippus of

---

[1] Ueberweg-Praechter, p. 195. Dr. Praechter's invaluable work does not, of course, represent the hypercritical fashion of the time of Ueberweg.
[2] *Plato*, p. 13. [3] Ueberweg-Praechter, p. 199. [4] *Plato*, p. 13.
[5] Arist., *Rhet.*, 1415 b 30. [6] *Topics* A 5, 102 a 6; E 5, 135 a 13; Z 6, 146 a 22.

Opus,[1] Praechter and Taylor deem it authentic. Of the *Epistles*, 6, 7 and 8 are generally accepted and Professor Taylor thinks that the acceptance of these *Epistles* leads logically to the acceptance of all the rest, except 1 and possibly 2. It is true that one would not like to relinquish the *Epistles*, as they give us much valuable information concerning Plato's biography; but we must be careful not to let this very natural desire influence unduly our acceptance of *Epistles* as genuine.[2]

(iii) The genuineness of the remaining dialogues may be accepted; so that the result of criticism would seem to be that of the thirty-six dialogues of the tetralogies, six are generally rejected, six others may be accepted until proved unauthentic (except probably *Alcibiades I* and certainly *Epistle I*), while twenty-four are certainly the genuine work of Plato. We have, therefore, a very considerable body of literature on which to found our conception of the thought of Plato.

B. *Chronology of Works*

1. *Importance* of determining the chronology of the works.

It is obviously important in the case of any thinker to see how his thought developed, how it changed—if it did change— what modifications were introduced in the course of time, what fresh ideas were introduced. The customary illustration in this connection is that of the literary production of Kant. Our knowledge of Kant would scarcely be adequate, if we thought that his Critiques came in his early years and that he later reverted to a "dogmatic" position. We might also instance the case of Schelling. Schelling produced several philosophies in the course of his life, and for an understanding of his thought it is highly desirable that one should know that he began with the standpoint of Fichte, and that his theosophical flights belong to his later years.

2. Method of determining the chronology of the works.[3]

(i) The criterion that has proved of most help in determining the chronology of the works of Plato is that of *language*. The argument from language is all the surer in that, while differences of content may be ascribed to the conscious selection and purpose of the author, development of linguistic style is largely

---

[1] *Aristotle*, e.g. p. 132. Cf. Diog. Laërt., 3, 37. Taylor (*Plato*, p. 497) thinks that Diog. only means that Philippus transcribed the *Epinomis* from wax tablets.

[2] Ritter accepts Epistles 3 and 8 and the main narrative of 7.

[3] Cf. Ueberweg-Praechter, pp. 199–218.

unconscious. Thus Dittenberger traces the frequent use of τί μήν; and the growing use of γε μήν and ἀλλα μήν, as formula of agreement, to the first Sicilian journey of Plato. The *Laws* certainly belong to Plato's old age,[1] while the *Republic* belongs to an earlier period. Now, not only is there a decreased vigour of dramatic power visible in the *Laws*, but we can also discern points of linguistic style which Isocrates had introduced into Attic prose and which do not appear in the *Republic*. This being so, we are helped in assessing the order of the intervening dialogues, according to the degree in which they approach the later style of writing.

But while the use of linguistic style as a criterion for determining the chronology of the dialogues has proved to be the most helpful method, one cannot, of course, neglect to make use of other criteria, which may often decide the matter at issue when the linguistic indications are doubtful or even contradictory.

(ii) One obvious criterion for assessing the order of the dialogues is that afforded by the direct testimony of the ancient writers, though there is not as much help to be had from this source as might perhaps be expected. Thus while Aristotle's assertion that the *Laws* were written later than the *Republic* is a valuable piece of information, the report of Diogenes Laërtius to the effect that the *Phaedrus* is the earliest of the Platonic dialogues cannot be accepted. Diogenes himself approves of the report, but it is evident that he is arguing from the subject-matter (love—in the first part of the dialogue) and from the poetic style.[2] We cannot argue from the fact that Plato treats of love to the conclusion that the dialogue must have been written in youth, while the use of poetic style and myth is not in itself conclusive. As Taylor points out, we should go far wrong were we to argue from the poetical and "mythical" flights of the second part of Faust to the conclusion that Goethe wrote the second part before the first.[3] A similar illustration might be taken from the case of Schelling, whose theosophical flights, as already mentioned, took place in his advanced age.

(iii) As for references within the dialogues to historical persons and acts, these are not so very many, and in any case they only furnish us with a *terminus post quem*. For example, if there were a reference to the death of Socrates, as in the *Phaedo*, the dialogue must clearly have been composed after the death of Socrates, but that does not tell us *how long after*. However, critics

---

[1] Arist., *Pol.*, B 6, 1264 b 27.   [2] Diog. Laërt., 3, 38.   [3] *Plato*, p. 18.

have obtained some help from this criterion. For instance, they have argued that the *Meno* was probably written when the incident of the corruption of Ismenias of Thebes was still fresh in people's memory.[1] Again, if the *Gorgias* contains a reply to a speech of Polycrates against Socrates (393/2), the *Gorgias* would probably have been written between 393 and 389, i.e. before the first Sicilian journey. It might, naïvely, be supposed that the age ascribed to Socrates in the dialogues is an indication of the date of composition of the dialogue itself, but to apply this criterion as a universal rule is clearly going too far. For instance, a novelist might well introduce his detective-hero as a grown man and as an already experienced police officer in his first novel, and then in a later novel treat of the hero's first case. Moreover, though one may be justified in supposing that dialogues dealing with the personal fate of Socrates were composed not long after his death, it would be clearly unscientific to take it for granted that dialogues dealing with the last years of Socrates, e.g. the *Phaedo* and the *Apology*, were all published at the same time.

(iv) References of one dialogue to another would obviously prove a help in determining the order of the dialogues, since a dialogue that refers to another dialogue must have been written after the dialogue to which it refers, but it is not always easy to decide if an apparent reference to another dialogue really *is* a reference. However, there are some cases in which there is a clear reference, e.g. the reference to the *Republic* that is contained in the *Timaeus*.[2] Similarly, the *Politicus* is clearly the sequel to the *Sophistes* and so must be a later composition.[3]

(v) In regard to the actual content of the dialogue, we have to exercise the greatest prudence in our use of this criterion. Suppose for instance, that some philosophical doctrine is found in a short summary sentence in dialogue X, while in dialogue Y it is found treated at length. A critic might say: "Very good, in dialogue X a preliminary sketch is given, and in dialogue Y the matter is explained at length." Might it not be that a short summary is given in dialogue X precisely because the doctrine has already been treated at length in dialogue Y? One critic[4] has maintained that the negative and critical examination of problems precedes the positive and constructive exposition. If this be taken as a criterion, then the *Theaetetus*, the *Sophistes*, the *Politicus*, the

---

[1] *Meno*, 90 a. [2] 17 ff. [3] *Polit.*, 284 b 7 ff., 286 b 10.
[4] K. Fr. Hermann.

Parmenides, should precede in date of composition the *Phaedo* and the *Republic*, but investigation has shown that this cannot be so.

However, to say that the content-criterion has to be used with prudence, is not to say that it has no use. For example, the attitude of Plato towards the doctrine of Ideas suggests, that the *Theaetetus*, *Parmenides*, *Sophistes*, *Politicus*, *Philebus*, *Timaeus*, should be grouped together, while the connection of the *Parmenides*, *Sophistes* and *Politicus* with the Eleatic dialectic suggests that these dialogues stand in a peculiarly close relation with one another.

(vi) Differences in the artistic construction of the dialogues may also be of help in determining their relation to one another in regard to order of composition. Thus in certain dialogues the setting of the dialogue, the characterisation of the personages who take part in it, are worked out with great care: there are humorous and playful allusions, vivid interludes and so on. To this group of dialogues belongs the *Symposium*. In other dialogues, however, the artistic side retreats into the background, and the author's attention is obviously wholly occupied with the philosophic content. In dialogues of this second group—to which the *Timaeus* and the *Laws* would belong—form is more or less neglected: content is everything. A probably legitimate conclusion is that the dialogues written with more attention to artistic form are earlier than the others, as artistic vigour flagged in Plato's old age and his attention was engrossed by the theoretic philosophy. (This does not mean that the use of poetic *language* necessarily becomes less frequent, but that the power of conscious artistry tends to decrease with years.)

3. Scholars vary in their estimate of the results obtained by the use of criteria such as the foregoing; but the following chronological schemes may be taken as, in the main, satisfactory (though it would hardly be acceptable to those who think that Plato did not write when he was directing the Academy in its early years).

1. *Socratic Period*

In this period Plato is still influenced by the Socratic intellectual determinism. Most of the dialogues end without any definite result having been attained. This is characteristic of Socrates' "not knowing."

i. *Apology*. Socrates' defence at his trial.
ii. *Crito*. Socrates is exhibited as the good citizen who, in spite of his unjust condemnation, is willing to give up his life in obedience to the laws of the State. Escape is suggested by Crito and others, and money is provided; but Socrates declares that he will abide by his principles.
iii. *Euthyphron*. Socrates awaits his trial for impiety. On the nature of piety. No result to the inquiry.
iv. *Laches*. On courage. No result.
v. *Ion*. Against the poets and rhapsodists.
vi. *Protagoras*. Virtue is knowledge and can be taught.
vii. *Charmides*. On temperance. No result.
viii. *Lysis*. On friendship. No result.
ix. *Republic*. Bk. I. On justice.
(The *Apology* and *Crito* must obviously have been written at an early date. Probably the other dialogues of this group were also composed before the first Sicilian journey from which Plato returned by 388/7.)

II. *Transition Period*

Plato is finding his way to his own opinions.

x. *Gorgias*. The practical politician, or the rights of the stronger versus the philosopher, or justice at all costs.
xi. *Meno*. Teachability of virtue corrected in view of ideal theory.
xii. *Euthydemus*. Against logical fallacies of later Sophists.
xiii. *Hippias* I. On the beautiful.
xiv. *Hippias* II. Is it better to do wrong voluntarily or involuntarily?
xv. *Cratylus*. On the theory of language.
xvi. *Menexenus*. A parody on rhetoric.
(The dialogues of this period were probably composed before the first Sicilian journey, though Praechter thinks that the *Menexenus* dates from after the journey.)

III. *Period of Maturity*

Plato is in possession of his own ideas.

xvii. *Symposium*. All earthly beauty is but a shadow of true Beauty, to which the soul aspires by Eros.
xviii. *Phaedo*. Ideas and Immortality.

xix. *Republic*. The State. Dualism strongly emphasised, i.e. metaphysical dualism.

xx. *Phaedrus*. Nature of love: possibility of philosophic rhetoric.

Tripartition of soul, as in *Rep*.

(These dialogues were probably composed between the first and second Sicilian journeys.)

IV. *Works of Old Age*

xxi. *Theaetetus*. (It may be that the latter part was composed *after* the *Parmenides*.) Knowledge is not sense-perception or true judgment.

xxii. *Parmenides*. Defence of ideal theory against criticism.

xxiii. *Sophistes*. Theory of Ideas again considered.

xxiv. *Politicus*. The true ruler is the *knower*. The legal State is a makeshift.

xxv. *Philebus*. Relation of pleasure to good.

xxvi. *Timaeus*. Natural science. Demiurge appears.

xxvii. *Critias*. Ideal agrarian State contrasted with imperialistic sea-power, "Atlantis."

xxviii. *Laws* and *Epinomis*. Plato makes concessions to real life, modifying the Utopianism of the *Republic*.

(Of these dialogues, some may have been written between the second and third Sicilian journeys, but the *Timaeus*, *Critias*, *Laws* and *Epinomis* were probably written after the third journey).

xxix. Letters 7 and 8 must have been written after the death of Dion in 353.

Note

Plato never published a complete, nicely rounded-off and finished philosophical system: his thought continued to develop as fresh problems, other difficulties to be considered, new aspects of his doctrine to be emphasised or elaborated, certain modifications to be introduced, occurred to his mind.[1] It would, therefore, be desirable to treat Plato's thought genetically, dealing with the different dialogues in their chronological order, so far as this can be ascertained. This is the method adopted by Professor A. E. Taylor in his outstanding work, *Plato, the Man and his Work*.

[1] Cf. the words of Dr. Praechter, *Platon ist ein Werdender gewesen sein Leben lang*. Ueberweg-Praechter, p. 260.

In a book such as this, however, such a course is scarcely practicable, and so I have thought it necessary to divide up the thought of Plato into various compartments. None the less, in order to avoid, as much as can be, the danger of cramming together views that spring from different periods of Plato's life, I will attempt not to lose sight of the gradual genesis of the Platonic doctrines. In any case, if my treatment of Plato's philosophy leads the reader to turn his attention to the actual dialogues of Plato, the author will consider himself amply rewarded for any pains he has taken.

CHAPTER XIX

THEORY OF KNOWLEDGE

PLATO'S theory of knowledge cannot be found systematically expressed and completely elaborated in any one dialogue. The *Theaetetus* is indeed devoted to the consideration of problems of knowledge, but its conclusion is negative, since Plato is therein concerned to refute false theories of knowledge, especially the theory that knowledge is sense-perception. Moreover, Plato had already, by the time he came to write the *Theaetetus*, elaborated his theory of degrees of "knowledge," corresponding to the hierarchy of being in the *Republic*. We may say, then, that the positive treatment preceded the negative and critical, or that Plato, having made up his mind what knowledge is, turned later to the consideration of difficulties and to the systematic refutation of theories which he believed to be false.[1] In a book like the present one, however, it seems best to treat first of the negative and critical side of the Platonic epistemology, before proceeding to consider his positive doctrine. Accordingly, we propose first of all to summarise the argument of the *Theaetetus*, before going on to examine the doctrine of the *Republic* in regard to knowledge. This procedure would seem to be justified by the exigencies of logical treatment, as also by the fact that the *Republic* is not primarily an epistemological work at all. Positive epistemological doctrine is certainly contained in the *Republic*, but some of the *logically prior* presuppositions of that doctrine are contained in the later dialogue, the *Theaetetus*.

The task of summarising the Platonic epistemology and giving it in systematic form is complicated by the fact that it is difficult to separate Plato's epistemology from his ontology. Plato was not a critical thinker in the sense of Immanuel Kant, and though it is possible to read into his thoughts an anticipation of the Critical Philosophy (at least, this is what some writers have endeavoured to do), he is inclined to assume that we can have knowledge and to be primarily interested in the question what

[1] We do not thereby mean to imply that Plato had not made up his mind as to the status of sense-perception long before he wrote the *Theaetetus* (we have only to read the *Republic*, for instance, or consider the genesis and implications of the Ideal Theory): we refer rather to systematic consideration in published writings.

is the true object of knowledge. This means that ontological and epistemological themes are frequently intermingled or treated *pari passu*, as in the *Republic*. We will make an attempt to separate the epistemology from the ontology, but the attempt cannot be wholly successful, owing to the very character of the Platonic epistemology.

1. *Knowledge is not Sense-perception*

Socrates, interested like the Sophists in practical conduct, refused to acquiesce in the idea that truth is relative, that there is no stable norm, no abiding object of knowledge. He was convinced that ethical conduct must be founded on knowledge, and that that knowledge must be knowledge of eternal values which are not subject to the shifting and changing impressions of sense or of subjective opinion, but are the same for all men and for all peoples and all ages. Plato inherited from his Master this conviction that there can be knowledge in the sense of objective and universally valid knowledge; but he wished to demonstrate this fact theoretically, and so he came to probe deeply into the problems of knowledge, asking what knowledge is and of what.

In the *Theaetetus* Plato's first object is the refutation of false theories. Accordingly he sets himself the task of challenging the theory of Protagoras that knowledge is perception, that what appears to an individual to be true is true for that individual. His method is to elicit dialectically a clear statement of the theory of knowledge implied by the Heraclitean ontology and the epistemology of Protagoras, to exhibit its consequences and to show that the conception of "knowledge" thus attained does not fulfil the requirements of true knowledge at all, since knowledge must be, Plato assumes, (i) infallible, and (ii) of what *is*. Sense-perception is neither the one nor the other.

The young mathematical student Theaetetus enters into conversation with Socrates, and the latter asks him what he thinks knowledge to be. Theaetetus replies by mentioning geometry, the sciences and the crafts, but Socrates points out that this is no answer to his question, for he had asked, not *of* what knowledge is, but *what* knowledge is. The discussion is thus meant to be epistemological in character, though, as has been already pointed out, ontological considerations cannot be excluded, owing to the very character of the Platonic epistemology.

Moreover, it is hard to see how in any case ontological questions can be avoided in an epistemological discussion, since there is no knowledge *in vacuo*: knowledge, if it is knowledge at all, must necessarily be knowledge of something, and it may well be that knowledge is necessarily related to some particular type of object.

Theaetetus, encouraged by Socrates, makes another attempt to answer the question proposed, and suggests that "knowledge is nothing but perception,"[1] thinking no doubt primarily of vision, though in itself perception has, of course, a wider connotation. Socrates proposes to examine this idea of knowledge, and in the course of conversation elicits from Theaetetus an admission of Protagoras' view that perception means appearance, and that appearances vary with different subjects. At the same time he gets Theaetetus to agree that knowledge is always of something that *is*, and that, as being knowledge, it must be infallible.[2] This having been established, Socrates next tries to show that the objects of perception are, as Heraclitus taught, always in a state of flux: they never *are*, they are always *becoming*. (Plato does not, of course, accept Heraclitus' doctrine that *all* is becoming, though he accepts the doctrine in regard to the objects of sense-perception, drawing the conclusion that sense-perception cannot be the same as knowledge.) Since an object may appear white to one at one moment, grey at another, sometimes hot and sometimes cold, etc., "appearing to" must mean "becoming for," so that perception is always of that which is in process of becoming. My perception is true for me, and if I know what appears to me, as I obviously do, then my knowledge is infallible. So Theaetetus has said well that perception is knowledge.

This point having been reached, Socrates proposes to examine the idea more closely. He raises the objection that if knowledge is perception, then no man can be wiser than any other man, for I am the best judge of my own sense-perception as such. What, then, is Protagoras' justification for setting himself up to teach others and to take a handsome fee for doing so? And where is our ignorance that makes us sit at his feet? For is not each one of us the measure of his own wisdom? Moreover, if knowledge and perception are the same, if there is no difference between seeing and knowing, it follows that a man who has come to know (i.e. see) a thing in the past and still remembers it, does not know it—although he remembers it—since he does not see it.

[1] 151 e 2–3.   [2] 152 c 5–7.

Conversely, granted that a man can remember something he has formerly perceived and can *know* it, even while no longer perceiving it, it follows that knowledge and perception cannot be equated (even if perception were a kind of knowledge).

Socrates then attacks Protagoras' doctrine on a broader basis, understanding "Man is the measure of all things," not merely in reference to sense-perception, but also to all truth. He points out that the majority of mankind believe in knowledge and ignorance, and believe that they themselves or others can hold something to be true which in point of fact is not true. Accordingly, anyone who holds Protagoras' doctrine to be false is, according to Protagoras himself, holding the truth (i.e. if the man who is the measure of all things is the individual man).

After these criticisms Socrates finishes the claims of perception to be knowledge by showing (i) that perception is not the whole of knowledge, and (ii) that even within its own sphere perception is not knowledge.

(i) Perception is not the whole of knowledge, for a great part of what is generally recognised to be knowledge consists of truths involving terms which are not objects of perception at all. There is much we know about sensible objects, which is known by intellectual reflection and not immediately by perception. Plato gives existence or non-existence as examples.[1] Suppose that a man sees a mirage. It is not immediate sense-perception that can inform him as to the objective existence or non-existence of the mirage perceived: it is only rational reflection that can tell him this. Again, the conclusions and arguments of mathematics are not apprehended by sense. One might add that our knowledge of a person's character is something more than can be explained by the definition, "Knowledge is perception," for our knowledge of a person's character is certainly not given in bare sensation.

(ii) Sense-perception, even within its own sphere, is not knowledge. We cannot really be said to know anything if we have not attained truth about it, e.g. concerning its existence or non-existence, its likeness to another thing or its unlikeness. But truth is given in reflection, in the judgment, not in bare sensation. The bare sensation may give, e.g. one white surface and a second white surface, but in order to judge the similarity between the two, the mind's activity is necessary. Similarly, the

[1] 185 c 4–e 2.

railway lines *appear* to converge: it is in intellectual reflection that we know that they are really parallel.

Sense-perception is not, therefore, worthy of the name of knowledge. It should be noted how much Plato is influenced by the conviction that sense-objects are not proper objects of knowledge and cannot be so, since knowledge is of what is, of the stable and abiding, whereas objects of sense cannot really be said to *be*—*qua* perceived, at least—but only to *become*. Sense-objects are objects of apprehension in some sort, of course, but they elude the mind too much to be objects of real knowledge, which must be, as we have said, (i) infallible, (ii) of what *is*.

(It is noteworthy that Plato, in disposing of the claim of perception to be the whole of knowledge, contrasts the private or peculiar objects of the special senses—e.g. colour, which is the object of vision alone—with the "common terms that apply to everything," and which are the objects of the mind, not of the senses. These "common terms" correspond to the Forms or Ideas which are, ontologically, the stable and abiding objects, as contrasted with the particulars or *sensibilia*).

11. *Knowledge is not simply "True Judgment"*

Theaetetus sees that he cannot say that judgment *tout simple* is knowledge, for the reason that false judgments are possible. He therefore suggests that knowledge is true judgment, at least as a provisional definition, until examination of it shows whether it is correct or false. (At this point a digression occurs, in which Socrates tries to find out how false judgments are possible and come to be made at all. Into this discussion I cannot enter at any length, but I will mention one or two suggestions that are made in its course. For example, it is suggested that one class of false judgments arises through the confusion of two objects of different sorts, one a present object of sense-perception, the other a memory-image. A man may judge—mistakenly—that he sees his friend some way off. There is someone there, but it is not his friend. The man has a memory-image of his friend, and something in the figure he sees recalls to him this memory-image: he then judges falsely that it is his friend who is over there. But, obviously, not all cases of false judgment are instances of the confusion of a memory-image with a present object of sense-perception: a mistake in mathematical calculation can hardly be reduced to this. The famous simile of the "aviary" is introduced, in an attempt to show how other kinds of false judgment may arise, but it is found to be unsatisfactory; and Plato concludes that the problem of false judgment cannot be advantageously treated until the nature of knowledge has been determined. The discussion of false judgment was resumed in the *Sophistes*.)

In the discussion of Theaetetus' suggestion that knowledge is true judgment, it is pointed out that a judgment may be true without the fact of its truth involving knowledge on the part of the man who makes the judgment. The relevance of this observation may be easily grasped. If I were to make at this moment the judgment, "Mr. Churchill is talking to President Truman over the telephone," it *might* be true; but it would not involve knowledge on my part. It would be a guess or random shot, as far as I am concerned, even though the judgment were objectively true. Similarly, a man might be tried on a charge of which he was actually not guilty, although the circumstantial evidence was very strong against him and he could not prove his innocence. If, now, a skilful lawyer defending the innocent man were able, for the sake of argument, so to manipulate the evidence or to play on the feelings of the jury, that they gave the verdict "Not guilty," their judgment would actually be a true judgment; but they could hardly be said to *know* the innocence of the prisoner, since *ex hypothesi* the evidence is against him. Their verdict would be a true judgment, but it would be based on persuasion rather than on knowledge. It follows, then, that knowledge is not simply true judgment, and Theaetetus is called on to make another suggestion as to the right definition of knowledge.

III. *Knowledge is not True Judgment plus an "Account"*

True judgment, as has been seen, may mean no more than true belief, and true belief is not the same thing as knowledge. Theaetetus, therefore, suggests that the addition of an "account" or explanation (λόγος) would convert true belief into knowledge. Socrates begins by pointing out that if giving an account or explanation means the enumeration of elementary parts, then these parts must be known or knowable: otherwise the absurd conclusion would follow that knowledge means adding to true belief the reduction of the complex to unknown or unknowable elements. But what does giving an account mean?

1. It cannot mean merely that a correct judgment, in the

sense of true belief, is expressed in words, since, if that were the meaning, there would be no difference between true belief and knowledge. And we have seen that there is a difference between making a judgment that happens to be correct and making a judgment that one *knows* to be correct.

2. If "giving an account" means analysis into elementary parts (i.e. knowable parts), will addition of an account in this sense suffice to convert true belief into knowledge? No, the mere process of analysing into elements does not convert true belief into knowledge, for then a man who could enumerate the parts which go to make up a wagon (wheels, axle, etc.) would have a scientific knowledge of a wagon, and a man who could tell you what letters of the alphabet go to compose a certain word would have a grammarian's scientific knowledge of the word. (N.B. We must realise that Plato is speaking of the mere enumeration of parts. For instance, the man who could recount the various steps that lead to a conclusion in geometry, simply because he had seen them in a book and had learnt them by heart, without having really grasped the necessity of the premisses and the necessary and logical sequence of the deduction, would be able to enumerate the "parts" of the theorem; but he would not have the scientific knowledge of the mathematician.)

3. Socrates suggests a third interpretation of "plus account." It may mean "being able to name some mark by which the thing one is asked about differs from everything else."[1] If this is correct, then to know something means the ability to give the distinguishing characteristic of that thing. But this interpretation too is disposed of, as being inadequate to define knowledge.

(a) Socrates points out that if knowledge of a thing means the addition of its distinguishing characteristic to a correct notion of that thing, we are involved in an absurd position. Suppose that I have a correct notion of Theaetetus. To convert this correct notion into knowledge I have to add some distinguishing characteristic. But unless this distinguishing characteristic were *already* contained within my correct notion, how could the latter be called a *correct* notion? I cannot be said to have a correct notion of Theaetetus, unless this correct notion includes Theaetetus' distinguishing characteristics: if these distinguishing characteristics are not included, then my "correct notion" of Theaetetus

[1] 208 c 7–8.

would equally well apply to all other men; in which case it would *not* be a correct notion of Theaetetus.

(*b*) If, on the other hand, my "correct notion" of Theaetetus includes his distinguishing characteristics, then it would also be absurd to say that I convert this correct notion into knowledge by adding the *differentia*, since this would be equivalent to saying that I convert my correct notion of Theaetetus into knowledge by adding to Theaetetus, as already apprehended in distinction from others, that which distinguishes him from others.

N.B. It is to be noted that Plato is not speaking here of *specific* differences, he is speaking of individual, sensible objects, as is clearly shown by the examples that he takes—the sun and a particular man, Theaetetus.[1] The conclusion to be drawn is not that no knowledge is attained through definition by means of a difference, but rather that the individual, sensible object is indefinable and is not really the proper object of knowledge at all. This is the real conclusion of the dialogue, namely, that true knowledge of sensible objects is unattainable, and—by implication—that true knowledge must be knowledge of the universal and abiding.

IV. *True Knowledge*

1. Plato has assumed from the outset that knowledge is attainable, and that knowledge must be (i) infallible and (ii) of the *real*. True knowledge must possess both these characteristics, and any state of mind that cannot vindicate its claim to both these characteristics cannot be true knowledge. In the *Theaetetus* he shows that neither sense-perception nor true belief are possessed of both these marks; neither, then, can be equated with true knowledge. Plato accepts from Protagoras the belief in the relativity of sense and sense-perception, but he will not accept a universal relativism: on the contrary, knowledge, absolute and infallible knowledge, is attainable, but it cannot be the same as sense-perception, which is relative, elusive and subject to the influence of all sorts of temporary influences on the part of both subject and object. Plato accepts, too, from Heraclitus the view that the objects of sense-perception, individual and sensible particular objects, are always in a state of becoming, of flux, and so are unfit to be the objects of true knowledge. They come into being and pass away, they are indefinite in number, cannot be clearly grasped in

[1] 208 c 7–e 4.

definition and cannot become the objects of scientific knowledge. But Plato does not draw the conclusion that there are no objects that are fitted to be the objects of true knowledge, but only that sensible particulars cannot be the objects sought. The object of true knowledge must be stable and abiding, fixed, capable of being grasped in clear and scientific definition, which is of the *universal*, as Socrates saw. The consideration of different states of mind is thus indissolubly bound up with the consideration of the different objects of those states of mind.

If we examine those judgments in which we think we attain knowledge of the essentially stable and abiding, we find that they are judgments concerning *universals*. If, for example, we examine the judgment "The Athenian Constitution is good," we shall find that the essentially stable element in this judgment is the concept of goodness. After all, the Athenian Constitution might be so changed that we would no longer qualify it as good, but as bad. This implies that the concept of goodness remains the same, for if we term the changed Constitution "bad," that can only be because we judge it in reference to a fixed concept of goodness. Moreover, if it is objected that, even though the Athenian Constitution may change as an empirical and historical fact, we can still say "The Athenian Constitution is good," if we mean the particular form of the Constitution that we once called good (even though it may in point of fact have since been changed), we can point out in answer that in this case our judgment has reference, not so much to the Athenian Constitution as a given empirical fact, as to a certain *type* of constitution. That this type of constitution happens at any given historical moment to be embodied in the Athenian Constitution is more or less irrelevant: what we really mean is that this universal type of constitution (whether found at Athens or elsewhere) carries with it the universal quality of goodness. Our judgment, as far as it attains the abiding and stable, really concerns a universal.

Again, scientific knowledge, as Socrates saw (predominantly in connection with ethical valuations), aims at the definition, at crystallising and fixing knowledge in the clear and unambiguous definition. A scientific knowledge of goodness, for instance, must be enshrined in the definition "Goodness is . . . ," whereby the mind expresses the essence of goodness. But definition concerns the universal. Hence true knowledge is knowledge of the universal. Particular constitutions change, but the concept of goodness remains the same, and it is in reference to this stable concept that we judge of particular constitutions in respect of goodness. It follows, then, that it is the universal that fulfils the requirements for being an object of knowledge. Knowledge of the highest universal will be the highest kind of knowledge, while "knowledge" of the particular will be the lowest kind of "knowledge."

But does not this view imply an impassable gulf between true knowledge on the one hand and the "real" world on the other— a world that consists of particulars? And if true knowledge is knowledge of universals, does it not follow that true knowledge is knowledge of the abstract and "unreal"? In regard to the second question, I would point out that the essence of Plato's doctrine of Forms or Ideas is simply this: that the universal concept is not an abstract form devoid of objective content or references, but that to each true universal concept there corresponds an objective reality. How far Aristotle's criticism of Plato (that the latter hypostatised the objective reality of the concepts, imagining a transcendent world of "separate" universals) is justified, is a matter for discussion by itself: whether justified or unjustified, it remains true that the essence of the Platonic theory of Ideas is not to be sought in the notion of the "separate" existence of universal realities, but in the belief that universal concepts have objective reference, and that the corresponding reality is of a higher order than sense-perception as such. In regard to the first question (that of the gulf between true knowledge and the "real" world), we must admit that it was one of Plato's standing difficulties to determine the precise relation between the particular and the universal; but to this question we must return when treating of the theory of Ideas from the ontological viewpoint: at the moment one can afford to pass it over.

2. Plato's positive doctrine of knowledge, in which degrees or levels of knowledge are distinguished according to objects, is set out in the famous passage of the *Republic* that gives us the simile of the Line.[1] I give here the usual schematic diagram, which I will endeavour to explain. It must be admitted that there are several important points that remain very obscure, but doubtless Plato was feeling his way towards what he regarded as the truth; and, as far as we know, he never cleared up his precise meaning

[1] *Rep.*, 509 d 6–511 e 5.

in unambiguous terms. We cannot, therefore, altogether avoid
conjecture.

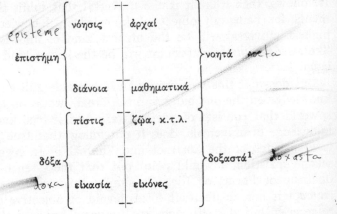

The development of the human mind on its way from ignorance
to knowledge, lies over two main fields, that of δόξα (opinion) and
that of ἐπιστήμη (knowledge). It is only the latter that can properly
be termed knowledge. How are these two functions of the mind
differentiated? It seems clear that the differentiation is based
on a differentiation of object. δόξα (opinion), is said to be concerned with "images," while ἐπιστήμη, at least in the form of
νόησις, is concerned with originals or archetypes, ἀρχαί. If a man
is asked what justice is, and he points to imperfect embodiments
of justice, particular instances which fall short of the universal
ideal, e.g. the action of a particular man, a particular constitution
or set of laws, having no inkling that there exists a principle of
absolute justice, a norm and standard, then that man's state of
mind is a state of δόξα: he sees the images or copies and mistakes
them for the originals. But if a man has an apprehension of justice
in itself, if he can rise above the images to the Form, to the Idea,
to the universal, whereby all the particular instances must be
judged, then his state of mind is a state of knowledge, of ἐπιστήμη
or γνῶσις. Moreover, it is possible to progress from one state of
mind to the other, to be "converted," as it were; and when a man
comes to realise that what he formerly took to be originals are in
reality only images or copies, i.e. imperfect embodiments of the

1 On the left side of the line are states of mind: on the right side are corresponding objects. In both cases the "highest" are at the top. The very close
connection between the Platonic epistemology and the Platonic ontology is at
once apparent.

ideal, imperfect realisations of the norm or standard, when he comes to apprehend in some way the original itself, then his state of mind is no longer that of δόξα, he has been converted to ἐπιστήμη.

The line, however, is not simply divided into two sections; each section is subdivided. Thus there are two degrees of ἐπιστήμη and two degrees of δόξα. How are they to be interpreted? Plato tells us that the lowest degree, that of εἰκασία, has as its object, in the first place, "images" or "shadows", and in the second place "reflections in water and in solid, smooth, bright substances, and everything of the kind."[1] This certainly sounds rather peculiar, at least if one takes Plato to imply that any man mistakes shadow and reflections in water for the original. But one can legitimately extend the thought of Plato to cover in general images of images, imitations at second hand. Thus we said that a man whose only idea of justice is the embodied and imperfect justice of the Athenian Constitution or of some particular man, is in a state of δόξα in general. If, however, a rhetorician comes along, and with specious words and reasonings persuades him that things are just and right, which in reality are not even in accord with the empirical justice of the Athenian Constitution and its laws, then his state of mind is that of εἰκασία. What he takes for justice is but a shadow or caricature of what is itself only an image, if compared to the universal Form. The state of mind, on the other hand, of the man who takes as justice the justice of the law of Athens or the justice of a particular just man is that of πίστις.

Plato tells us that the objects of the πίστις section are the real objects corresponding to the images of the εἰκασία section of the line, and he mentions "the animals about us, and the whole world of nature and of art."[2] This implies, for instance, that the man whose only idea of a horse is that of particular real horses, and who does not see that particular horses are imperfect "imitations" of the ideal horse, i.e. of the specific type, the universal, is in a state of πίστις. He has not got knowledge of the horse, but only opinion. (Spinoza might say that he is in a state of *imagination*, of inadequate knowledge.) Similarly, the man who judges that external nature is true reality, and who does not see that it is a more or less "unreal" copy of the invisible world (i.e. who does not see that sensible objects are imperfect realisations of the specific type) has only πίστις. He is not so badly off as the

[1] *Rep.*, 509 e 1–510 a 3.   [2] *Rep.*, 510 a 5–6.

dreamer who thinks that the images that he sees are the real world (εἰκασία), but he has not got ἐπιστήμη: he is devoid of real scientific knowledge.

The mention of art in the above quotation helps us to understand the matter a little more clearly. In the tenth book of the *Republic*, Plato says that artists are at the third remove from truth. For example, there is the specific form of man, the ideal type that all individuals of the species strive to realise, and there are particular men who are copies or imitations or imperfect realisations of the specific types. The artist now comes and paints a man, the painted man being an imitation of an imitation. Anyone who took the painted man to be a real man (one might say anyone who took the wax policeman at the entrance of Madame Tussaud's to be a real policeman) would be in a state of εἰκασία, while anyone whose idea of a man is limited to the particular men he has seen, heard of or read about, and who has no real grasp of the specific type, is in a state of πίστις. But the man who apprehends the ideal man, i.e. the ideal type, the specific form of which particular men are imperfect realisations, has νόησις.[1] Again, a just man may imitate or embody in his actions, although imperfectly, the idea of justice. The tragedian then proceeds to imitate this just man on the stage, but without knowing anything of justice in itself. He merely imitates an imitation.

Now, what of the higher division of the line, which corresponds in respect of object to νοητά, and in respect of state of mind to ἐπιστήμη? In general it is connected, not with ὁρατά or sensible objects·(lower part of the line), but with ἀορατά, the invisible world, νοητά. But what of the subdivision? How does νόησις in the restricted sense differ from διάνοια? Plato says that the object of διάνοια is what the soul is compelled to investigate by the aid of the imitations of the former segments, which it employs as images, starting from hypothesis and proceeding, not to a first principle, but to a conclusion.[2] Plato is here speaking of mathematics. In geometry, for instance, the mind proceeds from hypotheses, by the use of a visible diagram, to a conclusion. The geometer, says Plato, assumes the triangle, etc., as known, adopts these "materials" as hypotheses, and then, employing a visible diagram, argues to a conclusion, being interested, however, not in the diagram itself (i.e. in this or that particular triangle or particular square or particular diameter). Geometers thus employ

[1] Plato's theory of art is discussed in a later chapter.   [2] *Rep.*, 510 b 4-6.

figures and diagrams, but "they are really endeavouring to behold those objects which a person can only see with the eye of thought."[1]

One might have thought that the mathematical objects of this kind would be numbered among the Forms or ἀρχαί, and that Plato would have equated the scientific knowledge of the geometer with νόησις proper; but he expressly declined to do so, and it is impossible to suppose (as some have done) that Plato was fitting his epistemological doctrines to the exigencies of his simile of the line with its divisions. Rather must we suppose that Plato really meant to assert the existence of a class of "intermediaries," i.e. of objects which are the object of ἐπιστήμη, but which are all the same inferior to ἀρχάι, and so are the objects of διάνοια and not of νόησις.[2] It becomes quite clear from the close of the sixth book of the Republic[3] that the geometers have not got νοῦς or νόησις in regard to their objects; and that because they do not mount up above their hypothetical premisses, "although taken in connection with a first principle these objects come within the domain of the pure reason."[4] These last words show that the distinction between the two segments of the upper part of the line is to be referred to a distinction of state of mind and not only to a distinction of object. And it is expressly stated that understanding or διάνοια is intermediate between opinion (δόξα) and pure reason (διάνοῦς).

This is supported by the mention of hypotheses. Nettleship thought that Plato's meaning is that the mathematician accepts his postulates and axioms as if they were self-contained truth: he does not question them himself, and if anyone else questions them, he can only say that he cannot argue the matter. Plato does not use the word "hypothesis" in the sense of a judgment which is taken as true while it *might* be untrue, but in the sense of a judgment which is treated as if it were self-conditioned, not being seen in its ground and in its necessary connection with being.[5] Against this it might be pointed out that the examples of "hypotheses" given in 510 c are all examples of entities and not of judgments, and that Plato speaks of destroying hypotheses rather than of reducing them to self-conditioned or self-evident propositions. A further suggestion on this matter is given at the close of this section.

[1] Rep., 510 e 2–511 a 1.
[2] Cf. W. R. F. Hardie, A Study in Plato, p. 52 (O.U.P., 1936).
[3] Rep., 510 c.
[4] Rep., 511 c 8–d 2.
[5] Lectures on the Republic of Plato (1898), pp. 252 f.

In the *Metaphysics*,[1] Aristotle tells us that Plato held that mathematical entities are "between forms and sensible things." "Further, besides sensible things and forms, he says there are the objects of mathematics, which occupy an intermediate position, differing from sensible things in being eternal and unchangeable, from Forms in that there are many alike, while the Form itself is in each case unique." In view of this statement by Aristotle, we can hardly refer the distinction between the two segments of the upper part of the line to the state of mind alone. There must be a difference of object as well. (The distinction would be drawn between the states of mind exclusively, if, while τὰ μαθηματικά belonged *in their own right* to the same segment as αἱ ἀρχαί, the mathematician, acting precisely as such, accepted his "materials" hypothetically and then argued to conclusions. He would be in the state of mind that Plato calls διάνοια, for he treats his postulates as self-conditioned, without asking further questions, and argues to a conclusion by means of visible diagrams; but his reasoning would concern, not the diagrams as such but ideal mathematical objects, so that, if he were to take his hypotheses "in connection with a first principle," he would be in a state of νόησις instead of διάνοια, although the true object of his reasoning, the ideal mathematical objects, would remain the same. This interpretation, i.e. the interpretation that would confine the distinction between the two segments of the upper part of the line to states of mind, might well seem to be favoured by the statement of Plato that mathematical questions, when "taken in connection with a first principle, come within the domain of the pure reason"; but Aristotle's remarks on the subject, if they are a correct statement of the thought of Plato, evidently forbid this interpretation, since he clearly thought that Plato's mathematical entities were supposed to occupy a position between αἱ ἀρχαί and τὰ ὁρατά.)

If Aristotle is correct and Plato really meant τὰ μαθηματικά to constitute a class of objects on their own, distinct from other classes, in what does this distinction consist? There is no need to dwell on the distinction between τὰ μαθηματικά and the objects of the lower part of the line, τὰ ὁρατά, since it is clear enough that the geometrician is concerned with ideal and perfect objects of thought, and not with empirical circles or lines, e.g. cart-wheels or hoops or fishing-rods, or even with geometrical diagrams as such, i.e. as sensible particulars. The question, therefore, resolves

[1] 987 b 14 ff. Cf. 1059 b 2 ff.

itself into this: in what does the distinction between τὰ μαθηματικά, as objects of διάνοια, and αἱ ἀρχαί, as objects of νόησις, really consist?

A natural interpretation of Aristotle's remarks in the *Metaphysics* is that, according to Plato, the mathematician is speaking of intelligible particulars, and not of sensible particulars, nor of universals. For example, if the geometer speaks of two circles intersecting, he is not speaking of the sensible circles drawn nor yet of circularity as such—for how could circularity intersect circularity? He is speaking of intelligible circles, of which there are many alike, as Aristotle would say. Again, to say that "two and two make four" is not the same as to say what will happen if twoness be added to itself—a meaningless phrase. This view is supported by Aristotle's remark that for Plato "there must be a first 2 and 3, and the numbers must not be addable to one another."[1] For Plato, the integers, including 1, form a series in such a way that 2 is *not* made up of two 1's, but is a unique numerical form. This comes more or less to saying that the integer 2 is twoness, which is not composed of two "onenesses." These integer numbers Plato seems to have identified with the Forms. But though it cannot be said of the integer 2 that there are many alike (any more than we can speak of many circularities), it is clear that the mathematician who does not ascend to the ultimate formal principles, does in fact deal with a plurality of 2's and a plurality of circles. Now, when the geometer speaks of intersecting circles, he is not treating of sensible particulars, but of intelligible objects. Yet of these intelligible objects there are many alike, hence they are not real universals but constitute a class of intelligible particulars, "above" sensible particulars, but "below" true universals. It is reasonable, therefore, to conclude that Plato's τὰ μαθηματικά are a class of intelligible particulars.

Now, Professor A. E. Taylor,[2] if I understand him correctly, would like to confine the sphere of τὰ μαθηματικά to ideal spatial magnitudes. As he points out, the properties of e.g. curves can be studied by means of numerical equations, but they are not themselves numbers; so that they would not belong to the highest section of the line, that of αἱ ἀρχαί or Forms, which Plato identified with Numbers. On the other hand, the ideal spatial magnitudes, the objects which the geometrician studies, are not sensible

[1] *Metaph.*, 1083 a 33–5.
[2] Cf. *Forms and Numbers, Mind*, Oct. 1926 and Jan. 1927. (Reprinted in *Philosophical Studies*.)

objects, so that they cannot belong to the sphere of τὰ ὁρατά. They therefore occupy an intermediate position between Number-Forms and Sensible Things. That this is true of the objects with which the geometer deals (intersecting circles, etc.) I willingly admit; but is one justified in excluding from τὰ μαθηματικά the objects with which the arithmetician deals? After all, Plato, when treating of those whose state of mind is that of διάνοια, speaks not only of students of geometry, but also of students of arithmetic and the kindred sciences.[1] It would certainly not appear from this that we are justified in asserting that Plato confined τὰ μαθηματικά to ideal spatial magnitudes. Whether or not we think that Plato ought to have so confined the sphere of mathematical entities, we have to consider, not only what Plato *ought* to have said, but also what he *did* say. Most probably, therefore, he understood, as comprised in the class of τὰ μαθηματικά, the objects of the arithmetician as well as those of the geometer (and not only of these two, as can be inferred from the remark about "kindred sciences"). What, then, becomes of Aristotle's statement that for Plato numbers are not addable (ἀσύμβλητοι)? I think that it is certainly to be accepted, and that Plato saw clearly that numbers as such are unique. On the other hand, it is equally clear that we add groups or classes of objects together, and speaks of the characteristic of a class as a number. These we add, but they stand for the classes of individual objects, though they are themselves the objects, not of sense but of intelligence. They may, therefore, be spoken of as intelligible particulars, and they belong to the sphere of τὰ μαθηματικά, as well as the ideal spatial magnitudes of the geometer. Aristotle's own theory of number may have been erroneous, and he may thus have misrepresented Plato's theory in some respects; but if he definitely stated, as he did, that Plato posited an intermediate class of mathematical entities, it is hard to suppose that he was mistaken, especially as Plato's own writings would seem to leave no reasonable doubt, not only that he actually posited such a class, but also that he did not mean to confine this class to ideal spatial magnitudes.

(Plato's statement that the hypotheses of the mathematicians —he mentions "the odd and the even and the figures and three kinds of angles and the cognates of these in their several branches of science"[2]—when taken in connection with a first principle, are

[1] *Rep.*, 510 c 2 ff.   [2] *Rep.*, 510 c 4-5.

cognisable by the higher reason, and his statement that the higher reason is concerned with first principles, which are self-evident, suggest that he would welcome the modern attempts to reduce pure mathematics to their logical foundations.)

It remains to consider briefly the highest segment of the line. The state of mind in question, that of νόησις, is the state of mind of the man who uses the hypotheses of the διάνοια segment as starting-points, but passes beyond them and ascends to first principles. Moreover, in this process (which is the process of Dialectic) he makes no use of "images," such as are employed in the διάνοια segment, but proceeds in and by the ideas themselves,[1] i.e. by strictly abstract reasoning. Having clearly grasped the first principles, the mind then descends to the conclusions that follow from them, again making use only of abstract reasoning and not of sensible images.[2] The objects corresponding to νόησις are αἱ ἀρχάι, the first principles or Forms. They are not merely epistemological principles, but also ontological principles, and I will consider them more in detail later; but it is as well to point out the following fact. If it were merely a question of seeing the ultimate principles of the hypotheses of the διάνοια section (as e.g. in the modern reduction of pure mathematics to their logical foundations), there might be no very great difficulty in seeing what Plato was driving at; but he speaks expressly of dialectic as "destroying the hypotheses," ἀναιροῦσα τὰς ὑποθέσεις,[3] which is a hard saying, since, though dialectic may well show that the postulates of the mathematician need revision, it is not so easy, at first sight at least, to see how it can be said to destroy the hypotheses. As a matter of fact, Plato's meaning becomes clearer if we consider one particular hypothesis he mentions—the odd and the even. It would appear that Plato recognised that there are numbers which are neither even nor odd, i.e. irrational numbers, and that in the *Epinomis*[4] he demands the recognition of quadratic and cubic "surds" as *numbers*.[5] If this is so, then it would be the task of dialectic to show that the traditional hypotheses of the mathematician, that there are no irrational numbers, but that all numbers are integers and are either even or odd, is not strictly true. Again, Plato refused to accept the Pythagorean idea of the point-unit and spoke of the point as "the beginning of a line,"[6] so that the point-unit, i.e. the point as having magnitude of its

[1] *Rep.*, 510 b 6–9.   [2] *Rep.*, 511 b 3–c 2.   [3] *Rep.*, 533 c 8.
[4] *Epin.*, 990 c 5–991 b 4.   [5] Cf. Taylor, *Plato*, p. 501.   [6] *Metaph.*, 992 a 20 ff.

own, would be a fiction of the geometer, "a geometrical fiction,"[1] an hypothesis that needs to be "destroyed."

3. Plato further illustrated his epistemological doctrine by the famous allegory of the Cave in the seventh book of the *Republic*.[2] I will briefly sketch the allegory, since it is valuable as showing clearly, if any further proof be needed, that the ascent of the mind from the lower sections of the line to the higher is an epistemological progress, and that Plato regarded this process, not so much as a continuous process of evolution as a series of "conversions" from a less adequate to a more adequate cognitive state.

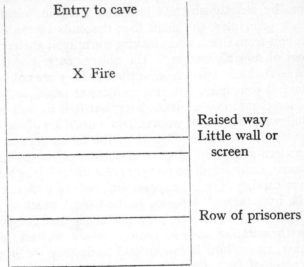

Plato asks us to imagine an underground cave which has an opening towards the light. In this cave are living human beings, with their legs and necks chained from childhood in such a way that they face the inside wall of the cave and have never seen the light of the sun. Above and behind them, i.e. between the prisoners and the mouth of the cave, is a fire, and between them and the fire is a raised way and a low wall, like a screen. Along this raised way there pass men carrying statues and figures of animals and other objects, in such a manner that the objects they carry appear over the top of the low wall or screen. The

[1] *Metaph.*, 992 a 20–1.   [2] *Rep.*, 514 a 1–518 d 1.

prisoners, facing the inside wall of the cave, cannot see one another nor the objects carried behind them, but they see the shadows of themselves and of these objects thrown on to the wall they are facing. They see only shadows.

These prisoners represent the majority of mankind, that multitude of people who remain all their lives in a state of εἰκασία, beholding only shadows of reality and hearing only echoes of the truth. Their view of the world is most inadequate, distorted by "their own passions and prejudices, and by the passions and prejudices of other people as conveyed to them by language and rhetoric."[1] And though they are in no better case than children, they cling to their distorted views with all the tenacity of adults, and have no wish to escape from their prison-house. Moreover, if they were suddenly freed and told to look at the realities of which they had formerly seen the shadows, they would be blinded by the glare of the light, and would imagine that the shadows were far more real than the realities.

However, if one of the prisoners who has escaped grows accustomed to the light, he will after a time be able to look at the concrete sensible objects, of which he had formerly seen but the shadows. This man beholds his fellows in the light of the fire (which represents the visible sun) and is in a state of πίστις, having been "converted" from the shadow-world of εἰκόνες, prejudices and passions and sophistries, to the real world of ζῷα, though he has not yet ascended to the world of intelligible, non-sensible realities. He sees the prisoners for what they are, namely prisoners, prisoners in the bonds of passion and sophistry. Moreover, if he perseveres and comes out of the cave into the sunlight, he will see the world of sun-illumined and clear objects (which represent intelligible realities), and lastly, though only by an effort, he will be able to see the sun itself, which represents the Idea of the Good, the highest Form, "the universal cause of all things right and beautiful—the source of truth and reason."[2] He will then be in a state of νόησις. (To this Idea of the Good, as also to the political considerations that concerned Plato in the *Republic*, I shall return in later chapters.)

Plato remarks that if someone, after ascending to the sunshine, went back into the cave, he would be unable to see properly because of the darkness, and so would make himself "ridiculous"; while if he tried to free another and lead him up to the light, the

[1] Nettleship, *Lectures on the Republic of Plato*, p. 260. [2] *Rep.*, 517 b 8–c 4.

prisoners, who love the darkness and consider the shadows to be true reality, would put the offender to death, if they could but catch him. Here we may understand a reference to Socrates, who endeavoured to enlighten all those who would listen and make them apprehend truth and reason, instead of letting themselves be misled by prejudice and sophistry.

This allegory makes it clear that the "ascent" of the line was regarded by Plato as a progress, though this progress is not a continuous and automatic process: it needs effort and mental discipline. Hence his insistence on the great importance of *education*, whereby the young may be brought gradually to behold eternal and absolute truths and values, and so saved from passing their lives in the shadow-world of error, falsehood, prejudice, sophistical persuasion, blindness to true values, etc. This education is of primary importance in the case of those who are to be statesmen. Statesmen and rulers will be blind leaders of the blind, if they dwell in the spheres of εἰκασία or πίστις, and the wrecking of the ship of State is a more terrible thing than the wreck of anyone's individual barque. Plato's interest in the epistemological ascent is thus no mere academic or narrowly critical interest: he is concerned with the conduct of life, tendence of the soul and with the good of the State. The man who does not realise the true good of man will not, and cannot, lead the truly good human life, and the statesman who does not realise the true good of the State, who does not view political life in the light of eternal principles, will bring ruin on his people.

The question might be raised, whether or not there are religious implications in the epistemology of Plato, as illustrated by the simile of the Line and the allegory of the Cave. That the conceptions of Plato were given a religious colouring and application by the Neo-Platonists·is beyond dispute: moreover, when a Christian writer, such as the Pseudo-Dicnysius, traces the mystic's ascent to God by the *via negativa*, beyond visible creatures to their invisible Source, the light of which blinds by excess of light, so that the soul is in a state of, so to speak, luminous obscurity, he certainly utilises themes which came from Plato *via* the Neo-Platonists. But it does not necessarily follow that Plato himself understood the ascent from a religious viewpoint. In any case this difficult question cannot be profitably touched on until one has considered the ontological nature and status of Plato's Idea of the Good; and even then one can scarcely reach definitive certainty.

CHAPTER XX

THE DOCTRINE OF FORMS

IN this chapter I propose to discuss the theory of Forms or Ideas in its ontological aspect. We have already seen that in Plato's eyes the object of true knowledge must be stable and abiding, the object of intelligence and not of sense, and that these requirements are fulfilled by the universal, as far as the highest cognitive state, that of νόησις, is concerned. The Platonic epistemology clearly implies that the universals which we conceive in thought are not devoid of objective reference, but we have not yet examined the important question, in what this objective reference consists. There is indeed plenty of evidence that Plato continued to occupy himself throughout his years of academic and literary activity with problems arising from the theory of Forms, but there is no real evidence that he ever radically changed his doctrine, still less that he abandoned it altogether, however much he tried to clarify or modify it, in view of difficulties that occurred to him or that were suggested by others. It has sometimes been asserted that the mathematisation of the Forms, which is ascribed to Plato by Aristotle, was a doctrine of Plato's old age, a relapse into Pythagorean "mysticism,"[1] but Aristotle does not say that Plato *changed* his doctrine, and the only reasonable conclusion to be drawn from Aristotle's words would appear to be that Plato held more or less the same doctrine, at least during the time that Aristotle worked under him in the Academy. (Whether Aristotle misinterpreted Plato or not is naturally another question.) But though Plato continued to maintain the doctrine of Ideas, and though he sought to clarify his meaning and the ontological and logical implications of his thought, it does not follow that we can always clearly grasp what he actually meant. It is greatly to be regretted that we have no adequate record of his lectures in the Academy, since this would doubtless throw great light on the interpretation of his theories as put forward in the dialogues, besides conferring on us the inestimable benefit of knowing what Plato's "real" opinions were, the opinions that he transmitted only through oral teaching and never published.

[1] Cf. Stace, *Critical History*, p. 191.

In the *Republic* it is assumed that whenever a plurality of individuals have a common name, they have also a corresponding idea or form.[1] This is the universal, the common nature or quality which is grasped in the concept, e.g. beauty. There are many beautiful things, but we form one universal concept of beauty itself: and Plato assumed that these universal concepts are not merely subjective concepts, but that in them we apprehend objective essences. At first hearing this sounds a peculiarly naïve view, perhaps, but we must recall that for Plato it is thought that grasps reality, so that the object of thought, as opposed to sense-perception, i.e. universals, must have reality. How could they be grasped and made the object of thought unless they were real? We *discover* them: they are not simply invented by us. Another point to remember is that Plato seems first to have concerned himself with moral and aesthetic universals (as also with the objects of mathematical science), as was only natural, considering the main interest of Socrates, and to think of Absolute Goodness or Absolute Beauty existing in their own right, so to speak, is not unreasonable, particularly if Plato identified them, as we believe that he did. But when Plato came to turn his attention more to natural objects than he had formerly done, and to consider class-concepts, such as those of man or horse, it was obviously rather difficult to suppose that universals corresponding to these class-concepts existed in their own right as objective essences. One may identify Absolute Goodness and Absolute Beauty, but it is not so easy to identify the objective essence of man with the objective essence of horse: in fact, to attempt to do so would be ludicrous. But some principle of unity had to be found, if the essences were not to be left in isolation one from another, and Plato came to devote attention to this principle of unity, so that all the specific essences might be unified under or subordinated to one supreme generic essence. Plato tackles this problem from the logical viewpoint, it is true, inquiring into the problem of logical classification; but there is no real evidence that he ever abandoned the view that universals have an ontological status, and he doubtless thought that in settling the problem of logical classification, he was also settling the problem of ontological unification.

To these objective essences Plato gave the name of Ideas or Forms (ἰδέαι or εἴδη), words which are used interchangeably.

[1] *Rep.*, 596 a 6–7; cf. 507 ab.

The word εἶδος in this connection appears suddenly in the *Phaedo*.[1] But we must not be misled by this use of the term "Idea." "Idea" in ordinary parlance means a subjective concept in the mind, as when we say: "That is only an idea and nothing real"; but Plato, when he speaks of Ideas or Forms, is referring to the objective content or reference of our universal concepts. In our universal concepts we apprehend objective essences, and it is to these objective essences that Plato applied the term "Ideas." In some dialogues, e.g. in the *Symposium*, the word "Idea" is not used, but the *meaning* is there, for in that dialogue Plato speaks of essential or absolute Beauty (αὐτο ὃ ἔστι καλόν), and this is what Plato would mean by the Idea of Beauty. Thus it would be a matter of indifference, whether he spoke of the Absolute Good or of the Idea of the Good: both would refer to an objective essence, which is the source of goodness in all the particular things that are truly good.

Since by Ideas or Forms Plato meant objective essences, it becomes of paramount importance for an understanding of the Platonic ontology to determine, as far as possible, precisely how he regarded these objective essences. Have they a transcendental existence of their own, apart from particular things, and, if so, what is their relation to one another and to the concrete particular objects of this world? Does Plato duplicate the world of sense-experience by postulating a transcendental world of invisible, immaterial essences? If so, what is the relation of this world of essences to God? That Plato's language often implies the existence of a separate world of transcendental essences cannot be denied, but it must be remembered that language is primarily designed to refer to the objects of our sense-experience, and is very often found inadequate for the precise expression of meta-physical truths. Thus we speak, and cannot well help speaking, of "God foreseeing," a phrase that, as it stands, implies that God is in time, whereas we know that God is not in time but is eternal. We cannot, however, speak adequately of the eternity of God, since we have no experience of eternity ourselves, and our language is not designed to express such matters. We are human beings and have to use human language—we can use no other: and this fact should make us cautious in attaching too much weight to the mere language or phrases used by Plato in dealing with abstruse, metaphysical points. We have to endeavour to

[1] *Phaedo*, 102 b 1.

get at the meaning behind those phrases. By this I do not mean to imply that Plato did not believe in the subsistence of universal essences, but simply to point out that, if we find that he did in fact hold this doctrine, we must beware of the temptation to put that doctrine in a ludicrous light by stressing the phrases used by Plato, without due consideration of the meaning to be attached to those phrases.

Now, what we might call the "vulgar" presentation of the Platonic theory of Ideas has generally been more or less as follows. In Plato's view the objects which we apprehend in universal concepts, the objects with which science deals, the objects corresponding to universal terms of predication, are objective Ideas or subsistent Universals, existing in a transcendental world of their own—somewhere "out there"—apart from sensible things, understanding by "apart from" practically spatial separation. Sensible things are copies or participations in these universal realities, but the latter abide in an unchanging heaven of their own, while sensible things are subject to change, in fact are always becoming and can never truly be said to *be*. The Ideas exist in their heaven in a state of isolation one from another, and apart from the mind of any Thinker. Plato's theory having been thus presented, it is pointed out that the subsistent universals either *exist* (in which case the real world of our experience is unjustifiably duplicated) or they do not exist, but have independent and *essential reality* in some mysterious way (in which case a wedge is unjustifiably driven between existence and essence.) (The Thomist School of Scholastic philosophers, be it remarked in passing, admit a "real distinction" between essence and the act of existence in created being; but, for them, the distinction is *within* the creature. Uncreated Being is Absolute Existence and Absolute Essence in identity.) Of the reasons which have led to this traditional presentation of the doctrine of Plato one may enumerate three.

(i) Plato's way of speaking about the Ideas clearly supposes that they exist in a sphere apart. Thus in the *Phaedo* he teaches that the soul existed before its union with the body in a transcendental realm, where it beheld the subsistent intelligible entities or Ideas, which would seem to constitute a plurality of "detached" essences. The process of knowledge, or getting to know, consists essentially in recollection, in remembering the Ideas which the soul once beheld clearly in its state of pre-existence.

(ii) Aristotle asserts in the *Metaphysics*[1] that Plato "separated" the Ideas, whereas Socrates had not done so. In his criticism of the theory of Ideas he constantly supposes that, according to the Platonists, Ideas exist apart from sensible things. Ideas constitute the reality or "substance" of things; "how, therefore," asks Aristotle, "can the Ideas, being the substance of things, exist apart?"[2]

(iii) In the *Timaeus* Plato clearly teaches that God or the "Demiurge" forms the things of this world according to the model of the Forms. This implies that the Forms or Ideas exist apart, not only from the sensible things that are modelled on them, but also from God, Who takes them as His model. They are therefore hanging in the air, as it were.

In this way, say the critics, Plato—

(a) Duplicates the "real" world;

(b) Posits a multitude of subsistent essences with no sufficient metaphysical ground or basis (since they are independent even of God);

(c) Fails to explain the relation between sensible things and the Ideas (except by metaphorical phrases like "imitation" or "participation"); and

(d) Fails to explain the relation of the Ideas to one another, e.g. of species to genus, or to find any real principle of unity. Accordingly, if Plato was trying to solve the problem of the One and the Many, he failed lamentably and merely enriched the world with one more fantastic theory, which was exploded by the genius of Aristotle.

It must be left to an examination of Plato's thought in more detail to show what truth there is in this presentation of the theory of Ideas; but we would point out at once that these critics tend to neglect the fact that Plato saw clearly that the plurality of Ideas needs some principle of unity, and that he tried to solve this problem. They also tend to neglect the fact that we have indications not only in the dialogues themselves, but also in the allusions of Aristotle to Plato's theory and Plato's lectures, how Plato tried to solve the problem, namely, by a new interpretation and application of the Eleatic doctrine of the One. Whether Plato actually solved the problems that arise out of his theorie is a matter for dispute, but it will not do to speak as though h

[1] *Metaph.*, A, 987 b 1–10; M, 1078 b 30–32.   [2] *Metaph.*, A, 991 b 2–3.

never saw any of the difficulties that Aristotle afterwards brought against him. On the contrary, Plato anticipated some of the very objections raised by Aristotle and thought that he had solved them more or less satisfactorily. Aristotle evidently thought otherwise, and he may have been right, but it is unhistorical to speak as though Aristotle raised objections which Plato had been too foolish to see. Moreover, if it is an historical fact, as it is, that Plato brought difficulties against himself, one should be careful in attributing to him an opinion that is fantastic—unless, of course, we are compelled by the evidence to believe that he held it.

Before going on to consider the theory of Ideas as presented in the dialogues, we will make some preliminary observations in connection with the three reasons that we enumerated in support of the traditional presentation of Plato's Ideal Theory.

(i) It is an undeniable fact that Plato's way of speaking about the Ideas very often implies that they exist "apart from" sensible things. I believe that Plato really did hold this doctrine; but there are two cautionary observations to be made.

(a) If they exist "apart from" sensible things, this "apart from" can only mean that the Ideas are possessed of a reality independent of sensible things. There can be no question of the Ideas being in a place, and, strictly speaking, they would be as much "in" as "out of" sensible things, for *ex hypothesi* they are incorporeal essences and incorporeal essences cannot be in a place. As Plato had to use human language, he would naturally express the essential reality and independence of the Ideas in spatial terminology (he could not do anything else); but he would not *mean* that the Ideas were spatially separate from things. Transcendence in this connection would mean that the Ideas do not change and perish with sensible particulars: it would no more mean that they are in a heavenly place of their own than God's transcendence implies for us that God is in a place, different from the places or spaces of the sensible objects He has created. It is absurd to speak as though the Platonic Theory involved the assumption of an Ideal Man with length, breadth, depth, etc., existing in the heavenly place. To do so is to make the Platonic theory gratuitously ridiculous: whatever the transcendence of the Ideas might mean, it could not mean *that*.

(b) We should be careful not to place too much weight on doctrines such as that of the pre-existence of the soul and the process of "recollection." Plato sometimes, as is well known, makes use of "Myth," giving a "likely account," which he does not mean to be taken with the same exactitude and seriousness as more scientifically argued themes. Thus in the *Phaedo* "Socrates" gives an account of the soul's future life, and then expressly declares that it does not become a man of sense to affirm that these things are exactly as he has described them.[1] But while it is clear enough that the account of the soul's future life is conjectural and admittedly "mythical" in character, it appears altogether unjustifiable to extend the concept of "myth" to include the whole doctrine of immortality, as some would do, for in the passage alluded to in the *Phaedo* Socrates declares that, though the picture of the future life is not to be understood literally or positively affirmed, the soul is "certainly immortal." And, as Plato couples together immortality after death with pre-existence, it hardly seems that one is warranted in dismissing the whole conception of pre-existence as "mythical." It may possibly be that it was no more than an hypothesis in Plato's eyes (so that, as I said, we should not attach too much weight to it); but, all things considered, we are not justified in simply asserting that it actually is myth, and, unless its mythical character can be demonstrated satisfactorily, we ought to accept it as a seriously-meant doctrine. Yet even if the soul pre-existed and contemplated the Forms in that state of pre-existence, it would *not* follow that the Forms or Ideas are in any *place*, save metaphorically. Nor does it even necessarily follow that they are "detached" essences, for they might all be included in some ontological principle of unity.

(ii) In regard to the statements of Aristotle in the *Metaphysics* it is as well to point out at once that Aristotle must have known perfectly well what Plato taught in the Academy and that Aristotle was no imbecile. It is absurd to speak as though Aristotle's insufficient knowledge of contemporary mathematical developments would necessarily lead to his essentially perverting Plato's doctrine of the Forms, at least in its non-mathematical aspects. He may or may not have fully understood Plato's mathematical theories: it does not follow from this alone that he made an egregious blunder in his interpretation of the Platonic ontology. If Aristotle declares that Plato "separated" the Forms, we cannot pass over this statement as mere ignorant criticism.

[1] *Phaedo,* 114 d 1–2.

All the same, we have to be careful not to assume *a priori* what
Aristotle meant by "separation," and in the second place we
have to inquire whether Aristotle's criticism of the Platonic
theory necessarily implies that Plato himself drew the conclusions
that Aristotle attacks. It *might* be that some of the conclusions
attacked by Aristotle were conclusions that he (Aristotle) considered to be logical consequences of the Platonic theory, although
Plato may 'not have drawn those conclusions himself. If this
were the case, then we should have to inquire whether the conclusions really did flow from Plato's premisses. But as it would
be impracticable to discuss Aristotle's criticism until we have
seen what Plato himself said about the Ideas in his published
works, it is best to reserve till later a discussion of Aristotle's
criticism, although it is true that, since one has to rely largely
on Aristotle for knowledge of what Plato taught in his lectures,
one cannot help drawing upon him in an exposition of the Platonic
doctrine. It is, however, important (and this is the burden of
these preliminary remarks) that we should put out of our heads
the notion that Aristotle was an incompetent fool, incapable of
understanding the true thought of the Master.[1] Unjust he may
have been, but he was no fool.

(iii) It can scarcely be denied that Plato in the *Timaeus* speaks
as though the Demiurge, the Efficient Cause of order in the world,
fashions the objects of this world after the pattern of the Forms
as Exemplary Cause, thus implying that the Forms or Ideas are
quite distinct from the Demiurge, so that, if we call the Demiurge
"God," we should have to conclude that the Forms are not only
"outside" the things of this world, but also "outside" God. But
though Plato's language in the *Timaeus* certainly implies this
interpretation, there is some reason, as will be seen later, to think
that the Demiurge of the *Timaeus* is an *hypothesis* and that
Plato's "theism" is not to be over-stressed. Moreover, and this
is an important fact to remember, Plato's doctrine, as given in
his lectures, was not precisely the same as that given in the
dialogues: or it might be better to say that Plato developed
aspects of his doctrine in his lectures that scarcely appear in the
dialogues. The remarks of Aristotle concerning Plato's lecture
on the Good, as recorded by Aristoxenus, would seem to indicate

---

[1] It is indeed the opinion of the writer that Aristotle, in his criticism of the
Ideal Theory, scarcely does justice to Plato, but he would ascribe this to the
polemical attitude Aristotle came to adopt towards the theory rather than to
any supposed imbecility.

that in dialogues such as the *Timaeus*, Plato revealed some of his thoughts only in a pictorial and figurative way. To this question I return later: we must now endeavour to ascertain, as far as possible, what Plato's doctrine of Ideas actually was.

1. In the *Phaedo*, where the discussion centres round the problem of immortality, it is suggested that truth is not to be attained by the bodily senses, but by reason alone, which lays hold of the things that "really are."[1] What are the things that "really are," i.e. that have true being? They are the essences of things, and Socrates gives as examples justice itself, beauty itself, and goodness itself, abstract equality, etc. These essences remain always the same, while particular objects of sense do not. That there really exist such essences is assumed by Socrates: he lays it down "as an hypothesis that there is a certain abstract beauty, and goodness, and magnitude," and that a particular beautiful object, for instance, is beautiful because it partakes of that abstract beauty.[2] (In 102 b the word Idea is applied to these essences; they are termed εἴδη.) In the *Phaedo* the existence of these essences is used as an aid in the proof of immortality. It is pointed out that the fact that a man is able to judge of things as more or less equal, more or less beautiful, implies knowledge of a standard, of the essence of beauty or equality. Now, men do not come into the world and grow up with a clear knowledge of universal essences: how is it, then, that they can judge of particular things in reference to a universal standard? Is it not because the soul pre-existed before its union with the body, and had knowledge of the essences in its state of pre-existence? The process of learning would thus be a process of reminiscence, in which particular embodiments of the essence acted as reminders of the essences previously beheld. Moreover, since rational knowledge of essences in this life involves transcending the bodily senses and rising to the intellectual plane, should we not suppose that the soul of the philosopher beholds these essences after death, when he is no longer hampered and shackled by the body?

Now, the natural interpretation of the doctrine of the Ideas as given in the *Phaedo* is that the Ideas are subsistent universals; but it is to be remembered that, as already mentioned, the doctrine is put forward tentatively as an "hypothesis," i.e. as a premiss which is assumed until connection with an evident first principle either justifies it or "destroys" it, or shows that it stands

---

[1] *Phaedo*, 65 c 2 ff.   [2] *Phaedo*, 100 b 5-7.

in need of modification or correction. Of course, one cannot exclude the possibility that Plato put forward the doctrine tentatively because he (Plato) was not yet certain of it, but it would appear legitimate to suppose that Plato makes Socrates put forward the doctrine in a tentative fashion precisely because he knew very well that the historical Socrates had not reached the metaphysical theory of the Ideas, and that in any case he had not arrived at Plato's final Principle of the Good. It is significant that Plato allows Socrates to divine the Ideal Theory in his "swan-song," when he becomes "prophetic."[1] This might well imply that Plato allows Socrates to divine a certain amount of his (i.e. Plato's) theory, but not all. It is also to be noted that the theory of pre-existence and reminiscence is referred, in the *Meno*, to "priests and priestesses,"[2] just as the sublimest part of the *Symposium* is referred to "Diotima." Some have concluded that these passages were avowedly "Myths" in Plato's eyes, but it might equally well be the case that these hypothetical passages (hypothetical for *Socrates*) reveal something of Plato's own doctrine, as distinct from that of Socrates. (In any case we should not use the doctrine of reminiscence as an excuse for attributing to Plato an explicit anticipation of Neo-Kantian theory. The Neo-Kantians may think that the *a priori* in the Kantian sense is the truth that Plato was getting at or that underlies his words, but they cannot be justified in fathering the explicit doctrine on to Plato, without much better evidence than they can offer.) I conclude, then, that the theory of Ideas, as put forward in the *Phaedo*, represents but a part of Plato's doctrine. It should not be inferred that for Plato himself the Ideas were *"detached"* subsistent universals. Aristotle clearly stated that Plato identified the One with the Good; but this unifying principle, whether already held by Plato when he composed the *Phaedo* (as is most probable) or only later elaborated, certainly does not appear in the *Phaedo*.

2. In the *Symposium*, Socrates is represented as reporting a discourse made to him by one Diotima, a "Prophetess," concerning the soul's ascent to true Beauty under the impulse of Eros. From beautiful forms (i.e. bodies), a man ascends to the contemplation of the beauty that is in souls, and thence to science, that he may look upon the loveliness of wisdom, and turn towards the "wide ocean of beauty" and the "lovely and majestic forms

---

[1] Cf. *Phaedo*, 84 e 3–85 b 7.   [2] *Meno*, 81 a 5 ff.

which it contains," until he reaches the contemplation of a Beauty that is "eternal, unproduced, indestructible; neither subject to increase nor decay; not partly beautiful and partly ugly; not at one time beautiful and at another time not; not beautiful in relation to one thing and deformed in relation to another; not here beautiful and there ugly; not beautiful in the estimation of some people and deformed in that of others. Nor can this supreme beauty be figured to the imagination like a beautiful face, or beautiful hands, or any other part of the body, nor like any discourse, nor any science. Nor does it subsist in any other thing that lives or is, either in earth, or in heaven, or in any other place; but it is eternally self-subsistent and monoeidic with itself. All other things are beautiful through a participation of it, with this condition, that although they are subject to production and decay, it never becomes more or less, or endures any change." This is the divine and pure, the monoeidic beautiful itself.[1] It is evidently the Beauty of the *Hippias Maior*, "from which all beautiful things derive their beauty."[2] .

The priestess Diotima, into whose mouth Socrates puts his discourse on Absolute Beauty and the ascent thereto under the impulse of Eros, is represented as suggesting that Socrates may not be able to follow her to such sublime heights, and she urges him to strain all his attention to reach the obscure depth of the subject.[3] Professor A. E. Taylor interprets this to mean that Socrates is too modest to claim the mystical vision for himself (although he has really experienced it), and so represents himself as but reporting the words of Diotima. Taylor will have nothing to do with the suggestion that the speech of Diotima represents *Plato's* personal conviction, never attained by the historical Socrates. "Much unfortunate nonsense has been written about the meaning of Diotima's apparent doubt whether Socrates will be able to follow her as she goes on to speak of the 'full and perfect vision . . .' It has even been seriously argued that Plato is here guilty of the arrogance of professing that he has reached philosophical heights to which the 'historical' Socrates could not ascend."[4] That such a procedure would be indicative of arrogance on Plato's part might be true, if there were question of a mystical vision, as Taylor apparently thinks there is; but it is by no means certain that there is any question of religious mysticism in the

[1] *Sympos.*, 210 e 1–212 a 7.   [2] *Hippias Maior*, 289 d 2–5.
[3] *Sympos.*, 209 e 5–210 a 4. Cf. 210 e 1–2.   [4] *Plato*, p. 229, note i.

speech of Socrates, and there seems no real reason why Plato should not be able to claim a greater philosophic penetration in regard to the ultimate Principle than Socrates, without thereby laying himself open to any justifiable charge of arrogance. Moreover, if, as Taylor supposes, the opinions put into the mouth of Socrates in the *Phaedo* and the *Symposium* are those of the historic Socrates, how does it come about that in the *Symposium* Socrates speaks as though he had actually grasped the ultimate Principle, the Absolute Beauty, while in the *Phaedo* the theory of Ideas (in which abstract beauty finds a place) is put forward as a tentative hypothesis, i.e. in the very dialogue that purports to give Socrates' conversation before his death? Might we not be justified in expecting that if the historic Socrates had really apprehended the final Principle for certain, some sure indication of this would have been given in his final discourse? I prefer, then, the view that in the *Symposium* the speech of Diotima does not represent the certain conviction of the historic Socrates. In any case, however, this is an academic point: whether the report of Diotima's words represents the conviction of the historic Socrates or of Plato himself, the evident fact remains that some hint (at the very least) of the existence of an Absolute is therein given.

Is this Beauty in itself, the very essence of Beauty, a subsistent essence, "separate" from beautiful things, or is it not? It is true that Plato's words concerning science might be taken to imply a scientific appreciation of the mere universal concept of Beauty which is embodied in varying degrees in various beautiful objects; but the whole tenor of Socrates' discourse in the *Symposium* leads one to suppose that this essential Beauty is no mere concept, but has objective reality. Does this imply that it is "separate?" Beauty in itself or Absolute Beauty is "separate" in the sense that it is real, subsistent, but not in the sense that it is in a world of its own, spatially separate from things. For *ex hypothesi* Absolute Beauty is spiritual; and the categories of time and space, of local separation, simply do not apply in the case of that which is essentially spiritual. In the case of that which transcends space and time, we cannot even legitimately raise the question, *where* it is. It is nowhere, as far as local presence is concerned (though it is not nowhere in the sense of being unreal). The Χωρισμός or separation would thus seem to imply, in the case of the Platonic essence, a reality beyond the subjective reality of the abstract concept—a subsistent reality, but not a local separation. It is, therefore, just as true to say that the essence is immanent, as that it is transcendent: the great point is that it is *real* and independent of particulars, unchanged and abiding. It is foolish to remark that if the Platonic essence is real, it must be some-where. Absolute Beauty, for instance, does not exist outside us in the sense in which a flower exists outside us—for it might just as well be said to exist inside us, inasmuch as spatial categories simply do not apply to it. On the other hand, it cannot be said to be inside us in the sense that it is purely subjective, is confined to us, comes into being with us, and perishes through our agency or with us. It is both transcendent and immanent, inaccessible to the senses, apprehensible only by the intellect.

To the means of ascent to Absolute Beauty, the signification of Eros, and the question whether a mystical approach is implied, we must return later: at the present I wish simply to point out that in the *Symposium* indications are not wanting that Absolute Beauty is the ultimate Principle of unity. The passage[1] concerning the ascent from different sciences to one science—the science of universal Beauty—suggests that "the wide ocean of intellectual beauty," containing "lovely and majestic forms," is subordinate to or even comprised in the ultimate Principle of Absolute Beauty. And if Absolute Beauty is a final and unifying Principle, it becomes necessary to identify it with the Absolute Good of the *Republic*.

3. In the *Republic* it is clearly shown that the true philosopher seeks to know the essential nature of each thing. He is not concerned to know, for example, a multiplicity of beautiful things or a multiplicity of good things, but rather to discern the essence of beauty and the essence of goodness, which are embodied in varying degrees in particular beautiful things and particular good things. Non-philosophers, who are so taken up with the multi-plicity of appearances that they do not attend to the essential nature and cannot distinguish, e.g. the essence of beauty from the many beautiful phenomena, are represented as having only opinion (δόξα) and as lacking in scientific knowledge. They are not concerned with not-being, it is true, since not-being cannot be an object of "knowledge" at all, but is completely unknowable; yet they are no more concerned with true being or reality, which is stable and abiding: they are concerned with fleeting phenomena or appearances, objects which are in a state of *becoming*,

[1] *Sympos.*, 210 a 4 ff.

constantly coming to be and passing away. Their state of mind is thus one of δόξα and the object of their δόξα is the phenomenon that stands half-way between being and not-being. The state of mind of the philosopher, on the other hand, is one of knowledge, and the object of his knowledge is Being, the fully real, the essential, the Idea or Form.

So far, indeed, there is no direct indication that the essence or Idea is regarded as subsistent or "separate" (so far as the latter term is applicable at all to non-sensual reality); but that it *is* so regarded may be seen from Plato's doctrine concerning the Idea of the Good, the Idea that occupies a peculiar position of pre-eminence in the *Republic*. The Good is there compared to the sun, the light of which makes the objects of nature visible to all and so is, in a sense, the source of their worth and value and beauty. This comparison is, of course, but a comparison, and as such should not be pressed: we are not to suppose that the Good exists as an object among objects, as the sun exists as an object among other objects. On the other hand, as Plato clearly asserts that the Good gives being to the objects of knowledge and so is, as it were, the unifying and all-comprehensive Principle of the essential order, while itself excelling even essential being in dignity and power,[1] it is impossible to conclude that the Good is a mere concept or even that it is a non-existent end, a teleological principle, as yet unreal, towards which all things are working: it is not only an epistemological principle, but also—in some, as yet, ill-defined sense—an *ontological* principle, a principle of being. It is, therefore, real in itself and subsistent.

It would seem that the Idea of the Good of the *Republic* must be regarded as identical with the essential Beauty of the *Symposium*. Both are represented as the high-peak of an intellectual ascent, while the comparison of the Idea of the Good with the sun would appear to indicate that it is the source not only of the goodness of things, but also of their beauty. The Idea of the Good gives being to the Forms or essences of the intellectual order, while science and the wide ocean of intellectual beauty is a stage on the ascent to the essentially beautiful. Plato is clearly working towards the conception of the Absolute, the absolutely Perfect and exemplary Pattern of all things, the ultimate ontological Principle. This Absolute is immanent, for phenomena embody it, "copy" it, partake in it, manifest it, in their varying degrees;

[1] *Rep.*, 509 b 6–10.

but it is also transcendent, for it is said to transcend even being itself, while the metaphors of participation (μέθεξις) and imitation (μίμησις)[1] imply a distinction between the participation and the Partaken of, between the imitation and the Imitated or Exemplar. Any attempt to reduce the Platonic Good to a mere logical principle and to disregard the indications that it is an ontological principle, necessarily leads to a denial of the sublimity of the Platonic metaphysic—as also, of course, to the conclusion that the Middle Platonist and Neo-Platonist philosophers entirely mis-understood the essential meaning of the Master.

At this point in the discussion there are two important obser-vations to be made:

(i) Aristotle in the *Eudemian Ethics*[2] says that Plato identifies the Good with the One, while Aristoxenus, recalling Aristotle's account of Plato's lecture on the Good, tells us that the audience, who went to the lecture expecting to hear something about human goods, such as wealth, happiness, etc., were surprised when they found themselves listening to a discourse on mathe-matics, astronomy, numbers and *the identity of the good and one*. In the *Metaphysics*, Aristotle says that "Of those who maintain the existence of the unchangeable substances, some say that the one itself is the good itself, but they thought its substance lay mainly in its unity."[3] Plato is not mentioned by name in this passage, but elsewhere[4] Aristotle distinctly says that, for Plato, "the Forms are the cause of the essence of all other things, and the One is the cause of the essence of the Forms." Now, in the *Republic*,[5] Plato speaks of the ascent of the mind to the first principle of the whole, and asserts that the Idea of the Good is inferred to be "the universal author of all things beautiful and right, parent of light and of the lord of light in this world, and the *source of truth and reason* in the other." Hence it would seem only reasonable to conclude that the One, the Good and the essential Beauty are the same for Plato, and that the intelligible world of Forms owes its being in some way to the One. The word "emanation" (so dear to the Neo-Platonists) is nowhere used, and it is difficult to form any precise notion how Plato derived the Forms from the One; but it is clear enough that the One is the unifying Principle. Moreover, the One itself, though immanent in the Forms, is also transcendent, in that it cannot

---

[1] These phrases occur in the *Phaedo*. [2] 1218 a 24. [3] *Metaph.*, 1091, b 13-15.
[4] *Metaph.*, 988 a 10-11. [5] 517 b 7-c 4.

be simply equated with the single Forms. Plato tells us that "the good is not essence, but far exceeds essence in dignity and power," while on the other hand it is "not only the source of intelligibility in all objects of knowledge, but also of their being and essence,"[1] so that he who turns his eye towards the Good, turns it towards "that place where is the full perfection of being."[2] The implication is that the Idea of the Good may rightly be said to transcend being, since it is above all visible and intelligible objects, while on the other hand, as the Supremely Real, the true Absolute, it is the Principle of being and essence in all things.

In the *Timaeus*, Plato says that "It is hard to find the maker and father of the universe, and having found him, it is impossible to speak of him to all."[3] That the position occupied by the Demiurge in the *Timaeus* suggests that these words apply to him, is true; but we must remember (*a*) that the Demiurge is probably a symbol for the operation of Reason in the universe, and (*b*) that Plato explicitly said that there were subjects on which he refused to write,[4] one of these subjects being without doubt his full doctrine of the One. The Demiurge belongs to the "likely account."[5] In his second letter, Plato says that it is a mistake to suppose that any of the predicates we are acquainted with apply to the "king of the universe,"[6] and in his sixth letter he asks his friends to swear an oath of loyalty "in the name of the God who is captain of all things present and to come, and of the Father of that captain and cause."[7] Now, if the "Captain" is the Demiurge, the "Father" cannot be the Demiurge too, but must be the One; and I think that Plotinus was right in identifying the Father with the One or Good of the *Republic*.

The One is thus Plato's ultimate Principle and the source of the world of Forms, and Plato, as we have seen, thinks that the One transcends human predicates. This implies that the *via negativa* of Neo-Platonist and Christian philosophers is a legitimate approach to the One, but it should not be immediately concluded that the approach to the One is an "ecstatic" approach, as in Plotinus. In the *Republic* it is definitely asserted that the approach is *dialectical*, and that a man attains the vision of the Good by "pure intelligence."[8] By dialectic the highest principle of the soul is raised "to the contemplation of that which is best in existence."[9] To this subject we must return later.

---

[1] *Rep.*, 509 b 6–10. [2] *Rep.*, 526 e 3–4. [3] *Tim.*, 28 c 3–5.
[4] Cf. *Ep.* 2, 314 b 7–c 4. [5] *Tim.*, 30 b 6–c 1. [6] *Ep.* 2, 312 e ff.
[7] *Ep.* 6, 323 d 2–6. [8] *Rep.* 532 a 5–b 2. [9] *Rep.*, 532 c 5–6.

(ii) If the Forms proceed from the One—in some undefined manner—what of particular sensible objects? Does not Plato make such a rift between intelligible and visible worlds that they can be no longer interconnected? It would appear that Plato, who in the *Republic*[1] appears to condemn empirical astronomy, was forced by the progress of empirical science to modify his views, and in the *Timaeus* he himself considers nature and natural questions. (Moreover, Plato came to see that the dichotomy between an unchanging, intelligible world of reality and a changing world of unreality is hardly satisfactory. "Shall we be easily persuaded that change and life and soul and wisdom are not really present to what completely is, that it is neither living nor intelligent but is something awful and sacred in its thoughtless and static stability?")[2] In the *Sophist* and *Philebus* it is implied that διάνοια and αἴσθησις (which belong to different segments of the Line) unite together in the scientific judgment of perception. Ontologically speaking, the sensible particular can become the object of judgment and knowledge only in so far as it is really subsumed under one of the Ideas, "partaking" in the specific Form: in so far as it is a class-instance, it is real and can be known. The sensible particular *as such*, however, considered precisely in its particularity, is indefinable and unknowable, and is not truly "real." To this conviction Plato clung, and it is obviously an Eleatic legacy. The sense-world is, therefore, not wholly illusion, but it contains an element of unreality. Yet it can hardly be denied that even this position, with its sharp distinction between the formal and material elements of the particular, would leave the problem of the "separation" of the intelligible world from the sensible world really unresolved. It is this "separation" that Aristotle attacked. Aristotle thought that determinate form and the matter in which it is embodied are inseparable, both belonging to the real world, and, in his opinion, Plato simply ignored this fact and introduced an unjustifiable separation between the two elements. The real universal, according to Aristotle, is the *determined* universal, and the determined universal is an inseparable aspect of the real: it is a λόγος ἔνυλος or definition embodied in matter. Plato did not see this.

(Professor Julius Stenzel made the brilliant suggestion[3] that when Aristotle criticised Plato's "separation," he was criticising Plato for his failure to see that there is no genus alongside the

---

[1] *Rep.*, 529–30.　[2] *Sophist*, 248 e 6–249 a 2.　[3] *Zahl und Gestalt*, pp. 133 ff.

species. He appeals to *Metaph.*, 1037 b 8 ff., where Aristotle attacks Plato's method of logical division for supposing that in the resulting definition the intermediate *differentiae* must be recapitulated, e.g. Plato's method of division would result in our defining man as a "two-footed animal." Aristotle objects to this on the ground that "footedness" is not something alongside "two-footedness." Now, that Aristotle objected to this method of division is true; but his criticism of the Platonic theory of Forms on the ground of the Χωρισμός it introduces, cannot be reduced to the criticism of a logical point, for Aristotle is not criticising Plato merely for putting a generic form alongside the specific form, but for putting Forms in general alongside particulars.[1] It may well be, however, that Aristotle considered that Plato's failure to see that there is no genus alongside the species, i.e. no merely determinable universal, helped to conceal from him the Χωρισμός he was introducing between Forms and particulars—and here Stenzel's suggestion is valuable; but the Χωρισμός attacked by Aristotle cannot be confined to a logical point. That is clear from the whole tenor of Aristotle's criticism.)

4. In the *Phaedrus* Plato speaks of the soul who beholds "real existence, colourless, formless and intangible, visible only to the intelligence" (ἡ ἀχρωματός τε καὶ ἀσχημάτιστος καὶ ἀναφὴς οὐσία ὄντως οὖσα, ψυχῆς, κυβερνήτῃ μόνῳ θεατὴ νῷ),[2] and which sees distinctly "absolute justice, and absolute temperance, and absolute science; not such as they appear in creation, nor under the variety of forms to which we nowadays give the name of realities, but the justice, the temperance, the science, which exist in that which is real and essential being" (τὴν ἐν τῷ ὅ ἐστιν ὂν ὄντως ἐπιστήμην οὖσαν). This would seem to me to imply that these Forms or *Ideals* are comprised in the Principle of Being, in the One, or at least that they owe their essence to the One. Of course, if we use the imagination and try to picture to ourselves absolute justice or temperance existing on its own account in a heavenly world, we shall no doubt think Plato's words childishly naïve and ludicrous; but we should ask ourselves what Plato *meant* and should beware of attributing hastily to him such an extraordinary conception. Most probably Plato means to imply, by his figurative account, that the Ideal of Justice, the Ideal of Temperance, etc., are objectively grounded in the Absolute Principle of Value, in the Good, which "contains" within itself the ideal of human nature

---

[1] Cf. Hardie, *A Study in Plato*, p. 75.   [2] *Phaedrus*, 247 c 6–8.

and so the ideal of the virtues of human nature. The Good or Absolute Principle of Value has thus the nature of a τέλος; but it is not an unrealised τέλος, a non-existent end-to-be-achieved; it is an existent τέλος, an ontological Principle, the Supremely Real, the perfect Exemplary Cause, the Absolute or One.

5. It is to be noted that at the beginning of the *Parmenides* the question is raised what Ideas Socrates is prepared to admit.[1] In reply to Parmenides, Socrates admits that there are Ideas of "likeness" and "of the one and many," and also of "the just and the beautiful and the good," etc. In answer to a further question, he says that he is often undecided, whether he should or should not include Ideas of man, fire, water, etc.; while, in answer to the question whether he admits Ideas of hair, mud, dirt, etc., Socrates answers, "Certainly not." He admits, however, that he sometimes gets disturbed and begins to think that there is nothing without an Idea, though no sooner has he taken up this position than he "runs away," afraid that he "may fall into a bottomless pit of nonsense and perish." He returns, therefore, "to the Ideas of which I was just now speaking."

Julius Stenzel uses this discussion in an attempt to prove that εἶδος had at first for Plato a definitely valuational connotation, as was but natural in the inheritor of Socrates. It was only later that the term came to be extended to cover all class-concepts. I believe that this is, in the main, correct, and that it was largely this very extension of the term Idea (i.e. *explicit* extension, since it already contained an implicit extension) which forced on Plato's attention difficulties of the type considered in the *Parmenides*. For, as long as the term εἶδος is "laden with moral and aesthetic qualities,"[2] as long as it has the nature of a valuational τέλος, drawing men under the impulse of Eros, the problem of its internal unity or multiplicity does not so obviously arise: it is the Good and the Beautiful in One. But once Ideas of man and other particular objects of our experience are explicitly admitted, the Ideal World threatens to become a Many, a reduplication of this world. What is the relation of the Ideas to one another, and what is their relation to particular things? Is there any real unity at all? The Idea of the Good is sufficiently remote from sensible particulars not to appear as an unwelcome reduplication of the latter; but if there is an Idea of man, for instance, "separate"

[1] 130 a 8 ff.
[2] *Plato's Method of Dialectic,* p. 55 (Trs. D. J. Allan, Oxford, Clarendon Press 1940.)

from individual men, it might well appear as a mere reduplication of the latter. Moreover, is the Idea wholly present in every individual man, or is it only partially present in every individual man? Again, if it is legitimate to speak of a likeness between individual men and the Idea of Man, must you not postulate a τρίτος ἄνθρωπος, in order to account for this resemblance and so proceed on an infinite regress? This type of objection was brought against the Ideal Theory by Aristotle, but it was already anticipated by Plato himself. The difference is, that while Plato (as we shall see later) thought that he had answered the objections, Aristotle did not think that Plato had answered them.

In the *Parmenides*, therefore, the question of the relation of individual objects to the Idea is discussed, objections being raised to the Socratic explanation. According to Socrates the relation may be described in two ways: (i) As a participation (μέθεξις, μετέχειν) of the particular object in the Idea; (ii) as an imitation (μίμησις) of the Idea by the particular object, the particular objects being ὁμοιώματα and μιμήματα of the Idea, the latter being the exemplar or παράδειγμα. (It does not seem possible to refer the two explanations to different periods of Plato's philosophical development—at least, not in any rigid way—since both explanations are found together in the *Parmenides*,[1] and both thoughts occur in the *Symposium*.)[2] The objections raised by Parmenides against these Socratic theories are, no doubt, intended to be serious criticism—as, indeed, they are—and not a mere *jeu d'esprit*, as has been suggested. The objections are real objections, and it would appear that Plato tried to develop his theory of Ideas in an attempt to meet some such criticisms as that which he puts into the mouths of the Eleatics in the *Parmenides*.

Do particular objects participate in the whole Idea or only in part of it? This is the dilemma proposed by Parmenides as a logical consequence of the participation-explanation of the relation between Ideas and particular objects. If the first of the alternatives be chosen, then the Idea, which is one, would be entirely in each of many individuals. If the second of the alternatives be chosen, then the Form or Idea is unitary and divisible (or many) at the same time. In either case a contradiction is involved. Moreover, if equal things are equal by the presence of a certain amount of equality, then they are equal by what is less than

[1] *Parm.*, 132 d 1 ff.
[2] *Sympos.*, 211 b 2 (μετέχοντα). In 212 a 4, sense-objects are spoken of as εἴδωλα, which implies "imitation."

equality. Again, if something is big by participation in bigness it is big by possessing that which is less than bigness—which seems to be a contradiction. (It is to be noted that objections of this kind suppose that the Ideas are what amount to individual objects on their own account, and so they serve to show the impossibility of regarding the Idea in this way.)

Socrates suggests the imitation-theory, that particular objects are copies of the Ideas, which are themselves patterns or exemplars; the resemblance of the particular objects to the Idea constitutes its participation in it. Against this Parmenides argues that, if white things are like whiteness, whiteness is also like white things. Hence, if the likeness between white things is to be explained by postulating a Form of whiteness, the likeness between whiteness and white things should also be explained by postulating an archetype, and so on indefinitely. Aristotle argued in much the same way, but all that really follows from the criticism is that the Idea is not simply another particular object, and that the relation between the particular objects and the Idea cannot be the same as that between different particular objects.[1] The objection, then, is to the point as showing the necessity for further consideration of the true relations, but this does not show that the Ideal Theory is totally untenable.

The objection is also raised that on Socrates' theory the Ideas would be unknowable. Man's knowledge is concerned with the objects of this world, and with the relations between individual objects. We can, for example, know the relation between the individual master and the individual slave, but this knowledge is insufficient to inform us as to the relationship between absolute mastership (the Idea of Mastership) and absolute slavery (the Idea of Slavery). For that purpose we should require absolute knowledge and this we do not possess. This objection, too, shows the hopelessness of regarding the Ideal World as merely parallel to this world: if we are to know the former, then there must be some objective basis in the latter which enables us to know it. If the two worlds are merely parallel, then, just as we would know the sensible world without being able to know the Ideal World, so a divine intelligence would know the Ideal World without being able to know the sensible world.

[1] Proclus pointed out that the relation of a copy to its original is a relation not only of resemblance, but also of derivation-from, so that the relation is not symmetrical. Cf. Taylor, *Plato*, p. 358: "My reflection in the glass is a reflection of my face, but my face is not a reflection of it."

7

The objections raised are left unanswered in the *Parmenides*, but it is to be noticed that Parmenides was not concerned to deny the existence of an intelligible world: he freely admits that if one refuses to admit the existence of absolute Ideas at all, then philosophic thinking goes by the board. The result of the objections that Plato raises against himself in the *Parmenides* is, therefore, to impel him to further exact consideration of the nature of the Ideal World and of its relation to the sensible world. It is made clear by the difficulties raised that some principle of unity is required which will, at the same time, not annihilate the many. This is admitted in the dialogue, though the unity considered is a unity in the world of Forms, as Socrates "did not care to solve the perplexity in reference to visible objects, but only in reference to thought and to what may be called ideas."[1] The difficulties are, therefore, not solved in the *Parmenides*; but the discussion must not be regarded as a destruction of the Ideal Theory, for the difficulties simply indicate that the theory must be expounded in a more satisfactory way than Socrates has expounded it hitherto.

In the second part of the dialogue Parmenides himself leads the discussion and undertakes to exemplify his "art," the method of considering the consequences which flow from a given hypothesis and the consequences which flow from denying that hypothesis. Parmenides proposes to start from the hypothesis of the One and to examine the consequences which are seen to flow from its assertion and its denial. Subordinate distinctions are introduced, the argument is long and complicated and no satisfactory conclusion is arrived at. Into this argument one cannot enter in a book like the present one, but it is necessary to point out that this second part of the *Parmenides* is no more a refutation of the doctrine of the One than the first part was of the Ideal Theory. A real refutation of the doctrine of the One would certainly not be put into the mouth of Parmenides himself, whom Plato greatly respected. In the *Sophist* the Eleatic Stranger apologises for doing violence to "father Parmenides,"[2] but, as Mr. Hardie aptly remarks, this apology "would hardly be called for if in another dialogue father Parmenides had done violence to himself."[3] Moreover, at the end of the *Parmenides* agreement is voted as to the assertion that, "If One is not, then nothing is." The participants may not be sure of the status of the many or

---

[1] 135 e 1–4.   [2] 241 a.   [3] *A Study in Plato*, p. 106.

of their relation to the One or even of the precise nature of the
One; but they are at least agreed that there *is* a One.

6. In the *Sophist* the object before the interlocutors is to
define the Sophist. They have a notion, of course, what the
Sophist is, but they wish to *define* the Sophist's nature, to pin
him down, as it were, in a clear formula (λόγος). It will be remembered that in the *Theaetetus* Socrates rejected the suggestion that
knowledge is true belief plus an account (λόγος); but in that
dialogue the discussion concerned particular sensible objects,
while in the *Sophist* the discussion turns on class-concepts. The
answer which is given to the problem of the *Theaetetus* is, therefore, that knowledge consists in apprehending the class-concept
by means of genus and difference, i.e. by *definition*. The method
of arriving at definition is that of analysis or division (διαίρεσις,
διαιρεῖν κατ'εἴδη), whereby the notion or name to be defined is
subsumed under a wider genus or class, which latter is then
divided into its natural components. One of these natural components will be the notion to be defined. Previous to the division
a process of synthesis or collecting (συνάγειν εἰς ἕν, συναγωγή) should
take place, through which terms that are at least *prima facie*
interrelated are grouped together and compared, with a view to
determining the genus from which the process of division is to
start. The wider class chosen is divided into two mutually-
exclusive sub-classes, distinguished from one another by the
presence or absence of some peculiar characteristic; and the process is continued until the *definiendum* is finally tracked down
and defined by means of its genus and differences. (There is an
amusing fragment of Epicrates, the comic poet, describing the
classification of a pumpkin in the Academy.)

There is no need to enter either upon the actual process of
tracking down the Sophist, or upon Plato's preliminary example
of the method of division (the definition of the angler); but it
must be pointed out that the discussion makes it clear that the
Ideas may be one and many at the same time. The class-concept
"Animal," for example, is one; but at the same time it is many,
in that it contains within itself the sub-classes of "Horse," "Fox,"
"Man," etc. Plato speaks as though the generic Form pervades
the subordinate specific Form or is dispersed throughout them,
"blending" with each of them, yet retaining its own unity. There
is a communion (κοινωνία) between Forms, and one Form partakes
of (μετέχειν) another (as in "Motion exists" it is implied that

Motion blends with Existence); but we should not suppose that
one Form partakes of another in the same sense in which the
individual partakes of the specific Form, for Plato would not
speak of the individual blending with the specific Form. The
Forms thus constitute a hierarchy, subordinate to the One as the
highest and all-pervading Form; but it is to be remembered that
for Plato the "higher" the Form is, the richer it is, so that his
point of view is the opposite to that of the Aristotelian, for whom
the more "abstract" the concept, the poorer it is.

There is one important point to be noticed. The process of
division (Plato, of course, believed that the logical division detects
the grades of real being) cannot be prolonged indefinitely, since
ultimately you will arrive at the Form that admits of no further
division. These are the *infimae species* or ἄτομα εἴδη. The Form
of Man, for instance, is indeed "many" in this sense, that it
contains the genus and all relative differences, but it is not many
in the sense of containing further subordinate specific classes into
which it could be divided. On the contrary, below the ἄτομον εἴδος
Man there stand *individual men*. The ἄτομα εἴδη, therefore, constitute the lowest rung of the ladder or hierarchy of Forms, and
Plato very probably considered that by bringing down the Forms,
by the process of division, to the border of the sensible sphere,
he was providing a connecting link between τὰ ἀόρατά and τὰ ὁρατά.
It may be that the relation between the individuals and the
infimae species was to be elucidated in the *Philosopher*, the
dialogue which, it is conjectured, was once intended by Plato to
follow the *Statesman* and which was never written; but it cannot
be said that the chasm was ever satisfactorily bridged, and the
problem of the Χωρισμός remained. (Julius Stenzel put forward
the suggestion that Plato adopted from Democritus the principle
of dividing until the atom is reached, which, in Plato's hands,
becomes the intelligible "atomic Form." It is certainly significant
that geometrical shape was a feature of the atom of Democritus,
while geometrical shapes play an important part in Plato's picture
of the formation of the world in the *Timaeus*; but it would seem
that the relation of Plato to Democritus must always remain
conjectural and something of a puzzle.)[1]

I have mentioned the "blending" of the Forms, but it is also
to be noticed that there are Forms which are incompatible, at
least in their "particularity," and will not "blend," e.g. Motion

[1] Cf. Chapter X, *Democritus*, in *Plato's Method of Dialectic*.

and Rest. If I say: "Motion does not rest," my statement is true, since it expresses the fact that Motion and Rest are incompatible and do not blend: if, however, I say: "Motion is Rest," my statement is false, since it expresses a combination that is not objectively verified. Light is thus thrown on the nature of false judgment which perplexed Socrates in the *Theaetetus*; though more relevant to the actual problem of the *Theaetetus* is the discussion of false statement in 262 e ff. of the *Sophist*. Plato takes as an example of a true statement, "Theaetetus sits," and as an example of a false statement, "Theaetetus flies." It is pointed out that Theaetetus is an existent subject and that Flying is a real Form, so that false statement is not a statement about *nothing*. (Every significant statement is about *something*, and it would be absurd to admit non-existent facts or objective falsehoods.) The statement has a meaning, but the relation of participating between the actual "sitting" of Theaetetus and the different Form "Flying" is missing. The statement, therefore, has a meaning, but the statement as a whole does not correspond with the fact as a whole. Plato meets the objection that there can be no false statement because there is nothing for it to mean, by an appeal to the Theory of Forms (which does not appear in the *Theaetetus*, with the consequence that in that dialogue the problem could not be solved). "We can have discourse only through the weaving together of Forms."[1] It is not meant that all significant statements must concern Forms exclusively (since we can make significant statements about singular things like Theaetetus), but that every significant statement involves the use of at least one Form, e.g. "Sitting" in the true statement, "Theaetetus sits."[2]

The *Sophist* thus presents us with the picture of a hierarchy of Forms, combining among themselves in an articulated complex; but it does not solve the problem of the relation of the particulars to the "atomic Forms." Plato insists that there are εἴδωλα or things which are not non-existent, but which at the same time are not fully real; but in the *Sophist* he realises that it is no longer possible to insist on the completely unchanging character

---

[1] *Soph.*, 259 e 5–6.

[2] To postulate Forms of Sitting and Flying may be a logical application of Plato's principles, but it obviously raises great difficulties. Aristotle implies that the upholders of the Ideal Theory did not go beyond postulating Ideas of natural substances (*Met.* 1079 a). He also asserts that according to the Platonists there are no Ideas of Relations, and implies that they did not believe in Ideas of Negation.

of all Reality. He still holds that the Forms are changeless, but somehow or other spiritual motion must be included in the Real. "Life, soul, understanding" must have a place in what is perfectly real, since, if Reality as a whole excludes all change, intelligence (which involves life) will have no real existence anywhere at all. The conclusion is that "we must admit that what changes and change itself are real things,"[1] and that "Reality or the sum of things is both at once—all that is unchangeable and all that is in change."[2] Real being must accordingly include life, soul and intelligence, and the change implied by them; but what of the εἴδωλα, the purely sensible and perpetually changing, mere becoming? What is the relation of this half-real sphere to Real Being? This question is not answered in the *Sophist*.

7. In the *Sophist*[3] Plato clearly indicates that the whole complex of Forms, the hierarchy of genera and species, is comprised in an all-pervading Form, that of Being, and he certainly believed that in tracing out the structure of the hierarchy of Forms by means of διαίρεσις he was detecting, not merely the structure of logical Forms, but also the structure of ontological Forms of the Real. But whether successful or not in his division of the genera and species, was it of any help to him in overcoming the Χωρισμός, the separation between the particulars and the *infimae species*? In the *Sophist* he showed how division is to be continued until the ἄτομον εἶδος is reached, in the apprehension of which δόξα and αἴσθησις are involved, though it is λόγος alone that determines the "undetermined" plurality. The *Philebus* assumes the same, that we must be able to bring the division to an end by setting a limit to the unlimited and comprehending sense-particulars in the lowest class, so far as they can be comprehended. (In the *Philebus* Ideas are termed ἑνάδες or μονάδες). The important point to notice is that for Plato the sense-particulars *as such* are the unlimited and the undetermined: they are limited and determined only in so far as they are, as it were, brought within the ἄτομον εἶδος. This means that the sense-particulars in so far as they are not brought within the ἄτομον εἶδος and cannot be brought within it, are not true objects at all: they are not fully real. In pursuing the διαίρεσις as far as the ἄτομον εἶδος Plato was, in his own eyes, comprehending all Reality. This enables him to use the words: "But the form of the infinite must not be brought near to the many until one has observed its full number,

[1] 249 b 2–3.   [2] 249 d 3–4.   [3] Cf. 253 b 8 ff.

the number between the one and the infinite; when this has been learnt, each several individual thing may be forgotten and dismissed into the infinite."[1] In other words, the division must be continued until particulars in their intelligible reality are comprehended in the ἄτομον εἶδος: when this has been done, the remainder, i.e. the sense-particulars, in their non-intelligible aspect, as impenetrable to λόγος, may be dismissed into the sphere of what is fleeting and only semi-real, that which cannot truly be said to *be*. From Plato's own point of view, therefore, the problem of the Χωρισμός may have been solved; but from the point of view of anyone who will not accept his doctrine of sense-particulars, it is very far from being solved.

8. But though Plato may have considered that he had solved the problem of the Χωρισμός, it still remained to show how the sense-particulars come into existence at all. Even if the whole hierarchy of Forms, the complex structure comprised in the all-embracing One, the Idea of Being, or the Good is an ultimate and self-explanatory principle, the Real and the Absolute, it is none the less necessary to show how the world of appearance, which is not simply not-being, even if it is not fully being, came into existence? Does it proceed from the One? If not, what is its cause? Plato made an attempt to answer this question in the *Timaeus*, though I can here only summarise very briefly his answer, as I shall return later to the *Timaeus* when dealing with the physical theories of Plato.

In the *Timaeus* the Demiurge is pictured as conferring geometrical shapes upon the primary qualities within the Receptacle or Space, and so introducing order into disorder, taking as his model in building up the world the intelligible realm of Forms. Plato's account of "creation" is most probably not meant to be an account of creation in time or *ex nihilo*: rather is it an analysis, by which the articulate structure of the material world, the work of a rational cause, is distinguished from the "primeval" chaos, without its being necessarily implied that the chaos was ever actual. The chaos is probably primeval only in the logical, and not in the temporal or historic sense. But if this is so, then the non-intelligible part of the material world is simply assumed: it exists "alongside of" the intelligible world. The Greeks, it would seem, never really envisaged the possibility of creation out of nothing (*ex nihilo sui et subiecti*). Just as the logical process of

---

[1] *Philebus*, 16 d 7–e 2.

διαίρεσις stops at the ἄτομον εἶδος and Plato in the *Philebus* dismisses the merely particular εἰς τὸ ἄπειρον, so in the physical analysis
of the *Timaeus* the merely particular, the non-intelligible element
(that which, logically considered, cannot be comprehended under
the ἄτομον εἶδος) is dismissed into the sphere of that which is "in
discordant and unordered motion,"[1] the factor that the Demiurge
"took over." Therefore, just as, from the viewpoint of the
Platonic logic, the sense-particulars as such cannot be deduced,
cannot be rendered fully intelligible (did not Hegel declare that
Herr Krug's pen could not be deduced?), so, in the Platonic
physics, the chaotic element, that into which order is "introduced"
by Reason, is not explained: doubtless Plato thought that it was
inexplicable. It can neither be *deduced* nor has it been *created
out of nothing*. It is simply there (a fact of experience), and that
is all that we can say about it. The Χωρισμός accordingly remains,
for, however "unreal" the chaotic may be, it is not not-being
tout simple: it is a factor in the world, a factor that Plato leaves
unexplained.

9. I have exhibited the Ideas or Forms as an ordered, intelligible structure, constituting in their totality a One in Many,
in such a way that each subordinate Idea is itself one in many,
as far as the ἄτομον εἶδος, below which is τὸ ἄπειρον. This complex
of Forms is the Logical-Ontological Absolute. I must now raise
the question, whether Plato regarded the Ideas as the Ideas of
God or as independent of God. For the Neo-Platonists, the Ideas
were the Thoughts of God: how far can such a theory be ascribed
to Plato himself? If it could be so ascribed, it would clearly go
a long way towards showing how the "Ideal World" is at once
a unity and a plurality—a unity as contained in the Divine Mind,
or Nous, and as subordinated to the Divine Plan, a plurality as
reflecting the richness of the Divine Thought-content, and as only
realisable in Nature in a multitude of existent objects.

In the tenth book of the *Republic*[2] Plato says that God is the
Author (Φυτουργός) of the ideal bed. More than that, God is the
Author of all other things—"things" in the context meaning
other essences. From this it might appear that God created the
ideal bed by *thinking* it, i.e. by comprising within His intellect
the Idea of the world, and so of man and of all his requirements.
(Plato did not, of course, imagine that there was a material ideal
bed.) Moreover, since Plato speaks of God as "king" and "truth"

---

[1] *Tim.*, 30 a 4-5.   [2] *Rep.*, 597 b 5-7.

(the tragic poet is at the third remove ἀπὸ βασιλέως καὶ τῆς ἀληθείας),
while he has already spoken of the Idea of the Good as κυρία
ἀλήθειαν καὶ νοῦν παραχομένη[1] and as Author of being and essence in
intelligible objects (Ideas),[2] it might well appear that Plato means
to Identify God with the Idea of the Good.[3] Those who wish to
believe that this was really Plato's thought, and who proceed to
interpret "God" in a theistic sense, would naturally appeal to
the *Philebus*,[4] where it is implied that the Mind that orders the
universe is possessed of soul (Socrates certainly says that wisdom
and mind cannot exist without soul), so that God would be a
living and intelligent being. We should thus have a personal God,
Whose Mind is the "place" of Ideas, and Who orders and rules
the universe, "king of heaven and earth."[5]

That there is much to be said for this interpretation of Plato's
thought, I would not deny: moreover, it is naturally attractive
to all those who desire to discover a tidy system in Plato and a
theistic system. But common honesty forces one to admit the
very serious difficulties against this tidy interpretation. For
example, in the *Timaeus* Plato pictures the Demiurge as introducing order into the world and forming natural objects according
to the model of the Ideas or Forms. The Demiurge is probably
a symbolic figure representing the Reason that Plato certainly
believed to be operative in the world. In the *Laws* he proposes
the institution of a Nocturnal Council or Inquisition for the
correction and punishment of atheists. Now, "atheist" means,
for Plato, first and foremost the man who denies the operation
of Reason in the world. Plato certainly admits that soul and
intelligence belong to the Real, but it does not seem possible to
assert with certainty that, in Plato's view, the Divine Reason is
the "place" of the Ideas. It might, indeed, be argued that the
Demiurge is spoken of as desiring that "all things should come
as near as possible to being like himself," and that "all things
should be good"[6]—phrases which suggest that the separation of
the Demiurge from the Ideas is a Myth and that, in Plato's real
thought, he is the Good and the ultimate Source of the Ideas.
That the *Timaeus* never says that the Demiurge created the Ideas
or is their Source, but pictures them as distinct from him (the

---

[1] *Rep.*, 517 c 4.   [2] *Rep.*, 509 b 6–10.
[3] The fact that Plato speaks of God as "king" and "truth," while the Idea of
the Good is "the source of truth and reason," suggests that God or Reason is *not* to
be identified with the Good. A Neo-Platonic interpretation is rather implied.
[4] *Phil.*, 30 c 2–e 2.   [5] *Phil.*, 28 c 6 ff.   [6] *Tim.*, 29 e 1–30 a 7.

Demiurge being depicted as Efficient Cause and the Ideas as
Exemplary Cause), does not seem to be conclusive evidence that
Plato did *not* bring them together; but it should at least make
us beware of asserting positively that he *did* bring them together.
Moreover, if the "Captain" and God of the sixth letter is the
Demiurge or Divine Reason, what of the "Father"? If the
"Father" is the One, then it would not look as though the One and
the whole hierarchy of the Ideas can be explained as thoughts
of the Demiurge.[1]

But if the Divine Reason is not the ultimate, is it possible that
the One is the ultimate, not only as ultimate Exemplary Cause,
but also as ultimate Productive Cause, being itself "beyond"
mind and soul as it is "beyond" essence? If so, can we say that
the Divine Reason proceeds in some way (timelessly, of course)
from the One, and that this Reason either contains the Ideas as
thoughts or exists "alongside" the Ideas (as depicted in the
Timaeus)? In other words, can we interpret Plato on Neo-
Platonic lines?[2] The remark about the "Captain" and the
"Father" in the sixth letter might be understood in support of
this interpretation, while the fact that the Idea of the Good is
never spoken of as a *soul* might mean that the Good is beyond
soul, i.e. more than soul, not less than soul. The fact that in the
Sophist Plato says, through the mouth of the Eleatic Stranger,
that "Reality or the sum of things" must include soul, intelligence
and life,[3] implies that the One or total Reality (the Father of
Ep. 6) comprises not only the Ideas but also mind. If so, what
is the relation of Mind to the World-soul of the *Timaeus*? The
World-soul and the Demiurge are distinct in that dialogue (for
the Demiurge is depicted as "making" the World-soul); but in
the *Sophist* it is said that intelligence must have life, and that
both these must have soul "in which they reside."[4] It is, however,
possible that the making of the World-soul by the Demiurge is not
to be taken literally at all, especially as it is stated in the *Phaedrus*
that soul is a beginning and uncreated,[5] and that the World-soul
and the Demiurge represent together the Divine Reason immanent
in the world. If this were so, then we should have the One, the
Supreme Reality, embracing and in some sense the Source (though
not the Creator in time) of the Divine Reason (=Demiurge=

---

[1] Though in *Timaeus*, 37 c, the "Father" means the Demiurge.
[2] The Neo-Platonists held that the Divine Reason was not ultimate, but
proceeded from the One.
[3] *Soph.*, 248 e 6–249 d 4.   [4] 249 a 4–7.   [5] 245 c 5–246 a 2.

World-soul) and the Forms. We might then speak of the Divine Reason as the "Mind of God" (if *we* equated God with the One) and the Forms as Ideas of God; but we should have to bear in mind that such a conception would bear a closer resemblance to later Neo-Platonism than to specifically Christian philosophy.

That Plato had some idea of what he meant hardly needs to be stressed, but in view of the evidence at our disposal we must avoid dogmatic pronouncements as to what he *did* mean. Therefore, although the present writer is inclined to think that the second interpretation bears some resemblance to what Plato actually thought, he is very far from putting it forward as certainly the authentic philosophy of Plato.

10. We must now touch briefly on the vexed question of the mathematical aspect of the Ideal Theory.[1] According to Aristotle,[2] Plato declared that:

   (i) The Forms are Numbers;

  (ii) Things exist by participation in Numbers;

 (iii) Numbers are composed of the One and the great-and-small or "indeterminate duality" (ἀόριστος δυάς) instead of, as the Pythagoreans thought, the unlimited (ἄπειρον) and limit (πέρας);

 (iv) τὰ μαθηματικά occupy an intermediate position between Forms and things.

With the subject of τὰ μαθηματικά or the "intermediates" I have already dealt when treating of the Line: it remains, therefore, to consider the following questions:

   (i) Why did Plato identify Forms with Numbers and what did he mean?

  (ii) Why did Plato say that things exist by participation in numbers?

 (iii) What is meant by composition from the One and the great-and-small?

With these questions I can only deal very briefly. Not only would an adequate treatment require a much greater knowledge of mathematics, both ancient and modern, than the present writer possesses; but it is also doubtful if, with the material at our disposal, even the mathematically-gifted specialist could give a really adequate and definitive treatment.

---

[1] My debt to Professor Taylor's treatment of the topic will be obvious to all those who have read his articles in *Mind* (Oct. 1926 and Jan. 1927). Cf. Appendix to *Plato*.

[2] *Metaph.*, A, 6, 9; M and N.

(i) Plato's motive in identifying Forms with Numbers seems to be that of rationalising or rendering intelligible the mysterious and transcendental world of Forms. To render intelligible in this case means to find the *principle of order*.

(ii) Natural objects embody the principle of order to some extent: they are, for example, instances of the logical universal and tend towards the realisation of their form: they are the handiwork of intelligence and exhibit design.

(*a*) This truth is expressed in the *Timaeus* by saying that the sensible characters of bodies are dependent on the geometrical structure of their corpuscles. This geometrical structure is determined by that of their faces, and that of their faces by the structure of the two types of triangles (isosceles right-angled and right-angled scalene) from which they are built up. The ratios of the sides of the triangles to one another may be expressed numerically.

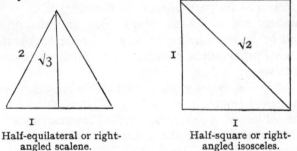

Half-equilateral or right-angled scalene.

Half-square or right-angled isosceles.

(*b*) Another expression of the same truth is the doctrine of the *Epinomis* that the apparently mazy movements of the heavenly bodies (the primary objects of official cult) really conform to mathematical law and so express the wisdom of God.[1]

(*c*) Natural bodies, therefore, embody the principle of order and may, to a greater or less extent, be "mathematicised." On the other hand, they cannot be entirely "mathematicised"—they are not Numbers—for they embody also contingency, an irrational element, "matter." They are thus not said to *be* Numbers, but to *participate* in Numbers.

(iii) This partly irrational character of natural objects gives us the key to the understanding of the "great and the small."

(*a*) The triplet of numbers which gives the ratio of the sides to one another is, in the case of the isosceles right-angled triangle,

[1] 990 c 5–991 b 4.

1, 1, $\sqrt{2}$, and in the case of the right-angled scalene, 1, $\sqrt{3}$, 2. In either case, then, there is an irrational element which expresses the *contingency* in natural objects.

(*b*) Taylor points out that in a certain sequence of fractions— nowadays derived from a "continual fraction," but actually alluded to by Plato himself[1] and by Theo of Smyrna[2]—alternate terms converge upwards to $\sqrt{2}$ as limit and upper bound, while alternate other terms converge downwards to $\sqrt{2}$ as limit and lower bound. The terms of the whole sequence, therefore, in their original order, are in consequence alternately "greater and less" than $\sqrt{2}$, while jointly converging to $\sqrt{2}$ as their unique limit. We have, then, the characteristics of the great and the small or the indeterminate duality. The "endlessness" of the continued fraction, the "irrationality," seems to be identified with the material element, the element of non-being, *in all that becomes*. It is a mathematical expression of the Heraclitean flux-character of natural entities.

This may seem fairly clear as regards natural bodies. But what are we to make of Aristotle's dictum that "from the great and the small, by participation in the One, come the Forms, i.e. the Numbers"?[3] In other words, how can we explain the extension of the form-matter composition to the integers themselves?

If we take the series $1 + \frac{1}{2} + \frac{1}{4} + \frac{1}{8} + \ldots + \frac{1}{2}n + \ldots$ we have a series that converges to the number 2. It is clear, then, that an infinite series of rational fractions may converge towards a rational limit, and examples could be given in which the μέγα καὶ μικρόν are involved. Plato would seem to have extended this composition from the μέγα καὶ μικρόν to the integers themselves, passing over, however, the fact that 2 as the limit of convergence cannot be identified with the integer 2, since the integers are *presupposed* as a series from which the convergents are formed. In the Platonic Academy the integers were derived or "educed" from One by the help of the ἀόριστος δυάς, which seems to have been identified with the *integer* 2, and to have been given the function of "doubling." The result is that the integers are derived in a non-rational series. On the whole we may say that, pending new light from philologically exact mathematical history, the theory of the composition of the integers from the One and the great-and-small will continue to look like a puzzling excrescence on the Platonic theory of Ideas.

---

[1] *Rep.*, 546 c.   [2] *Expositio*, ed. Hiller, 43, 5–45, 8.   [3] *Metaph.*, 987 b 21–2.

11. In regard to the whole tendency to pan-mathematisation I cannot but regard it as unfortunate. That the real is rational is a presupposition of all dogmatic philosophy, but it does not follow that the whole of reality can be rationalised by us. The attempt to reduce all reality to mathematics is not only an attempt to rationalise all reality—which is the task of philosophy, it may be said—but presupposes that all reality can be rationalised *by us*, which is an assumption. It is perfectly true that Plato admits an element in Nature that cannot be submitted to mathematisation, and so to rationalisation, but his attempt to rationalise reality and the extension of this attempt to the spiritual sphere has a flavour about it which may well remind us of Spinoza's deterministic and mechanistic view of reality (expressed in his *Ethica more geometrico demonstrata*) and of Hegel's attempt to comprehend the inner essence of ultimate Reality or God within the formulae of logic.

It may at first sight appear strange that the Plato who composed the *Symposium*, with its ascent to Absolute Beauty under the inspiration of Eros, should have been inclined to pan-mathematicism; and this apparent contrast might seem to support the view that the Socrates of the Platonic dialogues does not give Plato's opinions, but his own, that while Socrates invented the Ideal Theory as it appears in the dialogues, Plato "arithmetised" it. Yet, apart from the fact that the "mystical" and predominantly religious interpretation of the *Symposium* is very far from having been demonstrated as the certain interpretation, the apparent contrast between the *Symposium*—assuming for the moment that the "ascent" is a religious and mystical one—and Plato's mathematical interpretation of the Forms, as related to us by Aristotle, would hardly seem to be a compelling argument for the view that the Platonic Socrates is the historic Socrates, and that Plato reserved most of his personal views for the Academy, and, in the dialogues, for expression by other *dramatis personae* than the figure of Socrates. If we turn to Spinoza, we find a man who, on the one hand, was possessed by the vision of the unity of all things in God, and who proposed the ideal intuition of the *amor intellectualis Dei*, and who, on the other hand, sought to extend the mechanical aspect of Physics to all reality. Again, the example of Pascal should be sufficient to show us that mathematical genius and a deeply religious, even mystical, temperament are not at all incompatible.

Moreover, pan-mathematicism and idealism might even be held to lend support to one another. The more Reality is mathematicised, the more, in a sense, it is transferred on to an ideal plane, while, conversely, the thinker who desires to find the true reality and being of Nature in an ideal world might easily grasp the proffered hand of mathematics as an aid in the task. This would apply especially in the case of Plato, since he had before him the example of the Pythagoreans, who combined not only an interest in mathematics, but also a trend towards pan-mathematicism with religious and psychological interests. We are, therefore, in no way entitled to declare that Plato *could not* have combined in himself religious and transcendentalist tendencies with a tendency to pan-mathematicism, since, whether incompatible or not from the abstract viewpoint, history has shown that they are not incompatible from the psychological standpoint. If the Pythagoreans were possible, if Spinoza and Pascal were possible, then there is no reason why we should say, i.e. *a priori*, that Plato could not have written a mystical book and delivered the lecture on the Good in which, we learn, he spoke of arithmetic and astronomy and identified the One and the Good. But, though we cannot assert this *a priori*, it still remains to inquire whether in actual fact Plato meant such a passage as the speech of Socrates in the *Symposium* to be understood in a religious sense.

12. By what process does the mind arrive at the apprehension of the Ideas, according to Plato? I have already spoken briefly of the Platonic dialectic and method of διαίρεσις, and nobody will deny the importance of dialectic in the Platonic theory; but the question arises whether Plato did or did not envisage a religious, even a mystical, approach to the One or Good. *Prima facie* at least the *Symposium* contains mystical elements, and, if we come to the dialogue with our minds full of the interpretation given it by Neo-Platonist and Christian writers, we shall probably find in it what we are seeking. Nor can this interpretation be set aside *ab initio*, for certain modern scholars of great and deserved repute have lent their powerful support thereto.

Thus, referring to Socrates' speech in the *Symposium*, Professor Taylor comments: "In substance, what Socrates is describing is the same spiritual voyage which St. John of the Cross describes, for example, in the well-known song, *En una noche oscura*, which opens his treatise on the *Dark Night*, and Crashaw hints at more obscurely all through his lines on *The Flaming Heart*, and

Bonaventura charts for us with precision in the *Itinerarium Mentis in Deum*."[1] Others, however, will have none of this; for them Plato is no mystic at all, or if he does display any mystical leanings, it is only in the weakness of old age that he does so. Thus Professor Stace declares, that "the Ideas are rational, that is to say, they are apprehended through reason. The finding of the common element in the manifold is the work of inductive reason, and through this alone is the knowledge of the Ideas possible. This should be noted by those persons who imagine that Plato was some sort of benevolent mystic. The imperishable One, the absolute reality, is apprehended, not by intuition or in any kind of mystic ecstasy, but only by rational cognition and laborious thought."[2] Again, Professor C. Ritter says that he would like "to direct a critical remark against the recent attempts, oft repeated, to stamp Plato as a mystic. These are wholly based on forged passages of the *Epistles*, which I can only consider as inferior achievements of a spiritual poverty which seeks to take refuge in occultism. I am astonished that anyone can hail them as enlightened wisdom, as the final result of Platonic philosophising."[3] Professor Ritter is, needless to say, perfectly well aware that certain passages in the certainly authentic works of Plato lend themselves to interpretation in the mystical sense; but, in his view, such passages are not only poetical and mythical in character, but were understood as such by Plato himself. In his earlier works Plato throws out suggestions, is feeling his way, as it were, and sometimes clothes his half-formed thoughts in poetical and mythical language; but when, in later dialogues, he applies himself to a more scientific treatment of his epistemological and ontological doctrines, he no longer brings in priestesses or uses poetic symbolism.

It would seem that, if we regard the Good predominantly in its aspect as Ideal or τέλος, Eros might well be understood as simply the impulse of man's higher nature towards the good and virtue (or, in the language of the doctrine of pre-existence and reminiscence, as the natural attraction of man's higher nature towards the Ideal which he beheld in the state of pre-existence). Plato, as we have seen, would not accept a merely relativistic ethic: there are absolute standards and norms, absolute ideals. There is thus an ideal of justice, an ideal of temperance, an ideal

---

[1] *Plato*, p. 225.   [2] *Critical Hist.*, pp. 190-1.
[3] *The Essence of Plato's Philosophy*, p. 11.

of courage, and these ideals are real and absolute, since they do not vary but are the unchanging standards of conduct. They are not "things," for they are ideal; yet they are not merely subjective, because they "rule," as it were, man's acts. But human life is not lived out atomistically, apart from Society and the State, nor is man a being entirely apart from nature; and so we can arrive at the apprehension of an all-embracing Ideal and τέλος, to which all particular Ideals are subordinate. This universal Ideal is the Good. It is apprehended by means of dialectic, i.e. *discursively*; but in man's higher nature there is an attraction towards the truly good and beautiful. If man mistakenly takes sensible beauty and good, e.g. the beauty of physical objects, as his true good, then the impulse of attraction of Eros is directed towards these inferior goods, and we have the earthly and sensual man. A man may, however, be brought to see that the soul is higher and better than the body, and that beauty of soul is of more value than beauty of body. Similarly, he may be brought to see the beauty in the formal sciences[1] and the beauty of the Ideals: the power of Eros then attracts him "towards the wide ocean of intellectual beauty" and "the sight of the lovely and majestic forms which it contains."[2] Finally, he may come to apprehend how all the particular ideals are subordinate to one universal Ideal or τέλος, the Good-in-itself, and so to enjoy "the science" of this universal beauty and good. The rational soul is akin to the Ideal,[3] and so is able to contemplate the Ideal and to delight in its contemplation once the sensual appetite has been restrained.[4] "There is none so worthless whom Love cannot impel, as it were by a divine inspiration, towards virtue."[5] The true life for man is thus the philosophic life or the life of wisdom, since it is only the philosopher who attains true universal science and apprehends the rational character of Reality. In the *Timaeus* the Demiurge is depicted as forming the world according to the Ideal or Exemplary Pattern, and as endeavouring to make it as much like the Ideal as the refractory matter at his disposal will permit. It is for the philosopher to apprehend the Ideal and to endeavour to model his own life and that of others according to the Pattern. Hence the place accorded to the Philosopher-King in the *Republic*.

Eros or Love is pictured in the *Symposium*[6] as "a great god," holding an intermediate place between the divine and the mortal.

---

[1] Cf. *Philebus*, 51 b 9–d 1. [2] *Sympos.*, 210 d 3–5. [3] Cf. *Phaedo*.
[4] Cf: *Phaedrus*. [5] *Sympos.*, 179 a 7–8. [6] 201 d 8 ff.

Eros, in other words, "the child of Poverty and plenty," is *desire*, and desire is for what is not yet possessed, but Eros, though poor, i.e. not yet possessing, is the "earnest desire for the possession of happiness and that which is good." The term "Eros" is often confined to one species of Eros—and that by no means the highest —but it is a term of wider connotation than physical desire, and is, in general, "the desire of generation in the beautiful, both with relation to the body and the soul." Moreover, since Eros is the desire that good be for ever present with us, it must of necessity be also the desire for immortality.[1] By the lower Eros men are compelled to seek immortality through the production of children: through a higher Eros poets like Homer and statesmen like Solon leave a more enduring progeny "as the pledges of that love which subsisted between them and the beautiful." Through contact with Beauty itself the human being becomes immortal and produces true virtue.

Now all this might, it seems, be understood of a purely intellectualist, in the sense of discursive, process. None the less, it is true that the Idea of the Good or the Idea of Beauty is an ontological Principle, so there can be no *a priori* reason why it should not itself be the object of Eros and be apprehended intuitively. In the *Symposium* the soul at the summit of the ascent is said to behold Beauty "on a sudden," while in the *Republic* the Good is asserted to be seen last of all and only with an effort—phrases which might imply an intuitional apprehension. What we might call the "logical" dialogues may give little indication of any mystical approach to the One; but that does not necessarily mean that Plato never envisaged any such approach, or that, if he ever envisaged it, he had rejected it by the time he came to write the *Parmenides*, the *Theaetetus* and the *Sophist*. These dialogues deal with definite problems, and we have no right to expect Plato to present all aspects of his thought in any one dialogue. Nor does the fact that Plato never proposes the One or the Good as the object of official religious cult necessarily militate against the possibility of his admitting an intuitional and mystical approach to the One. In any case we would scarcely expect Plato to propose the radical transformation of the popular Greek religion (though in the *Laws* he does propose its purification, and hints that true religion consists in a virtuous life and recognition of Reason's operation in the universe, e.g. in the movements of the heavenly

[1] 206 a 7–207 a 4.

bodies); while, if the One is "beyond" being and soul, it might never occur to him that it could be the object of a popular cult. After all, Neo-Platonists, who certainly admitted an "ecstatic" approach to the One, did not hesitate to lend their support to the traditional and popular religion.

In view of these considerations, it would appear that we are forced to conclude that (*a*) we are certain as to the *dialectical* approach, and (*b*) we are uncertain as to any mystical approach, while not denying that some passages of Plato's writings could be understood as implying such an approach, and may *possibly* have been meant by Plato to be so understood.

13. It is evident that the Platonic Theory of Forms constitutes an enormous advance on pre-Socratic Philosophy. He broke away from the *de facto* materialism of the pre-Socratics, asserting the existence of immaterial and invisible Being, which is not but a shadow of this world but is real in a far deeper sense than the material world is real. While agreeing with Heraclitus, that sensible things are in a state of flux, of becoming, so that they can never really be said to *be*, he saw that this is but one side of the picture: there is also true Being, a stable and abiding Reality, which can be known, which is indeed the supreme object of knowledge. On the other hand, Plato did not fall into the position of Parmenides, who by equating the universe with a static One, was forced to deny all change and becoming. For Plato the One is transcendent, so that becoming is not denied but is fully admitted in the "created" world. Moreover, Reality itself is not without Mind and life and soul, so that there is spiritual movement in the Real. Again, even the transcendent One is not without the Many, just as the objects of this world are not entirely without unity, for they participate in or imitate the Forms and so partake in order to some extent. They are not fully real, but they are not mere Not-being; they have a share in being, though true Being is not material. Mind and its effect, order, are present in the world: Mind or Reason permeates, as it were, this world and is, not a mere *Deus ex machina*, like the Nous of Anaxagoras.

But if Plato represents an advance on the pre-Socratics, he represents an advance also on the Sophists and on Socrates himself. On the Sophists, since Plato, while admitting the relativism of bare αἴσθησις, refused, as Socrates had before him, to acquiesce in the relativity of science and moral values. On Socrates himself, since Plato extended his investigations beyond the sphere of ethical standards and definitions into those of logic and ontology. Moreover, while there is no certain indication that Socrates attempted any systematic unification of Reality, Plato presents us with a Real Absolute. Thus while Socrates and the Sophists represent a reaction to the foregoing systems of cosmology and to the speculations concerning the One and the Many (though in a true sense Socrates' pre-occupation with definiteness concerns the One and the Many), Plato took up again the problems of the Cosmologists, though on a much higher plane and without abandoning the position won by Socrates. He may thus be said to have attempted the synthesis of what was valuable, or appeared to him valuable, in the pre-Socratic and Socratic philosophies.

It must, of course, be admitted that the Platonic Theory of Forms is unsatisfactory. Even if the One or Good represents for him the ultimate Principle, which comprises all the other Forms, there remains the Χωρισμός between the intelligible and the purely sensible world. Plato may have thought that he had solved the problem of the Χωρισμός from the epistemological stand-point, by his doctrine of the union of λόγος, δόξα and αἴσθησις in the apprehension of the ἄτομα εἴδη; but, ontologically speaking, the sphere of pure Becoming remains unexplained. (It is, however, doubtful if the Greeks *ever* "explained" it.) Thus Plato does not appear to have cleared up satisfactorily the meaning of μέθεξις and μίμησις. In the *Timaeus*[1] he says explicitly that the Form never enters "into anything else anywhere," a statement which shows clearly that Plato did *not* regard the Form or Idea as an intrinsic constituent of the physical object. Therefore, in view of Plato's own statements, there is no point in trying to delete the difference between him and Aristotle. Plato may well have apprehended important truths to which Aristotle failed to do justice, but he certainly did not hold the same view of the universal as that held by Aristotle. Consequently, "participation" for Plato should not be taken to mean that there is an "ingredi-once" of "eternal objects" into "events." "Events" or physical objects are thus, for Plato, no more than imitations or mirror-images of the Ideas, and the conclusion is inescapable that the sensible world exists "alongside" the intelligible world, as the latter's shadow and fleeting image. The Platonic Idealism is a grand and sublime philosophy which contains much truth (for the purely sensible world is indeed neither the only world nor yet the

[1] 52 a 1-4.

highest and most "real" world); but, since Plato did not claim
that the sensible world is mere illusion and not-being, his philosophy inevitably involves a Χωρισμός, and it is useless to
attempt to slur over the fact. After all, Plato is not the only great
philosopher whose system has landed him in difficulties in regard
to "particularity," and to say that Aristotle was right in detecting
the Χωρισμός in the Platonic philosophy is not to say that the
Aristotelian view of the universal, when taken by itself, obviates
all difficulties. It is far more probable that these two great
thinkers emphasised (and perhaps over-emphasised) different
aspects of reality which need to be reconciled in a more complete
synthesis.

But, whatever conclusions Plato may have arrived at, and
whatever imperfections or errors there may be in his Theory of
Ideas, we must never forget that Plato meant to establish ascertained truth. He firmly held that we can, and do, apprehend
essences in thought, and he firmly held that these essences are
not purely subjective creations of the human mind (as though the
ideal of justice, for instance, were purely man's creation and
relative in character): we do not create them, we discover them.
We judge of things according to standards, whether moral and
aesthetic standards or generic and specific types: all judgment
necessarily implies such standards, and if the scientific judgment
is objective, then these standards must have objective reference.
But they are not found, and cannot be found, in the sense-world
as such: therefore they must be transcendent of the fleeting world
of sense-particulars. Plato really did not raise the "critical
problem," though he undoubtedly believed that experience is
inexplicable, unless the objective existence of the standards is
maintained. We should not attribute to Plato the position of a
Neo-Kantian, for even if (which we do not mean to admit) the
truth underlying the doctrines of pre-existence and reminiscence
is the Kantian *a priori*, there is no evidence that Plato himself
used these "myths" as figurative expressions for the doctrine of a
purely subjective *a priori*. On the contrary, all the evidence goes
to show that Plato believed in the truly objective reference of
concepts. Reality can be known and Reality is rational; what
cannot be known is not rational, and what is not fully real is not
fully rational. This Plato held to the last, and he believed that
if our experience (in a wide sense) is to be explained or rendered
coherent, it can only be explained on the basis of his theory. If

he was no Kantian, he was, on the other hand, no mere romancer or mythologist: he was a *philosopher*, and the theory of Forms was put forward as a philosophic and rational theory (a philosophic "hypothesis" for the explanation of experience), not as an essay in mythology or popular folklore, nor as the mere expression of the longing for a better world than this one.

It is, then, a great mistake to change Plato into a poet, as though he were simply an "escapist" who desired to create a supercorporeal world, an ideal world, wherein he could dwell away from the conditions of daily experience. If Plato could have said with Mallarmé, "La chair est triste, hélas! et j'ai lu tous les livres, Fuir! là-bas fuir . . . ,"[1] it would have been because he believed in the *reality* of a supersensual and intelligible world, which it is given to the philosopher to *discover*, not to create. Plato did not seek to transmute "reality" into dream, creating his own poetical world, but to rise from this inferior world to the superior world of the pure Archetypal Ideas. Of the subsistent reality of these Ideas he was profoundly convinced. When Mallarmé says: "Je dis: une fleur, et hors de l'oubli où ma voix relègue aucun contour, en tant que quelque chose d'autre, que les calices sus, musicalement se lève, idée même et suave, l'absente de tous bouquets," he is thinking of the creation of the ideal flower, not of the discovery of the Archetypal Flower in the Platonic sense. Just as in a symphony the instruments may transmute a landscape into music, so the poet transmutes the concrete flowers of experience into idea, into the music of dream-thought. Moreover, in actual practice Mallarmé's emptying-out of particular circumstances served rather the purpose of widening the associative, evocative and allusive scope of the idea or image. (And because these were so personal, it is so difficult to understand his poetry.) In any case, however, all this is foreign to Plato, who, whatever his artistic gifts may have been, is primarily a philosopher, not a poet.

Nor are we entitled to regard Plato's aim as that of transmuting reality in the fashion of Rainer Maria Rilke. There may be truth in the contention that we build up a world of our own by clothing it, as it were, from within ourselves—the sunlight on the wall may mean more to us than it means "in itself," in terms of atoms and electrons and light-waves, because of our subjective impressions, and the allusions, associations, overtones and undertones

[1] Stéphane Mallarmé, *Poems*. (Trans. by Roger Fry. Chatto & Windus, 1936.)

that we supply—but Plato's effort was not to enrich, beautify and transmute this world by subjective evocations, but to pass beyond the sensible world to the world of thought, the Transcendental Reality. Of course, it still remains open to us, if we are so inclined, to discuss the psychological origins of Plato's thought (it *might* be that he was psychologically an escapist); but, if we do so, we must at the same time remember that this is not equivalent to an interpretation of what Plato meant. Whatever "subconscious" motives he may or may not have had, he certainly meant to pursue a serious, philosophic and scientific inquiry.

Nietzsche accused Plato of being an enemy to this world, of setting up a transcendental world out of enmity to this world, of contrasting a "There" with a "Here" out of dislike of the world of experience and of human life and out of moral presuppositions and interests. That Plato was influenced by disappointments in actual life, e.g. by the political conduct of the Athenian State or by his disappointment in Sicily, is probably true; but he was not actively hostile to this world; on the contrary, he desired to train statesmen of the true type, who would, as it were, carry on the work of the Demiurge in bringing order into disorder. He was hostile to life and this world, only in so far as they are disordered and fragmentary, out of harmony with or not expressing what he believed to be stable realities and stable norms of surpassing value and universal significance. The point is not so much what influences contributed to the formation of Plato's metaphysic, whether as causes, conditions or occasions, as the question: "Did Plato prove his position or did he not?"—and with this question a man like Nietzsche does not concern himself. But we cannot afford to dismiss *a priori* the notion that what there is of order and intelligibility in this world has an objective foundation in an invisible and transcendent Reality, and I believe that Plato not only attained a considerable measure of truth in his metaphysic, but also went a long way towards showing that it *was* the truth. If a man is going to talk at all, he is certain to make valuational judgments, judgments which presuppose objective norms and standards, values which can be apprehended with varying degrees of insight, values which do not "actualise" themselves but depend for their actualisation on the human will, co-operating with God in the realisation of value and the ideal in human life. We have, of course, no direct intuition of the Absolute, as far as natural knowledge is concerned (and in so far as the Platonic theory implies such a knowledge it is inadmissible, while in so far as it identifies true knowledge with direct apprehension of the Absolute it might seem to lead, unwittingly, to scepticism), but by rational reflection we can certainly come to the knowledge of objective (and indeed transcendentally-grounded) values, ideals and ends, and this after all is Plato's main point.

CHAPTER XXI

THE PSYCHOLOGY OF PLATO

1. PLATO in no way fell a victim to the crude psychology of the former Cosmological Schools, in which the soul was reduced to air or fire or atoms: he was neither materialist nor epiphenomenalist, but an uncompromising spiritualist. The soul is clearly distinct from the body; it is man's most valuable possession, and the true tendance of the soul must be its chief concern. Thus at the close of the *Phaedrus*, Socrates prays: "Beloved Pan, and all ye other Gods who here are present, grant me to be beautiful in the inner man, and all I have of outer things to be consonant with those within. May I count the wise man only rich. And may my store of gold be such none but the temperate man can bear."[1] The reality of the soul and its pre-eminence over the body finds emphatic expression in Plato's psychological dualism, which corresponds to his metaphysical dualism. In the *Laws*[2] Plato defines the soul as "self-initiating motion" (τὴν δυναμένην αὐτὴν κινεῖν κίνησιν) or the "source of motion." This being so, the soul is prior to the body in the sense that it is superior to the body (the latter being moved without being the source of motion) and must rule the body. In the *Timaeus* Plato says that "the only existing thing which properly possesses intelligence is soul, and this is an invisible thing, whereas fire, water, earth and air are all visible bodies";[3] and in the *Phaedo* he shows that the soul cannot be a mere epiphenomenon of the body. Simmias suggests that the soul is only the harmony of the body and perishes when the body, of which it is the harmony, perishes; but Socrates points out that the soul can rule the body and its desires, whereas it is absurd to suppose that a mere harmony can rule that of which it is the harmony.[4] Again, if the soul were a mere harmony of the body, it would follow that one soul could be more of a soul than another (since a harmony will admit of increase or diminution), which is an absurd supposition.

But although Plato asserts an essential distinction between soul and body, he does not deny the influence that may be exercised on the soul by or through the body. In the *Republic* he includes

[1] 279 b 8–c 3. [2] 896 a 1–2. [3] 46 d 5–7. [4] 85 e 3–86 d 4, 93 c 3–95 a 2.

physical training among the constituents of true education, and he rejects certain types of music because of the deleterious effect they have on the soul. In the *Timaeus*, again, he admits the evil influence that can be wrought by bad physical education and by bodily habits of vice, which may even bring about an irremediable state in which the soul is enslaved,[1] and in the *Laws* he stresses the influence of heredity.[2] In fact, a defective constitution inherited from the parents and a faulty education or environment are responsible for most of the soul's ills. "No one is willingly bad; the bad man becomes bad because of some faulty habit of body and a stupid upbringing, and these are unwelcome evils that come to any man without his choice."[3] Even if, therefore, Plato speaks on occasion as though the soul merely dwelt in the body and used it, we must not represent him as denying any interaction of soul and body on one another. He may not have *explained* interaction, but this is a most difficult task in any case. Interaction is an obvious fact, and has to be accepted: the situation is certainly not bettered by denying interaction, because one cannot fully explain it, or by reducing soul to body in order to do away with the necessity of giving any explanation at all or of confessing that one has not got one to give.

2. In the *Republic* we find the doctrine of the tripartite nature of the soul,[4] a doctrine which is said to have been borrowed from the Pythagoreans.[5] The doctrine recurs in the *Timaeus*, so we can hardly be justified in supposing that Plato ever abandoned it.[6] The soul consists of three "parts"—the rational "part" (τὸ λογιστικόν), the courageous or spirited "part" (τὸ θυμοειδές) and the appetitive "part" (τὸ ἐπιθυμητικόν). The word "part" may justifiably be used in this connection, since Plato himself employs the term μέρος; but I put it just now in inverted commas in order to indicate that it is a metaphorical term and should not be taken to mean that the soul is extended and material. The word μέρος appears in 444 b 3 of the fourth book of the *Republic*, and before this Plato uses the word εἶδος, a word that shows that he regarded the three parts as forms or functions or principles of action, not as parts in the material sense.

τὸ λογιστικόν is what distinguishes man from the brute, and is the highest element or formality of the soul, being immortal and

---

[1] *Tim.*, 86 b ff.   [2] *Laws*, 775 b ff.   [3] *Tim.*, 86 d 7–e 3.   [4] Bk. 4.
[5] Cf. Cic., *Tusc. Disp.*, 4, 5, 10. (In this passage Cicero refers to *two* parts, the rational and the non-rational parts.)
[6] *Tim.*, 69 d 6–70 a 7.

akin to the divine. The two other formalities, τὸ θυμοειδές and τὸ ἐπιθυμητικόν, are perishable. Of these the spirited part is the nobler (in man more akin to moral courage), and is, or should be, the natural ally of reason, though is is found in animals. τὸ ἐπιθυμητικόν refers to bodily desires, for the rational part of the soul has its own desires, e.g. the passion for truth, Eros, which is the rational counterpart of the physical Eros. In the *Timaeus*[1] Plato locates the rational part of the soul in the head, the spirited part in the breast, and the appetitive part below the midriff. The location of the spirited element in heart and lungs was an ancient tradition, going back to Homer; but whether or not Plato understood these locations literally, it is hard to say. He may have meant that these locations are the points of interaction on the body of the several principles of the soul: did not Descartes (who certainly believed in the spirituality of the soul) locate the point of interaction in the pineal gland? But it is difficult to believe that Plato ever worked out his psychology systematically, as may be seen from the following considerations.

Plato declared that the soul is immortal, and the *Timaeus* certainly teaches that only the rational part of the soul enjoys this privilege.[2] But if the other parts of the soul are mortal and perishable, then they must be separable from the rational part in some mysterious way or they must form a different soul or souls. The apparent insistence on the simplicity of the soul in the *Phaedo* might be referred to the rational part; but in the Myths (e.g. of the *Republic* and the *Phaedrus*) it is implied that the soul survives in its totality, at least that it preserves memory in the state of separation from the body. I do not mean to suggest that all that is contained in the Myths is to be taken literally, but only to point out that their evident supposition that the soul after death retains memory and is affected by its previous life in the body, whether for good or evil, implies the possibility of the soul surviving in its totality and retaining at least the remote potentiality of exercising the spirited and appetitive functions, even though it could not exercise them actually in the state of separation from the body. However, this remains no more than a possible interpretation, and in view of Plato's own express statements and in view of his general dualistic position, it would seem probable that for him only τὸ λογιστικόν survives, and that the other parts of the soul perish entirely. If the conception of the

[1] *Tim., ibid.*   [2] *Tim.*, 69 c 2–e 4.

three elements of the souls as three μέρη conflicts with the conception of three εἴδη, then that is simply a proof that Plato never fully elaborated his psychology or worked out the implications of the statements he made.

3. Why did Plato assert the tripartite nature of the soul? Mainly owing to the evident fact of the conflict within the soul. In the *Phaedrus* occurs the celebrated comparison in which the rational element is likened to a charioteer, and the spirited and appetitive elements to two horses.[1] The one horse is good (the spirited element, which is the natural ally of reason and "loves honour with temperance and modesty"), the other horse is bad (the appetitive element, which is "a friend to all riot and insolence"); and, while the good horse is easily driven according to the directions of the charioteer, the bad horse is unruly and tends to obey the voice of sensual passion, so that it must be restrained by the whip. Plato, therefore, takes as his *point de départ* the fact of experience that there are frequently rival springs of action within man; but he never really discusses how this fact can be reconciled with the unity of consciousness, and it is significant that he expressly admits that "to explain what the soul is, would be a long and most assuredly a godlike labour," whereas "to say what it resembles is a shorter and a human task."[2] We may conclude, then, that the tendency to regard the three principles of action as principles of one unitary soul and the tendency to regard them as separable μέρη remain unreconciled in Plato's psychology.

Plato's main interest is, however, evidently the ethical interest of insisting on the right of the rational element to rule, to act as charioteer. In the *Timaeus* the rational part of the soul, the immortal and "divine" element, is said to be made by the Demiurge out of the same ingredients as the World-Soul, while the mortal parts of the soul, together with the body, are made by the celestial gods.[3] This is doubtless a mythical expression of the fact that the rational element of the soul is the highest and is born to rule, has a natural right to rule, because it is more akin to the divine. It has a natural affinity with the invisible and intelligible world, which it is able to contemplate, whereas the other elements of the soul are bound up essentially with the body, i.e. with the phenomenal world, and have no direct part in reason and rational activity and cannot behold the world of Forms.

[1] 246 a 6 ff.   [2] 246 a 4–6.   [3] 41 c 6–42 e 4, 69 b 8–c 8.

This dualistic conception reappears in Neo-Platonism, in St. Augustine, in Descartes, etc.[1] Moreover, in spite of the adoption of the Peripatetic doctrine of the soul by St. Thomas Aquinas and his School, the Platonic *way of speaking* remains and must always remain the "popular" way of speaking among Christians, since the *fact* that influenced Plato's thought, the fact of the interior conflict in man, naturally looms large in the minds of all those who support the Christian Ethic. It should, however, be noted that the fact that we feel this conflict *within ourselves* demands a more unified view of the soul than is afforded by the Platonic psychology. For, if there were a plurality of souls within man—the rational and irrational—then our consciousness of the conflict as taking place within ourselves and the consciousness of moral responsibility would be inexplicable. I do not mean to imply that Plato was entirely blind to the truth, but rather to suggest that he laid such stress on one aspect of the truth that he tended to neglect the other aspect, and so failed to give any really satisfactory rational psychology.

4. That Plato asserted the immortality of the soul is clear enough. From his explicit assertions it would appear, as we have seen, that this is confined to one part of the soul, τὸ λογιστικόν, though it is just possible that the soul survives in its totality, although it cannot, obviously enough, exercise its lower functions in a state of separation from the body. It is true, however, that the latter position might appear to lead to the conclusion that the soul is more imperfect and worse off in a state of separation from the body than it is in this mortal life—a conclusion which Plato would certainly refuse to accept.

Complete rejection of the Platonic Myths would seem to be prompted, to a certain extent at least, by the desire to get rid of any notion of sanctions after death, as if a doctrine of rewards and punishments were irrelevant—and even hostile—to morality. But is it fair or in accordance with principles of historical criticism to father this attitude on Plato? It is one thing to admit that the details of the Myths are not meant to be taken seriously (all admit this), and quite another thing to say that the conception of a future life, the character of which is determined by conduct in this life, is itself "mythical." There is no real evidence that Plato himself regarded the Myths in their entirety as mere moonshine:

[1] Cf. St. Aug.: *Homo anima rationalis est mortali atque terreno utens corpore.* (*De moribus Ecc. cath.*, I, 27.)

if he did, why did he put them forward at all? It seems to the present writer that Plato was by no means indifferent to the theory of sanctions, and that this was one of the reasons why he postulated immortality. He would have agreed with Leibniz that "in order to satisfy the hope of the human race, it must be proved that the God Who governs all is just and wise, and that He will leave nothing without recompense and without punishment. These are the great foundations of ethics."[1]

How did Plato attempt to prove immortality?

(i) In the *Phaedo*[2] Socrates argues that contraries are produced from contraries, as "from stronger, weaker," or "from sleeping, awaking, and from awaking, sleeping." Now, life and death are contraries, and from life is produced death. We must, therefore, suppose that from death life is produced.

This argument rests on the unproved assumption of an eternal cyclic process: it also supposes that a contrary is produced from a contrary, as the matter out of which it proceeds or is made. The argument would hardly satisfy us: besides, it says nothing of the condition of the soul in its state of separation from the body, and would, by itself, lead to the doctrine of the wheel of rebirth. The soul in one "period" on earth might have no conscious remembrance of any former period on earth, so that all that is "proved" is that the soul survives, not that the individual survives *qua* individual.

(ii) The next argument adduced in the *Phaedo*[3] is that from the *a priori* factor in knowledge. Men have a knowledge of standards and absolute norms, as is implied in their comparative judgments of value. But these absolutes do not exist in the sense-world: therefore man must have beheld them in a state of pre-existence. Similarly, sense-perception cannot give us knowledge of the necessary and universal. But a youth, even one who has had no mathematical education, can, by a process of questioning alone, without teaching, be induced to "give out" mathematical truths. As he has not learnt them from anybody and cannot get them from sense-perception, the implication is that he apprehended them in a state of pre-existence, and that the process of "learning" is simply a process of reminiscence (cf. *Meno*, 84 ff.).

As a matter of fact, the process of questioning employed by Socrates in the *Meno* is really a way of teaching, and in any case

[1] Letter to unknown correspondent about 1680, Duncan, *Philosophical Works of Leibniz*, p. 9.
[2] 70 d 7–72 e 2
[3] 72 e 3–77 d 5

a certain amount of mathematical knowledge is tacitly pre-supposed. However, even if the mathematical science cannot be accounted for by "abstraction," mathematics could still be an *a priori* science, without our being compelled to postulate pre-existence. Even supposing that mathematics could, theoretically at least, be worked out entirely *a priori* by the slave boy of *Meno*, that would not necessitate his having pre-existed: there is always an alternative on Kantian lines.[1]

Simmias points out[2] that this argument proves no more than that the soul existed before its union with the body: it does not prove that the soul survives death. Socrates accordingly observes that the argument from reminiscence must be taken in conjunction with the preceding argument.

(iii) The third argument in the *Phaedo* (or second, if the two previous arguments are taken together) is from the uncompounded and deiform nature of the soul—from its spirituality, as we would say.[3] Visible things are composite and subject to dissolution and death—and the body is of their number. Now, the soul can survey the invisible and unchanging and imperishable Forms, and by coming thus into contact with the Forms, the soul shows itself to be more like them than it is to visible and corporeal things, which latter are mortal. Moreover, from the fact that the soul is naturally destined to rule the body, it appears to be more like the divine than the mortal. The soul, as we may think, is "divine"—which for the Greeks meant immortal and unchanging.

(This argument has developed into the argument from the higher activities of the soul and the spirituality of the concept to the spiritual and uncompounded nature of the soul.)

(iv) Another argument of the *Phaedo* occurs in Socrates' answer to the objections of Cebes. (To Socrates' refutation of the "epiphenomenalism" suggested by Simmias, I have referred earlier.) Cebes suggests[4] that the expenditure of energy which is undergone by the soul in its successive bodily lives may "wear it out," so that in the end it will "perish altogether in some one of the deaths." To this Socrates replies with another proof of immortality.[5] The existence of Forms is admitted. Now, the presence of one Form will not admit of the presence of a contrary

---

[1] I do not mean to imply an acceptance of the Kantian Critique, but simply to point out that, even on Plato's assumption, his conclusion is not the only one possible.
[2] 77.   [3] 78 b 4–80 e 1.   [4] 86 e 6–88 b 8.   [5] 103 c 10–107 a 1.

Form, nor will a thing that is what it is by virtue of its participation in one Form admit of the simultaneous presence of a contrary Form, e.g. though we cannot say that fire is *warmth*, it is *warm*, and will not admit of the opposite predicate "cold" simultaneously. Soul is what it is by virtue of its participation in the Form of Life: therefore it will not admit of the presence of the contrary Form, "death." When, therefore, death approaches, the soul must either perish or withdraw. That it does not perish is assumed. Strictly speaking, then, this argument should not be termed an argument for the imperishability of the soul, once granted its spirituality. Cebes is understood by Socrates to accept the spirituality of the soul, but to be arguing that it might wear itself out. Socrates' answer practically comes to this, that a spiritual principle cannot wear itself out.

(v) In the *Republic*[1] Socrates assumes the principle that a thing cannot be destroyed or perish except through some evil that is inherent in it. Now, the evils of the soul are "unrighteousness, intemperance, cowardice, ignorance"; but these do not destroy it, for a thoroughly unjust man may live as long or longer than a just man. But if the soul is not destroyed by its own internal corruption, it is unreasonable to suppose that it can be destroyed by any external evil. (The argument evidently supposes dualism.)

(vi) In the *Phaedrus*[2] it is argued that a thing which moves another, and is moved by another, may cease to live as it may cease to be moved. The soul, however, is a self-moving principle,[3] a source and beginning of motion, and that which is a beginning must be uncreated, for if it were not uncreated, it would not be a beginning. But if uncreated, then indestructible, for if soul, the beginning of motion were destroyed, all the universe and creation would "collapse and come to a standstill."

Now, once granted that the soul is the principle of motion, it must always have existed (if motion is from the beginning), but obviously this does little to prove personal immortality. For all this argument shows, the individual soul might be an emanation from the World-Soul, to which it returns at bodily death. Yet on reading the *Phaedo* in general and the Myths of the *Phaedo*, *Gorgias* and *Republic*, one cannot avoid the impression that Plato believed in real personal immortality. Moreover, passages such as that in which Socrates speaks of this life as a preparation for

---

[1] 608 d 3–611 a 2.   [2] 245 c 5 ff.   [3] Cf. *Laws*, 896 a 1–b 3.

eternity,[1] and remarks like that made by Socrates in the *Gorgias*,[2] that Euripides might be right in saying that life here is really death and death really life (a remark which has an Orphic ring about it), can hardly permit one to suppose that Plato, in teaching immortality, meant to affirm a mere persistence of τὸ λογιστικόν without any personal consciousness or continued self-identity. It is far more reasonable to suppose that he would have agreed with Leibniz when the latter asks: "Of what use would it be to you, sir, to become king of China on condition of forgetting what you have been? Would it not be the same as if God at the same time that he destroyed you, created a king in China?"[3]

To consider the Myths in detail is not necessary, for they are but pictorial representations of the truth that Plato wished to convey, namely, that the soul persists after death, and that the soul's life hereafter will be in accordance with its conduct on this earth. How far Plato seriously intended the doctrine of successive reincarnations, which is put forward in the Myths, is uncertain: in any case it would appear that there is a hope for the philosophic soul of escaping from the wheel of reincarnation, while it would also appear that there may be incurable sinners who are flung for ever into Tartarus. As already mentioned, the presentation of the future life in the Myths is hardly consonant with Plato's assertion that only τὸ λογιστικόν survives, and in this sense I should agree with Ritter when he says: "It cannot be maintained with certainty that Plato was convinced of the immortality of the soul, as that is taught in the Myths of the *Gorgias*, the *Phaedo* and the *Republic*."[4]

Plato's psychological doctrine is, therefore, not a systematically elaborated and consistent body of "dogmatic" statements: his interest was undoubtedly largely ethical in character. But this is not to say that Plato did not make many acute psychological observations, which may be found scattered throughout the dialogues. We have only to think of the illustrations he gives in the *Theaetetus* of the process of forgetting and remembering, or the distinction between memory and recollection in the *Philebus*.[5]

[1] *Rep.*, 498 b 3–d 6.   [2] 492 e 8–11.   [3] Duncan, p. 9.   [4] *Essence*, p. 282.
[5] *Theaet.*, 191 c 8 and ff.; *Phil.*, 33 c 8–34 c 2.

1. *The Summum Bonum*

PLATO's ethic is eudaemonistic, in the sense that it is directed towards the attainment of man's highest good, in the possession of which true happiness consists. This highest good of man may be said to be the true development of man's personality as a rational and moral being, the right cultivation of his soul, the general harmonious well-being of life. When a man's soul is in the state it ought to be in, then that man is happy. At the beginning of the *Philebus* two extreme positions are taken up by Protarchus and Socrates *causa argumenti*. Though they are both agreed that the good must be a state of soul, Protarchus is prepared to maintain that the good consists in *pleasure*, while Socrates will maintain that the good consists in *wisdom*. Socrates proceeds to show that pleasure as such cannot be the true and sole human good, since a life of unmixed pleasure (bodily pleasure is understood), in which neither mind nor memory nor knowledge nor true opinion had any share, "would be, not a human life, but that of a *pulmo marinus* or an oyster."[1] Not even Protarchus can think such a life desirable for a human being. On the other hand, a life of "unmixed mind," which was destitute of pleasure, could not be the sole good of man; even if intellect is the highest part of man and intellectual activity (especially the contemplation of the Forms) is man's highest function, man is not pure intellect. Thus the good life for man must be a "mixed" life, neither exclusively the life of the mind nor yet exclusively the life of sense-pleasure. Plato, therefore, is prepared to admit those pleasures which are not preceded by pain, e.g. the intellectual pleasures,[2] but also pleasures which consist in the satisfaction of desire, provided that they are innocent and are enjoyed in moderation. Just as honey and water must be mixed in due proportion in order to make a pleasing drink, so pleasant feeling and intellectual activity must be mixed in due proportion in order to make the good life of man.[3]

First of all, Plato says, the good life must include all knowledge

---

[1] 21 c 1–8.   [2] Cf. 51.   [3] 61 b 4 ff.

of the truer type, the exact knowledge of timeless objects. But the man who was acquainted only with the exact and perfect curves and lines of geometry, and had no knowledge at all of the rough approximations to them which we meet with in daily life, would not even know how to find his way home. So second-class knowledge, and not only the first-class variety, must be admitted into the mixture: it will do a man no harm, provided that he recognises the second-class objects for what they are, and does not mistake the rough approximations for the exact truth. In other words, a man need not turn his back completely on this mortal life and the material world in order to lead the truly good life, but he must recognise that this world is not the only world, nor yet the highest world, but a poor copy of the ideal. (Music, says Protarchus, must be admitted, "if human life is to be a life at all," in spite of the fact that it is, according to Socrates, "full of guesswork and imitation" and "wanting in purity."[1])

All the "water" having thus been admitted to the mixing-bowl, the question arises, how much "honey" to put in. The deciding vote in this question, how much pleasure to admit, rests with knowledge. Now, knowledge, says Plato, would claim kinship with the class of "true" and "unmixed" pleasures; but, as to the rest, knowledge will accept only those which accompany health and a sober mind and any form of goodness. The pleasures of "folly and badness" are quite unfit to find a place in the blend.

The secret of the blend which forms the good life is thus measure or proportion: where this is neglected, there exists, not a genuine mixture, but a mess. The good is thus a form of the beautiful, which is constituted by measure and proportion, and συμμετρία, καλόν and ἀλήθεια will be the three forms or notes found in the good. The first place goes to "seasonableness," τὸ καίριον, the second to proportion or beauty or completeness (τὸ σύμμετρον καὶ καλόν καὶ τὸ τέλεον καὶ ἱκανον), the third to νοῦς καὶ φρόνησις, the fourth to ἐπιστῆμαι καὶ τέχναι καὶ δόξαι ὀρθαί, the fifth to the pleasures which have no pain mixed with them (whether involving actual sensation or not), and the sixth to the moderate satisfaction of appetite when, of course, this is harmless. Such, then, is man's true good, the good life, εὐδαιμονία, and the compelling motive in the search for it is Eros, the desire or longing for good or happiness.

[1] 62 c 1-4.

Man's *summum bonum* or happiness includes, of course, knowledge of God—obviously so if the Forms are the Ideas of God; while, even if the *Timaeus* were taken literally and God were supposed to be apart from the Forms and to contemplate them, man's own contemplation of the Forms, which is an integral constituent of his happiness, would make him akin to God. Moreover, no man could be happy who did not recognise the Divine operation in the world. Plato can say, therefore, that the Divine happiness is the pattern of man's happiness.[1]

Now, happiness must be attained by the pursuit of virtue, which means becoming as like to God as it is possible for man to become. We must become "like the divine so far as we can, and that again is to become righteous with the help of wisdom."[2] "The gods have a care of anyone whose desire is to become just and to be like God, as far as man can attain to the divine likeness, by the pursuit of virtue."[3] In the *Laws* Plato declares that "God is the measure of all things, in a sense far higher than any man, as they say, can ever hope to be." (He thus answers Protagoras.) "And he who would be dear to God, must as far as possible be like Him and such as He is. Wherefore the temperate man is the friend of God, for he is like Him. . . ." He goes on to say that to offer sacrifice to the gods and pray to them is "the noblest and best of all things, and also the most conducive to a happy life," but points out that the sacrifices of the wicked and impious are unacceptable to the gods.[4] Worship and virtue belong, therefore, to happiness, so that although the pursuit of virtue and the leading of a virtuous life is the means of attaining happiness, virtue itself is not external to happiness, but is integral to it. Man's good is a condition of soul primarily, and it is only the truly virtuous man who is a truly good man and a truly happy man.

II. *Virtue*

1. In general we may say that Plato accepted the Socratic identification of virtue with knowledge. In the *Protagoras*[5] Socrates shows, as against the Sophist, that it is absurd to suggest that justice can be impious or piety unjust, so that the several virtues cannot be entirely disparate. Furthermore, the intemperate man is one who pursues what is really harmful to man while the temperate

---

[1] *Theaet.*, 176 a 5–e 4.   [2] *Theaet.*, 176 b 1–3.   [3] *Rep.*, 613 a 7–b 1.
[4] *Laws*, 715 e 7–717 a 3.   [5] *Protag.*, 330 c 3 ff.

man pursues what is truly good and beneficial. Now, to pursue what is truly good and beneficial is wise, while to pursue what is harmful is foolish. Hence temperance and wisdom cannot be entirely disparate. Again, true valour or courage means, e.g. standing your ground in battle when you know the risks to which you are exposed; it does not mean mere foolhardiness. Thus courage can no more be separated from wisdom than can temperance. Plato does not, of course, deny that there are distinct virtues, distinguished according to their objects or the parts of the soul of which they are the habits; but all these distinct virtues form a unity, inasmuch as they are the expressions of the same knowledge of good and evil. The distinct virtues are, therefore, unified in prudence or the knowledge of what is truly good for man and of the means to attain that good. It is made clear in the *Meno* that *if* virtue is knowledge or prudence, it can be taught, and it is shown in the *Republic* that it is only the philosopher who has true knowledge of the good for man. It is not the Sophist, content with "popular" notions of virtue, who can teach virtue, but only he who has exact knowledge, i.e. the philosopher. The doctrine that virtue is knowledge is really an expression of the fact that goodness is not a merely relative term, but refers to something that is absolute and unchanging: otherwise it could not be the object of knowledge.

To the idea that virtue is knowledge and that virtue is teachable, Plato seems to have clung, as also to the idea that no one does evil knowingly and willingly. When a man chooses that which is *de facto* evil, he chooses it *sub specie boni*: he desires something which he imagines to be good, but which is, as a matter of fact, evil. Plato certainly allowed for the headstrong character of appetite, which strives to carry all before it, sweeping the charioteer along with it in its mad onrush to attain that which appears to it as a good; but if the bad horse overpowers the resistance of the charioteer, it can, on Plato's principles, only be because either the charioteer has no knowledge of the true good or because his knowledge of the good is obscured for the time being by the onrush of passion. It might well seem that such a doctrine, inherited from Socrates, conflicts with Plato's obvious admission of moral responsibility, but it is open to Plato to reply that a man who knows what is truly good may allow his judgment to be so obscured by passion, at least temporarily, that the apparent good appears to him as a true good, although he is responsible for having allowed passion so to darken reason. If it be objected that a man may deliberately choose evil because it is evil, Plato could only answer that the man has said: "Evil, be thou my good." If he chooses what is really evil or harmful, knowing it to be ultimately such, that can only be because he, in spite of his knowledge, fixes his attention on an aspect of the object which appears to him as good. He may indeed be responsible for so fixing his attention, but, if he chooses, he can only choose *sub ratione boni*. A man might very well know that to murder his enemy will be ultimately harmful to him, but he chooses to do it all the same, since he fixes his attention on what appears to be the immediate good of satisfying his desire for revenge or of obtaining some benefit by the elimination of his enemy. (It might be remarked that the Greeks needed a clearer view of *Good* and *Right* and their relation to one another. The murderer may know very well that murder is wrong, but he chooses to commit it as being, *in some respects*, a *good*. The murderer who knew that murder was wrong might also know, of course, that "wrong" and "ultimately harmful or evil" were inseparable, but that would not take away the aspect of "goodness" (i.e. usefulness or desirability) attaching to the act. When we use the word "evil," we often mean "wrong," but when Plato said that no one willingly chooses to do what he knows to be evil, he did not mean that no one chooses to do what he knows to be wrong, but that no one deliberately chooses to do what he knows to be in all respects harmful to himself.)

In the *Republic*[1] Plato considers four chief or cardinal virtues —wisdom (Σοφία), courage or fortitude ('Ανδρεία), temperance (Σωφροσύνη) and justice (Δικαιοσύνη). Wisdom is the virtue of the rational part of the soul, courage of the spirited part, while temperance consists in the union of the spirited and appetitive parts under the rule of reason. Justice is a general virtue consisting in this, that every part of the soul performs its proper task in due harmony.

2. In the *Gorgias* Plato argues against the identification of good and evil with pleasure and pain, and against the "Superman" morality propounded by Callicles. Against Polus, Socrates has tried to show that to do an injustice, e.g. to play the part of the tyrant, is worse than to suffer injustice, since to do injustice makes one's soul worse, and this is the greatest evil that a man

[1] *Rep.*, Bk. 4.

can suffer. Moreover, to do injustice and then to get off scot-free is the worst thing of all, because that only confirms the evil in the soul, whereas punishment may bring reformation. Callicles breaks in on the discussion in order to protest that Socrates is appealing "to the popular and vulgar notions of right, which are not natural, but only conventional":[1] to do evil may be disgraceful from the conventional standpoint, but this is simply herd-morality. The weak, who are the majority, club together to restrain "the stronger sort of men," and proclaim as *right* the actions that suit them, i.e. the members of the herd, and as *wrong* the actions that are harmful to them.[2] Nature, however, shows among both men and animals that "justice consists in the superior ruling and having more than the inferior."[3]

Socrates thanks Callicles for his frankness in openly stating his opinion that Might is Right, but he points out that if the weak majority do in fact tyrannise over the "strong," then they are actually the stronger and also are justified, on Callicles' own admission. This is not a mere verbal quibble, for if Callicles persists in maintaining his rejection of conventional morality, he must now show how the strong, the ruthless and unscrupulous individualist, is qualitatively "better" than the herd-man, and so has the right to rule. This Callicles tries to do by maintaining that his individualist is wiser than "the rabble of slaves and nondescripts," and so ought to rule and have more than his subjects. Irritated by Socrates' observation that, in this case, the physician should have more to eat and drink than anybody else, and the cobbler larger shoes than anybody, Callicles affirms that what he means is that those who are wise and courageous in the administration of the State ought to rule the State, and that justice consists in their having more than their subjects. Goaded by Socrates' question, whether the ruler should rule himself as well, Callicles roundly asserts that the strong man should allow his desires and passions full play. This gives Socrates his chance, and he compares Callicles' ideal man to a leaky cask: he is always filling himself with pleasure but never has enough: his life is the life of a cormorant not of a man. Callicles is prepared to admit that the scratcher who is constantly relieving his itch has a happy life, but he boggles at justifying the life of the

---

[1] *Gorgias*, 482 e 3-5.
[2] The resemblance to the opinions of Nietzsche is obvious, though Nietzsche's idea was very far from being that of the political and licentious tyrant.
[3] 483 d 5-6.

catamite, and in the end is driven to admit a *qualitative* difference in pleasures. This leads to the conclusion that pleasure is subordinate to the good, and that reason must, therefore, be judge of pleasures and admit them only in so far as they are consonant with health and harmony and order of soul and body. It is thus not the intemperate man but the temperate man who is truly good and happy. The intemperate man does evil to himself, and Socrates drives home his point by the "Myth" of the impossibility of escaping judgment after death.[1]

3. Plato expressly rejects the maxim that one should do good to one's friends and evil to one's enemies. To do evil can never be good. In the first Book Polemarchus puts forward the theory that "it is just to do good to our friend if he is a good man, and to hurt our enemy if he is a bad man."[2] Socrates (understanding by "to hurt" to do real harm, and not simply to punish—which he regarded as remedial) objects that to hurt is to make worse, and, in respect of human excellence, that means less just, so that, according to Polemarchus, it pertains to the just man to make the unjust man worse. But this is obviously rather the work of the unjust man than of the just man.

---

[1] *Gorgias*, 523 ff.   [2] *Rep.*, 335 a 7–8.

CHAPTER XXIII

THE STATE

PLATO's political theory is developed in close connection with his ethics. Greek life was essentially a communal life, lived out in the City-State and unthinkable apart from the City, so that it would not occur to any genuine Greek that a man could be a perfectly good man if he stood entirely apart from the State, since it is only in and through Society that the good life becomes possible for man—and Society meant the City-State. The rational analysis of this experimental fact results in the doctrine that organised Society is a "natural" institution, that man is essentially a social animal—a doctrine common to both Plato and Aristotle: the theory that Society is a necessary evil and results in the stunting of man's free development and growth would be entirely foreign to the genuine Greek. (It would, of course, be foolish to represent the Greek consciousness according to the analogy of the ant-heap or the beehive, since individualism was rife, showing itself both in the internecine wars between States and in the factions within the Cities themselves, e.g. in attempts on the part of an individual to establish himself as Tyrant; but this individualism was not a rebellion against Society as such—rather did it presuppose Society as an accepted fact.) For a philosopher like Plato, then, who concerned himself with man's happiness, with the truly good life for man, it was imperative to determine the true nature and function of the State. If the citizens were all morally bad men, it would indeed be impossible to secure a good State; but, conversely, if the State were a bad State, the individual citizens would find themselves unable to lead the good life as it should be lived.

Plato was not a man to accept the notion that there is one morality for the individual and another for the State. The State is composed of individual men and exists for the leading of the good life: there is an absolute moral code that rules all men and all States: expediency must bow the knee to Right. Plato did not look upon the State as a personality or organism that can or should develop itself without restraint, without paying any attention to the Moral Law: it is not the arbiter of right and wrong, the source of its own moral code, and the absolute justification of its own actions, be the latter what they may. This truth finds clear expression in the *Republic*. The interlocutors set out to determine the nature of justice, but at the close of the first Book Socrates declares that "I know not what justice is."[1] He then suggests in the second Book[2] that if they consider the State they will see the same letters "written larger and on a larger scale," for justice in the State "will be larger and more easily discernible." He proposes, therefore, that "we inquire into the nature of justice and injustice as appearing in the State first, and secondly in the individual, proceeding from the greater to the lesser and comparing them." The obvious implication of this is that the principles of justice are the same for individual and State. If the individual lives out his life as a member of the State, and if the justice of the one as of the other is determined by ideal justice, then clearly neither the individual nor the State can be emancipated from the eternal code of justice.

Now, it is quite obvious that not every actual Constitution or every Government embodies the ideal principle of Justice; but Plato was not concerned to determine what empirical States *are* so much as what the State *ought* to be, and so, in the *Republic*, he sets himself to discover the Ideal State, the pattern to which every actual State ought to conform itself, so far as it can. It is true that in the work of his old age, the *Laws*, he makes some concessions to practicability; but his general purpose remained that of delineating the norm or ideal, and if empirical States do not conform to the ideal, then so much the worse for the empirical States. Plato was profoundly convinced that Statesmanship is, or should be, a science; the Statesman, if he is to be truly such, must know what the State is and what its life ought to be; otherwise he runs the risk of bringing the State and its citizens to shipwreck and proves himself to be not a Statesman but a bungling "politician." Experience had taught him that actual States were faulty, and he turned his back on practical political life, though not without the hope of sowing the seeds of true statesmanship in those who entrusted themselves to his care. In the seventh Letter Plato speaks of his sad experience, first with the Oligarchy of 404 and then with the restored Democracy, and adds: "The result was that I, who had at first been full of eagerness for a public career, as I gazed upon the whirlpool of public life and

[1] 354 c 1.   [2] 368 e 2–369 a 3.

saw the incessant movement of shifting currents, at last felt dizzy
. . . and finally saw clearly in regard to all States now existing
that without exception their system of government is bad. Their
constitutions are almost without redemption, except through
some miraculous plan accompanied by good luck. Hence I was
forced to say in praise of the correct philosophy that it affords
a vantage-point from which we can discern in all cases what is
just for communities and for individuals; and that accordingly
the human race will not be free of evils until either the stock
of those who rightly and truly follow philosophy acquire political
authority, or the class who have power in the cities be led by
some dispensation of providence to become real philosophers."[1]

I shall outline Plato's political theory, first as it appears in the
Republic, and then as it appears in the *Statesman* and the *Laws*.

1. *The Republic*

1. The State exists in order to serve the wants of men. Men
are not independent of one another, but need the aid and co-
operation of others in the production of the necessaries of life.
Hence they gather associates and helpers into one dwelling-place
"and give this joint dwelling the name of City."[2] The original
end of the city is thus an economic end, and from this follows the
principle of the division and specialisation of labour. Different
people have different natural endowments and talents and are
fitted to serve the community in different ways: moreover, a
man's work will be superior in quality and also in quantity if he
works at one occupation alone, in accordance with his natural
gifts. The agricultural labourer will not produce his own plough
or mattock, but they will be produced for him by others, by
those who specialise in the production of such instruments. Thus
the existence of the State, which at present is being considered
from the economic viewpoint, will require the presence of husband-
men, weavers, shoemakers, carpenters, smiths, shepherds,
merchants, retail traders, hired labourers, etc. But it will be a
very rude sort of life that is led by these people. If there is to
be a "luxurious" city, something more will be required, and
musicians, poets, tutors, nurses, barbers, cooks, confectioners,
etc., will make their appearance. But with the rise of population
consequent on the growing luxury of the city, the territory will
be insufficient for the city's needs, and some of the neighbour's

---

[1] *Ep.*, 7, 325 d 6–326 b 4.   [2] *Rep.*, 369 c 1–4.

territory will have to be annexed. Thus Plato finds the origin of war in an economic cause. (Needless to say, Plato's remarks are not to be understood as a justification of aggressive war: for his remarks on this subject see the section on war under the heading of the *Laws*.)

2. But, if war is to be pursued, then, on the principle of the division and specialisation of labour, there will have to be a special class of guardians of the State, who will devote themselves exclusively to the conduct of war. These guardians must be spirited, gifted with the θυμοειδές element; but they must also be philosophic, in the sense of knowing who the true enemies of the State are. But if the exercise of their task of guardianship is to be based on knowledge, then they must undergo some process of education. This will begin with music, including narrative. But, says Plato, we will scarcely permit the children of the State to receive into their minds at their most impressionable age opinions the reverse of those which they should entertain when they are grown to manhood.[1] It follows, then, that the legends about the gods, as retailed by Hesiod and Homer, will not be taught to children or indeed admitted into the State, since they depict the gods as indulging in gross immorality, taking various forms, etc. Similarly, to assert that the violation of oaths and treaties was brought about by the gods is intolerable and not to be admitted. God is to be represented, not as the author of all things, whether good or bad, but only of such things as are good.[2]

It is to be noted in all this how, though Socrates starts off the discussion by finding the origin of the State in the need of supplying the various natural wants of man and asserts the economic origin of the State, the interest soon shifts to the problem of education. The State does not exist simply in order to further the economic needs of men, for man is not simply "Economic Man," but for their happiness, to develop them in the good life, in accordance with the principles of justice. This renders education necessary, for the members of the State are rational beings. But it is not any kind of education that will do, but only education to the true and the good. Those who arrange the life of the State, who determine the principles of education and allot the various tasks in the State to its different members, must have knowledge of what is really true and good—in other words, they must be philosophers. It is this insistence on truth that leads Plato to

[1] 377 a 12–c 5.   [2] 380 a 5–c 3.

the, as it appears to us, rather extraordinary proposal to exclude epic poets and dramatists from the ideal State. It is not that Plato is blind to the beauties of Homer or Sophocles: on the contrary, it is just the fact that the poets make use of beautiful language and imagery which renders them so dangerous in Plato's eyes. The beauty and charm of their words are, as it were, the sugar which obscures the poison that is imbibed by the simple. Plato's interest is primarily ethical: he objects to the way the poets speak about the gods, and the way in which they portray immoral characters, etc. In so far as the poets are to be admitted at all into the ideal State, they must set themselves to produce examples of good moral character, but, in general, epic and dramatic poetry will be banished from the State, while lyric poetry will be allowed only under the strict supervision of the State authorities. Certain harmonies (the Ionian and Lydian) will be excluded as effeminate and convivial. (We may think that Plato exaggerated the bad results that would follow from the admission of the great works of Greek literature, but the principle that animated him must be admitted by all who seriously believe in an objective moral law, even if they quarrel with his particular applications of the principle. For, granted the existence of the soul and of an absolute moral code, it is the duty of the public authorities to prevent the ruin of the morality of the members of the State so far as they can, and so far as the particular acts of prevention employed will not be productive of greater harm. To speak of the absolute rights of Art is simply nonsense, and Plato was quite justified in not letting himself be disturbed by any such trashy considerations.)

Besides music, gymnastics will play a part in the education of the young citizens of the State. This care of the body, in the case of those who are to be guardians of the State and athletes of war, will be of an ascetic character, a "simple, moderate system," not calculated to produce sluggish athletes, who "sleep away their lives and are liable to most dangerous illnesses if they depart, in ever so slight a degree, from their customary regimen," but rather "warrior athletes, who should be like wakeful dogs, and should see and hear with the utmost keenness."[1] (In these proposals for the State education of the young, both physically and mentally, Plato is anticipating what we have seen realised on a great scale, and which, we recognise, may be used for bad

[1] 403 e 11–404 b 8.

ends as well as for good. But that, after all, is the fate of most practical proposals in the political field, that while they may be used for the benefit of the State, i.e. its true benefit, they may also be abused and applied in a way that can only bring harm to the State. Plato knew that very well, and the selection of the rulers of the State was a matter of great concern to him.)

3. We have then so far two great classes in the State—the inferior class of artisans and the superior class of guardians. The question arises, who are to be the rulers of the State. They will, says Plato, be carefully chosen from the class of guardians. They are not to be young: they must be the best men of their class, intelligent and powerful, and careful of the State, loving the State and regarding the State's interests as identical with their own— in the sense, needless to say, of pursuing the true interests of the State without thought of their own personal advantage or disadvantage.[1] Those, then, who from childhood up have been observed to do that which is best for the State, and never to have deserted this line of conduct, will be chosen as rulers of the State. They will be the perfect guardians, in fact the only people who are rightly entitled to the name of "guardian": the others, who have hitherto been termed guardians, will be called "auxiliaries," having it as their office to support the decisions of the rulers.[2] (Of the education of the rulers I shall treat shortly.)

The conclusion is, therefore, that the ideal State will consist of three great classes (excluding the slave class, of whom more later), the artisans at the bottom, the Auxiliaries or military class over them, and the Guardians or Guardian at the top. However, though the Auxiliaries occupy a more honourable position than the artisans, they are not to be savage animals, preying on those beneath them, but even if stronger than their fellow-citizens, they will be their friendly allies, and so it is most necessary to ensure that they should have the right education and mode of life. Plato says that they should possess no private property of their own, but should receive all necessaries from their fellow-citizens. They should have a common mess and live together like soldiers in a camp: gold and silver they should neither handle nor touch. "And this will be their salvation and the salvation of the State."[3] But if they once start amassing property, they will very soon turn into tyrants.

4. It will be remembered that Plato set out at the beginning

[1] 412 c 9–413 c 7.   [2] 414 b 1–6.   [3] 417 a 5–6.

of the dialogue to determine the nature of justice, and that having found the task difficult, the suggestion was made that they might be able to see more clearly what justice is if they examined it as it exists in the State. At the present point of the discussion, when the different classes of the State have been outlined, it becomes possible to behold justice in the State. The wisdom of the State resides in the small class of rulers or Guardians, the courage of the State in the Auxiliaries, the temperance of the State consists in the due subordination of the governed to the governing, the justice of the State in this, that everyone attends to his own business without interfering with anyone else's. As the individual is just when all the elements of the soul function properly in harmony and with due subordination of the lower to the higher, so the State is just or righteous when all the classes, and the individuals of which they are composed, perform their due functions in the proper way. Political injustice, on the other hand, consists in a meddling and restless spirit, which leads to one class interfering with the business of another class.[1]

5. In the fifth Book of the *Republic* Plato treats of the famous proposal as to "community" of wives and children. Women are to be trained as men: in the ideal State they will not simply stay at home and mind the baby, but will be trained in music and gymnastics and military discipline just like men. The justification of this consists in the fact that men and women differ simply in respect to the parts they play in the propagation of the species. It is true that woman is weaker than man, but natural gifts are to be found in both sexes alike, and, as far as her nature is concerned, the woman is admissible to all pursuits open to man, even war. Duly qualified women will be selected to share in the life and official duties of the guardians of the State. On eugenic principles Plato thinks that the marriage relations of citizens, particularly of the higher classes of the State, should be under the control of the State. Thus the marriages of Guardians or Auxiliaries are to be under the control of the magistrates, with a view not only to the efficient discharge of their official duties, but also to the obtaining of the best possible offspring, who will be brought up in a State nursery. But be it noted that Plato does not propose any complete community of wives in the sense of promiscuous free love. The artisan class retains private property and the family: it is only in the two upper classes that

[1] 433 a 1 and ff.

private property and family life is to be abolished, and that for the good of the State. Moreover, the marriages of Guardians and Auxiliaries are to be very strictly arranged: they will marry the women prescribed for them by the relevant magistrates, have intercourse and beget children at the prescribed times and not outside those times. If they have relations with women outside the prescribed limits and children result, it is at least hinted that such children should be put out of the way.[1] Children of the higher classes, who are not suitable for the life of those classes, but who have been "legitimately" born, will be relegated to the class of the artisans.

(Plato's proposals in this matter are abhorrent to all true Christians. His intentions were, of course, excellent, for he desired the greatest possible improvement of the human race; but his good intentions led him to the proposal of measures which are necessarily unacceptable and repugnant to all those who adhere to Christian principles concerning the value of the human personality and the sanctity of human life. Moreover, it by no means follows that what has been found successful in the breeding of animals, will also prove successful when applied to the human race, for man has a rational soul which is not intrinsically dependent on matter but is directly created by Almighty God. Does a beautiful soul always go with a beautiful body or a good character with a strong body? Again, if such measures were successful—and what does "successful" mean in this connection? —in the case of the human race, it does not follow that the Government has the right to apply such measures. Those who to-day follow, or would like to follow, in the footsteps of Plato, advocating, e.g. compulsory sterilisation of the unfit, have not, be it remembered, Plato's excuse, that he lived at a period anterior to the presentation of the Christian ideals and principles.)

6. In answer to the objection that no city can, in practice, be organised according to the plans proposed, "Socrates" replies that it is not to be expected that an ideal should be realised in practice with perfect accuracy. Nevertheless he asks, what is the smallest change that would enable a State to assume this form of Constitution? and he proceeds to mention one—which is neither small nor easy—namely, the vesting of power in the hands of the philosopher-king. The democratic principle of government is, according to Plato, absurd: the ruler must govern in virtue of

[1] 461 c 4–7.

knowledge, and that knowledge must be knowledge of the truth. The man who has knowledge of the truth is the genuine philosopher. Plato drives home his point by the simile of the ship, its captain and crew.[1] We are asked to imagine a ship "in which there is a captain who is taller and stronger than anyone else in the ship, but he is a little deaf and is short-sighted, and his knowledge of navigation is not much better." The crew mutiny, take charge of the ship and, "drinking and feasting, they continue their voyage with such success as might be expected of them." They have, however, no idea of the pilot's art or of what a true pilot should be. Thus Plato's objection to democracy of the Athenian type is that the politicians really do not know their business at all, and that when the fancy takes the people they get rid of the politicians in office and carry on as though no special knowledge were required for the right guidance of the ship of State. For this ill-informed and happy-go-lucky way of conducting the State, he proposes to substitute rule by the philosopher-king, i.e. by the man who has real knowledge of the course that the ship of State should take, and can help it to weather the storms and surmount the difficulties that it encounters on the voyage. The philosopher will be the finest fruit of the education provided by the State: he, and he alone, can, as it were, draw the outline of the concrete sketch of the ideal State and fill up that outline, because he has acquaintance with the world of Forms and can take them as his model in forming the actual State.[2]

Those who are chosen out as candidates or possible rulers will be educated, not only in musical harmony and gymnastics, but also in mathematics and astronomy. They will not, however, be trained in mathematics merely with a view to enabling them to perform the calculations that everyone ought to learn to perform, but rather with a view to enabling them to apprehend intelligible objects—not "in the spirit of merchants or traders, with a view to buying or selling," nor only for the sake of the military use involved, but primarily that they may pass "from becoming to truth and being,"[3] that they may be drawn towards truth and acquire the spirit of philosophy.[4] But all this will merely be a prelude to Dialectic, whereby a man starts on the discovery of

---

[1] 488 a 1–489 a 2.

[2] Plato, like Socrates, considered the "democratic" practice of choosing magistrates, generals, etc., by lot or according to their rhetorical ability, irrational and absurd.

[3] 525 b 11–c 6.   [4] 527 b 9–11.

absolute being by the light of reason only, and without any
assistance of the senses, until he "attains at last to the absolute
good by intellectual vision and therein reaches the limit of the
intellectual world."[1] He will thus have ascended all the steps of
the "Line." The chosen rulers of the State, therefore, or rather
those who are chosen as candidates for the position of Guardians,
those who are "sound in limb and mind" and endowed with
virtue, will be gradually put through this course of education,
those who have proved themselves satisfactory by the time they
have reached the age of thirty being specially selected for training
in Dialectic. After five years spent in this study they will "be
sent down into the den and compelled to hold any military or
other office which the young are qualified to hold," in order that
they may get the necessary experience of life and show whether,
when confronted with various temptations, "they will stand firm
or flinch."[2] After fifteen years of such probation those who have
distinguished themselves (they will then be fifty years old) will
have reached the time "at which they must raise the eye of the
soul to the universal light which lightens all things, and behold
the absolute good; for that is the pattern according to which they
are to order the State and lives of individuals, and the remainder
of their own lives too, making philosophy their chief pursuit; but
when their turn comes, toiling also at politics and ruling for the
public good, not as if they were doing some great thing, but of
necessity; and when they have brought up others like themselves
and left them in their place to be governors of the State, then
they will depart to the Islands of the Blest and dwell there; and
the city will give them public memorials and sacrifices and honour
them, if the Pythian oracle consent, as demi-gods, and at any rate
as blessed and divine."[3]

7. In the eighth and ninth Books of the *Republic* Plato
develops a sort of philosophy of history. The perfect State is
the aristocratic State; but when the two higher classes combine
to divide the property of the other citizens and reduce them
practically to slavery, aristocracy turns into timocracy, which
represents the preponderance of the spirited element. Next the
love of wealth grows, until timocracy turns into oligarchy, political
power coming to depend on property qualifications. A poverty-
stricken class is thus developed under the oligarchs, and in the
end the poor expel the rich and establish democracy. But the

---

[1] 532 a 7–b 2.   [2] 539 e 2–540 a 2.   [3] 540 a 7–c 2.

extravagant love of liberty, which is characteristic of democracy, leads by way of reaction to tyranny. At first the champion of the common people obtains a bodyguard under specious pretences; he then throws off pretence, executes a *coup d'état* and turns into a tyrant. Just as the philosopher, in whom reason rules, is the happiest of men, so the aristocratic State is the best and happiest of States; and just as the tyrannical despot, the slave of ambition and passion, is the worst and most unhappy of men, so is the State ruled by the tyrant the worst and most unhappy of States.

II. *The Statesman* (*Politicus*)

1. Towards the close of the *Statesman*, Plato shows that the science of politics, the royal and kingly science, cannot be identical with e.g. the art of the general or the art of the judge, since these arts are ministerial, the general acting as minister to the ruler, the judge giving decisions in accordance with the laws laid down by the legislator. The royal science, therefore, must be superior to all these particular arts and sciences, and may be defined as "that common science which is over them all, and guards the laws, and all things that there are in the State, and truly weaves them all into one."[1] He distinguishes this science of the monarch or ruler from tyranny, in that the latter rests merely on compulsion, whereas the rule of the true king and statesman is "the voluntary management of voluntary bipeds."[2]

2. "No great number of persons, whoever they may be, can have political knowledge or order a State wisely," but "the true government is to be found in a small body, or in an individual,"[3] and the ideal is that the ruler (or rulers) should legislate for individual instances. Plato insists that laws should be changed or modified as circumstances require, and that no superstitious regard for tradition should hamper an enlightened application to a changed condition of affairs and fresh needs. It would be just as absurd to stick to obsolete laws in the face of new circumstances, as it would be for a doctor to insist on his patient keeping to the same diet when a new one is required by the changed conditions of his health. But as this would require divine, rather than human, knowledge and competence, we must be content with the second-best, i.e. with the reign of *Law*. The ruler will administer the State in accordance with fixed Law. The Law must be

[1] 305 e 2–4.   [2] 276 e 10–12   [3] 297 b 7–c 2.

absolute sovereign, and the public man who violates law should be put to death.[1]

3. Government may be government by one, by few, or by many. If we are speaking of well-ordered governments, then that of the one, monarchy, is the best (leaving out of account the ideal form, in which the monarch legislates for individual cases), that of the few the second-best, and that of the many the worst. If, however, we are speaking of lawless governments, then the worst is government by the one, i.e. tyranny (since that can do the most harm), the second-worst that by the few, and, the least bad that by the many. Democracy is thus, according to Plato, "the worst of all lawful governments, and the best of all lawless ones," since "the government of the many is in every respect weak and unable to do either any great good or any great evil when compared with the others, because in such a State the offices are parcelled out among many people."[2]

4. What Plato would think of demagogic Dictators is clear from his remarks on tyrants, as also from his observations on the politicians who are devoid of knowledge and who should be called "partisans." These are "upholders of the most monstrous idols, and themselves idols; and, being the greatest imitators and magicians, they are also Sophists *par excellence*."[3]

III. *The Laws*

1. In the composition of the *Laws* Plato would seem to have been influenced by personal experiences. Thus he says that perhaps the best conditions for founding the desired Constitution will be had if the enlightened Statesman meets with an enlightened and benevolent tyrant or sovereign, since the despot will be in a position to put the suggested reforms into practice.[4] Plato's (unhappy) experience at Syracuse would have shown him at least that there was a better hope of realising the desired constitutional reforms in a city ruled over by one man than in a democracy such as Athens. Again, Plato was clearly influenced by the history of Athens, its rise to the position of a commercial and maritime empire, its fall in the Peloponnesian war. For in Book Four of the *Laws* he stipulates that the city shall be about eighty stadia from the sea—although even this is too near—i.e. that the State should be an agrarian, and not a commercial State, a producing, and not an importing, community. The Greek prejudice against

[1] 297 e 1–5.   [2] 303 a 2–8.   [3] 303 b 8–c 5.   [4] 709 d 10–710 b 9.

trade and commerce comes out in his words, that "The sea is pleasant enough as a daily companion, but has a bitter and brackish quality; for it fills the streets with merchants and shopkeepers, and begets in the souls of men unfaithful and uncertain ways—making the State unfaithful and unfriendly both to her own citizens and also towards the rest of men."[1]

2. The State must be a true Polity. Democracy, oligarchy and tyranny are all undesirable because they are class-States, and their laws are passed for the good of particular classes and not for the good of the whole State. States which have such laws are not real polities but parties, and their notion of justice is simply unmeaning.[2] The government is not to be entrusted to any one because of considerations of birth or wealth, but for personal character and fitness for ruling, and the rulers must be subject to the law. "The State in which the law is above the rulers, and the rulers are the inferior of the law, has salvation and every blessing which the gods can confer." Plato here re-emphasises what he has already said in the *Statesman*.

The State exists, then, not for the good of any one class of men, but for the leading of the good life, and in the *Laws* Plato reasserts in unambiguous terms his conviction as to the importance of the soul and the tendance of the soul. "Of all the things which a man has, next to the gods, his soul is the most divine and the most truly his own," and "all the gold which is under or upon the earth is not enough to give in exchange for virtue."[3]

3. Plato had not much use for enormous States, and he fixes the number of the citizens at the number 5,040, which "can be divided by exactly fifty-nine divisors" and "will furnish numbers for war and peace, and for all contracts and dealings, including taxes and divisions."[4] But although Plato speaks of 5,040 citizens, he also speaks of 5,040 houses, which would imply a city of 5,040 families rather than individuals. However that may be, the citizens will possess house and land, since, though Plato expressly clings to communism as an ideal, he legislates in the *Laws* for the more practical second-best. At the same time he contemplates provisions for the prevention of the growth of a wealthy and commercial State. For example, the citizens should have a currency that passes only among themselves and is not accepted by the rest of mankind.[5]

[1] 705 a 2–7. [2] 715 a 8–b 6. [3] 726 a 2–3, 728 a 4–5.
[4] 737 e 1–738 b 1. [5] 742 a 5–6.

4. Plato discusses the appointment and functions of the various magistrates at length: I will content myself with mentioning one or two points. For example, there will be thirty-seven guardians of the law (νομοφύλακες), who will be not less than fifty years old when elected and will hold office up to their seventieth year at the latest. "All those who are horse or foot soldiers, or have taken part in war during the age for military service, shall share in the election of magistrates."[1] There shall also be a Council of 360 members, also elected, ninety from each property-class, the voting being designed apparently in such a way as to render unlikely the election of partisans of extreme views. There will be a number of ministers, such as the ministers who will have care of music and gymnastics (two ministers for each, one to educate, the other to superintend the contests). The most important of the ministers, however, will be the minister of education, who will have care of the youth, male and female, and who must be at least fifty years old, "the father of children lawfully begotten, of both sexes, or of one at any rate. He who is elected, and he who is the elector, should consider that of all the great offices of the State this is the greatest"; the legislator should not allow the education of children to become a secondary or accidental matter.[2]

5. There will be a committee of women to superintend married couples for ten years after marriage. If a couple have not had any children during a period of ten years, they should seek a divorce. Men must marry between the ages of thirty and thirty-five, girls between sixteen and twenty (later eighteen). Violations of conjugal fidelity will be punishable. The men will do their military service between the ages of twenty and sixty; women after bearing children and before they are fifty. No man is to hold office before he is thirty and no woman until she is forty. The provisions concerning the superintendence of married relations by the State are hardly acceptable to us; but Plato doubtless considered them the logical consequence of his conviction that "The bride and bridegroom should consider that they are to produce for the State the best and fairest specimens of children which they can."[3]

6. In Book Seven Plato speaks of the subject of education and its methods. He applies it even to infants, who are to be rocked frequently, as this counteracts emotions in the soul and

[1] 753 b 4-7.   [2] 765 d 5-766 a 6.   [3] 783 d 8-e 1.

produces "a peace and calm in the soul."[1] From the age of three
to the age of six boys and girls will play together in the temples,
supervised by ladies, while at the age of six they will be separated,
and the education of the two sexes will be conducted in isolation,
though Plato does not abandon his view that girls should have
more or less the same education as boys. They will be educated
in gymnastics and music, but the latter will be carefully watched
over, and a State anthology of verse will be composed. Schools
will have to be built, and paid teachers (foreigners) will be provided: children will attend daily at the schools, where they will
be taught not only gymnastics and music, but also elementary
arithmetic, astronomy, etc.

7. Plato legislates for the religious festivals of the State.
There will be one each day, that "one magistrate at least will
sacrifice daily to some god or demigod on behalf of the city and
citizens and their possessions."[2] He legislates, too, on the subject
of agriculture and of the penal code. In regard to the latter
Plato insists that consideration should be paid to the psychological
condition of the prisoner. His distinction between βλαβή and
ἀδικία[3] amounts pretty well to our distinction between a civil
action and a criminal action.

8. In the tenth Book Plato lays down his famous proposals
for the punishment of atheism and heresy. To say that the
universe is the product of the motions of corporeal elements,
unendowed with intelligence, is atheism. Against this position
Plato argues that there must be a source of motion, and that
ultimately we must admit a self-moving principle, which is soul
or mind. Hence soul or mind is the source of the cosmic movement. (Plato declares that there must be more than one soul
responsible for the universe, as there is disorder and irregularity
as well as order, but that there may be more than two.)

A pernicious heresy is that the gods are indifferent to man.[4]
Against this Plato argues:

(a) The gods cannot lack the power to attend to small
things.

(b) God cannot be too indolent or too fastidious to attend to
details. Even a human artificer attends to details.

(c) Providence does not involve "interference" with law.
Divine justice will at any rate be realised in the succession
of lives.

---

[1] 790 c 5–791 b 2.   [2] 828 b 2–3.   [3] 861 e 6 ff.   [4] 899 d 5–905 d 3.

A still more pernicious heresy is the opinion that the gods are
venal, that they can be induced by bribes to condone injustice.[1]
Against this Plato argues that we cannot suppose that the gods
are like pilots who can be induced by wine to neglect their duty
and bring ship and sailors to ruin, or like charioteers who can be
bribed to surrender the victory to other charioteers, or like
shepherds who allow the flock to be plundered on condition that
they share in the spoils. To suppose any of these things is to be
guilty of blasphemy.

Plato suggests penalties to be inflicted on those proved guilty
of atheism or heresy. A morally inoffensive heretic will be
punished with at least five years in the House of Correction,
where he will be visited by members of the "Nocturnal Council,"
who will reason with him on the error of his ways. (Presumably
those guilty of the two graver heresies will receive a longer term
of imprisonment.) A second conviction will be punished with
death. But heretics who also trade on the superstition of others
with a view to their own profits, or who found immoral cults, will
be imprisoned for life in a most desolate part of the country and
will be cast out unburied at death, their families being treated as
wards of the State. As a measure of safety Plato enacts that no
private shrines or private cults are to be permitted.[2] Plato
observes that before proceeding to prosecute an offender for
impiety, the guardians of the law should determine "whether the
deed has been done in earnest or only from childish levity."

9. Among the points of law dwelt on in Books Eleven and
Twelve we may mention the following as of interest:

(a) It would be an extraordinary thing, says Plato, if any
     well-behaved slave or freeman fell into the extremes of
     poverty in any "tolerably well-ordered city or government."
     There will, therefore, be a decree against beggars, and the
     professional beggar will be sent out of the country, "so that
     our country may be cleared of this sort of animal."[3]

(b) Litigiousness or the practice of conducting lawsuits with
     a view to gain, and so trying to make a court a party to
     injustice, will be punishable by death.[4]

(c) Embezzlement of public funds and property shall be
     punished by death if the offender is a citizen, since, if a
     man who has had the full benefit of the State-education
     behaves in this way, he is incurable. If, however, the

[1] 905 d 3–907 d 1.   [2] 909 d 7–8.   [3] 936 c 1–7.   [4] 937 d 6–938 c 5.

offender is a foreigner or a slave, the courts will decide the penalty, bearing in mind that he is probably not incurable.[1]

(d) A Board of εὔθυνοι will be appointed to audit the accounts of the magistrates at the end of their terms of office.[2]

(e) The Nocturnal Council (which is to meet early in the morning before the business of the day begins) will be composed of the ten senior νομοφύλακες, the minister and ex-ministers of education, and ten co-opted men between the ages of thirty and forty. It will consist of men who are trained to see the One in the Many, and who know that virtue is one (i.e. they will be men trained in Dialectic) and who have also undergone training in mathematics and astronomy, that they may have a firmly-grounded conviction as to the operation of divine Reason in the world. Thus this Council, composed of men who have a knowledge of God and of the ideal pattern of goodness, will be enabled to watch over the Constitution and be "the salvation of our government and of our laws."[3]

(f) In order to avoid confusion, novelties and restlessness, no one will be permitted to travel abroad without sanction of the State, and then only when he is over forty years of age (except, of course, on military expeditions). Those who go abroad will, on their return, "teach the young that the institutions of other States are inferior to their own."[4] However, the State will send abroad "spectators," in order to see if there is anything admirable abroad which might with profit be adopted at home. These men will be not less than fifty or more than sixty years old, and on their return they must make a report to the Nocturnal Council. Not only will visits of citizens to foreign countries be supervised by the State, but also visits of travellers from abroad. Those who come for purely commercial reasons will not be encouraged to mix with the citizens, while those who come for purposes approved of by the Government will be honourably treated as guests of the State.[5]

10. *Slavery.* It is quite clear from the *Laws* that Plato accepted the institution of slavery, and that he regarded the slave as the property of his master, a property which may be alienated.[6] Moreover, while in contemporary Athens the children of a

---

[1] 941 c 4–942 a 4.   [2] 945 b 3–948 b 2.   [3] 960 e 9 ff.   [4] 951 a 2–4.
[5] 949 e 3 ff.   [6] Cf. 776 b 5–c 3.

marriage between a slave woman and a freeman seem to have been considered as free, Plato decrees that the children always belong to the master of the slave woman, whether her marriage be with a freeman or a freedman.[1] In some other respects, too, Plato shows himself severer than contemporary Athenian practice, and fails to give that protection to the slave that was accorded by Athenian law.[2] It is true that he provides for the protection of the slave in his public capacity (e.g. whoever kills a slave in order to prevent the latter giving information concerning an offence against the law, is to be treated as though he had killed a citizen),[3] and permits him to give information in murder cases without being submitted to torture; but there is no explicit mention of permission to bring a public prosecution against a man guilty of ὕβρις against his slave, which was permitted by Attic law. That Plato disliked the free-and-easy way in which the slaves behaved in democratic Athens appears from the *Republic*,[4] but he certainly did not wish to advocate a brutal treatment of the slave. Thus in the *Laws*, although he declares that "slaves ought to be punished as they deserve, and not admonished as if they were freemen, which will only make them conceited," and that "the language used to a servant ought always to be that of command, and we ought not to jest with them, whether they are females or males"; he expressly says that "we should tend them carefully, not only out of regard to them, but yet more out of respect to ourselves. And the right treatment of slaves is not to maltreat them, and to do them, if possible, even more justice than those who are our equals; for he who really and naturally reverences justice and really hates injustice, is discovered in his dealings with that class of man to whom he can easily be unjust."[5] We must, therefore, conclude that Plato simply accepted the institution of slavery, and, in regard to the treatment of slaves, that he disliked Athenian laxity on the one hand and Spartan brutality on the other.

11. *War.* In the first Book of the *Laws*, Cleinias the Cretan remarks that the regulations of Crete were designed by the legislator with a view to war. Every city is in a natural state of war with every other, "not indeed proclaimed by heralds, but everlasting."[6] Megillus, the Lacedaemonian, agrees with him. The Athenian Stranger, however, points out (a) that, in regard to

---

[1] 930 d 1–e 2.
[2] Cf. *Plato and Greek Slavery*, Glenn R. Morrow, in *Mind*, April 1939, N.S. vol. 48, No. 190.
[3] 872 c 2–6.   [4] *Rep.*, 563.   [5] 776 d 2–718 a 5.   [6] 626 a 2–5.

external or international war, the best legislator will endeavour
to prevent it occurring in his State, or, if it does arise, will
endeavour to reconcile the warring factions in an abiding friendship, and (b), that in regard to external or international war, the
true statesman will aim at the best. Now, the happiness of the
State, secured in peace and goodwill, is the best. No sound
legislator, therefore, will ever order peace for the sake of war,
but rather, if he orders war it will be for the sake of peace.[1]
Thus Plato is not at all of the opinion that Policy exists for the
sake of War, and he would scarcely sympathise with the virulent
militarists of modern times. He points out that "many a victory
has been and will be suicidal to the victors, but education is
never suicidal."[2]

12. When man reflects on human life, on man's good and on
the good life, as Plato did, he clearly cannot pass by man's social
relations. Man is born into a society, not only into that of the
family but also into a wider association, and it is in that society
that he must live the good life and attain his end. He cannot
be treated as though he were an isolated unit, living to himself
alone. Yet, although every thinker who concerns himself with
the humanistic viewpoint, man's place and destiny, must form
for himself some theory of man's social relations, it may be well
that no theory of the State will result, unless a somewhat advanced
political consciousness has gone before. If man feels himself as
a passive member of some great autocratic Power—the Persian
Empire, for example—in which he is not called upon to play any
active role, save as taxpayer or soldier, his political consciousness
is scarcely aroused: one autocrat or another, one empire or
another, Persian or Babylonian, it may make very little difference
to him. But when a man belongs to a political community in
which he is called upon to shoulder his burden of responsibility,
in which he has not only duties but also rights and activities,
then he will become politically conscious. To the politically
unconscious man the State may appear as some thing set over
against him, alien if not oppressive, and he will tend to conceive
his way of salvation as lying through individual activity and
perhaps through co-operation in other societies than that of the
reigning bureaucracy: he will not be immediately stimulated to
form a theory of the State. To the politically conscious man, on
the other hand, the State appears as a body in which he has a

[1] 628 c 9-e 1.   [2] 641 c 2-7.

part, as an extension in some sort of himself, and so will be stimulated—the reflective thinker, that is to say—to form a theory of the State.

The Greeks had this political consciousness in a very advanced degree: the good life was to them inconceivable apart from the Πόλις. What more natural, then, than that Plato, reflecting on the good life in general, i.e. the good life of man as such, should reflect also on the State as such, i.e. the ideal Πόλις? He was a philosopher and was concerned, not so much with the ideal Athens or the ideal Sparta, as with the ideal City, the Form to which the empirical States are approximations. This is not, of course to deny that Plato's conception of the Πόλις was influenced to a great extent by the practice of the contemporary Greek City-State—it could not be otherwise; but he discovered principles which lie at the basis of political life, and so may truly be said to have laid the foundations of a *philosophical* theory of the State. I say a "philosophical" theory of the State, because a theory of immediate reform is not general and universal, whereas Plato's treatment of the State is based on the nature of the State as such, and so it is designed to be universal, a character which is essential for a philosophic theory of the State. It is quite true that Plato dealt with reforms which he thought to be necessitated by the actual conditions of the Greek States, and that his theory was sketched on the background of the Greek Πόλις; but since he meant it to be universal, answering to the very nature of political life, it must be allowed that he sketched a philosophical theory of the State.

The political theory of Plato and Aristotle has indeed formed the foundation for subsequent fruitful speculation on the nature and characteristics of the State. Many details of Plato's *Republic* may be unrealisable in practice, and also undesirable even if practicable, but his great thought is that of the State as rendering possible and as promoting the good life of man, as contributing to man's temporal end and welfare. This Greek view of the State, which is also that of St. Thomas, is superior to the view which may be known as the liberal idea of the State, i.e. the view of the State as an institution, the function of which is to preserve private property and, in general, to exhibit a negative attitude towards the members of the State. In practice, of course, even the upholders of this view of the State have had to abandon a completely *laissez-faire* policy, but their theory remains barren, empty and negative in comparison with that of the Greeks.

However, it may well be that individuality was insufficiently stressed by the Greeks, as even Hegel notes. ("Plato in his *Republic* allows the rulers to appoint individuals to their particular class, and assign to them their particular tasks. In all these relations there is lacking the principle of subjective freedom." Again, in Plato "the principle of subjective freedom does not receive its due.")[1] This was brought into strong light by the theorists of the modern era who stressed the Social Contract theory. For them men are naturally atoms, separate and disunited, if not mutually antagonistic, and the State is merely a contrivance to preserve them, so far as may be, in that condition, while at the same time providing for the maintenance of peace and the security of private property. Their view certainly embodies truth and value, so that the individualism of thinkers like Locke must be combined with the more corporate theory of the State upheld by the great Greek philosophers. Moreover, the State which combines both aspects of human life must also recognise the position and rights of the supernatural Society, the Church. Yet we have to be careful not to allow insistence on the rights of the Church and the importance of man's supernatural end to lead us to minimise or mutilate the character of the State, which is also a "perfect society," having man's temporal welfare as its end.

[1] Hegel, *The Philosophy of Right*, sect. 299 and sect. 185. Trans. Professor S. W. Dyde. (George Bell & Sons, 1896.)

CHAPTER XXIV

PHYSICS OF PLATO

1. THE physical theories of Plato are contained in the *Timaeus*, Plato's only "scientific" dialogue. It was probably written when Plato was about seventy years old, and was designed to form the first work of a trilogy, the *Timaeus*, the *Critias*, and the *Hermocrates*.[1] The *Timaeus* recounts the formation of the material world and the birth of man and the animals; the *Critias* tells how primitive Athens defeated the invaders from mythical Atlantis, and then was itself overwhelmed by flood and earthquake; and it is conjectured that the *Hermocrates* was to deal with the rebirth of culture in Greece, ending with Plato's suggestions for future reform. Thus the Utopian State or Socratic Republic[2] would be represented in the *Critias* as something realised in the past, while practical reforms for the future would be proposed in the *Hermocrates*. The *Timaeus* was actually written, the *Critias* breaks off before completion, and was left unfinished, while the *Hermocrates* was never composed at all. It has been very reasonably suggested that Plato, conscious of his advancing age, dropped the idea of completing his elaborate historical romance and incorporated in the *Laws* (Books 3 ff.) much of what he had wanted to say in the *Hermocrates*.[3]

The *Timaeus* was thus written by way of preface to two politico-ethical dialogues, so that it would be hardly correct to represent Plato as having suddenly conceived an intense interest in natural science in his old age. It is probably true that he was influenced by the growing scientific interest in the Academy, and there can be little doubt that he felt the necessity of saying something about the material world, with a view to explaining its relation to the Forms; but there is no real reason for supposing that the centre of Plato's interest underwent a radical shift from ethical, political and metaphysical themes to questions of natural science. As a matter of fact, he says expressly in the *Timaeus* that an account of the material world cannot be more than "likely," that we should not expect it to be exact or even altogether

---

[1] Cf. *Tim.*, 27 ab. [2] 26 c 7–e 5.
[3] See Introd. to Professor Cornford's edition of *Timaeus*.

self-consistent,[1] phrases which clearly indicate that in Plato's eyes Physics could never be an exact science, a science in the true sense. Nevertheless, some account of the material universe was called for by the peculiar character of the Platonic theory of Ideas. While the Pythagoreans held that things are numbers, Plato held that they participate in numbers (retaining his dualism), so that he might justly be expected to proffer some explanation from the physical standpoint of how this participation comes to be.

Plato doubtless had another important reason for writing the *Timaeus*, namely to exhibit the organised Cosmos as the work of Intelligence and to show that man partakes of both worlds, the intelligible and the sensible. He is convinced that "mind orders all things," and will not agree "when an ingenious individual (Democritus?) declares that all is disorder":[2] on the contrary, soul is "the oldest and most divine of all things," and it is "mind which ordered the universe."[3] In the *Timaeus*, therefore, Plato presents a picture of the intelligent ordering of all things by Mind, and exhibits the divine origin of man's immortal soul. (Just as the entire universe comprises a dualism of the intelligible and eternal on the one hand, and the sensible and fleeting on the other, so man, the microcosm, comprises a dualism of eternal soul, belonging to the sphere of Reality, and body which passes and perishes.) This exhibition of the world as the handiwork of Mind, which forms the material world according to the ideal pattern constitutes an apt preface to the proposed extended treatment of the State, which should be rationally formed and organised according to the ideal pattern and not left to the play of irrational and "chance" causes.

2. If Plato thought of his physical theories as a "likely account" (εἰκότες λόγοι), are we thereby compelled to treat the whole work as "Myth"? First of all, the theories of Timaeus, whether myth or not, must be taken as Plato's theories: the present writer entirely agrees with Professor Cornford's rejection of Professor A. E. Taylor's notion that the *Timaeus* is a "fake" on Plato's part, a statement of "fifth-century Pythagoreanism," "a deliberate attempt to amalgamate Pythagorean religion and mathematics with Empedoclean biology,"[4] so that "Plato was not likely to feel himself responsible for the details of any of his speaker's

---

[1] Cf. 27 d 5–28 a 4 and 29 b 3–d 3. This was a consequence of the epistemological and ontological dualism, which Plato never abandoned.
[2] *Philebus*, 28 c 6–29 a 5. [3] *Laws*, 966 d 9–e 4.
[4] *A Commentary on Plato's Timaeus*, pp. 18–19.

theories." Apart from the inherent improbability of such a fake on the part of a great and original philosopher, already advanced in years, how is it that Aristotle and Theophrastus and other ancients, as Cornford points out, have left us no hint as to the faked character of the work? If this was its real character, they cannot all have been ignorant of the fact; and can we suppose that, if they were aware of such an interesting fact, they would all have remained absolutely silent on the point? It is really too much to ask us to believe that the true character of the *Timaeus* was first revealed to the world in the twentieth century. Plato certainly borrowed from other philosophers (particularly the Pythagoreans), but the theories of Timaeus are Plato's own, whether borrowed or not.

In the second place, although the theories put into the mouth of Timaeus are Plato's own theories, they constitute, as we have seen, a "likely account," and should not be taken as meant to be an exact and scientific account—for the very simple fact that Plato did not consider such an exact scientific account to be possible. He not only says that we should remember that we "are only human," and so should accept "the likely story and look for nothing further"[1]—words which might imply that it is just human frailty which renders true natural science impossible; but he goes further than that, since he expressly refers this impossibility of an exact natural science to "the nature of the subject." An account of what is only a likeness "will itself be but likely": "what becoming is to being, that is belief to truth."[2] The theories are put forward, therefore, as "likely" or probable; but that does not mean that they are "mythical" in the sense of being consciously designed to symbolise a more exact theory that, for some reason or other, Plato is unwilling to impart. It may be that this or that feature of the *Timaeus* is conscious symbolism, but we have to argue each case on its own merits, and are not justified in simply dismissing the whole of the Platonic Physics as Myth. It is one thing to say: "I do not think an exact account of the material world possible, but the following account is as likely or more likely than any other"; and it is another thing to say: "I put forward the following account as a mythical, symbolic and pictorial expression of an exact account which I propose to keep to myself." Of course, if we care to call a confessedly "probable" account "Myth," then the *Timaeus* is certainly Myth; but it is

[1] *Tim.*, 29 d 1-3.   [2] *Tim.*, 29 c 1-3.

not Myth (in its entirety at least) if by "Myth" you mean a symbolic and pictorial representation of a truth clearly perceived by the author but kept to himself. Plato means to do the best he can, and says so.

3. Plato sets out to give an account of the generation of the world. The sensible world is becoming, and "that which becomes must necessarily become through the agency of some cause."[1] The agent in question is the divine Craftsman or Demiurge. He "took over"[2] all that was in discordant and unordered motion, and brought it into order, forming the material world according to an eternal and ideal pattern, and fashioning it into "a living creature with soul and reason"[3] after the model of the ideal Living Creature, i.e. the Form that contains within itself the Forms of "the heavenly race of gods, the winged things which fly through the air, all that dwells in the water, and all that goes on foot on the dry earth."[4] As there is but one ideal living Creature, the Demiurge made but one world.[5]

4. What was the motive of the Demiurge in so acting? The Demiurge is good and "desired that all things should come as near as possible to being like himself," judging that order is better than disorder, and fashioning everything for the best.[6] He was limited by the material at his disposal, but he did the best he could with it, making it "as excellent and perfect as possible."

5. How are we to regard the figure of the Demiurge? He must at least represent the divine Reason which is operative in the world; but he is not a Creator-God. It is clear from the *Timaeus* that the Demiurge "took over" a pre-existing material and did his best with it: he is certainly not said to have created it out of nothing. "The generation of this cosmos," says Plato, "was a mixed result of the combination of Necessity and Reason,"[7] Necessity being also called the Errant Cause. The word "Necessity" naturally suggests to us the reign of fixed law, but this is not precisely what Plato meant. If we take the Democritean or Epicurean view of the universe, according to which the world is built up out of atoms without the aid of Intelligence, we have an example of what Plato meant by Necessity, i.e. the *purposeless*, that which was not formed by Intelligence. If we also bear in mind that in the Atomistic System the world owes its origin to the "chance" collision of atoms, we can more easily see how Plato

---

[1] 28 c 2–3. [2] 30 a 3–4. [3] 30 b 1–c 1. [4] 39 e 3–40 a 2.
[5] 31 a 2–b 3. [6] 29 e 3–30 a 6. [7] 47 e 5–48 a 2.

9

could associate Necessity with Chance or the Errant Cause. For us these may seem to be opposed notions, but for Plato they were akin, since they both denote that in which Intelligence and conscious Purpose have no share. Thus it is that in the *Laws* Plato can speak of those who declare that the world originated "not by the action of mind, or of any God, or from art, but by nature and chance" (φύσει καὶ τύχη) or of necessity (ἐξ' ἀνάγκης).[1] Such a view of the universe is characterised by Aristotle[2] as the ascription of the world to Spontaneity (τὸ αὐτόματον), though inasmuch as motion is due to the previous motion of another atom, one could also say that the universe is due to Necessity. Thus the three notions of "spontaneously" and "by chance" and "of necessity" were allied notions. The elements, if considered as left to themselves, as it were, proceed spontaneously or by chance or necessarily, according to the point of view taken; but they do not subserve *purpose* unless the operation of Reason is introduced. Plato can, therefore, speak of Reason "persuading" necessity, i.e. making the "blind" elements subserve design and conscious purpose, even though the material is partly intractable and cannot be fully subordinated to the operation of Reason.

The Demiurge was, then, no Creator-God. Moreover, Plato most probably never thought of "chaos" as ever existing in actual fact, in the sense of there having been an historical period when the world was simply a disorderly chaos. At any rate this was the tradition of the Academy with but very few dissentient voices (Plutarch and Atticus). It is true that Aristotle takes the account of the world's formation in the *Timaeus* as an account of formation in time (or at least criticises it as so interpreted), but he expressly mentions that the members of the Academy declared that in describing the world's formation they were merely doing so for purposes of exposition, in order to understand the universe, without supposing that it ever really came into existence.[3] Among Neo-Platonists Proclus gave this interpretation[4] and Simplicius.[5] If this interpretation is correct, then the Demiurge is still less like a Creator-God: he is a symbol of the Intelligence operative in the world, the King of heaven and earth of the *Philebus*.[6] Moreover, it is to be noted that in the *Timaeus* itself Plato asserts that "it is hard to find the maker and father of the universe, and having found him it is impossible to speak of him

[1] *Laws*, 889 c 4–6.   [2] *Physics*, B. 4, 196 a 25.   [3] *De Caelo*, 279 b 33.
[4] i, 382; iii, 273.   [5] *Phys.*, 1122, 3.   [6] 28 c 7–8.

to all."[1] But if the Demiurge is a symbolic figure, it may also be that the sharp distinction implied in the *Timaeus* between the Demiurge and the Forms is only a pictorial representation. In treating of the Forms I inclined towards what might be called a Neo-Platonic interpretation of the relation between Mind, the Forms and the One, but I admitted that it *might* be that the Forms were Ideas of Mind or Intelligence. In any case it is not necessary to suppose that the picture of the Demiurge as a Divine Craftsman outside the world and also entirely distinct from the Forms is to be taken literally.

6. What did the Demiurge "take over"? Plato speaks of the "Receptacle—as it were, the nurse—of all Becoming."[2] Later he describes this as "Space, which is everlasting, not admitting destruction; providing a situation for all things which come into being, but itself apprehended without the senses by a sort of bastard reasoning, and hardly an object of belief."[3] It appears, therefore, that Space is not that out of which the primary elements are made, but that *in which* they appear. It is true that Plato makes a comparison with gold out of which a man moulds figures;[4] but he goes on to say that Space "never departs at all from its own character. For it is ever receiving all things, and never in any way whatsoever takes on any character which is like any of the things that enter it."[5] It is probable, then, that Space or the Receptacle is not the matter out of which the primary qualities are made, but that in which they appear.

Plato remarks that the four elements (earth, air, fire and water) cannot be spoken of as substances, since they are constantly changing: "for they slip away and do not wait to be described as 'that' or 'this' or by any phrase that exhibits them as having permanent being."[6] They are rather to be termed *qualities*, which make their appearance in the Receptacle, "in which (ἐν ᾧ) all of them are always coming to be, making their appearance and again vanishing out of it."[7] The Demiurge thus "took over" (*a*) the Receptacle, "a kind of thing invisible and characterless, all-receiving, partaking in some very puzzling way of the intelligible and very hard to apprehend,"[8] and (*b*) the primary qualities, which appear in the Receptacle and which the Demiurge fashions or builds up after the model of the Forms.

7. The Demiurge proceeds to confer geometrical shapes on the

[1] 28 c 3–5.   [2] 49 a 5–6.   [3] 52 a 8–b 2.   [4] 50 a 5–b 5.
[5] 50 b 7–c 2.   [6] 49 e 2–4.   [7] 49 e 7–50 a 1.   [8] 51 a 7–b 1.

four primary elements. Plato only takes things as far back as triangles, choosing the right-angled isosceles (half-square) and the right-angled scalene or half-equilateral, from which are to be built up the square and equilateral faces of the solids.[1] (If anyone asks why Plato makes a beginning with triangles, he answers that "the principles yet more remote, God knows and such men as are dear to Him."[2] In the *Laws*[3] he indicates that it is only when the third dimension is reached that things become "perceptible to sense." It is sufficient, therefore, for purposes of exposition to start with the surface or second dimension, and leave the remoter principles alone.) The solids are then constructed, the cube being assigned to earth (as the most immobile or hard to move), the pyramid to fire (as the "most mobile," having "the sharpest cutting edges and the sharpest points in every direction"), the octahedron to air, and the icosahedron to water.[4] These bodies are so small that no single one of them is perceptible by us, though an aggregate mass is perceptible.

The elementary solids or particles may be, and are, transformed into one another, since water, for example, may be broken down into its constituent triangles under the action of fire, and these triangles may recombine in Space into the same figure or into different figures. Earth, however, is an exception because, although it may be broken up, its constituent triangles (isosceles or half-square, from which the cube is generated) are peculiar to it alone, so that earth-particles "can never pass into any other kind."[5] Aristotle objects to this exception made in favour of earth, on the ground that it is unreasonable and unsupported by observation.[6] (The particles are spoken of as "motions or powers,"[7] and in the state of separation they have "some vestiges of their own nature."[8] Thus Ritter says that "Matter may be defined as that which acts in space."[9]) From the primary elements come substances as we know them: e.g. copper is "one of the bright and solid kinds of water," containing a particle of earth, "which, when the two substances begin to be separated again by the action of time," appears by itself on the surface as verdigris.[10] But Plato observes that to enumerate the genesis and nature of substances is not much more than a "recreation," a "sober and sensible pastime" that affords innocent pleasure.[11]

8. The Demiurge is depicted as creating the World-Soul

[1] Cf. 53 c 4 ff. [2] 53 d 6–7. [3] 894 a 2–5. [4] 55 d 6 ff. [5] 56 d 5–6. [6] *De Caelo*, 306 a 2. [7] 56 c 4. [8] 53 b 2. [9] *Essence*, p. 261. [10] 59 c 1–5. [11] 59 c 5–d 2.

(though it is unlikely that Plato meant this to be taken literally, for in the *Phaedrus* it is stated that soul is uncreated[1]), which is a mixture composed of (*a*) Intermediate Existence (i.e. intermediate between the Indivisible Existence of the Forms and the Divisible Existence or Becoming of purely sensible things); (*b*) Intermediate Sameness; and (*c*) Intermediate Difference.[2] As immortal souls are also fashioned by the Demiurge from the same ingredients as the World-Soul,[3] it follows that the World-Soul and all immortal souls share in both worlds—in the unchanging world, inasmuch as they are immortal and intelligible, and in the changing world, inasmuch as they are themselves living and changing. The stars and planets have intelligent souls which are the celestial gods,[4] made by the Demiurge and having assigned to them the office of fashioning the mortal parts of the human soul and the human body.[5] It would appear from the *Phaedrus* that human souls never really had a beginning, and Proclus interprets Plato in this sense, though it is true that in the *Laws* the question seems to be left open.[6]

As to the traditional Greek deities, whose genealogies were narrated by the poets, Plato remarks that "to know and to declare their generation is too high a task for us"; it is best to "follow established usage."[7] Plato seems to have been agnostic as regards the existence of the anthropomorphic deities,[8] but he does not reject them outright, and in the *Epinomis*[9] the existence of invisible spirits (who were to play a large part in post-Aristotelian Greek philosophy), in addition to that of the celestial gods, is envisaged. Plato, therefore, upholds the traditional worship, though he places little reliance on the stories of the generation and genealogy of the Greek deities, and was probably doubtful if they really existed in the form in which the Greeks popularly conceived them.

9. The Demiurge, having constructed the universe, sought to make it still more like its pattern, the Living Creature or Being. Now, the latter is eternal, but "this character it was not possible to confer completely on the generated things. But he took thought to make a certain moving likeness of eternity; and, at the same time that he ordered the Heaven, he made, of eternity that abides in unity, an everlasting likeness moving according to number—that

---

[1] 246 a 1–2.   [2] 35 a 1 ff. Cf. *Proclus*, ii, 155, Cornford's *Timaeus*, pp. 59 ff.
[3] 41 d 4 ff.   [4] 39 e 10–42 a 1.   [5] Cf. 41 a 7–d 3, 42 d 5–e 4.
[6] 781 e 6–782 a 3.   [7] *Tim.*, 40 d 6–41 a 3.   [8] Cf. *Phaedrus*, 246 c 6–d 3.
[9] 984 d 8–e 3.

which we have named Time."[1] Time is the movement of the sphere, and the Demiurge gave man the bright Sun to afford him a unit of time. Its brightness, relative to that of the other celestial bodies, enables man to differentiate day and night.

10. One cannot enter into details concerning the formation of the human body and its powers, or of the animals, etc. It must suffice to point out how Plato stresses finality, as in his quaint observation that "the gods, thinking that the front is more honourable and fit to lead than the back, gave us movement for the most part in that direction."[2]

The conclusion of the whole account of the formation of the world is that "having received its full complement of living creatures, mortal and immortal, this world has thus become a visible living creature embracing all things which are visible, an image of the intelligible, a perceptible god, supreme in greatness and excellence, in beauty and perfection, this Heaven, one and single in its kind."[3]

---

[1] *Tim.*, 37 d 3–7.   [2] *Tim.*, 45 a 3–5.   [3] *Tim.*, 92 c 5–9.

CHAPTER XXV

ART

1. *Beauty*

1. HAD Plato any appreciation of natural beauty? There is not
an abundance of material from which to form an opinion. However, there is a description of natural scenery at the beginning of
the *Phaedrus*,[1] and there are some similar remarks at the beginning
of the *Laws*,[2] though in both cases the beauty of the scene is
appreciated rather from a utilitarian standpoint, as a place of
repose or as a setting for a philosophic discussion. Plato had, of
course, an appreciation of human beauty.

2. Had Plato any real appreciation of Fine Art? (This question
only arises because of his dismissal of dramatists and epic poets
from the Ideal State on moral grounds, which might he held to
imply that he lacked any real appreciation of literature and art.)
Plato dismissed most of the poets from the *Republic* owing to
metaphysical and, above all, moral considerations; but there
certainly are not wanting indications that Plato was quite sensible
of the charm of their compositions. While the words at the
beginning of *Republic* 398 would not appear to be entirely
sarcastic, in No. 383 of the same dialogue Socrates affirms that
"although we praise much in Homer, this we shall not praise, the
sending by Zeus of a lying dream to Agamemnon." Similarly,
Plato makes Socrates say: "I must speak, although the love and
awe of Homer, which have possessed me from youth, deter me
from doing so. He seems to be the supreme teacher and leader
of this fine tragic band, but a man should not be reverenced before
the truth and I must needs speak out."[3] Again, "We are ready
to acknowledge that Homer is the greatest of poets and first of
tragedy writers; but we must recognise that hymns to the gods
and praises of the good are the only poetry which ought to be
admitted into our State."[4] Plato expressly says that if only
poetry and the other arts will prove their title to be admitted into
a well-ordered State, "we shall be delighted to receive her, knowing that we ourselves are very susceptible of her charms; but we
may not on that account betray the truth."[5]

Bearing these points in mind, it seems impossible to write Plato

[1] 230 b 2 ff.   [2] 625 b 1–c 2.   [3] 595 b 9–c 3.   [4] 607 a 2–5.   [5] 607 c 3–8.

253

down as a Philistine in regard to the arts and literature. And if it be suggested that his tributes of appreciation to the poets are but the grudging tributes of convention, we may point to Plato's own artistic achievement. If Plato himself had shown in no degree the spirit of the artist, it might be possible to believe that his remarks concerning the charms of the poets were due simply to convention or were even sarcastic in tone; but when we consider that it is the author of the *Symposium* and the *Phaedo* who speaks, it is really too much to expect anyone to believe that Plato's condemnation, or at least severe restriction, of art and literature was due to aesthetic insensibility.

3. What was Plato's theory of Beauty? That Plato regarded beauty as objectively real, is beyond all question. Both in the *Hippias Maior* and in the *Symposium* it is assumed that all beautiful things are beautiful in virtue of their participation in the universal Beauty, Beauty itself. So when Socrates remarks "Then beauty, too, is something real," Hippias replies, "Real, why ask?"[1]

The obvious consequence of such a doctrine is that there are degrees of beauty. For if there is a real subsistent Beauty then beautiful things will approximate more or less to this objective norm. So in the *Hippias Maior* the notion of relativity is introduced. The most beautiful ape will be ugly in comparison with a beautiful man, and a beautiful porridge-pot will be ugly in comparison with a beautiful woman. The latter in turn will be ugly in comparison with a god. Beauty itself, however, in virtue of a participation in which all beautiful things are beautiful, cannot be supposed to be something which "may just as well be called ugly as beautiful."[2] Rather is it "not partly beautiful and partly ugly; not at one time beautiful and at another time not; not beautiful in relation to one thing and deformed in relation to another; not here beautiful and there ugly, not beautiful in the estimation of some people and deformed in that of others; . . . but . . . eternally self-subsistent and monoeidic with itself."[3]

It follows also that this supreme Beauty, as being absolute and the source of all participated beauty, cannot be a beautiful *thing*, and so cannot be material: it must be supersensible and immaterial. We can see at once, then, that if true Beauty is supersensible, beautiful works of art or literature will, apart from

---

[1] *H.M.*, 287 c 8–d 2.   [2] *H.M.*, 289 c 3–5.   [3] *Sympos.*, 211 a 2–b 2.

any other consideration, necessarily occupy a comparatively low step on the ladder of beauty, since they are material, whereas Beauty itself is immaterial; they appeal to the senses, while absolute Beauty appeals to the intellect (and indeed to the rational will, if we bring into consideration the Platonic notion of Eros). Now, no one will wish to question the sublimity of Plato's idea of the ascent from the things of sense to the "divine and pure, the monoeidic beautiful itself"; but a doctrine of supersensible beauty (unless it is purely analogical) makes it very difficult to form any definition of beauty which will apply to the beautiful in all its manifestations.

The suggestion is offered in the *Hippias Maior*[1] that "whatever is useful is beautiful." Thus efficiency will be beauty: the efficient trireme or the efficient institution will be beautiful in virtue of its efficiency. But in what sense, then, can the Supreme Beauty be thought of as useful or efficient? It ought, if the theory is to be consistent, to be Absolute Usefulness or Efficiency—a difficult notion to accept, one might think. Socrates, however, introduces a qualification. If it is the useful or efficient which is beautiful, is it that which is useful for a good or for a bad purpose or for both? He will not accept the idea that what is efficient for an evil purpose is beautiful, and so it must be that the useful for a good purpose, the truly profitable, is the beautiful. But if the beautiful is the profitable, i.e. that which *produces* something good, then beauty and goodness cannot be the same, any more than the cause and its product can be the same. But since Socrates is unable to accept the conclusion that what is beautiful is not at the same time good, he suggests that the beautiful is that which gives pleasure to the eye or ear—e.g. beautiful men and colour-patterns and pictures and statues, beautiful voices and music and poetry and prose. This definition is, of course, not quite consistent with the characterisation of supreme Beauty as immaterial, but, quite apart from that fact, it is involved in another difficulty. That which gives pleasure through sight cannot be beautiful simply because it comes through *sight*, for then a beautiful tone would not be beautiful: nor can a tone be beautiful precisely because it gives pleasure to the sense of *hearing*, since in that case a statue, which is seen but not heard, would not be beautiful. The objects, therefore, which cause aesthetic pleasure of sight or hearing must share some common character which makes them beautiful, which

[1] 295 c 1 ff.

belongs to them both. What is this common character? Is it perhaps "Profitable pleasure," since the pleasures of sight and hearing are "the most harmless and the best of pleasures?" If this be so, then, says Socrates, we are back in the old position that beauty cannot be good nor the good beautiful.

If anything like the foregoing definition of beauty were maintained, it would be inconsistent with Plato's general metaphysical position. If Beauty is a transcendental Form, how can it possibly be that which gives pleasure to the senses of sight and hearing? In the *Phaedrus*[1] Plato declares that beauty alone, in distinction from wisdom, has the privilege of manifesting itself to the senses. But does it manifest itself through what is itself beautiful or not? If the latter, how can there be a real manifestation? If the former, then do the sensible manifesting beauty and the supersensible manifested beauty unite in a common definition or not? And if so, in what definition? Plato does not really offer any definition that will cover both types of beauty. In the *Philebus* he speaks of true pleasure as arising from beautiful shapes and colours and sounds and goes on to explain that he is referring to "straight lines and curves" and to "such sounds as are pure and smooth and yield a single pure tone." These "are not beautiful relatively to anything else but in their own proper nature."[2] In the passage in question Plato distinguishes between the pleasure attaching to the perception of beauty and beauty itself, and his words must be read in connection with his statement[3] that "measure and symmetry everywhere pass into beauty and virtue," which implies that beauty consists in μετριότης καὶ συμμετρία. Perhaps this is as near as Plato ever comes to offering a definition of beauty that would apply to sensible and to supersensible beauty (he certainly assumed that there are both, and that the one is a copy of the other); but if we take into account the remarks on beauty scattered about in the dialogues, it is probable that we must admit that Plato wanders "among so many conceptions, among which it is just possible to say that the identification of the Beautiful with the Good prevails,"[4] though the definition offered in the *Philebus* would seem to be the most promising.

---

[1] 250 d 6–8.   [2] 51 b 9–c 7.   [3] *Phil.*, 64 e 6–7.
[4] *Aesthetic*, by Benedetto Croce, pp. 165–6. (2nd edit., trs. by Douglas Ainslie, Macmillan, 1929.)

II. Plato's Theory of Art

1. Plato suggests that the *origin* of art is to be sought in the natural instinct of expression.[1]

2. In its metaphysical aspect or its essence, art is *imitation*. The Form is exemplary, archetypal; the natural object is an instance of μίμησις. Now, the painting of a man, for example, is the copy or imitation of a natural, particular man. It is, therefore, the imitation of an imitation. Truth, however, is to be sought properly in the Form; the work of the artist accordingly stands at two removes from the truth. Hence Plato, who was above all things interested in truth, was bound to depreciate art, however much he might feel the beauty and charm of statues, painting or literature. This depreciatory view of art comes out strongly in the *Republic*, where he applies it to the painter and the tragic poet, etc.[2] Sometimes his remarks are a little comical, as when he observes that the painter does not even copy objects accurately, being an imitator of appearance and not of fact.[3] The painter who paints a bed, paints it only from one point of view, as it appears to the senses immediately: the poet portrays healing, war and so on, without any real knowledge of the things of which he is speaking. The conclusion is that "imitative art must be a long way from truth."[4] It is "two grades below reality, and quite easy to produce without any knowledge of the truth—for it is mere semblance and not reality."[5] The man who gives up his life to producing this shadow of reality has made a very bad bargain.

In the *Laws* there appears what is perhaps a somewhat more favourable judgment concerning art, though Plato has not altered his metaphysical position. When saying that the excellence of music is not to be estimated merely by the amount of sense-pleasure it occasions, Plato adds that the only music which has real excellence is the kind of music "which is an imitation of the good."[6] Again, "those who seek for the best kind of song and music, ought not to seek for that which is pleasant, but for that which is true; and the truth of imitation consists, as we were saying, in rendering the thing imitated according to quantity and quality."[7] He thus still clings to the concept of music as imitative ("everyone will admit that musical compositions are all imitative

[1] Cf. *Laws*, 653–4, 672 b 8–c 6. [2] *Rep.*, 597 c 11 and ff. [3] *Rep.*, 597 e 10 ff.
[4] *Rep.*, 598 b 6. [5] *Rep.*, 598 e 6–599 a 3. [6] *Laws*, 668 a 9–b 2.
[7] *Laws*, 668 b 4–7.

and representative"), but admits that imitation may be "true" if
it renders the thing imitated as best as it can in its own medium.
He is ready to admit music and art into the State, not only for
educative purposes, but also for "innocent pleasure";[1] but he
still maintains the imitation-theory of art, and that Plato's idea
of imitation was somewhat narrow and literal must be clear to
anyone who reads the second Book of the *Laws* (though it must be
admitted, I think, that to make *music* imitative implies a widening
of imitation to include symbolism. That music is imitative is, of
course, a doctrine common to both the *Republic* and the *Laws*.)
It is through this concept of imitation that Plato arrives at the
qualities of a good critic, who must (*a*) know of what the imitation
is supposed to be; (*b*) know whether it is "true" or not; and
(*c*) know whether it has been well executed in words and melodies
and rhythms.[2]

It is to be noted that the doctrine of μίμησις would indicate
that for Plato art definitely has its own sphere. While ἐπιστήμη
concerns the ideal order and δόξα the perceptible order of natural
objects, εἰκασία concerns the imaginative order. The work of
art is a product of imagination and addresses itself to the emotional element in man. It is not necessary to suppose that the
imitative character of art maintained by Plato *essentially* denoted
mere photographic reproduction, in spite of the fact that his
words about "true" imitation indicate that this is what he was
often thinking of. For one thing, the natural object is not a
photographic copy of the Idea, since the Idea belongs to one
order and the perceptible natural object belongs to another order,
so that we may conclude by analogy that the work of art need
not necessarily be a mere reproduction of the natural object. It
is the work of imaginative creation. Again, Plato's insistence on
the imitative character of music makes it very difficult, as I
have mentioned, to suppose that imitation meant essentially mere
photographic reproduction. It is rather imaginative symbolism,
and it is precisely because of this fact that it does not assert truth
or falsehood, but is imaginative and symbolic and wears the
glamour of beauty, that it addresses itself to the emotional in man.

Man's emotions are varied, some being profitable, others harmful. Reason, therefore, must decide what art is to be admitted
and what is to be excluded. And the fact that Plato definitely
admits forms of art into the State in the *Laws* shows that art

---

[1] *Laws*, 670 d 6–7.   [2] *Laws*, 669 a 7–b 3.

occupies a particular sphere of human activity, which is irreducible to anything else. It may not be a high sphere, but it is
a sphere. This is borne out by the passage in which Plato, after
referring to the stereotyped character of Egyptian art, remarks
that "if a person can only find in any way the natural melodies,
he should confidently embody them in a fixed and legal form."[1]
It must, however, be admitted that Plato does not realise—or, if
he does realise, does not sufficiently exhibit—the specifically
disinterested character of aesthetic contemplation in itself. He
is much more concerned with the educational and moral effects
of art, effects which are irrelevant, no doubt, to aesthetic contemplation as such, but which are none the less real, and which
must be taken into account by anyone who, like Plato, values
moral excellence more than aesthetic sensibility.[2]

3. Plato recognises that the popular view of art and music is
that they exist to give pleasure, but it is a view with which he
will not agree. A thing can only be judged by the standard of
pleasure when it furnishes no utility or truth or "likeness"
(reference to imitation), but exists solely for the accompanying
charm.[3] Now, music, for instance, is representative and imitative, and good music will have "truth of imitation":[4] therefore
music, or at least good music, furnishes a certain kind of "truth,"
and so cannot exist solely for the sake of the accompanying charm
or be judged of by the standard of sense-pleasure alone. The
same holds good for the other arts. The conclusion is that the
various arts may be admitted into the State, provided that they
are kept in their proper place and subordinated to their educative
function, this function being that of giving *profitable* pleasure.
That the arts do not, or should not, give pleasure, Plato by no
means intends to assert: he allows that in the city there should
be "a due regard to the instruction and amusement which the
Muses give,"[5] and even declares that "every man and boy, free
and slave, both sexes, and the whole city, should never cease
charming themselves with the strains of which we have spoken,
and that there should be every sort of change and variation of
them in order to take away the effect of sameness, so that the
singers may always have an appetite for their hymns and receive
pleasure from them."[6]

[1] 657 b 2-3.
[2] For further treatment of Plato's philosophy of art, see e.g. Professor R. G.
Collingwood's article, "Plato's Philosophy of Art," in *Mind* for April 1925.
[3] *Laws*, 667 d 9-e 4.   [4] 668 b 4-7.   [5] 656 c 1-3.   [6] 665 c 2-7.

But though Plato in the *Laws* allows for the pleasurable and recreative functions of art, the "innocent pleasure"[1] that it affords, he most certainly stresses its educative and moral function, its character of providing profitable pleasure. The attitude displayed towards art in the *Laws* may be more liberal than that shown in the *Republic*, but Plato's fundamental attitude has not changed. As we have seen when treating of the State, a strict supervision and censorship of art is provided for in both dialogues. In the very passage in which he says that due regard should be paid to the instruction and amusement given by the Muses, he asks if a poet is to be allowed to "train his choruses as he pleases, without reference to virtue or vice."[2] In other words, the art admitted into the State must have that remote relation to the Form ("truth of imitation" *via* the natural object) which is possible in the creations of the imagination. If it has not got that, then the art will be not only unprofitable but also bad art, since good art must have this "truth of imitation," according to Plato. Once more, then, it becomes clear that art has a function of its own, even if not a sublime one, since it constitutes a rung on the ladder of education, fulfils a need of man (expression) and affords recreation and innocent amusement, being the expression of a definite form of human activity—that of the creative imagination (though "creative" must be understood in connection with the doctrine of imitation). Plato's theory of art was doubtless sketchy and unsatisfactory, but one can hardly be justified in asserting that he had no theory at all.

Note on the Influence of Plato

1. The example of Plato is an influence by itself. His life was one of utter devotion to truth, to the attainment of abiding, eternal and absolute truth, in which he firmly and constantly believed, being ready to follow, as Socrates was, wherever reason might lead. This spirit he endeavoured to stamp upon the Academy, creating a body of men who, under the ascendency of a great teacher, would devote themselves to the attainment of Truth and Goodness. But though he was a great speculative philosopher, devoted to the attainment of truth in the intellectual sphere, Plato, as we have seen, was no mere theorist. Possessed of an intense moral earnestness and convinced of the reality of absolute moral values and standards, he urged men to take

[1] 670 d 7.   [2] 656 c 5–7.

thought for their dearest possession, their immortal soul, and to strive after the cultivation of true virtue, which alone would make them happy. The good life, based on an eternal and absolute pattern, must be lived both in private and in public, realised both in the individual and in the State: as relativistic private morality was rejected, so was the opportunist, superficial, self-seeking attitude of the sophistic "politician" or the theory that "Might is Right."

If man's life *ought* to be lived under the dominion of reason according to an ideal pattern, in the world as a whole we must acknowledge the actual operation of Mind. Atheism is utterly rejected and the order in the world is ascribed to Divine Reason, ordering the cosmos according to the ideal pattern and plan. Thus that which is realised in the macrocosm, e.g. in the movements of heavenly bodies, should also be realised in man, the microcosm. If man does follow reason and strives to realise the ideal in his life and conduct, he becomes akin to the Divine and attains happiness in this life and the hereafter. Plato's "other-worldliness" did not spring from a hatred of this life, but was rather a consequence of his convinced belief in the reality of the Transcendent and Absolute.

2. Plato's personal influence may be seen from the impression he made on his great pupil, Aristotle. Witness the latter's verses to the memory

> Of that unique man
> Whose name is not to come from the lips of the wicked.
> Theirs is not the right to praise him—
> Him who first revealed clearly
> By word and by deed
> That he who is virtuous is happy.
> Alas, not one of us can equal him.[1]

Aristotle gradually separated himself from some of the Platonic doctrines that he had held at first; but, in spite of his growing interest in empirical science, he never abandoned metaphysics or his belief in the good life culminating in true wisdom—in other words, he never abandoned altogether the legacy of Plato, and his philosophy would be unthinkable apart from the work of his great predecessor.

3. Of the course of Platonism in the Academy and in the Neo-Platonic School I shall speak later. Through the Neo-Platonists

[1] Arist., Frag. 623. (Rose, 1870.)

Platonism made its influence felt on St. Augustine and on the formative period of mediaeval thought. Indeed, although St. Thomas Aquinas, the greatest of the Schoolmen, adopted Aristotle as "the Philosopher," there is much in his system that can be traced back ultimately to Plato rather than to Aristotle. Moreover, at the time of the Renaissance, the Platonic Academy of Florence endeavoured to renew the Platonic tradition, while the influence of the Platonic Republic may be seen in St. Thomas More's *Utopia* and Campanella's *City of the Sun*.

4. In regard to modern times, the influence of Plato may not be at first sight so obvious as it is in Antiquity and in the Middle Ages; but in reality he is the father or grandfather of all spiritualist philosophy and of all objective idealism, and his epistemology, metaphysics and politico-ethics have exercised a profound influence on succeeding thinkers, either positively or negatively. In the contemporary world we need only think of the inspiration that Plato has afforded to thinkers like Professor A. N. Whitehead or Professor Nicolai Hartmann of Berlin.

5. Plato, who stands at the head of European philosophy, left us no rounded system. That we do not possess his lectures and a complete record of his teaching in the Academy, we naturally regret, for we would like to know the solution of many problems that have puzzled commentators ever since; but, on the other hand, we may in a real sense be thankful that no cut and dried Platonic system (if ever there was such) has come down to us, a system to be swallowed whole or rejected, for this fact has enabled us to find in him, more easily perhaps than might otherwise be the case, a supreme example of the philosophic spirit. If he has not left us a complete system, Plato has indeed left us the example of a way of philosophising and the example of a life devoted to the pursuit of the true and the good.

CHAPTER XXVI

THE OLD ACADEMY

THE Platonic philosophy continued to exercise a profound influence throughout Antiquity; we must, however, distinguish various phases in the development of the Platonic School. The old Academy, which consisted of disciples and associates of Plato himself, held more or less to the dogmatic content of the Master's philosophy, though it is noticeable that it was the "Pythagorean" elements in the thought of Plato that received particular attention. In the Middle and New Academies an anti-dogmatic sceptical tendency is at first predominant, though it later gives way before a return to dogmatism of an eclectic type. This eclecticism is very apparent in Middle Platonism, which is succeeded at the close of the period of ancient philosophy by Neo-Platonism, an attempt at a complete synthesis of the original content of Platonism with those elements which had been introduced at various times, a synthesis in which those traits are stressed which are most in harmony with the general spirit of the time.

The Old Academy includes, together with men like Philippus of Opus, Heraclides Ponticus, Eudoxus of Cnidus, the following successors to Plato in the headship of the School at Athens: Speusippus (348/7–339/8), Xenocrates (339/8–315/4), Polemon (315/4–270/69) and Crates (270/69–265/4).

. Speusippus, Plato's nephew and immediate successor as Scholarch, modified the Platonic dualism by abandoning the Ideas as distinct from τὰ μαθηματικά and making Reality to consist in mathematical numbers.[1] The Platonic Number-Ideas were thus dismissed, but the essential χωρισμός remained. By his admission of scientific perception (ἐπιστημονικὴ αἴσθησις) Speusippus is sometimes said to have given up the Platonic dualism of knowledge and perception,[2] but it must be remembered that Plato had himself gone some way towards admitting this, inasmuch as he allowed that λόγος and αἴσθησις co-operate in the apprehension of the atomic idea.

It is difficult to tell exactly what the members of the Old

---

[1] Frag. 42, a–g.   [2] So Praechter, p. 343.

Academy taught, since (unless Philippus of Opus wrote the
Epinomis) no whole work of theirs has come down to us, and we
have only the remarks of Aristotle and the testimony of other
ancient writers to rely on. But apparently Speusippus held that
substances proceed from the One and the absolute Many, and
he placed the Good or τελεία ἕξις at the end of the process of
becoming and not at the beginning, arguing from the development of plants and animals. Among the animate beings that
proceed from the One is the invisible Reason or God,[1] which he
probably also identified with the World-Soul. (Possibly this might
afford an argument in favour of a "Neo-Platonic" interpretation
of Plato.) As for human souls, these are immortal in their entirety.
We may note that Speusippus interpreted the account of "creation" in the *Timaeus* as a mere form of exposition and not as
meant to be an account of an actual creation in time: the world
has no beginning in time. The traditional gods he interpreted as
physical forces, and thus brought upon himself a charge of
atheism.[2]

Xenocrates of Chalcedon, who succeeded Speusippus as Scholarch, identified the Ideas with mathematical numbers, and
derived them from the One and the Indeterminate Duality (the
former being Νοῦς or Zeus, the father of the gods, the latter being
the feminine principle, the mother of the gods).[3] The World-Soul,
produced by the addition of the Self and the Other to number, is
a self-moved number. Distinguishing three worlds—the sub-
lunar, the heavenly, and the super-celestial—Xenocrates filled all
three worlds with "demons," both good and bad. This doctrine
of evil demons enabled him to explain the popular myths, in
which evil actions are ascribed to "gods," and the existence of
immoral cults, by saying that the evil actions were the acts of
evil demons, and that the immoral cults were directed to these
demons and not to the gods.[4] In company with his predecessor,
Xenocrates held that even the irrational parts of the soul (which
was not created in time) survive after death, and, together with
his successor, Polemon, he deprecated the consumption of flesh-
meat on the ground that this might lead to the dominion of the
irrational over the rational. Like Speusippus and Crantor (and in
opposition to Aristotle), Xenocrates understood the priority of
the simple over the composite in the *Timaeus* to be a logical and

---

[1] Frag. 38–9.   [2] Cic., *De Nat. D.*, I, 13, 32.   [3] Frag. 34 ff.
[4] Frag. 24 ff.

not a temporal priority.[1] (The Περὶ ἀτόμων γραμμῶν, attributed to Aristotle, was directed against Xenocrates' hypothesis of tiny invisible lines, which he employed as an aid in the deduction of dimensions from numbers.)

Heraclides Ponticus adopted from the Pythagorean Ecphantus the theory that the world is composed of particles which he called ἄναρμοι ὄγκοι, probably meaning that they are separated from one another by space. From these material particles the world was composed through the operation of God. The soul is therefore corporeal (consisting of aether, an element added to the others by Xenocrates). While asserting the diurnal revolution of the earth on its axis, Heraclides also held that Mercury and Venus revolve round the sun, and he seems to have suggested that the earth may do likewise.

One of the most celebrated mathematicians and astronomers of Antiquity is *Eudoxus* (c. 497–355 B.C.). Philosophically speaking, he is noteworthy for having held (a) that the Ideas are "mixed" with things,[2] and (b) that pleasure is the highest good.[3]

The first commentary on Plato's *Timaeus* was written by *Crantor* (c. 330–270), in which he interpreted the account of "creation" as a timeless and not as a temporal event. It is depicted as taking place in time simply for the purpose of logical schematism. In this interpretation Crantor was in accord, as we have seen, with both Speusippus and Xenocrates. In his Περὶ πένθους Crantor upheld the doctrine of the moderating of the passions (Metriopathy) in opposition to the Stoic ideal of Apathy.[4]

---

[1] Frag. 54. [2] *Metaph.*, A 9, 991 a 8–19. [3] *Eth. Nic.*, 1101 b 27 ff.; 1172 b 9 ff.
[4] Cic., *Acad.*, 2, 44, 135; *Tusc.*, 3, 6, 12.

PART IV

ARISTOTLE

CHAPTER XXVII

LIFE AND WRITINGS OF ARISTOTLE

ARISTOTLE was born in 384/3 B.C. at Stageira in Thrace, and was the son of Nicomachus, a physician of the Macedonian king, Amyntas II. When he was about seventeen years old Aristotle went to Athens for purposes of study and became a member of the Academy in 368/7 B.C., where for over twenty years he was in constant intercourse with Plato until the latter's death in 348/7 B.C. He thus entered the Academy at the time when Plato's later dialectic was being developed and the religious tendency was gaining ground in the great philosopher's mind. Probably already at this time Aristotle was giving attention to empirical science (i.e. at the time of Plato's death), and it may be that he had already departed from the Master's teaching on various points; but there can be no question of any radical break between Master and pupil as long as the former was still alive. It is impossible to suppose that Aristotle could have remained all that time in the Academy had he already taken up a radically different philosophical position to that of his Master. Moreover, even after Plato's death Aristotle still uses the first person plural of the representatives of the Platonic doctrine of Ideas, and soon after Plato's death Aristotle eulogises him as the man "whom bad men have not even the right to praise, and who showed in his life and teachings how to be happy and good at the same time."[1] The notion that Aristotle was in any real sense an opponent of Plato in the Academy and that he was a thorn in the side of the Master, is scarcely tenable: Aristotle found in Plato a guide and friend for whom he had the greatest admiration, and though in later years his own scientific interests tended to come much more to the fore, the metaphysical and religious teaching of Plato had a lasting influence upon him. Indeed, it was this side of Plato's teaching that would have perhaps a special

[1] Frag. 623. (Rose, *Aristotelis Fragmenta*. Berlin, 1870 edit.)

value for Aristotle, as offsetting his own bent towards empirical studies. "In fact, this myth of a cool, static, unchanging and purely critical Aristotle, without illusions, experiences, or history, breaks to pieces under the weight of the facts which up to now have been artificially suppressed for its sake."[1] As I shall briefly indicate, when considering Aristotle's writings, the Philosopher developed his own personal standpoint only gradually; and this is, after all, only what one would naturally expect.

After Plato's death Aristotle left Athens with Xenocrates (Speusippus, Plato's nephew, had become head of the Academy, and with him Aristotle did not see eye to eye; in any case he may not have wished to remain in the Academy in a subordinate position under its new head), and founded a branch of the Academy at Assos in the Troad. Here he influenced Hermias, ruler of Atarneus, and married his niece and adopted daughter, Pythias. While working at Assos, Aristotle no doubt began to develop his own independent views. Three years later he went to Mitylene in Lesbos, and it was there that he was probably in intercourse with Theophrastus, a native of Eresus on the same island, who was later the most celebrated disciple of Aristotle. (Hermias entered into negotiations with Philip of Macedon, who conceived the idea of an Hellenic defeat of the Persians. The Persian general, Mentor, got hold of Hermias by treachery and carried him off to Susa, where he was tortured but kept silence. His last message was: "Tell my friends and companions that I have done nothing weak or unworthy of philosophy." Aristotle published a poem in his honour.[2])

In 343/2 Aristotle was invited to Pella by Philip of Macedon to undertake the education of his son Alexander, then thirteen years old. This period at the court of Macedon and the endeavour to exercise a real moral influence on the young prince, who was later to play so prominent a part on the political stage and to go down to posterity as Alexander the Great, should have done much to widen Aristotle's horizon and to free him from the narrow conceptions of the ordinary Greek, though the effect does not seem to have been so great as might have been expected: Aristotle never ceased to share the Greek view of the City-State as the centre of life. When Alexander ascended the throne in 336/5, Aristotle left Macedon, his pedagogical activity being now presumably at an

[1] Werner Jaeger, *Aristotle. Fundamentals of the History of His Development*, p. 34. (Trans. R. Robinson. Clarendon Press, 1934.)
[2] Diog. Laërt. 5, 7 and 8.

end, and probably went for a time to Stageira, his native city,
which Alexander rebuilt as payment of his debt to his teacher.
After a time the connection between the philosopher and his
pupil became weaker: Aristotle, though approving to a certain
extent of Macedonian politics, did not approve of Alexander's
tendency to regard Greeks and "barbarians" as on an equal footing.
Moreover, in 327, Callisthenes, nephew of Aristotle, who had been
taken into the service of Alexander on Aristotle's recommendation, was suspected of taking part in a conspiracy and was
executed.

In 335/4 Aristotle had returned to Atnens, where he founded
his own School. Apart from the fact of his absence from Athens
for some years, the development of his own ideas no doubt pre-
cluded any return to the Athenian Academy. The new School
was in the north-east of the city, at the Lyceum, the precincts of
Apollo Lyceus. The School was also known as the Περίπατος, and
the members as οἱ Περιπατητικοί, from their custom of carrying
on their discussions while walking up and down in the covered
ambulatory or simply because much of the instruction was given
in the ambulatory. The School was dedicated to the Muses.
Besides educational and tuitional work the Lyceum seems to
have had, in a more prominent way than the Academy, the
character of a union or society in which mature thinkers carried
on their studies and research: it was in effect a university or
scientific institute, equipped with library and teachers, in which
lectures were regularly given.

In 323 B.C. Alexander the Great died, and the reaction in
Greece against Macedonian suzerainty led to a charge of ἀσέβεια
against Aristotle, who had been so closely connected with the
great leader in his younger days. Aristotle withdrew from Athens
(lest the Athenians should sin against philosophy for the second
time, he is reported to have said) and went to Chalcis in Euboea,
where he lived on an estate of his dead mother. Shortly afterwards, in 322/1 B.C., he died of an illness.

The Works of Aristotle

The writings of Aristotle fall into three main periods, (i) the
period of his intercourse with Plato; (ii) the years of his activity
at Assos and Mitylene; (iii) the time of his headship of the Lyceum
at Athens. The works fall also into two groups or kinds,
(i) the exoteric works—ἐξωτερικοί, ἐκδεδομένοι λόγοι—which were

written for the most part in dialogue form and intended for general publication; and (ii) the pedagogical works—ἀκροαματικοὶ λόγοι, ὑπομνήματα, πραγματεῖα—which formed the basis of Aristotle's lectures in the Lyceum. The former exist only in fragments, but of the latter kind we possess a large number. These pedagogical works were first made known to the public in the edition of Andronicus of Rhodes (c. 60–50 B.C.), and it is these works which have earned for Aristotle a reputation for baldness of style unembellished by literary graces. It has been pointed out that, though a great inventor of philosophical terms, Aristotle was neglectful of style and of verbal beauty, while his interest in philosophy was too serious to admit of his employing metaphor instead of clear reason or of relapsing into myth. Now, this is true of the pedagogical works—that they lack the literary graces, but it is also true that the works which Aristotle himself published, and of which we possess only fragments, did not disdain the literary graces: their fluent style was praised by Cicero,[1] and even myths were occasionally introduced. They do, however, represent Aristotle's earlier work, when he was under direct Platonic influence or working his way towards his own independent position.

(i) In Aristotle's *first period* of literary activity he may be said to have adhered closely to Plato, his teacher, both in content and, in general at least, in form, though in the Dialogues Aristotle seems to have appeared himself as the leader of the conversation. "*. . . sermo ita inducitur ceterorum, ut penes ipsum sit principatus.*" (So Cic. *Ad Att.* 13, 19, 4.) It is most probable that in the Dialogues Aristotle held the Platonic philosophy, and only later changed his mind. Plutarch speaks of Aristotle as changing his mind (μετατίθεσθαι).[2] Moreover, Cephisodorus, pupil of Isocrates, saddles Aristotle with Plato's theories, e.g. concerning the Ideas.[3]

(a) To this period belongs the dialogue of *Eudemus*, or *On the Soul*, in which Aristotle shares Plato's doctrine of recollection and the apprehension of the Ideas in a state of pre-existence, and is in general dominated by the Master's influence. Aristotle argues for the immortality of the soul on lines suggested by the *Phaedo*—the soul is not a mere harmony of the body. Harmony has a contrary, namely, disharmony. But the soul has no contrary. Therefore the soul is not a harmony.[4] Aristotle supposes

---

[1] Cf. *De Orat.*, 1, xi, 49.
[2] *De virt. mor.*, c. 7.
[3] Euseb. *Prep. Evang.*, XIV, 6, following Numenius.
[4] Frag. 41. (Rose.)

pre-existence and the substantiality of the soul—also Forms. Just as men who fall ill may lose their memories, so the soul, on entering this life, forgets the state of pre-existence; but just as those who recover health after sickness remember their suffering, so the soul after death remembers this life. Life apart from the body is the soul's normal state (κατὰ φύσιν); its inhabitation of the body is really a severe illness.[1] This is a very different view from that afterwards put forward by Aristotle when he had taken up his own independent position.

(b) The *Protrepticus* also belongs to this period of Aristotle's development. This appears to have been an epistle to Themison of Cyprus and not a dialogue. In this work the Platonic doctrine of Forms is maintained, and the philosopher is depicted as one who contemplates these Forms or Ideas and not the imitations of them (αὐτῶν γὰρ ἐστι θεατὴς ἀλλ' οὐ μιμημάτων).[2] Again Phronesis retains the Platonic signification, denoting meta-physical speculation, and so having a theoretical meaning and not the purely practical significance of the *Nicomachean Ethics*. In the *Protrepticus* Aristotle also emphasises the worthlessness of earthly goods, and depicts this life as the death or tomb of the soul, which enters into true and higher life only through bodily death. This view certainly indicates direct Platonic influence, for in the *Nicomachean Ethics* Aristotle insists on the necessity of earthly goods, in some degree at least, for the truly happy life, and so even for the philosopher.

(c) It is probable that the oldest parts of the Logical Works, of the *Physics*, and perhaps also of the *De Anima* (book Γ) date back to this period. Thus if a preliminary sketch of the *Meta-physics* (including book A) dates back to Aristotle's *second* period, it is to be supposed that *Physics* (book 2) dates back to his *first* period, since in the first book of the *Metaphysics* there is a refer-ence to the *Physics*, or at least the setting-out of the theory of the causes is presupposed.[3] It is probable that the *Physics* fall into two groups of monographs, and the first two books and book 7 are to be ascribed to the earliest period of Aristotle's literary activity.

(ii) In his *second period* Aristotle began to diverge from his former predominantly Platonic position and to adopt a more

---

[1] Frag. 35. (Rose.)

[2] Iambl., *Protr.*, assuming that chapters 6–12 of Iamblichus' work consist of passages from Aristotle's *Protrepticus*. (Cf. Jaeger, *Aristotle*, pp. 60 ff.)

[3] *Metaph.*, A, 983 a 33–4.

critical attitude towards the teaching of the Academy. He still looked on himself as an Academician apparently, but it is the period of criticism or of growing criticism in regard to Platonism. The period is represented by the dialogue *On Philosophy*, Περὶ φιλοσοφίας, a work which combines clear Platonic influence with a criticism of some of Plato's most characteristic theories. Thus although Aristotle represents Plato as the culmination of previous philosophy (and indeed as regards pre-Aristotelian philosophy, Aristotle always held this idea), he criticises the Platonic theory of Forms or Ideas, at least under its later form of development at Plato's hands. "If the Ideas were another kind of number, and not the mathematical, we should have no understanding of it. For who understands another kind of number, at any rate among the majority of us?"[1] Similarly, although Aristotle adopts more or less Plato's stellar theology, the concept of the Unmoved Mover makes its appearance,[2] though Aristotle has not yet adopted the multitudinous movers of his later metaphysics. He applies the term visible god—τοσοῦτον ὁρατὸν θεόν—to the Cosmos or Heaven, a term which is of Platonic derivation.

It is interesting that the argument for the existence of the Divine drawn from the gradations of perfections is found in this dialogue. "In general, wherever there is a better there is also a best. Now, since among the things that are one is better than another, there is also a best thing, and this would be the divine." Aristotle supposes apparently the gradation of real forms.[3] The subjective belief in God's existence is derived by Aristotle from the soul's experience of ecstasies and prophecies in e.g. the state of sleep, and from the sight of the starry heavens, though such recognition of occult phenomena is really foreign to Aristotle's later development.[4] In this dialogue, then, Aristotle combines elements that can have no other source than Plato and his circle with elements of criticism of the Platonic philosophy, as when he criticises the Platonic theory of Ideas or the doctrine of "creation" as given in the *Timaeus*, asserting the eternity of the world.[5]

It appears that a first sketch of the *Metaphysics* goes back

[1] Frag. 11. (Rose.)
[2] Frag. 21. (Rose.) It must be admitted that this fragment implies that Aristotle had not yet definitely stated the existence of the First Mover or broken with his former views.
[3] Frag. 15. (Rose.) Professor Jaeger thinks that the dialogue contained also the proofs from motion and causality.
[4] Frags. 12 and 14. (Rose.) Cf. *Laws*, 966 d 9–967 a 5.
[5] Cf. Frag. 17. (Rose.)

to this second period in Aristotle's development, the period of transition. This would comprise Book A (the use of the term "we" denoting the transitional period), Book B, Book K, 1-8, Book Λ (except C 8), Book M, 9-10, Book N. According to Jaeger the attack in the original *Metaphysics* was directed mainly against Speusippus.[1]

The *Eudemian Ethics* are sometimes thought to belong to this period, and to date from Aristotle's sojourn at Assos. Aristotle still holds to the Platonic conception of Phronesis, though the object of philosophic contemplation is no longer the Ideal World of Plato but the transcendent God of the *Metaphysics*.[2] It is also probable that an original *Politics* dates from this second period, including Books 2, 3, 7, 8, which deal with the Ideal State. Utopias on the style of the Platonic Republic are criticised by Aristotle.

The writings *De Caelo* and *De Generatione et Corruptione* (Περὶ οὐρανοῦ and Περὶ γενέσεως καὶ φθορᾶς) are also ascribed to this period with probability.

(iii) Aristotle's *Third Period* (335-322) is that of his activity in the Lyceum. It is in this period that there appears Aristotle the empirical observer and scientist, who is yet concerned to raise a sure philosophical building upon a firm foundation sunk deep in the earth. We cannot but marvel at the power of organising detailed research in the provinces of nature and history that is shown by Aristotle in this last period of his life. There had, indeed, been in the Academy a practice of classification, mainly for logical purposes, that involved a certain amount of empirical observation, but there was nothing of the sustained and systematic investigation into details of nature and history that the Lyceum carried out under the direction of Aristotle. This spirit of exact research into the phenomena of nature and history really represents something new in the Greek world, and the credit for it must undoubtedly go to Aristotle. But it will not do to represent Aristotle as merely a Positivist in the last phase of his life, as is sometimes done, for there is really no evidence to show that he ever abandoned metaphysics, in spite of all his interest in exact, scientific research.

Aristotle's lectures in the School formed the basis of his "pedagogical" works, which were circulated among the members of the School, and were, as already mentioned, first given to the

---

[1] Jaeger, *Aristotle*, p. 192. [2] Cf. *Eud. Eth.*, 1249 b.

public by Andronicus of Rhodes. Most of the pedagogical works belong to this period, except, of course, those portions of works which are probably to be ascribed to an earlier phase. These pedagogical works have offered many difficulties to scholars, e.g. because of the unsatisfactory connections between books, sections that appear to break the logical succession of thought, and so on. It now appears probable that these works represent lectures of Aristotle which were equivalently published—so far as the School was concerned—by being given as lectures. But this does not imply that each work represents a single lecture or a continuous course of lectures: rather are they different sections or lectures which were later put together and given an external unity by means of a common title. This work of composition can have been only in part accomplished by Aristotle himself: it continued in the following generations of the School and was first completed by Andronicus of Rhodes, if not later.

These works of Aristotle's third period may be divided into:

(a) *Logical Works* (combined in Byzantine times as the *Organon*). The *Categories* or κατηγορίαι (Aristotelian in content at least), the *De Interpretatione* or Περὶ ἑρμενείας (on proposition and judgment), the *Prior Analytics* or 'Αναλυτικά Πρότερα (two books on inference), the *Posterior Analytics* or 'Αναλυτικά ὕστερα (two books on proof, knowledge of principles, etc.), the *Topics* or Τοπικά (eight books on dialectic or probable proof), the Sophistical Fallacies or Περὶ σοφιστικῶν ἐλέγχων.

(b) *Metaphysical Works.*
The *Metaphysics*, a collection of lectures of different dates, so called from its position in the Aristotelian Corpus, probably by a Peripatetic before the time of Andronicus.

(c) Works on Natural Philosophy, Natural Science, Psychology, etc. The *Physics* or φυσικὴ ἀκρόασις or φυσικά or τὰ περὶ φύσεως. This work consists of eight books, of which the first two must be referred to Aristotle's Platonic period. *Metaphysics* A 983 a 32–3 refers to the *Physics*, or rather presupposes explicitly the setting-out of the theory of causes in *Physics* 2. Book 7 of the *Physics* probably belongs also to the earlier work of Aristotle, while Book 8 is really not part of the *Physics* at all, since it quotes the *Physics*, with the remark 'as we have previously shown in the *Physics*."[1] The total work would then appear to have consisted originally of a

[1] *Physics*, VIII, 251 a 9, 253 b 8, 267 b 21.

number of independent monographs, a supposition borne out by the fact that the *Metaphysics* quotes as "Physics" the two works *De Caelo* and *De Generatione et Corruptione*.[1]

The *Meteorology* or Μετεωρολογικά or Περὶ μετεώρων (four books).

The *Histories of Animals* or Περὶ τὰ ζῷα ἱστορίαι (ten books on comparative anatomy and physiology, of which the last is probably post-Aristotelian).

The Ἀνατομαί in seven books, which is lost.

The *De Incessu Animalium* or Περὶ ζῴων πορείας (one book) and the *De Motu Animalium* or Περὶ ζῴων κινήσεως (one book).

The *De Generatione Animalium* or Περὶ ζῴων γενέσεως (five books).

The *De Anima* or Περὶ ψυχῆς, Aristotle's Psychology in three books.

The *Parva Naturalia*, a number of smaller treatises dealing with such subjects as perception (Περὶ αἰσθήσεως καὶ αἰσθητῶν), memory (Περὶ μνήμης καὶ ἀναμνήσεως), sleep and waking (Περὶ ὕπνου καὶ ἐγρηγόρσεως), dreams (Περὶ ἐνυπνίων), long life and short life (Περὶ μακροβιότητος καὶ βραχυβιότητος), life and death (Περὶ ζωῆς καὶ θανάτου, breathing (Περὶ ἀναπνοῆς), divination in sleep (Περὶ τῆς καθ' ὕπνον μαντικῆς).

The *Problemata* (Προβλήματα) seems to be a collection of problems, gradually formed, which grew up round a nucleus of notes or jottings made by Aristotle himself.

(d) *Works on Ethics and Politics.*

The *Magna Moralia* or Ἠθικὰ μεγάλα, in two books, which would seem to be a genuine work of Aristotle, at least so far as the content is concerned.[2] Part would appear to date from a time when Aristotle was still more or less in agreement with Plato.

The *Nicomachean Ethics* (Ἠθικὰ Νικομάχεια) in ten books, a work which was edited by Aristotle's son Nicomachus after the philosopher's death.

The *Politics* (Πολιτικά), of which books 2, 3, 7, 8, would appear to date from the second period of Aristotle's literary activity. Books 4–6 were, thinks Jaeger, inserted before the first book was prefixed to the whole, for Book 4 refers to 3 as the beginning of the work—ἐν τοῖς πρώτοις λόγοις. "The contents of 2 are merely negative."[3]

---

[1] *Metaph.*, 989 a 24.
[2] Cf. H. von Arnim, *Die drei arist. Ethiken.* (Sitz. Wien. Ak, 2 Abl., 1924.)
[3] Jaeger, *Aristotle*, p. 273.

Collection of Constitutions of 158 States. That of Athens was found in papyrus in 1891.

(e) *Works on Aesthetics, History and Literature.*

The *Rhetoric* (Τέχνη ῥητορική) in three books.

The *Poetics* (Περὶ ποιητικῆς), which is incomplete, part having been lost.

Records of dramatic performances at Athens, collection of Didascalia, list of victors at Olympic and Pythian games. Aristotle was engaged on a work concerning the Homeric problem, a treatise on the territorial rights of States (Περὶ τῶν τόπων δικαιώματα πόλεων), etc.

There is no need to suppose that all these works, for example the collection of the 158 Constitutions, were by Aristotle himself, but they would have been initiated by him and carried out under his superintendence. He entrusted others with the compilation of a history of natural philosophy (Theophrastus), of mathematics and astronomy (Eudemus of Rhodes), and medicine (Meno). One can but marvel at the catholicity of his interests and the scope of his aims.

The mere list of Aristotle's works shows a rather different spirit to that of Plato, for it is obvious that Aristotle was drawn towards the empirical and scientific, and that he did not tend to treat the objects of this world as semi-illusory or as unfitted to be objects of knowledge. But this difference in tendency, a difference which was no doubt accentuated as time went on, has, when coupled with consideration of such facts as the Aristotelian opposition to the Platonic theory of Ideas and to the Platonic dualistic psychology, led to the popular conception of a radical contrast between the two great philosophers. There is, of course, truth in this view, since there are clear cases of opposition between their tenets and also a general difference in atmosphere (at least if we compare Plato's exoteric works—and we have no other—with Aristotle's pedagogical works), but it can easily be exaggerated. Aristotelianism, historically speaking, is not the opposite of Platonism, but its development, correcting one-sided theories—or trying to do so—such as the theory of Ideas, the dualistic psychology of Plato, etc., and supplying a firmer foundation in physical fact. That something of value was omitted at the same time is true, but that simply shows that the two philosophies should not be considered as two diametrically opposed systems, but as two complementary philosophical spirits and bodies of doctrine. A synthesis was later attempted in Neo-Platonism, and mediaeval philosophy shows the same synthetic spirit. St. Thomas, for instance, though speaking of Aristotle as "the Philosopher," could not, and would not have wished to, cut himself off entirely from the Platonic tradition, while in the Franciscan School even St. Bonaventure, who awarded the palm to Plato, did not disdain to make use of Peripatetic doctrines, and Duns Scotus carried much further the impregnation of the Franciscan spirit with Aristotelian elements.

And it should not be supposed that Aristotle, in his enthusiasm for facts and his desire to set a firm empirical and scientific foundation, was lacking in systematic power or ever renounced his metaphysical interest. Both Platonism and Aristotelianism culminate in metaphysics. Thus Goethe can compare Aristotle's philosophy to a pyramid rising on high in regular form from a broad basis on the earth, and that of Plato to an obelisk or a tongue of flame which shoots up to heaven. Nevertheless, I must admit that, in my opinion, the direction of Aristotle's thought was increasingly directed away from the Platonic position to which he at first adhered, while the results of his new orientation of thought do not always combine harmoniously with those elements of the Platonic legacy which he seems to have retained to the last.

CHAPTER XXVIII

LOGIC OF ARISTOTLE

1. ALTHOUGH Aristotle divides philosophy systematically in different ways on different occasions,[1] we may say that the following is his considered view of the matter.[2] (i) *Theoretical Philosophy*,[3] in which knowledge as such is the end in view and not any practical purpose, is divided into (a) Physics or Natural Philosophy, which has to do with material things which are subject to motion; (b) Mathematics, which has to do with the unmoved but unseparated (from matter); (c) Metaphysics, which has to do with the separated (transcendent) and unmoved. (Metaphysics would thus include what we know as Natural Theology.[4]) (ii) *Practical* Philosophy (πρακτική) deals principally with Political Science, but has as subsidiary disciplines Strategy, Economics and Rhetoric, since the ends envisaged by these disciplines are subsidiary to and depend on that of Political Science.[5] (iii) *Poetical* Philosophy (ποιητική) has to do with production and not with action as such, as in the case with Practical Philosophy (which includes ethical action in the wider or political sense), and is to all intents and purposes the Theory of Art.[6]

2. The Aristotelian Logic is often termed "formal" logic. Inasmuch as the Logic of Aristotle is an analysis of the forms of thought (hence the term *Analytic*), this is an apt characterisation; but it would be a very great mistake to suppose that for Aristotle logic concerns the forms of human thinking in such an exclusive way that it has no connection with external reality. He is chiefly concerned with the forms of proof, and he assumes that the conclusion of a scientific proof gives certain knowledge concerning reality. For example, in the syllogism "All men are mortal, Socrates is a man, therefore Socrates is mortal," it is not merely that the conclusion is deduced correctly according to the

---

[1] Cf. *Top.*, A 14, 105 b 19 ff.
[2] Cf. *Top.*, Z 6, 145 a 15 ff.   *Metaph.*, E 1, 1025 b 25.
[3] Cf. *Metaph.*, K 7, 1064 b 1 ff.   [4] Cf. *Metaph.*, E 1, 1026 a 10 ff.
[5] Cf. *Eth. Nic.*, A 1, 1094 a 18 ff.
[6] Determining the rank of the branches of philosophy according to the rank of their object, Aristotle gives the palm to "Theology." Cf. *Metaph.*, K 7, 1064 b 1 ff. It has been argued that the threefold division has no adequate warrant in Aristotle's own words and that he conceived the *Poetics*, not as a philosophical aesthetic theory, but simply as a practical manual.

formal laws of logic: Aristotle assumes that the conclusion is verified in reality. He presupposes, therefore, a realist theory of knowledge and for him logic, though an analysis of the forms of thought, is an analysis of the thought that thinks reality, that reproduces it conceptually within itself, and, in the true judgment, makes statements about reality which are verified in the external world. It is an analysis of human thought in its thought about reality, though Aristotle certainly admits that things do not always exist in extramental reality precisely as they are conceived by the mind, e.g. the universal.

This may be clearly seen in his doctrine of the Categories. From the logical viewpoint the Categories comprise the ways in which we think about things—for instance, predicating qualities of substances—but at the same time they are ways in which things actually exist: things are substances and actually have accidents. The Categories demand, therefore, not only a logical but also a metaphysical treatment. Aristotle's Logic, then, must not be likened to the Transcendental Logic of Kant, since it is not concerned to isolate *a priori* forms of thought which are contributed by the mind alone in its active process of knowledge. Aristotle does not raise the "Critical Problem": he assumes a realist epistemology, and assumes that the categories of thought, which we express in language, are also the objective categories of extramental reality.

3. In the *Categories* and in the *Topics* the number of Categories or Praedicamenta is given as ten: οὐσία or τί ἐστι (man or horse); ποσόν (three yards long;) ποιόν (white); πρός τι (double); ποῦ (in the market-place); πότε (last year); κεῖσθαι (lies, sits); ἔχειν (armed, with shoes); ποιεῖν (cuts); πάσχειν (is cut or burnt). But in the *Posterior Analytics* they appear as eight, κεῖσθαι or *Situs* and ἔχειν or *Habitus* being subsumed under the other categories.[1] Aristotle, therefore, can hardly have looked upon the deduction of the Categories as definitive. Nevertheless, even if the tenfold division of the Categories was not looked upon as definitive by Aristotle, there is no reason to suppose that he regarded the list of Categories as a haphazard list, devoid of structural arrangement. On the contrary, the list of the Categories constitutes an orderly arrangement, a classification of concepts, the fundamental types of concepts governing our scientific knowledge. The word κατηγορεῖν means to predicate, and in the *Topics* Aristotle considers

---

[1] Cf. e.g. *Anal. Post.*, A 22, 83 a 21 ff., b 15 ff.

kategorein

the Categories as a classification of predicates, the ways in which we think of being as realised. For example, we think of an object either as a substance or as a determination of substance, as falling under one of the nine categories that express the way in which we think of substance as being determined. In the *Categories* Aristotle considers the Categories rather as the classification of genera, species and individuals from the *summa genera* down to individual entities. If we examine our concepts, the ways in which we represent things mentally, we shall find, for example, that we have concepts of organic bodies, of animals (a subordinate genus), of sheep (a species of animal); but organic bodies, animals, sheep, are all included in the category of substance. Similarly, we may think of colour in general, of blueness in general, of cobalt; but colour, blueness, cobalt, all fall under the category of quality.

The Categories, however, were not in Aristotle's mind simply modes of mental representation, moulds of concepts: they represent the actual modes of being in the extramental world, and form the bridge between Logic and Metaphysics (which latter science has Substance as its chief subject).[1] They have, therefore, an ontological as well as a logical aspect, and it is perhaps in their ontological aspect that their orderly and structural arrangement appears most clearly. Thus, in order that being may exist, substance must exist: that is, as it were, the starting-point. Only singulars actually exist outside the mind, and for a singular to exist independently in this way it must be a substance. But it cannot exist merely as a substance, it must have accidental forms. For instance, a swan cannot exist unless it has some colour, while it cannot have colour unless it has quantity, extension. At once, then, we have the first three Categories—substance, quantity, quality, which are intrinsic determinations of the object. But the swan is the same in specific nature as other swans, is equal in size or unequal in size to other substances; in other words, it stands in some relation to other objects. Moreover, the swan as a physical substance, must exist in a certain *place* and at a certain *period*, must have a certain *posture*. Again, material substances, as belonging to a cosmic system, *act* and are *acted upon*. Thus some of the Categories belong to the object considered in itself, as its *intrinsic* determinations, while others belong to it as *extrinsic* determinations, affecting it as standing in relation to other material objects. It will be seen, therefore, that even if the

---

[1] *Metaph.*, 1017 a 23–4. ὁσαχῶς γὰρ λέγεται, τοσαταυχῶς τὸ εἶναι σημαίνει.

10

number of the Categories could be reduced by subsuming certain Categories under others, the principle whereby the Categories are deduced is by no means merely a haphazard principle.

In the *Posterior Analytics* (in connection with definition) and in the *Topics*, Aristotle discusses the *Predicables* or various relations in which universal terms may stand to the subjects of which they are predicated. They are *genus* (γένος), *species* (εἶδος), *difference* (διαφορά), *property* (ἴδιον), *accident* (συμβεβηκός). In the *Topics* (I, c. 8), Aristotle bases his division of the predicables on the relations between subject and predicate. Thus if the predicate is co-extensive with the subject, it either gives us the essence of the subject or a property of the subject; while if it is not co-extensive with the subject, it either forms part of the attributes comprised in the definition of the subject (when it will be either a genus or a difference) or it does not do so (in which case it will be an accident).

Essential definitions are strict definitions by genus and difference, and Aristotle considered definition as involving a process of division down to the *infimae species* (cf. Plato).[1] But it is important to remember that Aristotle, aware that we are by no means always able to attain an essential or real definition, allows for nominal or descriptive definitions,[2] even though he had no high opinion of them, regarding as he did essential definitions as the only type of definition really worthy of the name. The distinction, however, is of importance, since in point of fact, we have to be content, in regard to the natural objects studied by physical science, with distinctive or characteristic definitions, which even if they approach the ideal more closely than Aristotle's nominal or descriptive definition, do not actually attain it.

(Some writers have emphasised the influence of language on philosophy. For instance, because we speak of the rose as being red (and this is necessary for purposes of social life and communication), we are naturally inclined to think that in the actual objective order there is a quality or accident, "redness," which inheres in a thing or substance, the rose. The philosophical categories of substance and accident can thus be traced back to the influence of words, of language. But it should be remembered that language follows thought, is built up as an expression of thought, and this is especially true of philosophical terms. When Aristotle laid down the ways in which the mind thinks about

---

[1] *Anal. Post.*, B 13.   [2] *Anal. Post.*, B 8 and 10.

things, it is true that he could not get away from language as the medium of thought, but the language follows thought and thought follows things. Language is not an *a priori* construction.)

4. Scientific knowledge *par excellence* means for Aristotle, deducing the particular from the general or the conditioned from its cause, so that we know both the cause on which the fact depends and the necessary connection between the fact and its cause. In other words, we have scientific knowledge when we know the cause on which the fact depends, as the cause of that fact and of no other, and further, that the fact could not be other than it is."[1]

But though the premisses are prior to the conclusion from the logical viewpoint, Aristotle clearly recognises that there is a difference between logical priority or priority *in se* and epistemological priority *quoad nos*. He expressly states that " 'prior' and 'better known' are ambiguous terms, for there is a difference between what is prior and better known in the order of being and what is prior and better known to man. I mean that objects nearer to sense are prior and better known to man; objects without qualification prior and better known are those further from sense."[2] In other words, our knowledge starts from sense, i.e. from the particular, and ascends to the general or universal. "Thus it is clear that we must get to know the primary premisses by induction; for the methods by which even sense-perception implants the universal is inductive."[3] Aristotle is thus compelled to treat not only of deduction, but also of induction. For instance, in the aforementioned syllogism the major premiss, "All men are mortal," is founded on sense-perception, and Aristotle has to justify both sense-perception and memory, since both are involved. Hence we have the doctrine that the senses *as such* never err: it is only the judgment which is true or false.

Thus if a patient who is suffering from *delirium tremens* "sees" pink rats, the senses as such do not err; error arises when the patient judges that the pink rats are "out there," as real extramentally-existing objects. Similarly, the sun *appears* smaller than the earth, but this is not an error on the part of the senses; indeed if the sun appeared as *larger* than the earth, the senses would be out of order. Error arises when, through a lack of

[1] *Anal. Post.*, I 2, 71 b.   [2] *Anal. Post.*, 71 b–72 a.
[3] *Anal. Post.*, II 19, 100 b.

astronomical knowledge, a man *judges* that the sun is objectively smaller than the earth.

5. In the *Analytics*, therefore, Aristotle treats, not only of scientific proof, demonstration or deduction, but also of induction (ἐπαγωγή). Scientific induction means for him *complete* induction, and he expressly states that "induction proceeds through an enumeration of all the cases."[1] *Incomplete* induction is of use especially to the orator. Aristotle used experiment but did not elaborate a scientific methodology of induction and the use of hypothesis. Although he admits that "syllogism through induction is clearer to us,"[2] his ideal remains that of deduction, of syllogistic demonstration. The analysis of deductive processes he carried to a very high level and very completely; but he cannot be said to have done the same for induction. This was no doubt only natural in the Ancient World, where mathematics was so much more highly developed than natural science. Nevertheless, after stating that sense-perception as such cannot attain the universal, Aristotle points out that we may observe groups of singulars or watch the frequent recurrence of an event, and so, by the use of the abstract reason, attain to knowledge of a universal essence or principle.[3]

6. In the *Prior Analytics* Aristotle inquires into the forms of inference, and he defines the syllogism as "discourse in which certain things being stated, something other than what is stated follows of necessity from their being so."[4] He discusses the three figures of the syllogism, etc..

(i) The Middle Term is Subject in one premiss and Predicate in the other. Thus: M is P, S is M, therefore S is P. Every animal is a substance. Every man is an animal. Therefore every man is a substance.

(ii) The Middle Term is Predicate in both premisses. P is M, S is not M, therefore S is not P.
Every man is risible. But no horse is risible. Therefore no horse is a man.

(iii) The Middle Term is Subject in both premisses. Thus: M is P, M is S, therefore S is P.
Every man is risible. But every man is an animal. Therefore some animals are risible.

In the *Topics*[5] Aristotle distinguishes *demonstrative* reasoning

---

[1] *Anal. Priora*, II 23, 68 b. [2] *Anal. Priora*, II, 23, 68 b. [3] *Anal. Post.*, I, 31.
[4] *Anal. Priora*, I, 1, 24 b. [5] I, 100 a b.

(i.e. "when the premisses from which the reasoning starts are true and primary, or are such that our knowledge of them has originally come through premisses which are primary and true") from _dialectical_ reasoning (i.e. reasoning "from opinions that are generally accepted," i.e. "by all, or by the majority, or by the most notable and illustrious of them"). He adds a third kind of reasoning, eristic or "contentious" reasoning (which "starts from opinions that seem to be generally accepted, but are not really such"). This third is dealt with at length in the _De Sophisticis Elenchis_, where Aristotle examines, classifies and solves the various kinds of fallacy.

7. Aristotle saw clearly that the premisses in deduction themselves need proof, while on the other hand if _every_ principle needs proof, we shall be involved in a _processus in infinitum_ and _nothing_ will be proved. He held, therefore, that there are certain principles which are known intuitively and immediately without demonstration.[1] The highest of these principles is the _principle of contradiction_. Of these principles no proof can be given. For example, the logical form of the principle of contradiction—"Of two propositions, one of which affirms something and the other denies the same thing, one must be true and the other false"—is not a proof of the principle in its metaphysical form—e.g. "The same thing cannot be an attribute and not an attribute of the same subject at the same time and in the same way." It simply exhibits the fact that no thinker can question the principle which lies at the basis of all thinking and is presupposed.[2]

We have, therefore, (i) first principles, perceived by νοῦς; (ii) what is derived necessarily from first principles, perceived by ἐπιστήμη; and (iii) what is contingent and could be otherwise, the subject of δόξα. But Aristotle saw that the major premiss of a syllogism, e.g. All men are mortal, cannot be derived immediately from the first principles: it depends also on induction. This involves a realist theory of universals, and Aristotle declares that induction exhibits the universal as implicit in the clearly known particular.[3]

8. In a book of this nature it would scarcely be desirable to enter upon a detailed exposition and discussion of the Aristotelian logic, but it is necessary to emphasise the very great contribution that Aristotle made to human thought in this branch of science,

[1] Cf. _Anal. Post._, I 3, 72 b.   [2] Cf. _Metaph._, 1005 b 35 ff.
[3] _Anal. Post._, A 1, 71 a.

especially in regard to the syllogism. That logical analysis and division had been pursued in the Academy, in connection with the theory of Forms, is quite true (one has only to think of the discussions in the *Sophist*); but it was Aristotle who first constituted logic ("Analytics") as a separate science, and it was Aristotle who discovered, isolated and analysed the fundamental form of inference, namely, the syllogism. This is one of his lasting achievements, and even if it were his only positive achievement, it would still be one for which his name would rightly be held in lasting memory. One could not justifiably assert that Aristotle made a complete analysis of all deductive processes, for the classical syllogism supposes (i) three propositions, each in subject and predicate form; (ii) three terms, from which each proposition takes both subject and predicate, and, given this situation, determines the cases in which two of the propositions entail the third in virtue, either (*a*) of logical form only, or (*b*) of an adjoined existence assertion, as with *Darapti*. Aristotle, for instance, did not consider that other form of inference discussed by Cardinal Newman in his *Grammar of Assent*, when the mind derives conclusions, not from certain propositions but from certain concrete facts. The mind considers these facts and, after forming a critical estimate of them, infers a conclusion, which is not a general proposition (as in induction proper), but a particular conclusion such as, e.g. "The prisoner is innocent." It is certainly true that general propositions are implied (e.g. evidence of a certain type is compatible, or incompatible, with the innocence of an accused man), but the mind is not actually concerned to elicit the implication of presupposed propositions so much as to elicit the implications of a number of concrete facts. St. Thomas Aquinas recognised this type of reasoning, and attributed it to the *vis cogitativa*, also called *ratio particularis*.[1] Moreover, even in regard to that form of inference which Aristotle analysed, he did not really consider the question, whether these general principles from which it starts are simply formal principles or have ontological import. The latter view seems to be assumed for the most part.

But it would be absurd to criticise Aristotle adversely for not having made a complete study of all the forms of inference, and for not having clearly raised and solved all the questions that might be raised in connection with the forms of human thought:

[1] Ia, 78, 4. Cf. IIa, IIae, 2, 1.

the task that he did undertake to accomplish, he accomplished very well, and the group of his logical treatises (later termed the *Organon*) constitute a masterpiece of the human mind. It is not without reason, we may be sure, that Aristotle represents himself as being a pioneer in logical analysis and systematisation. At the close of the *De Sophisticis Elenchis* he remarks, that while much had been said by others before him on the subject of Rhetoric, for instance, he had no anterior work to speak of on the subject of reasoning, which he might have used as a foundation, but was compelled to break what was practically new ground. It was not the case that systematic analysis of the reasoning-processes had been already completed in part: nothing at all existed in this line. The professors of rhetoric had given their pupils an empirical training in "contentious arguments," but they never worked out a scientific methodology or a systematic exposition of the subject: he had had to start from the beginning by himself. Aristotle's claim in reference to the particular subject-matter of the *De Sophisticis Elenchis* is doubtless substantially just in regard to the discovery and analysis of the syllogism in general.

Occasionally one hears people speak as though modern logical studies had deprived the traditional Aristotelian logic of all value, as though one could now relegate the traditional logic to the lumber-room of museum pieces, of interest only to the philosophical antiquarian. On the other hand, those who have been brought up according to the Aristotelian tradition may be tempted to display a mistaken loyalty to that tradition by attacking, e.g. modern symbolic logic. Either extreme is in fact unwarranted, and it is necessary to adopt a sane and balanced position, recognising indeed the incompleteness of the Aristotelian logic and the value of modern logic, but at the same time refusing to discredit the Aristotelian logic on the ground that it does not cover the whole province of logic. This sane and balanced position is the position maintained by those who have made a deep study of logic, a point that needs to be emphasised lest it be thought that it is only Scholastic philosophers, speaking *pro domo sua*, who in the present age still attach any value to the logic of Aristotle. Thus, while affirming, and rightly affirming, that "it is no longer possible to regard it as constituting the whole subject of deduction," Susan Stebbing admits that "the traditional syllogism retains its value";[1] while Heinrich Scholz declares that "the

[1] Susan Stebbing, *A Modern Introd. to Logic*, p. 102. (London, 1933.)

Aristotelian *Organon* is to-day still the most beautiful and instructive introduction to logic ever written by man."[1] Modern symbolic logic may be an addition, and a very valuable addition, to the logic of Aristotle, but it should not be regarded as a completely opposite counter thereto: it differs from non-symbolic logic by its higher degree of formalisation, e.g. by the idea of propositional functionality.

9. This necessarily brief and curtailed treatment of the Aristotelian logic may profitably be concluded by a summary of a *few characteristic topics* discussed in the *Organon*, a summary from which will appear the wide range of the Aristotelian logical analysis. In the *Categories*, Aristotle treats of the range of variability of Subject and *Predicate*, in the *De Interpretatione* of the opposition of propositions, modal and assertoric, which leads him into an interesting discussion of excluded middle in Chapters 7 and 10. In the first book of the *Prior Analytics* he discusses the conversion of pure propositions and of necessary and contingent propositions, analyses the syllogisms in the three figures, and gives rules for constructing or discovering syllogisms dealing with, e.g. oblique inference (Ch. 36), negation (Ch. 46), proofs *per impossibile* and *ex hypothesi* (Chs. 23 and 44). In the second book Aristotle deals with the distribution of truth and falsity between premisses and conclusion, the defects in the syllogism, induction in a narrow sense, through "enumeration of all the cases" (Ch. 23), the enthymeme, etc.

The first book of the *Posterior Analytics* treats of the structure of a deductive science and its logical starting-point, the unity, diversity, distinction and logical ranking of sciences, ignorance, error and invalidity; while the second book is concerned with definitions, essential and nominal, the difference between definition and demonstration, the indemonstrability of the essential nature, the way in which basic truths become known, etc. The *Topics* is concerned with the predicables, definition, the technique of proof or the practice of dialectic, the *De Sophisticis Elenchis* with the classification of fallacies and their solutions.

---

[1] *Geschichte der Logik*, p. 27. (Berlin, 1931.)

CHAPTER XXIX

THE METAPHYSICS OF ARISTOTLE

1. "ALL men by nature desire to know."[1] So does Aristotle optimistically begin the *Metaphysics*, a book, or rather collection of lectures, which is difficult to read (the Arabian philosopher Avicenna said that he had read the *Metaphysics* of Aristotle forty times without understanding it), but which is of the greatest importance for an understanding of the philosophy of Aristotle, and which has had a tremendous influence on the subsequent thought of Europe.[2] But though all men desire to know, there are different degrees of knowledge. For example, the man of *mere experience*, as Aristotle calls him, may know that a certain medicine had done good to X when he was ill, but without knowing the reason for this, whereas the man of *art* knows the reason, e.g. he knows that X was suffering from fever, and that the medicine in question has a certain property which abates fever. He knows a universal, for he knows that the medicine will tend to cure all who suffer from that complaint. Art, then, aims at production of some kind, but this is not Wisdom in Aristotle's view, for the highest Wisdom does not aim at producing anything or securing some effect—it is not utilitarian—but at apprehending the first principles of Reality, i.e. at knowledge for its own sake. Aristotle places the man who seeks for knowledge for its own sake above him who seeks for knowledge of some particular kind with a view to the attainment of some practical effect. In other words, that science stands higher which is desirable for its own sake and not merely with a view to its results.

This science, which is desirable for its own sake, is the science of first principles or first causes, a science which took its rise in wonder. Men began to wonder at things, to desire to know the explanation of the things they saw, and so philosophy arose out

[1] *Metaph.*, A, 980 a 1.

[2] The name *Metaphysics* simply refers to the position of the *Metaphysics* in the Aristotelian Corpus, i.e. as coming after the *Physics*. But the book is metaphysical also in the sense that it concerns the first and highest principles and causes, and so involves a higher degree of abstraction than does the *Physics*, which deals predominantly with a particular type of being—that which is subject to motion. Still, it is true to say that if we wish to know Aristotle's doctrine on the themes treated of to-day under the heading *Metaphysics*, we must consult not only the *Metaphysics* itself but also the *Physics*.

of the desire of understanding, and not on account of any utility that knowledge might possess. This science, then, is of all sciences to be called free or liberal, for, like a free man, it exists for its own sake and not for the sake of someone else. Metaphysics is thus, according to Aristotle, Wisdom *par excellence*, and the philosopher or lover of Wisdom is he who desires knowledge about the ultimate cause and nature of Reality, and desires that knowledge for its own sake. Aristotle is therefore a "dogmatist" in the sense that he supposes that such knowledge is attainable, though he is not of course a dogmatist in the sense of advancing theories without any attempt to prove them.

Wisdom, therefore, deals with the first principles and causes of things, and so is universal knowledge in the highest degree. This means that it is the science which is furthest removed from the senses, the most abstract science, and so is the hardest of the sciences as involving the greatest effort of thought. "Sense-perception is common to all and therefore easy and no mark of Wisdom."[1] But, though it is the most abstract of the sciences, it is, in Aristotle's view, the most *exact* of the sciences, "for those which involve fewer principles are more exact than those which involve additional principles, e.g. arithmetic than geometry."[2] Moreover, this science is in itself the most knowable, since it deals with the first principles of all things, and these principles are in themselves more truly knowable than their applications (for these depend on the first principles, and not vice versa), though it does not follow that they are the most knowable in regard *to us*, since we necessarily start with the things of sense and it requires a considerably effort of rational abstraction to proceed from what is directly known to us, sense-objects, to their ultimate principles.

2. The causes with which Wisdom or philosophy deals are enumerated in the *Physics* and are four in number: (i) the substance or essence of a thing; (ii) the matter or subject; (iii) the source of motion or the efficient cause; and (iv) the final cause or good. In the first book of the *Metaphysics* Aristotle investigates the views of his predecessors, in order, he says, to see if they discussed any other kind of cause besides the four he has enumerated. In this way he is led to give a brief sketch of the history of Greek philosophy up to his time, but he is not concerned to catalogue all their opinions, whether relevant or irrelevant to his purpose, for he wishes to trace the evolution of the notion of the

---

[1] *Metaph.*, 982 a 11-12.   [2] *Metaph.*, 982 a 26-8.

four causes, and the net result of his investigation is the conclusion, not only that no philosopher has discovered any other kind of cause, but that no philosopher before himself has enumerated the four causes in a satisfactory manner. Aristotle, like Hegel, regarded previous philosophy as leading up to his own position; there is none of the paraphernalia of the dialectic in Aristotle, of course, but there is the same tendency to regard his own philosophy as a synthesis on a higher plane of the thought of his predecessors. There is certainly some truth in Aristotle's contention, yet it is by no means completely true, and he is sometimes far from just to his predecessors.

Thales and the early Greek philosophers busied themselves with the material cause, trying to discover the ultimate substratum of things, the principle that is neither generated nor destroyed, but from which particular objects arise and into which they pass away. In this way arose, e.g. the philosophies of Thales, Anaximenes, Heraclitus, who posited one material cause, or Empedocles, who postulated four elements. But èven if elements are generated from one material cause, why does this happen, what is the source of the movement whereby objects are generated and destroyed? There must be some cause of the becoming in the world, even the very facts themselves must in the end impel the thinker to investigate a type of cause other than the material cause. Attempted answers to this difficulty we find in the philosophies of Empedocles and Anaxagoras. The latter saw that no material element can be the reason why objects manifest beauty and goodness, and so he asserted the activity of Mind in the material world, standing out like a sober man in contrast with the random talk of his predecessors.[1] All the same, he uses Mind only as a *deus ex machina* to explain the formation of the world, and drags it in when he is at a loss for any other explanation: when another explanation is at hand, he simply leaves Mind out.[2] In other words, Anaxagoras was accused by Aristotle of using Mind simply as a cloak for ignorance. Empedocles, indeed, postulated two active principles, Friendship and Strife, but he used them neither sufficiently nor consistently.[3] These philosophers, therefore, had succeeded in distinguishing two of Aristotle's four causes, the material cause and the source of movement; but they had not worked out their conceptions systematically or elaborated any consistent and scientific philosophy.

[1] *Metaph.*, 984 b 15–18. [2] *Metaph.*, 985 a 18–21. [3] *Metaph.*, 985 a 21–3.

After the philosophy of the Pythagoreans, who cannot be said to have contributed very much, came the philosophy of Plato, who evolved the doctrine of the Forms, but placed the Forms, which are the cause of the essence of things (and so, in a sense, the cause), apart from the things of which they are the essence. Thus Plato, according to Aristotle, used only two causes, "that of the essence and the material cause."[1] As to the final cause, this was not explicitly, or at least not satisfactorily, treated by previous philosophers, but only by the way or incidentally.[2] As a matter of fact, Aristotle is not altogether just to Plato, since the latter, in the *Timaeus*, introduces the concept of the Demiurge who serves as an efficient cause, and also makes use of the star-gods, besides maintaining a doctrine of finality, for the final cause of becoming is the realisation (in the sense of imitation) of the Good. Nevertheless, it is true that Plato, through the *chorismos*, was debarred from making the realisation of its immanent form or essence the final cause of the concrete substance.

3. After stating some of the main problems of philosophy in Book three (B) of the *Metaphysics*, Aristotle declares at the beginning of Book four (Γ) that metaphysical science is concerned with being as such, is the study of being *qua* being. The special sciences isolate a particular sphere of being, and consider the attributes of being in that sphere; but the metaphysician does not consider being of this or that particular characteristic, e.g. as living or as quantitative, but rather being itself and its essential attributes as being. Now, to say that something is, is also to say that it is *one*: unity, therefore, is an essential attribute of being, and just as being itself is found in all the categories, so unity is found in all the categories. As to goodness, Aristotle remarks in the *Ethics* (*E.N.* 1096) that it also is applicable in all the categories. Unity and goodness are, therefore, transcendental attributes of being, to use the phraseology of the Scholastic philosophers, inasmuch as, applicable in all the categories, they are not confined to any one category and do not constitute genera. If the definition of man is "rational animal," animal is the genus, rational the specific difference; but one cannot predicate animality of rationality, the genus of the specific difference, though one can predicate being of both. Being, therefore, cannot be a genus, and the same holds good of unity and goodness.

The term "being," however, is not predicated of all existent

---

[1] *Metaph.*, 988 a 8–10.   [2] *Metaph.*, 988 b 6–16.

things in precisely the same sense, for a substance is, possesses
being, in a way that a quality, for instance, which is an affection
of substance, cannot be said to be. With what category of being,
then, is metaphysics especially concerned? With that of substance,
which is primary, since all things are either substances or affections
of substances. But there are or may be different kinds of substances, and with which kind does first philosophy or metaphysics
deal? Aristotle answers that, if there is an unchangeable substance, then metaphysics studies unchangeable substance, since
it is concerned with being *qua* being, and the true nature of being
is shown in that which is unchangeable and self-existent, rather
than in that which is subject to change. That there is at least
one such unchangeable being which causes motion while remaining
itself unmoved, is shown by the impossibility of an infinite series
of existent sources of movement, and this motionless substance,
comprising the full nature of being, will have the character of
the divine, so that first philosophy is rightly to be called theology.
Mathematics is a theoretical science indeed and deals with motionless objects, but these objects, *though considered in separation from
matter*, do not exist separately: physics deals with things that are
both inseparable from matter and are subject to movement: it
is only metaphysics that treats of that which both exists in
separation from matter and is motionless.[1]

(In Book *E* of the *Metaphysics* Aristotle simply divides substances into changeable and unchangeable substances, but in
Book Λ he distinguishes three kinds of substances, (i) sensible
and perishable, (ii) sensible and eternal, i.e. the heavenly bodies,
(iii) non-sensible and eternal.)

Metaphysical science is, therefore, concerned with being, and it
studies being primarily in the category of substance, not "accidental being," which is the object of no science,[2] nor being as
truth, since truth and falsity exist in the judgment, not in things.[3]
(It also establishes the first principles or axioms, especially the
principle of contradiction, which, though not of course deducible,
is the ultimate principle governing all being and all knowledge.[4])
But, if metaphysics studies substance, non-sensible substance, it
is obviously of importance to determine what non-sensible substances there are. Are the objects of mathematics substances, or

[1] *Metaph.*, 1026 a 6–32. Cf. 1064 a 28–b 6.
[2] *Metaph.*, VI (E) 2. E.g. a confectioner aims at giving pleasure; if his productions produce health, that is "accidental."
[3] *Metaph.*, VI (E), 4.   [4] *Metaph.*, IV (Γ), 3 ff.

universals, or the transcendental ideas of being and unity? No, replies Aristotle, they are not: hence his polemic against the Platonic theory of ideas, of which a summary will now be given.

4. (i) The argument for Plato's theory that it makes scientific knowledge possible and explains it, proves, says Aristotle, that the universal is real and no mere mental fiction; but it does not prove that the universal has a subsistence apart from individual things. And, indeed, on Plato's theory, strictly applied, there should be Ideas of negations and relations. For if, whenever we conceive a common concept in relation to a plurality of objects, it is necessary to postulate a Form, then it follows that there must be Forms even of negations and relations. "Of the ways in which we prove that the Forms exist, none is convincing, for from some no inference necessarily follows, and from some it follows that there are Forms of things of which we think there are no Forms."[1]

(ii) The doctrine of Ideas or Forms is *useless.*

(*a*) According to Aristotle, the Forms are only a purposeless doubling of visible things. They are supposed to explain why the multitude of things in the world exist. But it does not help simply to suppose the existence of another multitude of things, as Plato does. Plato is like a man who, unable to count with a small number, thinks that he will find it easier to do so if he doubles the number.[2]

(*b*) The Forms are useless for our knowledge of things. "They help in no wise towards the knowledge of the other things (for they are not even the substance of these, else they would have been in them.[3])" This seems to be an expression of Aristotle's interest in the visible universe, whereas Plato was not really concerned with the things of this world for their own sake, but as stepping-stones to the Forms; though, by getting to know the Types, at which phenomena are, as it were, aiming or which they are trying to realise, we can, inasmuch as we are efficient causes, contribute to this approximate realisation. To this consideration Plato attached very considerable importance. For example, by coming to know the ideal Type of the State, to which actual States are, in a greater or less degree, approximations, we are enabled to contribute to the elevation of the actual State—for we know the goal.

(*c*) The Forms are useless when it comes to explaining the movement of things. Even if things exist in virtue of the Forms,

---

[1] *Metaph.*, 990 b 8–11.   [2] *Metaph.*, 990 a 34–b 8.   [3] *Metaph.*, 991 a 12–13.

how do the latter account for the movement of things and for
their coming-to-be and passing-away? "Above all one might
discuss the question what on earth the Forms contribute to
sensible things, either to those that are eternal or to those that
come into being and cease to be."[1] The Forms are motionless,
and the objects of this world, if they are copies of the Forms,
should be motionless too; or, if they move, as they do, whence
their motion?

Aristotle would not seem to be altogether just to Plato in
pursuing this line of criticism, since Plato fully realised that the
Forms are not moving causes, and it was precisely on this account
that he introduced the concept of the Demiurge. The latter may
be a more or less mythological figure, but, however that may be,
it is clear that Plato never considered the Forms to be principles
of motion and that he made an attempt to account for the
dynamism of the world on other lines.

(d) The Forms are supposed to explain sensible objects. But
they will themselves be sensible: the Ideal Man, for instance, will
be sensible, like Socrates. The Forms will resemble the anthropomorphic gods: the latter were only eternal men, and so the Forms
are only "eternal sensibles."[2]

This is not a very telling criticism. If the Ideal Man is conceived as being a replica of concrete man on the ideal plane, in
the common sense of the word "ideal," as being actual man raised
to the highest pitch of development, then of course Ideal Man
will be sensible. But is it at all likely that Plato himself meant
anything of this kind? Even if he may have implied this by the
phrases he used on certain occasions, such an extravagant notion
is by no means essential to the Platonic theory of Forms. The
Forms are subsistent concepts or Ideal Types, and so the subsistent concept of Man will contain the idea of corporeality, for
instance, but there is no reason why it should itself be corporeal:
in fact, corporeality and sensibility are *ex hypothesi* excluded
when it is postulated that the Ideal Man means an *Idea*. Does
anybody suppose that when later Platonists placed the Idea of
man in the Divine Mind, they were positing an actual concrete
man in God's Mind? The objection seems really to be a debating
point on Aristotle's part, i.e. so far as it is supposed to touch
Plato personally, and that not a particularly fair one. It would
be conclusive against a very gross rendering of the theory of

[1] *Metaph.*, 991 a 8-10.   [2] *Metaph.*, 997 b 5-12.

Forms; but it is useless to read into Plato the most gross and crude interpretation possible.

(iii) The theory of Ideas or Forms is an *impossible* theory.

(*a*) "It must be held to be impossible that the substance, and that of which it is the substance, should exist apart; how, therefore, can the Ideas, being the substance of things, exist apart?"[1] The Forms contain the essence and inner reality of sensible objects; but how can objects which exist apart from sensibles contain the essence of those sensibles? In any case, what is the relation between them? Plato tries to explain the relation by the use of terms such as "participation" and "imitation," but Aristotle retorts that "to say that they (i.e. sensible things) are patterns and the other things share in them, is to use empty words and poetical metaphors."[2]

This criticism would certainly be a very serious one if separation meant local separation. But does separation, in the case of the Forms, necessarily imply local separation? Does it not rather mean independence? Literal local separation would be impossible if the Forms are to be looked on as subsistent concepts or Ideas. It seems that Aristotle is arguing from the point of view of his own theory, according to which the form is the immanent essence of the sensible object. He argues that participation can mean nothing, unless it means that there is a real immanent form, co-constitutive of the object with matter—a conception not admitted by Plato. Aristotle rightly points out the inadequacy of the Platonic theory; but, in rejecting Platonic exemplarism, he also betrays the inadequacy of his own (Aristotle's) theory, in that he provides no real transcendental ground for the fixity of essences.

(*b*) "But, further, all things cannot come from the Forms in any of the usual senses of 'from'."[3] Here Aristotle again touches on the question of the relation of the Forms to that of which they are said to be Forms, and it is in this connection that he objects that the explanatory phrases used by Plato are merely poetical metaphors. This is of course one of the crucial points of the Platonic theory, and Plato himself seems to have felt the inadequacy of the attempted explanation. He cannot be said to have cleared up in any satisfactory manner what he actually meant by the metaphors he used and what the relation of sensible

---

[1] *Metaph.*, 991 b 1–3.   [2] *Metaph.*, M, 1079 b 24–6; A, 991 a 20–2.
[3] *Metaph.*, A, 991 a 19–20.

objects to the Forms really is. But it is curious that Aristotle, in his treatment of the Platonic theory in the *Metaphysics*, neglects the Demiurge altogether. One might suggest as a reason for this neglect, that the ultimate cause of motion in the world was, for Aristotle, a *Final* Cause. The notion of a super-terrestrial *efficient* Cause was for him unacceptable.

(*c*) The Forms will be individual objects like those other objects of which they are the Forms, whereas they should be not individuals but *universals*. The Ideal Man, for instance, will be an individual like Socrates. Further, on the supposition that when there is a plurality of objects possessing a common name, there must be an eternal pattern or Form, we shall have to posit a third man (τρίτος ἄνθρωπος), whom not only Socrates imitates, but also the Ideal Man. The reason is that Socrates and the Ideal Man have a nature in common, therefore there must be a subsistent universal beyond them. But in this case the difficulty will always recur and we shall proceed to infinity.[1]

This criticism of Aristotle would hold good if Plato held that the Forms are things. But did he? If he held them to be subsistent concepts, they do not turn into individual objects in the same sense that Socrates is an individual object. Of course they are individual concepts, but there are signs that Plato was trying to systematise the whole world of concepts or Ideas, and that he envisaged them as forming one articulated system—the rational structure of the world, as we might say, that the world, to speak metaphorically, is always trying to embody, but which it cannot fully embody, owing to the contingency which is inevitable in all material things. (We are reminded of Hegel's doctrine of the universal Categories in relation to the contingent objects of Nature.)

(iv) Against the theory that the Forms are Numbers.

(*a*) It scarcely seems necessary to treat of Aristotle's objections and criticisms in detail, since the Form-Number theory was perhaps an unfortunate adventure on Plato's part. As Aristotle remarks, "mathematics has come to be the whole of philosophy for modern thinkers, though they say that it should be studied for the sake of other things."[2]

For Aristotle's general treatment of number and pertinent questions, one should see *Metaphysics* A, 991 b 9 to 993 a 10 and M and N.

---

[1] *Metaph.*, A, 990 b 15–17; K, 1059 b 8–9. [2] *Metaph.*, 992 a 32–b 1.

(b) If the Forms are Numbers, how can they be causes?[1] If it is because existing things are other numbers (e.g. "one number is man, another is Socrates, another Callias"), then why "are the one set of numbers causes of the other set"? If it is meant that Callias is a numerical ratio of his elements, then his Idea will also be a numerical ratio of elements, and so neither will be, properly speaking, a number. (Of course, for Plato the Forms were exemplary causes, but not efficient causes.)

(c) How can there be two kinds of numbers?[2] If besides the Form-numbers it is also necessary to posit another kind of numbers, which are the mathematical objects, then what is the basis of differentiation between the two kinds of numbers? We only know one kind of numbers, thinks Aristotle, and that is the kind of numbers with which the mathematician deals.

(d) But whether there are two classes of numbers, i.e. Forms and mathematical objects (Plato) or simply one class, i.e. mathematical numbers existing, however, apart from sensible objects (Speusippus), Aristotle objects (i) that if the Forms are numbers, then they cannot be unique, since the elements of which they are composed are the same (as a matter of fact, the Forms were not supposed to be unique in the sense that they were without inner relation to one another); and (ii) that the objects of mathematics "cannot in any way exist separately."[3] One reason for the latter assertion is that a *processus in infinitum* will be unavoidable if we accept the separate existence of mathematical objects, e.g. there must be separate solids corresponding to the sensible solids, and separate planes and lines corresponding to the sensible planes and lines. But there must also be other separate planes and lines corresponding to the planes and lines of the separate solid. Now, "the accumulation becomes absurd, for we find ourselves with one set of solids apart from the sensible solids; three sets of planes apart from the sensible planes—those which exist apart from the sensible planes, and those in the mathematical solids, and those which exist apart from those in the mathematical solids; four sets of lines; and five sets of points. With which of these, then, will the mathematical sciences deal?"[4]

(e) If the substance of things is mathematical, then what is the source of movement? "If the great and the small are to *be* movement, evidently the Forms will be moved; but if they are not,

[1] *Metaph.*, 991 b 9 ff. [2] *Metaph.*, e.g. 991 b 27–31. [3] *Metaph.*, b 1077 –1214. [4] *Metaph.*, 1076 b 28–34.

whence did movement come? If we cannot answer this, the whole study of Nature has been annihilated."[1] (As already remarked, Plato tried to provide a source of movement other than the Forms themselves, which are motionless.)

(v) Some of what Aristotle has to say on the subject of Plato's mathematical objects and the Form-numbers implies a rather crude interpretation of Platonic doctrine, as though for example Plato imagined that mathematical objects or the Forms are things. Moreover, Aristotle has himself to meet the great difficulty against the abstraction theory of mathematics (for Aristotle the geometrician, for instance, considers, not separate mathematical objects but sensible things abstractly, i.e. according to one particular point of view), namely, that we cannot abstract e.g. the perfect circle from nature, since there is no perfect circle in nature which we could abstract, while on the other hand it is difficult to see how we could form the idea of a perfect circle by "correcting" the imperfect circles of nature, when we should not know that the circles of nature *were* imperfect unless we *previously* knew what a perfect circle was. To this Aristotle might answer either that, though perfect circles are not given really, i.e. as regards measurement, in nature, yet they are given *quoad visum*, and that this is sufficient for the abstraction of the idea of the perfect circle, or that mathematical figures and axioms are more or less arbitrary hypotheses, so that the cardinal requisite in mathematics is to be consistent and logical, without its being necessary to suppose that e.g. every type of geometry will fit the "real" world, or, on the other hand, that it has an ideal world corresponding to it, of which it is the mental reflection or perception.

In general, we would point out that we cannot well dispense with either Plato or Aristotle, but that the truth in both of them has to be combined. This the Neo-Platonists attempted to do. For example, Plato posited the Forms as Exemplary Causes: the later Platonists placed them in God. With due qualifications, this is the correct view, for the Divine Essence is the ultimate Exemplar of all creatures.[2] On the other hand, Plato assumes that we

---

[1] *Metaph.*, A, 992 b 7–9.

[2] St. Thomas Aquinas, who quotes St. Augustine as to the Divine Ideas, teaches that there is a plurality of ideas in the Divine Mind (*S.T.*, I, 15, 2), rejecting the opinion of Plato that they are "outside" the Divine Mind (cf. *S.T.*, I, 15, 1, ad 1). He explains that he does not mean that there is a plurality of accidental *species* in God, but that God, knowing perfectly His Essence, knows it as imitable (or *participabilis*) by a plurality of creatures.

have, or can have, direct knowledge of the Forms. Now, we certainly have not got a direct knowledge of the Divine Ideas, as Malebranche supposed we have. We have direct knowledge only of the expressed universal, and this expressed universal exists externally, i.e. as universal, only in the particulars. We have therefore the external exemplary Idea in God, the foundation in the particular object, i.e. its specific essence, and the abstract universal in our minds. From this point of view Aristotle's criticism of Plato would seem to be justified, for the universal, of which we have direct knowledge, simply is the nature of the individual thing. It would appear, therefore, that we require both Plato and Aristotle in order to form anything like a complete philosophical view. Plato's Demiurge must be identified with the Aristotelian νόησις νοήσεως, the eternal Forms must be referred to God, and Aristotle's doctrine of the concrete universal must be accepted, together with the Aristotelian doctrine of abstraction. Neither of these two great thinkers can be accepted precisely as he stands, and while it is right to value Aristotle's criticism of the Platonic theory of Forms, it is a great mistake to suppose that that theory was a mass of crude absurdity, or that it can be dispensed with altogether. The Augustinian philosophy was, through Neo-Platonism, strongly impregnated with the thought of Plato.

Although it has been admitted that Aristotle's fundamental criticism of the Platonic theory of Forms, that the theory involves the *chorismos*, is justified, and that the Platonic theory cannot stand by itself but needs to be supplemented by Aristotle's doctrine of the immanent Form (which we consider abstractly in its universality), we have not given an altogether sympathetic treatment of Aristotle's criticisms. "How, then," it might be asked, "can you say that Aristotle's statements concerning what Plato taught must be taken seriously? If Aristotle's account of what Plato taught is correct, then his criticisms of the Platonic theory were perfectly justified, while if his criticisms misrepresent the Platonic theory, then he either deliberately misrepresented that theory or he did not understand it."

First of all, it must be admitted that Aristotle was attacking, in his own mind at least, the theory of Plato himself, and not merely that of some Platonists as distinct from Plato: a careful reading of the *Metaphysics* hardly permits any other supposition. Secondly, it must be admitted that Aristotle, though primarily perhaps attacking the form of the Platonic theory that was taught in the Academy, was perfectly well acquainted with the content of the published dialogues, and knew that some of his own criticisms had already been raised in the *Parmenides*. Thirdly, there is no real reason for supposing that the Platonic theory as taught in the Academy involved a retraction or rejection of the theory developed in the published works of Plato: if this had been the case, we might reasonably have expected Aristotle to make some reference to the fact; while conversely, if he makes no reference to such a change of view on Plato's part, we have no right to affirm such a change without better evidence than can be offered. The mathematical form of the theory was probably meant to be a supplement to the theory, or, rather, a speculative justification and elucidation of it, an 'esoteric' version of it (if one may use a word with somewhat unfortunate associations, without at the same time wishing to imply that the mathematical version was *another* and *different* theory). Aristotle, therefore, was attacking, under both its aspects, what he regarded as the *Platonic* theory of Ideas. (It must, however, be remembered that the *Metaphysics* is not a continuous book, written for publication, and that we cannot assume without more ado that all the objections raised against the Platonic theory in Aristotle's lectures were regarded with equal seriousness by Aristotle himself. A man may say things in his lectures that he would not say, in the same form at least, in a work intended for publication.)

It would seem, then, that we are faced by an awkward dilemma. Either Plato, in spite of the difficulties that he himself saw and proposed in the *Parmenides*, held the theory in the exact form under which it was attacked by Aristotle (in which case Plato appears in a foolish light), or Aristotle grossly misunderstood the Platonic theory (in which case it is Aristotle who appears as the fool). Now, we are not willing to admit that either Plato or Aristotle was a fool, and any treatment of the problem that necessarily involves either supposition is to our mind thereby ruled out of court. That Plato on the one hand never really solved satisfactorily the problem of the *chorismos*, and that Aristotle on the other hand was not perfectly *au fait* with contemporary higher mathematics, does not show either of them to be a fool and can easily be admitted; but this admission obviously does not dispose of the difficulty involved by Aristotle's criticisms, that the Platonic theory is therein depicted as excessively naïve, and that

Aristotle makes little reference to the dialogues and is silent as to the Demiurge. But perhaps a way out of the difficulty can be found. Aristotle, well aware that Plato had not satisfactorily solved the problem of the *chorismos*, had broken away from his Master's theory and adopted a quite different standpoint. When he regarded the theory *from that standpoint*, it could not but appear to him as extravagant and bizarre under any form: he might, therefore, have easily considered himself justified in attempting to put this bizarre character of the theory in an exaggerated light for polemical purposes. One might cite as a parallel the case of Hegel. To one who believes that the Hegelian system is a mere intellectual *tour de force* or an *extravaganza*, nothing is easier than to overstate and even to misrepresent the undoubtedly weak elements in that system for polemical purposes, even though the critic, believing the system to be fundamentally false, could not be justly accused of deliberate misrepresentation. We would wish that the critic had acted otherwise in the interests of historical accuracy, but we could hardly dub him an imbecile because he had chosen to overdo the rôle of critic. While refusing to believe that Aristotle felt towards Plato any of the animus that Schelling and Schopenhauer felt towards Hegel, I would suggest that Aristotle overdid the rôle of critic and exaggerated weak points in a theory that he considered false. As to his silence concerning the Demiurge, that can be explained, in part at least, if we remember that Aristotle was criticising Plato from his own (i.e. Aristotle's) standpoint, and that the conception of the Demiurge was unacceptable to him: he did not take it seriously. If, in addition, Aristotle had reason to believe that the actual Demiurge of the *Timaeus* was largely a symbolic figure, and *if* Plato never worked out thoroughly, even in the Academy, the precise nature or status of Mind or Soul, then it is not so difficult to understand how Aristotle, who did not believe in any formation of the world *a tergo*, could neglect the figure of the Demiurge altogether in his criticism of the Ideal Theory. He may have been unjustified in neglecting it to the extent that he did, but the foregoing considerations may make it easier to understand how he could do so. The suggestions we have made may not be altogether satisfactory, and no doubt remain open to serious criticism, but they have at least this advantage, that they make it possible for us to escape from the dilemma of holding either Plato or Aristotle to have been a fool. And after all, Aristotle's root criticism of

Plato's theory is perfectly justified, for by using the terms "imitation" and "participation," Plato clearly implies that there is some formal element, some principle of comparative stability, in material things, while on the other hand, by failing to provide a theory of substantial form, he failed to explain this immanent formal element. Aristotle rightly provided this element, but, seeing (rightly again) that the Platonic Forms, being "separate," *could not* account for this element, he unfortunately went too far by rejecting the Platonic exemplarism altogether: looking on the Platonic theory from the point of view of a *biologist* primarily (with a biologist's insistence on the immanent entelechy) and from the theological standpoint envisaged in the *Metaphysics* (xii), he had no use for Platonic exemplarism, Platonic mathematicism and the Platonic Demiurge. Thus, when regarded in the light of his own system, Aristotle's attitude towards Plato's theory is quite understandable.

5. But although Aristotle passes an adverse criticism on the Platonic theory of separate Ideas or Forms, he is in full agreement with Plato that the universal is not merely a subjective concept or a mode of oral expression (*universale post rem*), for to the universal in the mind there corresponds the specific essence in the object, though this essence does not exist in any state of separation *extra mentem*: it is separated only in the mind and through the mind's activity. Aristotle was convinced, as Plato was, that the universal is the object of science: it follows, then, that if the universal is in no way real, if it has no objective reality whatsoever, there is no scientific knowledge, for science does not deal with the individual as such. The universal is real, it has reality not only in the mind but also in the things, though the existence in the thing does not entail that formal universality that it has in the mind. Individuals belonging to the same species are real substances, but they do not partake in an objective universal that is numerically the same in all members of the class. This specific essence is numerically different in each individual of the class, but, on the other hand, it is specifically the same in all the individuals of the class (i.e. they are all alike in species), and this objective similarity is the real foundation for the abstract universal, which has numerical identity in the mind and can be predicated of all the members of the class indifferently. Plato and Aristotle are, then, at one as to the character of true science, namely, that it is directed to the universal element in things, i.e.

to the specific similarity. The scientist is not concerned with individual bits of gold as individual, but with the essence of gold, with that specific similarity which is found in all individual bits of gold, i.e. supposing that gold is a species. "Socrates gave the impulse to this theory" (i.e. the Platonic theory) "by means of his definitions, but he did not separate them" (i.e. the universals) "from the particulars; and in this he thought rightly in not separating them. This is plain from the results, for without the universal it is not possible to get knowledge, but the separation is the cause of the objections that arise with regard to the Ideas."[1] *Strictly* speaking, therefore, there is no objective Universal for Aristotle, but there is an objective foundation in things for the subjective universal in the mind. The universal "horse" is a subjective concept, but it has an objective foundation in the substantial forms that inform particular horses.

The individuals are truly substance (οὐσία). Are the universals substances, i.e. is the specific element, the formal principle, that which places the individual in its specific class, to be called substance? No, says Aristotle, except in a secondary and derived sense. It is the individual alone which is the subject of predication and is itself not predicated of others. The species may, however, be called substance in a secondary sense and it has a claim to this title, since the essential element has a higher reality than the individual *qua* individual and is the object of science. Aristotle, therefore, terms the individuals πρῶται οὐσίαι and the species δεύτεραι οὐσίαι.[2] In this way Aristotle has brought upon himself the charge of contradiction. The alleged contradiction consists in this, that if only the individual is truly substance and if science is concerned with the οὐσία, it necessarily follows that the individual is the true object of science, whereas Aristotle teaches in point of fact the very opposite, namely, that science is not concerned with the individual as such but with the universal. In other words, Aristotle teaches that science is concerned with substance and that the individual is substance in the primary sense, while on the other hand he teaches that the universal is of

---

[1] *Metaph.*, M, 1086 b 2–7. We may compare K, 1059 b 25–6 ("every formula and every science is of universals") and Z 1036 a 28–9 ("definition is of the universal and of the form").

[2] *Categ.* 5. It is to be noted that the terms *first* and *second* in this respect are not valuations but mean first or second *in regard to us*, πρὸς ἡμᾶς. We come to know the individuals first and the universals only secondarily by abstraction, but Aristotle does not depart from his view that the universal is an object of science and has a higher reality than the individual as such.

superior quality and is the true object of science, which would seem to be the exact opposite of what he should teach on his premisses.

In answer to this accusation of self-contradiction, we might answer two things. (i) There is no real contradiction, if we consider what Aristotle *means*. When he says that the individual is truly substance and that it alone is truly substance, he means to reject Plato's doctrine that the universal is a separate substance on its own, but he does not mean to deny that the universal, in the sense of the formal or specific element in things, is real. The individual is truly substance, but that which makes it a substance of this or that kind, that which is the chief element in the thing and is the object of science, is the universal element, the form of the thing, which the mind abstracts and conceives in formal universality. So when he says that the universal is the object of science he is not contradicting himself, for he has not denied that the universal has some objective reality but only that it has a separate existence. It is real in the individual: it is not transcendent, if considered in its objective reality, but immanent, the concrete universal. The individual alone is substance in the true sense, but the individual sensible thing is compound, and the intellect, in scientific knowledge, goes straight to the universal element, which is really there, though existing only concretely, *as an element of the individual*. Aristotle was no doubt influenced by the fact that individuals perish, while the species persists. Thus individual horses perish, whereas the nature of horses remains the same (specifically, though not numerically) in the succession of horses. It is the nature of horses that the scientist considers, and not merely Black Beauty or any other individual horse. (ii) Nor does Aristotle really contradict himself even in terminology, for he expressly distinguishes the two meanings of οὐσία or substance. Substance in the primary sense is the individual substance, composed of matter *and* form: substance in the secondary sense is the formal element or specific essence that corresponds to the universal concept. πρῶται οὐσίαι are objects which are not predicated of another, but of which something else (i.e. accident or τὸ συμβεβηκός) is predicated. Substances in the secondary sense (δεύτεραι οὐσίαι) are the nature, in the sense of specific essence, that which corresponds to the universal concept, ἡ κατὰ τὸν λόγον οὐσία. Moreover, when Aristotle speaks of primary and secondary substances, he does not mean primary and secondary in nature, dignity, or time, but primary and secondary in regard to us.[1]

The individual substance, οὐσία αἰσθητή, is a compound (σύνολον) of the subject or substratum (ὑποκείμενον or ὕλη) and the essence of form. To the individual substance belong the conditions (πάθη) and the relations (πρός τι), which are distinguished according to the nine accidental categories. The universal becomes pre-eminently the object of science, because it is the essential element and so has reality in a higher sense than what is *merely* particular. The universal certainly exists only in the particular, but from this it follows, not that we are unable to make the universal an object of science in its universality, but that we cannot apprehend the universal except through apprehension of the individual.

Is it true, as Aristotle thinks it is true, that universals are necessary for science? (i) If by science is meant knowledge of the universal, the answer is obvious. (ii) If by science is meant Wisdom in the sense in which Aristotle uses the term, then it is perfectly true to say that the philosopher is not concerned with the particular as particular. If, for example, the philosopher is arguing about contingent being, he is not thinking of this or that particular contingent being as such, but with contingent being in its essential nature, even if he uses particular contingent beings as an illustration. If he were confined to the particular contingent beings that have actually been experienced, either by himself or by others whose testimony he could trust, then his conclusion would be limited to those particular beings, whereas he desires as philosopher to reach a universal conclusion which will apply to all possible contingent beings. (iii) If by science is meant "science" in the sense in which we use the term generally to-day, then we must say that, although knowledge of the true universal essence of a class of beings would certainly be desirable and remains the ideal, it is hardly *necessary*. For example, botanists can get along very well in their classification of plants without knowing the essential definition of the plants in question. It is enough for them if they can find phenomena which will suffice to

[1] Professor Zeller remarks: "It is, of course, a contradiction to attribute a higher reality to form, which is always a universal, in comparison to that which is a compound of form and matter, and at the same time to assert that only the universal is the object of knowledge which is in itself the prior and better known. The results of this contradiction are to be observed throughout the whole Aristotelian system." (*Outlines*, p. 274.) This is scarcely a fortunate statement of the alleged contradiction.

delimit and define a species, irrespective of whether the real specific essence is thereby defined or not. It is significant that when Scholastic philosophers wish to give a definition which is representative they so often say "Man is a rational animal." They would scarcely take it upon themselves to give an essential definition of the cow or the buttercup. We frequently have to be content with what we might call the "nominal" essence as opposed to the real essence. Yet even in this case knowledge of *some* universal characteristics is necessary. For even if you cannot assign the difference of some species, yet you have got to define it, if you define it at all, in function of some universal characteristics possessed by the whole class. Suppose that "Rational Animal" is the real definition of man. Now, if you could not attain this definition but had to describe man as e.g. a featherless significantly-speaking biped, you imply a knowledge of the universals "featherlessness" and "significantly-speaking." So even classification or description by accidental characteristics would seem to imply a discerning of the universal in some way, for one discerns the type even if one cannot adequately define it. It is as though one had a dim realisation of the universal, but could not adequately define or grasp it clearly. Universal definition, in the sense of real essential definition, would thus remain the ideal at any rate, even if in practice empirical science can get along without attaining the ideal, and Aristotle is of course speaking of science in its ideal type. He would never agree with the empiricist and nominalist views of e.g. J. S. Mill, although he would doubtless admit that we often have to content ourselves with description instead of true definition.

6. Aristotle, therefore, refuses to admit that the objects of mathematics or universals are substances. In the *Metaphysics*, where he wishes to refute the Platonic theory, he simply denies flatly that they are substances, though in the *Categories*, as we have seen, he called them secondary substances or substances in a secondary and derived sense. In any case, it is the individual that is truly substance, and only the individual. There is, however, this further point to be observed. According to Aristotle,[1] the sensible individuals cannot be defined owing to the material element in them, which renders them perishable and makes them obscure to our knowledge. On the other hand, substance is primarily the definable essence or form of a thing, the principle

[1] *Metaph.*, VII (Z), 15.

in virtue of which the material element is some definite concrete object.[1] It follows from this that substance is primarily form which is, in itself, immaterial, so that if Aristotle begins by asserting that individual sensible objects are substances, the course of his thought carries him on towards the view that pure form alone is truly and primarily substance. But the only forms that are really independent of matter are God, the Intelligences of the spheres and the active intellect in man, so that it is these forms which are primarily substance. If metaphysics studies substance, then, it is easily seen that it is equivalent to "theology." It is certainly not unreasonable to discern here the influence of Platonism, since, in spite of his rejection of the Platonic theory of Ideas, Aristotle evidently continued to look on matter as the element which is impenetrable to thought and on pure form as the intelligible. It is not suggested that Aristotle was wrong in thinking this, but, right or wrong, it is clearly a legacy of Platonism.

7. Aristotle, as we have seen, gives four principles: ἡ ὕλη or matter, τὸ εἶδος or the form, τὸ ὅθεν ἡ κίνησις—the source of movement or the efficient cause, and τὸ οὗ ἕνεκα or the final cause. Change or motion (i.e. motion in the general sense of the term, which includes every passage from a *terminus a quo* to a *terminus ad quem*, such as the change of the colour of a leaf from green to brown) is a fact in the world, in spite of the dismissal of change as illusory by Parmenides, and Aristotle considered this fact of change. He saw that several factors are involved, to each of which justice must be done. There must, for example, be a substratum of change, for in every case of change which we observe there is something that changes. The oak comes from the acorn and the bed from the wood: there is something which is changed, which receives a new determination. First of all, it is in potentiality (δύναμις) to this new determination; then under the action of some efficient cause (τὸ ὅθεν ἡ κίνησις) it receives a new actualisation (ἐντελέχεια). The marble upon which the sculptor works is in potency to receiving the new form or determination which the sculptor gives it, namely, the form of the statue.

Now, when the marble receives the form of the statue, it is indeed changed, but this change is only accidental, in the sense that the substance is still marble, but the shape or figure is

[1] *Ibid.*, 17.

different. In some cases, however, the substance by no means remains the same: thus when the cow eats grass, the grass is assimilated in the process of digestion and takes on a new substantial form. And since it would seem that, absolutely speaking, anything might ultimately change into anything else, it would appear that there is an ultimate substratum which has no definite characteristics of its own, but is simply potentiality as such. This is what Aristotle means by ἡ πρώτη ἑκάστῳ ὑποκειμένη ὕλη[1]— the *materia prima* of the Scholastics—which is found in all material things and is the ultimate basis of change. Aristotle is, of course, perfectly aware that no efficient agent ever acts directly on prime matter as such: it is always some definite thing, some already actualised substratum, that is acted upon. For example, the sculptor works upon the marble; this is his matter, the substratum of the change which he initiates: he does not act upon prime matter as such. Similarly, it is grass which becomes cow, and not prime matter as such. This means that prime matter never exists precisely as such—as bare prime matter, we might say—but always exists in conjunction with form, which is the formal or characterising factor. In the sense that prime matter cannot exist by itself, apart from all form, it is only logically distinguishable from form; but in the sense that it is a real element in the material object, and the ultimate basis of the real changes that it undergoes, it is really distinguishable from form. We should not, therefore, say that prime matter is the simplest body in the material universe, for it is not a body at all, but an element of body, even of the simplest body. Aristotle teaches in the *Physics*[2] that the apparently simplest bodies of the material sublunary world, the four elements, earth, air, fire and water, themselves contain contraries and can be transmuted into one another. But if they can change, then they presuppose composition of potentiality and act. Air, for instance, *is* air, but *can become* fire. It has the form or *actuality* of air, but has also the *potentiality* of becoming fire. But it is logically necessary to

---

[1] Cf. *Physics*, 193 a 29 and 191 a 31-2. λέγω γάρ ὕλην τὸ πρῶτον ὑποκείμενον ἑκάστῳ, ἐξ οὗ γίγνεταί τι ἐνυπάρχοντος μὴ κατὰ συμβεβηκός.
One might also approach prime matter from this point of view. Take any material substance and think away all its definite characteristics, all that it possesses in common with other substances—colour, shape, etc. You are ultimately left with a substratum that is absolutely formless, characterless, that cannot exist by itself, but is logically to be presupposed. This is prime matter. Cf. Stace, *Critical History*, p. 276.

[2] Cf. e.g. *Physics*, I, 6; III, 5.

presuppose, prior to the potentiality of becoming fire or any other particular and definite kind of thing, a potentiality of becoming at all, i.e. a bare potentiality.

Now, change is the development of a previously existing body, not precisely as that definite body, but as a body capable of becoming something else, though as not yet that something else. It is the actualisation of a potentiality; but a potentiality involves an actual being, which is not yet that which it could be. Steam, for example, does not come from nothing, it comes from water. But it does not come from water precisely as water: water precisely as water is water and nothing else. Steam comes from water, which could be steam and "demands" to be steam, having been heated to a certain temperature, but is not yet steam, which is as yet "deprived" of the form of steam—not merely in the sense that it has not got the form of steam, but in the sense that it could have the form of steam and ought to have it but has not yet got it. There are, then, three, and not merely two, factors in change, since the product of change contains two positive elements —form and matter—and presupposes a third element—privation (στέρησις). Privation is not a positive element in the same sense that matter and form are positive elements, but it is, nevertheless, necessarily presupposed by change. Aristotle accordingly gives three presuppositions of change, matter, form and privation or exigency.[1]

8. The concrete sensible substance is thus an individual being, composed of matter and form. But the formal element in such a being, that which makes it this definite thing, is specifically the same in all the members of an *infima species*. For instance, the specific nature or essence of man is the same (though not, of course, numerically the same) in Socrates and in Plato. This being so, it cannot be that the formal element renders the concrete sensible substance this individual, i.e. form cannot be the principle of individuation in sensible objects. What is the individuating principle according to Aristotle? It is matter. Thus Callias and Socrates are the same in form (i.e. the human form or nature), but they are different in virtue of the different matter that is informed.[2] This view of the principle of individuation was adopted by St. Thomas Aquinas, but seeing the difficulty involved in holding that completely characterless prime matter is the principle of individuation, he said that it is *materia signata*

---

[1] *Physics*, I, 7 ff.   [2] *Metaph.*, 1034 a 5–8.

quantitate which individualises matter considered as having an anticipatory exigency for the quantity that it will afterwards actually possess in virtue of its union with form. This theory, that it is matter that individualises, would appear to be a consequence or legacy of Platonism, according to which Form is the universal.

From this theory it logically follows that each pure form must be the only member of its species, must exhaust the possibilities of its species, since there is no matter which can act as a principle of individuation within the species. St. Thomas Aquinas drew this conclusion, and did not hesitate to say (a point in which he was at variance with St. Bonaventure) that the pure intelligences or angels constitute so many species, that there cannot be a plurality of angels or immaterial forms belonging to one species. This conclusion was one that had already occurred to Aristotle himself, for, after observing that plurality depends on matter, he goes on to comment that the immovable first mover, having no matter, must be numerically one, and not only one in formula or definition.[1] It is true that the passage in question seems to be by way of objection against Aristotle's theory of a plurality of unmoved movers, but it at least clear that he was not unaware of the consequence that follows from his doctrine of matter as principle of individuation within the species.

There is a further and a more serious consequence, which would appear to follow from this doctrine. According to Aristotle, matter is at once the principle of individuation and unknowable in itself. Now, from this it appears to follow, that the individual concrete thing is not fully knowable. Moreover, Aristotle, as has been mentioned, explicitly stated that the individual cannot be defined, whereas science is concerned with the definition or essence. The individual as such, therefore, is not the object of science and is not fully knowable. Aristotle does indeed remark[2] concerning individual intelligible (i.e. mathematical circles) and sensible circles (e.g. of bronze or wood) that, though they cannot be defined, they are apprehended by intuition (μετὰ νοήσεως) or perception (αἰσθήσεως); but he did not elaborate this hint or work out any theory of the intuition of the individual. Yet such a theory is surely necessary. For example, we are fully convinced that we can and do know an individual person's character, but we do not arrive at the knowledge by discursive and scientific

[1] *Metaph.*, 1074 a 33–8.   [2] *Metaph.*, 1036 a 2–6.

reasoning. In fact, one can hardly avoid the impression that Aristotle's exaltation of scientific definition, of knowledge of substance in the sense of specific essence, and his depreciation of knowledge of the sensible individual, were little more than a relic of his Platonic education.

9. In the ninth book of the *Metaphysics* Aristotle discusses the notions of potency and act. This is an extremely important distinction, as it enables Aristotle to admit a doctrine of real development. The Megaric School had denied potentiality, but, as Aristotle remarks, it would be absurd to say that the builder who is not actually building cannot build. It is true, of course, in one sense, that he cannot build when he is not actually building, i.e. if "cannot build" be understood as "cannot be actually building" (that is an obvious application of the principle of contradiction); but he has a potentiality for building, a power to build, even when he is not actually employing that power. That potentiality is not simply the negation of actuality can be shown by a simple illustration. A man in a state of deep sleep or coma is not actually thinking, but, being a man, he has the potentiality of thinking, whereas a stone, though it is not actually thinking, has no potentiality for thinking. A natural object is in potency in regard to the full realisation of its form, e.g. an acorn or a small tree in regard to its full development. This potency may be the power to effect a change in another or it may be a power of self-realisation: in either case it is something real, something between not-being and actuality.

Actuality, says Aristotle, is prior to potency.[1] The actual is always produced from the potential, the potential is always reduced to act by the actual, that which is already in act, as man is produced by man. In this sense the actual is *temporally* prior to the potential. But the actual is also prior to the potential *logically*, in principle, since the actuality is the end, that for the sake of which the potency exists or is acquired. Thus, although a boy is temporally prior to his actualisation as man, his manhood is logically prior, since his boyhood is for the sake of his manhood. Moreover, that which is eternal is prior in substance to that which is perishable; and that which is eternal, imperishable, is in the highest sense actual. God, for example, exists necessarily, and that which exists necessarily must be fully actual: as the eternal Source of movement, of the reduction of potentiality to act, God

[1] *Metaph.*, 1049 b 5.

must be full and complete actuality, the Unmoved First Mover. Eternal things, says Aristotle,[1] must be good: there can be in them no defect or badness or perversion. Badness means defect or perversion of some kind, and there can be no defect in that which is fully actual. It follows that there can be no separate bad principle, since that which is without matter is pure form. "The bad does not exist apart from bad things."[2] It is clear from this that God, in the thought of Aristotle, took on something of the character of Plato's Idea of the Good, and indeed he remarks that the cause of all goods is the good itself.[3] The First Unmoved Mover, being the source of all movement, as *final* cause, is the ultimate cause why potentiality is actualised, i.e. why goodness is realised.

It is through the distinction between potency and act that Aristotle answers Parmenides. Parmenides had said that change is impossible, because being cannot come out of not-being (out of nothing comes nothing), while equally it cannot come from being (for being already *is*). Thus fire could not come out of air, since air is air and not fire. To this Aristotle would reply that fire does not come out of air as air, but out of air which can be fire and is not yet fire, that has a potentiality to become fire. Abstractly put, a thing comes into being from its privation. If Parmenides were to object that this is tantamount to saying that a thing comes into being from not-being, Aristotle would answer that it does not come into being from its privation merely (i.e. from bare privation), but from its privation *in a subject*. Were Parmenides to retort that in this case a thing comes into being from being, which is a contradiction, Aristotle could answer that it does not come into being from being precisely as such, but from being which is also not-being, i.e. not the thing which it comes to be. He thus answers the Parmenidean difficulty by recourse to the distinction between form, matter and privation, or (better and more generally), between act, potency and privation.[4]

10. The distinction of potency and act leads to the doctrine of the hierarchy or scale of existence, for it is clear that an object which is in act as regards its own *terminus a quo* may be in potency as regards a further *terminus ad quem*. To use a hackneyed illustration, the hewn stone is in act as regards the unhewn stone—in respect to the latter's potentiality of being hewn—but in potency

---

[1] *Metaph.*, 1051 a 20–1. [2] *Metaph.*, 1051 a 17–18. [3] *Metaph.*, 985 a 9–10.
[4] For a discussion of potentiality and act, cf. *Metaph.*, Δ, 12 and Θ.

as regards the house, in respect to the part it will play in the house that is yet to be built. Similarly, the soul or ψυχή, i.e. the soul in its sensitive aspect and functions, is act in regard to the body, but potency in respect to the higher function of νοῦς. At the bottom of the ladder, so to speak, is prime matter, in itself unknowable and never actually existing apart from form. In union with the contraries, with heat or cold and with dryness or wetness, it forms the four bodies—earth, air, water and fire. These relatively, though not absolutely, simple bodies form in turn inorganic bodies, such as gold, and the simple tissues of living beings (both together called homoemerous bodies). Anomoemerous beings, organisms, are formed of homoemerous bodies as their material. Thus the rungs of the ladder are gradually ascended, until we come to the active intellect of man, unmixed with matter, the separate intelligence of the spheres and finally God. (The doctrine of the scale of existence should not, of course, be understood as involving "evolution." Pure forms do not evolve out of matter. Moreover, Aristotle held that species are eternal, though individual sensible objects perish.)

11. How is change initiated? Stone that is unhewn remains unhewn so far as the stone itself is concerned: it does not hew itself. No more does hewn stone build itself into a house. In both cases an external agent, source of the change or movement, is required. In other words, besides the formal and material causes an *efficient* cause is requisite, τὸ ὅθεν ἡ κίνησις. But this is not necessarily *external* to the thing that undergoes the change: for instance, according to Aristotle, each of the four elements has a natural movement towards its own proper place in the universe (e.g. fire goes "up"), and the element in question will move in accord with its natural motion unless it is hindered. It belongs to the form of the element to tend towards its natural region,[1] and thus the formal and efficient causes coincide. But this does not mean that the efficient cause is always identical with the formal cause: it is identical in the case of the soul, formal principle of the organism, regarded as initiator of movement; but it is not identical in the case of the builder of the house, while in that of the generation of the human being, for example, the efficient cause, the father, is only specifically, and not numerically, the same as the formal cause of the child.

12. It will be remembered that Aristotle thought of himself as

[1] *De Caelo*, 311 a 1–6.

being the first thinker to give real consideration to the final cause, τὸ οὖ ἕνεκα. But though he lays great stress on finality, it would be a mistake to suppose that finality, for Aristotle, is equivalent to *external* finality, as though we were to say, for instance, that grass grows in order that sheep may have food. On the contrary, he insists much more on internal or immanent finality (thus the apple tree has attained its end or purpose, not when the fruit forms a healthy or pleasant food for man or has been made into cider, but when the apple tree has reached that perfection of development of which it is capable, i.e. the perfection of its form), for in his view the formal cause of the thing is normally its final cause as well.[1] Thus the formal cause of a horse is the specific form of horse, but this is also its final cause, since the individual of a species naturally strives to embody as perfectly as may be the specific form in question. This natural striving after the form means that the final, formal and efficient causes are often the same. For example, in the organic substance the soul or ψυχή is the formal cause or determining element in the *compositum*, while at the same time it is also the efficient cause, as source of movement, and final cause, since the immanent end of the organism is the individual embodiment of the specific form. Thus the acorn, in the whole process of its development into a full-grown tree, is tending towards the full realisation of its final cause. In Aristotle's view it is the final cause itself which moves, i.e. by attraction. In the case of the oak tree its final cause, which is also its formal cause, causes the development of the acorn into the oak-tree by drawing up, as it were, the acorn towards the term of its process of development. It might of course be objected that the final cause, the perfected form of the oak, does not as yet exist and so cannot cause, while on the other hand it cannot cause as conceived in the mind (as the idea of the picture in the artist's mind is said to have a causal action), since the acorn is without mind and power of reflection. He would answer, no doubt, by recalling the fact that the form of the acorn is the form of the oak in germ, that it has an innate and natural tendency towards its own full evolution. But difficulties might arise for Aristotle if one were to continue asking questions.

(Of course, in spite of the tendency to run the causes together, Aristotle does not deny that the causes may be physically distinct from one another. For instance, in the building of a house, the

[1] *Metaph.*, H, 1044 a 36-b 11. Cf. *Physics*, B, 7, 198 a 24 ff.

formal cause of the house—so far as one can talk of the formal
cause of a house—is not only conceptually but also physically
distinct from the final cause, the idea or plan of the house in the
architect's mind, as also from the efficient cause or causes. In
general, however, one can say that the efficient, final, formal and
material causes tend to melt, into two, that Aristotle inclines to
reduce the four causes to two, namely, the formal cause and the
material cause (though in our modern use of the term "cause" we
naturally think first of all of efficient causality, and then perhaps
of final causes).

This emphasis on finality does not mean that Aristotle excludes
all mechanical causality, and this in spite of the anthropomorphic
language he uses concerning teleology in nature, e.g. in his famous
saying that "Nature does nothing in vain, nothing superfluous,"[1]
language which is scarcely consistent with the theology of the
Metaphysics at least. Sometimes finality and mechanism combine,
as in the fact that light cannot but pass through the lantern,
since its own particles are finer than those of the horn, though it
thereby serves to preserve us from stumbling;[2] but in other cases
there may be, he thinks, only mechanical causality at work (as in
the fact that the colour of the eyes of the animal has no purpose,
but is due simply to circumstances of birth).[3] Moreover, Aristotle
says explicitly that we must not always look for a final cause,
since some things have to be explained only by material or
efficient causes.[4]

13. Every motion, every transit from potentiality to act,
requires some principle in act, but if every becoming, every object
in movement, requires an actual moving cause, then the world in
general, the universe, requires a First Mover.[5] It is important,
however, to note that the word "First" must not be understood
temporally, since motion, according to Aristotle, is necessarily
eternal (to initiate it or cause it to disappear would itself require
motion). Rather is it to be understood as meaning *Supreme*: the
First Mover is the eternal source of eternal motion. Moreover,
the First Mover is not a Creator-God: the world existed from all
eternity without having been created from all eternity. God
forms the world, but did not create it, and He forms the world, is

---

[1] *De Caelo*, A 4, 271 a 33.
[2] *Anal. Post.*, 94 b 27–31. Cf. *De Gen. An.*, 743 b 16 f.
[3] *De Gen. An.*, 778 a 16–b 19; 789 b 19 f. *De Part. An.*, 642 a 2; 677 a 17–19.
[4] *Metaph.*, 1049 b 24 ff.
[5] For First Mover, see *Metaph.*, Δ and *Physics*, Θ, 6, 258 b 10 f.

the source of motion, by *drawing* it, i.e. by acting as *final* cause. In Aristotle's view, if God caused motion by efficient physical causation—"shoving" the world, as it were—then He Himself would be changed: there would be a reaction of the moved on the mover. He must act, therefore, as Final Cause, by being the object of desire. To this point we shall return in a moment.

In *Metaphysics*, Λ 6 ff., Aristotle shows that this moving Principle must be of such a kind that it is pure act, ἐνέργεια, without potentiality. Presupposing the eternity of the world (if time could come into being there would, he thinks, be a time before time was—which is contradictory—and since time is essentially connected with change, change too must be eternal) he declares that there must be a First Mover which causes change without itself being changed, without having any potentiality, for if, for instance, it could cease from causing motion, then motion or change would not be necessarily eternal—which it is. There must accordingly be a First Mover which is pure act, and if it is pure act, then it must be immaterial, for materiality involves the possibility of being acted upon and changed. Moreover, experience, which shows that there exists the ceaseless, circular motion of the heavens, confirms this argument, since there must be a First Mover to move the heavens.

As we have seen, God moves the universe as Final Cause, as being the object of desire. Apparently God is conceived as moving directly the first heaven, causing the daily rotation of the stars round the earth. He moves by inspiring love and desire (the desirable and the intelligible are the same in the immaterial sphere), and so there must be an Intelligence of the first sphere, and other Intelligences in the other spheres. The Intelligence of each sphere is spiritual, and the sphere desires to imitate the life of its Intelligence as closely as may be. Not being able to imitate it in its spirituality, it does the next best thing by performing a circular movement. In an earlier period Aristotle maintained the Platonic conception of star souls, for in the Περὶ Φιλοσοφίας the stars themselves possess souls and move themselves; but he abandoned the conception in favour of that of the Intelligences of the spheres.

It is a curious fact that Aristotle does not seem to have had any very definite conviction as to the *number* of unmoved movers. Thus in the *Physics* there are three passages which refer to a plurality of unmoved movers,[1] while in the *Metaphysics* a plurality also appears.[2] According to Jaeger, chapter eight of *Metaphysics*, Λ is a later addition on Aristotle's part. In chapters seven and nine (continuous and forming part of the "original" *Metaphysics*) Aristotle speaks of the One Unmoved Mover. But in chapter eight the fifty-five transcendent movers make their appearance. Plotinus afterwards objected that the relation of these to the First Mover is left wholly obscure. He also asks how there can be a plurality of them, if matter is the principle of individuation—as Aristotle held it to be. Now, Aristotle himself saw this last objection, for he inserts the objection in the middle of chapter eight without giving a solution.[3] Even in Theophrastus' time some Aristotelians clung to *one* Unmoved Mover —not seeing how the independent movements caused by the plurality of movers could be harmonised.

It was ultimately due to this notion of a plurality of movers that mediaeval philosophers supposed there were Intelligences or Angels that move the spheres. By making them subordinate to and dependent on the First Mover or God, they were taking up the only possible position, since, if any harmony is to be achieved, then the other movers must move in subordination to the First Mover and should be related by intelligence and desire to Him, whether directly or indirectly, i.e. hierarchically. This the Neo-Platonists saw.

The First Mover, being immaterial, cannot perform any bodily action: His activity must be purely spiritual, and so intellectual. In other words, God's activity is one of thought. But what is the object of His thought? Knowledge is intellectual participation of the object: now, God's object must be the best of all possible objects, and in any case the knowledge enjoyed by God cannot be knowledge that involves change or sensation or novelty. God therefore knows Himself in an eternal act of intuition or self-consciousness. Aristotle, then, defines God as "Thought of Thought," νόησις νοήσεως.[4] God is subsistent thought, which eternally thinks itself. Moreover, God cannot have any object of thought outside Himself, for that would mean that He had an end outside Himself. God, therefore, knows only Himself. St.

---

[1] *Physics*, 258 b 11; 259 a 6–13; 259 b 28–31. (Jaeger thinks that these three passages are later additions, but as it is only in the third passage that A. assumes the actual existence of a plurality of unmoved movers, Ross (*Physics*, pp. 101–2) reasonably concludes that this passage alone was added after the completion of *Metaph.*, Λ).

[2] *Metaph.*, Λ 8.   [3] *Metaph.*, 1074 a 31–8.   [4] *Metaph.*, Λ 9, 1074 b 33–5.

Thomas[1] and others, e.g. Brentano,. have tried to interpret Aristotle in such a way as not to exclude knowledge of the world and the exercise of Divine Providence; but, though St. Thomas is right as to the true view of God, it does not follow that this was the view of Aristotle. "Aristotle has no theory either of divine creation or of divine providence."[2] He does indeed speak in rather a different strain on occasion, as when he speaks of God as the captain of an army who brings about order in the army, or says that God provides for the continuance of generation in the case of those beings which, unlike the stars, are incapable of permanent existence: but such remarks should hardly be pressed in view of his treatment of the First Mover.[3]

Is the God of Aristotle a Personal God? Aristotle sometimes speaks of God as the First Unmoved Mover (τὸ πρῶτον κινοῦν ἀκίνητον), sometimes as ὁ θεός,[4] while in the *Nicomachean Ethics* he also speaks about οἱ θεοί.[5] Like most Greeks, Aristotle does not seem to have worried much about the number of the gods, but if we are to say that he was definitely and exclusively monotheist, then we would have to say that his God is personal. Aristotle may not have spoken of the First Mover as being personal, and certainly the ascription of anthropomorphic personality would be very far indeed from his thoughts, but since the First Mover is Intelligence or Thought, it follows that He is personal in the philosophic sense. The Aristotelian God may not be personal *secundum nomen*, but He is personal *secundum rem*. We should add, however, that there is no indication that Aristotle ever thought of the First Mover as an object of worship, still less as a Being to Whom prayers might profitably be addressed. And indeed, if Aristotle's God is entirely self-centred, as I believe Him to have been, then it would be out of the question for men to attempt personal intercourse with Him. In the *Magna Moralia* Aristotle says expressly that those are wrong who think that there can be a friendship towards God. For (a) God could not return our love, and (b) we could not in any case be said to *love* God.[6]

---

[1] *In Met.*, xii, lect. xi: *Nec tamen sequitur quod omnia alia a se ei sunt ignota; nam intelligendo se intelligit omnia alia.*
[2] Ross, *Aristotle*, p. 184.
[3] *In De Caelo*, A 4, 271 a 33. Aristotle says that God and nature do nothing in vain, but he had not yet elaborated his theory of the Unmoved Mover.
[4] *Metaph.* Λ 7.
[5] *Eth. Nic.*, e.g. 1170 b 8 ff. and 1179 a 24–5. Cf. *Eth. Nic.*, 1179 a 24–5.
[6] *M.M.*, 1208 b 26–32.

14. Other arguments for the existence of God are found in rudimentary form in Aristotle's works. Thus in the fragments of the Περὶ Φιλοσοφίας he pictures men who behold for the first time the beauty of the earth and sea and the majesty of the heavens, and conclude that they are the work of gods. This is an adumbration of the teleological argument.[1] In the same work Aristotle hints at least at a line of argument which was later to develop into the "fourth way" of St. Thomas Aquinas (through various intermediaries, of course). Aristotle there argues that "where there is a better, there is a best; now, among existing things one is better than another, therefore there is a best, which must be the divine."[2] This line of argument leads directly only to a *relatively* best: in order to arrive at the absolutely best, or the Perfect, it is necessary to introduce the idea of causality, arguing that all finite perfections ultimately spring from or are "participations" in Absolute Perfection, which is the fount of all finite perfections. This St. Thomas does, referring to a passage in the *Metaphysics*,[3] and even making use of Aristotle's illustration of fire, which is said to be the hottest of all things, inasmuch as it is the cause of the heat of all other things.[4] As far as Aristotle himself is concerned, the use of the degrees of perfection in order to prove God's existence would seem to be confined to his earlier period, when he is still strongly under Platonic influence: in the *Metaphysics* he does not use this line of argument in reference to the existence of the divine. In general, we must say that Aristotle, when he came to compose the *Metaphysics*, had moved a good way from the popular religious conceptions that appear, for example, in the fragments of the Περὶ Φιλοσοφίας. He continued on occasion to use language that hardly fits the conceptions of *Metaphysics*, Λ; but in any case we would not expect Aristotle to avoid all popular language, expressions and notions with an absolute and rigorous consistency, while it is also extremely probable that he never really attempted any final systematisation of his doctrine concerning God or to harmonise the expressions he sometimes employs implying Divine Providence and activity in the world with the speculations of the *Metaphysics*.

15. From what has been said, it should be apparent that Aristotle's notion of God was far from satisfactory. It is true that he shows a clearer apprehension of the ultimate Godhead

---

[1] Frag. 14. (Rose.)   [2] Frag. 15. (Rose.)
[3] *Metaph.*, 993 b 23–31. Cf. 1008 b 31–1009 a 5.
[4] St. Thomas, *Summa Theologica*, Ia, q., 2, art. 3, in corp.

than Plato does, but in Book Λ of the *Metaphysics* at least, Aristotle leaves out of account that Divine operation in the world which was so insisted on by Plato, and which is an essential element in any satisfactory rational theology. The Aristotelian God is efficient Cause *only* by being the final Cause. He does not know this world and no Divine plan is fulfilled in this world: the teleology of nature can be nothing more than unconscious teleology (at least this is the only conclusion that will really fit in with the picture of God given in the *Metaphysics*). In this respect, therefore, the Aristotelian metaphysic is inferior to that of Plato. On the other hand, while not a few of Aristotle's doctrines must be traced to a Platonic origin, he certainly succeeded, by his doctrine of immanent teleology, of the movement of all concrete sensible objects towards the full realisation of their potentialities, in establishing the reality of the sensible world on a firmer foundation than was possible for his great predecessor, and at the same time attributed a real meaning and purpose to becoming and change, even if in the process he abandoned valuable elements of Plato's thought.

CHAPTER XXX

PHILOSOPHY OF NATURE AND PSYCHOLOGY

1. NATURE is the totality of objects which are material and subject to movement. As a matter of fact, Aristotle does not really define what he means by nature, but it is clear from what he writes in the *Physics*[1] that he regards Nature as the totality of natural objects, i.e. of objects which are capable of initiating change and of bringing it to an end, of objects which have an inner tendency to change. Artificial objects, a bed for instance, have not the power of self-movement. The "simple" bodies of which the bed is composed have this power of initiating change or movement, but they do so as natural bodies, not as components of a bed as such. This position has, of course, to be qualified by the doctrine that the passage of lifeless bodies from a state of rest to a state of movement must be initiated by an external agent. But, as we have seen, when the agent removes an obstacle, e.g. makes a hole in the bottom of a cauldron, the water responds with a movement of its own, its natural downward motion. This may seem a contradiction, namely, that natural objects are spoken of as having in themselves a principle of movement; while, on the other hand, Aristotle makes use of the maxim, that whatever is moved is moved in virtue of the action of an external agent.[2] Aristotle, however, holds that the apparent initiation of movement by animals, e.g. when an animal goes for food, is not an absolute initiation, for there would be no movement were the food not an external attractive agent. Similarly, when the water falls through the hole in the cauldron, this downward movement may indeed be spoken of as though it were a natural movement of the element, yet it is incidentally caused

[1] *Physics*, B 1, 192 b 13 ff.
[2] Aristotle's words in *Physics*, H 1, 241 b 39 ff. and Θ 4, 254 b 7 ff., may seem to be somewhat ambiguous. He says that whatever is moved is moved by something, either by itself or by something else, not that every moving thing is moved by something else; but the discussion that follows these words, when understood in the light of his principle of the priority of act to potency and in the light of his arguments for the existence of the Unmoved Mover shows clearly enough that in his eyes no moving thing can be the *absolute* initiator of motion. Whatever initiates motion *absolutely* must be itself *unmoved*. Whether there is a plurality of unmoved movers or not is, of course, another question. The principle, however, is clear.

by the external agent who makes the hole and so removes the obstacle to the natural motion of the water, while it is directly caused by that which generated the water and made it heavy, presumably by the primary contraries, hot or cold. Aristotle expresses the matter by saying that inanimate bodies have in themselves "a beginning of being moved" but not "a beginning of causing movement."[1]

2. Movement in the wider sense is divided into coming-to-be and passing-away on the one hand, and κίνησις or movement in the narrower sense on the other. This latter (κίνησις) is to be divided into its three kinds—qualitative movement (κίνησις κατὰ τὸ ποιόν or κατὰ πάθος), quantitative movement (κατὰ τὸ ποσόν or κατὰ μέγεθος) and local movement (κίνησις κατὰ τὸ ποῦ or κατὰ τόπον). The first is ἀλλοίωσις or qualitative change, the second αὔξησις καὶ φθίσις or quantitative change, the third φορά or motion in our ordinary sense of the word.[2]

3. Presuppositions of local motion, and indeed of all motion, are Place and Time. That Place (τόπος) exists is proved[3] (a) by the fact of displacement, e.g. by the fact that where there is water, there may come to be air; and (b) by the fact that the four elements have their natural places. These distinctions of natural place are not simply relative to us but exist independently: for instance "up" is the place whither fire moves and "down" the place whither earth moves. Place, therefore, exists and it is defined by Aristotle as τὸ τοῦ περιέχοντος πέρας ἀκίνητον πρῶτον,[4] the *Terminus continentis immobilis primus* of the Scholastics. Aristotle's τόπος, then, is the limit within which a body is, a limit considered as immobile. If this definition is adopted then obviously there can be no empty place nor any place outside the universe or world, for place is the inner limit of the containing body. But Aristotle distinguished between the vessel or container of a body and its place. In the case of a boat carried down by a stream, the stream—itself moving—is the vessel rather than the place of the boat. Place, then, is the first unmoved limit of the container, reckoning outwards. In the actual case in point the whole river, according to Aristotle, is the place of the boat and of whoever is in the boat, on the ground that the whole river is at rest, ὅτι ἀκίνητον ὁ πᾶς.[5] Everything in the physical universe

[1] *Physics*, 254 b 33–256 a 3. Cf. *De Caelo*, 311 a 9–12.
[2] *Physics*, E 2, 226 a 24 ff.; Θ 7, 260 a 26 ff.
[3] *Physics*, Δ 1, 208 a 27 ff.   [4] *Physics*, Δ 4, 212 a 20 ff.
[5] *Physics*, Δ 4, 212 a 19–20.

is thus in a place, while the universe itself is not. Since, therefore, motion occurs through change of place, the universe itself cannot move *forwards*, but only by turning.

4. According to Aristotle a body can only be moved by a present mover in contact with the moved. What, then, are we to say of projectiles?[1] The original mover communicates to the medium, e.g. air or water, not only motion but also the power of moving. The first particles of air moved move other particles *and* the projectiles. But this power of moving decreases in proportion to the distance, so that in the end the projectile comes to rest irrespective of opposing forces. Aristotle is thus no believer in the law of inertia: he thought of compulsory movement as tending to decelerate, whereas "natural" movement tends to accelerate. (Cf. *Physics*, 230 a 18 ff.) In this he was followed by e.g. St. Thomas, who rejected the *impetus* theory of Philoponus, Al Bitrogi, Olivi, etc.

5. In regard to Time, Aristotle points out that it cannot be simply identified with movement or change, for movements are many, while time is one.[2] However, time is clearly connected with movement and change: if we are unaware of change, we are also unaware of time. The definition of time given by Aristotle is ὁ χρόνος ἀριθμός ἐστι κινήσεως κατὰ τὸ πρότερον καὶ ὕστερον.[3] He does not refer in this definition to pure number but to number in the sense of that which is numbered, i.e. to the numerable aspect of movement. Time, however, is a *continuum*, as movement is a continuum: it does not consist of discrete points.

Only things which are in movement or at rest in such a way that they are capable of movement, are in time: what is eternal *and* immobile is not in time. (Movement is eternal but obviously it is not immobile: therefore it is in time, and it necessarily follows that time also is eternal, in the sense that it never first began and will never end.) It is to be noted that the movement referred to is not of necessity local motion, for Aristotle expressly allows that the recognition even of a change in one's own state of mind may enable us to recognise a lapse of time. As to Aristotle's assertion that time is that in movement which is *counted*, it is not meant to be understood as though we could count the *nows* involved in change, as though the period of change were made up of discrete points of time: he means that, when one is conscious of time, one

---

[1] *Physics*, 215 a 14 ff.; 266 b 27 ff.   [2] *Physics*, Δ 10-11, 218 a 30 ff.
[3] *Physics*, Δ 11, 219 b 1-2 ff.; 220 a 24-5 ff.

is recognising plurality, i.e. a plurality of phases. Time, then, is that aspect of element of change or movement, which makes it possible for the mind to recognise a plurality of phases.[1]

If we are to measure time, we must have a standard of measurement. According to Aristotle, movement in a straight line is not satisfactory for this purpose, for it is not uniform. If it is natural movement, it accelerates; if it is unnatural, it decelerates. What movement, then, is both natural and uniform? In Aristotle's view movement in a circle is naturally uniform, and the rotation of the heavenly spheres is a natural movement. So it is thus the best suited for our purpose—and telling time by the sun will be justified.[2]

Aristotle raises the question,[3] though he does not treat it at length, whether there would be time if there were no mind. In other words, as time is the measure of movement or movement *qua* countable, would there be any time if there were no mind to count? He answers that there would be no time, properly speaking, though there would be the substratum of time. Professor Ross comments that this position is consistent with Aristotle's general account of the *continuum*.[4] In the continuum there are no actual parts, but only potential parts. These are brought into actual existence when some event breaks up the *continuum*. So with time or duration. The "nows" within duration are brought into actual existence by a mind which distinguishes the "nows" within that duration. The difficulty that time may have existed when there were as yet no minds in existence, is at first sight no difficulty for Aristotle, since he thought of animals and men as having always existed. But a more pertinent difficulty is that counting is not the creation of parts, but the recognition of parts already there.[5] In any case, how could there be change if there were no time? We might suggest in answer that since, according to Aristotle, time is not really distinguished from the *prius* and *posterius* of motion, time exists independently of the mind, because motion does, though it receives a complement, as it were, from mind. "Parts" of time are potential in the sense that they are not formally distinguished from one another save by the "counting" mind; but they are not potential in the sense that they have no real existence apart from mind. Aristotle's position is not that of Kant, nor does it, of itself, lead to the position of Kant.

[1] Cf. Ross, *Physics*, p. 65.   [2] *Physics*, 223 a 29–224 a 2.
[3] *Physics*, 223 a 21–9.   [4] Ross, *Physics*, p. 68.   [5] Ross, *Physics*, p. 69.

6. Aristotle raises the question of the possibility of the infinite.

(a) An infinite body, he says, is impossible,[1] since every body is bounded by a surface, and no body which is bounded by a surface can be infinite. He also proves the impossibility of an existent actually infinite body by showing that it could be neither composite nor simple. For example, if it is supposed to be composite, the elements of which it is composed are themselves either infinite or finite. Now, if one element is infinite and the other element or elements finite, then the latter are deleted by the first, while it is impossible for both elements to be infinite, since one infinite element would equal the whole body. As to finite elements, composition of such elements would certainly not form one actually infinite body. Aristotle also considered that the existence of absolute "up," "down," etc., which he accepted, shows that there cannot be an existent actually infinite body, for such distinctions would be meaningless in the case of an infinite body. Nor can there be an actual infinite number, since number is that which can be numbered, whereas an infinite number could not be numbered.[2]

(b) On the other hand, though Aristotle rejected an existent actually infinite body or number, he admitted the infinite in another sense.[3] The infinite exists potentially. For example, no spatial extension is an actual infinite, but it is potentially infinite in the sense that it is infinitely divisible. A line does not consist of an actual infinite of points, for it is a *continuum* (it is in this way that Aristotle attempts, in the *Physics*, to meet the difficulties raised by Zeno the Eleatic), but it is infinitely divisible, though this potentially infinite division will never be completely realised in actuality. Time, again, is potentially infinite, since it can be added to indefinitely; but time never exists as an actual infinite, for it is a *successive continuum* and its parts never coexist. Time, therefore, resembles spatial extension in being infinitely divisible (though no actual infinity is ever realised), but is also potentially infinite by way of addition, and in this it differs from extension, since extension, according to Aristotle, has a maximum, even if it has no minimum. A third potential infinity is that of Number, which resembles time in being potentially infinite by way of addition, since you cannot count up to a number beyond which all counting and addition is impossible. Number, however, differs

[1] *Physics*, 5, 204 a 34–206 a 7.   [2] *Physics*, 204 b 7–10.   [3] *Physics*, 206 a 9 ff.

from both time and extension in being insusceptible of infinite division, for the reason that it has a minimum—the unit.

7. According to Aristotle, all natural motion is directed towards an end.[1] What is the end that is sought in nature? It is the development from a state of potentiality to one of actuality, the embodiment of form in matter. With Aristotle, as with Plato, the teleological view of nature prevails over the mechanical, even if it is difficult to see how Aristotle could logically admit any conscious teleology in regard to nature in general. The teleology is not, however, all-pervasive and all-conquering, since matter sometimes obstructs the action of teleology (as, for instance, in the production of monsters, which must be ascribed to defective matter.[2]) Thus the working of teleology in any particular instance may suffer interference from the occurrence of an event which does not serve the end in question at least, but the occurrence of which cannot be avoided owing to certain circumstances. This is τὸ αὐτόματον or the "fortuitous," consisting of those events which are "by nature," though not "according to nature," e.g. the production of a monster by generation. Such occurrences are undesirable and are distinguished by Aristotle from luck (τύχη), which denotes the occurrence of a desirable event, e.g. which might be the willed end of a purposive agent, as in the case of the finding of a treasure in a field.[3]

With what justification does Aristotle speak of "Nature" as having ends? Plato had made use of the conceptions of a World-Soul and of the Demiurge, and so was enabled to speak of ends in nature, but Aristotle talks as though there were some teleological activity inherent in nature itself. He does indeed speak on occasion of ὁ θεός, but he never gives any satisfactory treatment of the relation of nature to God, and what he says about God in the *Metaphysics* would seem to preclude any purposive activity in nature on the part of God. Probably it is true to say that Aristotle's increasing interest in empirical science led him to neglect any real systematisation of his position, and even lays him open to a justified accusation of inconsistency with his metaphysical presuppositions. While having no wish to reject or question Aristotle's view that there is teleology in nature, we are, it seems, compelled to admit that Aristotle's metaphysical system, his theology, gives him little justification for speaking of nature,

---

[1] *De Caelo*, A 4, 217 a 33. ὁ θεός καὶ ἡ φύσις οὐδὲν μάτην ποιοῦσιν.
[2] *De Gen. An.*, 767 b 13–23.   [3] *Physics*, B, 4–6. Cf. *Metaph.*, E, 2–3.

as he not infrequently does, as though it were a consciously operating and organising principle. Such language bears an unmistakably Platonic flavour.

8. According to Aristotle the universe consists of two distinct worlds—the superlunary and the sublunary. In the superlunary world are the stars, which are imperishable and undergo no change other than that of local motion, their motion being circular and not rectilinear, as is the natural movement of the four elements. Aristotle concludes that the stars are composed of a different material element, *aether*, which is the fifth and superior element, incapable of any change other than change of place in a circular movement.

Aristotle maintained the view that the earth, spherical in shape, is at rest in the centre of the universe, and that round it lie the layers, concentric and spherical, of water, air and fire or the warm (ὑπέκκαυμα). Beyond these lie the heavenly spheres, the outermost of which, that of the fixed stars, owes its motion to the First Mover. Accepting from Calippus the number thirty-three as the number of spheres which must be presupposed in order to explain the actual motion of the planets, Aristotle assumed also twenty-two backward-moving spheres, interposed between the other spheres, in order to counteract the tendency of a sphere to disturb the motion of the planet in the next encompassed sphere. He thus obtained fifty-five spheres, excluding the outermost sphere; and this is the explanation of his suggestion in the *Metaphysics* that there are fifty-five unmoved movers, in addition to the First Mover that moves the outermost sphere. (He remarks that if the computation of Eudoxus be accepted instead of that of Calippus, then the number will be forty-nine).[1]

9. Particular things in this world come into being and pass away, but species and genera are eternal. There is, therefore, no evolution in the modern sense to be found in the system of Aristotle. But although Aristotle cannot develop any theory of temporal evolution, an evolution of species, he can and does develop a theory of what may be called "ideal" evolution, namely, a theory concerning the structure of the universe, a theory of the scale of being, in which form is ever more predominant as the scale is ascended. At the bottom of the scale comes inorganic matter, and above this organic matter, the plants being less perfect than the animals. Nevertheless, even the plants possess

[1] Cf. *Metaph.*, Λ, 8.

soul, which is the principle of life, and which Aristotle defines as "the entelechy of a natural body endowed with the capacity of life" or as "the first entelechy of a natural organic body." (So in *De Anima* Β I, 412 a 27-b 4, ψυχή ἐστιν ἐντελέχεια ἡ πρώτη σώματος φυσικοῦ δυνάμει ζωὴν ἔχοντος· τοιοῦτο δέ, ὃ ἂν ᾖ ὀργανικόν, or ἐντελέχεια ἡ πρώτη σώματος φυσικοῦ ὀργανικοῦ.) Being the act of the body, the soul is at the same time form, principle of movement, and end. The body is for the soul, and every organ has its purpose, that purpose being an activity.

At the beginning of the *De Anima* Aristotle points out the importance of an investigation concerning the soul, for the soul is, as it were, the vital principle in living things.[1] This problem is, however, he says, a difficult one, for it is not easy to ascertain the right method to be employed: but he insists—and how wisely —that the speculative philosopher and the naturalist have different standpoints, and so frame their definitions differently. It is not every thinker that has recognised that different sciences have their different methods, and that because a particular science cannot employ the method of the chemist or the natural scientist, it does not follow that all its conclusions must necessarily be vitiated.[2]

The composite substance, says Aristotle,[3] is a natural body endowed with life, the principle of this life being called the soul (ψυχή). Body cannot be soul, for body is not life but what has life. (In the first book of the *De Anima*, where Aristotle gives a history of Psychology, he remarks, apropos of the views of different philosophers concerning the soul, that "the most far-reaching difference is that between the philosophers who regard the elements as corporeal and those who regard them as incorporeal." Aristotle ranges himself with the Platonists as against the followers of Leucippus and Democritus.) The body, then, must be as matter to the soul, while the soul is as form or act to the body. Hence Aristotle, in his definition of the soul, speaks of it as the entelechy or act of the body that possesses life in potency —"potentiality of life," as he remarks, not referring to a thing which has become dispossessed of soul, but to that which possesses it. The soul is thus the realisation of the body and is inseparable from it (though there may be—as Aristotle held there were— parts which can be separated, because they are not precisely realisations of the body). The soul is thus the cause and principle

[1] *De An.*, 402 a 1-9.　　[2] *De An.*, 402 a 10 ff.　　[3] *De An.*, 412 a.

of the living body, (a) as source of movement,[1] (b) as final cause, and (c) as the real substance (i.e. formal cause) of animate bodies.

The different types of soul form a series of such a kind that the higher presupposes the lower, but not vice versa. The lowest form of soul is the nutritive or vegetative soul, τὸ θρεπτικόν, which exercises the activities of assimilation and reproduction. It is found, not only in plants, but also in animals; yet it can exist by itself, as it does in plants. In order that any living thing should continue to exist, these functions are necessary: they are found, therefore, in all living things, but in plants they are found alone, without the higher activities of soul. For plants sensation is not necessary, for they do not move but draw their nourishment automatically. (The same holds good, indeed, of motionless animals.) But animals endowed with the power of movement must have sensation, for it would be useless for them to move after their food, if they could not recognise it when they found it.

Animals, then, possess the higher form of soul, the sensitive soul, which exercises the three powers of sense-perception (τὸ αἰσθητικόν), desire (τὸ ὀρεκτικόν), and local motion (τὸ κινητικόν κατὰ τόπον).[2] Imagination (φαντασία) follows on the sensitive faculty, and memory is a further development of this.[3] Just as Aristotle has pointed out the necessity of nutrition for the preservation of life at all, so he shows the necessity of touch in order that an animal should be able to distinguish its food, at least when it is in contact with it.[4] Taste, whereby that which is food attracts the animal, and what is not food repels it, is also necessary. The other senses, though not strictly necessary, are for the well-being of the animal.

10. Higher in the scale than the merely animal soul is the human soul. This soul unites in itself the powers of the lower souls, τὸ θρεπτικόν, τὸ αἰσθητικόν, τὸ ὀρεκτικόν, τὸ κινητικόν κατὰ τόπον, but has a peculiar advantage in the possession of νοῦς, τὸ διανοητικόν. The latter is active in two ways, as the power of scientific thought (λόγος, νοῦς θεωρητικός = τὸ ἐπιστημονικόν) and as the power of deliberation (διάνοια πρακτική = λογιστικόν). The former has truth as its object, truth for its own sake, while the latter aims at truth, not for its

---

[1] Aristotle insists that the soul is badly defined if it is assigned motion as its characteristic. The soul moves actively but does not itself move. This is against the Platonic doctrine of the soul as a self-moving entity. Cf. *De An.*, A, 3.

[2] *De An.*, B 3.

[3] *De An.*, 3, 427 b 29 ff.; *Rhet.*, A 11, 1370 a 28–31; *De Mem.*, 1; *Anal. Post.*, B 19, 99 b 36 ff.

[4] *De An.*, 3, 12. Cf. *De Sensu*, 1.

own sake but for practical and prudential purposes. All the powers of the soul, with the exception of νοῦς, are inseparable from the body and perishable: νοῦς, however, pre-exists before the body and is immortal. λείπεται δὲ τὸν νοῦν μόνον θύραθεν ἐπεισιέναι καὶ θεῖον εἶναι μόνον.[1] This νοῦς, however, which enters into the body, requires a potential principle—a *tabula rasa*, on which it may imprint forms; and so we have the distinction between the νοῦς ποιητικός and the νοῦς παθητικός. (Aristotle speaks himself of τὸ ποιοῦν: the phrase νοῦς ποιητικός is first found in Alexander Aphrodisiensis, *c*. A.D. 220). The active intellect abstracts forms from the images or *phantasmata*, which, when received in the passive intellect, are actual concepts. (Aristotle considered that the use of imagery is involved in all thinking.) Only the active intellect is immortal. οὗτος ὁ νοῦς χωριστὸς καὶ ἀπαθὴς καὶ ἀμιχὴς τῇ οὐσίᾳ ὢν ἐνέργεια, ἀεὶ γὰρ τιμιώτερον τὸ ποιοῦν τοῦ πάσχοντος καὶ ἡ ἀρχὴ τῆς ὕλης . . . καὶ τοῦτο μόνον ἀθάνατον καὶ ἀίδιον, . . . ὁ δὲ παθητικὸς νοῦς φθαρτός.[2] To this point I shall return in a moment.

11. If we leave out of account the question of the νοῦς ποιητικός, it is clear that Aristotle does not uphold the Platonic dualism in the *De Anima*, for he makes soul to be the entelechy of the body, so that the two form one substance. Altogether Aristotle allows a much closer union between soul and body than did the Platonists: the tendency to look on the body as the tomb of the soul is not that of Aristotle. Rather is it for the good of the soul to be united with the body, since only so can it exercise its faculties. This was the view adopted by the mediaeval Aristotelians, such as St. Thomas, although many great Christian thinkers had spoken and continue to speak, in language very reminiscent of ͡the Platonic tradition—we have only to think of St. Augustine. Aristotle insisted that the Platonic School failed to give any satisfactory explanation of the soul's union with the body. They seem, he says, to suppose that any soul can fit itself into any body. This cannot be true, for every body appears to have a distinct form and character.[3] "A notion like that of Descartes, that the existence of the soul is the first certainty and the existence of matter a later inference, would have struck Aristotle as absurd. The whole self, soul and body alike, is something given and not questioned."[4] Needless to say, if Aristotle would have opposed the Cartesian view, he would also have opposed the

---

[1] *De Gen. et Corrupt.*, B 3, 738 b 27 ff.   [2] *De An.*, 3, 5, 430 a 17 ff.
[3] *De An.*, 414 a 19 ff.   [4] Ross, *Aristotle*, p. 132.

position of those who would reduce the whole human soul and all its activities to the condition of an epiphenomenon of the body, making the highest activity of human thought a mere efflorescence of the brain, though the direction of Aristotle's psychology, as it developed, would seem to have been towards a position suspiciously resembling an epiphenomenalist position, especially if one is right in supposing that the active intellect of man was not, in Aristotle's eyes, an individualised principle, which persisted after death as the individual mind of, e.g. Socrates or Callias. The absence of a doctrine of historical organic evolution would, however, naturally preclude Aristotle from accepting epiphenomenalism in the modern sense.

12. The well-worn question arises, "What was Aristotle's precise doctrine as to the Active Intellect?" Aristotle's *precise* doctrine one cannot give: it is a matter of interpretation, and different interpretations have been advanced both in the ancient and in the modern world. What Aristotle says in the *De Anima* is as follows: "This Nous is separable and impassible and unmixed, being essentially an actuality. For the active is always of higher value than the passive, and the originative principle than the matter. Actual knowledge is identical with its object; potential knowledge is prior in time in the individual, but in general it is not temporally prior; but Nous does at one time function and at another not. When it has been separated it is that only which it is in essence, and this alone is immortal and eternal. We do not remember, however, because active reason is impassible, but the passive reason is perishable, and without the active reason nothing thinks."[1]

Of this much-disputed passage various interpretations have been given. Alexander of Aphrodisias (*flor. c.* A.D. 220) identified "reason," i.e. the Active Intellect, with God, being followed in this by Zabarella (end of sixteenth and early seventeenth century A.D.), who would make God's function in the soul to be the illumination of the potentially known, as the sun's light makes what is visible to be actually seen. Now, although, as Sir David Ross points out,[2] it would not be necessarily inconsistent on Aristotle's part to speak of God's immanence in the *De Anima*, while speaking of His transcendence in the *Metaphysics*, while on the other hand it might be possible for the two books to represent divergent views of God, the interpretation of Alexander of Aphrodisias and

[1] *De An.*, 3, 5, 430 a 17 ff. [2] *Aristotle*, p. 153.

Zabarella, as Ross allows, is most unlikely. For is it probable that Aristotle, having described God as the Unmoved Mover Whose causal activity is one of attraction—as *Finis*—and as knowing only Himself, should go on, in another book, to depict God as immanent in man in such a way as actually to impart knowledge to him?

If the Active Intellect is not to be identified with God, is it to be regarded as individual and particular in each single man or as an identical principle in all men? Aristotle's words, "We do not remember," when taken together with his assertion[1] that memory and loving and hating perish at death, as belonging to the whole man and not to Reason, which is "impassable," seem to indicate that the Active Intellect in its separate existence has no memory. Although this does not prove with certainty that the Active Intellect of each man is not individual in its state of separation, it does seem to raise a difficulty in accepting such an interpretation. Moreover, when Aristotle asserts that "potential knowledge is prior in time in the individual, but in general it is not temporally prior, but Nous does not at one time function and at another not," he seems to be drawing a distinction between the individual, who at one time knows and at another not, and the Active Intellect, which is an essentially active principle. Perhaps, then, Aristotle regarded the Active Intellect as a principle which is identical in all men, an Intelligence that has above it the hierarchy of the other separate Intelligence, that enters into man and functions within him, and that survives the death of the individual. If this were correct, then the conclusion would necessarily follow that the individualised human soul perishes with the matter it informed.[2] (Yet, even if one is inclined to such an interpretation, one must admit that there is very considerable difficulty in supposing that, in Aristotle's opinion, the active intellect of Plato was numerically the same as that of Socrates. All the same, if he believed in the individual character of the active intellect in each single man, what did he mean when he said that it came "from outside"? Was this simply a relic of Platonism?)

---

[1] *De An.*, 408 b 24–30.

[2] St. Thomas Aquinas, in his Commentary on Aristotle's *De Anima* (3, lect. 10), does not interpret Aristotle in the Averroistic sense, i.e. as denying individual immortality. The active intellect is essentially and only an *active* principle: hence it is unaffected by passions and emotions and is not retentive of *species*. The separated human reason cannot, therefore, function as it does in the state of union with the body, and the mode of its functioning after death is not treated by Aristotle in the *De Anima*; but this omission does not mean that Aristotle denied individual immortality or condemned the separated intellect to a state of enforced and absolute inactivity.

CHAPTER XXXI

ARISTOTLE'S ETHICS

1. THE Ethics of Aristotle are frankly teleological. He is concerned with action, not as being right in itself irrespective of every other consideration, but with action as conducive to man's good. What conduces to the attainment of his good or end will be a "right" action on man's part: the action that is opposed to the attainment of his true good will be a "wrong" action.

"Every art and every inquiry, every action and choice, seems to aim at some good; whence the good has rightly been defined as that at which all things aim."[1] But there are different goods, corresponding to different arts or sciences. Thus the doctor's art aims at health, seamanship at a safe voyage, economy at wealth. Moreover, some ends are subordinate to other and more ultimate ends. The end of giving a certain medicine might be to produce sleep, but this immediate end is subordinate to the end of health. Similarly, the making of bits and reins for cavalry horses is the end of a certain craft, but it is subordinate to the wider and more comprehensive end of conducting warlike operations efficiently. These ends, therefore, have further ends or goods in view. But if there is an end which we desire for its own sake and for the sake of which we desire all other subordinate ends or goods, then this ultimate good will be the best good, in fact, *the* good. Aristotle sets himself to discover what this good is and what the science corresponding to it is.

As to the second question, Aristotle asserts that it is political or social science which studies the good for man. The State and the individual have the same good, though this good as found in the State is greater and nobler.[2] (Here we see an echo of the *Republic*, that in the ideal State we see justice writ large.) Ethics, then, are regarded by Aristotle as a branch of political or social science: we might say that he treats first of individual ethical science and secondly of political ethical science, in the *Politics*.

As to the question what is the good of man, Aristotle points out that it cannot be answered with the exactitude with which

[1] *E.N.*, 1094 a 1–3.   [2] *E.N.*, 1094 a 27–b 11. Cf. *M.M.*, 1181 a and b.

a mathematical problem can be answered, and that owing to the nature of the subject-matter, for human action is the subject-matter of ethics, and human action cannot be determined with mathematical exactitude.[1] There is also this big difference between mathematics and ethics, that while the former starts from general principles and argues to conclusions, the latter starts with the conclusions. In other words, in ethics we start from the actual moral judgments of man, and by comparing, contrasting and sifting them, we come to the formulation of general principles.[2] This view presupposes that there are natural tendencies implanted in man, the following of which in a general attitude of consistent harmony and proportion, i.e. recognising relative importances and unimportances, is the ethical life for man. This view affords a basis for a natural as opposed to an arbitrary ethic, but considerable difficulties arise as to the theoretical establishment of moral *obligation*, especially in a system such as that of Aristotle, who cannot link up his ethic of human action with the Eternal Law of God, as Christian philosophers of the Middle Ages, who accepted so much from Aristotle, tried to do. However, in spite of such defects, Aristotle's ethic is eminently common-sense for the most part, founded as it is on the moral judgments of the man who was generally looked upon as a good and virtuous man. Aristotle intended his ethic to be a justification and supplementation of the natural judgments of such a man, who is, he says, best qualified to judge in matters of this kind.[3] It may be thought that the taste of the intellectual and professor comes out strongly in his picture of the ideal life, but one can scarcely accuse Aristotle of attempting a purely *a priori* and deductive ethic, or an *Ethica more geometrico demonstrata*. Moreover, although we can discern evidence of contemporary Greek taste in matters of human conduct, e.g. in Aristotle's account of the moral virtues, the philosopher certainly considered himself to be dealing with human nature as such, and to be founding his ethic on the universal characteristics of human nature—in spite of his opinion of the "barbarians." If he were alive to-day and had to answer, e.g. Friedrich Nietzsche, he would no doubt insist on the basic universality and constancy of human nature and the necessity

---

[1] *E.N.*, 1094 b 11-27. Cf. *E.E.*, I, 6.

[2] In the *Eudemian Ethics* Aristotle says that we start with "true but obscure judgments" (1216 b 32 ff.) or "the first confused judgments" (1217 a 18 ff.), and go on to form clear ethical judgments. In other words Aristotle starts with the ordinary moral judgments of men as the basis of argument.

[3] *E.N.*, 1094 b 27 ff.

of constant valuations, which are not merely relative but are founded in nature.

What do people generally view as the end of life? Happiness, says Aristotle, and he, like a true Greek, accepts this view. But obviously this does not take us very far by itself, for different people understand very different things by happiness. Some people identify it with pleasure, others with wealth, others again with honour, and so on. More than that, the same man may have different estimations of what happiness is at different times. Thus when he is ill he may regard health as happiness, and when he is in want he may regard wealth as happiness. But pleasure is rather an end for slaves than freemen, while honour cannot be the end of life, for it depends on the giver and is not really our own. Honour, moreover, seems to be aimed at assuring us of our virtue (hence, perhaps, the Victorian attachment to "respectability"); so perhaps moral virtue is the end of life. No, says Aristotle, for moral virtue can go with inactivity and misery; and happiness, which is the end of life, that at which all aim, must be an activity and excludes misery.[1]

Now, if happiness is an activity and an activity of man, we must see what activity is peculiar to man. It cannot be the activity of growth or reproduction, nor yet of sensation, since these are shared by other beings below man: it must be the activity of that which is peculiar to man among natural beings, namely, the activity of reason or activity in accordance with reason. This is indeed an activity of virtue—for Aristotle distinguished, besides the moral virtues, the intellectual virtues—but it is not what people ordinarily mean when they say that happiness consists in being virtuous, since they are generally thinking of moral virtues, such as justice, temperance, etc. In any case, happiness, as the ethical end, could not consist simply in virtue as such: it consists rather in activity according to virtue or in virtuous activity, understanding by virtue both the intellectual and the moral virtues. Moreover, says Aristotle, it must, if it really deserves the name of happiness, be manifested over a whole life and not merely for brief periods.[2]

But if happiness is essentially activity in accordance with virtue, Aristotle does not mean by this simply to exclude all the common notions about happiness. For instance, the activity to which virtue is the tendency is necessarily accompanied by

[1] *E.N.*, A 4 and ff.   [2] *E.N.*, 1100 a 4 ff.; 1101 a 14–20.

pleasure, since pleasure is the natural accompaniment of an unimpeded and free activity. Again, without some external goods a man cannot well exercise that activity—an Aristotelian view to which the Cynics took exception, for the most part at least.[1] The character of happiness as an activity, and an activity peculiar to man, is therefore preserved without at the same time having to sacrifice or exclude pleasure and external prosperity. Once more Aristotle shows the common-sense character of his thought, and that he is not "over-transcendental" or hostile to this earth.

This being established, Aristotle goes on to consider, first the general nature of good character and good action, then the leading moral virtues, the virtues of that part of man which can follow the plan laid down by reason, then the virtues of the intellect. At the end of the *Nicomachean Ethics* he considers the ideal life, or the ideal life of activity in accordance with virtue, which life will be the truly happy life for man.

2. As to goodness of character in general, Aristotle says that we start by having a capacity for it, but that it has to be developed by practice. How is it developed? By doing virtuous acts. At first sight this looks like a vicious circle. Aristotle tells us that we become virtuous by doing virtuous acts, but how can we do virtuous acts unless we are already virtuous? Aristotle answers[2] that we begin by doing acts which are objectively virtuous, without having a reflex knowledge of the acts and a deliberate choice of the acts as good, a choice resulting from an habitual disposition. For instance, a child may be told by its parents not to lie. It obeys without realising perhaps the inherent goodness of telling the truth, and without having yet formed a habit of telling the truth; but the acts of truth-telling gradually form the habit, and as the process of education goes on, the child comes to realise that truth-telling is right in itself, and to choose to tell the truth for its own sake, as being the right thing to do. It is then virtuous in this respect. The accusation of the vicious circle is thus answered by the distinction between the acts which *create* the good disposition and the acts which *flow from* the good disposition once it has been created. Virtue itself is a disposition which has been developed out of a capacity by the proper exercise

---

[1] Aristotle remarks that the truly happy man must be sufficiently equipped with external goods. He thus rejects extreme Cynicism, but he warns us (cf. *E.E.*, 1214 b 25 f.) not to mistake indispensable conditions of happiness for essential elements of happiness.

[2] *E.N.*, B 1, 1103 a 14–b 26; B 4, 1105 a 17–b 18.

of that capacity. (Further difficulties might arise, of course, concerning the relation between the development of moral valuations and the influence of social environment, suggestion of parents and teachers, etc., but with these Aristotle does not deal.[1])

3. How does virtue stand to vice? It is a common characteristic of all good actions that they have a certain order or proportion, and virtue, in Aristotle's eyes, is a mean between two extremes, the extremes being vices, one being a vice through excess, the other being a vice through defect.[2] Through excess or defect of what? Either in regard to a feeling or in regard to an action. Thus, in regard to the feeling of confidence, the excess of this feeling constitutes rashness—at least when the feeling issues in action, and it is with human actions that ethics are concerned—while the defect is cowardice. The mean, then, will be a mean between rashness on the one hand and cowardice on the other hand: this mean is courage and is the virtue in respect to the feeling of confidence. Again, if we take the action of giving of money, excess in regard to this action is prodigality—and this is a vice—while defect in regard to this action is illiberality. The virtue, liberality, is the mean between the two vices, that of excess and that of defect. Aristotle, therefore, describes or defines moral virtue as "a disposition to choose, consisting essentially in a mean relatively to us determined by a rule, i.e. the rule by which a practically wise man would determine it."[3] Virtue, then, is a disposition, a disposition to choose according to a rule, namely, the rule by which a truly virtuous man possessed of moral insight would choose. Aristotle regarded the possession of practical wisdom, the ability to see what is the right thing to do in the circumstances, as essential to the truly virtuous man, and he attaches much more value to the moral judgments of the enlightened conscience than to any *a priori* and merely theoretical conclusions. This may seem somewhat naïve, but it must be remembered that for Aristotle the prudent man will be the man who sees what is truly good for a man in any set of circumstances: he is not required to enter upon any academic preserve, but to see what truly befits human nature in those circumstances.

When Aristotle speaks of virtue as a mean, he is not thinking

---

[1] Aristotle thus insists that a completely right action must be not only "externally" the right thing to do in the circumstances, but also done from a right motive, proceeding from a moral agent acting precisely as a moral agent. (Cf. *E.N.*, 1105 b 5 ff.).

[2] *E.N.*, B, 6 ff.   [3] *E.N.*, 1106 b 36–1107 a 2.

of a mean that has to be calculated arithmetically: that is why he says in his definition "relatively to us." We cannot determine what is excess, what mean and what defect by hard-and-fast, mathematical rules: so much depends on the character of the feeling or action in question: in some cases it may be preferable to err on the side of excess rather than on that of defect, while in other cases the reverse may be true. Nor, of course, should the Aristotelian doctrine of the mean be taken as equivalent to an exaltation of mediocrity in the moral life, for as far as excellence is concerned virtue is an extreme: it is in respect of its essence and its definition that it is a mean. One may illustrate this important point by a diagram given in the *Ethics* of Professor Nicolai Hartmann of Berlin,[1] in which the horizontal line at the bottom of the figure represents the ontological dimension, and the vertical line the axiological dimension.

Goodness

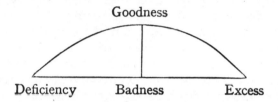

Deficiency   Badness   Excess

This diagram illustrates the important point that virtue (ἀρετή) has a double position. (i) As regards the ontological dimension, it is a mean (μεσότης); as regards the axiological dimension, it is an excellence or extreme (ἀκρότης). It is not as though virtue were a composition of vices from a valuational point of view, since, from this point of view, it stands in opposition to both vices; but it is nevertheless a mean from the ontological viewpoint, since it combines in itself both the good points which, run to excess, constitute vices. For example, courage is not boldness alone, nor is it cool foresight alone, but a synthesis of both—this character of a synthesis preventing courage from degenerating into the daring of the foolhardy man on the one hand or the prudence of the coward on the other hand. "What Aristotle so strongly felt in the lower moral values, without being able to formulate it, was just this, that all valuational elements, taken in isolation, have in them a point beyond which they are dangerous, that they are tyrannical, and that for the true fulfilment

<hr />

[1] *Ethics*, by Nicolai Hartmann, vol. 2, p. 256. (Trans., Dr. Stanton Coit George Allen & Unwin, Ltd.)

of their meaning in their real carrier there is always a counter-weight. Because of this profoundly justified feeling, he assigned virtue to no one of these elements but to their synthesis. It is precisely in their synthesis that the danger in values is diminished, their tyranny in consciousness paralysed. In this matter Aristotle's procedure is a model for every further treatment of the problem of contrasts."[1]

One must, however, admit that Aristotle's treatment of the virtues betrays the fact that he was under the influence of the predominantly *aesthetic* attitude of the Greek towards human conduct, a fact that appears in a clear light in his treatment of the "great-souled" man. The notion of a crucified God would have been abhorrent to him: it would most probably have seemed in his eyes at once unaesthetic and irrational.

4. A presupposition of moral action is Freedom, since it is only for voluntary actions that a man incurs responsibility, i.e. voluntary in a wide sense. If a man acts under physical external compulsion or in ignorance, he cannot be held responsible. Fear may lessen the voluntary character of an action, but an action such as throwing the cargo overboard in a storm, though not one that a sane man would perform in ordinary circumstances, is yet voluntary, since it springs from the agent himself.[2]

In regard to ignorance Aristotle certainly makes some pertinent observations, as when he points out that while a man who acts in rage or under the influence of drink may be said to act *in* ignorance, he cannot be said to act *from* ignorance, for that ignorance is itself due to rage or drink.[3] However, his assertion that an action done through ignorance is involuntary if it is subsequently regretted by the agent, non-voluntary if not subsequently regretted, can scarcely be accepted, for although the agent's subsequent attitude may reveal his general character, i.e. whether he is on the whole a good or bad man, it cannot serve to differentiate between unwilling and merely involuntary acts.[4]

In regard to the Socratic position that no man acts against knowledge, Aristotle does on occasion show that he is alive to the reality of the moral struggle[5] (he was too good a psychologist to disregard the point), but when he is treating formally of the question, in reference to continence and incontinence,[6] he tends

---

[1] Hartmann, *Ethics*, 2, p. 424. [2] *E.N.*, Γ 1, 1100 a 8–19.
[3] *E.N.*, Γ1, 1110 b 24–7. [4] *E.N.*, Γ 1110 b 18 ff. [5] *E.N.*, e.g. 1102 b 14 ff.
[6] *E.N.*, H.

to overlook this and to emphasise the view that the man who does a wrong act does not know at the moment of action that the act is wrong. This may certainly happen sometimes, e.g. in the case of actions done under the stress of passion, but Aristotle does not allow sufficiently for the truth that a man may do deliberately what he knows to be wrong, and, moreover, what he knows to be wrong at the moment that he does it. It might be remarked that, owing to what might be called the strictly human character of Aristotle's ethic, by which "right" is explained in terms of "good," he could answer that even the incontinent man acts *sub ratione boni*. This is true, but all the same the incontinent man may know well enough that the action he performs is morally wrong. In fact, Aristotle, while professedly rejecting the Socratic theory, was none the less dominated by it to a certain extent. He lacked a proper concept of duty, though in this he seems to have been at one with other Greek theorists before the rise of the Stoics, with certain reservations in the case of Plato. An action may be good or contributory to good without thereby being strictly obligatory, a duty, and Aristotle's ethical theory does not account for this distinction.

5. Aristotle, like Plato before him, had no really distinct concept of will, but his description or definition of choice as "desireful reason" or "reasonable desire"[1] or as "the deliberate desire of things in our power,"[2] shows that he had some idea of will, for he does not identify preferential choice (προαίρεσις) with either desire by itself or with reason by itself. His description of it would seem to indicate that he regarded it as substantially *sui generis*. (Aristotle does indeed declare that προαίρεσις has to do with means and not with ends, but in his use of the word, both in the *Ethics* itself and also elsewhere, he is not consistent.[3])

Aristotle's analysis of the moral process is as follows. (i) The agent desires an end. (ii) The agent deliberates, seeing that B is the means to A (the end to be obtained), C the means to B, and so on, until (iii) he perceives that some particular means near to the end or remote from it, as the case may be, is something that he can do here and now. (iv) The agent chooses this means that presents itself to him as practicable *hic et nunc*, and (v) does the act in question. Thus a man might desire happiness (in fact, he always does, Aristotle thought). He then sees that health is a

---

[1] *E.N.*, 1139 b 4-5. [2] *E.N.*, 1113 a 9-11.
[3] *E.N.*, e.g. 1111 b 26 ff. But cf. e.g. 1144 a 20 ff.

means to happiness, and that exercise is a means to health. He then perceives that to go for a walk is something that he can do here and now. He chooses this act and does it, i.e. takes the walk. This analysis may be a very good statement of the way in which we fix on actions in view of an end: the difficulty is to allow for any real moral obligation in Aristotle's system, at least if considered in itself and without any of the supplementary treatment that later philosophers have given it.

From the doctrine that virtuous activity is voluntary and in accordance with choice, it follows that virtue and vice are in our power, and that Socrates' doctrine is false. True, a man may have formed a bad habit of such strength that he cannot cease to perform the intrinsically bad actions that naturally flow from that habit, but he could have refrained from contracting that habit in the first place. A man may have so blinded his conscience that he fails now to discern the right, but he is himself responsible for his blindness and for bringing about his ignorance. This may be said to be the general thought of Aristotle, though, as we have seen, in his formal treatment of the Socratic position he does not do sufficient justice to moral weakness and to sheer wickedness.

6. Aristotle's treatment of the moral virtues is often enlightening and shows his common-sense moderation and clear judgment. For example, his characterisation of courage as a mean between rashness or foolhardiness and cowardice, seems, when developed, to set the true nature of courage in relief and to distinguish it from forms of pseudo-courage. Similarly, his description of the virtue of temperance as a mean between profligacy and "insensibility," serves to bring out the truth that temperance or self-control in regard to the pleasures of touch does not of itself involve a puritanical attitude towards sense and the pleasures of sense. Again, his insistence that the mean is a mean "relatively to us" and cannot be arithmetically determined, brings out his practical, empirical and common-sense outlook. As he pertinently remarks, "If ten pounds of food are too much for a man and two are too little, the trainer in gymnastics will not order six pounds, for this may be too much or too little for the special case: for a Milo it may be too little, but for one who is beginning to train it may be too much."[1]

It can hardly be denied, however (and who would expect anything else?) that his treatment of the virtues is, to a certain

[1] *E.N.*, 1106 a 36–b 4.

extent, determined by contemporary Greek taste.[1] Thus his view that the "great-souled" and self-respecting man will be ashamed of receiving benefits and so putting himself in the position of an inferior, while on the contrary he will always pay back benefits received with greater ones in order to make his friend his debtor, may be in accordance with Greek taste (or with those of Nietzsche), but will scarcely be acceptable in all quarters. Again, Aristotle's pictures of the "great-souled" man as slow in step, deep in voice and sedate in speech is largely a matter of aesthetic taste.[2]

7. In Book Five of the *Ethics* Aristotle treats of Justice. Under Justice he understands (*a*) what is lawful and (*b*) what is fair and equal. (τὸ μὲν δίκαιον ἄρα τὸ νόμιμον καὶ τὸ ἴσον, τὸ δ᾽ ἄδικον τὸ παράνομον καὶ τὸ ἄνισον (*E.N.*, 1129 a 34)). The first kind of justice, "universal" justice, is practically equivalent to obedience to law, but since Aristotle envisages the law of the State—ideally, at least—as extending over the whole of life and enforcing virtuous actions in the sense of materially virtuous actions (since of course law cannot enforce virtuous actions, formally or subjectively considered), universal justice is more or less coterminous with

---

[1] The conception of a man claiming honour from others as a due to his "virtue" and nobility is somewhat repugnant to us, but it was a lineal descendant of the Homeric hero's expectation of honour as due to his ἀρετή.

[2] *E.N.*, 1124 b 9–1125 a 16.

Sir David Ross gives the following tabulation of the moral virtues as treated by Aristotle. (*Aristotle*, p. 203.)

Feeling	Action	Excess	Mean	Defect
Fear } Confidence }		{ Cowardice Rashness	Courage Courage	Unnamed Cowardice
Certain pleasures of touch		Profligacy	Temperance	Insensibility
(Pain arising from desire of such pleasures)	Giving of money } Taking of money }	{ Prodigality Illiberality	Liberality Liberality	Illiberality Prodigality
	Giving of money on large scale	Vulgarity	Magnificence	Meanness
	Claiming of honour on large scale	Vanity	Self-respect	Humility
	Pursuit of honour on small scale	Ambition	Unnamed	Unambition
Anger		Irascibility	Gentleness	Unirascibility
Social Intercourse {	Telling truth about oneself	Boastfulness	Truthfulness	Self-depreciation
	Giving of pleasure: By way of amusement	Buffoonery	Wittiness	Boorishness
	in life generally	Obsequiousness	Friendliness	Sulkiness
Shame		Bashfulness	Modesty	Shamelessness
Pains at good or bad fortune of others		Envy	Righteous Indignation	Malevolence

virtue, looked at in its social aspect at any rate. Aristotle, like Plato, is firmly convinced of the positive and educative function of the State. This is diametrically opposed to theories of the State, such as those of Herbert Spencer in England and Schopenhauer in Germany, who rejected the positive functions of the State and confined the functions of law to the defence of personal rights, above all the defence of private property.

"Particular" justice is divided into (a) Distributive Justice, whereby the State divides goods among its citizens according to geometrical proportions, i.e. according to merit (as Burnet says, the Greek citizen regarded himself as a shareholder in the State, rather than as a taxpayer), and (b) Remedial Justice. This latter is subdivided into two types, (i) that dealing with voluntary transactions (Civil Law), and (ii) that dealing with involuntary transactions (Criminal Law). Remedial Justice proceeds according to arithmetical proportion. Aristotle added to these two main divisions of particular justice Commercial or Commutative Justice.

According to Aristotle, Justice is a mean between acting unjustly and being unjustly treated.[1] But this is hardly acceptable and is obviously asserted merely in order to bring justice into line with the other virtues already discussed. For the business man, for instance, who is just in his dealings, is the man who chooses to give the other fellow his due and to take exactly his own share without further extortion, rather than to give the other man less than his due or to take for himself more than what is owing to him. To give the other fellow more than his share or to accept for himself less than his own due, is scarcely a vice—or even, necessarily, to be unjustly treated. However, Aristotle goes on to say, rather more happily, that justice is not really a mean as the other virtues are, but is a mean in the sense that it produces a state of affairs that stand midway between that in which A has too much and that in which B has too much.[2]

Finally[3] Aristotle draws the very valuable distinction between various types of action that are materially unjust, pointing out that to do an action which results in damage to another, when the damage was not foreseen or intended—and still more if the damage would not ordinarily result from that action—is very different from doing an action which would naturally result in

---

[1] *E.N.*, 1133 b 30-2.   [2] *E.N.*, 1133 b 32 ff.
[3] *E.N.*, E, 8, 1135 a 15-36 a 9. Cf. *Rhet.*, 1374 a 26-b 22.

damage to another, particularly if that damage was foreseen and intended. The distinctions drawn afford room for equity as a type of justice superior to legal justice, the latter being too general for application to all particular cases. καὶ ἔστιν αὕτη ἡ φύσις ἡ τοῦ ἐπιεικοῦς, ἐπανόρθωμα νόμου, ᾗ ἐλλείπει διὰ τὸ καθόλου.[1]

8. Discussing the intellectual virtues Aristotle divides them according to the two rational faculties, (i) the scientific faculty— τὸ ἐπιστημονικόν, by which we contemplate objects that are necessary and admit of no contingency, and (ii) the calculative faculty— τὸ λογιστικόν, or faculty of opinion, which is concerned with objects that are contingent. The intellectual virtues of the scientific faculty are ἐπιστήμη, "the disposition by virtue of which we demonstrate,"[2] and which has regard to proof, and νοῦς or intuitive reason, whereby we grasp a universal truth after experience of a certain number of particular instances and then see this truth or principle to be self-evident.[3] The union of νοῦς and ἐπιστήμη is theoretical wisdom or σοφία, and it is directed to the highest objects—probably including not only the objects of Metaphysics, but also those of Mathematics and Natural Science. The contemplation of these objects belongs to the ideal life for man. "Wisdom or philosophy may be defined as the combination of intuitive reason and science, or as scientific knowledge of the most precious things, with the crown of perfection, so to speak, upon it." Knowledge is dignified by its object, and Aristotle remarks that it would be absurd to call political science the highest type of knowledge, unless indeed men were the highest of all beings—and that he did not believe.[4] "There are other things in the universe of a nature far more divine than his, as, for example, the starry heavens of which the universe is built. From all of which it is clear that wisdom is a combination of science and the speculative reason, directed to the noblest objects in creation."[5]

The virtues of τὸ λογιστικόν are τέχνη or art, "the disposition by which we make things by the aid of a true rule,"[6] and practical wisdom or φρόνησις, "a true disposition towards action, by the aid of a rule, with regard to things good or bad for men."[7] φρόνησις is subdivided according to the objects with which it is concerned. (i) As concerned with the individual's good, it is φρόνησις in the narrow sense. (ii) As concerned with the family, with household

[1] *E.N.*, 1137 b 26–7. [2] *E.N.*, 1139 b 31–2. [3] *E.N।*, Z, 6, 1140 b 31–1141 a 8.
[4] *E.N.*, 1141 a 9–2. [5] *E.N.*, 1141 a 33–b 3. [6] *E.N.*, 1140 a 9–10, 20–21.
[7] *E.N.*, 1140 b 4–6.

management, it is called Economics (οἰκονομία). (iii) As concerned with the State, it is called Political Science in the wider sense. This latter, Politics in a wide sense, is again subdivided into (a) the Architectonic or Legislative faculty, Politics in the narrower sense, and (b) the Subordinate or Administrative faculty. The last again subdivides into (α) Deliberative and (β) Judicial. (It is important to note that, in spite of these divisions, it is really the same virtue that is called practical wisdom in connection with the individual and Politics in connection with the good of the State.)

Practical wisdom, says Aristotle, is concerned with the practical syllogism, e.g. A is the end, B is the means, therefore B should be done. (If Aristotle were confronted with the difficulty that this only gives us an hypothetical imperative and not a categorical imperative, he might answer that in ethical matters the end is happiness, and as happiness is an end that all seek and cannot help seeking, that they seek by nature, the imperative that bears on our choice of means to this end is different from the imperatives that bear on the means to some freely-chosen end, and that while the latter are hypothetical, the former is a categorical imperative.) But Aristotle, with his customary good sense, expressly recognises that some people may have knowledge of the right action to do from their experience of life, although they have not got a clear idea of the general principles. Hence it is better to know the conclusion of the practical syllogism, without the major premiss, than to know the major premiss without knowing the conclusion.[1]

In reference to Socrates' view that all virtue is a form of prudence, Aristotle declares that Socrates was partly right and partly wrong. "He was wrong in holding that all virtue is a form of prudence, but right in holding that no virtue can exist without prudence."[2] Socrates held that all the virtues were forms of reason (as being forms of knowledge), but Aristotle declares that the truth is rather that they are all *reasonable*. "Virtue is not only the right and reasonable attitude, but the attitude which leads to right and reasonable choice, and right and reasonable choice in these matters is what we mean by prudence."[3] Prudence, therefore, is necessary for the truly virtuous man, (a) as being "the excellence of an essential part of our nature," and (b) inasmuch as "there can be no right choice without both prudence

[1] *E.N.*. 1141 b 14-22. [2] *E.N.*, 1144 b 19-21. [3] *E.N.*, 1144 b 26-8.

and virtue, seeing that the latter secures the choice of the right end, and the former the choice of the right means to its attainment."[1] But prudence or practical wisdom is not the same thing as cleverness (δεινότης). Cleverness is the faculty by which a man is enabled to find the right means to any particular end, and a rogue may be very clever in discovering the right means to attain his ignoble end. Mere cleverness is, then, different from prudence, which presupposes virtues and is equivalent to moral insight.[2] Prudence cannot exist without cleverness, but it cannot be reduced to cleverness, for it is a moral virtue. In other words, prudence is cleverness as dealing with the means that lead to the attainment, not of any sort of end, but of the true end of man, what is best for man, and it is moral virtue that enables us to choose the right end, so that prudence presupposes moral virtue. Aristotle is quite well aware that it is possible for a man to do what is right, what he ought to do, without being a good man. He is good only if his action proceeds from moral choice and is done because it is good.[3] For this prudence is necessary.

Aristotle admits that it is possible to have "natural" virtues in separation from one another (e.g. a child might be naturally courageous, without being at the same time gentle), but in order to have a moral virtue in the full sense, as a reasonable disposition, prudence is necessary. Moreover, "given the single virtues of prudence, all the virtues necessarily follow from it."[4] Socrates was then right in holding that no virtue can exist without prudence, though he was wrong in supposing that all virtues are forms of prudence. In the *Eudemian Ethics*[5] Aristotle remarks that for Socrates all the virtues were forms of knowledge, so that to know what justice is, for example, and to be just would come simultaneously, just as we are geometers from the moment we have learned geometry. In reply Aristotle says that it is necessary to distinguish between theoretical science and productive science. "We do not wish to know what bravery is but to be brave, nor what justice is but to be just." Similarly, he observes in the *Magna Moralia*[6] that "any one who knows the essence of justice is not forthwith just," while in the *Nicomachean Ethics* he compares those who think they will become good by mere theoretical knowledge, to patients who listen attentively to what the doctor says, but carry out none of his orders.[7]

[1] *E.N.*, 1145 a 2–6. [2] *E.N.*, 1144 a 23 ff. [3] *E.N.*, 1144 a 13 ff.
[4] *E.N.*, 1144 b 32–45 a 2. [5] *E.E.*, 1216 b 3–26. [6] *M.M.*, 1183 b 15–16.
[7] *E.N.*, 1105 b 12–18.

9. Aristotle refuses to admit that pleasures as such are bad. Pleasure cannot indeed be *the* good, as Eudoxus thought, for pleasure is the natural accompaniment of an unimpeded activity (as a sort of colouring attached to the activity), and it is the activity that should be aimed at, not the accompanying pleasure. We ought to choose certain activities, even if no pleasure resulted from them.[1] Nor is it true to say that all pleasures are desirable, for the activities to which certain pleasures are attached are disgraceful.

But if pleasure is not *the* good, we must not fall into the opposite extreme and say that all pleasure is wrong because some pleasures are disgraceful. As a matter of fact, says Aristotle, we might really say that disgraceful pleasures are not really pleasant, just as what appears white to a man with bad eyes, may not be really white. This observation is perhaps not very convincing: more convincing is Aristotle's remark that the pleasures themselves may be desirable, but not when obtained in such a way: and still more convincing is his suggestion that pleasures differ specifically according to the activities from which they are derived.[2]

Aristotle will not allow that pleasure is simply a replenishment, i.e. that pain represents a falling-short in the natural state, and that pleasure is a replenishment of the deficiency. It is true, indeed, that where there is replenishment there is pleasure, and that where there is exhaustion there is pain, but we cannot say universally of pleasure that it is a replenishment after antecedent pain. "The pleasures of mathematics, among the pleasures of sense those of smell as well as many sights and sounds, lastly, hopes and memories, are instances of pleasure which involve no antecedent pain."[3]

Pleasure, then, is something positive, and its effect is to perfect the exercise of a faculty. Pleasures differ specifically according to the character of the activities to which they are attached, and the good man must be our standard as to what is truly pleasant and unpleasant. (Aristotle remarks on the importance of training children to delight in and dislike the proper things, for which purpose the educator uses pleasure and pain "as a species of rudder."[4]) Some pleasures are pleasant only to those whose nature is corrupt: the true pleasures for man are those that accompany the activities that are proper to man. "All others, like the activities which they accompany, are so only in a partial and secondary sense."[5]

[1] *E.N.*, 1174 a 7–8.   [2] *E.N.*, 1173 b 20–31.   [3] *E.N.*, 1173 b 16–19.
[4] *E.N.*, 1172 a 19–25.   [5] *E.N.*, 1176 a 22–9.

In all this discussion of Pleasure, Aristotle's good sense and psychological insight are evident. He may be thought by some to over-emphasise the pleasures of theoretical and purely intellectual activity, but he sedulously avoids all extreme positions, refusing to agree with Eudoxus on the one hand that pleasure is *the* good, or with Speusippus on the other hand that all pleasures are bad.

10. Aristotle devotes Books Eight and Nine of the *Ethics* to the subject of Friendship. Friendship, he says, "is one of the virtues, or at any rate implies virtue. Moreover, it is one of the prime necessities of life."[1] Aristotle tends to give a somewhat self-centred picture of friendship. Thus he emphasises our need for friends at different periods of our life, and suggests that in friendship a man is loving himself—at first hearing a rather egoistic viewpoint. But he attempts the reconciliation of egoism and altruism by pointing out that it is necessary to distinguish the uses of the term "self-loving." Some men seek to get as much as possible for themselves of money, honour or the pleasures of the body, and these we call self-loving by way of reproach: others, i.e. good men, are anxious to excel in virtue and noble actions, and these, though "self-loving," we do not blame as such. The latter type of man "will give away money in order that his friend may have more. For the money goes to the friend, but the noble deed to himself, and in this way he appropriates the greater good. Similarly with regard to honours and offices."[2] The picture of a man relinquishing money or office to his friend in order that he himself may have the noble action to his credit, is not altogether pleasing; but Aristotle is doubtless right in observing that there can be a good type of self-love as well as a bad type. (Indeed we are bound to love ourselves and to make ourselves as good as possible.) A happier thought is Aristotle's saying that a man's relations to his friend are the same as his relations to himself, since the friend is a second self.[3] In other words, the concept of the self is capable of extension and may grow to include friends, whose happiness or misery, success or failure, become as our own. Moreover, incidental observations, such as "friendship consists in loving rather than in being loved,"[4] or that "men wish well to their friends for their sake,"[5] show that his view of friendship was not so egoistic as his words would sometimes lead one to suppose.

---

[1] *E.N.*, 1155 a 3–5.   [2] *E.N.*, 1169 a 27–30.   [3] *E.N.*, 1166 a 30–2.
[4] *E.N.*, 1159 a 27–8.   [5] *E.N.*, 1157 b 31–2.

That Aristotle's concept of friendship was a very wide one can be seen from the divisions that he makes between different types of friendship. (i) On the lowest level are friendships of utility, in which men do not love their friends for what they are in themselves, but only for the advantage which they receive from them.[1] Such friendships are necessary to man, since man is not economically self-sufficient. A business friendship would be of this type. (ii) Friendships of pleasure. These are founded on the natural delight that men take in the society of their fellow-men, and. are characteristic of the young, for "young people live by feeling, and have a main eye to their own pleasure and to the present moment."[2] But both these types of friendship are unstable, for when the motive of the friendship—utility or pleasure—is gone, the friendship also is destroyed. (iii) Friendships of the good. This type of friendship is perfect friendship and endures as long as both retain their character—"and virtue," says Aristotle, "is a lasting thing."

As we would expect, Aristotle makes not a few observations on the subject of friendship, which, if not profound, are shrewd and to the point, and which are applicable not only to natural friendship, but also to supernatural friendship with Christ Our Lord. For example, he observes that friendship differs from affection in that the latter is a feeling, the former a trained habit of mind,[3] and that "the wish for friendship is of rapid growth, but friendship itself is not."[4]

11. "If happiness is activity in accordance with virtue, it is reasonable that it should be in accordance with the highest virtue, and this will be that of the best thing in us."[5] The faculty, the exercise of which constitutes perfect happiness, is, according to Aristotle, the contemplative faculty, by which he means the faculty of intellectual or philosophic activity, thus showing the intellectualist standpoint which he shared with Plato. The precise relation of moral action to the highest type of human happiness is left obscure, but of course Aristotle makes it quite clear in the *Ethics* that without moral virtue true happiness is impossible.

Aristotle gives several reasons for saying that man's highest happiness consists in τὸ θεωρῆσαι.[6] (i) Reason is the highest faculty

---

[1] *E.N.*, 1156 a 10–12.   [2] *E.N.*, 1156 a 31–3.   [3] *E.N.*, 1157 b 28–31.
[4] *E.N.*, 1156 b 31–2.
God, says Aristotle, does not need a friend, since "the deity is his own well-being," but we need a friend or friends, since "with us welfare involves a something beyond us." (*E.E.*, 1245 b 14–19.)
[5] *E.N.*, 1177 a 12–13.   [6] *E.N.*, K, 7.

of man, and theoretic contemplation is the highest activity of reason. (ii) We can keep up this form of activity longer than any other, e.g. than bodily exercise. (iii) Pleasure is one of the elements of happiness, and "philosophy is admittedly the pleasantest of the activities in which human excellence manifests itself." (The last remark may have seemed a trifle unusual even to Aristotle himself, for he adds, "the pleasures of philosophy at least appear to be wonderfully pure and reliable, nor indeed is it surprising if the life of him who knows is pleasanter than that of the learner.") (iv) The philosopher is more self-sufficient than any other man. He cannot indeed dispense with the necessaries of life any more than others can (and Aristotle considered that the philosopher needs external goods in moderation and friends); but all the same "the thinker is able to pursue his studies in solitude, and the more of a thinker he is, the more capable he is of doing so." The co-operation of others is a great assistance to him, but if it be wanting, the thinker is better able than other men to get along without it. (v) Philosophy is loved for its own sake and not for the sake of any results that accrue from it. In the field of practical activity, it is not the action itself that is desirable, but some result to be attained by means of the activity. Philosophy is no mere means to a further end. (vi) Happiness would seem to imply leisure. Now, "the practical virtues find the field of their exercise in war or politics, which cannot be said to be leisurely employments, least of all war."

It is in the exercise of reason, then, and in the exercise of that reason concerning the noblest objects, that man's complete happiness is found, provided that it is extended over "a complete term of years." Such a life expresses the divine element in man, but we shall refuse to listen to those who advise us, being human and mortal, to mind things that are human and mortal. On the contrary, as far as possible, we ought to try to put off our mortality and do all we can to live the life to which the highest element in us points. For though it be but a small part of us, yet in power and value it far surpasses all the others. Moreover, it would seem to be the real self in each of us, since it is sovereign over all and better than all. And accordingly it would be strange if we were not to choose the life of our own true selves, but of something other than ourselves.[1]

What objects does Aristotle include among the objects of

---

[1] *E.N.*, 1177 b 26–1178 a 8.

theoretic contemplation? He certainly includes the invariable objects of metaphysics and mathematics, but does he include the objects of natural science? Probably only so far as they are non-contingent, since the highest activity of man is, as we have already seen, concerned with objects that are not contingent. In the *Metaphysics*[1] Aristotle makes physics a branch of theoretic wisdom, though in another place in the *Metaphysics*[2] he implies that it is also the study of contingent events. Physics therefore can belong to "contemplation" only in so far as it studies the invariable or necessary element in the contingent events that constitute the object of physics.

The highest object of metaphysics is God, but in the *Nicomachean Ethics* Aristotle does not expressly include the religious attitude expressed in the definition of the ideal life contained in the *Eudemian Ethics*, namely, "the worship and contemplation of God."[3] Whether Aristotle meant this attitude of religious adoration to be understood in the picture of the ideal life given in the *Nicomachean Ethics*, or had come to lose sight of this earlier religious attitude, we cannot well decide. In any case his treatment of contemplation exercised a great influence on posterity, not least on Christian philosophers, who naturally found it well adapted to their purpose. The intellectualist attitude of Aristotle finds its echo in the teaching of St. Thomas Aquinas, that the essence of the Beatific Vision consists in the act of the intellect rather than in the will's act, on the ground that the intellect is the faculty by which we *possess*, the will the faculty by which we enjoy the object already possessed by the intellect.[4]

[1] *Metaph.*, 1005 b 1–2, 1026 a 18–19.
[2] Cf. e.g. *Metaph.*, 1069 a 30 ff., where Aristotle says that physics has to do not only with eternal objects, but also with perishable sensible objects.
[3] *E.E.*, 1249 b 20. I have already mentioned (when treating of Aristotle's metaphysics) the philosopher's dictum in the *Magna Moralia* (1208 b 26–32) that there can be no question of friendship towards God, since, even if it were possible for us to love Him, He could not return our love.
[4] Cf. e.g. *Summa Theologica*, Ia, q. 26, art. 2.

CHAPTER XXXII

POLITICS

1. THE State (and by State Aristotle is thinking of the Greek City-State), like every other community, exists for an end. In the case of the State this end is the supreme good of man, his moral and intellectual life. The family is the primitive community that exists for the sake of life, for the supply of men's everyday wants,[1] and when several families join together and something more than the mere supply of daily needs is aimed at, the village comes into existence. When, however, several villages are joined together to form a larger community that is "nearly or quite self-sufficing,"[2] there comes into existence the State. The State comes into existence for the bare ends of life, but it continues in existence for the sake of the good life, and Aristotle insists that the State differs from family and village, not merely quantitatively but qualitatively and specifically.[3] It is only in the State that man can live the good life in any full sense, and since the good life is man's natural end, the State must be called a natural society. (The Sophists were therefore wrong in thinking that the State is simply the creation of convention.) "It is evident that the State is a creature of nature, and that man is by nature a political animal. And he who by nature and not by mere accident is without a State, is either above humanity or below it."[4] Man's gift of speech shows clearly that nature destined him for social life, and social life in its specifically complete form is, in Aristotle's view, that of the State. The State is prior to the family and to the individual in the sense that, while the State is a self-sufficing whole, neither the individual nor the family are self-sufficient. "He who is unable to live in society, or who has no need because he is sufficient for himself, must be either a beast or a god."[5]

The Platonic-Aristotelian view of the State as exercising the positive function of serving the end of man, the leading of the good life or the acquisition of happiness, and as being *natura prior* (to be distinguished from *tempore prior*) to the individual and the family, has been of great influence in subsequent philosophy.

---

[1] *Pol.*, 1252 b 13-14.   [2] *Pol.*, 1252 b 28 ff.   [3] *Pol.*, 1252 a 8-23.
[4] *Pol.*, 1253 a 1-4.   [5] *Pol.*, 1253 a 27-9.

Among Christian mediaeval philosophers it was naturally tempered by the importance they rightly attached to individual and family, and by the fact that they accepted another "perfect society," the Church, whose end is higher than that of the State (also by the fact that the nation-State was comparatively undeveloped in the Middle Ages); but we have only to think of Hegel in Germany and of Bradley and Bosanquet in England, to realise that the Greek conception of the State did not perish along with Greek freedom. Moreover, though it is a conception that can be, and has been, exaggerated (especially where Christian truth has been absent and so unable to act as a corrective to one-sided exaggeration), it is a richer and truer conception of the State than that of, e.g. Herbert Spencer. For the State exists for the temporal well-being of its citizens, i.e. for a positive and not merely for a negative end, and this positive conception of the State can quite well be maintained without contaminating it with the exaggerations of Totalitarian State mysticism. Aristotle's horizon was more or less bounded by the confines of the Greek City-State (in spite of his contacts with Alexander), and he had little idea of nations and empires; but all the same his mind penetrated to the essence and function of the State better than did the *laissez-faire* theorists and the British School from Locke to Spencer.

2. In the *Politics*, as we have it, Aristotle's treatment of the family is practically confined to discussion of the master-slave relationship and to the acquisition of wealth. Slavery (the slave, according to Aristotle, is a living instrument of action, i.e. aid to his master's life) is founded on nature. "From the hour of their birth, some are marked out for subjection, others for rule."[1] "It is clear that some men are by nature free, and others slaves, and that for these slavery is both expedient and right."[2] This view may well seem to us monstrous, but it must be remembered that the essence of Aristotle's doctrine is that men differ in intellectual and physical capacities and are thereby fitted for different positions in society. We regret that Aristotle canonised the contemporary institution of slavery, but this canonisation is largely an historical accident. Stripped of its historic and contemporary accidentals, what is censurable in it is not so much the recognition that men differ in ability and in adaptability (the truth of this is too obvious to need elaboration), but the over-rigid

[1] *Pol.*, 1254 a 23–4.   [2] *Pol.*, 1255 a 1–3.

dichotomy drawn between two types of men and the tendency
to regard the "slave-nature" as something almost less than human.
However, Aristotle tempered his acceptance and rationalisation
of slavery by insisting that the master should not abuse his
authority, since the interests of master and slave are the same,[1]
and by saying that all slaves should have the hope of emancipa-
tion.[2] Moreover, he admitted that the child of a natural slave
need not himself be a natural slave, and rejected slavery by right
of conquest on the ground that superior power and superior
excellence are not equivalent, while on the other hand the war
may not be a just war.[3] Nevertheless, regarded in itself, this
rationalisation of slavery is regrettable and betrays a limited
outlook on the part of the philosopher. In fact, Aristotle rejected
the legitimacy of the historical origin of slavery (conquest), and
then proceeded to give a philosophic rationalisation and justification of slavery!

3. There are, in general, two distinct modes of acquiring wealth,
and an intermediate mode.[4]

(i) The "natural" mode consists in the accumulation of things
needed for life by, e.g. grazing, hunting, agriculture. Man's needs
set a natural limit to such accumulation.

(ii) The intermediate mode is that of barter. In barter a thing
is used apart from its "proper use," but in so far as it is employed
for the acquisition of the needs of life, barter may be called a
natural mode of acquiring wealth.

(iii) The second, and "unnatural," mode of acquiring wealth
is the use of money as a means of exchange for goods. It seems
very odd to us that Aristotle should condemn retail trade, but
his prejudice is largely determined by the ordinary Greek attitude
towards commerce, which was regarded as illiberal and unfit for
the free man. Of importance is Aristotle's condemnation of
"usury," the breeding of money out of money, as he calls it.
"Money was intended to be used in exchange, but not to increase
at interest." This, literally taken, would condemn all taking of
interest on money, but Aristotle was probably thinking of the
practice of money-lenders, or usurers in our sense, who make
victims of the needy, credulous and ignorant: though he certainly
found a rationalisation of his attitude in his doctrine about the

---

[1] *Pol.*, cf. 1255 b 9–15, 1278 b 33–8. (In 1260 b 5–7 Aristotle criticises Plato's
notion that masters should not converse with their slaves.)
[2] *Pol.*, 1330 a 32–3.   [3] *Pol.*, 1254 b 32–4, 1255 a 3–28.
[4] *Pol.*, 1256 a ff. (A, 8–11).

"natural" purpose of money. Cows and sheep have a natural increase, as have fruit-trees, but money has no such natural increase: it is meant to be a means of exchange and nothing else. To serve as a means of exchange is its natural purpose, and if it is used to get more wealth merely by a process of lending it, without any exchange of goods for money and without any labour on the part of the lender, then it is being used in an unnatural way. Needless to say, Aristotle did not envisage modern finance. If he were alive to-day, we cannot say how he would react to our financial system, and whether he would reject, modify or find a way round his former views.

4. Aristotle, as one might expect, refused to allow himself to be carried away by Plato's picture of the ideal State. He did not think that such radical changes as Plato proposed were necessary; nor did he think that they would all, if feasible, be desirable. For instance, he rejected the Platonic notion of the crèche for the children of the Guardian-class, on the ground that he who is a child of all is a child of none. Better to be a real cousin than a Platonic son![1] Similarly, he criticised the notion of communism, on the ground that this would lead to disputes, inefficiency, etc. The enjoyment of property is a source of pleasure, and it is of no use for Plato to say that the State would be made happy if the Guardians were deprived of this source of happiness, for happiness is either enjoyed by individuals or it is not enjoyed at all.[2] In general, Plato aimed at excessive unification. Aristotle had no sympathy for the accumulation of wealth as such; but he saw that there is a need, not so much of equalising all property as of training citizens not to desire excessive wealth and, if any are incapable of being trained, then of preventing them acquiring it.

5. The qualifications of citizenship are taken by Aristotle from the practice of the Athenian democracy, which was not the same as the modern democracy with its representative system. In his view all the citizens should take their share in ruling and being ruled by turn,[3] and the minimum of citizen-rights is the right to participate in the Assembly and in the administration of justice. A citizen, therefore, is he ᾧ ἐξουσία κοινωνεῖν ἀρχῆς βουλευτικῆς καὶ κριτικῆς.[4]

The fact that Aristotle considered it essential for the citizen to sit in the Assembly and in the Law Courts, led him to exclude

---

[1] *Pol.*, 1262 a 13–14.   [2] *Pol.*, 1264 b 15–23.   [3] *Pol.*, cf. 1277 b.
[4] *Pol.*, 1275 b 18–19.

the class of mechanics and artisans from the citizenship, for they had not got the necessary leisure. Another reason is that manual toil deliberalises the soul and makes it unfit for true virtue.[1]

6. Discussing various types of Constitution Aristotle divides governments into those which aim at the common interest and those which aim at their own private interest.[2] Each of these broad divisions has three subdivisions, so that there are three good types of Constitution and three wrong or deviation-types of Constitution. To the right form Kingship corresponds the deviation-form Tyranny, to Aristocracy Oligarchy, and to Polity Democracy, and in his treatment of the comparative merits of the various Constitutions appears Aristotle's political sense. For him the ideal is that one man should so transcend all the other citizens individually and in the mass in respect of excellence that he would be the natural monarch and ruler. But in point of fact the perfect man does not appear, and, in general, pre-eminent heroes are found only among primitive peoples. This being so, aristocracy, i.e. the rule of many good men, is better than monarchy. Aristocracy is the best form of government for a body of people who can be ruled as freemen by men whose excellence makes them capable of political command. However, Aristotle recognises that even Aristocracy is perhaps too high an ideal for the contemporary State, and so he advocates "Polity," in which "there naturally exists a warlike multitude able to obey and to rule in turn by a law which gives office to the well-to-do according to their desert."[3] This is practically equivalent to rule by the middle-class, and is more or less a half-way house between Oligarchy and Democracy, since in a Polity it is indeed a multitude that rules—in distinction from Oligarchy—yet it is not a property-less mob, as in Democracy, for ability to serve as a warrior, i.e. as a heavily-armed hoplite, presupposes a certain amount of property. Aristotle is probably thinking—though he does not refer to it— of the Constitution at Athens in 411 B.C., when power rested with the Five Thousand who possessed heavy armour and the system of payment for attendance at meetings had been abolished. This was the Constitution of Theramenes.[4] Aristotle admired this type of Constitution, but his contention that the middle-class is the most stable, since both rich and poor are more likely to trust the middle-class than one another (so that the middle-class need

---

[1] *Pol.*, cf. 1277 a 33–1278 a 15, 1328 b 33–1329 a 21.   [2] *Pol.*, 1279 a 17–21.
[3] *Pol.*, 1288 a 12–15.   [4] Cf. *Athen. Polit.*, 28 and 33.

fear no coalition against it) may not sound so convincing to us as it did to him, though there is doubtless some truth in the view.[1]

7. Aristotle treats acutely of the various kinds and degrees of revolution which tend to occur under different Constitutions, of their causes and the means of preventing them; and, owing to his great historical knowledge, he was able to give apt historical illustrations of the points he wished to make.[2] He points out, for instance, that the revolutionary state of mind is largely brought about by one-sided notions of justice—democrats thinking that men who are equally free should be equal in everything, oligarchs thinking that because men are unequal in wealth they should be unequal in everything. He emphasises the fact that rulers should have no opportunity of making money for themselves out of the offices they hold, and stresses the requisites for high office in the State, namely, loyalty to the Constitution, capacity for administrative work and integrity of character. Whatever be the type of Constitution, it must be careful not to go to extremes; for if either democracy or oligarchy is pushed to extremes the ensuing rise of malcontent parties will be sure to lead in the end to revolution.

8. In Books Seven and Eight of the *Politics* Aristotle discusses his positive views of what a State should be.

(i) The State must be large enough to be self-sufficing (of course Aristotle's notion of what a self-sufficing community actually is would be altogether inadequate for modern times), but not so large that order and good government are rendered impracticable. In other words, it must be large enough to fulfil the end of the State and not so large that it can no longer do so. The number of citizens requisite for this purpose cannot of course be arithmetically determined *a priori*.[3]

(ii) Similarly with the territorial extent of the State. This should not be so small that a leisured life is impossible (i.e. that culture is impracticable) nor yet so large that luxury is encouraged. The city should not aim at mere wealth, but at importing her needs and exporting her surplus.[4]

(iii) Citizens. Agricultural labourers and artisans are necessary, but they will not enjoy citizen rights. Only the third class, that of the warriors, will be citizens in the full sense. These will be warriors in youth, rulers or magistrates in middle-age and priests

[1] *Pol.*, 1295 b 1–1296 a 21. [2] *Pol.*, Bk. 5. [3] *Pol.*, 1325 b 33–1326 b 24.
[4] *Pol.*, 1326 b 25–1327 b 18.

in old age. Each citizen will possess a plot of land near the city and another near the frontier (so that all may have an interest in the defence of the State). This land will be worked by the non-citizen labourers.[1]

(iv) Education. Aristotle, like Plato, attached great importance to education and, again like Plato, he considered it to be the work of the State. Education must begin with the body, since the body and its appetites develop earlier than the soul and its faculties; but the body is to be trained for the sake of the soul and the appetites for the sake of the reason. Education is therefore, first and foremost, a moral education—the more so because the citizen will never have to earn his living by work as husbandman or artisan, but will be trained to be, first a good soldier, and then a good ruler and magistrate.[2] This emphasis on moral education shows itself in Aristotle's views concerning pre-natal care and the games of the children. The Directors of Education will take all these matters very seriously, and will not consider the games of the children and the stories that are told them as things too insignificant for them to attend to. (In regard to musical education Aristotle makes the amusing remark, that "The rattle is a toy suited to the infant mind, and musical education is a rattle or toy for children of a larger growth."[3])

As the *Politics* is unfortunately incomplete—the sections dealing with education in science and philosophy being missing—we cannot say what precise directions Aristotle would have given in regard to the higher education of the citizens. One thing, however, is obvious, that both Plato and Aristotle had a lofty and noble conception of education and of the ideal of the citizen. They would have but scant sympathy with any scheme of education that laid the emphasis on technical and utilitarian training, since such a scheme leaves the higher faculties of the soul un-tended and so fails to fit man to attain his proper end, which is the purpose of education. For although it may sometimes look as though Aristotle wanted to educate men merely to be cogs in the State machine, this is really not the case: in his eyes the end of the State and the end of the individual coincide, not in the sense that the individual should be entirely absorbed in the State but in the sense that the State will prosper when the individual citizens are good, when they attain their own proper end. The only real guarantee of the stability and prosperity of the State is

[1] *Pol.*, 1328 b 2–1331 b 23.   [2] *Pol.*, 1332 b–1333 a 16.   [3] *Pol.*, 1340 b 29–31.

the moral goodness and integrity of the citizens, while conversely, unless the State is good and the system of its education is rational, moral and healthy, the citizens will not become good. The individual attains his proper development and perfection through his concrete life, which is a life in Society, i.e. in the State, while Society attains its proper end through the perfection of its members. That Aristotle did not consider the State to be a great Leviathan beyond good and evil is clear from the criticism he passes on the Lacedaemonians. It is a great mistake, he says, to suppose that war and domination are the be-all and end-all of the State. The State exists for the good life, and it is subject to the same code of morality as the individual. As he puts it, "the same things are best for individuals and states."[1] Reason and history both show that the legislator should direct all his military and other measures to the establishment of peace. Military States are safe only in wartime: once they have acquired their empire, they rust away like iron and fall. Both Plato and Aristotle, in their preoccupation with the fostering of a truly cultural political life, set their faces against imperialist dreams of military aggrandisement.

[1] *Pol.*, 1333 b 37.

CHAPTER XXXIII

AESTHETICS OF ARISTOTLE

1. *Beauty*

1. ARISTOTLE distinguishes the beautiful from the merely pleasant. For example, in the *Problemata*[1] he contrasts sexual preference with aesthetic selection, thus distinguishing real objective beauty from "beauty" that has reference only to desire. Again in the *Metaphysics*[2] he says that the mathematical sciences are not unrelated to the beautiful. The beautiful, therefore, for him cannot be the merely pleasant, that which pleasantly stimulates the senses.

2. Does Aristotle distinguish beauty from the good? He would seem not to have been very clear on this point.

(a) In the *Rhetoric*[3] he states that "the beautiful is that good which is pleasant because it is good," a definition which would not seem to admit of any real distinction between the beautiful and the moral. (Professor W. Rhys Roberts translates τὸ καλόν as Noble, cf. *Oxford Trans.*, Vol. XI.)

(b) In the *Metaphysics*, however, he expressly states that "the good and the beautiful are different (for the former always implies conduct as its subject, while the beautiful is found also in motionless things)."[4] This statement seems to differentiate between the beautiful and the moral at least, and may be taken to imply that the beautiful as such is not simply the object of desire. This should allow of a doctrine of aesthetic contemplation and of the *disinterested* character of such contemplation—as stated by e.g. Kant and Schopenhauer.

3. A further definition or description—and a more satisfactory one—is found in the *Metaphysics*[5] where Aristotle says that "the chief forms of beauty are order and symmetry and definiteness." It is the possession of these three properties that confers on mathematics a certain diagnostic value in regard to beautiful objects. (Aristotle seems to have been conscious of his obscurity, for he goes on to promise a more intelligible treatment, though, if the promise was ever fulfilled, its fulfilment is not extant.)

[1] 896 b 10–28. [2] 1078 a 31–b 6. [3] 1366 a 33–6. [4] 1078 a 31–2.
[5] 1078 a 36–b 1.

Similarly in the *Poetics*[1] Aristotle says that "beauty is a matter of size and order" or consists in size and order. Thus he declares that a living creature, in order to be beautiful, must present a certain order in its arrangement of parts and also possess a certain definite magnitude, neither too great nor too small. This would tally more or less with the definition in the *Metaphysics* and would imply that the beautiful is the object of contemplation and not of desire.

4. It is interesting to note that Aristotle in the *Poetics*[2] makes the subject-matter of Comedy to be the ridiculous, "which is a species of the ugly." (The ridiculous is "a mistake or deformity not productive of pain or harm to others.") This would imply that the ugly may be employed in a work of art, subordinated to the total effect. Aristotle does not, however, treat expressly of the relation of the ugly to the beautiful nor of the question, how far the "ugly" may become a constitutive element of the beautiful.[3]

II. *Fine Art in General*

1. Morality aims at conduct itself (πράττειν), Art at producing something, not at activity itself. But Art in general (τέχνη) must be subdivided[4] into:

(a) Art that aims at completing the work of nature, e.g. producing tools, since nature has provided man only with his hands.

(b) Art that aims at *imitating* nature. This is Fine Art, the essence of which Aristotle, like Plato, finds in imitation. In other words, in art an imaginary world is created which is an imitation of the real world.

2. But "imitation" has not, for Aristotle, the rather contemptuous colouring that it has for Plato. Not believing in Transcendental Concepts, Aristotle would naturally not make art a copy of a copy, at the third remove from truth. In fact, Aristotle inclines to the opinion that the artist goes rather to the ideal or the universal element in things, translating it into the medium of whatever art is in question. He says[5] that Tragedy makes its personages better, Comedy worse, than the "men of the present

---

[1] 1450 b 40–1.   [2] 1449 a 32–4.

[3] Cf. "Beautiful art shows its superiority in this, that it describes as beautiful things which may be in nature ugly or displeasing." Kant, *Critique of Judgment*, I. 1, 48.

[4] *Physics*, B 8, 199 a 15 ff.   [5] *Poetics*, 1448 a 16–18.

day." According to Aristotle, Homer's personages are better than we are. (Homer, it will be remembered, came in for some very hard knocks at the hands of Plato.)

3. Imitation, Aristotle insists, is natural to man, and it is also natural for man to delight in works of imitation. He points out that we may delight to view artistic representations of what is, in reality, painful to us to see.[1] (Cf. Kant, in passage already quoted in footnote.) But the explanation of this fact he seems to find in the purely intellectual pleasure of recognising that this man in the picture, for example, is someone we know, e.g. Socrates. This pleasure in recognition is no doubt a fact, but it hardly goes far towards constructing a theory of art: in fact, it is really irrelevant.

4. Aristotle expressly states that poetry "is something more philosophic and of graver import than history, since its statements are of the nature rather of universals, whereas those of history are singulars."[2] He goes on to explain that by a singular statement he means what e.g. Alcibiades did or had done to him, and by an universal statement "what such or such a kind of man will probably or necessarily say or do." The poet's function is, therefore, "to describe, not the thing that has happened, but a kind of thing that might happen, i.e. what is possible as being probable or necessary." It is in this that Aristotle finds the distinction between poet and historian, not in the one writing verse and the other prose. As he remarks: "you might put the work of Herodotus into verse, and it would still be a species of history."

On this theory, then, the artist deals rather with *types*, which are akin to the universal and ideal. An historian might write the life of Napoleon, telling what the historic figure Napoleon said and did and suffered: the poet, however, though he called the hero of his epic Napoleon, would rather portray universal truth or "probability." Adherence to historic fact is of minor importance in poetry. The poet may indeed take a subject from real history, but if what he describes is in—to use Aristotle's words—"the probable and possible order of things," he is none the less a poet. Aristotle even says that it is much better for the poet to describe what is probable but impossible than what is possible but improbable. This is simply a way of emphasising the universal character of poetry.

5. It is to be noted that Aristotle says that the statements of

---

[1] *Poetics*, 1448 b 10–19.   [2] *Poetics*, 1451 b 5–8.

poetry are of the nature *rather* of universals. In other words, poetry is not concerned with the abstract universal: poetry is not philosophy. Aristotle accordingly censures didactic poetry, for to give a system of philosophy in verse is to write versified philosophy; it is not to produce poetry.

6. In the *Poetics* Aristotle confines himself to a consideration of Epic, Tragedy and Comedy, particularly Tragedy: painting and sculpture and music are only mentioned incidentally, as when he tells us[1] that the painter Polygnotus portrayed personages "better than we are," Pauson worse, and Dionysius "just like ourselves." But what he does have to say on the subject of the other arts is important for his theory of imitation.

Thus *Music* (which is treated more or less as an accompaniment to the drama) was declared by Aristotle to be the most imitative of all the arts. Pictorial art only indicates mental or moral moods through external factors such as gesture or complexion, whereas musical tunes contain *in themselves* imitations of moral moods. And in the *Problemata*[2] he asks, "Why does what is heard alone of the objects of sense possess emotional import?" Aristotle would seem to be thinking of the direct stimulative effect of music which, though a fact, is hardly an aesthetic fact; yet the theory that music is the most imitative of the arts would none the less seem to extend the concept of imitation so far as to include *symbolism*, and to open the way to the romantic conception of music as a direct embodiment of spiritual emotion. (In the *Poetics* Aristotle remarks that "rhythm alone, without harmony, is the means in the dancer's imitations; for even he, by the rhythms of his attitudes, may represent men's characters, as well as what they do and suffer."[3])

7. In the *Politics*[4] Aristotle observes that drawing is useful in the education of the young, to acquire a "more correct judgment of the works of artists," and he argues also[5] that "music has a power of forming the character, and should therefore be introduced into the education of the young." It might seem, then, that Aristotle's interest in Fine Art is mainly educational and moral; but, as Bosanquet remarks, "to introduce aesthetic interest into education is not the same as to introduce educational interest into aesthetic."[6] Aristotle certainly regarded both music and the drama as having as one of their functions that of moral

---

[1] 1448 a 5–6. [2] 919 b 26. [3] 1447 a 26–8. [4] 1338 a 17–19.
[5] 1340 b 10–13. [6] *A History of Aesthetic*, p. 63.

education; but it does not necessarily follow that a person who recognises this function thereby makes the moral effect of an art a characteristic of its essence.

But though Aristotle dwells on the educational and moral aspect of art, that does not mean that he was blind to its recreative nature or effect.[1] If by allowing to music and the drama a recreative function he had referred merely to sense-pleasure or a tickling of the fancy, this would have been irrelevant to aesthetic; but higher recreation might well mean something more.

III. *Tragedy*

1. Aristotle's famous definition of tragedy is as follows:[2] "A tragedy—is the imitation of an action that is serious (σπουδαίας) and also, as having magnitude, complete in itself; in language with pleasurable accessories, each kind brought in separately in the parts of the work; in a dramatic, not in a narrative form; with incidents arousing pity and fear, wherewith to accomplish its catharsis (κάθαρσις) of such emotions."

I may add in explanation one or two points:

(i) "Serious," "noble," "good," indicate the character of the content of tragedy. This it shares with Epic poetry, and by it both are distinguished from Comedy and Satire, which deal with the inferior or ugly or ridiculous.

(ii) "Complete in itself," i.e. having beginning, middle and— being an organic whole. This *unity of plot* or organic unity of structure is the only unity strictly demanded by Aristotle.

In the *Poetics*[3] Aristotle does indeed observe that tragedy, in distinction from epic poetry, "endeavours to keep as far as possible within a single circuit of the sun or something near that"; but this is simply a statement of fact and he does not expressly state a demand for Unity of Time. As for Unity of Place, it is not mentioned. It is incorrect, therefore, to say that Aristotle demanded the three Unities in drama.

(iii) "Language with pleasurable accessories." Aristotle tells us himself that he means "with rhythm and harmony or song superadded."

[1] Aristotle certainly regarded the giving of enjoyment as one of the functions of tragedy. The question is, how far was this enjoyment specifically aesthetic in character?

[2] *Poetics*, 1449 b 25–9.　　　　　　　　　　　　[3] 1449 b 12–14.

(iv) "Each kind brought in separately," i.e. "some portions are worked out with verse only, and others in turn with song." Aristotle is naturally thinking of Greek tragedy with its alternations of spoken verse and choral songs.

(v) "In a dramatic, not in a narrative form." This distinguishes tragedy from epic poetry.

(vi) Catharsis. This states the psychological end or aim of tragedy, and I shall return to it presently.

2. Aristotle enumerates six formative elements of tragedy . . . fable or plot, characters, diction, thought, spectacle and melody.[1]

(i) The most important of these elements, in Aristotle's opinion, is the Plot, which is "the end and purpose of the tragedy." It is more important than Character, for "in a play—they do not act in order to portray the characters; they include the characters for the sake of action." Aristotle gives his reason for this somewhat strangely sounding dictum. "Tragedy is essentially an imitation not of persons but of action and life, of happiness and misery. All human happiness or misery takes the form of action; the end for which we live is a certain kind of activity, not a quality. Character gives us qualities, but it is in our actions—what we do—that we are happy or the reverse—a tragedy is impossible without action, but there may be one without Character."[2] (It is true perhaps that we can enjoy a good story in which the character-drawing is defective better than one in which the character-drawing is good but the plot is ridiculous.)

(ii) Aristotle, however, does not mean to belittle the importance of character-delineation in the drama: he admits that a tragedy without it is a defective tragedy and esteems it the most important element after the Plot.

(iii) "Thirdly comes the element of Thought, i.e. the power of saying whatever can be said, or what is appropriate to the occasion." Aristotle is thinking here, not of speech as revealing character directly but of speech "on a purely indifferent subject," i.e. Thought shown "in all they say when proving or disproving some particular point, or enunciating some universal proposition." Euripides certainly used tragedy as an opportunity for discussions on

---

[1] *Poetics*, 1450 a 4–16.   [2] *Poetics*, 1450 a 17–26.

various topics; but we may well feel that the drama is scarcely the place for Socratic disquisitions.

(iv) Diction, i.e. the verse and prose. This is important, but, as Aristotle wisely remarks, "one may string together a series of characteristic speeches of the utmost finish as regards Diction and Thought, and yet fail to produce the true tragic effect."

(v) Melody is "the greatest of the pleasurable accessories of Tragedy."

(vi) The Spectacle is indeed an attraction; but it is "the least of all the parts, and has least to do with the art of poetry." The getting-up of the *mise en scène* is "more a matter for the costumier than for the poet." It is a pity that Aristotle's words on this matter have not been heeded in later times. Elaborate scenery and spectacular effect are poor substitutes for plot and character-drawing.

3. Aristotle demands, as we have seen, unity of plot, in the sense of organic, structural unity. The plot must be neither so vast that it cannot be taken in at once by the memory nor so short that it is small and insignificant. But he points out that unity of plot "does not consist, as some suppose, in its having one man as its subject," nor in describing everything that happens to the hero. The ideal is that the several incidents of the plot should be so connected "that the transposal or withdrawal of any one of them will disjoin and dislocate the whole. For that which makes no perceptible difference by its presence or absence is no real part of the whole." The incidents must follow one another, not "episodically" but with probability or necessity. As Aristotle observes, "there is a great difference between a thing happening *propter hoc* and *post hoc*" (διὰ τάδε ἢ μετὰ τάδε).

4. Aristotle thought of Tragedy (complex, at least) as involving Peripety or Discovery, or both: (i) Περιπέτεια is the change from one state of things to the opposite, e.g. when the Messenger reveals the secret of Oedipus' birth, the whole state of affairs is changed within the play, for Oedipus realises that he has, unwittingly committed incest, (ii) Ἀναγνώρισις is "a change from ignorance to knowledge, and thus to either love or hate, in the personages marked for good or evil fortune."[1] In the case of Oedipus the Discovery is of course attended by Peripety, and this is, according to Aristotle, the finest form of Discovery.

[1] *Poetics*, 1451 b 32–5.

Thus is attained the tragic effect, the arousing of pity and fear.

5. Since tragedy is an imitation of actions arousing pity and fear, there are three forms of plot that must be avoided:

(i) A good man must not be seen passing from happiness to misery, as this is, in Aristotle's opinion, simply odious and will distract our minds by such disgust and horror that the tragic effect will not be realised.

(ii) A bad man must not be seen passing from misery to happiness. This is quite "untragic," appealing neither to our pity nor to our fear.

(iii) An extremely bad man must not be seen falling from happiness to misery. This may arouse human feeling but neither pity nor fear, for pity is occasioned by undeserved misfortune and fear by the misfortune of one like ourselves.

It remains, then, that tragedy should portray an "intermediate" type of person passing through misfortune, brought about by some error of judgment and not by vice or depravity. Aristotle accordingly refuses to agree with critics who censured Euripides for giving an unhappy ending to many of his plays, for this is the proper thing for tragedy, though not for Comedy. (Though there were occasional comic interludes in Greek tragedies, the tendency was to have unmixed tragedy or unmixed comedy, and Aristotle's views rather reflect this tendency.)

6. Tragic pity and fear should be aroused by the plot itself, and not by extraneous elements, e.g. by the portrayal of a brutal murder on the stage. (Aristotle would of course thoroughly approve of the way in which the murder of Agamemnon took place behind the scenes. Presumably he would censure the murder of Desdemona on the stage.)

7. We come now to the consideration of the psychological aim of tragedy, the arousing of pity and fear for the κάθαρσις of these emotions. The exact meaning to be attached to this famous doctrine of the κάθαρσις has been a subject of constant discussion: as Professor Ross says, "a whole library has been written on this famous doctrine."[1] The solution of the difficulty is rendered all the harder by the fact that the second book of the *Poetics* is missing—in which, it is conjectured, Aristotle explained what he meant by *catharsis* (and probably also treated of Comedy).

[1] Ross, *Aristotle*, p. 282. On this subject see e.g. *Aristotle's Theory of Poetry and Fine Art*, by S. H. Butcher (Macmillan); *Aristotle on the Art of Poetry*, by Ingram Bywater (Oxford).

Two main lines of explanation have been defended. (i) The catharsis in question is a *purification* of the emotions of pity and fear, the metaphor being drawn from ceremonial purification (the view of Lessing); (ii) the catharsis is a *temporary elimination* of the emotions of pity and fear, the metaphor being drawn from medicine (the view of Bernays). This latter view is the one that is most acceptable, i.e. from the exegetic standpoint, and now generally holds the field. According to this view the proximate object of tragedy, in Aristotle's eyes, is to arouse the emotions of pity and fear, i.e. pity for the past and actual sufferings of the hero, fear for those which loom before him. The ulterior object of tragedy then would be to relieve or purge the soul of these emotions through the harmless and pleasurable outlet afforded by the medium of art. The implication is that these emotions are undesirable, or rather that they are undesirable when in excess, but that all men, or at any rate most men, are subject to them, some in an excessive degree, so that it is a healthy and beneficial practice for all—necessary in the case of some—to give them a periodic opportunity of excitation and outlet through the medium of art, the process being at the same time a pleasurable one. This would be Aristotle's answer to Plato's criticism of tragedy in the *Republic*: tragedy has not a demoralising effect but is a harmless pleasure. How far Aristotle recognised an intellectual element in this recreation, is a question we cannot answer with only a truncated *Poetics* before us.

That Aristotle had in mind a purgative effect and not a moral purificative effect seems to be borne out by the *Politics*.

(i) According to Aristotle the flute has an exciting, and not an ethical effect, and should be left to professionals and kept for times when the hearing of music is a κάθαρσις rather than a form of education.[1] The inference is that catharsis is connected, not with ethical effect but with emotional effect.

(ii) Aristotle admits the "enthusiastic" harmonies in a well-ordered State, because they restore those who are subject to fits of enthusiasm to the normal condition. He then goes on to enumerate three purposes for which music should be studied: (a) "education," (b) "purification" ("the word 'purification' we use at present without explanation, but when hereafter we speak of poetry, we will treat the subject

[1] *Pol.*, 1341 a 17 ff.

with more precision"), (c) "for intellectual enjoyment, for relaxation and for recreation after exertion." From this enumeration alone one might suppose, applying what is said to tragedy, that the tragic effect might be ethical and purgative at the same time. But Aristotle proceeds to make a distinction. "In education ethical melodies are to be performed, but we may listen to the melodies of action and passion when they are performed by others. For feelings such as pity and fear, or again, enthusiasm, exist very strongly in some souls, and have more or less influence over all. Some persons fall into a religious frenzy whom we see disenthralled by the use of mystic melodies, which bring healing and purification to the soul. Those who are influenced by pity or fear and every emotional nature have a like experience, others in their degree are stirred by something which specially affects them, and all are in a manner purified and their souls lightened and delighted. The melodies of purification likewise give an innocent pleasure to mankind."[1] From this it would appear that the catharsis of pity and fear, though an "innocent pleasure," is not looked upon by Aristotle as ethical in character; and if it is not ethical in character, then "purification" should not be interpreted as purification in an ethical sense, but in a non-ethical sense, i.e. as a metaphor from medicine.

This interpretation is not acceptable to all. Thus Professor Stace declares that "The theory of certain scholars, based upon etymological grounds, that it means that the soul is purged, not *through*, but *of* pity and terror, that by means of a diarrhoea of these unpleasant emotions we get rid of them and are left happy, is the thought of men whose scholarship may be great, but whose understanding of art is limited. Such a theory would reduce Aristotle's great and illuminating criticism to the meaningless babble of a philistine."[2] The question, however, is not what is the *right* view of tragedy, but what was *Aristotle's* view. In any case, even the upholders of the "diarrhoea" theory could agree with Stace's own interpretation of Aristotle's meaning ("the representation of truly great and tragic sufferings arouses in the beholder pity and terror which purge his spirit, and render it serene and pure"), provided that "pure" is not understood as the term of an educational process.

[1] *Pol.*, 1342 a 1–16.   [2] *Crit. Hist.*, p. 331.

IV. *Origins of Tragedy and Comedy*

1. According to Aristotle,[1] tragedy began with "improvisation" on the part of the leader of the Dithyramb, no doubt between the two halves of the chorus. In origin, therefore, it would be connected with the worship of Dionysus, just as the renaissance of the drama in Europe was connected with the mediaeval mystery plays.

2. Comedy began in a parallel manner, from the phallic songs, "which still survive as institutions in many of our cities." He thought no doubt of the leader coming to improvise some scurrilous piece.

3. The most significant thing in the development of the drama is for Aristotle the increasing importance of the actor. Aeschylus first increased the number of actors to two, curtailing the business of the Chorus. Sophocles added a third actor and scenery.

4. When spoken parts were introduced, the iambic metre was brought in as "the most speakable of metres." ("The reason for their original use of the trochaic tetrameter was that their poetry was satyric and more connected with dancing than it now is.")

Discussion of the highly problematic question of the origins of tragedy and comedy scarcely belongs to the history of philosophy; so I will content myself with the foregoing brief indication of the view of Aristotle, which bristles with difficulties (i) as to interpretation, (ii) as to its correctness.

Note on the Older Peripatetics

The old Academy continued the mathematical speculation of Plato: the older Peripatetics continued Aristotle's empirical trend, while adhering closely to the general philosophical position of their Master, though they made slight modifications and developments, e.g. in the field of logic. Thus both Theophrastus and Eudemus of Rhodes adhered pretty faithfully to the metaphysical and ethical tenets of Aristotle, this being especially true of Eudemus who was termed by Simplicius the γνησιώτατος of Aristotle's disciples.[2] Theophrastus ardently defended the Aristotelian doctrine of the eternity of the world against Zeno the Stoic.

Theophrastus of Eresus in Lesbos succeeded Aristotle as head of the Peripatetic School in 322/1 and continued in that office until his death in 288/7 or 287/6.[3] He is chiefly remarkable for

---

[1] *Poetics*, 1449 a 9-30.   [2] Simplic. *Phys.*, 411, 14.   [3] Diog. Laërt., 5, 36.

his continuation of Aristotle's work in the field of empirical science. Applying himself particularly to Botany, he left works on that subject which made him the botanical authority up to the end of the Middle Ages, while through his zoological studies he seemed to have grasped the fact that changes of colour in the animal world are partly due to "adaptation to environment." A scholar of wide interests, like Aristotle himself, Theophrastus also composed a history of philosophy (the famous φυσικῶν δόξαι) and works on the history and nature of religion, Περὶ θεῶν, Περὶ εὐσεβείας and Περὶ τὸ θεῖον ἱστορία.. Of these works only part of the history of philosophy has come down to us, while Porphyry has preserved some of the Περὶ εὐσεβείας.[1] Believing that all living beings are akin, Theophrastus rejected animal-sacrifices and the eating of flesh-meat and declared that *all* men are related to one another and not merely the fellow-members of a nation. One may also mention his celebrated work, the *Characters*, a study of thirty types of character.

Aristoxenus of Tarentum brought with him into the Peripatetic School certain of the later Pythagorean theories, e.g. the doctrine that the soul is the harmony of the body, a doctrine that led Aristoxenus to deny the soul's immortality.[2] He thus championed the view suggested by Simmias in the *Phaedo* of Plato. But he followed in the footsteps of Aristotle by his empirical work on the nature and history of music.

Aristoxenus' theory of the soul was shared by Dicaearchus of Messene,[3] who composed a βίος Ἑλλάδος, in which he traced the civilisation of Greece through the stages of primitive savagery, nomadic life and agriculture. He differed from Aristotle in that he accorded the practical life the preference over the theoretical.[4] In his Τριπολιτικός he declared that the best constitution is a mixture of the three types of government, monarchy, aristocracy and democracy, and considered that this type of mixed constitution was realised at Sparta.

Demetrius of Phaleron, a pupil of Theophrastus, and a prolific writer[5] is remarkable for his political activity (he was head of the government at Athens from 317 until 307) and for having urged Ptolemy Soter to found the library and School of Alexandria (whither Demetrius betook himself about 297). As this project

---

[1] Porph., Περὶ ἀποχῆς ἐμψύχων.   [2] Cic., *Tusc.*, 1, 10, 19.
[3] Cic., *Tusc.*, 1, 10, 21; 31, 77.   [4] Cic., *Ad Att.*, 2, 16, 3.
[5] Diog. Laërt., 5, 80-1.

was realised by Ptolemy Philadelphus, the successor of Ptolemy Soter, shortly after 285, Demetrius furnished the link between the work of the Peripatos at Athens and the scientific and research work of the Greeks at Alexandria, the city which was to become a celebrated centre of scholarship and learning.

CHAPTER XXXIV

PLATO AND ARISTOTLE

PLATO and Aristotle are, without a shadow of doubt, not only the two greatest Greek philosophers, but also two of the greatest philosophers the world has seen. They had much in common with one another (how should it not be so, when Aristotle was for many years a pupil of Plato and began from the Platonic standpoint?); but there is also a marked difference of outlook between them, which, if one prescinds from the very considerable common element, enables one to characterise their respective philosophies as standing to one another in the relation of thesis (Platonism) to antithesis (Aristotelianism), a thesis and an antithesis which need to be reconciled in a higher synthesis, in the sense that the valuable and true elements in both need to be harmoniously developed in a more complete and adequate system than the single system of either philosopher taken in isolation. Platonism may be characterised by reference to the idea of Being, in the sense of abiding and steadfast reality, Aristotelianism by reference to the idea of Becoming; but, if unchanging being is real, so also are change and becoming real, and to both aspects of reality must justice be done by any adequate system of philosophy.

To characterise the philosophy of Plato by reference to the idea of Being and that of Aristotle by reference to the idea of Becoming, is to be guilty of a generalisation, a generalisation which does not, of course, represent the whole truth. Did not Plato treat of Becoming, did he not propound a theory of teleology, it may be asked with justice; did he not recognise the material world as the sphere of change and did he not even explicitly admit that change or movement (so far as this is involved by the nature of life or soul) must belong to the sphere of the real? On the other hand, did not Aristotle find a place, and a very important place, for unchanging being, did he not, even in the changing, material world, discover an element of stability, of fixity, did he not declare that the sublimest occupation of man is the contemplation of unchanging objects? One cannot but give an affirmative answer to these questions; yet the truth of the generalisation is not disposed of, since it refers to what is peculiarly characteristic in each system, to its general tone or flavour, to the general orientation of the philosopher's thought. I will attempt briefly to justify this generalisation, or at least to indicate the lines along which I should attempt to justify it in detail, did space permit.

Plato, like Socrates, assumed the validity of ethical judgments; like Socrates again, he attempted to reach a clear apprehension of ethical values dialectically, to enshrine their nature in definition, to crystallise the ethical idea. He came to see, however, that if ethical concepts and ethical judgments are objective and universally valid, these concepts must possess some objective foundation. Obviously enough moral values are ideals, in the sense that they are not concrete things like sheep or dogs: they are what ought to be realised in the concrete world, or what it is desirable to realise in the concrete world, through human conduct: hence the objectivity attaching to values cannot be the same kind of objectivity that attaches to sheep or dogs, but must be an ideal objectivity or an objectivity in the ideal order. Moreover, material things in this world change and perish, whereas moral values, Plato was convinced, are unchanging. He concluded, therefore, that moral values are ideal, yet objective, essences, apprehended intuitively at the end of a process of dialectic. These moral values, however, have a common share in goodness or perfection, so that they are rightly said to participate in, to derive their goodness or perfection from, the supreme ideal essence, absolute goodness or perfection, the Idea of the Good, the "sun" of the ideal world.

In this way Plato elaborated a metaphysic on the basis of the Socratic ethic, and, being based on the thought of Socrates, it could, without undue propriety, be put into the mouth of Socrates. But, in the course of time, Plato came to apply his dialectic, not only to moral and aesthetic values, but to the common concept in general, maintaining that, just as good things participate in goodness, so individual substances participate in the specific essence. This new viewpoint cannot be said to constitute a radical break in Plato's thought, inasmuch as the theory of values itself rested to a certain extent on a logical foundation (that the common name must have an objective reference), it is rather an extension of the theory; but the new viewpoint forced Plato to consider more closely, not only the relation between the Ideas themselves, but also between sensible objects and the Ideas or exemplary essences. He thus developed his theory of the hierarchic noetic structure and the "communion" between the Ideas and explained participation as imitation, with the result that, in place of pure values on the one hand and bearers of values on the other, there was substituted the dichotomy between true essential Reality, the objective noetic structure and sensible particulars, between the original and the mirrored or "copy." This division came to have the force of a division between Being on the one hand and Becoming on the other, and there can be no question on which side of the dividing line Plato's chief interest lay.

It may be objected that Plato regarded the specific essence of e.g. man as an ideal and that the true meaning of Becoming is to be sought in the gradual approximation to and realisation of the ideal in the material world, in human personality and society, a realisation which is the task of God and of God's human co-operators. This is perfectly true, and I have not the slightest wish to belittle the importance of teleology in the Platonic philosophy; but none the less, the emphasis was most decidedly placed by Plato on the sphere of Being, of true Reality. Through his doctrine of teleology he certainly admitted some relation between the changing world and the unchanging world of Being; but becoming as such and particularity as such were to him the irrational, the factor that must be dismissed into the sphere of the indeterminate. How could it be otherwise for a thinker to whom logic and ontology are one, or at least parallel? Thought is concerned with the universal and thought apprehends Being: the universal, then, is Being and the particular as such is not Being. The universal is unchanging, so that Being is unchanging, the particular changes, becomes, perishes, and in so far as it changes, becomes, perishes, it is not Being. Philosophical activity or dialectic is an activity of thought and is thus concerned with Being primarily and only secondarily with Becoming, in so far as it "imitates" Being, so that Plato, as philosopher, was primarily interested in essential and unchanging Being. He was also interested, it is true, in the moulding of the world according to the pattern of Being; but the emphasis is placed unmistakably on Being rather than on Becoming.

It might seem that much of what I have said in regard to Plato would apply equally well, perhaps even better, to Aristotle, who asserted that the metaphysician is concerned with being as being, who referred change and becoming to the final causality of the unmoved First Mover, who taught that man's highest activity is the theoretic contemplation of unchanging objects, of those beings which are *par excellence* being, actuality, form. Nevertheless, this very real side of the Aristotelian philosophy represents rather the Platonic legacy, even if elaborated and developed by Aristotle himself. I do not intend for a moment to question the fact that Aristotle attributed great importance to this aspect of his philosophy or the fact that Aristotle accomplished a great deal in this line of speculation, e.g. by bringing out clearly the intellectual and immaterial nature of pure form and so making a contribution of tremendous value to natural theology; but I wish to inquire into the character of Aristotle's peculiar contribution to philosophy in so far as he deviated from Platonism, to ask what was the antithesis that Aristotle set over against the Platonic thesis.

What was Aristotle's chief objection against the Platonic theory of Ideas? That it left an unbridged chasm between sensible objects and the Ideas. As the sensible objects were said to imitate or participate in the Ideas, one would expect to find Plato admitting some internal essential principle, some formal cause within the object itself, placing it in its class, constituting it in its essence, whereas in point of fact Plato did not allow for an interior formal principle of this sort, but left a dualism of pure universal and pure particular, a dualism which resulted in depriving the sensible world of most of its reality and meaning. What was Aristotle's answer to this objection? While admitting the general Platonic position that the universal element, or essential form, is the object of science, of rational knowledge, he identified this universal element with the immanent essential form of the sensible object, which, together with its matter, constitutes the object and which is the intelligible principle in the object. This formal principle realises itself in the activity of the object, e.g. the formal principle in an organism, its entelechy, expresses itself in organic functions, unfolds itself in matter, organises, moulds and shapes matter, tends towards an end, which is the adequate manifestation of the essence, of the "idea," in the phenomenon. All nature is conceived as a hierarchy of species, in each of which the essence tends towards its full actualisation in a series of phenomena, drawn, in some rather mysterious way, by the ultimate final causality of the supreme Unmoved Mover, which is itself complete actuality, pure immaterial Being or Thought, self-subsistent and self-contained. Nature is thus a

13

dynamical process of self-perfection or self-development, and the series of phenomena has meaning and value.

From this brief statement of Aristotle's position it should be quite clear that his philosophy is not simply a philosophy of Becoming. Being may truly be predicated of something in so far as it is actual, and that which is *par excellence* Being is also *par excellence* Actuality, unmixed with potency; the world of becoming, being a world of realisation, of reduction of potency to act, is a world in which actuality or being is being constantly realised in matter, in phenomena, under the final attraction of ultimate Actuality or Being; so that the explanation of Becoming is to be found in Being, for Becoming is for the sake of Being, which is always logically, even when it is not temporally, prior. If I say, then, that Aristotle was possessed by the concept of Becoming, that his philosophy, as peculiarly his, may justly be characterised by reference to his doctrine of Becoming, I do not mean to deny that Being was, for him as for Plato, of supreme importance or that he gave a metaphysic of Being which was, in some respects, greatly superior to that of Plato: what I mean is, that Aristotle, through his theory of the entelechy, the immanent substantial form, which tends to its realisation in the processes of nature, was enabled to attach a meaning and reality to the sensible world which are missing in the philosophy of Plato and that this particular contribution to philosophy gives a characteristic tone and flavour to Aristotelianism as distinct from Platonism. Aristotle said that the end of man is an activity, not a quality, whereas one has the impression that for Plato quality would take precedence of activity: Plato's "Absolute" was not the immanent activity of Aristotle's "self-thinking Thought" and Plato's "Absolute" was the supreme Exemplar. (That Aristotle's characterisation of matter tended to diminish the reality and intelligibility of the material world is no objection against my main thesis, since his doctrine of matter was very largely an effect of his Platonic education, and my main thesis is concerned with Aristotle's *peculiar* contribution to the philosophy of nature.)

Aristotle thus made a most important contribution to the philosophy of nature and he certainly regarded himself as having broken fresh ground. In the first place, he regarded his doctrine of the *immanent* essence as an antithesis to, or correction of, Plato's doctrine of the transcendental essence, and, in the second place, his remarks concerning the emergence of the idea of finality in philosophy, even if those remarks are to some extent patently unjust to Plato, show clearly that he regarded his theory of immanent teleology as something new. But though Aristotle provided a needed correction or antithesis to Platonism in this respect, he discarded much that was of value in the process of correcting his predecessor. Not only was Plato's conception of Providence, of Divine Reason immanent in the world and operating in the world, discarded by Aristotle, but also Plato's conception of exemplary causality. Plato may have failed to work out a systematised view of Absolute Being as exemplary Cause of essences, as Ground of value; he may have failed to realise, as Aristotle realised, that the immaterial form is intelligent, that supreme Actuality is supreme Intelligence; he may have failed to bring together and identify the supreme Efficient, Exemplary and Final Causes; but, in his opposition to Plato's inadequate view of the concrete object of this world, Aristotle allowed himself to miss and pass over the profound truth in the Platonic theory. Each thinker, then, has his high-points, each made an invaluable contribution to philosophy, but neither thinker gave the complete truth, even so far as that is attainable. One may be drawn towards either Plato or Aristotle by temperamental affinity, but one would not be justified in rejecting Aristotle for Plato or Plato for Aristotle: the truths contained in their respective philosophies have to be integrated and harmoniously combined in a complete synthesis, a synthesis which must incorporate and build upon that cardinal tenet, which was held in common by both Plato and Aristotle, namely, the conviction that the fully real is the fully intelligible and the fully good, while utilising also the peculiar contributions of each philosopher, in so far as these contributions are true and so compatible.

In the pages devoted to Neo-Platonism we shall witness an attempt, successful or unsuccessful as the case may be, to accomplish such a synthesis, an attempt which has been repeated in the course of both mediaeval and modern philosophy; but it might be as well to point out that, if such a synthesis is possible, it is made possible largely through the Platonic elements which are contained in Aristotelianism. Let me give one example, to illustrate my meaning. If Aristotle, in correcting what he considered to be the excessively dualistic character of the Platonic anthropology (I refer to the soul-body relationship), had explicitly rejected the supersensible character of the rational principle in man and had reduced thought, for example, to matter in motion, he would indeed have posited an antithesis to the Platonic theory, but this antithesis would have been of such a character that it could not combine with the thesis in a higher synthesis. As it was, however, Aristotle never, as far as we know, rejected the presence of a supersensible principle in man—he affirms it in his *De Anima* —even though he insisted that the soul cannot inhabit *any* body but is the entelechy of a particular body. A synthesis was, therefore, rendered possible, which would include the Aristotelian idea of the soul as the form of the body, while allowing, with Plato, that the *individual* soul is more than the body and survives death in individual self-identity.

Again, it might appear perhaps at first sight that the Aristotelian God, the Thought of Thought, constitutes an incompatible antithesis to the Platonic Idea of the Good, which, though intelligible, is not depicted as intelligent. Yet, since pure form is not only the intelligible but also the intelligent, the Platonic Absolute Good cried out, as it were, to be identified with the Aristotelian God, an identification which was accomplished in the Christian synthesis at least, so that both Plato and Aristotle contributed different, though complementary, facets of theism.

(In the foregoing remarks I have spoken of a synthesis of Platonism and Aristotelianism; but one is entitled to speak of the necessity of a synthesis only when there is question of two "antithetical" theories, each of them being more or less true in what it affirms and false in what it denies. For example, Plato was correct in affirming exemplarism, wrong in neglecting immanent substantial form, while Aristotle was correct in asserting his theory of the immanent substantial form, wrong in neglecting exemplarism. But there are other aspects of their philosophies in regard to which one can hardly speak of the necessity for a synthesis, since Aristotle himself accomplished the synthesis. For instance, the Aristotelian logic, that marvellous creation of genius, does not need to be synthesised with the Platonic logic, owing to the simple fact that it was a tremendous advance on Plato's logic (or what we know of it, at least) and itself comprised what was valuable in the Platonic logic).

PART V

POST-ARISTOTELIAN PHILOSOPHY

CHAPTER XXXV

INTRODUCTORY

1. With the reign of Alexander the Great the day of the free and independent Greek City-State had really passed away. During his reign and that of his successors, who fought with one another for political power, any freedom that the Greek cities possessed was but nominal—at least it depended on the goodwill of the paramount sovereign. After the death of the great Conqueror in 323 B.C. we must speak rather of Hellenistic (i.e. in opposition to National-Hellenic) than of Hellenic civilisation. To Alexander the sharp distinction between Greek and "Barbarian" was unreal: he thought in terms of Empire, not in terms of the City: and the result was, that while the East was opened up to the influence of the West, Greek culture on its side could not remain uninfluenced by the new state of affairs. Athens, Sparta, Corinth, etc.—these were no longer free and independent units, united in a common feeling of cultural superiority to the barbarian darkness round about them: they were merged in a larger whole, and the day was not far distant when Greece was to become but a Province of the Roman Empire.

The new political situation could not be without its reaction on philosophy. Both Plato and Aristotle had been men of the Greek City, and for them the individual was inconceivable apart from the City and the life of the City: it was in the City that the individual attained his end, lived the good life. But when the free City was merged in a greater cosmopolitan whole, it was but natural that not only cosmopolitanism, with its ideal of citizenship of the world, as we see it in Stoicism, but also individualism should come to the fore. In fact these two elements, cosmopolitanism and individualism, were closely bound together. For when the life of the City-State, compact and all-embracing, as Plato and Aristotle had conceived it, had broken down and citizens were merged in a much greater whole, the individual was inevitably cast adrift by himself, loosed from his moorings in the City-State. It was but to be expected, then, that in a cosmopolitan society philosophy should centre its interest in the individual, endeavouring to meet his demand for guidance in life, which he had to live out in a great society and no longer in a comparatively small City-family, and so displaying a predominantly ethical and practical trend—as in Stoicism and Epicureanism. Metaphysical and physical speculation tend to drop into the background: they are of interest not for their own sake but as providing a basis and preparation for ethics. This concentration on the ethical makes it easy to understand why the new Schools borrowed their metaphysical notions from other thinkers, without attempting fresh speculation on their own. Indeed it is to the pre-Socratics that they return in this respect, Stoicism having recourse to the Physics of Heraclitus and Epicureanism to the Atomism of Democritus. More than that, the post-Aristotelian Schools returned to the pre-Socratics, at least in part, even for their ethical ideas or tendencies, the Stoics borrowing from Cynic ethics and the Epicureans from the Cyrenaics.

This ethical and practical interest is particularly marked in the development of the post-Aristotelian Schools in the Roman period, for the Romans were not, like the Greeks, speculative and metaphysical thinkers; they were predominantly men of practice. The old Romans had insisted on *character*—speculation was somewhat foreign to them—and in the Roman Empire, when the former ideals and traditions of the Republic had been swamped, it was precisely the philosopher's task to provide the individual with a code of conduct which would enable him to pilot his way through the sea of life, maintaining a consistency of principle and action based on a certain spiritual and moral independence. Hence the phenomenon of philosopher-directors, who performed a task somewhat analogous to that of the spiritual director as known to the Christian world.

This concentration on the practical, the fact that philosophy took as its office the provision of standards of life, naturally led to a wide diffusion of philosophy among the cultured classes of the Hellenistic-Roman world and so to a kind of Popular Philosophy. Philosophy in the Roman period became more and more part of the regular course of education (a fact which demanded its presentation in an easily apprehended form), and it was in this way that philosophy became a rival to Christianity, when the new Religion began to lay claim to the allegiance of the Empire. Indeed one may say that philosophy, to a certain extent at least, offered to satisfy the religious needs and aspirations of man. Disbelief in the popular mythology was common, and where this disbelief reigned—among the educated classes—those who were not content to live without religion at all had either to attach themselves to one of the many cults that were introduced into the Empire from the East and which were definitely more calculated to satisfy man's spiritual aspirations than the official State religion with its businesslike attitude, or to turn to philosophy for the satisfaction of those needs. And so it is that we can discern religious elements in such a predominantly ethical system as Stoicism, while in Neo-Platonism, the last flower of Ancient Philosophy, the syncretism of religion and philosophy reaches its culmination. More than that, we may say that in Plotinian Neo-Platonism, in which the mystical flight of the spirit or ecstasy is made the final and highest point of intellectual activity, philosophy tends to pass over into religion.

Insistence on ethics alone leads to an ideal of spiritual independence and self-sufficiency such as we find in both Stoicism and Epicureanism, while insistence on religion tends rather to assert dependence on a Transcendental Principle and to ascribe the purification of the self to the action of the Divine, an attitude that we find in a mystery-cult like that of Mithras. It is to be noted, however, that both tendencies, the tendency to insist on the ethical, the self-sufficient perfection of the personality or the acquisition of a true moral personality, and the tendency to insist on the attitude of the worshipper towards the Divine or the need of the non-self-sufficient human being to unite himself with God, contributed to meet the same want, the want of the individual in the Greco-Roman world to find a sure basis for his individual life, since the religious attitude too brought with it a certain independence vis-à-vis the secular Empire. In practice, of course, the two attitudes tended to coalesce, the emphasis being placed sometimes on the ethical (as in Stoicism), sometimes on the religious factor (as in the mystery-cults), while in Neo-Platonism there was an attempt at a comprehensive synthesis, the ethical being subordinated to the religious, but without losing its importance.

2. In the development of the Hellenistic-Roman philosophy it is usual to distinguish several phases:[1]

[1] Cf. Ueberweg-Praechter, pp. 32–3.

(i) The first phase or period extends from about the end of the fourth century B.C. to the middle of the first century B.C. This period is characterised by the founding of the Stoic and Epicurean philosophies, which place the emphasis on conduct and the attainment of personal happiness, while harking back to pre-Socratic thought for the cosmological bases of their systems. Over against these "dogmatic" systems stands the Scepticism of Pyrrho and his followers, to which must be added the sceptical vein in the Middle and New Academies. The interaction between these philosophies led to a certain Eclecticism, which showed itself in a tendency on the part of the Middle Stoa, the Peripatetic School and the Academy to eclectic assimilation of one another's doctrines.

(ii) Eclecticism on the one hand and Scepticism on the other hand continue into the second period (from about the middle of the first century B.C. to the middle of the third century A.D.), but this period is characterised by a return to philosophical "orthodoxy." Great interest is taken in the founders of the Schools, their lives, works and doctrines, and this tendency to philosophical "orthodoxy" is a counterpart to the continuing eclecticism. But the interest in the past was also fruitful in scientific investigation, e.g. in editing the works of the old philosophers, commenting on them and interpreting them. In such work the pre-eminence belongs to the Alexandrians.

This scientific interest is not, however, the sole characteristic of the second period. Over against the scientific interest we find the tendency to religious mysticism, which becomes ever stronger. It has been pointed out (e.g. Praechter, p. 36) that this tendency has a common root with the scientific tendency, namely, the disappearance of productive speculation. While the latter factor might lead to scepticism or to devotion to scientific pursuits, it might equally result in a tendency to religious mysticism. This tendency was of course favoured by the growing religious consciousness of the time and by acquaintance with religions of eastern origin. Western philosophers, e.g. the Neo-Pythagoreans, endeavoured to incorporate these religious-mystical elements into their speculative systems, while eastern thinkers, e.g. Philo of Alexandria, tried to systematise their religious conceptions in a philosophic framework. (Thinkers like Philo were, of course, also influenced by the desire to win over the Greeks for their un-Greek doctrines by presenting the latter in philosophic guise.)

(iii) The third period (from about the middle of the third

century A.D. to the middle of the sixth century A.D.—or, in Alexandria, to the middle of the seventh century) is that of Neo-Platonism. This final speculative effort of Ancient Philosophy attempted to combine all the valuable elements in the philosophic and religious doctrines of East and West in one comprehensive system, practically absorbing all the philosophic Schools and dominating philosophical development for a number of centuries, so that it cannot justifiably be overlooked in a history of philosophy or be relegated to the dustbin of esoteric mysticism. Moreover, Neo-Platonism exercised a great influence on Christian speculation: we have only to think of names like those of St. Augustine and the Pseudo-Dionysius.

3. A feature of the Hellenistic world that must not be passed over is the increased cultivation of the special sciences. We have seen how philosophy and religion tended to become united: with regard to philosophy and the special sciences the opposite holds good. Not only had the domain of philosophy become more sharply delineated than it was in the early days of Greek thought, but the different sciences had themselves reached such a pitch of development that they required special treatment. Moreover, the improvement in the external conditions for research and study, though itself largely an outcome of specialisation, reacted in turn on the cultivation of the sciences, promoting an intensification of departmental work and research. The Lyceum had, of course, greatly contributed to the growth and development of the sciences, but in the Hellenistic age there arose scientific Institutes, Museums and Libraries in the great capital cities of Alexandria, Antioch, and Pergamon, with the result that philological and literary research, mathematical, medical and physical studies, were enabled to make great strides. Thus according to Tzetzes, the "outer" library at Alexandria contained 42,800 volumes, while the main library in the Palace contained some 400,000 "mixed" and some 90,000 "unmixed" or "simple" volumes, the latter being probably small papyrus rolls while the former were bigger rolls. Later on the larger volumes, divided into books, were reduced to "simple" volumes. We are told that when Antony presented Cleopatra with the Pergamene library, he gave her 200,000 "simple" volumes.

It may be, of course, that the influence of philosophy on the special sciences was not always favourable to their advance, for speculative assumptions sometimes took a place which did not belong to them and led to hasty and precipitate conclusions, when experiment and exact observation should have exercised the decisive rôle. On the other hand, however, the special sciences were helped by being given a philosophical foundation, for they were thereby rescued from crude empiricism and from an exclusively practical and utilitarian orientation.

CHAPTER XXXVI

THE EARLY STOA

1. THE founder of the Stoic School was Zeno, who was born about 336/5 B.C. at Citium in Cyprus and died about 264/3 at Athens. He seems to have at first followed his father in commercial activity.[1] Coming to Athens about 315–313 he read the *Memorabilia* of Xenophon and the *Apology* of Plato and was filled with admiration for Socrates' strength of character. Thinking that Crates the Cynic was the man who most resembled Socrates, he became his disciple. From the Cynics he seemed to have turned to Stilpo,[2] though Zeno is also reported to have listened to Xenocrates and, after Xenocrates' death, to Polemon. About the year 300 B.C. he founded his own philosophic School, which takes its name from the Στοὰ Ποικίλη, where he lectured. He is said to have taken his own life. Of his writings we possess only fragments.

Zeno was succeeded in the leadership of the School by Cleanthes of Assos (331/30–233/2 or 231) and Cleanthes by Chrysippus of Soloi in Cilicia (281/278–208/205), who was called the second founder of the School because of his systematisation of the Stoic doctrines. Εἰ μὴ γὰρ ἦ Χρύσιππος, οὐκ ἂν ἦν Στόα.[3] He is said to have written more than 705 books and was famed for his dialectic, though not for his style of composition.

Among Zeno's pupils were Ariston of Chios, Herillus of Carthage, Dionysius of Heracleia, Persion of Citium. A pupil of Cleanthes was Sphairus of the Bosphorus. Chrysippus was succeeded by two pupils, Zeno of Tarsus and Diogenes of Seleucia. The latter came to Rome in 156/5 B.C., together with other philosophers, as ambassadors of Athens in an attempt to obtain remission of the fine. The philosophers gave lectures in Rome, which excited admiration among the youth of the City, though Cato thought that such philosophical interests were not consonant with the military virtues and he advised the Senate to get rid of the embassy as soon as possible.[4] Diogenes was succeeded by Antipater of Tarsus.

---

[1] Diog. Laërt., 7, 2 and 31.   [2] Diog. Laërt., 7, 2.   [3] Diog. Laërt., 7, 183.
[4] Plut., *Cat. Mai.*, 22.

II. *Logic of the Stoa*

Logic was divided by the Stoics into Dialectic and Rhetoric, to which some added the Theory of Definitions and the Theory of the Criteria of Truth.[1] Something will be said here of the Stoic epistemology, omitting their account of formal logic, though we may note the fact that the Stoics reduced the ten Categories of Aristotle to four, namely, the substrate (τὸ ὑποκείμενον), the essential constitution (τὸ ποιόν or τὸ ποιὸν ὑποκείμενον), the accidental constitution (τὸ πῶς ἔχον or τὸ πῶς ἔχον ποιὸν ὑποκείμενον) and the relative accidental constitution (τὸ πρός τι πῶς ἔχον, τὸ πρός τι πῶς ἔχον ποιὸν ὑποκείμενον). A further feature of the formal logic of the Stoa may also be mentioned. Propositions are simple if their terms are non-propositions, otherwise compound. The compound proposition, "if X, then Y" (τὸ συνημμένον), is declared to be (i) true, if X and Y are both true; (ii) false, if X is true and Y is false; (iii) true, if X is false and Y is true; (iv) true, if X and Y are both false. Thus our "material" implication is separated from our "formal" implication and our "strict" implication, and from entailment by ontological necessitation.[2]

The Stoics rejected not only the Platonic doctrine of the transcendental universal, but also Aristotle's doctrine of the concrete universal. Only the individual exists and our knowledge is knowledge of particular objects. These particulars make an impression on the soul (τύπωσις—Zeno and Cleanthes—or ἑτεροίωσις —Chrysippus), and knowledge is primarily knowledge of this impression. The Stoics adopted, therefore, the opposite position to that of Plato, for, while Plato depreciated sense-perception, the Stoics founded all knowledge on sense-perception. They would doubtless re-echo the words of Antisthenes, to the effect that he saw a horse but not "horseness." (Zeno, as we have seen, became a pupil of Crates the Cynic.) The soul is originally a *tabula rasa*, and, in order for it to know, there is need of perception. The Stoics did not of course deny that we have knowledge of our interior states and activities, but Chrysippus reduced this knowledge, too, to perception, which was rendered all the easier in that these states and activities were considered to consist of material processes. After the act of perception a memory (μνήμη) remains behind, when the actual object is no longer there, and experience arises from a plurality of similar recollections (ἐμπειρία).

[1] Diog. Laërt., 7, 41–2.   [2] Sext. Emp., *Pyrr. Hyp.*, 2, 105; *Adv. Math.*, 8, 449.

The Stoics were therefore Empiricists, even "Sensualists"; but they also maintained a Rationalism which was scarcely consistent with a thoroughly empiricist and nominalist position. For although they asserted that reason (λόγος, νοῦς) is a product of development, in that it grows up gradually out of perceptions and is formed only about the fourteenth year, they also held, not only that there are deliberately-formed general ideas, but also that there are general ideas (κοιναὶ ἔννοιαι or προλήψεις), which are apparently antecedent to experience (ἔμφυτοι προλήψεις) in that we have a natural predisposition to form them—virtually innate ideas, we might call them. What is more, it is only through Reason that the system of Reality can be known.

The Stoics devoted a good deal of attention to the question of the criterion of truth. This they declared to be the φαντασία καταληπτική, the apprehensive perception or representation. The criterion of truth lies, therefore, in the perception itself, namely, in the perception that compels the assent of the soul, i.e. to all intents and purposes in clear perception. (This is scarcely consistent with the view that it is science alone that gives us certain knowledge of Reality.) However, the difficulty arose that the soul can withhold assent from what is objectively a true perception. Thus when the dead Alcestis appeared to Admetus from the underworld, her husband had a clear perception of her, yet he did not assent to this clear perception because of subjective hindrances, namely, the belief that dead people do not rise again, while on the other hand there may be deceptive apparitions of the dead. In view of this sort of objection the later Stoics, as Sextus Empiricus tells us, added to the criterion of truth, "which has no hindrance." Objectively speaking, the perception of the dead Alcestis has the value of a criterion of truth—for it is objectively a καταληπτικὴ φαντασία—but subjectively speaking, it cannot act as such, because of a belief which acts as a subjective hindrance.[1] This is all very well, but the difficulty still remains of ascertaining when there is such a hindrance and when there is not.

III. *Cosmology of the Stoa*

In their cosmology the Stoics had recourse to Heraclitus for the doctrine of the Logos and of Fire as the world-substance, but elements are also present which are borrowed from Plato and

[1] Sext. Emp., *Adv. Math.*, 7, 254 ff.

Aristotle. Thus the λόγοι σπερματικοί seem to be a transposition on to the material plane of the ideal theory.

According to the Stoics there are two principles in Reality, τὸ ποιοῦν and τὸ πάσχον. But this is not dualism as we find it in Plato, since the active principle, τὸ ποιοῦν, is not spiritual but material. In fact it is hardly dualism at all, since the two principles are both material and together form one Whole. The Stoic doctrine is therefore a monistic materialism, even if this position is not consistently maintained. It is uncertain what Zeno's view was, but Cleanthes and Chrysippus would seem to have regarded the two factors as ultimately one and the same.

> "All are but parts of one stupendous whole,
> Whose body Nature is and God the soul,"[1]

The passive principle is matter devoid of qualities, while the active principle is immanent Reason or God. Natural beauty or finality in Nature point to the existence of a principle of thought in the universe, God, Who, in His Providence, has arranged everything for the good of man. Moreover, since the highest phenomenon of nature, man, is possessed of consciousness, we cannot suppose that the whole world is devoid of consciousness, for the whole cannot be less perfect than the part. God, therefore, is the Consciousness of the world. Nevertheless God, like the substrate on which He works, is material. "(Zeno) *Nullo modo arbitrabatur quidquam effici posse ab ea (natura) quae expers esset corporis—nec vero aut quod efficeret aut quod efficeretur, posse esse non corpus.*"[2] ὄντα γὰρ μόνα τὰ σώματα καλοῦσιν.[3] Like Heraclitus the Stoics make Fire to be the stuff of all things. God is the active Fire (πῦρ τεχνικόν), which is immanent in the universe (πνεῦμα διῆκον δι' ὅλου τοῦ κόσμου), but He is at the same time the primal Source from which the crasser elements, that make the corporeal world, come forth. These crasser elements proceed from God and are at length resolved into Him again, so that all that exists is either the primal Fire—God in Himself—or God in His different states. When the world is in existence God stands to it as soul to body, being the soul of the world. He is not something entirely different from the stuff of the world, His Body, but is a finer stuff, the moving and forming principle—the crasser stuff, of which the world is formed, being itself motionless and unformed, though capable of receiving all sorts of movement and form.

---

[1] Pope, *Essay on Man*, I, 267.   [2] Cic., *Acad. Post.*, I, 11, 39.
[3] Plut., *De Comm. Notit.*, 1073 ε.

"Zenoni et reliquis fere Stoicis aether videtur summus deus, mente praeditus, qua omnia reguntur." [1]

God therefore, ὁ Λόγος, is the Active Principle which contains within itself the active forms of all the things that are to be, these forms being the λόγοι σπερματικοί. These active forms—but material—are as it were "seeds," through the activity of which individual things come into being as the world develops; or rather they are seeds which unfold themselves in the forms of individual things. (The conception of λόγοι σπρερματικοί is found in Neo-Platonism and in St. Augustine, under the name of *rationes seminales*.) In the actual development of the world part of the fiery vapour, of which God consists, is transformed into air and from air is formed water. From part of the water comes earth, while a second part remains water and a third part is transformed into air, which through rarefaction becomes the elementary fire. Thus does the "body" of God come into being.

Now Heraclitus, as we have seen, most probably never taught the doctrine of the universal conflagration, in which the whole world returns to the primeval fire, from which it was born. The Stoics, however, certainly added this doctrine of the ἐκπύρωσις, according to which God forms the world and then takes it back into Himself through a universal conflagration, so that there is an unending series of world-constructions and world-destructions. Moreover, each new world resembles its predecessor in all particulars, every individual man, for example, occurring in each successive world and performing the identical actions that he performed in his previous existence. (Cf. Nietzsche's idea of the "Eternal Recurrence.") Consistently with this belief the Stoics denied human freedom, or rather liberty for them meant doing consciously, with assent, what one will do in any case. (We are reminded somewhat of Spinoza.) This reign of necessity the Stoics expressed under the concept of Fate ('Ειμαρμένη), but Fate is not something different from God and universal reason, nor is it different from Providence (Πρόνοια) which orders all things for the best. Fate and Providence are but different aspects of God. But this cosmological determinism is modified by their insistence on interior freedom, in the sense that a man can alter his judgment on events and his attitude towards events, seeing them and welcoming them as the expression of "God's Will." In this sense man is free.

[1] Cic., *Acad. Prior.*, 2, 41, 126.

Evil

Since the Stoics held that God orders all things for the best, they had to explain the evil in the world or at least to bring it into harmony with their "optimism." Chrysippus especially undertook the perennial difficulty of formulating a theodicy, taking as his fundamental tenet the theory that the imperfection of individuals subserves the perfection of the whole. It would follow that there is really no evil when things are looked at *sub specie aeternitatis*. (If we are reminded here of Spinoza, we are reminded also of Leibniz, not only by Stoic optimism, but also by their doctrine that no two individual phenomena of Nature are completely alike.) Chrysippus, in his fourth book on Providence, argues that goods could not have existed without evils, on the ground that of a pair of contraries neither can exist without the other, so that if you take away the one, you take away both.[1]

Physical

There is certainly a great deal of truth in this contention. For instance, the existence of a sensible creature capable of pleasure implies also the capacity for feeling pain—unless, of course, God determines otherwise; but we are now speaking of the natural state of affairs and not of preternatural Divine ordinances. Moreover, pain, though spoken of as an evil, would seem to be—in a certain aspect—a good. For example, given the possibility of our teeth decaying, toothache would seem to be a definite good or benefit. The privation of right order in the teeth is certainly an evil, but—given the possibility of decay—we should be worse off if toothache were impossible, since it serves as a danger-signal, warning us that it is time that we had our teeth examined by a dentist. Similarly, if we never felt hungry—a pain—we might ruin our health by insufficient nourishment. Chrysippus saw this clearly and argued that it is good for man to have his head of delicate construction, though the very fact of its delicate construction involves at the same time the possibility of danger from a comparatively slight blow.

Moral

But though physical evil is not so great a difficulty, what of moral evil? According to the Stoics no act is evil and reprehensible *in itself*: it is the intention, the moral condition of the agent from whom the act proceeds, that makes the act evil: the act as a physical entity is indifferent. (If this were taken to mean that a good intention justifies any act, then such an act is in the moral order and will be either good or bad—though if the agent performs a bad act with a sincerely good intention in a state of inculpable

[1] Apud Gellium, *Noctes Atticae*, 6, 1.

ignorance of the fact that the act is contrary to right reason, the action is only *materialiter* evil and the agent is not guilty of formal sin.[1] However, if the act be considered merely in itself, as a positive entity, apart from its character as a human act, then Chrysippus is right in saying that the act as such is not evil —in fact, it is good. That it cannot of itself be evil, can easily be shown by an example. The physical action, the positive element, is precisely the same when a man is murderously shot as when he is shot in battle during a just war: it is not the positive element in the murder, the action considered merely abstractly, that is the *moral* evil. Moral evil, considered precisely as such, cannot be a positive entity, since this would reflect on the goodness of the Creator, the Source of all being. Moral evil consists essentially in a privation of right order in the human will, which, in the human bad act, is out of harmony with right reason.) Now, if a man can have a right intention, he can also have a wrong intention; hence, in the moral sphere, no less than in the physical sphere, contraries involve one another. How, asked Chrysippus, can courage be understood apart from cowardice or justice apart from injustice? Just as the capacity of feeling pleasure implies the capacity of feeling pain, so the capacity of being just implies the capacity of being unjust.

In so far as Chrysippus simply meant that the capacity for virtue implies *de facto* the capacity for vice, he was enunciating a truth, since for man in his present state in this world, with his limited apprehension of the *Summum Bonum*, freedom to be virtuous implies also freedom to commit sin, so that, if the possession of moral freedom is a good thing for man and if it is better to be able to choose virtue freely (even though this implies the possibility of vice) than to have no freedom at all, no valid argument against Divine Providence can be drawn from the possibility, or even the existence, of moral evil in the world. But in so far as Chrysippus implies that the presence of virtue in the universe necessarily implies the presence of its contrary, on the ground that opposites always involve one another, he is implying what is false, since human moral freedom, while involving the *possibility* of vice in this life, does not necessarily involve its

---

[1] An act, i.e. a human act, one proceeding from the free will of the human agent, is *materialiter* (or *objectively*) good or evil, in so far as it is objectively in conformity with, or not in conformity with, right reason, with the objective Natural Law. The agent's conscious intention cannot alter the objective or material character of a human act, even though, in the case of an objectively evil act, it may excuse him from formal moral fault.

actuality. (The apology for moral evil, as also for physical evil, which consists in saying that the good is thrown into higher relief through the presence of the bad, might, if pressed, imply the same false view. Given this present order of the world, it is certainly better that man should be free, and so *able* to sin, than that he should be without freedom; but it is better that man should use his freedom to choose virtuous actions, and the best condition of the world would be that all men should always do what is right, however much the presence of vice may set the good in high relief.)

Chrysippus was not so happy when he speculated whether external misfortunes might not be due to oversight on the part of Providence, as when trifling accidents occur in a large household that is, in general, well administered, through neglect of some kind;[1] but he rightly saw that those physical evils that befall the good may be turned into a blessing, both through the individual (through his interior attitude towards them) or for mankind at large (e.g. by stimulating medical investigation and progress). Further, it is interesting to notice, that Chrysippus gives an argument which recurs later in, e.g. Neo-Platonism, St. Augustine, Berkeley and Leibniz, to the effect that evil in the universe throws the good into greater relief, just as the contrast of light and shadow is pleasing in a picture or, to use an actual example employed by Chrysippus, as "Comedies have in them ludicrous verses which, though bad in themselves, nevertheless lend a certain grace to the whole play."[2]

In inorganic objects the Universal Reason or πνεῦμα operates as a ἕξις or principle of cohesion, and this holds good also for plants—which have no soul—though in them the ἕξις has the power of movement and has risen to the rank of φύσις. In animals there is soul (ψυχή), which shows itself in the powers of φαντασία and ὁρμή, and in human beings there is reason. The soul of man is therefore the noblest of souls: indeed it is part of the divine Fire which descended into men at their creation and is then passed on at generation, for, like all else, it is material. τὸ ἡγεμονικόν the dominant part of the soul, has its seat in the heart according to Chrysippus, apparently on the ground that the voice, which is the expression of thought, proceeds from the heart. (Some other Stoics placed τὸ ἡγεμονικόν in the head.) Personal immortality was

---

[1] Plut., *De Stoic. Repugn.*, 1051 c.
[2] Plut., *De Comm. Notit.*, 1065 d; Marcus Aurel., *To Himself*, VI, 42.

scarcely possible in the Stoic system, and the Stoics admitted that all souls return to the primeval Fire at the conflagration. The only dispute was on the subject of what souls persist after death until the conflagration; and while Cleanthes considered that this held good for all human souls, Chrysippus admitted it only in regard to the souls of the wise.

In a monistic system such as that of the Stoics we would hardly expect to find any attitude of personal devotion towards the Divine Principle; but in point of fact such a tendency is indubitably visible. This tendency is particularly observable in the celebrated hymn to Zeus by Cleanthes:

> O God most glorious, called by many a name,
> Nature's great King, through endless years the same;
> Omnipotence, who by thy just decree
> Controllest all, hail, Zeus, for unto thee
> Behoves thy creatures in all lands to call.
> We are thy children, we alone, of all
> On earth's broad ways that wander to and fro,
> Bearing thy image wheresoe'er we go.
> Wherefore with songs of praise thy power I will forth show.
> Lo! yonder heaven, that round the earth is wheeled,
> Follows thy guidance, still to thee doth yield
> Glad homage; thine unconquerable hand
> Such flaming minister, the levin-brand,
> Wieldeth, a sword two-edged, whose deathless might
> Pulsates through all that Nature brings to light;
> Vehicle of the universal Word, that flows
> Through all, and in the light celestial glows
> Of stars both great and small. O King of Kings
> Through ceaseless ages, God, whose purpose brings
> To birth, whate'er on land or in the sea
> Is wrought, or in high heaven's immensity;
> Save what the sinner works infatuate.
> Nay, but thou knowest to make the crooked straight:
> Chaos to thee is order: in thine eyes
> The unloved is lovely, who did'st harmonise
> Things evil with things good, that there should be
> One Word through all things everlastingly.
> One Word—whose voice alas! the wicked spurn;
> Insatiate for the good their spirits yearn:
> Yet seeing see not, neither hearing hear
> God's universal law, which those revere,
> By reason guided, happiness who win.
> The rest, unreasoning, diverse shapes of sin
> Self-prompted follow: for an idle name
> Vainly they wrestle in the lists of fame:

Others inordinately Riches woo,
Or dissolute, the joys of flesh pursue.
Now here, now there they wander, fruitless still,
For ever seeking good and finding ill.
Zeus the all-beautiful, whom darkness shrouds,
Whose lightning lightens in the thunder clouds;
Thy children save from error's deadly sway:
Turn thou the darkness from their souls away:
Vouchsafe that unto knowledge they attain;
For thou by knowledge art made strong to reign
O'er all, and all things rulest righteously.
So by thee honoured, we will honour thee,
Praising thy works continuously with songs,
As mortals should; nor higher meed belongs
E'en to the gods, than justly to adore
The universal law for evermore.[1]

But this attitude of personal devotion towards the Supreme Principle on the part of some of the Stoics does not mean that they rejected the popular religion; on the contrary, they took it under their protection. Zeno did indeed declare that prayers and sacrifices are of no avail, but polytheism was nevertheless justified by the Stoics on the ground that the one Principle or Zeus manifests itself in phenomena, e.g. the heavenly bodies, so that divine reverence is due to these manifestations—a reverence which is also to be extended to deified man or "heroes." Moreover, Stoicism found a place for divination and oracles. This fact need really cause no great surprise, if we reflect that the Stoics maintained a deterministic doctrine and held that all the parts and events of the universe are mutually interconnected.

IV. *The Stoic Ethic*

The importance of the ethical part of philosophy for the Stoics may be exemplified by the description of philosophy given by Seneca. Seneca belongs, of course, to the later Stoa, yet the emphasis laid by him on philosophy as the science of conduct was common to the early Stoa as well. *Philosophia nihil aliud est quam recta vivendi ratio vel honeste vivendi scientia vel ars rectae vitae agendae. non errabimus, si dixerimus philosophiam esse legem bene honesteque vivendi, et qui dixerit illam regulam vitae, suum illi nomen reddidit.*[2] Philosophy, therefore, is primarily concerned with conduct. Now the end of life, happiness, εὐδαιμονία, consists

[1] Trans. by Dr. James Adam, quoted in Hicks' *Stoic and Epicurean*, pp. 14–16 (Longmans, 1910).
[2] Seneca, Frag. 17.

in Virtue (in the Stoic sense of the term), i.e. in the natural life or life according to nature (ὁμολογουμένως τῇ φύσει ζῆν), the agreement of human action with the law of nature, or of the human will with the divine Will. Hence the famous Stoic maxim, "Live according to nature." For man to conform himself to the laws of the universe in the wide sense, and for man to conform his conduct to his own essential nature, reason, is the same thing, since the universe is governed by the law of nature. While earlier Stoics thought of "Nature," the Φύσις which man should follow, rather as the nature of the universe, later Stoics—from Chrysippus—tended to conceive nature from a more anthropological point of view.

The Stoic conception of life according to nature differs therefore from the old Cynic conception, as exemplified in the conduct and teaching of Diogenes. For the Cynics "nature" meant rather the primitive and instinctive, and so life according to nature implied a deliberate flouting of the conventions and traditions of civilised society, a flouting that externalised itself in conduct that was eccentric and not infrequently indecent. For the Stoics on the other hand, life according to nature meant life according to the principle that is active in nature, λόγος, the principle shared in by the human soul. The ethical end, therefore, according to the Stoics, consists essentially in submission to the divinely appointed order of the world, and Plutarch informs us that it was a general principle of Chrysippus to begin all ethical inquiries with a consideration of the order and arrangement of the universe.[1]

The fundamental instinct implanted in the animal by nature is the instinct of self-preservation, which means for the Stoics pretty well what we would call self-perfection or self-development. Now, man is endowed with reason, the faculty which gives him his superiority over the brute: therefore for man "life in accordance with nature is rightly understood to mean life in accordance with reason. Hence Zeno's definition of the end is to live in conformity with nature, which means to live a life of virtue, since it is to virtue that nature leads. On the other hand, a virtuous life is a life which conforms to our experience of the course of nature, our human natures being but parts of universal nature. Thus the end is a life which follows nature, whereby is meant not only our own nature, but the nature of the universe, a life wherein we do nothing that is forbidden by the universal, i.e. by right reason, which pervades all things and is identical with Zeus, the

[1] Plut., De Stoic. Repugn., c. 9 (1035 a 1-f 22).

guide and governor of the universe."[1] Diogenes Laërtius' account of the ethical teaching of the Stoics thus declares that virtue is a life in accordance with nature, while a life in conformity with nature is, i.e. for man, life in accordance with right reason. (As has been pointed out by others, this does not tell us very much, since the statements that it is reasonable to live in accordance with nature and natural to live in accordance with reason do not give much help to determining the content of virtue.)

Since the Stoics held that everything necessarily obeys the laws of nature, the objection was bound to be raised: "What is the good in telling man to obey the laws of nature, if he cannot help doing so in any case?" The Stoics answered that man is rational and so, though he will follow the laws of nature in any case, he has the privilege of knowing these laws and of assenting to them consciously. Hence there is a purpose in moral exhortation: man is free to change his interior attitude. (This involves, of course, a modification of the deterministic position, to say the least of it —but then no determinists are or can be really consistent, and the Stoics are no exception to the rule.) The consequence is that, strictly speaking, no action is in itself right or wrong, for determinism leaves no place for voluntary action and moral responsibility, while in a monistic system evil is really only evil when seen from some particular standpoint—*sub specie aeternitatis* all is right and good. The Stoics seem to have accepted—theoretically at least—the notion that no actions are wrong in themselves, as when Zeno admitted that not even cannibalism, incest or homosexuality are wrong in themselves.[2] Zeno did not, of course, mean to commend such actions: he meant that the physical act is indifferent, moral evil pertaining to the human will and intention.[3] Cleanthes declared that the human being necessarily follows the path of Destiny: "—if, to evil prone, my will rebelled, I needs must follow still."[4] And the same thought occurs in the celebrated dictum of Seneca, *Ducunt volentem fata, nolentem trahunt.*[5] However, the determinism of the Stoics was greatly modified in practice, since the doctrine that the wise man is he who *consciously* follows the path of Destiny (a doctrine brought out in the dictum of Seneca just quoted), when coupled with their exhortatory ethic,

[1] Diog. Laërt., 7, 86 ff.
[2] Von Arnim, *Stoic. Vet. Frag.*, Vol. I, pp. 59–60. (Pearson, pp. 210 ff.)
[3] Cf. Origen, *c. Cels*, 4, 45 (*P.G.*, 11, 1101).
[4] Frag. 91. (Pearson, *The Fragments of Zeno and Cleanthes*, 1891.)
[5] Seneca, *Ep.*, 107, 11.

implies liberty to a certain extent, as we have already remarked—a man is free to change his inner attitude and to adopt one of submission and resignation rather than of rebellion. Moreover, they admitted a scale of values, as we shall see, and it is at least tacitly implied that the wise man is free to choose the higher values and eschew the lower. But no deterministic system can be consistent in practice, a fact which need cause no surprise, since freedom is an actuality of which we are conscious, and even if it be theoretically denied, it creeps in again through the back door.

According to the Stoics virtue alone is a good in the full sense of the word: everything which is neither virtue nor vice is also neither good nor evil but indifferent· (ἀδιάφορον). "Virtue is a disposition conformable to reason, desirable in and for itself and not because of any hope or fear or any external motive."[1] It was in accord with this view of the self-sufficiency and self-desirability of virtue that the Platonic myths concerning rewards and punishments in the next life were ridiculed by Chrysippus. (We may compare therewith the doctrine of Kant.) However, in regard to this middle realm of the indifferent the Stoics admitted that some things are preferable (προηγμένα) and others to be rejected (ἀποπροηγμένα), while others again are indifferent in a narrower sense. This was a concession to practice, perhaps at the expense of theory, but it was doubtless demanded by the Stoic doctrine, that virtue consists in conformity to nature. Hence among the morally indifferent things the Stoics introduced a division into (i) those things which are in accordance with nature and to which a value may therefore be ascribed (τὰ προηγμένα); (ii) those things which are contrary to nature and so valueless (τὰ ἀποπροηγμένα); and (iii) those things which possess neither value nor "disvalue" (τὰ ἀπαξία). In this way they constructed a scale of values. Pleasure is a result or accompaniment of activity and may never be made into an end. On this all the Stoics were agreed, though they did not all go so far as Cleanthes, who held that pleasure is not according to nature.

The Cardinal Virtues are Moral Insight (φρόνησις), Courage, Self-control or Temperance, and Justice. These virtues stand or fall together, in the sense that he who possesses one possesses all. Zeno found the common source of all virtues in φρόνησις, while for Cleanthes it was self-mastery, φρόνησις being replaced by ἐγκράτεια,

[1] Diog. Laërt., 7, 89.

In spite of differences, however, the Stoics in general adhered to the principle that the Virtues are indissolubly connected as expressions of one and the same character, so that the presence of one virtue implies the presence of all. Conversely, they thought that when one vice is present, all the vices must be present. Character, then, is the chief point stressed and truly virtuous conduct—which is fulfilment of duty (τὸ καθῆκον, a term apparently invented by Zeno, but denoting rather what is suitable than duty in our sense) in the right spirit—is performed only by the wise man. The wise man is without passions, and in respect of his interior worth he takes second place to none, not even to Zeus. Moreover, he is lord over his own life, and may commit suicide.

If all the virtues are so bound up with one another that he who possesses the one must possess the others, it is an easy step to supposing that there are no degrees in virtue. Either a man is virtuous, i.e. completely virtuous, or he is not virtuous at all. And this would seem to have been the position of the early Stoics. Thus, according to Chrysippus, a man who has *almost* completed the path of moral progress is not yet virtuous, has not yet that virtue which is true happiness. A consequence of this doctrine is that very few attain to virtue and then only late in life. "Man walks in wickedness all his life, or, at any rate, for the greater part of it. If he ever attains to virtue, it is late and at the very sunset of his days."[1] But while this strict moral idealism is characteristic of the earlier Stoicism, later Stoics emphasised much more the conception of progress, devoting their attention to encouraging man to begin and continue in the path of virtue. Admitting that no individual actually corresponds to the ideal of the wise man, they divided mankind into fools and those who are progressing towards virtue or wisdom.

Characteristic of the Stoic ethic is their doctrine in regard to the passions and affections. These—pleasure (ἡδονή), sorrow or depression (λύπη), desire (ἐπιθυμία) and fear (φόβος) are irrational and unnatural; and so it is not so much a question of moderating and regulating them as of getting rid of them and inducing a state of Apathy. At least when the passions or affections become habits (νόσοι ψυχῆς) they have to be eliminated. Hence the Stoic ethic is in practice largely a fight against the "affections," an endeavour to attain to a state of moral freedom and sovereignty. (The Stoics tended, however, to moderate somewhat this extreme

[1] Von Arnim, I, 529, p. 119 (i.e. Sext. Empir., *Adv. Math.*, 9, 90, of Cleanthes).

position, and we find some admitting rational emotions—εὐπάθειαι
—in the wise man.) A quotation from Seneca well illustrates the
Stoic attitude in regard to self-conquest.

"*Quid praecipuum in rebus humanis est ? non classibus maria
complesse nec in rubri maris litore signa fixisse nec deficiente ad
iniurias terra errasse in oceano ignota quaerentem, sed animo
omnia vidisse et, qua maior nulla victoria est, vitia domuisse.
Innumerabiles sunt, qui populos, qui urbes habuerunt in
potestate, paucissimi qui se. quid est praecipuum ? erigere
animum supra minas et promissa fortunae, nihil dignam illam
habere putare, quod speres: quid enim habet dignum, quod
concupiscas ? qui a divinorum conversatione, quotiens ad
humana recideris, non aliter caligabis, quam quorum oculi in
densam umbram ex claro sole redierunt. quid est praecipuum ?
posse laeto animo tolerare adversa. quidquid acciderit, sic ferre,
quasi volueris tibi accidere. debuisses enim velle, si scires omnia
ex decreto dei fieri: flere, queri, gemere desciscere est.quid est
praecipuum ? in primis labris animam habere. haec res efficit
non e iure Quirium liberum, sed e iure naturae. liber enim est,
qui servitutem effugit. haec est assidua et ineluctabilis et per
diem et per noctem aequaliter premens. sine intervallo, sine
commeatu. sibi servire gravissima est servitus: quam discutere
facile est, si desieris multa te posceris, si desieris tibi referre
mercedem, si ante oculos et naturam tuam et aetatem posueris,
licet prima sit, ac tibi ipsi dixeris: quid insanio ? quid anhelo ?
quid sudo ? Quid terram, quid forum verso ? nec multo opus
est, nec diu.*"[1]

This side of the Stoic ethic—namely the endeavour to acquire
complete independence of all externals—represents its Cynic
heritage; but it has another side, whereby it passes beyond
Cynicism and that is its Cosmopolitanism. Every man is naturally
a social being, and to live in society is a dictate of reason. But
reason is the common essential nature of all men: hence there is
but one Law for all men and one Fatherland. The division of
mankind into warring States is absurd: the wise man is a citizen,
not of this or that particular State, but of the World. From this
foundation it follows that all men have a claim to our goodwill,
even slaves having their rights and even enemies having a right
to our mercy and forgiveness. Now, this transcendence of narrow

[1] Seneca, *Nat. Quaest.*, III, Praef., 10-17.

social limits was obviously favoured by the monism of the Stoic
system, but an ethical basis for the Stoic Cosmopolitanism was
found in the fundamental instinct or tendency of self-preservation
or self-love (οἰκείωσις). In the first place, of course, this instinctive
tendency to self-preservation shows itself in the form of self-love,
i.e. the individual's self-love. But it extends beyond self-love in
the narrow sense to embrace all that belongs to the individual,
family, friends, fellow-citizens and, finally, the whole of humanity.
It is naturally stronger in regard to what stands closer to the
individual, and grows weaker in proportion as the object is more
remote, so that the individual's task, from the ethical viewpoint,
is to raise the οἰκείωσις to the same pitch of intensity in regard
to the remote objects as it manifests in regard to the nearer
objects. In other words, the ethical ideal is attained when we
love all men as we love ourselves or when our self-love embraces
all that is connected with the self, including humanity at large,
with an equal intensity.

CHAPTER XXXVII

EPICUREANISM

1. The founder of the Epicurean School, Epicurus, was born at Samos in 342/1 B.C. At Samos he listened to Pamphilus, a Platonist,[1] and then at Teos to Nausiphanes, a follower of Democritus, who exercised considerable influence upon him, in spite of Epicurus' later contentions.[2] When eighteen, Epicurus came to Athens for his military service, and then seems to have given himself to study at Colophon. In 310 he taught at Mitylene— though he afterwards transferred to Lampsacus—and in 307/6 he moved to Athens and there opened his School.[3] This School was instituted in Epicurus' own garden, and we learn from Diogenes Laërtius that the philosopher in his will bequeathed the house and garden to his disciples. From the situation of the School the Epicureans got the name of οἱ ἀπὸ τῶν κήπων. Almost divine honours were paid to Epicurus even in his lifetime, and this cult of the founder is no doubt responsible for the fact that philosophic orthodoxy was maintained among the Epicureans more than in any other School. The chief doctrines were given the pupils to learn by heart.[4]

Epicurus was a voluminous writer (according to Diog. Laërt. he wrote about 300 works), but most of his writings are lost. However, Diogenes Laërtius has given us three didactic letters, of which the letters to Herodotus and Menoeceus are considered authentic while that to Pythocles is considered to be an extract from Epicurus' writing made by a pupil. Fragments have also been preserved of his chief work, Περὶ Φύσεως, from the library of the Epicurean Piso (thought to be L. Piso, Consul in 58 B.C.).

Epicurus was succeeded as Scholarch by Hermarchus of Mitylene, who was in turn succeeded by Polystratus. An immediate disciple of Epicurus, together with Hermarchus and Polyaenus, was Metrodorus of Lampsacus. Cicero heard Phaedrus (Scholarch at Athens about 78–70) at Rome about 90 B.C. But the best-known disciple of the School is the Latin poet, T. Lucretius Carus (91–51 B.C.), who expressed the Epicurean philosophy in

Diog. Laërt., 10, 14.   [2] Cic., *De Nat. D.*, I, 26, 73; Diog. Laërt., 10, 8.
    [3] Diog. Laërt., 10, 2.   [4] Diog. Laërt., 10, 12.

his poem *De Rerum Natura*, having as his chief aim the liberation of men from the fear of the gods and of death and the leading of them to peace of soul.

11. *The Canonic*

Epicurus was not interested in dialectic or logic as such, and the only part of logic to which he paid any attention was that dealing with the criterion of truth. That is to say, he was interested in dialectic only in so far as it directly subserved Physics. But Physics again interested him only in so far as it subserved Ethics. Epicurus therefore concentrated on Ethics even more than did the Stoics, depreciating all purely scientific pursuits and declaring mathematics useless, since it has no connection with the conduct of life. (Metrodorus declared that "It need not trouble any one, if he had never read a line of Homer and did not know whether Hector was a Trojan or a Greek.")[1] One of Epicurus' reasons for objecting to mathematics was that it is not substantiated by sense-knowledge, since in the real world the geometer's points, lines and surfaces are nowhere to be found. Now, sense-knowledge is the fundamental basis of all knowledge. "If you fight against all your sensations, you will have no standard to which to refer and thus no means of judging even those sensations which you pronounce false."[2] Lucretius asks what can be accounted of higher certainty than sense. Reason, by which we judge of sense-data, is itself wholly founded on the senses, and if the senses are untrue, then all reason as well is rendered false.[3] Moreover, the Epicureans pointed out that in astronomical questions, for instance, we cannot attain certainty, as we can argue for this position just as well as for that position, e.g. "For the heavenly phenomena may depend for their production on many different causes."[4] (It must be remembered that the Greeks lacked our modern scientific appliances, and that their opinions on scientific subjects were, very largely, of the nature of guesses, unsubstantiated by exact observation.)

Epicurus' Logic or Canonic deals with the norms or canons of knowledge and the criteria of truth. The fundamental criterion of truth is Perception (ἡ αἴσθησις), in which we attain what is clear (ἡ ἐνάργεια). Perception takes place when images (εἴδωλα)

---

[1] Frag. 24. (Metrodori Epicurei Fragmenta, A. Körte, 1890.) But cf. Sext. Emp., *Adv. Math.*, I, 49.
[2] Diog. Laërt., 10, 146.   [3] Cf. *De Rerum Nat.*, IV, 478–99.
[4] Diog. Laërt., 10, 86.

of objects penetrate the sense-organs (cf. Democritus and Empedocles), and is always true. It is to be noted that the Epicureans included under perception imaginative representations (φανταστιϰαὶ ἐπιβολαὶ τῆς διανοίας), *all* perception taking place through the reception of εἴδωλα. When these images stream continuously from the same object and enter by the sense-organs, we have perception in the narrower sense: when, however, individual images enter through the pores of the body they become, as it were, mixed up and imaginative pictures arise, e.g. of a centaur. In either case we have "perception," and, as both sorts of images arise from objective causes, both types of perception are true. How then does error arise? Only through *judgment*. If, for instance, we judge that an image corresponds exactly to an external object, when in point of fact it does not so correspond, we are in error. (The difficulty, of course, is to know when the image corresponds to an external object and when it does not, and when it corresponds perfectly or imperfectly; and on this point the Epicureans give us no help.)

The first criterion is therefore Perception. A second criterion is afforded by Concepts (προλήψεις). The concept, according to the Epicureans, is simply a memory image (μνήμη τοῦ πολλάϰις ἔξωθεν φανέντος).[1] After we have had perception of an object, e.g. of a man, the memory image or general image of man arises when we hear the word "man." These προλήψεις are always true, and it is only when we proceed to form opinions or judgments that the question of truth or falsity arises. If the opinion or judgment (ὑπόληψις) has reference to the future, then it must be confirmed by experience, while if it has reference to hidden and unperceived causes (e.g. the atoms) it must at least not contradict experience.

There is yet a third criterion, namely feelings or πάθη, which are criteria for conduct. Thus the feeling of pleasure is the criterion of what we should choose, while the feeling of pain shows us what we should avoid. Hence Epicurus could say that "the criteria of truth are the senses, and the preconceptions, and the passions."[2]

III. *The Physics*

Epicurus' choice of a physical theory was determined by a practical end, that of freeing man from the fear of the gods and of the afterworld and so giving them peace of soul. While not

---

[1] Diog. Laërt., 10, 33.   [2] Diog. Laërt., 10, 31.

denying the existence of the gods he wished to show that they do not interfere in human affairs and that man need not therefore occupy himself with propitiation and petition and "superstition" in general. Moreover, by rejecting immortality he hoped to free man from fear of death—for what reason is there to fear death when it is mere extinction, absence of all consciousness and feeling, when there is no judgment and when no punishment awaits one in the afterworld? "Death is nothing to us; for that which is dissolved is devoid of sensation, and that which is devoid of sensation is nothing to us."[1] Moved by these considerations Epicurus chose the system of Democritus (which he adopted with but slight modifications), since this system seemed best calculated to serve his end. Did it not explain all phenomena by the mechanical motions of atoms, thus rendering any recourse to divine intervention superfluous and did it not afford an easy handle for the rejection of immortality—the soul, as well as the body, being composed of atoms? This practical aim of the Epicurean Physics appears in a marked manner in Lucretius' *De Rerum Natura*, clothed in the splendid language and imagery of the poet.

Nothing proceeds from nothing, nothing passes into nothingness, declared Epicurus, re-echoing the thought of the old Cosmologists. "And, first of all, we must admit that nothing can come out of that which does not exist; for, were the fact otherwise, everything would be produced from everything and there would be no need of any seed. And if that which disappeared were so absolutely destroyed as to become non-existent, then everything would soon perish, as the things with which they would be dissolved would have no existence."[2] We may compare the lines of Lucretius, *Nunc age, res quoniam docui non posse creari de nilo neque item genitas ad nil revocari.*[3] The bodies of our experience are composed of pre-existing material entities—atoms—and their perishing is but a resolution into the entities of which they are composed. The ultimate constituents of the universe are therefore atoms, Atoms and the Void. "Now the universal whole is a body; for our senses bear us witness in every case that bodies have a real existence; and the evidence of the senses, as I have said before, ought to be the rule of our reasonings about everything which is not directly perceived. Otherwise, if that which we call the vacuum, or space, or intangible nature, had not a real

[1] Diog. Laërt., 10, 139. [2] Diog. Laërt., 10, 38–9. [3] *De Rerum Nat.*, I, 265–6.

existence, there would be nothing in which the bodies could be
contained, or across which they could move, as we see that they
really do move. Let us add to this reflection that one cannot
conceive, either in virtue of perception, or of any analogy founded
on perception, any general quality peculiar to all beings which is
not either an attribute, or an accident of the body, or of the
vacuum."[1] These atoms vary in size, form and weight (the
Epicureans certainly attributed weight to the atoms, whatever
the earlier atomists may have done) and are indivisible and
infinite in number. In the beginning they rained down through
the void or empty space, though Lucretius compares their motion
to that of motes in a sunbeam, and it may be that the Epicureans
did not think of the atoms as ever in actuality raining down in
parallel straight lines—a conception which would make the
"collision" very much of a *deus ex machina*.

In order to account for the origin of the world, Epicurus had
to allow for a collision of atoms: moreover he wished at the same
time to afford some explanation of human freedom (which the
School maintained). He postulated, therefore, a spontaneous
oblique movement or declination from the straight line of descent
on the part of individual atoms. Thus occurred the first collision
of atoms, and from the collision and the entanglements consequent
on the deviation the rotary movements were set up which led to
the formation of innumerable worlds, separated from one another
by empty spaces (the μετακόσμια or *intermundia*). The human
soul is also composed of atoms, smooth and round, but in distinction to the animals it possesses a rational part which is seated in
the breast, as is shown by the emotions of fear and joy. The
irrational part, the principle of life, is spread throughout the
whole body. At death the atoms of the soul are separated, and
there can be no more perception: death is the privation of perception (στέρησις αἰσθήσεως).

The world is, therefore, due to mechanical causes and there is no
need to postulate teleology. On the contrary, the Epicureans
entirely rejected the anthropocentric teleology of the Stoics and
would have nothing to do with the Stoic theodicy. The evil with
which human life is afflicted is irreconcilable with any idea of
divine guidance in the universe. The gods dwell in the *intermundia*, beautiful and happy and without thought of human
affairs, eating and drinking and speaking Greek!

[1] Diog. Laërt., 10, 39–40.

Apparet divinum numen sedesque quietae
Quas neque concutiunt venti nec nubila nimbis
Aspergunt neque nix acri concreta pruina
Cana cadens violat semperque innubilus aether
Integit, et largo diffuso lumine rident.[1]

The gods are anthropomorphically conceived, for they too are composed of atoms—even if of the finest atoms and possessing only ethereal or quasi-bodies—and are divided sexually: they are like to mankind in appearance and breathe and eat as we do. Epicurus not only needed the gods in order to present them as an embodiment of his ethical ideal of calm tranquillity, but he also considered that the universality of belief in the gods can only be explained on the hypothesis of their objective existence. εἴδωλα come to us from the gods, especially in sleep, but perception presents us only with the existence and anthropomorphic character of the gods: knowledge of their happy condition is attained by reason or λόγος. Men may honour the gods for their excellence and may even take part in the customary ceremonial worship, but all fear of them is out of place and also all attempts to win their favour by sacrifices. True piety consists in right thought.

nec pietas ullast velatum saepe videri
vertier ad lapidem atque omnis accedere ad aras
nec procumbere humi prostratum et pandere palmas
ante deum delubra nec aras sanguine multo
spargere quadrupedum nec votis nectere vota,
sed mage pacata posse omnia mente tueri.'[2]

The wise man, therefore, does not fear death—for death is mere extinction—nor the gods—for they are unconcerned with human affairs and exact no retribution. We may recall the celebrated lines of Virgil:

felix qui potuit rerum cognoscere causas:
atque metus omnes et inexorabile fatum
subiecit pedibus strepitumque Acherontis avari.[3]

IV. *The Epicurean Ethic*

Like the Cyrenaics Epicurus made *pleasure* the end of life. Every being strives after pleasure, and it is in pleasure that happiness consists. ". . . we affirm that pleasure is the beginning and

---

[1] *De Rerum Nat.*, III, 18–22.   [2] *De Rerum Nat.*, V, 1198–1203.
[3] *Georgics*, II, 490–2.

end of living happily; for we have recognised this as the first good, being connate with us; and it is with reference to it that we begin every choice and avoidance; and to this we come as if we judged of all good by passion as the standard . . ."[1] The question then arises what Epicurus understands by pleasure, when he makes it the end of life. Two facts are to be noted: first, that Epicurus meant, not the pleasures of the moment, individual sensations, but the pleasure which endures throughout a lifetime; and secondly, that pleasure for Epicurus consisted rather in the absence of pain than in positive satisfaction. This pleasure is to be found pre-eminently in serenity of soul (ἡ τῆς ψυχῆς ἀταραξία). With this serenity of soul Epicurus conjoined also health of body, but the emphasis is rather on intellectual pleasure, for, while very severe bodily pains are of short duration, less severe pains may be overcome or rendered endurable by intellectual pleasures. ". . . a correct theory . . . can refer all choice and avoidance to the health of the body and the freedom from disquietude of the soul." ". . . at times we pass over many pleasures when any difficulty is likely to ensue from them; and we think many pains better than pleasures when a greater pleasure follows them, if we endure the pain for a time."[2] When Epicurus speaks of choice among pleasures and rejects certain pleasures, it is to the permanence of pleasure that he is looking, and to the presence or absence of subsequent pain, for there is really no room in his ethic for a discrimination between pleasures that is based on a difference of moral value. (Though we may well discern a differentiation of pleasures on grounds of moral value creeping in unawares—as it is bound to do in any hedonistic ethic, unless the hedonist is prepared to admit that the "basest" pleasures are on the same level as the more refined pleasures. And what serious moral philosopher has ever been prepared to admit that, without introducing qualifications that suggest another criterion beside pleasure?) "Every pleasure is therefore a good on account of its own nature, but it does not follow that every pleasure is worthy of being chosen; just as every pain is an evil, and yet every pain must not be avoided." "When, therefore, we say that pleasure is a chief good, we are not speaking of the pleasures of the debauched man, or those which lie in sensual enjoyment, as some think who are ignorant, and who do not entertain our opinions, or else interpret them perversely; but we mean the freedom of the body from pain

[1] Diog. Laërt., 10, 129.   [2] Diog. Laërt., 10, 128 and 129.

14

and of the soul from confusion. For it is not continued drinkings and revels . . . that make life pleasant, but sober contemplations, which examine into the reasons for all choice and avoidance, and which put to flight the vain opinions from which the greater part of the confusion arises which troubles the soul."[1] "No pleasure is intrinsically bad: but the efficient causes of some pleasures bring with them a great many perturbations of pleasure."[2]

In practice we have to consider whether any individual pleasure may not be productive of greater pain and any individual pain may not be productive of greater pleasure. For instance, an individual pleasure might be very intense for the moment but might lead to ill-health or to enslavement to a habit; in which case it would be productive of greater pain. Conversely, a pain might be intense for the moment—as in an operation—and yet be productive of a greater good, health. Therefore, although every pain, abstractly considered, is an evil, and every pleasure is a good, we must in practice look to the future and endeavour to attain the maximum of durable pleasure—in Epicurus' opinion, health of body and tranquillity of soul. Epicurean hedonism would not then result in libertinism and excess, but in a calm and tranquil life; for a man is unhappy either from fear or from unlimited and vain desires, and if he but bridle these he may secure for himself the blessings of reason. The wise man will not multiply his needs, since that is to multiply sources of pain: he will rather reduce his needs to a minimum. (The Epicureans even went so far as to say that the wise man can be perfectly happy even when undergoing bodily torture. Thus Epicurus declared that, "Though he is being tortured on the rack, the wise man is still happy."[3] An extreme statement of this position is found in the saying: "If the wise man is being burned, if he is being tortured—nay, within the very bull of Phalaris, he will say: 'How delightful this is! How little I care for it'!"[4]) Hence the Epicurean ethic leads to a moderate asceticism, self-control and independence. "To accustom one's self, therefore, to simple and inexpensive habits is a great ingredient in the perfecting of health, and makes a man free from hesitation with respect to the necessary uses of life."[5]

Virtue is a condition of ἀταραξία or tranquillity of soul, though

[1] Diog. Laërt., 10, 129 and 131–2.   [2] Diog. Laërt., 10, 141.
[3] Diog. Laërt., 10, 118.   [4] Cic., Tusc., 2, 7, 17.   [5] Diog. Laërt., 10, 131.

of course its value is estimated by Epicurus according to its power of producing pleasure. Virtues such as simplicity, moderation, temperance, cheerfulness, are much more conducive to pleasure and happiness than are unbridled luxury, feverish ambition and so on. "It is not possible to live pleasantly without living prudently, and honourably, and justly; nor to live prudently, and honourably, and justly, without living pleasantly. But he to whom it does not happen to live prudently, honourably, and justly, cannot possibly live pleasantly." "The just man is the freest of all men from disquietude; but the unjust man is a perpetual prey to it." "Injustice is not intrinsically bad; it has this character only because there is joined with it a fear of not escaping those who are appointed to punish actions marked with that character." "When, without any fresh circumstances arising, a thing which has been declared just in practice does not agree with the impressions of reason, that is a proof that the thing was not really just. In the same way, when in consequence of new circumstances, a thing which has been pronounced just does not any longer appear to agree with utility, the thing which was just, inasmuch as it was useful to the social relations and intercourse of mankind, ceases to be just at the moment when it ceases to be useful."[1] Moreover, in spite of the fact that the ethic of the Epicureans is fundamentally selfish or egocentric, in that it is based on the individual's pleasure, it was not in practice so selfish as it might sound. Thus the Epicureans thought that it is really pleasanter to do a kindness than to receive one, and the founder himself was commended for his contented and kind character. "He who desires to live tranquilly without having anything to fear from other men, ought to make himself friends; those whom he cannot make friends of, he should, at least, avoid rendering enemies; and if that is not in his power, he should, as far as possible, avoid all intercourse with them, and keep them aloof, as far as it is for his interest to do so." "The happiest men are they who have arrived at the point of having nothing to fear from those who surround them. Such men live with one another most agreeably, having the firmest grounds of confidence in one another, enjoying the advantages of friendship in all their fullness, and not lamenting, as a pitiable circumstance, the premature death of their friends."[2] It is probably true to say that Epicurus' practical moral judgment was sounder than the theoretical

---

[1] Diog. Laërt., 10; Maxims, 5, 17, 37, 42.   [2] Diog. Laërt., 10, 154.

responsibility?

foundations of his ethic, an ethic which could obviously give little account of moral obligation.

Owing to the fact that man should not pursue heedlessly the first pleasure that offers itself, there is need of an art of calculation or mensuration in the conduct of life. We must therefore practise συμμέτρησις, and it is in the right mensuration of pleasures and pains, in the ability to take into account and balance one against another present or future happiness and unhappiness, that the essence of insight or φρόνησις, the highest virtue, consists. If a man is to live a truly happy, pleasurable and contented life, he must possess this insight, he must be φρόνιμος. "Now, the beginning and the greatest good of all these things is prudence, on which account prudence is something more valuable than even philosophy, inasmuch as all the other virtues spring from it, teaching us that it is not possible to live pleasantly unless one also lives prudently, and honourably, and justly; and that one cannot live prudently, and honourably, and justly, without living pleasantly; for the virtues are connate with living agreeably, and living agreeably is inseparable from the virtues."[1] When a man is φρόνιμος, he is virtuous, for the virtuous man is not so much the person who is actually enjoying pleasure at any given moment as the man who knows how to conduct himself in the search for pleasure. Once virtue has been thus defined, it is obvious that it is an absolutely necessary condition for lasting happiness.

Epicurus laid great stress on *Friendship.* "Of all the things which wisdom provides for the happiness of the whole life, by far the most important is the acquisition of friendship."[2] This may seem strange in a fundamentally egoistic ethic, but the emphasis on friendship is itself based on egoistic considerations, namely that without friendship a man cannot live a secure and tranquil life, while on the other hand friendship gives pleasure. Friendship rests, therefore, on an egoistic basis, the thought of personal advantage. This egoism was, however, modified through the Epicurean doctrine that an unselfish affection arises in the course of the friendship and that in a friendship a wise man loves the friend as he does himself. Nevertheless it remains true that the social theory of the Epicureans is egoistic in character, a fact that comes out clearly in their teaching that the wise man will not mix himself up in politics, as this disturbs tranquillity of soul. There are, however, two exceptions: the first, that of the man

[1] Diog. Laërt., 10, 132.   [2] Diog. Laërt., 10, 148.

who needs to take part in politics in order to ensure his own personal security, the second, that of a man who has such an urge towards a political career that ἀταραξία would be quite impossible for him, were he to remain in retirement.

Pleasure and personal advantage are again decisive for the Epicurean theory of law. It is pleasanter to live in a society where law reigns and "rights" are respected than in a condition of *bellum omnium contra omnes*. The latter condition would be by no means favourable to tranquillity of soul or to ἀταραξία.

The Epicureans, as we have seen, went back to the School of Leucippus and Democritus for their Physics, as the Stoa went back to the Cosmology of Heraclitus. The Epicurean ethics, on the other hand, are more or less in agreement with that of the Cyrenaics. Both Aristippus and Epicurus make pleasure the end of life, and in both Schools attention is paid to the future, to calculation, to the "measuring" of pleasures and pains. There are, however, differences between the Epicureans and the Cyrenaics. For while the latter—in general, that is to say—considered *positive* pleasure (the smooth movement or λεία κίνησις) to be the end, the Epicureans stressed more the negative side, calm and tranquillity, ἡ καταστηματικὴ ἡδονή. Again, while the Cyrenaics considered bodily suffering worse than mental suffering, the Epicureans accounted mental suffering worse than bodily suffering, on the ground that the body suffers only from present evil whereas the soul can suffer also from the recollection of past evil and the expectation or fear of future evil. All the came it can be truly said that Cyrenaicism was absorbed in Epicureanism. Did not Epicurus agree with the Cyrenaic Hegesias in laying the emphasis on absence of suffering and with Anniceris in recommending to the wise the cultivation of friendship?

The Epicurean philosophy is, therefore, not a philosophy of heroes, nor has it the moral grandeur of the Stoic creed. Yet it is neither so selfish nor so "immoral" as its fundamental tenet might at first sight imply, and its attraction for certain types of men is easily understandable. It is certainly not a heroic creed or philosophy; but it was not meant by its author to be an incentive to base living, whatever its tenets might lead to in popular application to practice.

Note on Cynicism in the First Period of the Hellenistic Epoch

Cynicism in this period tended to lose its serious character of emphasis on independence, suppression of desire and physical endurance, and to give itself rather to mockery of convention and tradition and prevailing beliefs and modes of behaviour. Not of course that this tendency was absent from the earlier Cynicism —we have only to think of Diogenes—but it showed itself in this period through the new literary genre of the satire or σπουδογέλοιον. In the first half of the third century B.C., *Bion of Borysthenes*, influenced by Cyrenaicism (he had listened to the Cyrenaic Theodorus at Athens), propagated the so-called "hedonistic Cynicism" in his "diatribes," dwelling on the happiness and pleasurable character of the simple Cynic life. *Teles*, who taught at Megara about 240 B.C., followed Bion in the composition of such "diatribes"—popular and anecdotal pieces—dealing with appearance and reality, poverty and riches, cynical "apathy," etc.

Menippus of Gadara (about 250 B.C.) created the Satire, in which he combined poetry with prose, criticised under various forms—e.g. journeys to Hades, letters to the gods—natural philosophy and specialist learning, and mocked at the idolatrous honour paid to Epicurus by his followers. He was imitated by Varro, Seneca in his *Apocolocyntosis*, and Lucian.

Cercides of Megalopolis, composer of meliambs, displayed the same satyric tone, declaring, for example, that he would leave to the μετεωροσκόποι the solution of the ticklish question, why Cronus showed himself a father to some people and a stepfather to others.

CHAPTER XXXVIII

THE OLDER SCEPTICS, THE MIDDLE AND NEW ACADEMIES

I. *The Older Sceptics*

JUST as in the Stoa and in the Garden of Epicurus theory was subordinated to practice, so in the School of Pyrrho, the founder of Scepticism, though there is of course this big difference, that whereas the Stoics and Epicureans looked to science or positive knowledge as a means to peace of soul, the Sceptics sought to attain the same end by the disavowal of knowledge, i.e. by scepticism, the opposite of science.

Pyrrho of Elis (*c.* 360–*c.* 270), who is said to have accompanied Alexander on his march to India,[1] was apparently influenced by the Democritean theory of the sense-qualities, the relativism of the Sophists and the Cyrenaic epistemology. He taught that the human reason cannot penetrate to the inner substance of things (things are ἀκατάληπτα in our regard):[2] we can only know how things appear to us. The same things appear differently to different people, and we cannot know which is right: to any assertion we could oppose the contradictory assertion with equally good grounds (ἰσοσθένεια τῶν λόγων). We cannot, therefore, be certain of anything and the wise man will withhold his judgment (ἐπέχειν). Rather than say, "This is so," we should say, "So it appears to me" or "It may be so."

The same scepticism and consequent suspension of judgment is extended to the practical sphere. Nothing is in itself ugly or beautiful, right or wrong, or at least we cannot be sure of it: all external things in our lives are indifferent and the wise man will aim simply at tranquillity of soul and endeavour to preserve his soul in that condition. It is true that even the wise man cannot avoid acting and taking part in practical life, but he will follow in practice probable opinion, custom and law, conscious that absolute truth is unattainable.

Diogenes Laërtius informs us that Pyrrho expressed his philosophical views only by word of mouth,[3] but his views are known through those of his pupil *Timon of Phlius* (*c.* 320–230 B.C.), who

---

[1] Diog. Laërt., 9, 61.   [2] Diog. Laërt., Proem., 16.
[3] Diog. Laërt., Proem., 16; 9, 102.

is called by Sextus Empiricus ὁ προφήτης τῶν Πύρρωνος λόγων.[1] Timon composed Σίλλοι or mocking verses, in which he parodied Homer and Hesiod and made fun of the Greek philosophers, with the exception of Xenophanes and Pyrrho himself. According to Timon we can trust neither sense-perception nor reason. We must accordingly suspend all judgment, not allowing ourselves to be caught in any theoretical assertion, and then we shall attain to true ἀταραξία or tranquillity of soul.

(Cicero apparently did not know of Pyrrho as a Sceptic, but considered him rather as a moralist who preached and practised indifference towards external things. It may be, then, that Pyrrho did not personally develop the Sceptic position. But as he left no writings, we can hardly attain certainty on this point.)

II. *The Middle Academy*

Plato had held that the objects of sense-perception are not the objects of true knowledge, but he was very far from being a Sceptic, the whole point of his Dialectic being the attainment of true and certain knowledge of the eternal and abiding. A sceptical current of thought manifests itself, however, in what is known as the Second or Middle Academy, a scepticism directed principally against the Stoic dogmatism but also expressed in universal terms. Thus *Arcesilaus* (315/14–241/40), the founder of the Middle Academy, is reputed to have said that he was certain of nothing—not even of the fact that he was certain of nothing,[2] thus going further than Socrates, who knew that he knew nothing. He practised therefore a similar suspension of judgment or ἐποχή to that of the Pyrrhonists.[3] While trying to support his position by the example and practice of Socrates, Arcesilaus made the Stoic epistemology a special object of attack. No representation is given that might not be false: none of our sense-perceptions or presentations possess the guarantee of their own objective validity, for we may feel an equally intense subjective certainty even when the presentation is objectively false. We can therefore never be certain.

III. *The New Academy*

1. The founder of the Third or New Academy was *Carneades of Cyrene* (214/12–129/8 B.C.), who accompanied the Stoic

---

[1] *Adv. Math.*, 1, 53.   [2] Cic., *Acad. Post* I, 12, 45.   [3] Cic., *de Orat.*, 3, 18, 67.

Diogenes on the embassy to Rome in 156/5. Following the scepticism of Arcesilaus, Carneades taught that knowledge is impossible and that there is no criterion of truth. Against the Stoics he maintained that there is no sense-presentation by the side of which we could not place a false presentation that is indistinguishable from the true, appealing to the influence upon us of presentations in e.g. dreams, presentations which are, however, unreal, and to the facts of hallucination and delusion. Impressions of sense are, therefore, not infallible, and the Stoics cannot look to reason as a remedy, since they themselves admit that concepts are founded on experience.[1]

We are unable to prove anything, since any proof rests on assumptions which must themselves be proved. But this latter proof will itself rest on assumptions, and so on indefinitely. All dogmatic philosophy is accordingly out of the question: for either side in a question equally good—or equally bad—reasons can be adduced. Carneades attacked the Stoic theology, trying to show that their proofs for God's existence are not conclusive and that their doctrine as to God's Nature contained antinomies.[2] For example, the Stoics appealed to the *consensus gentium* as an argument for the divine existence. Now, if they can prove this *consensus gentium*, then they have proved a universal *belief* in the divine existence, but that does not prove that there *are* gods. And on what grounds do the Stoics assert that the Universe is wise and rational? It must first be proved to be *animate*, and this they have not proved. If they argue that there must be a universal Reason, from which man's reason proceeds, they have first to prove that the human mind cannot be the spontaneous product of nature. Again, the argument from design is not conclusive. If the universe is a designed product, then there must be a Designer; but the whole point at issue is, whether the universe is a designed product or not. Might it not be the undesigned product of natural forces?

The Stoic God is animate and so must be possessed of feeling. But if he can feel and receive impressions, then he can suffer from impressions and is ultimately liable to disintegration. Moreover, if God is rational and perfect, as the Stoics suppose Him to be, He cannot be "virtuous," as the Stoics also suppose Him to be. How, for example, can God be brave or courageous? What dangers

[1] Cf. Sext. Emp., *Adv. Math.*, 7, 159 and 166 ff.; Civ., *Acad. Prior.*, 2, 30, 98 ff.
[2] Cf. Sext. Emp., *Adv. Math.*, 9, 13 ff.; Cic., *De Nat. D.*, 3, 17, 44; 3, 29 ff.

or pains or labours affect Him, in respect of which He can show courage?

The Stoics maintain a doctrine of Divine Providence. But if this be so, how can they explain the presence of e.g. poisonous snakes? The Stoics say that God's Providence is manifested in His gift of reason to man. Now, the great majority of men use this reason to degrade themselves, so that to such men the possession of reason is an injury and not a benefit. If God really exercised Providence over all men, He should have made all men good and given all *right* reason. Moreover, it is useless for Chrysippus to speak of "neglect" on the part of God—i.e. in regard to "little" matters. In the first place what Providence has neglected to provide for, is not a little matter: in the second place, the neglect could not be intentional in God (for intentional neglect is a fault even in an earthly ruler); while in the third place unintentional neglect is inconceivable in respect of the Infinite Reason.

These and other criticisms of Carneades are directed against the Stoic doctrines, and so they are, in part, of but academic interest. By maintaining a materialistic doctrine of God the Stoics involved themselves in insurmountable difficulties, for if God were material He could disintegrate, and if He were the Soul of the world—possessed of a body—He could feel pleasure and pain. Criticisms against such a conception of the Deity can have for us no more than academic interest. Moreover, we would not dream of ascribing virtues to God in the anthropomorphic manner that the line of criticism adopted by Carneades pre-supposes. Nor would we undertake to prove in philosophy that everything is created for the good of man. Yet some of the difficulties raised by Carneades are of lasting interest, and an attempt must be made to meet them in every Theodicy, e.g. the presence of physical suffering and of moral evil in the world. I have already made some remarks on this subject when treating of the Stoic theodicy, and I hope to show later on, how other philosophers, mediaeval and modern, tried to answer these questions; but it must always be remembered that, even if the human reason is unable to answer fully and with complete satisfaction all the difficulties that can be raised against a position, that does not compel us to abandon that position, if it rests on valid argument.

Carneades saw that complete suspension of judgment is

impossible, and so he elaborated a theory of Probability (πιθανότης). Probability has various grades and is both necessary and sufficient for action. He showed, for example, how we may approximate to the truth—even if we can never attain certainty—by the accumulation of reasons for accepting some position. If I merely saw the shape of someone I knew, it might be an hallucination, but if I hear the person speak, if I touch him, if he eats, I may for all practical purposes accept the presentation as true. It enjoys a very high degree of probability, especially if it is also intrinsically probable that the person should be in that place at that time. If a man leaves his wife in England and goes to India on business, he might well doubt the objective validity of the presentation, if he seems to see his wife on the quay when he disembarks at Bombay. But if, on returning to England, he finds his wife waiting for him on the landing-stage, the validity of the presentation bears its own inherent probability.

2. The Academy returned to dogmatism under *Antiochus* of Ascalon (d. *c.* 68 B.C.), who apparently started as an agnostic but later came to abandon this position,[1] and whose lectures were heard by Cicero in the winter of 79/8. He pointed out the contradiction involved in asserting that nothing is knowable or that all is doubtful; for, in asserting that all is doubtful, I am at any rate asserting my knowledge that all is doubtful. His own criterion of truth he apparently found in the agreement of eminent philosophers and endeavoured to show that the Academic, Peripatetic and Stoic systems were in essential agreement with each other. In fact he openly taught Stoic doctrines, shamelessly asserting that Zeno had borrowed them from the old Academy. He thus tried to deprive the Sceptics of one of their principal arguments, namely, the contradiction between the various philosophic systems. He shows himself at the same time to be an Eclectic.

This eclectic tendency comes out in his moral teaching. For, while holding with the Stoics that virtue is sufficient for happiness, he also taught with Aristotle that for happiness in its highest degree external goods and health of the body are also necessary. In spite of the fact, then, that Cicero declares him to have been more of a Stoic than an Academician,[2] Antiochus was undoubtedly an Eclectic.

3. A Roman Eclectic was *M. Terentius Varro* (116–27 B.C.),

[1] Cic., *Acad. Prior.*, 2, 22, 69; Numenius cited by Euseb., *Prep. Evang.*, 614, 9, 2 (*P.G.* 21, 1216–17); Aug., *contra Acad.*, 2, 6, 15; 3, 18, 41.
[2] Cic., *Acad. Prior.*, 2, 43, 132.

scholar and philosopher. The only true theology in Varro's opinion is that which recognises *one* God, Who is the Soul of the world, which He governs according to reason. The mythical theology of the poets is to be rejected on the ground that it attributed unworthy characteristics and actions to the gods, while the physical theologies of the natural philosophers contradict one another. We must not, however, neglect the official cult of the State, since this has a practical and popular value. Varro even suggested that the popular religion was the work of earlier statesmen, and that if the work had to be done over again, it might be done better in the light of philosophy.[1]

Varro seems to have been greatly influenced by Poseidonius. From the latter he accepted many theories concerning the origin and development of culture, geography, hydrology, etc., and by his exposition of these theories he influenced later Romans such as Vitruvius and Pliny. Varro's tendency to Pythagorean "number-mysticism" also derives from the thought of Poseidonius and thereby he influenced later writers like Gellius, Macrobius and Martianus Capella. Cynic influence is visible in Varro's *Saturae Menippeae*, of which we possess only fragments. Therein he opposed Cynic simplicity to the luxury of the rich, whose gluttony he subjected to mockery, and he made fun of the philosophers' squabbles.

4. The most celebrated of all Roman eclectics is *M. Tullius Cicero*, the great orator (Jan. 3rd 106–Dec. 7, 43 B.C.). In his youth Cicero was a pupil of Phaedrus the Epicurean, Philon the Academician, Diodotus the Stoic, Antiochus of Ascalon, and Zeno the Epicurean. In Rhodes he listened to the teaching of Poseidonius the Stoic. To the philosophic studies of his youth at Athens and Rhodes there succeeded years spent in public life and official activity, but in the last three years of his life Cicero returned to philosophy. The majority of his philosophic writings date from these later years (e.g. the *Paradoxa*, the *Consolatio*, the *Hortensius*, the *Academica*, the *De Finibus*, the *Tusculana*, the *De Natura Deorum*, the *De Senectute*, the *De Divinatione*, the *De Fato*, the *De Amicitia*, the *De Virtutibus*). The *De Republica* (54 B.C. seq.) and the *De Legibus* (*c.* 52 seq.) are earlier compositions. The writings of Cicero are scarcely to be called original in content, as Cicero himself openly admits—"ἀπόγραφα *sunt, minore labore fiunt, verba tantum affero, quibus abundo.*"[2] He had,

---

[1] *De Civit. Dei*, 6, 4.   [2] *Ad. Att.*, 12, 52, 3.

however, the gift of presenting the doctrine of the Greeks to Roman readers in a clear style.

While Cicero was unable to effect a scientific refutation of Scepticism (he was inclined to the latter, owing to the conflict of opposing philosophical Schools and doctrines), he found a refuge in the intuitions of the moral consciousness, which are immediate and certain. Realising the danger of Scepticism for morality, he sought to place the moral judgment beyond its corroding influence and speaks of *notiones innatae, natura nobis insitae*. These moral concepts proceed therefore from our nature, and they are confirmed by general agreement—*consensus gentium*.

In his ethical doctrine Cicero was inclined to agree with the Stoics that virtue is sufficient for happiness, but he could not bring himself to reject altogether the Peripatetic teaching, which attributed value to external goods as well, though he seems to have hesitated somewhat in his opinion on this matter.[1] He agreed with the Stoics that the wise man should be without πάθη[2] and combated the Peripatetic teaching that virtue is a mean between opposite πάθη. (But it is to be noted that Cicero's notion of πάθος or *perturbatio* is that of *aversa a recta ratione contra naturam animi commotio*.[3]) For Cicero again, as for the Stoics, practical, and not speculative, virtue is the higher.[4]

In the sphere of natural philosophy Cicero was inclined to scepticism, though he by no means despised this province of human thought.[5] He was particularly interested in the proof of God's existence from nature and rejected the doctrine of atheistic atomism. "*Hoc* (i.e. the formation of the world from the chance collision of atoms) *qui existimat fieri potuisse non intelligo cur non idem putet, si innumerabiles unius et viginti formae litterarum vel aureae vel qualeslibet aliquo coiciantur, posse ex iis in terram excussis annales Enni ut deinceps legi possint, effici.*"[6]

Cicero considered that the popular religion should be preserved in the interests of the community at large, while at the same time it should be purified from gross superstition and the practice of attributing immorality to the gods (e.g. the story of the rape of Ganymede).[7] Especially should we preserve belief in Providence and the immortality of the soul.[8]

---

[1] *De Fin.*, 5, 32, 95; *De Off.*, 3, 3, 11; cf. *De Fin.*, 5, 26, 77 ff, and *Tusc.*, 5, 13, 39 ff.
[2] *Tusc.*, 4, 18, 41 ff.   [3] *Tusc.*, 4, 6, 11; 4, 21, 47.   [4] *De Off.*, 1, 44, 158.
[5] *Acad. Prior.*, 2, 41, 127.   [6] *De Nat. D*, 2, 37, 93.   [7] *Tusc.*, 1, 26, 65; 4, 33, 71.
[8] *Tusc.*, 1, 12, 26 ff.; 1, 49, 117 ff.

Cicero stressed the ideal of human fellowship (cf. the Stoa), and appealed to the ninth letter of Plato. "—*ut profectus a caritate domesticorum ac suorum serpat longius et se implicet primum civium, deinde omnium mortalium societate atque, ut ad Archytam scripsit Plato, non sibi se solum natum meminerit sed patriae, sed suis, ut perexigua pars ipsi relinquatur.*"[1]

[1] *De Fin.*, 2, 14, 45.

CHAPTER XXXIX

THE MIDDLE STOA

In the second and third centuries before Christ the Stoic philosophers show a marked tendency to Eclecticism, admitting Platonic and Aristotelian elements into the School and departing from orthodox Stoicism. They were impelled to this course, not only by the attacks levelled against the Stoic dogmatism by the Academicians, but also by their contact with the Roman world, which was much more interested in the practical application of philosophic doctrines than in speculation. The dominant names of the Middle Stoa are those of Panaetius and Poseidonius.

1. *Panaetius of Rhodes* (c. 185–110/9 B.C.) lived for some time in Rome, where he interested the younger Scipio and Laelius in Greek philosophy and greatly influenced the Roman historian Q. Mucius Scaevola and the Greek historian Polybius. Cicero made use of his works, especially in the first two books of the *De Officiis*.[1] In 129 B.C. he succeeded Antipater of Tarsus as Scholarch at Athens.

While Panaetius modified certain Stoic doctrines on the one hand, he did not hesitate on the other hand to jettison altogether some of the cargo of Stoic orthodoxy. Thus he modified Stoic "puritanism" by allowing that the end of life in the case of ordinary men is simply the rational perfection of their individual nature. Stoicism thus became rather less "idealistic" in the hands of Panaetius, especially as he seems to have denied the existence of the truly wise man, the old Stoic ideal, and to have set the proficient (προκόπτων) to all intents and purposes in the first place. Moreover, he attached more value to external goods than did the early Stoa and rejected the ideal of "Apathy."

While thus modifying the Stoic ethic Panaetius cast overboard the Stoic theory of divination (which the early Stoics maintained on a philosophical basis of determinism), rejected astrology and jettisoned the doctrines of the world-conflagration and of the relative "immortality" of the soul.[2] He had little sympathy with popular theology.[3] In his political teaching he appears to have been influenced by Plato and Aristotle, though he advocated a

[1] *Ad. Att.*, 16, 11, 4. [2] Cic., *Tusc.*, 1, 32, 79. [3] Cic., *De Div.*, 1, 3, 6.

wider ideal, in accordance with Stoic doctrine, than that of the two Greek philosophers.

It was apparently from Panaetius that Scaevola got his three-fold division of theology (cf. Varro). He distinguished (i) the theology of the poets, which is anthropomorphic and false, (ii) the theology of the philosophers, which is rational and true, but unfitted for popular use, and (iii) the theology of the states-men, which maintains the traditional cult and is indispensable for public education.[1]

2. The greatest of the disciples of Panaetius was *Poseidonius of Apamaea* (*c.* 135–51 B.C.). At first a pupil of Panaetius at Athens, Poseidonius then made extensive journeys, to Egypt, for example, and to Spain, after which he opened a School at Rhodes in 97 B.C. It was here that Cicero came to hear him in 78 B.C., and he was twice visited by Pompey. His works have disappeared and it is only recently, through the critical analysis of the literature that was indebted to his influence, that some idea has been obtained—even if not in all points a very clear idea—of the greatness of Poseidonius. Historian and geographer, rationalist and mystic, he bound together various philosophic currents in a framework of Stoic monism, tried to support his speculative doctrines by a wealth of empirical knowledge, and infused into the whole the warmth of religious inspiration. Indeed Zeller does not hesitate to call him "the most universal mind that Greece had seen since the time of Aristotle."[2] Proclus (*in Eukleiden*) mentions Poseidonius and his School seven times in connection with the philosophy of mathematics, e.g. on parallels, on the distinction between theorems and problems, and on existence theorems.

Stoic monism is fundamental to the philosophy of Poseidonius, and he tries to display the articulated unity of Nature in detail. The phenomenon of the tide's ebb and flow, as caused by the moon, revealed to him the "sympathy" that prevails between all parts of the cosmic system. The world is a hierarchy of grades of being, from inorganic entities, as in the mineral kingdom, through plants and animals up to man, and so to the super-organic sphere of the Divine, the whole being bound together in one great system and every detail being arranged by Divine Providence. This universal harmony and structural ordering of the universe postulates Absolute Reason, God, at the summit of

---

[1] *St. Aug., De Civit. Dei*, 4, 27. [2] *Outlines*, p. 249.

the hierarchy and as the all-pervading Rational Activity.[1] The world is permeated by a vital force (ζωτικὴ δύναμις) which proceeds from the sun, and God Himself is represented by Poseidonius, following in the footsteps of the orthodox Stoicism, as a rational, fiery breath. Moreover, in contradistinction to his teacher Panaetius, Poseidonius reaffirmed the Stoic doctrine of the conflagration or ἐκπύρωσις, a doctrine which emphasises the monistic character of the universe.

But, though his philosophy was monistic, Poseidonius admitted a dualism, apparently under the influence of Platonism. There are two divisions of the Cosmos, the supralunar world and the infralunar world. While the latter world is earthly and perishable, the former is heavenly and "imperishable" and sustains the lower world through the forces which it imparts. These two worlds are, however, bound together in man, who is the bond (δεσμός) between them.[2] Composed of body and spirit, he stands on the borderline between the perishable and the imperishable or the earthly and the heavenly; and as man is the ontological bond, so is knowledge of man the epistemological bond, binding together in itself all knowledge, knowledge of the heavenly and knowledge of the earthly. Moreover, just as man from the *corporeal* viewpoint is the *highest* grade, so, conversely, from the *spiritual* viewpoint he is the *lowest* grade. In other words, between man and the Supreme Godhead there exist "demons" or higher spiritual beings, who form an intermediate gradation between man and God. The hierarchical character of the universe is thus uninterrupted, though the dualism remains. This dualism is emphasised in the psychology of Poseidonius, for, although with the older Stoics he makes the soul a fiery πνεῦμα—and so material like the body—he then proceeds to emphasise the dualism of soul and body in a manner reminiscent of Plato. Thus the body is a hindrance to the soul, impeding the free development of its knowledge.[3] Further than that, Poseidonius readopted the Platonic theory of the pre-existence of the soul, which naturally underlined the dualism, and also admitted—against Panaetius—the immortality of the soul. This immortality, however, could be no more than a relative immortality (i.e. relative to the body) in the philosophy of Poseidonius, since he had reaffirmed the Stoic world-conflagration. His teaching on "immortality" thus followed that of the older Stoics.

[1] Cic., *De Nat. D.*, 2, 33 ff.   [2] Cf. *Plat. Tim.*, 31 b c.
[3] Cic., *De Div.*, 1, 49, 110; 1, 57, 129-30.

In spite of this dualism in his psychology of man Poseidonius'
influenced by Plato and Aristotle, emphasised the gradation-
aspect in his general psychology. Thus the plants, which in the
earlier Stoic view possess only φύσις and not ψυχή, enjoy τὸ
ἐπιθυμητικόν, and also the θρεπτική and αὐξητικὴ δύναμεις, while the
animals possess in addition τὸ θυμοειδές, ἡ αἴσθησις, τὸ ὀρεκτικόν, and τὸ
κινητικὸν κατὰ τόπον. Man, higher than the animals, possesses τὸ
λογιστικόν and so the capacity of λόγος, νοῦς and διάνοια.

Thus, although Poseidonius admits the Platonic dualism, he
subordinates it to an ultimate monism, influenced by the Heraclitean theory of opposition in harmony or unity in difference.
In this attempt at a synthesis of dualism and monism he marks
a stage on the way to Neo-Platonism.

In contrast to Panaetius, Poseidonius reaffirmed the Stoic
theory of divination. Because of the universal harmony of the
Cosmos and the reign of Fate the future can be divined in the
present: moreover, the Providence of God would not have with-
held from men the means of divining future events.[1] In states
like sleep and ecstasy the soul, free from the body's hindrance,
may see the underlying connection of events and divine the future.
We have already mentioned that Poseidonius admitted the
existence of "demons": he believed too that man can enter into
communication with them.

Poseidonius propounded a theory of history or of cultural
development. In the primitive golden age the wise, i.e. the
philosophers, ruled (corresponding in mankind to the natural
leadership of the strongest beast in the herd within the animal
kingdom), and it was they who made those inventions which
raised man from his primitive way of life to more refined conditions of material civilisation. Thus the wise discovered metals
and founded the art of making tools, etc.[2] In the moral sphere
the primitive stage of innocence was followed by decadence, and
the prevalence of violence necessitated the institution of laws.
The philosophers accordingly, leaving to others the elaboration
of technical appliances, set themselves to the task of raising the
moral condition of mankind, first of all through practical and political activity and later by a self-dedication to the life of speculation
or θεωρία. Yet all these activities, from the lowest to the highest,
were but different grades of one and the same wisdom or σοφία.

[1] Cic., *De Div.*, I, 49, 110; I, 55, 125.
[2] Cf. Seneca, *Epist.*, 90; Lucr., *De Rerum Nat.*, V.

Poseidonius also interested himself in ethnographical questions, stressing the influence of climate and natural conditions on the character and way of life of a people, his travels affording him material for observation on this matter. In addition, his empirical bent led him to extend his activity over a wide field in the domain of the special sciences, e.g. in mathematics, astronomy, history and literature. But his outstanding characteristic is his ability for reducing all this wealth of empirical knowledge to the unity of a philosophical system, discovering everywhere connections, interactions and harmonies, trying to penetrate and exhibit the rational structure of the universe and the rational development of history.

Note on the Peripatetic School in the Hellenistic-Roman Period

1. *Strato of Lampsacus*, ὁ φυσικός, succeeded Theophrastus as head of the Peripatetic School at Athens and occupied that position from about 287–269 B.C. His philosophic teaching betrays the influence of Democritus, which impelled him towards a monistic view of the universe. The world consists of particles, between which there is empty space. These particles, however, are endlessly divisible, and appear to possess qualities, since Strato assumes ultimate characteristics or qualities, namely the Warm and the Cold. The world was formed by natural necessity or the laws of nature, and can be ascribed to God only so far as God is to be identified with the unconscious forces of Nature itself. Thus, although Strato does not follow Democritus in matters of detail, the inspiration of his materialistic monism and his denial of the Aristotelian dualism must be attributed to the influence of the Democritean philosophy. This transformation of the Peripatetic system in the hands of Strato is consonant with the latter's special interest in physical science—it was this that won him the title of ὁ φυσικός. He appears to have influenced the medicine, astronomy and mechanics of the Alexandrian period.

In Strato's eyes all psychical activities, such as thought and feeling, are reducible to *motion*, and they are activities of the one rational soul, which is situated between the eyebrows. We can have as objects of our thought only that which has been the cause of a previous sense-impression,[1] and, conversely, every perception involves intellectual activity.[2] This might seem at first sight to be but a repetition of Aristotelian epistemology, but Strato seems

[1] Simplic., *Phys.*, 965, 16 a.　　[2] Plut., *de sol. animal.*, 3 (961 a).

to have meant it in a sense which involves the denial of a rational principle in man, essentially distinct from the animal soul. His denial of immortality was, therefore, a logical conclusion, for, if all thinking is essentially dependent on sense, there can be no question of a principle of thought surviving independently of the body.

2. Under Strato's successors—Lycon of Troas, Ariston of Chios, Critolaus of Phaselis, Diodorus of Tyre and Erymneus—the Peripatetic School does not seem to have made any real contribution to philosophy. Moreover, an eclectic tendency made itself visible in the School. Thus although Critolaus defended Aristotle's doctrine of the eternity of the world against the Stoics, he accepted the Stoics' reduction of God and the human soul to matter (Aether) and adopted the Cynic attitude in regard to pleasure.

3. With *Andronicus of Rhodes* the School took a new turn. Andronicus was the tenth Scholarch at Athens (i.e. excluding Aristotle himself) and occupied the post from about 70 B.C. to 50 B.C. He published the "pedagogical" works of Aristotle, investigated their authenticity, and commented on many of the works, giving special attention to logic. The line of commentators culminated in *Alexander of Aphrodisias*, who lectured on the Peripatetic philosophy at Athens between A.D. 198 and 211. Alexander was the most celebrated of the commentators of Aristotle, but he did not hesitate to depart from the latter's teaching. For instance, he adopted a nominalist position in regard to universals and denied anthropocentric teleology. Moreover, he identified the νοῦς ποιητικός with τὸ πρῶτον αἴτιον. Man possesses at birth only the νοῦς φυσικός or ὑλικός and later acquires the νοῦς ἐπίκτητος under the influence of the νοῦς ποιητικός. A consequence of this is the denial of the human soul's immortality. While in denying the immortality of the human soul Alexander is probably at one with Aristotle, it must be admitted that the denial follows much more obviously from Alexander's teaching than it does from the somewhat ambiguous remarks of Aristotle.

4. Alexander's eloquent defence of the study of logic in his commentary on the *Prior Analytics* is worthy of mention. He there declares that logic is not less deserving of our attention and study owing to the fact that it is an instrument of philosophy rather than an actual part of philosophy. For if man's greatest good is to become like to God, and if this likeness is attained through contemplation and knowledge of truth, and the knowledge

of truth through demonstration, then we should hold demonstration in the greatest honour and esteem, and so syllogistic reasoning also, inasmuch as demonstration is a form of syllogistic reasoning.[1] Together with this scholarly tendency grew the tendency to eclecticism. Thus the famous physician *Galen* (A.D. 129 to about A.D. 199) and *Aristocles* of Messana (*c.* A.D. 180) inclined to Stoicism with their doctrine of the immanent and active Nous, that pervades all nature.

5. The Peripatetics of the latest period can indeed hardly be called Peripatetics—certainly not without qualification: to all intents and purposes the School was absorbed in Neo-Platonism, the last great effort of Greek philosophy, and the late Peripatetics either inclined to eclecticism or contented themselves with commenting on the works of Aristotle. Thus Anatolius of Alexandria, who became bishop of Laodicea about A.D. 268 and may be identical with the Anatolius who was the teacher of Iamblichus,[2] combined, in his treatise on the numbers one to ten, consideration of the real properties of numbers with Pythagorean "number-mysticism."

Themistius (*c.* A.D. 320–*c.* 390), who taught at Constantinople and other places in the East and never became a Christian, affirmed indeed that he had chosen Aristotle as his guide to wisdom, and either paraphrased or commented on some of Aristotle's works, but was in fact much influenced by Platonism. With the later Platonism he defined philosophy as ὁμοίωσις θεοῦ κατὰ τὸ δυνατὸν ἀνθρώπῳ. (Cf. Plat. *Theaet.* 176 b.)

---

[1] *C.A.G.*, 11/1, 4; 30 and 6 : 8.   [2] Eunap., *Vit. Soph.*, II.

CHAPTER XL

THE LATER STOA

IN the early Roman Empire the chief characteristic of the Stoa is its insistence on the practical and moral principles of the School, which take on a religious colouring, being bound up with the doctrine of man's kinship with God and his duty of love towards his fellow-men. The noble morality of the Stoa is strikingly displayed in the teaching of the great Stoics of the period, Seneca, Epictetus and the Emperor Marcus Aurelius. At the same time a certain tendency to eclecticism is visible in the Stoa as in other Schools. Nor was the contemporary scientific interest absent from the Stoa: we may think, for example, of the geographer Strabo. We are fortunate in possessing an extensive Stoic literature from this period, which enables us to form a clear idea of the teaching of the School and the characteristics of its great personalities. Thus we are well provided in regard to Seneca's writings and we have four of the eight books in which Flavius Arrianus reported the lectures of Epictetus, while the Meditations of Marcus Aurelius show us the Stoic philosopher on the Roman throne.

1. *L. Annaeus Seneca* of Córdoba was tutor and minister to the Emperor Nero, and it was in obedience to the latter's command that the philosopher opened his veins in A.D. 65.

As we would expect of a Roman, Seneca emphasises the practical side of philosophy, ethics, and—within the sphere of ethics—is more concerned with the practice of virtue than with theoretical investigations into its nature. He does not seek intellectual knowledge for its own sake, but pursues philosophy as a means to the acquirement of virtue. Philosophy is necessary, but it is to be pursued with a practical end in view. *Non delectent, verba nostra, sed prosint—non quaerit aeger medicum eloquentem.*[1] His words on this topic not infrequently recall those of Thomas à Kempis, e.g. *plus scire quam sit satis, intemperantiae genus est.*[2] To spend one's time in the so-called liberal studies without having a practical end in view is waste of time—*unum studium vere liberale est quod liberum facit.*[3] and he calls on Lucilius to abandon

[1] *Ep.*, 75, 5   [2] *Ep.*, 88, 36.   [3] *Ep.*, 88, 2.

the literary game of reducing sublime themes to grammatical and dialectical jugglery.[1] Seneca is interested to a certain extent in physical theories, but he insists that it is the conquest of the passions that is the really important point and which makes man equal to God,[2] and he often uses physical subjects simply as an opportunity for moralising conclusions, as when he makes use of the earthquakes in Campania (A.D. 63) to furnish matter for a moral discourse.[3] However, he certainly praises the study of Nature (under the influence of Poseidonius) and even declares that knowledge of Nature is to be sought for its own sake,[4] but even here the practical and human interest is visible.

Seneca adheres theoretically to the old Stoic materialism,[5] but in practice he certainly tends to regard God as transcending matter. This tendency to metaphysical dualism was a natural consequence or accompaniment of his marked tendency to psychological dualism. True, he affirms the materiality of the soul, but he proceeds to speak in Platonic strain of the conflict between soul and body, between the aspirations of the higher man and the doctrines of the flesh. *Nam corpus hoc animi pondus ac poena est, premente illo urgetur, in vinculis est.*[6] True virtue and true worth rest within: external goods do not confer true happiness but are transitory gifts of Fortune in which it would be foolish to place our trust. *Brevissima ad divitias per contemptum divitiarum via est.*[7] Seneca, as courtier of Caligula and Claudius and the wealthy tutor and minister of the young Nero, has been accused of practical inconsistency and hypocrisy, but it must be remembered that his very experience of the contrast between great wealth and splendour on the one hand and the constant fear of death on the other would very much help a man of his temperament to realise the ephemeral character of wealth, position and power. Moreover, he had unrivalled opportunities of observing human degradation, lust and debauchery at close quarters. Some ancient writers accumulated gossip about Seneca's private life, calculated to show that he did not live up to his own principles.[8] But, even if, allowing for the exaggeration and gossip of opponents, he did not pass through life without falls from his moral ideal—as is indeed only too likely in a man of his position

---

[1] *Ep.*, 71, 6. [2] *Ep.*, 73, 13. [3] *Nat. Q.*, 6, 32. [4] *Nat. Q.*, 6, 4.
[5] *Ep.*, 66, 12; 117, 2; 57, 8.
[6] *Ep.*, 120, 14; 65, 16. Cf. *Dies iste, quem tamquam extremum reformidas, aeterni natalis est. Ep.*, 102, 26.
[7] *Ep.*, 62, 3. [8] Cf. Dion Cassius, 61, 10.

and connections, attached to a depraved Court[1]—that does not mean that he was insincere in his teaching and preaching. His knowledge of the force of temptation and of the degradation to which avarice, ambition and lust could lead—to a certain extent perhaps from personal experience, but far more from his observation of others—lent power and force to his pen and to his moral exhortation. In spite of all rhetoric Seneca knew what he was talking about.

Although theoretically adhering to the traditional Stoic determinism, Seneca maintained that, as rational, every man has the power to take the path of virtue if he will only *will* to do so. *Satis natura dedit roboris si illo utamur.*[2] Moreover, God will help those who strive to help themselves. *Non sunt di fastidiosi: adscendentibus manum porrigunt*, and *O te miserum si contemnis hunc testem.*[3] The man who does help himself, conquer his passions and lead a life in accordance with right reason, is better off than our ancestors of the Golden Age, for, if they were innocent, they were innocent from ignorance and absence of temptation. *Non fuere sapientes—ignorantia rerum innocentes erant.*[4]

Since he aimed at encouraging men to set their feet upon the path of virtue and to continue therein in spite of temptation and fall, Seneca was naturally forced to temper the strict moral idealism of the earlier Stoics. He knew too much about the moral struggle to suppose that man can become virtuous by sudden conversion. And so we find him distinguishing three classes of *proficientes.* (i) Those who have abandoned some of their sins, but not all; (ii) those who have formed the resolution to renounce evil passions in general, even if still liable to occasional relapse; (iii) those who have got beyond possibility of relapse, but still lack confidence in themselves and the consciousness of their own wisdom. They *approximate*, therefore, to wisdom and perfect virtue.[5] Moreover, Seneca admits that external goods, e.g. wealth, may be used for good ends. The wise man will be the master of his wealth and not its slave. He gives practical counsel as to how to secure moral progress, e.g. by the use of the daily self-examination, which he himself practised.[6] It is useless to retire into solitude, if you do not attempt at the same time to change yourself: change of place does not necessarily mean change of

---

[1] Does he not himself admit, *Non de me loquor, qui multum ab homine tolerabili nedum a perfecto absum? Ep.* 57, 3.
[2] *Ep.*, 116, 7.   [3] *Ep.*, 73, 15; 43, 5.   [4] *Ep.*, 90, 46.   [5] *Ep.*, 75, 8.
[6] *De Ira*, 3, 36, 3.

heart, and wherever you go, you will still have to struggle with yourself. It is easy to understand, how the legend of Seneca's correspondence with St. Paul could grow up, when we read such phrases as *Nos quoque evincamus omnia, quorum praemium non corona nec palma est.*[1]

Seneca lays emphasis on the Stoic doctrine of the relationship that exists among all human beings, and instead of the self-sufficiency of the wise man—a self-sufficiency tinged with contempt for others—he calls on us to help our fellow-men and to forgive those who have injured us. *Alteri vivas oportet, si vis tibi vivere.*[2] He stresses the necessity of active benevolence. "Nature bids me to be of use to men whether they are slave or free, freedmen or free born. Wherever there is a human being there is room for benevolence."[3] "See that you are beloved by all while you live and regretted when you die."

Yet punishment of evil-doers is necessary. *Bonis nocet qui malis parcet.*[4] The most effective punishment, however, for the purpose of reformation is the mildest. Punishment should not be inflicted out of rage or the desire of revenge (cf. *De Ira* and *De Clementia*).

2. *Epictetus of Hierapolis* (c. A.D. 50–138) was at first a slave belonging to a member of Nero's bodyguard, and, when he became a freedman, continued to live in Rome until the expulsion of the philosophers by the Emperor Domitian (A.D. 89 or 93). He then founded a School at Nicopolis in Epirus and probably continued at its head until his death. It was at Nicopolis that his lectures were attended by Flavius Arrianus, who composed eight books of Διατριβαί on the basis of the lectures. Of these eight books we possess four. Arrian also published a small catechism or handbook of his master's doctrines, the Ἐγχειρίδιον.

Epictetus insists that all men have the capacity for virtue and that God has given to all men the means of becoming happy, of becoming men of steadfast character and self-control. "What then is a man's nature? To bite, to kick, to throw into prison, and to behead? No, but to do good, to co-operate with others, to wish them well."[5] All men have the sufficient initial moral intuitions on which they can build up the moral life. "Observe whom you yourself praise when you praise without partiality? Do you praise the just or the unjust, the moderate or the immoderate, the temperate or the intemperate?"[6] "There are

---

[1] *Ep.*, 78, 16, 4.   [2] *Ep.*, 48, 2.   [3] *De Vita Beata*, 24, 3.   [4] Fr. 114.
[5] *Disc.*, 4, 1, 22.   [6] *Disc.*, 3, 1, 8.

certain things which men who are not altogether perverted see by the common notions which all possess."[1]

Yet, though all men possess sufficient basis for the building-up of the moral life, philosophic instruction is necessary for all, in order that they may be able to apply their primary conceptions (προλήψεις) of good and evil to particular circumstances. "Primary conceptions are common to all men,"[2] but a conflict or difficulty may arise in the application of these primary conceptions to particular facts. It is this which explains the diversity of ethical notions, in the sense of applied notions, among different peoples and between various individuals.[3] Education is, therefore, necessary and, inasmuch as the right application of principles depends on reasoning and reasoning on logic, a knowledge of logic is not to be despised. The important thing, however, is not that a man should possess a knowledge of formal dialectic, but that he should be able to apply his principles to practice and, above all, that he should actually carry them into practice in his conduct. There are two factors in which education chiefly consists: (i) in learning to apply the natural primary conceptions to particular circumstances in accordance with "nature", and (ii) in learning to distinguish between things in our power and things not in our power.[4] Epictetus, in common with the Stoic School in general, makes a great deal of this latter distinction. To acquire honours and wealth, to enjoy continual health, to avoid physical mal-treatment or the disfavour of the Emperor, to ward off death or disaster from himself or his friends and relatives, all this does not depend solely on the efforts of any individual man: he must be careful, then, not to set his heart on any of these things, but to accept all that happens to himself or his relatives and friends as Fate, as the will of God: he must accept all events of this kind without rebellion or discontent, as being the expression of the Divine Will. What, then, is in man's power? His judgments on events and his will: these he can control, and his self-education consists in attaining true judgment and a right will. "The essence of good and evil lies in an attitude of the will,"[5] and this will lies within a man's power, for "the will may conquer itself, but nothing else can conquer it."[6] That which is really necessary for man is, therefore, to *will* virtue, to *will* victory over sin. "Be well assured that nothing is more tractable than the human soul. You must exercise your will and the thing is done, it is set right;

---

[1] *Disc.*, 3, 6, 8.   [2] *Disc.*, 1, 22.   [3] *Ibid.*   [4] *Ibid.*   [5] *Disc.*, 1, 29.   [6] *Ibid.*

as on the other hand relax your vigilance and all is lost, for from within comes ruin and from within comes help."[1] Sins differ from the material standpoint, but from the moral standpoint they are equal in that they all involve a perverted will. To overcome and set right this perverted will is within the power of all. "Now will you not help yourself? And how much easier is this help? There is no need to kill or imprison any man or to treat him with contumely or to go into the law-courts. You must just talk to yourself. You will be most easily persuaded; no one has more power to persuade you than you yourself."[2]

As practical means to moral progress Epictetus advises the daily examination of conscience (the faithful use of which leads to the substitution of good habits for bad ones), avoidance of bad companions and occasions of sin, constant self-vigilance, etc. We must not be discouraged by falls but must persevere, setting before our eyes some ideal of virtue, e.g. Socrates or Zeno. Again, ". . . remember that Another looks from above on what is happening and that you must please Him rather than this man."[3] In the course of moral progress he distinguishes three stages:

(i) A man is taught to order his *desires* in accordance with right reason, freeing himself from morbid emotions and attaining to tranquillity of soul.

(ii) A man is trained to action, to performance of his duty (τὸ καθῆκον), coming to act as a true son, brother, citizen, etc.

(iii) The third stage relates to judgment and assent, and "its aim is to make the other two secure, so that even in sleep, intoxication, or hypochondria we may not let any presentation pass untested."[4] An unerring moral judgment is produced.

Duties towards oneself must begin with cleanliness of the body. "I indeed would rather that a young man, when first moved to philosophy, should come to me with his hair carefully trimmed, than with it dirty and rough."[5] That is to say, if a man has a feeling for natural cleanliness and beauty there is more hope of elevating him to the perception of moral beauty. Epictetus inculcates temperance, modesty, and chastity, censuring, for example, the adulterer. Simplicity is to be cultivated, though there is no harm in pursuing wealth, if this is done for good ends. "If I can acquire money, and also keep myself modest and faithful and magnanimous, point out the way and I will acquire it. But

[1] *Disc.*, 4, 9, 16.   [2] *Disc.*, 4, 9, 13.   [3] *Disc.*, 1, 30.
[4] *Disc.*, 3, 2; cf. 1, ch. 18 (end).   [5] *Disc.*, 4, 11, 25.

if you ask me to lose the things which are good and my own, in order that you may gain the things which are not good, see how unfair and silly you are."[1] (This to people who urge a friend to acquire money that they also may have some.) Like all the Stoics, Epictetus lauded veracity and loyalty.

True piety is to be encouraged. "Of religion towards the Gods, know that the chief element is to have right opinions concerning them, as existing and governing the whole in fair order and justice, and then to set thyself to obey them, and to yield to them in each event, and submit to it willingly, as accomplished under the highest counsels."[2] Atheism and denial of Divine Providence, both general and particular, are condemned. "Concerning the Gods, there are some who say that a Divine Being does not exist; and others, that it exists indeed, but is idle and uncaring, and hath no forethought for anything; and a third class say that there is such a Being, and he taketh forethought also, but only in respect of great and heavenly things, but of nothing that is on the earth; and a fourth class, that he taketh thought of things both in heaven and earth, but only in general, and not of each thing severally. And there is a fifth class, whereof are Odysseus and Socrates, who say, 'Nor can I move without thy knowledge.' "[3]

Marriage and the family are in accordance with right reason, though the "missionary" may remain celibate in order to be free for his work.[4] The child must always obey the father, unless the latter commands something immoral. Patriotism and active sharing in public life are encouraged—somewhat inconsistently —but war is condemned and the ruler should win the allegiance of his subjects by his example and by his self-sacrificing care for them.

Yet cosmopolitanism and the love of humanity transcend narrow patriotism. All men have God for their Father and are brothers by nature. "Will you not remember who you are and whom you rule? That they are kinsmen, that they are brethren by nature, that they are the offspring of Zeus?"[5] To all men we owe love and should not return evil for evil. "To suppose that we shall be easily despised by others unless in every possible way we do injury to those who first show us hostility, is the work of very ignoble and foolish men, for this implies that inability to

---

[1] Ench., 24. [2] Ench., 31. [3] Disc., 1, 12. [4] Cf. Disc., 3, 22; 3, 26, 67.
[5] Disc., 1, 13.

do injury is the reason why we are thought contemptible, whereas the really contemptible man is not he who cannot do injury but he who cannot do benefit."[1] Epictetus does not, however, reject punishment any more than the other Stoics. They insist that violation of law must be punished, but that this punishment must proceed from mature deliberation and not from hasty anger, and that it should be tempered with mercy, calculated to be, not merely a deterrent, but also a remedy for the offender.

In *Disc.* 3, 22, Epictetus devotes a chapter to Cynicism, in which the Cynic philosopher appears as the preacher of the truth concerning good and evil, as the ambassador of God. Without sharing the Cynic contempt for science, Epictetus seems to have admired the Cynic's indifference towards external goods. This is all the more natural in that for Epictetus happiness depends on that which alone is in our power and independent of external conditions —namely, our will, our ideas concerning things, and the use that we make of our ideas. If we seek our happiness in goods which do not depend entirely on ourselves for attainment or continued possession, we invite unhappiness: we must practise abstinence therefore—ἀνέχου καὶ ἀπέχου—and seek our happiness within.

(Dr. Praechter tells of the Director of a Swiss sanatorium, who was accustomed to hand to his neurasthenic and psychasthenic patients a copy of the Enchiridion in a German translation, and who found it to be a valuable aid in effecting a cure.[2])

3. *Marcus Aurelius*, Roman Emperor from A.D. 161 to 180, composed his Meditations (in the Greek language) in twelve books in aphoristic form. For Epictetus he had a lively admiration,[3] and he was at one with Epictetus and Seneca in giving a religious colouring to his philosophy. With Marcus Aurelius, too, we find stress laid on Divine Providence and a wise ordering of the universe, the close relationship between man and God, the duty of love towards one's fellow-men. Thus the Emperor teaches compassion for human infirmity. "When any one does you a wrong, set yourself at once to consider what was the point of view, good or bad, that led him wrong. As soon as you perceive it you will be sorry for him, not surprised or angry. For your own view of good is either the same as his or something like in kind, and you will make allowance. Or, supposing your own view of good and bad has altered, you will find charity for his mistake

---

[1] Stob., *Flor.*, 20, 61.   [2] Ueberweg-Praechter, p. 498, Note.
[3] *Med.*, I, 7.

comes easier."[1] "It is man's special gift to love even those who fall into blunders; this takes effect the moment we realise that men are our brothers, that sin is ignorance and unintentional, that in a little while we shall both be dead, that, above all, no injury is done us; our inner self is not made worse than it was before."[2] Active benevolence is stressed. "Does the eye demand a recompense for seeing, or the feet for walking? Just as this is the end for which they exist, and just as they find their reward in realising the law of their being, so, too, man is made for kindness, and whenever he does an act of kindness or otherwise helps forward the common good, he thereby fulfils the law of his being and comes by his own."[3] "Love mankind, follow God."[4]

Marcus Aurelius shows a decided tendency to break through the Stoic materialism. He adheres indeed to the Stoic monism, as in the following passage: "All harmonises with me which is in harmony with thee, O universe. Nothing for me is too early nor too late which is in due season for thee. For thee are all things, in thee are all things, to thee all things return. The poet says, Dear City of Cecrops; and wilt not thou say, Dear City of Zeus?"[5] Moreover, the Emperor was punctiliously observant of the forms of polytheistic worship, a fact which will partly explain the persecution of Christians during his reign, since he clearly looked upon the fulfilment of the requirements of State-worship as implied in good citizenship. But although Marcus Aurelius adheres to the Stoic monism, he tends to transcend materialism by his division of man into three parts—σῶμα, ψυχή and νοῦς, ψυχή being material but νοῦς being expressly distinguished from all four elements, and so—logically speaking at least—from matter. The human νοῦς or τὸ νοερόν comes from the νοερόν of the Universe, it is an ἀπόσπασμα of God,[6] it is τὸ ἡγεμονικόν.[7] The influence of Platonism is clear, but it is possible that the Emperor, who had Claudius Severus, a Peripatetic, as one of his teachers,[8] was influenced also by the doctrine of Aristotle.

The νοῦς is the δαίμων which God has given to every man to be his guide, and this δαίμων is an emanation of the Divinity. It follows, then, that whoever disobeys the commands of the δαίμων which are the commands of reason, acts not only irrationally but also impiously. Immorality is thus impiety.[9] "Live with the gods, And he lives with the gods whoever presents to them his

---

[1] *Med.*, 7, 26. [2] *Med.*, 7, 22. [3] *Med.*, 9, 42. [4] *Med.*, 7, 31. [5] *Med.*, 4, 23.
[6] *Med.*, 5, 27.   [7] *Med.*, 12, 1.   [8] Capitol, *Vit. M. Ant.*, 3, 3.
[9] *Med.*, 2, 13 : 11, 20: 9, 1.

soul accepting their dispensations and busied about the will of God, even that particle of Zeus which Zeus gives to every man for his controller and governor—to wit, his mind and reason."[1] Man has it in his power to avoid wickedness. "As for those things which are truly evil, as vice and wickedness, such things they (the gods) have put in a man's own power, that he might avoid them if he would."[2]

Marcus Aurelius, after the Stoic tradition, admits only limited immortality. Although he stresses, as Seneca did, the dualism between soul and body and depicts death as a liberation,[3] he allows not only the possibility of the soul's "reabsorption" at the world-conflagration, but also the possibility that the soul is reabsorbed in the Cosmic Reason in virtue of the constant change in nature—a theme dwelt upon by the Emperor, who compares the flow of phenomena to a river.[4] In any case the soul enjoys but a limited persistence after death.[5]

[1] *Med.*, 5, 27.   [2] *Med.*, 2, 11.   [3] *Med.*, 9, 3; 11, 3.
[4] *Med.*, 4, 14; 4, 43; 5, 23.   [5] *Med.*, 4, 21.

CHAPTER XLI

CYNICS, ECLECTICS, SCEPTICS

1. *Cynics*

THE moral corruption in the Roman Empire not unnaturally prompted a revival of Cynicism, and the writing of letters under the names of ancient Cynics seems to have been calculated to forward this revival. Thus we have 51 letters under the name of Diogenes and 36 under that of Crates.

Roman Stoics of the type of Seneca addressed themselves mainly to members of the highest classes in society, to men who belonged to that circle which was naturally drawn into court-life, to men, above all, who possessed some hankering after virtue and tranquillity of soul, but who were at the same time bewildered by the luxurious and sensation-loving life of the aristocracy, who felt the power of the flesh and the attractions of sin and yet were also weary of self-indulgence and ready to grasp and hold the helping hand that might be held out to them. But beside the aristocracy and the men of wealth there were the masses, who may have benefited to a certain extent by the humanitarian ideals propagated among their masters by the Stoics, but who were not directly touched by men like Seneca. To meet the spiritual and moral needs of the masses there grew up a different type of "apostle," that of the Cynic preacher or missionary. These men led the life of itinerant preachers, poor and self-denying, aiming at the "conversion" of the masses who came to listen to them—as when the celebrated Apollonius of Tyana (who belongs rather to the story of Neo-Pythagoreanism), mystic and reported miracle-worker, preached a rivalry of public spirit to the inhabitants of Smyrna, who were torn apart by faction, or discoursed on virtue to the crowd gathered at Olympia to witness the games and races[1] —as when Musonius (who, in spite of his affinity with Cynicism, actually belonged to the Stoic School and was the teacher of Epictetus), harangued the troops of Vespasian and Vitellius on the blessings of peace and the horrors of civil war at the risk of his own life[2] or denounced impiety and demanded virtue from men and women alike. They were often men of undaunted courage, as may be seen from the example of Musonius, just

[1] Philostr., *Apoll. Tyan.*, 4, 8; 4, 31.   [2] Tac., *Hist.*, 3, 81.

described, or from Demetrius' defiance of Nero: "You threaten me with death, but nature threatens you."[1] Demetrius, praised by Seneca in his writings, consoled the last hours of Thrasea by discoursing on the soul and its destiny.[2]

Lucian criticises the Cynic preachers unmercifully, particularly for their bad manners, their lack of culture, their coarseness and buffoonery, their vulgarity and obscenity. Lucian was a foe to all enthusiasm, and religious fervour and "mystic" exaltation were repugnant to him, so that he often doubtless does an injustice to the Cynics owing to his lack of sympathy and understanding; but it must be remembered that Lucian was not alone in his criticism, for Martial, Petronius, Seneca, Epictetus, Dion Chrysostom and others are agreed in condemning abuses which were undoubtedly real. Some of the Cynics were certainly impostors and buffoons who brought the name of philosophy into contempt, as Dion Chrysostom states plainly.[3] Moreover, some of them betrayed a repulsive egoism and lack of good taste and proper respect, as when that same Demetrius, who had denounced Nero, took it upon himself to insult the Emperor Vespasian—who was no Nero—or as when Peregrinus attacked the Emperor Antoninus Pius.[4] (Vespasian took no notice of Demetrius, while Peregrinus was merely told by the Prefect to leave the city. The Cynic who publicly attacked Titus in the theatre for his intercourse with Berenice was scourged, however, while Heros, who repeated the performance, was beheaded.[5]) Lucian is inclined to put the worst interpretation on the conduct of the Cynics. Thus, when Peregrinus—called Proteus—who had become a Christian in Palestine, but who had subsequently joined the ranks of the Cynics, publicly burnt himself to death at Olympia in order to give an example of contempt for death, to imitate the Cynic patron Heracles and to unite himself with the divine element, Lucian assumes that his action was due simply to a love of notoriety—κενοδοξία.[6] The motive of vainglory may very well have entered in, but it may not have been the sole motive operative with Peregrinus.

Nevertheless, in spite of extravagance and in spite of the existence of impostors and buffoons, Cynicism cannot be condemned root and branch. *Demonax* (c. A.D. 50–150) was universally honoured at Athens for his goodness,[7] and when the Athenians proposed to institute gladiatorial shows in the city he advised

---

[1] Epict., *Disc.*, I, 25.   [2] Tac., *Ann.*, 16, 34.   [3] e.g. *Or.*, 32, 9.
[4] Suet., *Vesp.*, 13; Dion Cass., 66, 13; Luc., *De morte Peregr.*, c. 18.
[5] Cf. Dio. Cass., 66, 15.   [6] *De Morte Peregr.*, 4; 20 ff.   [7] Cf. *Demonax* (Lucian).

15

them first of all to demolish the altar of Pity. Though simple
and frugal in his ways he seems to have avoided ostentatious
singularity. Brought before the Athenian courts on a charge of
impiety, since he declined to offer sacrifice and refused to seek
initiation into the Eleusinian Mysteries, he replied that God has
no need of sacrifices, while, as for the Mysteries, if they contained
a revelation of good tidings to man, he would have to publish it,
whereas, if they were of no value, he would feel bound to warn
the people against them.[1] *Oenomaus* of Gadara dismissed the
pagan anthropomorphic fables concerning the gods and fiercely
attacked the revival of belief in divination and oracles. The
oracles, he said, were mere deception, while in any case man is
possessed of free will and man alone is responsible for his actions.
Julian the Apostate, champion of paganism, was aroused to
indignation by the very memory of such a man as Oenomaus,
who had attacked the pagan oracles.[2]

A celebrated and honourable Cynic preacher was *Dion Chrysostom*, who was born about A.D. 40 and lived, at any rate, well
into the reign of the Emperor Trajan. He came of an aristocratic
family of Prusa (Bithynia) and was at first a rhetorician and
Sophist. Condemned to banishment from Bithynia and Italy in
A.D. 82 during the reign of the Emperor Domitian, he led a
wandering life of poverty. During the period of exile he underwent a sort of "conversion" and became an itinerant Cynic
preacher with a mission to the submerged masses of the Empire.
Dion retained his rhetorical manner and liked, in his Orations,
to clothe the moral truths he expressed in an attractive and
elegant form; but though true to the rhetorical tradition, he
insisted in his preaching on living in conformity with the Divine
Will, on the moral ideal, on the practice of true virtue and on the
insufficiency of purely material civilisation. In the Ἐυβοϊκός he
depicts the life of the poor countryman as being more natural,
freer and happier than that of the rich town-dweller; but he
occupies himself also with the question, how the poor in the cities
can most satisfactorily live their lives without hankering after
luxury or involving themselves in what is harmful to soul or body.
He warned the people of Tarsus that they had a wrong sense of
values. Happiness is to be found, not in stately buildings, wealth
and delicate living, but in temperance, justice and true piety.
The great materialistic civilisations of the past—Assyria, for

---

[1] *Demonax*, 11.   [2] Julian, *Or.*, 7, 209.

example—have perished, while the great Empire of Alexander is gone and Pella is a heap of bricks.[1] He harangues the people of Alexandria on their vices and lust for sensation, on their lack of dignity and their trivial interests.[2]

Dion's social interests led him towards Stoicism and he made use of the Stoic doctrines of world-harmony and of cosmopolitanism. As God rules over the world, so should the Monarch rule over the State, and as the world is a harmony of many phenomena, so should individual States be preserved, but in such a way that they live in peace and harmony and free intercourse with one another. Besides the influence of Stoicism Dion seems to have undergone the influence of Poseidonius, taking from him, the division of a threefold theology, that of the philosophers, that of the poets and that of the official or State cult. He became, after the end of his period of banishment under Domitian, a favourite of Trajan, who used to invite the philosopher to his table and take him as a companion in his carriage, though he did not pretend to understand Dion's rhetoric. τί μὲν λέγεις, οὐκ οἶδα. φιλῶ δε σε ὡς ἐμαυτόν.[3] It was before the court of Trajan that Dion delivered some of his orations, contrasting the ideal monarch with the tyrant. The true monarch is the shepherd of his people, appointed by God for the good of his subjects. He must be a truly religious[4] and virtuous man, the father of his people, a hard worker, hostile to flatterers.

For Dion Chrysostom the idea of God is innate and universal among all men, brought into full consciousness by the contemplation of the design and providence in the universe. Yet God is hidden from us, and we are like little children stretching out their hands for father or mother.[5] Yet though God in Himself is veiled from us, we naturally try to imagine Him as best we can, and this is best accomplished by the poets. Artists, too, attempt the same task, though more inadequately, for no sculptor or painter can portray the Nature of God. All the same, in portraying God in human form they do not do wrong, since it is only natural to have recourse to the highest being of which we have direct experience as an image of the Divine.

Later we find evidence of a Christianised Cynicism, e.g. in the person of Maximus of Alexandria, who came to Constantinople

---

[1] *Or.* 33.   [2] *Or.* 32.   [3] Philostr., *Vit. Soph.*, 1, 7.   [4] Cf. *Or.* 1–4.
[5] *Or.* 12, 61. ὥσπερ νήπιοι παῖδες πατρὸς ἢ μητρὸς ἀπεσπασμένοι δεινὸν ἵμερον ἔχοντες καὶ πόθον ὀρέγουσι χεῖρας . . .

in A.D. 379 or 380 and formed an intimate friendship with St. Gregory Nazianzen, though he afterwards had himself consecrated bishop behind St. Gregory's back. Maximus imitated the ways of the Stoics, though there does not seem to have been much consistency in his behaviour.[1]

II. *Eclectics*

A professedly Eclectic School was founded by *Potamon* of Alexandria in the time of the Emperor Augustus. According to Diogenes Laërtius the School was named Ἐκλεκτικὴ αἵρεσις[2] and it seems to have combined Stoic and Peripatetic elements, though Potamon also wrote a commentary on Plato's *Republic*.

Eclectic tendencies were also shown by the School of *Q. Sextius* (b. *c.* 70 B.C.). They adopted Stoic and Cynic principles, with which they combined Pythagorean and Platonico-Aristotelian elements. Thus Sextius adopted the Pythagorean customs of self-examination and abstinence from flesh-meat, while his disciple Sotion of Alexandria took over from the Pythagoreans the theory of metempsychosis. The School does not appear to have been of any great consequence, though Seneca was a disciple of Sotion.[3]

III. *Sceptics*

Although the Academy before the time of Antiochus of Ascalon had shown, as we have seen, a marked sceptical tendency, it was to the School of Pyrrho that the revived Scepticism looked as its ancestor rather than to the Academy. Thus the founder of the revived School, Aenesidemus of Knossos, wrote eight books Πυρρωνείων λόγων. The members of the School attempted to show the relative character of all judgments and opinions, embodying their arguments for this position in what they called Τρόποι. However, though they naturally opposed philosophic dogmatism, they did not fail to recognise the claims of practical life, and stated norms according to which man should act in practice. This was not alien to the spirit of Pyrrho who, in spite of his scepticism, declared that custom, tradition, State law, afforded a norm for practical life.

Aenesidemus of Knossos (who taught at Alexandria and probably composed his work round about 43 B.C.) gave ten Τρόποι or arguments for the sceptical position.[4] They were:

---

[1] Greg., *Adv. Maxim.*, *P.G.*, 37, 1339 ff. [2] Diog. Laërt., *Proem.*, 21.
[3] Sen., *Ep.*, 108, 17. [4] Sext. Emp., *Pyrr. Hyp.*, 1, 36 ff.

(1) Difference between types of living beings imply different—and so relative—"ideas" of same object.

(2) Differences between individual men imply the same.

(3) The different structure and presentation of our various senses (e.g. there is an eastern fruit that smells unpleasant but tastes delicious).

(4) The difference between our various states, e.g. waking or sleeping, youth or age. For example, a current of air may seem a pleasant breeze to a young man, while to an old man it is a detestable draught.

(5) Differences of perspective, e.g. the stick immersed in water appears bent, the square tower appears round from a distance.

(6) The objects of perception are never presented in their purity, but a medium is always involved, such as air. Hence the mixing or ἐπιμιξία. For example, grass appears green at noon, golden in the evening light. A lady's dress looks different in sunlight to what it looks in electric light.

(7) Differences in perception due to differences of quality, e.g. one grain of sand appears rough, while if sand is allowed to slip through the fingers it appears smooth and soft.

(8) Relativity in general, ὁ ἀπὸ τοῦ πρός τι.

(9) Difference in impression due to frequency or infrequency of perception, e.g. the comet, seldom seen, makes more impression than the sun.

(10) Different ways of life, moral codes, laws, myths, philosophic systems, etc. (cf. Sophists).

These ten Τρόποι of Aenesidemus were reduced to five by Agrippa.[1]

(1) The variation of views concerning the same objects.

(2) The infinite process involved in proving anything (i.e. the proof rests on assumptions that require to be proved, and so on indefinitely).

(3) The relativity involved in the fact that objects appear differently to people according to the temperament, etc., of the percipient and according to their relation with other objects.

(4) The arbitrary character of dogmatic assumptions, assumed as starting-points, in order to escape the *regressus in infinitum*.

---

[1] Sext. Emp., *Pyrr. Hyp.*, 1, 164 ff.

(5) The vicious circle or the necessity of assuming in the proof of anything the very conclusion that has to be proved.

Other Sceptics meanwhile reduced the Τρόποι to two:[1]

(1) Nothing can be rendered certain through itself. Witness the variety of opinions, between which no choice can be made with certainty.
(2) Nothing can be rendered certain through anything else, since the attempt to do so involves either the *regressus in infinitum* or the vicious circle.

(It is clear that these arguments for relativism have, for the most part at least, to do with perception. But perception does not err, since perception does not judge, and error lies in the false judgment. Moreover, it is in the power of reason to prevent error by avoiding precipitate judgment, by considering the matter more closely, by suspending judgment in certain cases, etc.)

Sextus Empiricus (c. A.D. 250), who is our main source for the details of Sceptic doctrine, argued against the possibility of proving any conclusion syllogistically.[2] The major premiss—for instance, "All men are mortal"—can be proved only by a complete induction. But the complete induction involves a knowledge of the conclusion—"Socrates is a mortal." For we cannot say, that *all* men are mortal unless we already know that Socrates is mortal. The Syllogism is, therefore, an instance of a vicious circle. (We may note that this objection against the syllogism, which was revived by John Stuart Mill in the nineteenth century, would only be valid if the Aristotelian doctrine of the specific essence were rejected in favour of Nominalism. It is in virtue of our perception of the essence or universal nature of man that we are entitled to assert that all men are mortal and not because we lay claim to any perfect and complete enumeration of particulars through actual observation, which in the case in point would be out of the question. The major premiss is founded, therefore, on the nature of man, and does not require explicit knowledge of the conclusion of the syllogism. The conclusion is contained *implicitly* in the major premiss, and the syllogistic process renders this implicit knowledge clear and explicit. The nominalist standpoint demands, of course, a new logic, and this Mill attempted to supply.) The Sceptics also argued against the validity of the notion of Cause, but they do not seem to have anticipated the

[1] Sext. Emp., *Pyrr. Hyp.*, 1, 178 ff.　　[2] Sext. Emp., *Pyrr. Hyp.*, 2, 193 ff.

epistemological difficulties raised by David Hume.[1] Cause is essentially *relative*, but the relative is not objective but is attributed extrinsically by the mind. Again, the cause must be either simultaneous with the effect or prior or posterior. It cannot be simultaneous, since then B might just as well be called the cause of A as A of B. Nor could the cause be prior to the effect, since then it would first exist without relation to its effect, and cause is essentially relative to the effect. Nor could the cause be posterior to the effect—for obvious reasons.

The Sceptics also attempted to prove the existence of antinomies in theology. For instance, God must be either infinite or finite.[2] Not the former, for He would then be unmoved and so without life or soul: not the latter, as He would then be less perfect than the Whole, whereas God is *ex hypothesi* perfect. (This is an argument against the Stoics for whom God is material: it does not affect those for whom God is Infinite Spirit. Infinite Spirit cannot move, but is living, or rather is Infinite Life.) Again, the Stoic doctrine of Providence is necessarily involved in a dilemma. There is much evil and suffering in the world. Now, either God has the will and power to stop this evil and suffering or He has not. The latter supposition is incompatible with the notion of God (though J. S. Mill arrived at the strange notion of a finite God, with Whom we co-operate). He has, therefore, the will and power to stop the evil and suffering in the world. But this He obviously does not do. It follows that there is at least no *universal* Providence on the part of God. But we can give no explanation why Divine Providence should extend to this being and not to that. We are forced, therefore, to conclude that there is *no* Providence at all.[3]

In regard to practical life the Sceptics taught that we should follow the presentations of perception and thought, satisfy our natural instincts, adhere to law and tradition, and pursue science. We can never indeed attain to certainty in science, but we can go on *seeking*.[4]

---

[1] Sext. Emp., *Adv. Math.*, 9, 207 ff. Cf. 8, 453 ff.
[2] Sext. Emp., *Adv. Math.*, 9, 148 ff. [3] Sext. Emp., *Pyrr. Hyp.*, 3, 9 ff.
[4] Sext. Emp., *Pyrr. Hyp.*, 1, 3; 1, 226; *Adv. Math.*, 7, 435 ff.

CHAPTER XLII

NEO-PYTHAGOREANISM

THE old Pythagorean School seems to have become extinct in
the fourth century B.C.: if it did continue, we have certainly no
evidence of effective and vigorous life. But in the first century B.C.
the School came to life again under the form of what is known
as Neo-Pythagoreanism. It was related to the old School, not
only by reverence for the Founder, but also by a certain interest
in scientific pursuits and, above all, by its religious colouring.
Much of the old Pythagorean asceticism was adopted by the new
School, which naturally adhered to the soul-body dualism—a
salient feature, as we have seen, of the Platonic philosophy—and
to this it added mystical elements, which answered the contemporary demand for a purer and more personal religion. Direct
intuition of the Deity was claimed, and revelation—so much so that
the philosopher is sometimes depicted as prophet and wonder-
worker, e.g. Apollonius of Tyana.[1] The new School was very far,
however, from being a mere reproduction of the former Pythagorean system, for it followed the current tendency to Eclecticism,
and we find the Neo-Pythagoreans drawing widely on the Platonic,
Aristotelian and Stoic philosophies. These borrowed elements
were not fused together into one synthesis, common to all the
members of the School, for the various members constructed their
different syntheses, in one of which Stoic themes might predominate, in another themes from the Platonic philosophy.
Neo-Pythagoreanism is of some historical importance, however,
not only because it stands in close relation to the religious life of
the time (it seems to have originated in Alexandria, the meeting-
point of Hellenistic philosophy, special science and Oriental
religion), but also because it marks a step on the way to Neo-
Platonism. Thus Numenius taught the doctrine of the Divine
Hierarchy—the first god, the πρῶτος θεός, being the οὐσίας ἀρχή or
πατήρ, the second god being the Demiurge and the third god being
the World, τὸ ποίημα.

Sextus Empiricus tells us of various tendencies within Neo-
Pythagoreanism. Thus in one form of Neo-Pythagoreanism

[1] See Note on Apoll. Tyana, pp. 449–50.

446

everything is derived from the monad or point (ἐξ ἑνὸς σημείου). The point generates the line in its flow, while from lines are generated surfaces, and from surfaces three-dimensional bodies. Here we have a monistic system, though obviously influenced by older mathematical conceptions. In another form of Neo-Pythagoreanism, although everything is derived ultimately from the point or μονάς, the greatest emphasis is laid on the dualism of the μονάς, and the ἀόριστος δυάς. All "unities" participate in the μονάς and all dualities in the ἀόριστος δυάς.[1] There is nothing particularly original in these forms of Neo-Pythagoreanism, but the notion of "emanation" is clearly present, which was to play a leading rôle in Neo-Platonism.

One of the motives that prompted the Neo-Platonic theory of emanation and the assertion of beings intermediary between the corporeal world and the supreme God was the desire of maintaining God's purity free from all contact with the things of sense. God's utter transcendence, His position "beyond being," is brought into sharp relief. Now, this theme of the transcendence of God is already discernible in Neo-Pythagoreanism. It may have been influenced by the Judaeo-Alexandrian philosophy and by Oriental tradition, though we may discern its latent germs within the thought of Plato himself. The noted wonder-worker Apollonius of Tyana (who flourished about the end of the first century A.D.), whose "life" was written by Philostratus, distinguished the first god from the other gods. To this first god men should not offer any material sacrifice, since all material things are tainted with impurity. We should sacrifice to the other gods, but not to the first god, to whom we should offer none but the service of our reason, without outward speech or offering.

An interesting figure is that of *Nicomachus of Gerasa* (in Arabia), who lived about A.D. 140, and was author of an ἀριθμητικὴ εἰσαγωγή. In his system the Ideas existed before the formation of the world (Plato), and the Ideas are numbers (Plato again). But the Number-Ideas did not exist in a transcendental world of their own: rather were they Ideas in the Divine Mind, and so patterns or archetypes according to which the things of this world were formed (cf. Philo the Jew, Middle Platonism and Neo-Platonism). The transposition of the Ideas into the Mind of God had, therefore, taken place before the rise of Neo-Platonism, from which it passed over into the Christian tradition.

[1] *Adv. Math.*, 10, 281 ff.

A similar transposition is to be observed in the philosophy of *Numenius of Apamea* (Syria), who lived in the second half of the second century A.D. and seems to have been well acquainted with the Jewish philosophy of Alexandria. According to Clement he spoke of Plato as Μωϋσῆς ἀττικίζων.[1] In Numenius' philosophy the πρῶτος θεός is the Principle of Being (οὐσίας ἀρχή) and the βασιλεύς.[2] He is also the activity of Pure Thought (νοῦς), and has no direct share in the formation of the world. Moreover, He is the Good. Numenius thus seems to have identified the Platonic Form of the Good with the Aristotelian God or νόησις νοήσεως. The second god is the Demiurge (*Timaeus*), who is good by participation in the being of the First God and who, as γενέσεως ἀρχή, forms the world. He does this by working on matter and forming it on the pattern of the archetypal Ideas. The world itself, the production of the Demiurge, is the third god. These three gods are also characterised by Numenius as πατήρ, ποιητής and ποίημα respectively, or as πάππος, ἔγγονος and ἀπόγονος.[3]

Dualism is very apparent in the psychology of Numenius, since he postulates two souls in man, a rational soul and an irrational soul, and declares the entry of the soul into the body as something evil, as a "fall." He seems also to have taught the existence of a good and a bad world-soul.[4]

The philosophy of Numenius was thus a syncretism or harmonisation of elements taken from preceding thinkers, a philosophy which laid great emphasis on the divine transcendence and which, in general, asserted a sharp antithesis between "higher" and "lower," both in reality as a whole and in human nature in particular.

In connection with Neo-Pythagoreanism stand the so-called *Hermetic Literature* and the *Chaldaic Oracles*. The former is the name given to a type of "mystical" literature that arose in the first century A.D. and that may, or may not, owe a debt to previous Egyptian writings. The Greeks found in Hermes the Egyptian god Thoth, and their appellation "Hermes Trismegistos" is derived from the Egyptian "Great Thoth." But whatever be the truth concerning the supposed influence of Egyptian tradition on the Hermetic literature, the latter owes its main contents to earlier Greek philosophy, and seems to have been indebted particularly to Poseidonius. The fundamental notion expressed in this

---

[1] Clem. Alex., *Strom.*, I, 22, 148. (*P.G.*, 8, 895.)   [2] Cf. Plato, *Ep.*, 2.
[3] Procl. *in Tim.*, I, 303, 27 ff.   [4] Chalcid., *in Tim.*, c. 295.

literature is that of *salvation through knowledge of God*—γνῶσις—
a notion that played a great part in "Gnosticism." A similar
doctrine of salvation formed the content of the Chaldaic Oracles,
a poem that was composed about A.D. 200, and which, like the
Hermetic literature, combines Orphic-Pythagorean, Platonic and
Stoic elements.

In its close relation to the religious interest and needs of the
time, and in the work of preparing the ground for Neo-Platonism,
Neo-Pythagoreanism resembles Middle Platonism, to which we
must now turn.

Note on Apollonius of Tyana

The rhetorician Philostratus undertook the composition of the
life of Apollonius at the request of Julia Domna, second wife of
Septimius Severus. The book was composed about A.D. 200. The
story given by Philostratus about the Memoirs of Apollonius by
his disciple Damis, an Assyrian, which are said to have been
given to Julia Domna by a relative of Damis, is probably a literary
fiction.[1] In any case the motive of Philostratus seems to have
been that of representing Apollonius as a wise man, as a true
servant of the gods and a miracle-worker, instead of the magician
or conjurer depicted by Moeragenes in his *Memorabilia* of
Apollonius.[2] There are indications that Philostratus knew and
utilised the Gospels, Acts of the Apostles and Lives of the Saints,
but it remains uncertain how far it was his conscious intention
to substitute the ideal of a "Hellenistic Christ" for the Christian
Christ: resemblances have been greatly exaggerated. If the
intention of Philostratus remains obscure, so does the foundation
of truth at the base of his narrative: it is practically impossible
to say exactly what sort of a man the historic Apollonius actually
was.

The work of Philostratus had a great success and led to a cult
of Apollonius. Thus Caracalla raised a shrine to the wonder-
worker,[3] while Alexander Severus included him in his *Lararium*
along with his Penates, Abraham, Orpheus and Christ.[4] Aurelian
spared the city of Tyana, which he had vowed to destroy, out
of respect for the birthplace of Apollonius.[5] Eunapius honours
him in his Lives of the Sophists,[6] while Ammianus Marcellinus,

---

[1] Cf. Ed. Meyer, *Hermes*, 197, pp. 371 ff.
[2] Orig., *Contra Celsum*, 6, 41 (*P.G.*, 11, 1357).
[3] Dion Cass., 77, 18. [4] Lamprid., *Alex.*, 29. [5] Lamprid., *Aurel.*, 24.
[6] Ed. Boissonade, p. 500, Didot.

companion of the Emperor Julian, cites him along with Plotinus as one of the privileged mortals who were visited by the *familiares genii*.[1]

Whatever the intention of Philostratus himself may have been, it is certain that the pagan apologists made use of the figure of Apollonius in their fight against Christianity. Thus Hierocles, Governor of Lower Egypt under Diocletian and a ferocious enemy of Christianity, tried to lessen the importance of the miracles of Christ by citing the "miracles" of Apollonius and tried to show the superiority of pagan wisdom in that they refrained from elevating Apollonius to the rank of God because of these miracles.[2] Porphyry also made use of Apollonius, citing his miracles and opposing his bold defiance of Domitian to the humiliations of Christ in His Passion.[3] St. Augustine bears testimony to this sort of apologetic exploitation of Apollonius on the part of the pagans.[4]

Towards the end of the fourth century Virius Nicomachus Flavianus, a pagan, translated Philostratus' book into Latin, and it was repolished by the grammarian Tascius Victorinus. It seems to have excited some interest in Christian circles, since Sidonius Apollinaris revised it also and speaks of Apollonius with great deference.[5]

[1] *Rerum gest.*, 21, 14, 5. [2] Lact., *Div. Inst.*, V, 3; *P.L.* 6, 556 ff.
[3] St. Jerome, in Ps. 81 (*P.L.* 26, 1130). [4] Cf. *Ep.*, 136, I; 102, 32; 138, 18.
[5] *Ep.*, 8, 3; ed. Mohr, p. 173.

CHAPTER XLIII

MIDDLE PLATONISM

WE have already seen how the Middle and New Academies inclined to scepticism, and how, when the Academy returned to dogmatism under Antiochus of Ascalon, the latter maintained the theory of the fundamental unity of the Platonic and Peripatetic philosophies. It is, therefore, not surprising to find Eclecticism as one of the leading characteristics of Middle Platonism. Platonists did not possess the lectures of Plato, but the more popular dialogues, and this fact made it more difficult for any rigid orthodoxy to assert itself: it was not as though the founder had left a systematised and carefully-articulated philosophic deposit, which could be passed on as the norm and canon of Platonism. There is no reason, then, to be astonished that Middle Platonism took over the Peripatetic logic, for example, since the Peripatetics had a more carefully-elaborated logical foundation than the Platonists possessed.

Platonism, no less than Neo-Pythagoreanism, felt the influence of contemporary religious interests and demands and the result was that Platonism borrowed from Neo-Pythagoreanism or developed germs latent in itself under the influence of the latter School. Hence we find in Middle Platonism the same insistence on the divine transcendence that we have already observed in Neo-Pythagoreanism, together with the theory of intermediary beings and a belief in mysticism.

On the other hand—and here again Middle Platonism was in line with the contemporary tendencies—much attention was devoted to the work of studying and commenting on the Platonic dialogues.[1] The result of this was a more intense reverence for the person and actual *dicta* of the founder and, consequently, a tendency to stress the differences between Platonism and the other philosophical systems. Thus we find writings directed against the Peripatetics and the Stoics. These two movements, the one towards philosophic "orthodoxy" and the other towards eclecticism, were obviously in conflict, and the consequence is

[1] The tetralogic arrangement of the Platonic Dialogues was attached to the name of Thrasyllus, the court-astronomer of Tiberius, who joined the Platonic School.

that Middle Platonism does not present the character of a unitary whole: different thinkers amalgamated the various elements in different ways. Middle Platonism is accordingly *Middle* Platonism; that is to say, it bears the mark of a transition-stage: it is only in Neo-Platonism that anything like a real synthesis and fusion of the various currents and tendencies can be found. Neo-Platonism is thus like the sea, to which the various contributing rivers are flowing and in which their waters are at length mingled.

1. The eclectic tendency of Middle Platonism and the orthodox tendency of the same School may be observed together in the thought of *Eudorus of Alexandria* (about 25 B.C.). In accordance with the *Theaetetus* (176 b) Eudorus affirmed that the end of philosophy is ὁμοίωσις θεῷ κατὰ τὸ δυνατόν. In this conception of the end of philosophy Socrates, Plato and Pythagoras are in agreement, said Eudorus. This shows the eclectic side of Eudorus' thought and, in particular, the influence of Neo-Pythagoreanism, in accordance with which he distinguished a threefold One or ἕν. The first is the supreme Godhead and is the ultimate source of being, and from Him proceeds the second ἕν (also called μονάς,, together with the ἀόριστος δυάς, the second ἕν being τεταγμένο), περιττόν, φῶς, etc., the ἀόριστος δυάς being ἄτακτον, ἄρτιον, σκότονς etc. But though Eudorus obviously felt the influence of Neo-Pythagoreanism and to this extent was eclectic, we learn that he composed a work against the Aristotelian κατηγορίαι, thus showing the "orthodox" as over against the eclectic tendency.

2. A prominent figure of Middle Platonism is the author of the celebrated lives of Greek and Roman worthies, *Plutarch of Chaeronea*. This distinguished man was born about A.D. 45 and was educated at Athens, where he was stimulated to mathematical studies by the Platonist Ammonius. He often visited Rome and was on terms of friendship with important personages in the imperial city. According to Suidas[1] the Emperor Trajan gave him the consular dignity and told the officials of Achaea to ask for Plutarch's approval for all their measures. Plutarch also became Archon Eponymos of his native city and was for some years priest to the Delphic Apollo. Besides the *Lives* and the *Moralia* Plutarch wrote commentaries on Plato (e.g. Πλατωνικὰ ζητήματα), books against the Stoics and the Epicureans (e.g. Περὶ Στοικῶν ἐναντιωμάτων and Ὅτι οὐδὲ ζῆν ἔστιν ἡδέως κατ' Ἐπίκουρον), works

---

[1] Suid., Πλούταρχος.

on psychology and astronomy, on ethics and on politics. To these must be added compositions on family life, on pedagogy and on religion (e.g. Περὶ τῶν ὑπὸ τοῦ θείου βραδέως τιμωρουένων and Περὶ δεισιδαιμονίας). A number of works that pass under his name are not by Plutarch (e.g. the *Placita* and the Περὶ εἱμαρμένης).

Plutarch's thought was decidedly eclectic in character, for he was influenced not only by Plato but also by the Peripatetics, the Stoics and especially the Neo-Pythagoreans. Moreover, while on the one hand the scepticism of the Middle and New Academies led him to adopt a somewhat distrustful attitude towards theoretical speculation and a strong opposition to superstition (the latter due more, perhaps, to his desire for a purer conception of the Deity), he combined therewith a belief in prophecy and "revelation" and "enthusiasm." He speaks of an immediate intuition or contact with the Transcendental, which doubtless helped to prepare the way for the Plotinian doctrine of ecstasy.[1]

Plutarch aimed at a purer conception of God. "While we are here below, encumbered by bodily affections, we can have no intercourse with God save as in philosophic thought we may faintly touch Him, as in a dream. But when our souls are released, and have passed into the region of the pure, invisible, and changeless, this God will be the guide and king of those who depend on Him and gaze with insatiable longing on the beauty which may not be spoken of by the lips of man."[2] This desire for a purer conception of God led him to deny God's authorship of evil. Some other cause had to be found for the evil in the world, and this Plutarch found in the World-Soul. This is postulated as the cause of evil and imperfection in the world and is set over against God as the pure Good, so that a dualism is asserted of two principles, the good and the bad. The evil principle, however, seems to have become the divine World-Soul at creation by participating in, or being filled with, reason, which is an emanation from the Godhead. The World-Soul is therefore not destitute of reason and harmony, but on the other hand it continues to act as the evil principle and thus the dualism is maintained.

Since God, freed from all responsibility for evil, is elevated far above the world, it is but natural that Plutarch should introduce intermediary beings below God. Thus he accepted the star-gods and followed Xenocrates and Poseidonius in postulating a number

---

[1] *De Is. et Osir.*, 77.　　　　[2] *De Is. et Osir.*, 78.

of "Demons" who form the connecting link between God and man. Some of these are more akin to God, others are tainted by the evil of the lower world.[1] Extravagant rites, barbarous and obscene sacrifices are really offered to the evil demons. The good demons are the instruments of Providence (on which Plutarch lays great stress). Plutarch, as I have already mentioned, professed himself a foe to superstition and condemned myths that were unworthy of God (like Poseidonius, he distinguished a threefold theology); but that did not prevent him from showing considerable sympathy for the popular religion. Thus according to him the various religions of mankind all worship the same God under different names, and he makes use of allegorical interpretation, in order to justify popular beliefs. For instance, in his *De Iside et Osiride* he tries to show that Osiris represents the good principle and Tryphon the bad principle, while Isis represents matter, which is not evil in Plutarch's view but, though neutral in itself, has a natural tendency and love for the Good.

Plutarch's psychology gives evidence of mythological and fantastic notions of the origin of the soul and its relation with the Demons, into which it is unnecessary to enter. One may, however, point out the dualism asserted between ψυχή and νοῦς, that is superimposed upon the soul-body dualism. Just as ψυχή is better and more divine than the body, so is νοῦς better and more divine than ψυχή, the latter being subject to passions, the former being the "Demon" in man and the element which should rule. Immortality is affirmed by Plutarch and he depicts the happiness of the after-life, when the soul not only attains to a knowledge of the truth but also enjoys once more the company of relatives and friends.[2] In his ethic the philosopher was clearly influenced by the Peripatetic tradition, since he emphasises the need of attaining the happy mean between ὑπερβολή and ἔλλειψις, excess and defect. To get rid of the affections is neither possible nor desirable; we should aim rather at moderation and the golden mean. Plutarch, however, follows the Stoics in permitting suicide, and he was influenced too by their Cosmopolitanism, especially when seen under the light of his experience of the Roman Empire. The ruler represents God.

The world was created in time, for this is necessitated by the principle of the soul's priority over the body and of God's priority

---

[1] *De Is. et Osir.*, 26.   [2] *Non p. suav.*, 28 ff.; *De ser. num. vind.*, 18.

in regard to the world.¹ There are five elements (adding aether) and five worlds.²

3. *Albinus* (A.D. second century), a disciple of Gaius the Middle Platonist, distinguished the πρῶτος θεός, νοῦς and ψυχή. The πρῶτος θεός is unmoved (Aristotle) but is not mover, and he would appear to be identical with the ὑπερουράνιος θεός. The first god does not operate immediately—since he is unmoved but not mover —but operates through the Νοῦς or World-Intellect.³ Between God and the world are the star-gods and others, οἱ γεννητοί θεοί. The Platonic Ideas are made eternal ideas of God and are patterns or exemplary causes of things: the Aristotelian εἴδη are subordinated to them as copies.⁴ The conception of God as unmoved and as not acting through efficient causality is, of course, Aristotelian in origin, though elements in the conception of God are developments of Platonic doctrine, e.g. the transposition of the Ideas into Ideas of God, a doctrine which we have already met in Neo-Pythagoreanism. Albinus also makes use of the gradual elevation to God through the various degrees of beauty, an ascent suggested by Plato's *Symposium*, while the conception of the World-Soul is obviously to be connected with the *Timaeus*.⁵ In this fusion of Platonic and Aristotelian elements Albinus, like Numenius the Neo-Pythagorean, helped to prepare the way for Neo-Platonism. His distinction of πρῶτος θεός, νοῦς and ψυχή was also a direct step on the way to the Neo-Platonic distinction of τὸ ἕν, νοῦς and ψυχή. (In his psychology and ethics Albinus combined Platonic, Aristotelian and Stoic elements, e.g. identifying the Stoic ἡγεμονικόν with the Platonic λογιστικόν, introducing the Aristotelian παθητικόν over against the λογιστικόν, distinguishing with Plato τὸ θυμικόν (Plat. θυμοειδές) and τὸ ἐπιθυμητικόν, making use of the Stoic οἰκείωσις, declaring the end of ethics to be the Platonic end of ὁμοίωσις θεῷ κατὰ τὸ δυνατόν, following the Stoics in making φρόνησις the first of the cardinal virtues and Plato in making δικαιοσύνη the general virtue, opposing the Stoic "Apathy" in favour of the Platonic- Aristotelian "Metriopathy." An eclectic indeed!)

4. Among other Middle Platonists we may mention *Apuleius* (b. *c.* A.D. 125), *Atticus* (*c.* A.D. 176), *Celsus* and *Maximus of Tyre* (*c.* A.D. 180). Atticus represented the more orthodox Platonic tradition in contrast to the eclectic tendency, as we have observed

---

¹ *De anim. procr.*, 4 ff.
² *De def. orac.*, 32 ff., 37; cf. Plat., *Tim.*, 31 a b, 34 b, 55 cd, where Plato opts for one world.
³ *Didaskalikos*, 164, 21 ff.   ⁴ *Didask.*, 163–4.   ⁵ *Didask.*, 169, 26 ff.

it in Albinus. Thus he attacked Aristotle for neglecting Divine Providence, teaching the eternity of the world, and for denying immortality or not expressing it clearly. But he seems to have been influenced by Stoic doctrine, as he emphasises the Divine Immanence and stresses the all-sufficiency of virtue, in contrast to the Peripatetic doctrine that corporeal and external goods are necessary for happiness. He naturally maintained the Platonic Ideas, but, characteristically of his time, made them thoughts or ideas of God. In addition he identified the Demiurge of the *Timaeus* with the Form of the Good, and he attributed to matter an evil soul as its principle.

Celsus is best known to us as a determined opponent of Christianity: we are acquainted with the content of his Ἀληθὴς λόγος (written about A.D. 179) through Origen's reply to it. He emphasised God's utter transcendence and would not allow that the corporeal is the work of God. To bridge the gulf between God and the world he admitted "Demons," angels and heroes. God's Providence has the universe as its object and is not, as the Christians believe, anthropocentric.

A similar emphasis on the Divine Transcendence, together with the admission of inferior gods and demons, as also the referring of evil to matter, is found in the case of Maximus of Tyre (c. A.D. 180). Maximus speaks of the vision of the transcendent God. "Thou shalt see Him fully only when He calls thee, in age or death, but meantime glimpses of the Beauty which eye hath not seen nor can tongue speak of, may be won, if the veils and wrappings which hide His splendour be torn away. But do not thou profane Him by offering vain prayers for earthly things which belong to the world of chance or which may be obtained by human effort, things for which the worthy need not pray, and which the unworthy will not obtain. The only prayer which is answered is the prayer for goodness, peace, and hope in death."[1] The angels are servants of God and helpers of men; "thrice ten thousand are they upon the fruitful earth, immortal, ministers of Zeus."[2]

---

[1] *Diss.*, 17, 11: 11, 2 and 7.　　　　[2] *Diss.*, 14, 8.

CHAPTER XLIV

JEWISH-HELLENISTIC PHILOSOPHY

IT was at Alexandria particularly that the influence of Greek speculation on the Jewish mind became most apparent, although traces of such influence may be seen in Palestine itself, as in the doctrine of the sect of the Essenes (mentioned by Josephus for the first time in his picture of the period of Jonathan the Hasmonaean, about 160 B.C.),[1] which shows Orphic-Pythagorean traits. For example, the Essenes maintained a clear dualism of soul and body, with which they coupled a belief, not only in the soul's survival after death but also in its pre-existence before birth. Blood-offerings and the consumption of flesh and wine were banned, and great importance was attached to the belief in angels or intermediary beings. Moreover it is a significant feature—even if not to be overstressed—that when Antiochus Epiphanes attempted a forcible Hellenisation of the Palestinian Jews, he was able to rely on a certain amount of support among the Jews themselves, though he encountered a determined opposition on the part of the more orthodox, who resolutely adhered to the tradition of their fathers and were naturally irreconcilable enemies of the moral abuses that they considered accompaniments of Hellenism. However, Alexandria, that great cosmopolitan city set on the confines of East and West, became the real centre of the Jewish-Hellenistic philosophy, which culminated in the thought of Philo. Away from their native home the Jews were naturally more prone to accept Greek influence, and this showed itself largely in an attempt to reconcile Greek philosophy with Jewish theology, an attempt that led on the one hand to the selection of those elements in Greek speculation that harmonised best with Jewish religion and on the other hand to the practice of allegorising the Jewish Scriptures and interpreting them in such a way that they would harmonise with Greek thought. Thus we even find Jews asserting that the great Greek philosophers were indebted to the Scriptures for their leading ideas. This notion is of course void of historical foundation as it concerns Plato, for instance, but it is symptomatic

[1] *Ant. Jud.*, 13, 5, 9.

457

of the syncretistic tendencies of the Hellenised Jews of the Empire.[1]

The chief figure of the Jewish-Hellenistic philosophy is *Philo of Alexandria*, who was born about 25 B.C. and died some time after A.D. 40, the year in which he was at Rome as ambassador of the Alexandrian Jews to the Emperor Gaius. We possess a large number of his works, though some have perished.[2]

Filled with admiration for the Greek philosophers Philo maintained that the same truth is to be found in both the Greek philosophy and Jewish Scriptures and tradition. While believing that the philosophers had made use of the Sacred Scriptures, he at the same time did not hesitate to interpret the Scriptures allegorically when he deemed it necessary. Thus in his work Ὅτι ἄτρεπτον τὸ θεῖον he shows that God cannot properly be said to move, since He is in no way corporeal. We must accordingly recognise two senses in the anthropomorphic passages of the Scriptures, a higher and non-anthropomorphic sense and a lower or anthropomorphic sense, which is suited to ordinary people. It might be supposed that this work of allegorisation and of discerning "higher" meanings would, if pushed far enough, lead to a denial of the necessity of observing literally the ceremonial precepts of the Law, at least for those who are capable of discerning the higher sense. But this Philo would not allow. Soul is above body, yet body is part of man; and though the allegorical sense is higher than the literal, we are not entitled to disregard the literal sense—rather should we pay heed to both letter and spirit. His intention was therefore not that of destroying or superseding Jewish orthodoxy but rather that of reconciling it with philosophy, while at the same time preserving the observance of the Law intact.[3]

God is personal, as the Jewish theology teaches, but He is at the same time Pure Being (τὸ ὄντως ὄν), absolutely simple (φύσις ἁπλῆ), free and self-sufficient.[4] He does not occupy space or place but rather contains all things within Himself.[5] Yet He is absolutely transcendent, transcending even the Idea of the Good and

---

[1] Consideration of the question, What influence was exercised by Greek speculation on Jewish Apocryphal writings and even on certain books of the O.T. itself, is here omitted.

[2] Cf. Euseb., *Hist. Eccles.*, 2, 18. References to the works of Philo are given according to the edition of Leopold Cohen and Paul Wendland, Berlin (Vol. 6, Cohen and Reiter).

[3] Cf. *De migrat. Abrah.*, 16, 92.

[4] Cf. *De post. Caini*, 48, 167; *Leg. alleg.*, 2, 1, 2 f.; *De Mutat nom.*, 4, 27.

[5] *De conf. ling.*, 27, 136; *De somniis*, I, 11; 63.

the Idea of Beauty (αὐτὸ τὸ ἀγαθὸν καὶ αὐτὸ τὸ καλόν).[1] Man attains to God, not through scientific understanding (λόγων ἀποδείξει)—"In order to comprehend God we must first become God, which is impossible"[2]—but in immediate intuition (ἐνάργεια).[3] God is thus ineffable Being, Who is above thought and can be attained only through ecstasy or intuition. We see how Philo was influenced by the contemporary tendency to exalt the Divine Transcendence—though we must not forget that the transcendence of the Divine Being was clearly maintained in Jewish scriptural theology, even if not expressed in philosophic terminology.

This insistence on the Divine Transcendence and on God's elevation above everything material not unnaturally led, as later on, for example, in Albinus the Middle Platonist and Numenius the Neo-Pythagorean, to the conception of intermediary beings, in order to bridge the gulf between God Himself and the material cosmos. The highest of these intermediary beings is the Logos or Nous. The Logos is spoken of as the first-born of God, being πρεσβύτατος καὶ γενικώτατος τῶν ὅσα γέγονε.[4] The Logos is for Philo definitely inferior to God and is to be placed in the rank of ὅσα γέγονε, which includes many other beings besides the Logos, even if the latter has the primacy. The Philonic conception of the Logos is therefore not identical with the dogma of the Logos as maintained in Christian theology, even if it influenced early Christian thinkers. Sometimes indeed the Logos seems to be conceived as an aspect of God, but even in this case there would still be a clear distinction between the Philonic and the Christian idea of the Logos. It has been well said, that Philo wavered between "Monarchianism" and "Arianism" but never asserted "Athanasianism"—provided, of course, that it is understood that in the Philonic doctrine of the Logos there is no reference to an historic Man. The Platonic Ideas are placed in the Logos, so that the Logos is the Τόπος or place in which the ideal world (ὁ ἐκ τῶν ἰδεῶν κόσμος) is situated.[5] In this conception Philo is at one with Neo-Pythagoreanism, which placed the Ideas in Nous. (Numenius was influenced by the Philonic philosophy.) Generally speaking Philo speaks simply of the Logos, though he distinguishes two aspects or functions of Logos, ὁ λόγος ἐνδιάθετος and ὁ λόγος προφορικός, the first consisting in the immaterial world of the

---

[1] De opif. mundi., 2, 8.   [2] Frag. a 654.   [3] De post. Caini, 48, 167.
[4] Leg. alleg., 3, 61, 175.   [5] De opif. mundi., 4, 17 ff.

Ideas, the second in the visible things of this world, in so far as they are copies of the immaterial Ideas.[1] This division of the Logos corresponds to the vision in man between the λόγος ἐνδιάθετος or faculty of reason itself and the λόγος προφορικός or spoken word, which proceeds from the λόγος ἐνδιάθετος as the stream from its source. An example of Philo's allegorising is to be found in the fact that he discovers a symbol of this twofold Logos in the double breastplate of the High Priest. The Logos is God's instrument in the formation of the world, and Philo found a reference to this in the words of the Pentateuch, καὶ ἐποίησεν ὁ θεὸς τὸν ἄνθρωπον κατ εἰκόνα θεοῦ.[2]

It is to be noted that, when the Old Testament mentions the angel of God in describing the theophanies, Philo identifies the angel with the Logos, just as, when several angels are mentioned, he identifies them with the Powers (see below). This Logos is an incorporeal substance, the immaterial Word or Voice of God; but, in so far as it is conceived as really distinct from God, it is conceived as subordinate to God, as God's instrument. Philo utilised, not only the conception of the Divine Wisdom, as found in the Sapiential Books, but also Platonic exemplarism (the Logos is the image, the shadow, of God and is itself the exemplar of creation) and Stoic themes (the Logos is the immanent, yet at the same time, transcendent, principle of law in the world and organising bond of creatures); but the general conception seems to be that of a descending scale of being. In other words, the Philonic Logos, so far as it is really distinct from the ultimate Godhead, Yahweh, is a subordinate and intermediary being, through which God expresses Himself and acts: it is not the consubstantial Word of the Father, the Second Person of the Blessed Trinity. The Philonic philosophy, in respect to the Logos, is more akin to Neo-Platonism than to Christian Trinitarianism.[3]

Besides the Logos there are other Powers (δύναμεις) or intermediary beings subordinate to God, such as ἡ ποιητική and ἡ βασιλική or κύριος (sometimes named ἀγαθότης and ἐξουσία), ἡ προνοητική, ἡ νομοθητική, etc. But just as Philo seems to have wavered between conceiving the Logos as an aspect of God and conceiving it as an independent being, so he wavered between conceiving the other Powers as attributes or powers of God,

---

[1] *Quod Deus sit immut.*, 7, 34; cf. *De vita Mos.*, 2 (3), 13, 127.
[2] *De opif. mundi.*, 6, 25.
[3] On this subject, cf. Jules Lebreton, S.J., *Histoire du Dogme de la Trinité.* (Beauchesne, 1910.)

corresponding to the Ideas (i.e. as operative functions of the Ideas) and conceiving them as relatively independent beings. They all appear to be comprehended in the Logos, but this does not help much in settling the question as to their personality or lack of it. If the Logos is conceived as an aspect of God, then the Powers will be qualities or ideas of God, while if the Logos is conceived as a relatively independent being, subordinate to God, then the Powers may be minor subordinate beings or forces; but it does not appear that Philo ever came to a settled or clear decision on the matter. Dr. Praechter can thus say, that "Philo wavers between two conceptions, the 'Analoga' of which recur in the Christian Church as Monarchianism and Arianism; but a doctrine analogous to that of Athanasius is wholly foreign to him and would contradict both his religious and his philosophic consciousness."[1] Moreover, it does not require much thought to recognise that the Philonic philosophy could never admit the Christian doctrine of the Incarnation—at least if Philonism were to remain self-consistent—since it lays such stress on the Divine Transcendence that direct "contact" with matter is excluded. It is indeed perfectly true that Christianity itself insists on the Divine Transcendence and that the Incarnation is a mystery; but on the other hand the spirit of the Christian attitude towards matter is not that of the Philonic or Neo-Platonic philosophies.

Influenced by Platonism, Philo maintains a sharp dualism of soul and body or of the rational and sensual elements in man, and insists on the necessity of man's liberating himself from the power of the sensual.[2] Virtue is the only true good, and in regard to the passions apathy is to be aimed at. But though Philo was influenced by Stoic and Cynic ethical teaching, he emphasised trust in God rather than trust in oneself. Virtue then is to be pursued and man's task is to attain the greatest possible likeness to God.[3] This is an interior task and so public life is discouraged because of its distracting influence, while science is to be pursued only so far as it is an aid to the soul's inner life. In this development there are stages, for above conceptual knowledge of God is to be ranked heavenly wisdom or the immediate intuition of the ineffable Godhead. The passive state of ecstasy thus becomes the highest stage of the soul's life on earth, as it was later to be in the Neo-Platonic philosophy.[4]

---

[1] Ueb.-P., p. 577.　　　[2] E.g. *De somn.*, 123, 149.
[3] *De opif. mundi.*, 50, 144; *De human.*, 23, 168.
[4] Cf. *Quis rer. div. her.*, 14, 68 ff.; *De gigant.*, II, 52 f.

While Philo's influence on early Christian thought has doubtless been exaggerated,[1] it will be recognised that Philonism helped to prepare the way for Neo-Platonism through its insistence on the utter Transcendence of God, the existence of intermediary beings, and the soul's ascent to God culminating in ecstasy.

[1] It is probable, however, that Origen's habit of allegorising is due in large measure to Philo.

CHAPTER XLV

PLOTINIAN NEO-PLATONISM

1. *Life of Plotinus*

THE birthplace of Plotinus is uncertain, since it is given as Lycon by Eunapius and as Lycopolis by Suidas.[1] In any case he was born in Egypt about A.D. 203 or 204 (Porphyry gives 205/6). Plotinus, we are told by Porphyry, attended the lectures of various professors at Alexandria in turn, but did not find what he was looking for until he came upon Ammonius Saccas, when he was about twenty-eight. He remained a pupil of Ammonius until the year 242 when he joined the Persian expedition of the Emperor Gordian, in order to make the acquaintance of Persian philosophy. However, the expedition came to grief when Gordian was assassinated in Mesopotamia, and Plotinus made his way to Rome where he arrived in his fortieth year. At Rome he opened a school and soon came to enjoy the favour of the highest officials, even of the Emperor Gallienus and his wife. Plotinus conceived the notion of founding a city, Platonopolis, in the Campagna, which was to be the concrete realisation of Plato's Republic, and he seems to have obtained the Emperor's consent to the project; but for some reason or other the Emperor withdrew his consent after a while and so the plan fell through.

When Plotinus was about sixty years old he received as a pupil the celebrated Porphyry, who afterwards wrote the life of the Master whom he so greatly admired. It was Porphyry who attempted to arrange the writings of Plotinus in systematic form, dividing them into six books, each of which contained nine chapters. Hence the name *Enneads*, which is applied to the works of Plotinus. Although the philosopher is said to have had a pleasant and eloquent oral style, his written composition was somewhat difficult and the difficulty was not lessened by the fact that his weak eyesight prevented him from correcting the manuscript. Porphyry had therefore no easy task to start with, and as he made a point of preserving the style of the writer, Plotinus' treatises have always been a source of difficulty to later editors.

At Rome, Plotinus was frequently approached for help and

[1] Eunap., *Vit. Soph.*, 6; Porph., *Isag.*, 12b; Suid., *Plot.*

advice, and so exercised the office of a sort of "spiritual director."
Moreover he took into his house orphaned children and acted as
their guardian—an example of his kindness and amiability. He
made many friends and no enemies, and though his personal life
was ascetic, he was gentle and affectionate in character. We are
told that he was somewhat diffident and nervous, a fact that
tended to show itself in his lectures. He led a deep spiritual life
and Porphyry relates that his Master experienced ecstatic union
with God four times in the six years in which he was his disciple.[1]
Plotinus did not enjoy strong health, and his infirmities had a
fatal termination in A.D. 269/70, when he died at a country-house
in the Campagna. Porphyry was at that time in Sicily, whither
he had gone on Plotinus' advice, in order to recover from a state
of melancholy and depression into which he had fallen; but a
friend of Plotinus, the physician Eustochius, arrived from Puteoli
in time to hear the philosopher's last words: "I was waiting for
you, before that which is divine in me departs to unite itself with
the Divine in the universe."

Although Plotinus attacked the Gnostics, he is silent about
Christianity, which he must have known to some extent. But
though he never became a Christian, he was a resolute witness to
spiritual and moral ideals, not only in his writings but also in his
own life, and it was the spiritual idealism of his philosophy that
enabled it to exercise such an influence on the great Latin doctor,
St. Augustine of Hippo.

II. *Doctrine of Plotinus*

God is absolutely transcendent: He is the One, beyond all
thought and all being, ineffable and incomprehensible, οὖ μὴ
λόγος, μηδὲ ἐπιστήμη, ὃ δὴ καὶ ἐπέκεινα λέγεται εἶναι οὐσίας.[2] Neither
essence nor being nor life can be predicated of the One,
not of course that it is less than any of these things but because
it is *more*, τὸ ὑπὲρ πάντα ταῦτα εἶναι.[3] The One cannot be
identical with the sum of individual things, for it is these individual things which require a Source or Principle, and this
Principle must be distinct from them and logically prior to them.
(We might say that, however much you increase the number of
contingent things, you cannot thus arrive at a Necessary Being.)

---

[1] Ἔτυχε δὲ τετράκις που, ὅτε συνήμην αὐτῷ, τοῦ σκόπου, ἐνεργείᾳ ἀρρήτῳ, καὶ
οὐ δυνάμει. *Plotini Vita*, 23, 138

[2] *Enn.*, 5 4, 1 (516 b-c).   [3] *Enn.*, 3, 8, 9 (352 b).

Moreover, if the One were identical with each individual thing taken separately, then each thing would be identical with every other and the distinction of things, which is an obvious fact, would be illusion. "Thus the One cannot be any existing thing, but is prior to all existents."[1] The One of Plotinus is not, therefore, the One of Parmenides, a monistic principle, but is the One, whose transcendence we have seen emphasised in Neo-Pythagoreanism and Middle Platonism. Indeed, just as Albinus had set the πρῶτος θεός above νοῦς and distinguished the ὑπερουράνιος θεός from the ἐπουράνιος θεός, and as Numenius had set the πρῶτος θεός above the Demiurge, and as Philo had set God above the world-forming Powers, so Plotinus sets the ultimate Deity, the One or πρῶτος θεός,, beyond being, ἐπέκεινα τῆς οὐσίας.[2] This does not mean, however, that the One is nothing or non-existent; rather does it mean that the One transcends all being of which we have experience. The concept of being is drawn from the objects of our experience, but the One transcends all those objects and consequently transcends also the concept that is founded on those objects.

Since God is one, without any multiplicity or division, there can be in the One no duality of substance and accident, and Plotinus is accordingly unwilling to ascribe to God any positive attributes. We should not say that the One is "thus" or "not thus," for if we say this we thereby delimit it and make it a particular thing, whereas in reality, it is beyond all things which can be delimited by such predication, ἄλλο τοίνυν παρ᾽ ἅπαντα τὸ οὕτως.[3] Nevertheless, Goodness may be attributed to the One, provided that it is not attributed as an inhering quality. God is accordingly *The Good* rather than "good."[4] Moreover, we can legitimately ascribe to the One neither thought nor will nor activity. Not thought, since thought implies a distinction between the thinker and the object of his thought;[5] not will, since this also implies distinction: not activity, for then there would be a distinction between the agent and the object on which he acts. God is the One, beyond all distinctions whatsoever: He cannot even distinguish Himself from Himself, and so is beyond self-consciousness. Plotinus allows, as we have seen, the predicates of unity and goodness to be ascribed to God (in the sense that God is the

---

[1] *Enn.*, 3, 8, 8 (351 d).   [2] Cf. *Rep.*, 509 b 9.   [3] *Enn.*, 6, 8, 9 (743 e).
[4] *Enn.*, 6, 7, 38.
[5] *Enn.*, 3, 8, 8. Ἐὰ οὖν τοῦτο νοῦν ἐγγένησεν, ἁπλούστερον νοῦ δεῖ αὐτὸ εἶναι (351 c).

One and the Good); yet he stresses the fact that even these predicates are inadequate and can be applied to God only analogously. For unity expresses the denial of plurality and goodness expresses an effect on something else. All we can say is that the One is—though, indeed, God is beyond being, One, indivisible, unchanging, eternal, without past or future, a constant self-identity.

On this view of God, the ultimate Principle, how can Plotinus account for the multiplicity of finite things? God cannot limit Himself to finite things, as though they were part of Him; nor can He create the world by a free act of His Will, since creation is an activity and we are not justified in ascribing activity to God and so impairing His unchangeability. Plotinus, therefore, had recourse to the metaphor of emanation. But although he makes use of metaphorical terms like ῥεῖν and ἀπορρεῖν, Plotinus expressly rejects the notion that God becomes in any way less through the process of emanation: He remains untouched, undiminished, unmoved. A free creative act would imply that God issues forth from His state of tranquil self-containedness, and this Plotinus would not admit: he maintained, then, that the world issues from God or proceeds from God by necessity, there being a principle of necessity that the less perfect should issue from the more perfect. It is a principle that every nature should make that which is immediately subordinate to it (τὸ μετ' αὐτὴν ποιεῖν), unfolding itself, as a seed unfolds itself, the procession being from an undivided source or principle to a goal in the universe of sense. The prior Principle, however, remains always in its own place (μένοντος μὲν ἀεὶ τοῦ προτέρου ἐν τῇ οἰκείᾳ ἕδρᾳ), the consequent being engendered out of an ineffable power (ἐκ δυνάμεως ἀφάτου) which is in the prior Principles, it being unfitting that this power should be stayed in its operation by any jealousy or selfishness.[1] (Plotinus also uses the metaphors περίλαμψις, ἔλλαμψις, likening the One to the sun, which illuminates, itself undiminished. He also employs the comparison of the mirror, since the object which is mirrored is reduplicated, yet without itself undergoing any change or any loss.)

We have, therefore, to be careful, if we wish to make the

---

[1] *Enn.*, 4, 8, 6 (474 b–c). The assertion that the prior Principle is not stayed by jealousy is an echo of Plato's words in the *Timaeus*. Plotinus' comparison of the One or the Good with the sun is a development of the comparison already given by Plato in the *Republic*. The view of God as the uncreated Light and of creatures as participated lights, hierarchically ordered according to their degree of luminosity, which we find in some Christian philosophers comes from Neo-Platonism.

statement that the process of emanation in Plotinus is pantheistic in character. It is quite true that for Plotinus the world proceeds from God *secundum necessitatem naturae* and that he rejects free creation *ex nihilo*; but it should also be remembered that for him the prior Principle remains "in its own place," undiminished and unimpaired, always transcending the subordinate being. The truth of the matter would seem to be that, while rejecting free creation out of nothing on the ground that this would involve change in God, Plotinus equally rejects a fully pantheistic self-canalisation of the Deity in individual creatures, a self-diremption of God. In other words he tries to steer a middle course between theistic creation on the one hand and a fully pantheistic or monistic theory on the other hand. We may well think that (since an ultimate dualism does not enter into the question) no such compromise is possible; but that is no reason for calling Plotinus a pantheist without due qualification.

The first emanation from the One is Thought or Mind, Νοῦς, which is intuition or immediate apprehension, having a twofold object, (a) the One, (b) itself. In Nous exist the Ideas, not only of classes but also of individuals,[1] though the whole multitude of Ideas is contained indivisibly in Nous. (τὴν δὲ ἐν τῷ νοητῷ ἀπειρίαν, οὐ δεῖ δεδιέναι πᾶσα γὰρ ἐν ἀμερεῖ, καὶ οἷον προείσιν, ὅταν ἐνεργῇ.) Nous is identified with the Demiurge of the Platonic *Timaeus*, and Plotinus uses the phrase πατὴρ τοῦ αἰτίου of the One, identifying the αἴτιον with the Nous and the Demiurge. That Nous is itself ὁ κόσμος νοητός[2] is a point insisted on by Plotinus against Longinus, who had made the Ideas to be apart from Nous, appealing to the *Timaeus* of Plato, where the Ideas are depicted as being distinct from the Demiurge. (Porphyry held the same opinion as Longinus, until Plotinus persuaded him to change it.) It is in Nous, therefore, that multiplicity first appears, since the One is above all multiplicity, above even the distinction of νοεῖν and νοητόν; yet the distinction in Nous is not to be understood absolutely, for it is one and the same Nous that is both τὸ νοοῦν and τὸ νούμενον. The Demiurge of Plato and the νόησις νοήσεως of Aristotle thus come together in the Plotinian Nous. Nous is eternal and beyond time, its state of blessedness being not an acquired state but an eternal possession. Nous

---

[1] *Enn.*, 5, 7, 1 ff.
[2] *Enn.*, 5, 9, 9. ἀναγκαῖον καὶ ἐν νῷ τὸ ἀρχέτυπον πᾶν εἶναι, καὶ κόσμον νοητὸν τοῦτον τὸν νοῦν εἶναι, ὃν φησὶν ὁ Πλάτων, ἐν τῷ ὅ ἐστι ζῷον.

enjoys, therefore, that eternity which time does but mimic.[1] In the case of Soul its objects are successive, now Socrates, now a horse, now some other thing; but Nous knows all things together, having neither past nor future but seeing all in an eternal present.

From Nous, which is Beauty, proceeds Soul, corresponding to the World-Soul of the *Timaeus*. This World-Soul is incorporeal and indivisible, but it forms the connecting-link between the super-sensual world and the sensual world, and so looks not only upwards to the Nous but also downwards towards the world of nature. Whereas Plato, however, had posited only one World-Soul, Plotinus posited two, a higher and a lower, the former standing nearer to Nous and being in no immediate contact with the material world, the latter (γέννημα ψυχῆς προτέρας) being the real soul of the phenomenal world. This second soul Plotinus termed nature or φύσις.[2] Moreover, although the phenomenal world owes all the reality it possesses to its participation in the Ideas, which are in Nous, these Ideas do not operate in the sensible world and have no direct connection with it, so that Plotinus posited reflections of the Ideas in the World-Soul, calling them λόγοι σπερματικοί and saying that they are comprised within the λόγος—an obvious adoption of Stoic doctrine. In order to fit in this conception with his distinction of two World-Souls, he further distinguished πρῶτοι λόγοι, comprised within the higher Soul, from the derivate λόγοι, comprised within the lower Soul.[3]

Individual human souls proceed from the World-Soul, and, like the World-Soul, they are subdivided into two elements (in accordance with the Pythagorean-Platonic tripartition Plotinus admits also a third and mediating element), a higher element which belongs to the sphere of Nous (cf. the Aristotelian Nous) and a lower element, which is directly connected with the body. The soul pre-existed before its union with the body, which is represented as a fall, and survives the death of the body, though apparently without memory of the period of earthly existence. (Transmigration is also admitted.) But although Plotinus speaks of individual souls as bound together in the unity of the World-Soul,[4] he is not prepared to deny personal immortality: the soul is real and nothing that is real will perish. Can we suppose that Socrates, who existed as Socrates on this earth, will cease to be

---

[1] *Enn.*, 5, 1, 4. ὁ ὄντως αἰὼν ὃ μιμεῖται χρόνος περιθέων ψυχὴν (485 b).
[2] *Enn.*, 3, 8, 3. ἡ λεγομένη φύσις ψυχὴ οὖσα γέννημα ψυχῆς προτέρας (345 e).
[3] *Enn.*, 4, 3, 10; 5, 9, 3; 5, 9, 9; 2, 3, 17.
[4] *Enn.*, 3, 5, 4. οὐκ ἀποτετμημένη, ἐμπεριεχομένη δὲ, ὡς εἶναι πάσας μίαν.

Socrates, just because he has reached the best of all abodes? In the after-life, therefore, each individual soul will persist, each remaining one, yet all being one together.[1]

Below the sphere of Soul is that of the material world. In accord with his conception of the emanative process as radiation of light, Plotinus pictures light as proceeding from the centre and passing outwards, growing gradually dimmer, until it shades off into that total darkness which is matter-in-itself, conceived as the privation of light, as στέρησις.[2] Matter, then, proceeds from the One (ultimately), in the sense that it becomes a factor in creation only through the process of emanation from the One; but in itself, at its lowest limit, it forms the lowest stage of the universe and is the antithesis to the One. In so far as it is illumined by form and enters into the composition of material objects (Aristotle's ὕλη) it cannot be said to be complete darkness; but in so far as it stands over against the intelligible and represents the ἀνάγκη of the *Timaeus*, it is unilluminated, darkness. Plotinus thus combined Platonic with Aristotelian themes, for though he adopted the Platonic conception of matter as ἀνάγκη, as the antithesis to the intelligible, as the privation of light, he also adopted the Aristotelian conception of matter as the substrate of form, as an integral component of material objects. The transmutation of one element into another shows that there must be some substrate of bodies, which is distinct from the bodies themselves.[3] If we consider bodies and make complete abstraction of form, then the residuum is what we mean by matter.[4] Matter is thus partially illuminated by its information and does not exist separately in the concrete as complete darkness, the principle of not-being. Moreover, just as the phenomenal world in general has its pattern in the intelligible, so does matter in nature correspond to a νοητὴ ὕλη.[5]

In addition to this fusion of Platonic and Aristotelian cosmological themes Plotinus asserts the Orphic and Neo-Pythagorean view of matter as the principle of evil. At its lowest grade, as devoid of quality, as unilluminated privation, it is evil itself (not, however, having evil as an inhering quality any more than the Good has goodness as an inhering quality), and so stands over against the Good as its radical antithesis. (The evil of matter does

---

[1] *Enn.*, 4, 3, 5 (375 c–f). [2] *Enn.*, 2, 4; 3, 67; 6, 3, 7.
[3] *Enn.*, 2, 4, 6 (162 c–e). [4] *Enn.*, 1, 8, 9 (79 a b)
[5] *Enn.*, 2, 4, 4–5; 3, 5, 6 (ὕλην δεῖ νοητὴν ὑποθέσθαι, 296 e).

not, of course, pertain to the νοητὴ ὕλη.) Plotinus thus comes perilously near to asserting a dualism which would be opposed to the real character of his system, though it must be remembered that matter itself is privation and not a positive principle. In any case we might suppose that Plotinus would be led logically to depreciate the visible universe, though in point of fact he does not do so. It is true that a certain tendency to depreciate the visible universe does show itself in his psychological and ethical teaching; but this is offset, so far as his cosmology is concerned, by his insistence on the unity and harmony of the cosmos. Plotinus opposed the Gnostic contempt for the world and praised the latter as the work of the Demiurge and the World-Soul: it is an eternal and unified creature, bound together in a harmony of parts, governed by Divine Providence. He expressly says that we must not allow that the universe is an evil creation, in spite of all the vexatious things that are in it. It is the image of the intelligible, but it is too much to demand that it should be the precise counterpart of the intelligible. What cosmos, he asks, could be better than the one we know, with the exception of the intelligible cosmos?[1] The material world is the exteriorisation of the intelligible, and the sensible and the intelligible are bound together for ever, the former reproducing the latter according to the measure of its capacity.[2] This universal harmony and cosmic unity form the rational basis for prophecy and for the magical influencing of superhuman powers. (Besides the star-gods Plotinus admitted other "gods" and "demons," which are invisible to man.)

In his psychology Plotinus assigns three parts to the individual soul. The highest of these (corresponding to the Nous of Aristotle) is uncontaminated by matter and remains rooted in the intelligible world,[3] but in so far as the soul enters into real union with the body, to form the compositum (τὸ κοινόν), it is contaminated by matter, and so there follows the necessity of an ethical ascent, with the θεῷ ὁμοιωθῆναι as the proximate goal and union with the One as the ultimate goal. In this ascent the ethical element (πρᾶξις) is subservient to the theoretical or intellectual element (θεωρία), as in Aristotle. The first stage of the ascent, undertaken under the impulse of Eros (cf. Plato's *Symposium*) consists in κάθαρσις, the process of purification by which man frees himself from the dominion of the body and the senses

---

[1] *Enn.*, 2, 9, 4 (202 d–e).   [2] *Enn.*, 4, 8, 6 (474 d–e).   [3] *Enn.*, 4, 8, 8 (476 a–d).

and rises to the practice of the πολιτικαὶ ἀρεταί, by which Plotinus means the four cardinal virtues. (The highest of these is Φρόνησις.[1]) Secondly the soul must rise above sense-perception, turning towards Nous and occupying herself with philosophy and science.[2] A higher stage, however, carries the soul beyond discursive thought to union with Nous which Plotinus characterises as πρώτως καλός. In this union the soul retains her self-consciousness. But all these stages are but a preparation for the final stage, that of mystical union with God or the One (Who transcends beauty) in an ecstasy characterised by the absence of all duality. In thought *of* God or *about* God the Subject is separated from the Object; but in ecstatic union there is no such separation. "There shall a man see, as seeing may be in Heaven, both God and himself: himself made radiant, filled with the intelligible light, or rather grown one with that light in its purity, without burden or any heaviness, transfigured to godhead, nay, being in essence God. For that hour he is enkindled; but when once more he is become heavy, it is as though the fire were quenched." "That sight is hard to put into words. For how should a man bring back report of the Divine, as of a thing distinct, when in the seeing he knew it not distinct but one with his own consciousness?"[3] (Needless to say, the ascent to God is not meant to imply that God is spatially present "out there." In meditation on God it is not necessary to cast one's thought outwards, as though God were present in any one place in such a way that He leaves other places destitute of Himself.[4] On the contrary, God is everywhere present. He is "outside" no one but is present to all, even if they know it not.[5]) This ecstatic union is, however, of brief duration so far as this life is concerned: we look for its complete and permanent possession in the future state, when we are freed from the hindrance of the body. "He will lapse again from the vision: but let him again awaken the virtue which is in him, again know himself made perfect in splendour; and he shall again be lightened of his burden, ascending through virtue to the Intelligence, and thence through wisdom to the Supreme. This is the life of gods and of the godlike and happy among men; a quittance from things alien and earthly, a life beyond earthly pleasure, a flight of the alone to the Alone."[6]

---

[1] *Enn.*, I, 2, I.   [2] *Enn.*, I, 3, 4.
[3] *Enn.*, 6, 9, 9 (768 f–769 a); 6, 9, 10 (769 d). (Professor Dodds' translation.)
[4] *Enn.*, 6, 9, 7 (765 c).   [5] *Enn.*, 6, 9, 7 (766 a).
[6] *Enn.*, 6, 9, 11 (771 b). (Professor Dodds' translation.)

In the system of Plotinus, then, the Orphic-Platonic-Pythagorean strain of "otherworldliness," intellectual ascent, salvation through assimilation to and knowledge of God, reach their most complete and systematic expression. Philosophy now includes, not only logic, cosmology, psychology, metaphysics and ethics, but also the theory of religion and mysticism: in fact, since the highest type of knowledge is the mystical knowledge of God and since Plotinus, who most probably based his theory of mysticism on his own experience as well as on past speculation, evidently regards mystical experience as the supreme attainment of the true philosopher, we may say that in Plotinian Neo-Platonism philosophy tends to pass into religion—at least it points beyond itself: speculation does not set itself up as the ultimate goal to be achieved. This made it possible for Neo-Platonism to act as a rival to Christianity, though on the other hand its complicated philosophic system and its "anhistorical" spirit prevented it from proving the rival that it might have been: it lacked the popular appeal exercised by the mystery religions, for instance. Neo-Platonism was really the intellectualist reply to the contemporary yearning for personal salvation, those spiritual aspirations of the individual, which are so marked a feature of the period. "Truly the words of counsel 'Let us flee to our own fatherland,'[1] might be uttered with a deep meaning. The Fatherland to us is that place from whence we came; and in that place is the Father."[2] Christianity, rooted in history, combining popular appeal with a growing speculative background, insistence on the Beyond with a sense of a mission to be accomplished in the Here, mystical communion with ethical probity, asceticism with a consecration of the natural, would have a far wider and deeper appeal than the transcendental philosophy of the Neo-Platonists or the fashionable devotions of the mystery cults. Yet, from the point of view of Christianity itself, Neo-Platonism had an important function to fulfil, that of contributing to the intellectual statement of the Revealed Religion, and so the convinced Christian cannot but look with sympathy, and a certain reverence, on the figure of Plotinus, to whom the greatest of the Latin Fathers (and so the Universal Church) owed no inconsiderable debt.

III. *School of Plotinus*

The tendency to increase the intermediary beings between

---

[1] *Iliad*, 2, 140.   [2] *Enn.*, 1, 6, 8 (56 g). (Professor Dodds' translation.)

God and corporeal objects is already observable in Plotinus' disciple *Amelius*, who distinguished three hypostases in Nous, namely τὸν ὄντα, τὸν ἔχοντα, and τὸν ὁρῶντα.[1] A more important philosopher, however, was *Porphyry of Tyre* (A.D. 232/3—after 301), who joined Plotinus in Rome in 262/3. Porphyry's life of his master I have already mentioned: in addition to this he wrote a great number of other works and on a great variety of subjects, his most celebrated book being his *Isagoge* or introduction to the *Categories* of Aristotle. This was translated into Latin (e.g. by Boethius), Syrian, Arabic and Armenian and exercised great influence, not only in Antiquity but on into the Middle Ages, being itself made the subject of many commentaries. The work treats of 'Aι πέντε φωναί—genus (γένος), species (εἶδος), difference (διαφορά), property (ἴδιον) and accident (συμβεβηκός). Porphyry composed many other commentaries both on Plato (e.g. on the *Timaeus*) and on Aristotle (mainly on his logical works), and tried to show—in his Περὶ τοῦ μίαν εἶναι τὴν Πλάτωνος Ἀριστοτέλους αἵρεσιν—that the Platonic and Aristotelian philosophies are in essential agreement.

Porphyry set himself to propound the doctrine of Plotinus in a clear and comprehensible manner, but he laid more stress on the practical and religious sides than even Plotinus had done. The end of philosophy is salvation (ἡ τῆς ψυχῆς σωτερία), and the soul must purify itself by turning its attention from what is lower to what is higher, a purification to be accomplished by asceticism and knowledge of God. The lowest stage of virtue consists in the practice of the πολιτικαὶ ἀρεταί, which are essentially "metriopathic" virtues, i.e. consisting in the reduction of the affections of the soul to the golden mean under the dominion of reason, and concerning man's intercourse with his fellow men. Above these virtues stand the cathartic or purifying virtues, which aim rather at "Apathy." This is realised in the πρὸς θεὸν ὁμοίωσις. In the third stage of virtue the soul turns towards Nous (for Porphyry evil does not lie in the body as such but rather in the soul's conversion to inferior objects of desire),[2] while the highest stage of virtue, that of the παραδειγματικαὶ ἀρεταί, belongs to the νοῦς as such. The four cardinal virtues recur at each stage, but of course at different degrees of elevation. In order to facilitate the soul's ascent Porphyry stresses the need for ascetic practices, such as abstinence from flesh-meat, celibacy, abstinence from theatrical

---

[1] Procl., *in Plat. Tim.*, I, 306, 1 ff.   [2] *Ad Marcellam*, 29.

performances, etc. Positive religion occupies an important place in his philosophy. While issuing a warning against the misuse of divination and other such superstitions (which he, however, accepted and permitted in themselves, since he believed in demonology), Porphyry at the same time lent his support to the popular and traditional religion, making the pagan myths allegorical representations of philosophic truth. He insisted on the importance of works, affirming that God does not prize the wise man's words, but his deeds.[1] The truly pious man is not for ever at prayer and sacrifice, but practises his piety in works: God does not accept a man for his reputation or for the empty formulae he employs, but for a life in accordance with his professions.[2]

During his residence in Sicily Porphyry composed fifteen books against the Christians. These polemical works were burnt in the year A.D. 448 under the Emperors Valentinian III and Theodosius II, and only fragments have come down to us: we have to rely largely on the writings of Christians for testimony as to the line of attack adopted by Porphyry. (Answers were composed by, among others, Methodius and Eusebius of Caesarea.) St. Augustine says that if Porphyry had ever had a true love of wisdom and had known Jesus Christ ". . . *nec ab eius saluberrima humilitate resiluisses.*"[3] This phrase would not seem to be conclusive evidence that Porphyry was ever actually a Christian or even a catechumen, for the Saint gives no further evidence that he looked on Porphyry as an apostate, though it is true that the historian Socrates affirms that Porphyry abandoned Christianity (τὸν χριστιανισμὸν ἀπέλειτε) and attributed the apostasy to the philosopher's indignation at being assaulted by some Christians at Caesarea in Palestine.[4] It seems that we cannot attain absolute certainty on the question whether or not Porphyry ever was a Christian: he is not quoted as saying himself that he ever adhered to the Christian religion. Porphyry wanted to prevent the conversion of cultured people to Christianity, and he endeavoured to show that the Christian religion was illogical, ignoble, involved in contradictions, etc. He made a special point of attacking the Bible and the Christian exegesis, and it is interesting to observe his anticipation of Higher Criticism, e.g. by denying the authenticity of the book of Daniel and declaring the prophecies therein

---

[1] *Ad Marc.*, 16.   [2] *Ad Marc.*, 17.
[3] *De Civit. Dei.*, 10, 28. (P. knew Origen while a youth. Euseb., *Hist. Ecc.*, 6, 19, 5.)
[4] *Hist. Eccl.*, 3, 23, (*P.G.*, 67, 445).

contained to be *vaticinia ex eventu*, denying that the Pentateuch was by Moses, pointing out apparent inconsistencies and contradictions in the Gospels, etc. The Divinity of Christ was a particular point of attack, and he brought many arguments against the Divinity of Christ and the doctrines of Christ.[1]

[1] "Obscurity, incoherence, illogicality, lying, abuse of confidence and stupidity, Porphyry saw scarcely anything else in Christianity, to judge by the *membra disiecta* of his work." (Pierre de Labriolle, *La Réaction Païenne*, p. 286, 1934.)

CHAPTER XLVI

OTHER NEO-PLATONIC SCHOOLS

1. *The Syrian School*

THE chief figure of the Syrian School of Neo-Platonism is Iamblichus (d. *c.* A.D. 330), a pupil of Porphyry. Iamblichus carried much further the Neo-Platonic tendency to multiply the members of the hierarchy of beings, which he combined with an insistence on the importance of theurgy and occultism in general.

1. The tendency to multiply the members of the hierarchy of being was present in Neo-Platonism from the very beginning, as a consequence of the desire to emphasise the transcendence of the Supreme Godhead and remove God from all contact with the world of sense. But while Plotinus had restrained this tendency within reasonable bounds, Iamblichus gave it wings. Thus above the One of Plotinus he asserted yet another One, which exceeds all qualifications whatsoever and stands beyond the good.[1] This One, which transcends all predicates or indeed any statements on our part—except that of unity—is therefore superior to the One of Plotinus, which is identical with the Good. From the One proceeds the world of ideas or intelligible objects—ὁ κόσμος νοητός—and from this again the world of intellectual beings—ὁ κόσμος νοερός[2]—consisting of Νοῦς, an intermediary hypostasis and the Demiurge, though Iamblichus seems not to have been content with this complication, but to have distinguished further the members of the κόσμος νοερός.[3] Below the κόσμος νοερός is the Super-terrestrial Soul, and from this Soul proceeds two others. As for the gods of the popular religion and the "heroes," these—together with a host of angels and demons—belong to the world, and Iamblichus tried to arrange them according to numbers. But while endeavouring to establish this fantastic scheme by means of the speculative reason, Iamblichus insisted on the immediate and innate character of our knowledge of the gods, which is given us together with our innate psychical impulse towards the Good.

2. The religious interest of Iamblichus is apparent in his

---

[1] ἡ πάντη ἄρρητος ἀρχή Damasc., *Dubit.*, 43.   [2] Procl., *in Tim.*, 1308, 21 d.
[3] Procl., *in Tim.*, 1308, 21 ff. d. Damasc., *Dubit.*, 54.

ethical doctrine. Accepting Porphyry's distinction of the political, cathartic and paradigmatic virtues he then proceeds to introduce, between the two last, the *theoretical* virtues, by which the soul contemplates Nous as its object and views the procession of the orders from the final Principle. By the paradigmatic virtues the soul identifies herself with Nous, the place of ideas and παράδειγμα of all things. Finally, above these four types of virtue stand the *priestly* virtues, in the exercise of which the soul is ecstatically united to the One. (These virtues are therefore also called ἑνιαῖαι). As we must look to divine revelation in order to ascertain the means of entering upon union with God, the priest is superior to the philosopher. Purification from the sensual, theurgy, miracles, divination, play an important part in the system of Iamblichus.

II. *The School of Pergamon*

The Pergamene School was founded by *Aedesius*, a pupil of Iamblichus, and is characterised mainly by its interest in theurgy and in the restoration of polytheism. Thus while *Maximus*, one of the Emperor Julian's tutors, gave particular attention to theurgy, Sallustius wrote a work *On the gods and the world* as propaganda for polytheism, while the rhetorician Libonius, another of Julian's tutors, wrote against Christianity, as did also *Eunapius* of Sardes. *Julian* (322–363) was brought up as a Christian but became a pagan. In his short reign (361–363), Julian showed himself to be a fanatical opponent of Christianity and adherent of polytheism, combining this with Neo-Platonic doctrines, for which he relied largely on Iamblichus. He interpreted, for example, the worship of the sun according to the Neo-Platonic philosophy, by making the sun the intermediary between the intelligible and the sensible realms.[1]

III. *The Athenian School*

In the Athenian School of Neo-Platonism there flourished a lively interest in the writings of Aristotle, as well of course as in those of Plato, an interest that showed itself in the commentary on the *De Anima* composed by Plutarch of Athens, the son of Nestorius and Athenian Scholarch (d. A.D. 431/2) and in the commentaries on the *Metaphysics* by Syrianus (d. *c.* 430), the successor of Plutarch in the headship of the School at Athens.

[1] Julian, *Or.*, 4.

But Syrianus was no believer in the agreement of Plato and Aristotle: on the contrary not only did he account the study of the philosophy of Aristotle merely a preparation for the study of Plato, but—in his commentary on the *Metaphysics*—he defended the Platonic ideal theory against Aristotle's attacks, clearly recognising the difference between the two philosophers on this point. Yet that did not prevent him from trying to show the agreement between Plato, the Pythagoreans, the Orphics and the "Chaldaic" literature. He was succeeded by *Domninus*, a Syrian of Jewish origin, who wrote on mathematics.

Much more important, however, than any of these men is the celebrated *Proclus* (410–485), who was born at Constantinople and was Athenian Scholarch for many years. He was a man of untiring diligence, and though much of his work has perished, we still possess his commentaries on the *Timaeus, Republic, Parmenides, Alcibiades I* and *Cratylus*, in addition to his works Στοιχείωσις Θεολογική, 'Εἰς τὴν Πλάτωνος Θεολογίαν and the *De decem dubitationibus circa providentiam*, the *De providentia et fato et eo quod in nobis* and the *De malorum subsistentia*—the last three works being preserved in the Latin translation of William of Moerbeke. Possessed of a wide knowledge concerning the philosophies of Plato and Aristotle and of his Neo-Platonic predecessors, Proclus combined with this knowledge a great interest in and enthusiasm for all sorts of religious beliefs, superstitions and practices, even believing that he received revelations and was the reincarnation of the Neo-Pythagorean Nicomachus. He had, therefore, an immense wealth of information and learning at his disposal, and he attempted to combine all these elements in one carefully articulated system, a task rendered all the easier by his dialectical ability. This has won for him the reputation of being the greatest Scholastic of Antiquity, in that he brought his dialectical ability and genius for subtle systematisation to bear on the doctrines that he had received from others.[1]

The main *motif* of Proclus' dialectical systematisation is that of triadic development. This principle was certainly used by Iamblichus, but Proclus employed it with considerable dialectical subtlety and made it the dominant principle in the procession of beings from the One, i.e. in the emanation of the orders of being from the highest 'Αρχή down to the most inferior stage. The

---

[1] In his commentary on Euclid I Proclus gives much valuable information concerning Platonic, Aristotelian, Neo-Platonic and other positions in mathematical philosophy (ed. Friedlein, Leipzig, 1873).

effect, or being that proceeds, is partly similar to the cause or source of emanation and partly dissimilar. In so far as the being that proceeds is similar to its origin, it is regarded as being in some degree identical with its principle, for it is only in virtue of the self-communication of the latter that the procession takes place. On the other hand, since there *is* a procession, there must be something in the proceeding being that is not identical with, but different from, the principle. We have, therefore, at once two moments of development, the first being that of remaining in the principle (μονή), in virtue of partial identity, the second being that of difference, in virtue of external procession (πρόοδος). In every being that proceeds, however, there is a natural tendency towards the Good, and, in virtue of the strictly hierarchical character of the development of beings, this natural tendency towards the Good means a turning-back towards the immediate source of emanation on the part of the being that emanates or proceeds. Proclus thus distinguishes three moments of development, (i) μονή or remaining in the principle; (ii) πρόοδος or proceeding out of the principle, and (iii) ἐπιστροφή or turning-back towards the principle. This triadic development, or development in three moments dominates the whole series of emanations.[1]

The original principle of the whole process of development is the primary one, τὸ αὐτὸ ἕν.[2] Beings must have a cause, and cause is not the same as effect. Yet we cannot admit a *regressus ad infinitum*. There must be, therefore, a First Cause, whence the multiplicity of beings proceed "as branches from a root," some being nearer to the First Cause, others more remote. Moreover, there can be only one such First Cause, for the existence of a multiplicity is always secondary to unity.[3] This must exist since we are logically compelled to refer all multiplicity back to unity, all effects to an ultimate Cause and all participated good to an Absolute Good; yet as a matter of fact the primary Principle transcends the predicates of Unity, Cause and Good, just as it transcends Being. It follows that we are really not entitled to predicate anything positively of the ultimate Principle: we can only say what it is *not*, realising that it stands above all discursive thought and positive predication, ineffable and incomprehensible.

From the primary One proceed the Units or ἑνάδες, which are nevertheless looked on as super-essential and incomprehensible

---

[1] *Instit. Theol..* 30 ff.; *Theol. Plat.*, 2, 4; 3, 14; 4, 1.
[2] *Instit. Theol.*, 4, 6; *Theol. Plat.*, 2, 4.   [3] *Instit. Theol.*, 11.

gods, the source of providence, and of which goodness is to be predicated. From the Henads proceeds the sphere of Nous, which subdivides into the spheres of the νοητοί, the νοητοί καί νοεροί and the νοεροί (cf. Iamblichus), the spheres corresponding respectively to the concepts of Being, Life and Thought.[1] Not content with these divisions Proclus introduces further sub-divisions in each of the three spheres of Nous, the first two being sub-divided into three triads, the third into seven hebdomads, and so on.

Below the general sphere of Nous is the sphere of the Soul, which is the intermediary between the supersensible and the sensible worlds, mirroring the former as a copy (εἰκονικῶς) and serving as a pattern for the latter (παραδειγματικῶς). This sphere of soul is subdivided into three sub-spheres, that of divine souls, that of "demonic" souls, and that of ψυχαί or human souls. Each sub-sphere is again sub-divided. The Greek gods appear in the sphere of divine souls, but the same name is found in different groups according to the different aspect or function of the god in question. For instance, Proclus seems to have posited a threefold Zeus. The sphere of demonic souls, which serves as a bridge between gods and men, is subdivided into angels, demons and heroes.

The world, a living creature, is formed and guided by the divine souls. It cannot be evil—nor can matter itself be evil—since we cannot refer evil to the divine. Rather is evil to be thought of as imperfection, which is inseparable from the lower strata of the hierarchy of being.[2]

In this process of emanation the productive cause, Proclus insists, remains itself unaltered. It brings into actuality the subordinate sphere of being, but it does so without movement or loss, preserving its own essence, "neither transmuted into its consequents nor suffering any diminution." The product, therefore, does not arise through the self-diremption of the producer, nor by its transformation. In this way Proclus tries, like Plotinus, to steer a middle course between *creatio ex nihilo* on the one hand and true monism or pantheism on the other hand, for, while the productive being is neither altered nor diminished through the production of the subordinate being, it nevertheless furnishes the subordinate being out of its own being.[3]

---

[1] *Theol. Plat.*, 3, 14; 4, 1.   [2] *Theol. Plat.*, 1, 17; in *Remp.*, I, 37, 27 ff.
[3] *Instit. Theol.*, 27.

On the principle that like can only be attained by like, Proclus attributed to the human soul a faculty above thought, by which it can attain the One.[1] This is the unitary faculty, which attains the ultimate Principle in ecstasy. Like Porphyry, Iamblichus, Syrianus and others, Proclus also attributed to the soul an ethereal body composed of light, which is midway between the material and the immaterial and is imperishable. It is with the eyes of this ethereal body that the soul can perceive theophanies. The soul ascends through the different grades of virtue (as in Iamblichus) to ecstatic union with the primary One. Proclus distinguishes three general stages in the soul's ascent, Eros, Truth and Faith. Truth leads the soul beyond love of the beautiful and fills it with knowledge of true reality, while Faith consists in the mystical silence before the Incomprehensible and Ineffable.

Proclus was succeeded in the headship of the School by *Marinus*, a native of Samaria. Marinus distinguished himself in mathematics and through his sober and restrained interpretation of Plato. For instance, in his commentary on the *Parmenides* he insisted that the One and so on denote *ideas* and not gods. However, that did not prevent him from following the contemporary fashion of attributing great importance to religious superstitions, and at the summit of the scale of virtues he placed the θεουργικαὶ ἀρεταί. Marinus was succeeded as Scholarch by Isidorus.

The last of the Athenian Scholarchs was Damascius (Sch. from c. A.D. 520), whom Marinus had instructed in mathematics. Having been forced to the conclusion that the human reason cannot understand the relation of the One to the proceeding beings, Damascius seems to have considered that human speculation cannot really attain the truth. All the words we employ in this connection, "cause" and "effect," "processions," etc., are but analogies and do not properly represent the actuality.[2] Since on the other hand he was not prepared to abandon speculation, he gave full rein to theosophy, "Mysticism" and superstition.

A well-known disciple of Damascius is *Simplicius*, who wrote valuable commentaries on the *Categories*, *Physics*, *De Caelo* and *De Anima* of Aristotle. That on the *Physics* is particularly valuable because of the fragments of the pre-Socratics therein contained.

In the year 529 the Emperor Justinian forbade the teaching of

---

[1] *In Alcib.*, III; *de Prov.*, 24.
[2] *Dubit.*, 38, I 79, 20 ff.; 41, I 83, 26 ff.; 42 I 85, 8 ff.; 107 I 278, 24 f.

philosophy at Athens, and Damascius, together with Simplicius and five other members of the Neo-Platonic School, went to Persia, where they were received by king Chosroes. In 533, however, they returned to Athens, apparently disappointed with the cultural state of Persia. It does not appear that there were any more pagan Neo-Platonists surviving shortly after the middle of the century.

iv. *The Alexandrian School*

1. The Alexandrian School of Neo-Platonism was a centre for investigation in the department of the special sciences and for the labour of commenting on the works of Plato and Aristotle. Thus *Hypatia* (best known for her murder in A.D. 415 by a fanatical mob of Christians) wrote on mathematics and astronomy and is said to have lectured on Plato and Aristotle, while *Asclepiodotus* of Alexandria (second half of A.D. fifth century), who later resided at Aphrodisias in Caria, studied science and medicine, mathematics and music. *Ammonius, Ioannes Philoponus, Olympiodorus* and others commented on works of Plato and Aristotle. In the commentaries of the School special attention was paid to the logical works of Aristotle, and in general it may be said of these commentaries that they show moderation and a desire on the part of their authors to give the natural interpretation of the works on which they are commenting. Metaphysical and religious interests tend to retreat from the foreground, the multiplication of intermediary beings, so characteristic of Iamblichus and Proclus, being abandoned and little attention being paid to the doctrine of ecstasy. Even the pious and somewhat mystically inclined Asclepiodotus, who was a pupil of Proclus, avoided the latter's complicated and highly speculative metaphysic.

2. Characteristic of Alexandrian Neo-Platonism is its relation to Christianity and the thinkers of the celebrated Catechetical School. The result of the abandonment of the speculative extravagancies of Iamblichus and Proclus was that the Neo-Platonic School at Alexandria gradually lost its specifically pagan character and became rather a "neutral" philosophical institute: logic and science were obviously subjects on which Christians and pagans could meet on more or less common ground. It was this growing association of the School with Christianity which made possible the continuation of Hellenic thought at Constantinople. (Stephanus of Alexandria migrated to Constantinople and there

expounded Plato and Aristotle in the university in the first half of the seventh century, during the reign of the Emperor Heraclius, i.e. a century after Justinian had closed the School at Athens.) An instance of the close relation between Neo-Platonists and Christians at Alexandria is the life of Hypatia's disciple, Synesius of Cyrene, who became bishop of Ptolemais in A.D. 411. Another striking instance is the conversion of Ioannes Philoponus to Christianity. As a convert he wrote a book against Proclus' conception of the eternity of the world and supported his own view by an appeal to Plato's *Timaeus* which he interpreted as teaching creation in time. Philoponus also held the view that Plato drew his wisdom from the Pentateuch. One may mention also *Nemesius*, bishop of Emesa in Phoenicia, who was influenced by the Alexandrian School.

3. But if Neo-Platonism exercised a profound influence on Christian thinkers at Alexandria, it is also true that Christian thinkers were not without influence on non-Christian philosophers. This can be seen in the case of *Hierocles of Alexandria*, who lectured at Alexandria from about A.D. 420. Hierocles shows affinity with Middle Platonism rather than with his Neo-Platonist predecessors, for, neglecting the Plotinian hierarchy of beings which had been so exaggerated by Iamblichus and Proclus, he admits only one super-terrestrial being, the Demiurge. But what is particularly striking is that Hierocles asserts *voluntary creation out of nothing* by the Demiurge.[1] He rejects indeed creation in time, but that does not militate against the very great probability of Christian influence, especially as Fate or 'Αιμαρμένη denotes for Hierocles, not mechanical determinism, but the apportioning of certain effects to man's free actions. Thus petitionary prayer and providential 'Αιμαρμένη are not mutually exclusive,[2] and the doctrine of Necessity or Fate is brought more into harmony with the Christian insistence on human freedom on the one hand and Divine Providence on the other.

v. *Neo-Platonists of the Latin West*

One would scarcely be justified in speaking of a "School" of Neo-Platonism in the Latin West. However, there is a characteristic common to those thinkers who are usually classed as "Neo-Platonists of the Latin West" and that is, that the speculative side of Neo-Platonism is no longer in evidence while the learned

---

[1] Phot., 460 b 23 ff.; 461 b 6 ff.   [2] Phot., 465 a 16 ff.

side is very much to the fore. By their translation of Greek works into Latin and by their commentaries on Platonic and Aristotelian writings, as well as on writings of Latin philosophers, they helped to spread the study of philosophy in the Roman world and at the same time constructed a bridge whereby Ancient Philosophy passed to the Middle Ages. Thus in the first half of the fourth century A.D. *Chalcidius* (who probably was or became a Christian) made a Latin translation of Plato's *Timaeus* and wrote a Latin commentary on it—apparently in dependence on Poseidonius' commentary (with the possible use of intermediate writings). This translation and its commentary were much used in the Middle Ages.[1] In the same century *Marius Victorinus* (who became a Christian when of advanced years) translated into Latin Aristotle's *Categories* and *De Interpretatione*, Porphyry's *Isagoge* and some Neo-Platonist works. He also wrote commentaries on Cicero's *Topics* and *De Inventione* and composed original works *De Definitionibus* and *De Syllogismis Hypotheticis*. As a Christian he also composed some theological works, of which a great part are still extant. (St. Augustine was influenced by Marius Victorinus.) One may also mention *Vettius Agonius Praetextatus* (d. 384), who translated Themistius' paraphrase of Aristotle's *Analytics*, and *Macrobius* (he seems to have become a Christian in later years), who wrote the *Saturnalia* and also a commentary on Cicero's *Somnium Scipionis* about A.D. 400. In this commentary the Neo-Platonist theories of emanation appear and it seems that Macrobius made use of Porphyry's commentary on the *Timaeus*, which itself made use of that of Poseidonius.[2] Fairly early in the fifth century *Martianus Capella* composed his (still extant) *De Nuptiis Mercurii et Philologiae*, which was much read in the Middle Ages. (For instance, it was commented on by Remigius of Auxerre.) This work, which is a kind of Encyclopaedia, treats of each of the seven liberal arts, books three to nine being each devoted to one of the arts. This was of importance for the Middle Ages, which made the seven liberal arts the basis of education as the *Trivium* and *Quadrivium*.

[1] As this work contains extracts from other dialogues of Plato, as well as extracts and texts and opinions from other Greek philosophers, it came about that up to the twelfth century A.D. Chalcidius was regarded as one of the chief sources for a knowledge of Greek philosophy.

[2] As Macrobius introduces into his Commentary ideas on number-symbolism, emanation, the Plotinian gradation of virtues, and even polytheism, the work is "really a syncretic product of Neo-Platonist paganism." (Maurice De Wulf, *Hist. Med. Phil.*, I, p. 79. Trans. E. Messenger, Ph.D., Longmans, 3rd Eng. edit., 1935.)

More important, however, than any of the afore-mentioned writers is the Christian *Boethius* (*c.* A.D. 480–524/5), who studied at Athens, held high office under Theodoric, king of the Ostrogoths, and was finally executed on a charge of treason after a term of imprisonment, during which he composed the famous *De Consolatione Philosophiae*. As it is more convenient to treat of the philosophy of Boethius by way of introduction to Mediaeval Philosophy, I shall content myself here with mentioning some of his works.

Although it was the aim of Boethius to translate into Latin, and to furnish with commentaries, all the works of Aristotle (*De Interpret.* 1, 2), he did not succeed in carrying his project to completion. He did, however, translate into Latin the *Categories*, the *De Interpretatione*, the *Topics*, both *Analytics* and the *Sophistical Arguments*. It may be that Boethius translated other works of Aristotle besides the *Organon*, in accordance with his original plan; but this is uncertain. He translated Porphyry's *Isagoge*, and the dispute concerning universals which so agitated the early Middle Ages took its *point de départ* in remarks of Porphyry and Boethius.

Besides furnishing the *Isagoge* (in the translation of Marius Victorinus) with a double commentary, Boethius also commented on the *Categories*, the *De Interpretatione*, the *Topics*, the *Analytics* and *Sophistical Arguments* (probably) and on Cicero's *Topics*. In addition to these commentaries he composed original treatises, the *Introductio ad categoricos syllogismos*, *De categoricis syllogismis*, *De hypotheticis syllogismis*, *De divisione*, *De topicis differentiis*, *De Consolatione Philosophiae*, *De Institutione arithmetica*, etc. In the last period of his life several theological opuscula came from his pen.

On account of this extensive labour expended on translation and commenting, Boethius may be called the principal mediator between Antiquity and the Middle Ages, "the last Roman and the first Scholastic," as he has been called. "Down to the end of the twelfth century he was the principal channel by which Aristotelianism was transmitted to the West."[1]

---

[1] M. De Wulf, *Hist. Med. Phil.*, I, p. 109.

CHAPTER XLVII

CONCLUDING REVIEW

WHEN we look back at the philosophy of Greece and of the Greco-Roman world, as we watch its naïve beginnings on the shore of Asia Minor, as we see the intellectual power and comprehensive mind of a Heraclitus or a Parmenides struggling with a crippling poverty of philosophic language, as we trace the development of two of the greatest philosophies the world has ever seen, the philosophies of Plato and of Aristotle, as we see the broadening influence of the Stoic School and witness the evolution of the final creative effort of ancient thought, the system of Plotinian Neo-Platonism, we cannot but acknowledge that we have before us one of the supreme achievements of the human race. If we gaze with admiration at the Greek temples of Sicily, at the Gothic cathedrals of the Middle Ages, at the work of a Fra Angelico or a Michelangelo, a Rubens or a Velasquez, if we treasure the writings of a Homer or a Dante, a Shakespeare or a Goethe, we should pay the tribute of a like admiration to what is great in the realm of pure thought and count it as one of the greatest treasures of our European heritage. Mental effort and perseverance are no doubt required in order to penetrate the riches of Greek thought, but any effort that is expended in the attempt to understand and appreciate the philosophy of those two men of genius, Plato and Aristotle, is amply rewarded: it can no more be wasted than the effort we expend to appreciate at its full value the music of Beethoven or Mozart or the beauty of the cathedral at Chartres Greek drama, Greek architecture, Greek sculpture, are imperishable memorials of the Greek genius and culture, of the glory of Hellas; but that glory would be incomplete without Greek philosophy and we cannot appreciate fully the culture of the Greeks unless we know something of Greek philosophy. It may be of help towards the appreciation of that philosophy if, in these concluding remarks, I make a few suggestions (some of them already touched upon) concerning different ways in which we may regard Greek philosophy as a whole.

 1. I have already mentioned, particularly in connection with the Pre-Socratic philosophers, the problem of the One and the

Many; but the theme of the relation between the One and the Many and of the character of both may be discerned running through the whole of Greek philosophy, just as it runs indeed through the whole of philosophy, owing to the fact that while the Many are given in experience, the philosopher strives to see the Many with a synoptic vision, to arrive, so far as is possible, at a comprehensive view of Reality, i.e. to see the Many in the light of the One or in some sense to reduce the Many to the One. This attempt at a synoptic vision is very clear in the case of the pre-Socratic cosmologists and there is no need to dwell on this point again, beyond recalling to mind that their attempt to reconcile the Many of experience with the One demanded by thought was pursued predominantly on the material plane; the Many are material and the One also, the Unity-in-difference is material, water or the indeterminate or air or fire. Sometimes the aspect of Unity is predominant, as in the Eleatic system, sometimes the Many are triumphant, as in the atomistic philosophy of Leucippus and Democritus; but mind, partly no doubt owing to poverty of language, hardly rises above the material plane, though in Pythagoreanism we see, for example, a much clearer distinction between soul and body, while with Anaxagoras the concept of Nous tends to liberation from materialism.

So far as we can speak of the Sophists as occupying themselves at all with this problem, it is rather the aspect of multiplicity that is stressed (the multiplicity of ways of life, of ethical judgments, of opinions), while with Socrates the aspect of unity is stressed, inasmuch as the basic unity of true judgments of value is set in clear light; but it is Plato who really develops the complexity and richness of the problem. The fleeting multiplicity of phenomena, the data of experience, is seen against the background of the unitary realities of the exemplary Ideas, apprehended by the human mind in the concept, and this assertion of the Ideal realm of reality forces the philosopher to consider the problem of the One and the Many not only in the logical sphere, but also in the ontological sphere of immaterial being. The result is that the immaterial unities (themselves a multiplicity) are viewed in function of the One, the synthesising reality of the transcendental sphere and the ultimate Exemplar. Moreover, although the particulars of sense-experience, the Many of the older Cosmologists, are "dismissed," precisely in regard to their particularity considered as impenetrable by conceptual thought, into the infinite or indeterminate, the whole material world is regarded as ordered and informed by Mind or Soul. On the other hand a "chorismos" is left between exemplary Reality and the fleeting particulars, while—apparently at least—no satisfactory answer is given as to the precise relation between the Exemplary and Efficient Causes, so that, although Plato brings the complexity of the problem into greater relief and definitely transcends the pre-Socratic materialism, he fails to give any adequate solution to the problem and leaves us with a dualism, the sphere of Reality on the one hand and the sphere of semi-reality or Becoming on the other hand. Not even his assertion of the immaterial, which sets him above both Parmenides and Heraclitus, can suffice to explain the relation of Being and Becoming or of the One and the Many.

With Aristotle we find a greater realisation of the wealth and richness of the material world and he attempts, through his doctrine of immanent substantial form, to effect some synthesis of the realities of the One and the Many, the multiplicity of members within a species being united in the possession of a similar specific form, though there is no numerical identity. Again, the doctrine of hylomorphism enabled Aristotle to assert a real unifying principle in the terrestrial world, while at the same time he avoided any over-emphasis of unity, such as would conflict with the evident multiplicity given in experience: he thus provided a principle of stability and a principle of change and so did justice to both Being and Becoming. Moreover, Aristotle's Unmoved Mover, the ultimate Final Cause of the universe, served in some degree as a unifying and harmonising Principle, drawing the multiplicity of phenomena into an intelligible unity. On the other hand, however, Aristotle's dissatisfaction with the Ideal Theory of Plato and his perception of its weaknesses led him into an unfortunate rejection of the Platonic Exemplarism as a whole, while his insistence on final causality to the apparent exclusion of cosmic efficient causality meant the assertion of an ultimate dualism between God and an *independent* world.

In post-Aristotelian philosophy it is perhaps not fanciful to see in Stoicism an over-stressing of the One, resulting in cosmic pantheism (which has its noble reflection in ethical cosmopolitanism), and in Epicureanism an over-assertion of the Many, appearing in a cosmology built on an atomistic basis and in a (theoretically at least) egoistic ethic. In Neo-Pythagoreanism and Middle

Platonism we see that growing syncretism of Pythagorean, Platonic, Aristotelian and Stoic elements which culminated in the Neo-Platonic system. In that system the only possible way of settling the problem of the One and the Many is apprehended, namely that the Many must issue in some way from the One, the dualism between God and an independent world being avoided on the one hand and monism being avoided on the other hand, so that justice could be done to the reality of the One and the Many, to the supreme reality of the One and the dependent reality of the Many. But, while the Neo-Platonists rejected cosmic monism through their doctrine of the hierarchy of being and rejected any self-diremption of the transcendent One and while they admitted a "manifold Many" and did not attempt to dismiss the cosmos and the subordinate degrees of Being as illusory, they failed to see the unsatisfactory character of their attempt to steer a middle way between a true creation and monism and that their theory of "emanation," given their denial of creation out of nothing on the one hand and their denial of the self-diremption of God on the other hand, could possess no intelligible significance, but remained a mere metaphor. It was left for Christian philosophy to assert the true solution of *creatio ex nihilo sui et subiecti*.

2. Under a slightly different aspect we might regard Greek philosophy in its totality as an attempt to discover the ultimate cause or causes of the world. The pre-Socratics in general, as Aristotle observes, were concerned with the material cause, the *Urstoff* of the world, that which remains permanent beneath the constant changes. Plato, however, gave special emphasis to the Exemplary Cause, ideal and supra-material Reality, while he also asserted the Efficient operative Cause, Mind and Soul, developing the first steps of the pre-Socratic Anaxagoras. Nor did he, in spite of what Aristotle says, neglect final causality, since the exemplary causes are also final causes: they are not only Ideas, but also Ideals. God acts in the world with a view to an end, as is clearly stated in the *Timaeus*. But Plato seems to have left a dichotomy between the Exemplary Cause and the Efficient Cause (at least this is suggested by what he actually says and we have not sufficient warrant to state categorically that he brought the two ultimate Causes together), while in the terrestrial world he does not give that clear place to the immanent formal cause that Aristotle supplied. Yet while Aristotle developed a clear theory concerning the immanent formal and material causes in the

terrestrial world, his system is sadly deficient in relation to the ultimate Efficient and Exemplary Causes. The Aristotelian God works as ultimate Final Cause, but, since the philosopher did not see how God's changelessness and self-sufficiency could be reconciled with the exercise of efficient causality, he neglected to provide an ultimate Efficient Cause. He thought, no doubt, that the exercise of final causality by the Unmoved Mover was also all the ultimate efficient causality that was requisite; but this meant that for Aristotle the world was not only eternal, but also ontologically independent of God: the Unmoved Mover could scarcely be regarded as drawing the world into existence through the unconscious exercise of final causality.

A synthesis of Plato and Aristotle was, therefore, necessary, and in Neo-Platonism (as also, to a greater or less extent, in the intermediate philosophies leading up to it) the God of Aristotle and the Exemplary and Efficient Causes of Plato were brought more or less together, even if not in a thoroughly satisfactory manner. In Christian philosophy on the other hand the ultimate Efficient, Exemplary and Final Causes are explicitly identified in the one spiritual God, supreme Being and Reality and the Source of all created and dependent being.

3. Again, we might look on Greek philosophy as a whole from the humanistic viewpoint, according to the position attributed to man in the individual systems. The pre-Socratic cosmology, as I pointed out earlier, was particularly concerned with the Object, the material cosmos and man was regarded as an item in that cosmos, his soul being, for example, a contraction of the primal Fire (Heraclitus) or composed of a particular type of atoms (Leucippus). On the other hand, the doctrine of transmigration of souls, as found for instance in the Pythagorean philosophy and in the teaching of Empedocles, implied that there was in man a principle superior to matter, an idea which bore splendid fruit in the philosophy of Plato.

With the Sophists and with Socrates we find a swing-over, due to various causes, from the Object to the Subject, from the material cosmos as such to man. But it is in the Platonic philosophy that the first real attempt is made to combine both realities in a comprehensive synthesis. Man appears as the knowing and willing subject, the being who realises, or should realise, true values in his individual life and in the life of society, the being endowed with an immortal soul; and human knowledge, human nature, human conduct and human society, are made the subject of profound and penetrating analyses and considerations. On the other hand man appears as a being set between two worlds, the full immaterial world of Reality above him and the merely material limit below him: he thus appears, in his dual character of embodied spirit, as what Poseidonius, the outstanding thinker of the Middle Stoa, was later to term the δεσμός or bond between the two worlds of the immaterial and the material.

In Aristotle's philosophy man is again a midway being, as it were, for neither Plato nor Aristotle considered man to be the highest being: the founder of the Lyceum, no less than the founder of the Academy, was convinced that above men there is unchanging Being and that contemplation of unchanging Being is the exercise of man's highest faculty. Again, Aristotle, no less than Plato, gave profound consideration to human psychology, human conduct and human society. Yet of Aristotle's philosophy we may perhaps say that it was at once more and also less human than that of Plato: more human in that, for example, he knits together soul and body more closely than does Plato and so produces a more "realistic" epistemology, attributes a greater value to human aesthetic experience and artistic production, and is more "commonsense" in his treatment of political society, less human in that his identification of the active intellect in all man (according to what seems the more probable interpretation of the De Anima) would result in denial of personal immortality. Moreover, there is nothing in Aristotle to suggest that man can ever become united to God in any real sense.

Yet, although it is true that Plato and Aristotle attribute an important position to the study of man and his conduct, as individual and as a member of society, it is also true that both of them (notwithstanding Aristotle's trend towards empirical science) are great metaphysicians and speculative philosophers and of neither of them could we say that he fixes his attention exclusively in man. In the Hellenistic and Roman periods, however, man comes to occupy more and more the centre of the picture: cosmological speculation tends to flag and is unoriginal in character, while in Epicureanism and the developed Stoa the philosopher is concerned above all with human conduct. This preoccupation with man produces the noble doctrine of the later Stoa, of Seneca, Marcus Aurelius and—most strikingly perhaps —of Epictetus, in which all men, as rational beings, appear as brethren, children of "Zeus." But if it is man's moral conduct that is most insisted on in the Stoic School, it is man's religious capacity, need and yearning that come to occupy a prominent position in the Schools and thinkers that are influenced by the Platonic tradition: a doctrine of "salvation," of knowledge of God and assimilation to God, culminates in the Plotinian doctrine of ecstatic union with the One. If Epicureanism and Stoicism (the latter with some qualification perhaps) concern themselves with man on what we might call the horizontal level, Neo-Platonism concerns itself rather with the vertical, with man's ascent to God.

4. Epistemology or the theory of knowledge is generally regarded as a branch of philosophy, the study of which is peculiar to our modern era, and for some modern thinkers it has constituted practically the whole of philosophy. There is, of course, a good deal of truth in the assertion that it was modern philosophy that first made epistemology a really serious and critical study, but it is not a completely true statement, if asserted without qualification. Leaving out of account the philosophy of the Middle Ages, which also dealt with epistemological themes, it can scarcely be denied that the great thinkers of Antiquity concerned themselves to some extent with epistemological questions, even if it was not recognised as a separate branch of philosophy or accorded that critical importance which has generally been attributed to it in modern times, since the time of Immanuel Kant at least. Without attempting to give anything like a complete survey of the development of epistemology in ancient philosophy, I will suggest one or two points which may help to throw into relief the fact that important epistemological problems at least raised their heads above the ground in the ancient world, even if they did not emerge into full light of day and receive that close attention which they deserve.

The pre-Socratic philosophers were, in the main, "dogmatists," in the sense that they assumed that man can know reality objectively. It is true that the Eleatic philosophy made a distinction between the way of truth and the way of belief or opinion or appearance; but the Eleatics themselves did not realise the importance of the problems involved in their philosophy. They adopted a monistic position on rationalistic grounds and, since this position conflicted with the data of sense-experience, cavalierly denied the objective reality of phenomena: they did not question their general philosophical position or the power of the human mind to transcend phenomena, but rather assumed this power. Nor did they realise apparently that, by rejecting the objective reality of appearance, they were undermining their metaphysic. In general, therefore, the thinkers of the Eleatic School cannot be termed exceptions to the generally uncritical attitude of the pre-Socratics, in spite of the dialectical ability of a man like Zeno.

The Sophists did indeed assert relativism to a greater or less extent, and the assertion of relativism involved an implicit epistemology. If Protagoras' dictum that man is the measure of all things is to be taken in a broad sense, it is tantamount to an assertion, not only of the independence of man in the ethical sphere, as a creator of moral values, but also of the inability of man to attain metaphysical truth. Did not Protagoras adopt a sceptical attitude in regard to theology and did not the Sophists in general regard cosmological speculation as little more than waste of time? Now, if the Sophists had gone on to institute a critique of human knowledge and had attempted to show why human knowledge is necessarily confined to phenomena, they would have been epistemologists; but in point of fact their interests were, for the most part, other than philosophical and their relativistic theories do not seem to have been based on any profound consideration either of the nature of the subject or of that of the object. The epistemology involved in their general position remained, therefore, implicit and was not elaborated into an explicit theory of knowledge. *We*, of course, can discern the germs of epistemological theories or problems, not only in Sophism but also in pre-Socratic philosophy; but that is not to say that either the Sophists or the pre-Socratic cosmologists had a reflective realisation of these problems.

When we turn to Plato and Aristotle, however, we find explicit theories of knowledge. Plato had a clear notion what he meant by knowledge and sharply distinguished the nature of true knowledge from the nature of opinion and of imagination, he possessed a clear reflective knowledge of the relativistic and variable elements in sense-perception and he discussed the question, how error of judgment takes place and in what it consists. His whole theory of the ascending degrees of knowledge and the corresponding objects of knowledge entitles him without a doubt to rank as an epistemologist. The same is true of Aristotle, who asserted a theory of abstraction, of the function of the image, of the active and passive principle in cognition, of the distinction between sense-perception and conceptual thought, of the different functions of reason. Of course, if we wished to restrict the scope of epistemology to consideration of the question, *"Can* we attain knowledge?"*, then the Aristotelian epistemology would belong rather to psychology, since it purports to answer the question, *"How* do we come to know?"*, rather than the question, *"Can* we know?"*; but if we are willing to extend the scope of epistemology to cover the nature of the process of coming to know, then we must certainly reckon Aristotle an epistemologist. He may have treated the questions he raises in his psychology and we might to-day include most of them under the heading of psychology, but, labels apart, it remains an undoubted fact that Aristotle had a theory of knowledge.

On the other hand, though both Plato and Aristotle elaborated theories of knowledge, there is no use in pretending that they were not "dogmatists." Plato, as I have said, had a clear idea of what he meant by knowledge; but that such knowledge was possible for man, he assumed. If he accepted from Heraclitus his insistence on the changing character of the material world and from the Sophists the relativity of sense-perception, he accepted also from the Eleatics and the Pythagoreans the rationalistic assumption that the human mind can transcend phenomena and from Socrates the starting-point of his metaphysics of essence. Moreover, it was essential for Plato's ethical and political aims that the possibility of knowing the unchanging values and exemplary essences should be admitted: he never really questioned this possibility nor did he ever seriously raise the question of a purely subjective *a priori* element in human cognition: he attributed the *a priori* element (which he admitted) to "reminiscence," i.e. to previous objective knowledge. Nor did Aristotle ever raise the "critical problem": he assumed that the human mind can transcend phenomena and attain to a certain knowledge of unchanging and necessary objects, the objects of theoretic contemplation. Plato was an untiring dialectician, Aristotle was always ready to consider fresh problems and was careful in the statement of his own theories, even if not in that of other people's theories; but of neither the one nor the other can we say that he was the Kant or the anti-Kantian of the ancient world, for Kant's problem was not considered by them. Nor is this really surprising, since both men were dominated by the problem of Being (whereas in modern philosophy so many thinkers have started from *Consciousness*), so that their theories of knowledge were elaborated in function of their metaphysics and general philosophic positions rather than as a necessary *prolegomenon* to any metaphysic.

In the post-Aristotelian philosophy, if we except the Sceptics, we find in general the same "dogmatic" attitude, though it is also true that considerable attention was devoted to the question of the criteria of truth, e.g. by the Stoics and Epicureans. In other words, thinkers were alive to the difficulty that arises through the variability of sense-perception and attempted to meet this difficulty; in fact they had to meet it, in order to be able to erect their several philosophical structures. They were much more critical than the pre-Socratics; but that does not mean that they were critical philosophers in the Kantian sense, for they confined themselves more or less to a particular problem and tried to differentiate between, e.g. objective sense-perception, imagination and hallucination. In the New Academy, however, a radical scepticism showed itself, as when Carneades taught that there is no criterion of truth and that knowledge is impossible, on the ground that no sense-presentation is certainly true and that conceptual reasoning, since it is founded on sense-experience, is no more reliable than the latter, and the later Sceptics elaborated a systematic criticism of dogmatism and argued the relative character of both sensation and judgment, so that they were determined anti-metaphysicians. Dogmatism indeed won the final victory in ancient philosophy; but in view of the attacks of the Sceptics it cannot be said that ancient philosophy was altogether uncritical or that epistemology had no place in the consideration of Greek philosophers. This is the point I want to make: I am not concerned to admit that the attacks on metaphysics were justified, for I believe that they can be answered. I only wish to point out that not all Greek philosophers were naïve "dogmatists" and that, even if this can be legitimately asserted of the pre-Socratics, it would be a far too sweeping assertion in regard to Greek philosophers in general.

5. Closely allied with epistemology is psychology, and it may be as well to make a few remarks on the development of psychology in ancient philosophy. It is the Pythagorean School which stands out among the pre-Socratics as possessing a definite concept of the soul as a permanent principle, persisting in its individuality,

even after death. The philosophy of Heraclitus recognised, of course, a part of man which is more akin to the ultimate Principle of the universe than the body, and Anaxagoras asserted that Nous is present in man; but the latter did not succeed in transcending, *verbally* at least, the materialism of the pre-Socratic system, while for Heraclitus the rational element in man was but a purer manifestation of the fiery Principle. The Pythagorean psychology, however, by its distinction between soul and body at least implied a distinction between the spiritual and corporeal. Indeed, the doctrine of metempsychosis over-emphasised the distinction between soul and body, since it involved the conclusion that the soul stands in no intrinsic relation to any particular body. Moreover, acceptance of metempsychosis involves the acceptance of the theory that memory and reflective consciousness of continued self-identity are not essential to individual persistence. (If Aristotle held that there is a separate active intellect in each man and that the active intellect persists in its individuality, his notion that memory perishes with death may have been due not only to his own psychology and physiology, but to relics of the Pythagorean doctrine and its implication.) As to the Pythagorean theory of the tripartite nature of the soul, this was doubtless ultimately due to empirical observation of man's rational and emotional functions and of the conflict between reason and passion.

The Pythagorean conception of the soul exercised a very considerable influence on the thought of Plato. Rejecting epiphenomenalism, he made the soul the principle of life and movement in man, a principle that does not depend essentially on the body for the exercise of its highest intellectual functions, a principle that comes from "without" and survives the death of the body. Tripartite in nature, the soul has various functions or "parts," the hierarchy of which was fitted by Plato into his general metaphysical position. The lower parts or functions depend essentially on the body, but the rational soul belongs to the sphere of abiding Reality: in its proper dialectical and intuitive processes its activity is on a higher plane than that of phenomena and demonstrates the "divine" or immortal character of the soul. But Plato was not primarily interested in the soul from the strictly psychological aspect, still less from the point of view of the biologist: he was interested first and foremost in the soul as apprehending values and as realising values, in its ethical aspect. Hence the tremendous importance that he attached to education and culture of the soul.

If he sharpened, as he did, the antithesis between soul and body and spoke of the soul as inhabiting the body, as being lodged in the body like a captain in a ship, destined to rule the body, it was mainly his ethical interest that led him to do so. It is true that he attempted to prove the soul's pre-existence, intrinsic independence of the body and immortality, with epistemological arguments, arguing, e.g. from the *a priori* element in human knowledge; but all the time he was under the sway of ethical, and to a certain extent religious interests, and at the close of his life we find him still insisting that the soul is man's dearest possession and tendance of the soul man's highest task and duty. This is what we might call the characteristic side of Plato's psychology, for, though he certainly attributed a biological function to the soul, i.e. as source of movement and vital principle, he placed the emphasis on ethical and metaphysical aspects to such a degree that it may well be doubted if his treatment of these aspects really squares with his treatment of the soul in its biological function.

Aristotle began with the Platonic conception of the soul and the Platonic metaphysico-ethical picture of the soul and features of this conception are salient features of his psychology as represented in the pedagogical works. Thus, according to Aristotle, the highest part of man's soul, the active intellect, comes from without and survives death, while insistence on education and on moral culture is prominent in the philosophy of Aristotle as in that of Plato. Nevertheless, one can hardly avoid the impression that this aspect of his doctrine of the soul is not the really characteristic aspect of the Aristotelian psychology. However much he may have insisted on education and however prominent his intellectualist attitude may be in the picture of the ideal life for man as given in the *Ethics*, it would seem true to say that Aristotle's characteristic contribution to psychology is to be found rather in his treatment of the soul in its biological aspects. The sharp antithesis drawn by Plato between soul and body tends to retreat into the background, to give place to the conception of the soul as the immanent form of the body, as wedded to this particular body. The active intellect (whether monistically conceived or not) survives death, but the soul in its generality, including the passive intellect and including the functions of memory, etc., depends on the bodily organism and perishes at death. Where does it come from, this soul of man (excluding the active intellect)? It does not come from "without," it is not "made" by any Demiurge: is it perhaps a function of the body, little more than an epiphenomenon? Aristotle gave an extensive empirical treatment of such psychical functions as memory, imagination, dreams, sensations, and it would appear that his realisation of the dependence of so many of these functions on physiological factors and conditions was leading him towards an epiphenomenalist view of the soul, even if he never explicitly repudiated the totality of his Platonic inheritance or realised the tension between what he had retained of the Platonic psychology and that view of the soul to which his own researches and bent of mind were leading him.

The most important contribution of post-Aristotelian philosophy to psychology in a broad sense was perhaps the emphasis it laid on the religious aspect of the human soul: this is true at least of Neo-Platonism and of the Schools that led up to Neo-Platonism, though not, of course, of all post-Aristotelian Schools. The thinkers of the movement which culminated in Neo-Platonism working from the viewpoint of the Platonic tradition, set in clear relief man's kinship to the Divine, the soul's transcendental orientation and destiny. In other words, it was the characteristically Platonic attitude that triumphed in ancient philosophy rather than the characteristically Aristotelian attitude. As for the Stoics and Epicureans, the former could not achieve a really unified psychology owing to the simple fact that their dogmatic materialism demanded one psychology and their ethic another. Moreover, they did not investigate the nature and function of the psyche for their own sake and endeavour to establish a rational psychology on sure empirical foundations; but, adopting and adapting a pre-Socratic cosmology and centering their attention on ethical conduct, fitted a rationalist psychology, as best they could, to a hybrid system. Nevertheless, the tendency of Stoic doctrine and the effect of its influence was certainly to increase the direction of interest to the ethical and religious aspects of the soul rather than to its biological aspects. The Epicureans denied the immortality of the soul and asserted its atomic character; but they did so in the interest of their own ethic and not, of course, because they had discovered that the soul is in reality composed of atoms, though it must be admitted that the Epicurean psychology fits in better with their banal ethic than the Stoic psychology with the Stoic idealist ethic. Both Stoic psychology and Stoic ethic were constantly striving, as it were, to break the bonds of the traditional materialistic monism in which they were bound, and the Stoics could no more explain rational thought in terms of their system than the Epicureans could explain thought in terms of the motion of atoms. The Epicureans may have anticipated to some extent the psychology of Hobbes or of thinkers of the French Enlightenment, but neither in the ancient world nor in eighteenth-century France, nor even in the twentieth century, can the psychical be satisfactorily explained in terms of the corporeal, the rational in terms of irrational, the conscious in terms of the unconscious. On the other hand, if the psychical cannot be reduced to the corporeal, no more can the corporeal be reduced to the psychical: the two remain distinct, though in man, the bond between the purely spiritual and the purely material spheres, the two elements are intimately related. Plato laid the emphasis on the fact of distinction, Aristotle on that of the intimate relationship: both factors need to be borne in mind if one would avoid occasionalism or modern idealism on the one hand and epiphenomenalism on the other hand.

6. A few remarks on the development of ethics in ancient philosophy, particularly in regard to the relationship between ethical norms and a transcendental foundation of morality. I am quite aware that the question of the relation between ethics and metaphysics is hotly debated, and I do not propose to discuss the problem on its own merits: I wish to do no more than indicate what I consider one of the main trends in Greek ethical thought.

We have to distinguish between moral philosophy as such and the unsystematised moral judgments of mankind. Moral judgments had been made by Greeks long before the Sophists, Socrates, Plato, Aristotle, the Stoics, etc., reflected on them, and the fact that the ordinary moral judgments of man formed the material for their reflection meant that the theories of the philosophers mirrored to a greater or less extent the ordinary moral consciousness of the time. These moral judgments, however, are in turn dependent, in part at least, on education, social tradition and environment, are moulded by the community, so that it is only natural that they should differ somewhat from community to community, nation to nation. Now, in face of this difference two ways of reaction at any rate lie open to the philosopher.

(i) Perceiving that a given community holds fast to its own traditional code and considers it the only one, the "natural" one, while on the other hand not all communities have exactly the

same code, he may react by drawing the conclusion that morals
are relative, that though one code may be more useful, more
expedient, than another, there exists no absolute code of morals.
This was the line taken by the Sophists.

(ii) The philosopher may attribute a good deal of the observed
differences to *error* and assert a sure standard and norm of
morality. This was the way taken by Plato and Aristotle. In
fact the ethical intellectualism, particularly characteristic of
Socrates, though also of Plato to a less extent, bears witness
to the fact that they ascribed differences in moral judgment to
mistake, to error. Thus to the man who thinks, or professes
to think, that the natural and proper procedure is to injure one's
enemies or to pursue a career of unabashed egoism, Plato attempts
to show that he is quite mistaken in his notion. He may at times
appeal to self-interest, even if only in *argumentum ad hominem*;
but, whatever he appeals to in order to prove his view, Plato was
certainly no relativist in ethics: he believed in abiding standards,
objectively true and universally valid.

Now, if we look at the moral philosophies of Plato and Aristotle,
this fact is apparent, that in either case the standard of conduct
is measured by their conception of human nature. The ideal was
regarded by Plato as something fixed, eternal and transcendent,
not subject to relativity and variation. The different faculties
of man are faculties of activity according to certain habits or
virtues, and of each virtue there is an ideal pattern, comprised
in the all-embracing ideal, the Ideal of the Good. There is an
ideal of man and ideals of man's virtues, and it is man's moral
function to conform himself to those ideals. When he does so,
when his nature is harmoniously developed and perfected according to the ideal, he is a "just" or good man, he is a true example
of a man and has attained true well-being. Moreover, for Plato
God is constantly operative in the world, striving to realise the
ideal in the concrete and actual world. God Himself never departs
from the ideal, but always has the ideal, the best, in view: He is
the Reason, Divine Providence, operative in the cosmos. God is
also the source of the human reason and is depicted symbolically
in the *Timaeus* as forming the human reason Himself, so that
man's rational soul is akin to the Divine and has as its task the
same task as the Deity, the realisation of the ideal, of value, in
the world. Man is thus by nature a co-operator with God: in that
consists his vocation, to work towards the realisation of the ideal,

of value, in his personal life and in that of society or the State. It is God Who sets the standard, not man, says Plato against Protagoras, and man's end is the greatest possible likeness to God. Plato says little of moral obligation, it is true, but he evidently considered, even if without a fully reflective consciousness of the fact, that man is under an obligation to act as truly befits a man. The ethical intellectualism which he inherited from Socrates, was doubtless a hindrance in the way of a clear realisation of moral obligation and responsibility; but do not the myths of the future life, of reward and punishment, clearly imply some realisation of moral obligation? Plato certainly gave a transcendental foundation to the *content* of the moral law and, though the same cannot be said in regard to the *form* of the moral law, the categorical imperative, he does seem to have had a dim awareness of the fact that a moral law, if its morally binding and universally valid character is to be substantiated, must be given a transcendental foundation, not only in regard to its content, but also in regard to its form.

When we turn to Aristotle, we find a very fine analysis of the good life, of the moral and intellectual virtues, which were analysed by Aristotle much more completely and systematically than by Plato; but the transcendental values of Plato have been swept away or been replaced by the immanent form. It is true that Aristotle calls on man to think divine things, to imitate, as far as he can, God's contemplation of the highest object, so that in a sense there is, even for Aristotle, an eternal pattern of human life; but the theoretic life is inaccessible to most men, while on the other hand Aristotle affords no ground for a man thinking that he is called upon to co-operate with the Divine, since the God of the *Metaphysics* at least does not operate consciously and efficiently in the world. Aristotle never really synthesised satisfactorily the life of the moral virtues and the theoretic life, and the moral law for Aristotle is, it would seem, devoid of any real transcendental foundation, in regard to both content and form. What could he say to anyone who questioned the obligation of living in the manner proposed in the *Ethics*? He could appeal to aesthetic standards, to good form, to "fairness," and he could reply that to act otherwise is to miss the goal of happiness, which all necessarily seek, with the consequence that one would be acting irrationally; but he left no place for an appeal to a specifically moral obligation with a firm foundation in absolute Reality.

Later Greek philosophers, if we except, e.g. the Epicureans, seem to have seen the necessity of founding a standard morality on an absolute basis. The Stoics insist on duty, on the Divine Will, on the life of reason which is life in accordance with nature, since man's rational nature proceeds from God, the all-pervasive Reason, and returns to Him. Their pantheism certainly involved them in ethical difficulties; but, none the less, they viewed morality as ultimately the expression of the Divine in man and in human life. As God is one, as human nature is constant, there can be but one morality. It would be an anachronism to read into their expression for "duty" all the meaning that the term has acquired in modern times; but at least they had some conception of duty and of moral obligation, even if the clear statement of this conception was hampered by the determinism consequent on their pantheism. In the Neo-Platonic system or systems ethics proper was subordinated to insistence on the religious aspect of human life and man's ascent to God; but the practice of the moral life was regarded as an integral part of that ascent and, in practising it, man conforms himself to transcendentally-grounded standards. Moreover, the fact that those Romans who aspired to a moral life and attached importance to moral values, saw the necessity of purifying the idea of God and of emphasising Divine Providence serves to illustrate the practical benefit of founding ethics ultimately on metaphysics and so serves as an empirical confirmation of the theoretical assertion of that foundation.

7. The mention of ethics and of an ascription to morality of a transcendental foundation naturally leads one on to a brief consideration of Greek philosophy viewed as a preparatory intellectual instrument for Christianity, as a *preparatio evangelica*. Only a few suggestions can be made, however: any adequate treatment of the subject would require more space than I can devote to it in this concluding chapter. (Consideration of the doctrines actually borrowed directly or indirectly by Christian philosophy from Greek thinkers is best reserved for the next volume, that dealing with mediaeval philosophy.)

In the philosophy of Heraclitus we find the beginnings of the doctrine of an immanent Reason operative in the world, though the Logos is conceived on the material plane, as identical with the primal Fire (a conception that was elaborated in later times by the Stoics), while Anaxagoras contributes the theory of Nous as the primary moving Principle. But in both cases there is but a hint of the developments that were to come later, and it is not until Plato that we find anything like a natural theology. But, if among the pre-Socratics we find little more than hints of the doctrine of (what we would call) God, as First Efficient Cause (Anaxagoras) and as Providence or immanent Reason (Heraclitus), we find in Pythagoreanism a somewhat clearer enunciation of the distinction between soul and body, the superiority of soul to body and the necessity of tending the former and preserving it from contamination. However, in regard to pre-Socratic philosophy as a whole, it is the search for the ultimate nature of the world and its conception of the world as a law-ordered world, rather than any specific doctrines (with the exception perhaps of the Orphic-Pythagorean psychology), which entitles it to be regarded in any sense as a remote *preparatio evangelica,* a preparation of the pagan mind for the reception of the revealed religion. For it is the conception of a law-ordered world that naturally leads on to the conception of a Lawgiver and Orderer. Before this further step could be taken, however, it was necessary to arrive at a clear distinction between soul and body, the immaterial and the material, and for the apprehension of this distinction the Orphics and Pythagoreans paved the way, though it was really Plato who extended the Pythagorean anthropological distinction between the transcendental and the phenomenal, the immaterial and the material.

It would be difficult to exaggerate the importance of Plato in the intellectual *preparatio evangelica* of the pagan world. By his doctrine of exemplarism, his theory of the transcendental Exemplary Cause, by his doctrine of Reason or Mind operative in the world and forming the world for the best, he obviously remotely paved the way for the ultimate acceptance of the one Transcendent-Immanent God. Again, by his doctrine of the immortal and rational soul of man, of retribution, of moral purification, he made easier the intellectual acceptance of Christian psychology and asceticism, while his insistence on absolute moral standards in accordance with the teaching of his great Master, Socrates, and the hints he drops as to the assimilation with God were a remote preparation for the acceptance of the Christian ethic. Nor must we forget that in the *Laws* Plato gave reasons why we should admit the existence of Mind operative in the universe, thus foreshadowing the later natural theologies. But it is rather the total attitude fostered by the Platonic philosophy—I refer to the belief

17

in transcendental Reality, eternal values, immortality, righteous-
ness, Providence, etc., and the characteristic mental and emotional
attitude that is logically fostered by such belief—rather than any
specific arguments which helped to lead up to the acceptance of
Christianity. It is true that the doctrine of the Transcendental,
as developed in Middle and Neo-Platonism, was used *against*
Christianity, under the plea that the dogma of the Incarnation
is incompatible with the transcendent character of God: but the
transcendent character of God is an integral doctrine of Christianity and it can scarcely be denied that the Platonic ascent
above pre-Socratic materialism was a predisposing factor towards
the acceptance of a religion which insists on the supreme reality
of the transcendental and on the abiding character of spiritual
values. Early Christian thinkers certainly recognised in Platonism
a certain kinship, even if more or less remote, with their own
Weltanschauung and, though Aristotle was later to become the
philosopher *par excellence* of Scholasticism, Augustinianism stands
rather in the line of the Platonic tradition. Moreover, Platonic-
Augustinian elements are very far from being entirely absent in
the philosophy of that very Scholastic who adopted—and adapted
—Aristotelianism, St. Thomas Aquinas. Thus, if Platonism helped
in some degree to prepare the way for Christianity, even if largely
through succeeding Schools that developed the Platonic tradition,
Christianity may also be said to have borrowed some of its
philosophic "outfit" from Platonism.

By mediaeval philosophers of the Augustinian tradition, such
as St. Bonaventure (one of whose main objections against Aristotle
was that he rejected exemplarism), Aristotelianism tended to be
regarded as inimical to the Christian religion, largely because he
became known to the West principally through the Arabian
commentators. (Thus Averroes interpreted Aristotle—probably
rightly—as denying, for example, the *personal* immortality of the
human soul.) But though it is true, for instance, that the conception of God in the *Metaphysics* as entirely self-engrossed and
caring nought for the world and man, is not that of Christianity,
it must surely be admitted that the natural theology of Aristotle
was a preparation for the acceptance of Christianity. God appears
as transcendent, immaterial Thought, the absolute Final Cause,
and when the Platonic Ideas came later to be placed in the Mind
of God and a certain syncretism of Platonism and Aristotelianism
took place, the ultimate Efficient, Exemplary and Final Causes

tending to coalesce, a conception of reality was provided that made it easier than it might otherwise have been to accept Christianity from the intellectual standpoint.

Of the post-Aristotelian philosophy much might be said in the present connection; I can but select a few points for mention. Stoicism, with its doctrine of the immanent Logos and its "providential" operation in the world, with its noble ethic, was an important factor in the world in which Christianity was implanted and grew. It is quite true that the Stoic philosophy remained theoretically materialist and more or less determinist; but, from the practical viewpoint, the insistence on man's kinship with God, on purification of the soul by self-control and moral education, on submission to the "Divine Will," together with the broadening influence of its cosmopolitanism, served as a preparation in some minds for the acceptance of the universal religion which, while transcending the materialism of the Stoics, insisted on the brotherhood of men as children of God and introduced a dynamic influence which was wanting in the Stoic system. Moreover, in so far as ethical Stoicism was an answer to the contemporary need for moral guidance and direction as to the right course to be pursued by the individual, swamped in the great cosmopolitan Empire, this need was far better met by the Christian doctrine, which could appeal to the uneducated and simple in a way that Stoicism could hardly do and which held out the prospect of complete happiness in the future life as the term of moral endeavour in a way that Stoicism, by its very system, was debarred from doing.

Besides the strictly ethical needs of man there were also his religious capacity and need to be satisfied. While the State cult was unable to meet this need, the mystery-religions and even philosophy (in a far less popular form, e.g. in Neo-Platonism) catered for its satisfaction. By attempting to cater for man's deeper spiritual aspirations they at the same time tended to develop and intensify those aspirations, with the result that Christianity fell on an already prepared ground. Christianity, with its doctrine of salvation, its sacramental system, its dogmas, its doctrine of incorporation with Christ through membership of the Church and of the final vision of God, its offer of supernatural life, was *the* "mystery-religion"; but it had the inestimable advantage over all pagan mystery-religions that it was an *historical* religion, based on the Life, Death and Resurrection of the God-Man, Jesus Christ, Who lived and suffered in Palestine in a certain historical period: it was based on historical fact, not on myth. As to the doctrine of "salvation" as found in philosophical Schools and the doctrine of ecstatic union with God as developed in Neo-Platonism, this was far too intellectualist in character to admit of its having a popular appeal. Through the Sacraments and the reception of the supernatural life Christianity offered to *all* men, educated and uneducated alike, union with God, imperfect in this life, perfect in the next, and so, even from the purely natural viewpoint, was obviously destined to exercise a far wider influence than philosophy as such could ever exercise, even a philosophy that was strongly tinctured with religious elements. Moreover, the Neo-Platonic philosophy was unhistorical, in the sense that a doctrine like that of the Incarnation was alien to its spirit, and an historical religion is bound to have a wider popular appeal than a metaphysical philosophy. Nevertheless, in spite of the shocked and scandalised attitude that some early Christian writers adopted (very naturally) in regard to the mystery-religions, particularly that of Mithras, with its quasi-sacramental rites, both the more or less popular mystery-religions and intel-lectualist Neo-Platonism served the purpose of preparing men's minds for the acceptance of Christianity. They may have tended to set themselves up as rivals to Christianity and they may have kept some individuals from embracing Christianity who would otherwise have done so; but that does not mean that they could not and did not serve as a way to Christianity. Porphyry attacked Christianity, but was not St. Augustine brought to Christianity by way of Plotinus? Neo-Platonism was the last breath, the last flower, of ancient pagan philosophy; but in the thought of St. Augustine it became the first stage of Christian philosophy. Christianity was not, of course, in any sense the outcome of ancient philosophy, nor can it be called a philosophic system, for it is the revealed religion and its historical antecedents are to be found in Judaism; but when Christians began to philosophise, they found ready at hand a rich material, a store of dialectical instruments and metaphysical concepts and terms, and those who believe that divine Providence is operative in history will hardly suppose that the provision of that material and its elaboration through the centuries was simply and solely an accident.

APPENDIX I

SOME ABBREVIATIONS USED IN THIS VOLUME

AËTIUS. Collectio placitorum (philosophorum).
ALBINUS. Didask. (Didaskalikos).
AMMIANUS MARCELLINUS. Rerum gest. (Rerum gestarum libri 18).
AUGUSTINE. Contra Acad. (Contra Academicos).
           C.D. (De Civitate Dei).
BURNET. E.G.P. (Early Greek Philosophy).
        G.P., I. (Greek Philosophy. Part I, Thales to Plato).
CAPITOLINUS, JULIUS.. Vit. M. Ant. (Vita Marci Antonini Pii).
CHALCIDIUS. In Tim. (Commentary on Plato's *Timaeus*).
CICERO. Acad. Prior. (Academica Priora).
      Acad. Post. (Academica Posteriora).
      Ad Att. (Letters to Atticus).
      De Div. (De Divinatione).
      De Fin. (De Finibus).
      De Nat. D. (De Natura Deorum).
      De Off. (De Officiis).
      De Orat. (De Oratore).
      De Senect. (De Senectute).
      Somn. Scip. (Somnium Scipionis).
      Tusc. (Tusculanae Disputationes).
CLEMENS ALEXANDRINUS. Protrep. (Protrepticus).
                 Strom. (Stromata).
DAMASCIUS. Dubit. (Dubitationes et solutiones de primis principiis).
DIOGENES LAËRTIUS. Lives of the Philosophers.
EPICTETUS. Disc. (Discourses).
        Ench. (Enchiridion).
EUDEMUS. Phys. (*Physics*, of which only fragments remain).
EUNAPIUS. Vit. Soph. (Lives of the Sophists).
EUSEBIUS. Hist. Eccl. (Historia Ecclesiastica).
        Prep. Evan. (Preparatio Evangelica).
GELLIUS, AULUS. Noct. Att. (Noctes Atticae).
GREGORY OF NAZIANZEN. adv. Max. (adversus Maximum).
HIPPOLYTUS. Ref. (Refutationis omnium haeresium libri X).
JOSEPHUS. Ant. Jud. (Jewish Antiquities).
LACTANTIUS. Div. Inst. (Institutiones divinae).
LAMPRIDIUS. Alex. (Life of Alexander Severus).
          Aurel. (Life of Aurelian).
LUCIAN. De morte Peregr. (De morte Peregrini).

Marcus Aurelius. Med. (Meditations or To Himself).

Maximus of Tyre. Diss. (Dissertationes).

Origen. c. Cels. (Contra Celsum).

P.G. Patrologia Graeca (ed. Migne).

P.L. Patrologia Latina (ed. Migne).

Philo. De conf. ling. (De confusione linguarum).
  De gigant. (De gigantibus).
  De human. (De humanitate).
  De migrat. Abrah. (De migratione Abrahami).
  De mutat. nom. (De mutatione nominum).
  De opif. mundi (De opificio mundi).
  De post. Caini (De posteritate Caini).
  De somn. (De somniis).
  De vita Mos. (De vita Moysis).
  Leg. alleg. (Legum allegoriarum libri).
  Quis rer. div. her. (Quis rerum divinarum heres sit).
  Quod Deus sit immut. (Quod Deus sit immutabilis).

Photius. Bibliotheca (about A.D. 857).

Plutarch. Cat. Mai. (Cato Maior).
  De anim. proc. (De animae procreatione in Timaeo).
  De comm. notit. (De communibus notitiis adversus Stoicos).
  De def. orac. (De defectu oraculorum).
  De gloria Athen. (Bellone an pace clariores fuerint Athenienses).
  De Is. et Osir. (De Iside et Osiride).
  De prim. frig. (De primo frigido).
  De ser. num. vind. (De sera numinis vindicta).
  De sol. animal. (De sollertia animalium).
  De Stoic repug. (De repugnantiis Stoicis).
  Non p. suav. (Ne suaviter quidem vivi posse secundum Epicurum).

Pseudo-Plutarch. Strom. (Fragments of the stromateis conserved in Eusebius' *Preparatio Evangelica*).

Porphyry. Isag. (Isagoge, i.e. introd. to Aristotle's *Categories*).

Proclus. De Prov. (De providentia et fato et eo quod in nobis).
  In Alcib. (Commentary on *Alcibiades* I of "Plato").
  In Remp. (Commentary on *Republic* of Plato).
  In Parmen. (Commentary on *Parmenides* of Plato).
  In Tim. (Commentary on *Timaeus* of Plato).
  Instit. Theol. (Institutio Theologica).
  Theol. Plat. (In Platonis Theologiam).

Seneca. Nat. Quaest. (Naturalium Quaestionum libri VII).

Sextus Empiricus. adv. math. (Adversus mathematicos).
    Pyrr. Hyp. (Pyrrhonenses Hypotyposes).

Simplicius. In Arist. Categ. (Commentary on Aristotle's *Categories*).
   Phys. (Commentary on Aristotle's *Physics*).
Stace, W. T. Crit. Hist. (A Critical History of Greek Philosophy).
Stobaeus. Flor. (Florilegium).
Tacitus. Ann. (Annales).
   Hist. (Historiae).
Theophrastus. Phys. Opin. (Physicorum Opiniones).
Xenophon. Cyneg. (Cynegeticus).
   Mem. (Memorabilia).

APPENDIX II

A NOTE ON SOURCES

Since on the one hand some philosophers did not write at all, while on the other hand the works of many philosophers who did write have been lost, we have to rely in very many cases on the testimony of later writers for information as to the course of Greek philosophy.

The chief source of knowledge in the ancient world concerning the pre-Socratic philosophy was the work of Theophrastus entitled *Physicorum Opiniones*, a work which, unfortunately, we possess only in fragmentary form. Theophrastus' work became the source of various other compilations, epitomes or "doxographies," in some of which the opinions of the philosophers were arranged according to theme, while in others the opinions were set forth under the names of the respective philosophers. Of the former type were the *Vetusta Placita*, written by an unknown disciple of Poseidonius in the first half of the first century A.D. We do not possess this work, but that it existed and that it was based on Theophrastus' work, has been shown by Diels. The *Vetusta Placita* in turn formed the main source of the so-called *Aëtii Placita* or Συναγωγὴ τῶν 'Αρεσκόντων (about A.D. 100). Aetiüs' work in turn served as a basis for the *Placita philosophorum* of the Pseudo-Plutarch (compiled about A.D. 150) and the doxographical extracts given by John Stobaeus (A.D. fifth century) in the first book of his *Eclogae*. These two last works are the most important doxographical compilations which we possess, and it has become evident that the main ultimate source for both was the work of Theophrastus, which was also ultimately the chief, though not the only, source for the first book of Hippolytus' *Refutation of all heresies* (in which the subject-matter is arranged under the names of the respective philosophers concerned), and for the fragments, falsely attributed to Plutarch, which are quoted in the *Preparatio Evangelica* of Eusebius.

Further information on the opinions of Greek philosophers is provided by such works as the *Noctes Atticae* of Aulus Gellius (about A.D. 150), the writings of philosophers like Plutarch, Cicero and Sextus Empiricus, and the works of the Christian Fathers and early Christian writers. (Care must be exercised, however, in the use of such historical sources, since, for example, Cicero drew his knowledge of early Greek philosophers from intermediate sources, while Sextus Empiricus was mainly concerned to support his own sceptical position by drawing attention to the contradictory opinions of the dogmatic philosophers. In regard to Aristotle's testimony as to the opinions of his predecessors we must not forget that Aristotle tended to look on earlier philosophies simply from the viewpoint of his own system and to see in them preparatory work for his own achievement. His attitude on this matter was doubtless largely justified, but it does mean that he was not always concerned to give what we should consider a purely objective and scientific account of the course of philosophic thought.) The commentaries composed by authors of Antiquity on the works of eminent philosophers are also of considerable importance, for instance, the commentary by Simplicius on the Physics of *Aristotle*.

In regard to the lives of the philosophers the most important work which we possess is that of Diogenes Laërtius (A.D. third century). This work is a compilation of material taken from various sources and is of very unequal merit, much of the biographical material being anecdotal, legendary and valueless in character, "tall stories" and different, sometimes contradictory, accounts of an event being included by the author, accounts which he had collected from previous writers and compilers. On the other hand it would be a great mistake to allow the unscientific character of the work to obscure its importance and very real value. The indices of the works of the philosophers are important, and we are indebted to Diogenes for a considerable amount of valuable information on the opinions and lives of the Greek philosophers. In assessing the historical value of Diogenes' statements it is obviously necessary to know (as far as this is possible) the particular source to which he was indebted on any given occasion, and no little painstaking and fruitful labour has been expended by scholars, in order to attain this knowledge.

For the chronology of the Greek philosophers the chief source is the *Chronica* of Apollodorus, who based the first part of his chronicle on the *Chronographia* of Eratosthenes of Cyrene (third century before Christ), but added a supplement, carrying it down to about the year 110 B.C. Apollodorus had not, of course, exact material at his disposal, and he had recourse to the arbitrary method of linking up some event of importance which was supposed to have occurred during the period of a philosopher's life, with the philosopher's prime or ἀκμή (taken as the fortieth year) and then reckoning backward to the date of the philosopher's birth. Similarly, it was taken as a general rule that a disciple was forty years younger than his master. Accuracy, therefore, was not to be expected.

(On the general subject of sources see e.g. Ueberweg-Praechter, *Die Philosophie des Altertums*, pp. 10–26 (Apollodorus' Chronicle is given on pp. 667–71), A. Fairbanks, *The First Philosophers of Greece*, pp. 263–88, L. Robin, *Greek Thought and the Origins of the Scientific Spirit*, pp. 7–16, and the *Stellenregister* to Diels' *Fragmente der Vorsokratiker*.

APPENDIX III

A FEW BOOKS

1. *General Histories of Greek Philosophy*

ADAMSON, R. (ed. Sorley and Hardie). The Development of Greek Philosophy. London, 1908.

BENN, A. W. The Greek Philosophers. London, 1914.

BRÉHIER, E. Histoire de la philosophie. Tome I. Paris, 1943.

BURNET, J. Greek Philosophy, Part I. Thales to Plato. Macmillan.
  (This scholarly work is indispensable to the student).

ERDMANN, J. E. A History of Philosophy, vol. I. Swan Sonnenschein, 1910.
  (Erdmann was an eminent historian of the Hegelian School.)

GOMPERZ, TH. Greek Thinkers, 4 vols. (Trs. L. Magnus.) John Murray.

ROBIN, L. La pensée grecque et les origines de l'esprit scientifique. Paris, 1923.
  Greek Thought and the Origins of the Scientific Spirit. London, 1928.

RUGGIERO, G. DE. La filosofia greca. 2 vols. Bari, 1917.
  (Professor de Ruggiero writes from the viewpoint of an Italian Neo-Hegelian.)

STACE, W. T. A Critical History of Greek Philosophy. Macmillan, 1920.

STENZEL, J. Metaphysik des Altertums. Berlin, Oldenbourg, 1929.
  (Particularly valuable for the treatment of Plato.)

STOCKL, A. A Handbook of the History of Philosophy. Part I. Pre-Scholastic Philosophy. Trs. by T. A. Finlay, S.J. Dublin, 1887.

UEBERWEG-PRAECHTER. Die Philosophie des Altertums. Berlin, Mittler, 1926.

WERNER, C. La philosophie grecque. Paris, Payot, 1938.

Z ELLER, E. Outlines of the History of Greek Philosophy. Kegan Paul, 1931.
  (Revised by W. Nestle, translated by L. R. Palmer.)

2. *Pre-Socratic Philosophy*

Th e best collection of the fragments of the Pre-Socratics is to be found in Hermann Diels' *Vorsokratiker*, fifth edition. Berlin, 1934–5.

BURNET, J. Early Greek Philosophy. Black, 3rd edition, 1920; 4th edition, 1930. (This extremely useful work includes very many fragments.)

COVOTTI, A. I Presocratici. Naples, 1934.

FAIRBANKS, A. The First Philosophers of Greece. London, 1898.

ZELLER, E. A History of Greek Philosophy from the earliest period to the time of Socrates. Trs. S. F. Alleyne. 2 vols. Longmans, 1881.

3. *Plato*

The Works of Plato are published, under the editorship of J. Burnet, in the *Oxford Classical Texts*. A well-known translation, in five volumes, is that by B. Jowett, O.U.P., 3rd edition, 1892. There are also more literal translations.

ARCHER-HIND, R. D. The Timaeus of Plato. Macmillan, 1888.

CORNFORD, F. M. Plato's Theory of Knowledge. Kegan Paul, 1935.
　　　　　　(A translation of the *Theaetetus* and *Sophist*, with commentary.)
　　　　　Plato's Cosmology. Kegan Paul, 1937.
　　　　　　(A translation of the *Timaeus*, with running commentary.)
　　　　　Plato and Parmenides. Kegan Paul, 1939.
　　　　　　(Translation of the *Parmenides*, with commentary and discussion.)
　　　　　The Republic of Plato. Translated with Introduction and Notes. O.U.P.

DEMOS, R. The Philosophy of Plato. Scribners, 1939.

DIÈS, AUGUSTE. Autour de Platon. Beauchesne, 1927.
　　　　　Platon. Flammarion, 1930.

FIELD, G. C. Plato and his Contemporaries. Methuen, 1930.

GROTE, C. Plato and the other Companions of Socrates. John Murray, 2nd edition, 1867.

HARDIE, W. F. R. A Study in Plato. O.U.P., 1936.

HARTMANN, N. Platons Logik des Seins. Giessen, 1909.

LODGE, R. C. Plato's Theory of Ethics. Kegan Paul, 1928.

LUTOSLAWSKI, W. The Origin and Growth of Plato's Logic. London, 1905.

MILHAUD, G. Les philosophes-géomètres de la Grèce. 2nd edition, Paris, 1934.

NATORP, P. Platons Ideenlehre. Leipzig, 1903.

NETTLESHIP, R. L. Lectures on the Republic of Plato. Macmillan, 1898.

RITTER, C. The Essence of Plato's Philosophy. George Allen & Unwin, 1933.
(Translated by Adam Alles.)
Platon, sein Leben, seine Schriften, seine Lehre. 2 vols. Munich, 1910 and 1923.

ROBIN, L. La théorie Platonicienne des idées et des nombres. Paris, 1933.
Platon. Paris, 1936.
La physique de Platon. Paris, 1919.

SHOREY, P. The Unity of Plato's Thought. Chicago, 1903.

STENZEL, J. Plato's Method of Dialectic. O.U.P., 1940.
(Translated by D. G. Allan.)
Zahl und Gestalt bei Platon und Aristoteles. 2nd edition. Leipzig, 1933.
Platon der Erzieher. 1928.
Studien zur Entwicklung der Platonischen Dialektik. Breslau, 1917.

STEWART, J. A. The Myths of Plato. O.U.P., 1905.
Plato's Doctrine of Ideas. O.U.P., 1909.

TAYLOR, A. E. Plato, the Man and his Work. Methuen, 1926.
(No student of Plato should be unacquainted with this masterly work.)
A Commentary on Plato's Timaeus. O.U.P., 1928.
Article on Plato in Encyc. Brit., 14th edition.
Platonism and its Influence. U.S.A. 1924 (Eng. Harrap).

WILAMOWITZ-MOELLENDORF, U. VON. Platon. 2 vols. Berlin, 1919.

ZELLER, E. Plato and the Older Academy. Longmans, 1876.
(Translated by S. F. Alleyne and A. Goodwin.)

4. *Aristotle*

The Oxford translation of the works of Aristotle is published in eleven volumes, under the editorship of J. A. Smith and W. D. Ross.

BARKER, E. The Political Thought of Plato and Aristotle. Methuen, 1906.
Article on Aristotle in the Encyc. Brit., 14th edition.

CASE, T. Article on Aristotle in the Encyc. Brit., 11th edition.

GROTE, G. Aristotle. London, 1883.

JAEGER, WERNER. Aristotle. Fundamentals of the History of his Development. O.U.P., 1934.
(Translated by R. Robinson.)

LE BLOND, J. M. Logique et Méthode chez Aristote. Paris, Vrin, 1939

MAIER, H. Die Syllogistik des Aristoteles. Tübingen, 1896.
New edition, 1936.

MURE, G. R. G. Aristotle. Benn, 1932.

PIAT, C. Aristote. Paris, 1912.

ROBIN, L. Aristote. Paris, 1944.

ROSS, SIR W. D. Aristotle. Methuen, 2nd edition, 1930.
                (A survey of Aristotle's thought by a great
                    Aristotelian scholar.)
                Aristotle's Metaphysics. 2 vols. O.U.P., 1924.
                Aristotle's Physics. O.U.P., 1936.
                (These two commentaries are invaluable.)

TAYLOR, A. E. Aristotle. Nelson, 1943.

ZELLER, E. Aristotle and the earlier Peripatetics. 2 vols. Longmans,
1897.

5. Post-Aristotelian Philosophy

ARMSTRONG, A. P. The Architecture of the Intelligible Universe in
                the Philosophy of Plotinus. Cambridge, 1940.
                (A very careful study of the origins and nature
                of Plotinian Neo-Platonism.)

ARNOLD, E. V. Roman Stoicism. 1911.

BAILEY, C. The Greek Atomists and Epicurus. O.U.P.

BEVAN, E. E. Stoics and Sceptics. O.U.P., 1913.
                Hellenistic Popular Philosophy. Cambridge, 1923.

BIGG, C. Neoplatonism. S.P.C.K., 1895.

BRÉHIER, E. Philon d'Alexandrie. Paris, 1908.
                La philosophie de Plotin. Paris, 1928.

CAPES, W. W. Stoicism. S.P.C.K., 1880.

DILL, SIR S. Roman Society from Nero to Marcus Aurelius. Macmillan, 1905.

DODDS, E. R. Select Passages illustrating Neoplatonism. S.P.C.K.,
1923.

FULLER, B. A. G. The Problem of Evil in Plotinus. Cambridge, 1912.

HENRY, PAUL (S.J.). Plotin et l'Occident. Louvain, 1934.
                Vers la reconstitution de l'enseignement oral
                de Plotin. Bulletin de l'Academie royale de
                Belgique, 1937.

HICKS, R. D. Stoic and Epicurean. Longmans, 1910.

INGE, W. R. The Philosophy of Plotinus. 2 vols. 3rd edition. Longmans, 1928.

KRAKOWSKI, E. Plotin et le Paganisme Religieux. Paris, Denoël et Steele, 1933

LEBRETON, J. (S.J.). Histoire du Dogme de la Trinité. Beauchesne, 1910.

MARCUS AURELIUS. The Meditations of the Emperor Marcus Aurelius Edited with Translation and Commentary by A. S. L. Farquharson. 2 vols., O.U.P. 1944.

PLOTINUS. The *Enneads* have been translated into English, in five vols. by S. MacKenna and B. S. Page. 1917–30.

PROCLUS. The Elements of Theology. O.U.P.
(A Revised Text with Translation, Introduction and Commentary by E. R. Dodds.)

REINHARDT, K. Poseidonios. Munich, 1921.

ROBIN, L. Pyrrhon et le Scepticisme Grec. Paris, 1944.

TAYLOR, T. Select Works of Plotinus (ed. G. R. S. Mead). G. Bell & Sons, 1929.

WHITTAKER, T. The Neo-Platonists. 2nd edition, Cambridge, 1901.

WITT, R. E. Albinus and the History of Middle Platonism. Cambridge,

ZELLER, E. The Stoics, Epicureans and Sceptics. Longmans, 1870.
(Translated by O. J. Reichel.)
A History of Eclecticism in Greek Philosophy. Longmans, 1883.
(Translated by S. F. Alleyne.)

INDEX

(A small *n* after a number indicates that the reference is to a footnote on the page in question.)

517